# GATEWAY BEER

# GATEWAY BEER

## ST. LOUIS CRAFT BREWING IN THE SHADOW OF ANHEUSER-BUSCH

JOEL BITTLE

Foreword by Cheryl Baehr

3 FIELDS BOOKS
An imprint of the University of Illinois Press

3 Fields Books is an imprint of the
University of Illinois Press.


Manufactured in the United States of America
P 5 4 3 2 1
∞ This book is printed on acid-free paper.

Cataloging data available from the Library of Congress
LCCN 2026015209
ISBN 978-0-252-08958-9 (paper : alk.)
ISBN 978-0-252-04908-8 (ebook)

The manufacturer's authorized representative in the EU for product safety is Mare Nostrum Group B.V., Mauritskade 21D, 1091 GC Amsterdam, The Netherlands. Email: gpsr@mare-nostrum.co.uk

For Megan, Clara, Kate,
and Cecilia

**gateway beer** [geyt-wey beer]

noun

1. a beer lover's entry point into the world of craft beer
2. a beer from the world beer capital of St. Louis

# CONTENTS

# FOREWORD

Every year, the Bellefontaine Cemetery and Arboretum's Historic Beer Barons Tour sells out almost as quickly as tickets go on sale. In any other city, a walk through the final resting places of its industry titans might be a solemn affair, but in St. Louis it's downright celebratory, filled with music, historical reenactments, snacks, and, of course, a lot of beer.

Perhaps St. Louisans' ability to revel in joy when thinking about the beer spirits that have gone before us is due to the idea that they never really left. Beer flows through the city's veins—physically, if you consider the arteries of underground caves and passageways underneath the South St. Louis streets that were used to store and transport beer beginning in the 1800s; figuratively, when you hear people on the street continue to refer to Augustus Anheuser Busch Jr. as "Gussie," even a decade and a half after the homegrown brewery was sold to the Belgian conglomerate InBev.

As someone who has been in and adjacent to the St. Louis food and beverage community since the 1990s—as a front-of-house professional, dining critic, and editor for *The Riverfront Times*, and now dining writer and podcast host for *St. Louis Magazine*—I've always marveled at the way beer has captured the city's soul. It's not just a preference; it's an identity, though one that has changed tremendously since the Falstaff, Busch, and Lemp barons first set up shop. But as Joel Bittle elegantly outlines in the following pages, that change has been vital to St. Louis remaining a beer city in the wake of so much tumult. And that change is craft beer.

I met Joel in the most St. Louis way possible: through mutual friends. That those friends are a prominent local food journalist and the owner of one of the area's most acclaimed restaurants speaks to just how much Joel has ingrained himself in the St. Louis food and beverage community since moving to town many years ago. Hailing from California, the land of Sierra Nevada and Anchor Steam, he has the perfect view from which to understand, and then lay out, craft beer's role in not only how St. Louis drinks but also how it defines itself. Joel is able to tell this story with the knowledge and experiences of a true insider thanks to his clear passion for his adopted hometown and the relationships he has developed with its craft beer community; he also has the ability to pan out and put St. Louis's beer past and present into a broader context—and ask the why of it all—in a way that only someone with the benefit of some distance can.

The result is the definitive exploration of St. Louis's craft beer scene, from its roots to the present day. It's a story for anyone interested in the beverage and who is curious about the key players and moments that lit the spark and then tended the fire until it became the force that it is today. But Joel has done something even more special. In telling the story of craft beer's birth, rise, sort-of fall, stabilization, and present moment in St. Louis, he has told the story of any other city in the United States that has experienced the loss of an industry that has been so connected to the way it sees itself. In St. Louis that industry is beer and the loss of the homegrown Anheuser-Busch to InBev; in Akron it's rubber; in Buffalo and Pittsburgh it's steel. Joel positions St. Louis craft beer as a blueprint for how a city can get back up after being dealt a blow and create something just as vibrant out of the remains of what has been lost. In this sense, I found *Gateway Beer* to be hopeful, not just for beer enthusiasts but for everyone with a strong sense of civic pride and a belief that the creative spirit can move us forward.

Joel's writing also helped me see just how ironic it is that craft beer is what has aided in the preservation of St. Louis's brewing heritage. Though he does not go so far as to present them as gadflies, Joel explores the, at times, tense relationship between the Goliath Anheuser-Busch and the Davids who were the craft breweries fighting for their share of the market in a city that was the last place anyone would have thought would become a craft beer mecca. Where once Schlafly could not get a tap handle at a South City dive bar, the brewery has now become one of the defining names in St. Louis beer—the fact that its corporate name is *The* Saint Louis Brewery underscores just how far the mighty have fallen and the little guy has risen up. I found Joel's illumination of this struggle and how it ultimately played out to be insightful and inspiring for underdogs everywhere.

A beer lover might pick up *Gateway Beer* expecting to read the interesting story of one city's craft brewing industry. And they'll find that. A history buff might go in wanting to learn about the rise and fall of an industry titan and what sprung up in its wake. That's there too. But the appeal of this book is much bigger than for either of those niche audiences. It's a story of tenacity, of collaboration, of realizing that by throwing in your lot with those who could be your competitors, you are instead creating something bigger than what you could achieve on your own. I've seen that firsthand in the St. Louis restaurant community as chefs and restaurateurs built up the city's modern dining scene through a coordinated and collegial effort. As Joel shows, this same ethos underpins the city's craft beer community, making it one of the brightest chapters in St. Louis's ongoing story—and one of the most hopeful examples of the true spirit of St. Louis.

Cheryl Baehr
Food writer, *St. Louis Magazine*

# ACKNOWLEDGMENTS

This project is a testament to the family that is the St. Louis craft beer community. It would not have been possible without many hours of guidance, interviews, and follow-ups. Thank you to every brewer and brewery owner who gave their time. I would like to single out Abbey Spencer and Benn Overkamp, whose early discussions and encouragement provided the spark, and Phil Wymore, who connected me with other beer writers across the country. Thank you to Tom Schlafly for his time and detailed review of the project, to Dan Kopman for the economics of beer and hard alcohol sales, to John Witte for the deep dive into St. Charles history, to Marc Gottfried for his experience in both craft beer and Kräftig, and to Jake Hafner for pulling the curtain back and showing the challenges breweries face. Fran Caradonna, who was present from the early St. Louis craft beer scene as a distributor, cofounded O'Fallon Brewery, and finished her career at Schlafly, was a unique and valuable resource. Thank you to Cheryl Baehr for taking the time to get to know me and my project, then interviewing members of the craft beer community before writing the prologue. Finally, thank you to Martha Bayne and her colleagues at the University of Illinois Press. They have made the process easy and enjoyable, and I could not have done it without their guidance.

# GATEWAY BEER

# PROLOGUE

There's a myth slowly lumbering toward fact that President Jimmy Carter is responsible for the rise of craft beer as we know it. If not for his deregulation of the beer industry, we would still today live under the bland yoke of Big Beer. Every taproom in America should have a backlit Saint Jimmy prominently displayed. Or so the story goes.

It's an easy story to believe and within the character of the peanut-farming, solar panel–installing former president. Who better to shift power away from giant breweries into the hands of the emerging microbrewers? But that's not what happened.

Homebrewing, once a common practice before the big German brewers arrived in the United States two centuries ago, never made it out of Prohibition. The Twenty-First Amendment legalized commercial beer and wine production, but homebrewing remained a crime. As a result, little innovation occurred in beer making for the next half century. In that time, a rapid consolidation of large breweries left consumers with little choice beyond a lager from St. Louis or a lager from Milwaukee.

The first bubbles of change emerged in the mid-1960s, when Fritz Maytag III bought San Francisco's Anchor Brewing Company, turning the brewery in decline into the model for craft breweries to come. Anchor Brewing had once supplied beer for the California Gold Rush, their open fermenting containers of hot beer meeting the cool San Francisco air, throwing steam into the air. Anchor Steam's malty, slightly caramel flavor provided the Bay Area an alternative to the lagers of the big beer companies, but by the 1960s the brewery was struggling to compete. Maytag took over, expanded Anchor Steam distribution, and continued to push the boundaries of beer, influencing the waves of craft brewers to come.

Jack McAuliffe found a taste for beer while stationed overseas in the navy. Inspired by the new styles Anchor Steam offered, he began to brew at home. With assistance from Suzanne Stern and Jane Zimmerman, McAuliffe built New Albion Brewing Company in Sonoma, California, in 1976. As Anchor Brewing Company had existed since 1897, New Albion is considered America's first modern craft brewery. Fellow homebrewer Ken Grossman followed three years later with Sierra Nevada Brewing Company.

On the opposite coast, Charlie Papazian studied nuclear engineering at the University of Virginia, but it was a friendship with an elderly man who had homebrewed his way through Prohibition that changed Papazian's life. Papazian brought what he had learned to Boulder, Colorado, in the early 1970s and taught anyone interested—and many were interested—how to brew their own beer. Papazian's two-page instructions for homebrewing later expanded into his first book, *The Joy of Home Brewing*, holy scripture in the beer making world. The brew spoon he used in that decade is now hanging in the Smithsonian's National Museum of American History. In 1978 Papazian founded the American Homebrewers Association.

Pockets of homebrewers appeared around the country, but they had to do it quietly as they operated in a legal gray area, more akin to bootleggers than brewmasters. Hobbyists lobbied their state representatives to legalize homebrewing. The time had come to move beyond the kitchens and basements.

The pivotal year of 1979 started America down the road to the Craft Beer America we have today, but President Carter, who didn't drink, was only tangentially involved. It was Wisconsin congressman Bill Steiger and California senator Alan Cranston who shaped legislation that allowed for legal, tax-free homebrewing. Individuals could now brew up to one hundred gallons a year at home, two hundred gallons per household. Jimmy Carter signed into law H.R. 1337, legalizing homebrewing beer and winemaking for personal use, but that was the extent of his involvement.

True deregulation of the brewing industry happened on a state-by-state basis. Colorado's Boulder Brewing Company opened in 1979 in the shadow of Coors. Two years later, Charlie Papazian and others turned the region into a beer capital by hosting the first annual Great American Beer Festival (GABF), where twenty-four breweries came together to showcase the new trend. Today, more than nine hundred breweries compete in over one hundred categories. Washington and its fertile hops became a beer destination in 1982. Seattle's Independent Ale Brewing Company brewed Redhook Ale, a British pub–style beer brewed with a Belgian yeast that imparted spicy, fruity notes. It proved so popular that the brewery changed its name to Redhook. Their Extra Special Bitter became even more popular. In Yakima, Washington, Bert Grant opened Grant's Brewery Pub, the first brewpub in America since Prohibition. Grant believed drinkers wanted hoppier, bitterer beer, and he poured more hops into his fermenters than anyone else at the time. Grant's Brewery Pub is credited with the first beer labeled as an India pale ale (IPA). A beer revolution was under way.

By 1982, fourteen American microbreweries had opened. California led the way with eight. States like Massachusetts and Michigan created environments where microbreweries could grow to distribute beyond their states' borders: Boston Beer Company with their Samuel Adams Boston Lager in 1984; Kalamazoo Brewing Company, which changed its name to Bell's in 1985; and Harpoon Brewery in 1986. Other states, like Utah, Alabama, and Mississippi, established hard ceilings for alcohol content, limiting their breweries' development.

And then there was Missouri. In any study of beer in America, all roads lead to St. Louis. Anheuser-Busch, brewer of Budweiser, was the biggest beer company in the world by volume. And after Falstaff Brewing closed in 1977, it was the only brewery in St. Louis. Its growing dominance had wiped out smaller breweries both locally and nationally.

The line graph of total breweries in the United States reads like an inverted bell curve. At its beginning, Anheuser-Busch was one of over four thousand, most of them tiny. That number was already quickly declining when Prohibition hit, eliminating the majority of American breweries. Around seven hundred remained by Prohibition's end. What survived held on against the big boys until they went under or were bought up. By 1979 the number was down to one hundred.

Before the dominance of national lagers like Budweiser, beer styles were varied and were brewed for consumption in the local neighborhood. For much of beer history, from the time of priestesses and monks, of alewives and brewsters, it was not uncommon for beer drinkers to know personally the person brewing their beer.

While Big Beer did a lot of things right—namely, quality, consistency, and freshness—their supremacy removed much of the diversity in beer making. Did the lager dominate because it was the superior style, or did the dominance of the companies cause the homogenization? Whatever the answer, commercials in the 1970s and '80s tried to convince Americans that their brand of lager was better than all the other brands of lagers. The choice came down to the label, not the type of beer.

Legendary Chicago newspaper columnist Mike Royko drew the ire of American beer drinkers in 1973 by writing, "America's beer tastes as if it were brewed through a horse." The angry responses Royko received prompted him to hold an official taste test at Chicago's Old Town Ale House. Eleven judges found that of the twenty-two domestic and imported beers they blind taste tested, America's number one selling beer came in dead last. Budweiser, judges claimed, smelled and tasted bad. It wasn't quite the horse piss Royko claimed, but his point stood. Schlitz, number two at the time, came in second to last. None of the top-selling American beers did well in the competition. German pilsner Würzburger took top marks, followed by England's Bass Pale Ale. Point Special, a lager from Wisconsin brewery Stevens Point, came in third, making it officially the best beer made in America.

The Wisconsin brewery's reaction to the honor is remarkable in retrospect and still offers lessons for today's beer climate. Though Stevens Point received orders from across the country, including one to supply Trans World Airlines (TWA), the brewery turned them all down to focus on their local market. They would not sacrifice quality for quantity, and they would not leave behind the members of their community who loved their beer. As breweries closed or sold to the big guys over the next decades, Stevens Point carried on and years later replicated the feat by winning gold at the Great American Beer Festival in the Premium Lager category.

Most of the beers in the 1973 competition had national distribution and could be picked up from a local store, but Stevens Point did not distribute to Chicago. Someone had to drive bottles of Point Special, no doubt fresh from the brewery, to the Ale House. Did proximity give Stevens Point an advantage in the competition? From the moment a beer comes off the line, the quality begins to decline. Beer made nearby is fresher. Fresher beer is better beer. It's a simple concept, one that provided the foundation for craft beer.

Because of the bill signed by Jimmy Carter, small breweries and brewpubs offering styles that had all but disappeared reappeared across the country, and many more followed. It was a return to neighborhood-based brewing. Beer making began as a local activity, and to its roots it slowly returned.

Too big to notice the activities of so many ants, Anheuser-Busch (A-B) had spent the last century establishing and maintaining their top position in the global beer market. In 1979 they were uniquely positioned for a corporate dominance unseen in other industries. They controlled over 25 percent of the market share, on their way to 49 percent at their peak in 2002.

St. Louis was the population center of the country. Almost exactly as many people lived east of the city as lived west, as many north as south. The location was perfect for the national distribution system created by A-B founder Adolphus Busch. Early use of ice-car rail systems gave way to a complex web of relationships with regional distributors.

A scattering of small breweries opened in A-B's shadow. Boulevard Brewing Company opened across the state in Kansas City in 1989. Schlafly was the first in the city of St. Louis in 1991. The obstacles Schlafly overcame, both culturally and legally, are discussed in chapter 2, but they cleared the way for the breweries that followed. Despite Schlafly's steady expansion into area bars and refrigerators, craft beer's growth in St. Louis was slow compared to other parts of the United States. It would take almost two decades, and a corporate takeover that shocked the beer world, for the craft beer wave to hit St. Louis.

"On a national level it was happening," says Schlafly cofounder Dan Kopman. "But it was like someone had a thumb in a dike in St. Louis, and the dike was going to break. The river was cresting. Anheuser-Busch was the thumb."

Following the sale of Anheuser-Busch to the international conglomerate InBev in 2008, St. Louis saw an explosion of craft breweries. Were they a natural result of the vacuum created by the sale, or was the craft beer movement going to hit St. Louis anyway? Opinions are divided. Some craft brewers blame "The Brewery" and its distributor lieutenants for stifling craft beer growth. Others hold a more generous view, crediting the beer giant for turning St. Louis into a beer mecca, for revolutionizing technology, and for training several of the brewers who went on to open craft breweries.

2nd Shift Brewing opened in 2010, followed by the big four of 2011: Urban Chestnut, Perennial, Civil Life, and 4 Hands. Side Project Brewing, rated the number two brewery in the world in 2020 by the website

RateBeer, began in 2014 and quickly developed a national following. A release of a new Side Project beer brings blocks-long lines of fans. Narrow Gauge started in the basement of an Italian restaurant in 2016 just as the New England IPA (NEIPA) style was gaining popularity. In a short time, they went from best new Missouri brewery to earning the national title "Best NEIPA Brewer" in 2018. At festivals and competitions all over the country, St. Louis craft breweries poured beer and won medals. Beer drinkers were paying attention and came to St. Louis to visit breweries that were not named Anheuser-Busch.

For three years in a row, 2018 to 2020, St. Louis was named "Best Beer Scene" by *USA Today*. Locals had witnessed a city dominated in so many ways by the King of Beers, whose influence had spread into every facet of St. Louis life, shift into the top craft beer town in America. And then COVID hit, changing the industry in ways no one could expect.

By the mid-2020s the craft beer world was on the other side of something. Call it post-COVID, call it something akin to a hangover, but the landscape had shifted, growth had slowed, and drinking trends moved toward spirits. Breweries that had expanded rapidly, counting on continued growth, found themselves in a tough position. Others came into their own with business models that favored hyperlocalism. With the market tightening and oversaturated, quality and consistency became more important than chasing trends, relationships more important than reach.

Of the highs and lows the city of St. Louis has experienced over the past 150 years, it is not hyperbole to say that beer has played a vital role. Beers and brewers are woven into the tapestry. Here are their stories. This is an account not just about beer but about a city's resilience and triumph, its collective memory, collective consciousness, and, at times, collective trauma.

# 1

# FERMENTATION

Budweiser was America's beer, brewed in perhaps the most American of cities. St. Louis bore witness to the heights of the American ascendancy, felt the economic flow and ebb as manufacturing jobs flooded the area only to dry up, and to this day bears the scars of complicated and, at times, incendiary race relations.

It is difficult to overstate the influence Anheuser-Busch had on the city of St. Louis in the century leading up to 2008, when the company was sold to the Brazilian/Belgian conglomerate InBev. Ask a local about growing up in the Gateway City and you'll hear accounts of corporate sponsorship of events and organizations that go beyond reasonable expectations for a local business. Cases of Budweiser showed up at family BBQs or were delivered to doorsteps on Christmas Eve. In times of disaster, which around St. Louis usually meant flooding, A-B delivered pallets of water stamped with their logo to assist relief efforts.

Here it was normal for a beer company to sponsor children's sports teams, its A&Eagle logo, an eagle sitting on the letter "A" with a gold star above it, prominent on uniforms. More than one future craft brewer played soccer as a teenager wearing the "Busch" logo across his chest, branding that crossed the line in most other cities. Also normal is carrying and drinking alcohol on the streets of St. Louis. Missouri laws are notoriously alcohol-friendly. Open containers of alcohol are legal in a vehicle, and passengers are allowed to consume alcohol.

The city's relationship with Anheuser-Busch went beyond the usual type of corporate citizenship, where buying local products kept that money in the community. The company's economic impact began with the brewery and its thousands of jobs but spread out to the bars and restaurants, local suppliers, distributors, delivery, and so on. The money circulated within the community, where its tax income paid for better infrastructure, schools, police, and fire services. But for St. Louis, there was a deeper bond, one forged through more than a century of goodwill between St. Louisans and the beer company. There was a social contract: Support the brewery and the brewery will support the city. In many ways, Anheuser-Busch and the Busch family were more important to the city than its civic leaders. Politicians came and went; there would always be a Busch. To St. Louis, they were royalty.

Pity the transplant to St. Louis at the turn of the millennium—perhaps from a state rich in craft beer like California—who disparaged the taste of Budweiser in public. There might as well have been a loud record scratch as heads turned, faces disapproving. At the very least, our Californian got a lecture on who among present company worked for The Brewery (somehow St. Louisans capitalize it verbally), what family members worked their whole lives there, and all A-B has done for the city. Everyone had a story, a connection to The Brewery. Few St. Louisans were more than one degree removed from Anheuser-Busch.

The locals' defense of everything Anheuser-Busch comes across as a kind of corporate nationalism, beyond just civic identity. Some would fight for it. This was an intended result of 150 years of marketing.

It may be difficult to imagine now, but St. Louis was once one of the most populous US cities, peaking at number four in the late 1800s. German immigrants, known as "Forty-Eighters" after the failed German revolution of 1848, fueled the city's rise. Their strong opposition to slavery led many to fight for the Union in the Civil War. Craving German beer, they turned St. Louis into the brewing center of America, ideal due to its abundance of water, a natural cave system for aging and storing beer, and the proximity of the Mississippi River for transportation of incoming supplies and outgoing deliveries. Ice houses built along the shores ensured consistent temperatures.

A brewery that opened as the Western Brewery grew and changed its name to the Lemp Brewery. The Cherokee Brewery on Cherokee Street would, over 150 years later, reopen as Earthbound Beer. Eberhard Anheuser, a German immigrant who owned a soap and candle company, lent money to the Bavarian Brewery. When it faltered in 1860, Anheuser purchased other creditors' interests, taking over ownership.

Adolphus Busch was a twenty-one-year-old recent immigrant whose wealthy family sold winery and brewing supplies. His two older brothers, Henry and John, had already founded a brewery in nearby Washington, Missouri. After serving as a corporal in the Union Army during the Civil War, Busch worked for a brewing supply company in St. Louis. Through his dealings with Anheuser's brewery, Busch met and married Lilly Anheuser, Eberhard's daughter. With the families joined, Adolphus Busch began to work for Anheuser's Bavarian Brewery as a salesman and later as company secretary. Eberhard Anheuser died in 1880, passing the brewery down to his daughter Lilly and son-in-law Adolphus Busch. Anheuser-Busch was born.

Photo of Adolphus Busch as a young man, circa 1869. (Courtesy of the Missouri Historical Society.)

Around this time citizens of the city of St. Louis voted to separate themselves from St. Louis County, a mostly empty westward sprawl. The rationale was that 310,000 city residents didn't want to pay the taxes to develop and maintain a county filled with only 27,000 people. It was perhaps the worst decision in the city's history, for reasons that wouldn't become clear for another seventy-five years.

Back in the late nineteenth century, it turned out that Adolphus Busch was something of a beer visionary. Even before he had settled on a style for his beer, he saw Anheuser-Busch growing beyond the local market to become a national brand. To do so, the brewery needed to innovate. Busch utilized recent scientific breakthroughs.

French scientist Louis Pasteur discovered in 1860 that spoilage in beer was not a result of the death and putrefaction of beer cells, as was believed at the time, but rather the presence of new, harmful contaminants like bacteria, fungi, and other yeasts. He experimented with heat, discovering a sweet spot for beer between 55 and 60 degrees Celsius that inhibited harmful organisms. Beer, the world soon discovered, could sit on shelves for up to nine months because of Pasteur's revelations.

A kind of beer arms race took place in St. Louis in the late 1800s between Adolphus Busch and William J. Lemp of the Lemp Brewery. Anheuser-Busch was the first brewery to use pasteurization to extend shelf life and one of the first to bottle its beer. Busch extended his railway distribution to reach new markets by setting up icehouses along the way. Both Busch and Lemp took advantage of new technologies in refrigerated rail cars to distribute coast to coast, with Lemp Brewing reaching that goal first.

Adam Lemp, William's father, had introduced the lager style to St. Louis—and possibly all of America—as early as 1838. Lager yeasts differ from ale yeasts in that they ferment at lower temperatures. The term "lager" comes from a German verb meaning "to store," referring to the cooling caves used during the summer for both fermentation and storage. Multiple cavern systems under the city of St. Louis provided the perfect environment. The process, called "lagering," improves the flavor by

Wood engraved advertisement for William J. Lemp's Western Brewery, 1883. (Courtesy of the Missouri Historical Society.)

allowing the beer to settle. What results is a bright and sparkling beer that does not have to be consumed quickly before it goes bad.

During a tour of European breweries in the 1870s, Adolphus Busch decided to brew new lager styles at his growing brewery, capitalizing on the growing demand. But it was a style of Czech pilsner that Busch brewed and packaged, known as "contract brewing," for a liquor importer named Carl Conrad that became what came to be known as the King of Beers. Originally called Conrad's Budweiser Beer after the Czech city of Budweis, the beer's popularity spread across the nation. Carl Conrad's other ventures were not as popular, and bankruptcy forced him to sell Budweiser to the company that brewed it. Adolphus Busch made it his flagship beer. The timing couldn't have been better for Busch. As immigration increased from beer-drinking countries, beer consumption in America increased fourfold in the late 1800s, with more and more of the beer coming from St. Louis.

Ironically, Adolphus Busch did not drink his own beer, referring to it as "that slop," or, with his thick German accent, "*dot schlop*." The founder of the biggest beer company in the world preferred wine. Fellow St. Louis brewer Louis Koch leaned into the common sentiment by naming his Sydney Street brewery Schlop Brewery. Though Koch's brewery didn't last long, his recipes were passed down to his children and grandchildren, eventually ending up in the hands of his great-grandson Jim Koch. One recipe in particular would help spark the craft beer movement under the new name Samuel Adams Boston Lager.

Budweiser may be a German lager, but cofounder Adolphus Busch spent considerable effort tying the beer to American patriotism. In 1896 he commissioned a repainting of *Custer's Last Fight* from the Battle of Little Big Horn for an advertising campaign, initially spreading fifteen thousand prints across Budweiser's distribution network. In it, a defiant General Custer fights back a wave of Native Americans while his men lay dead or dying around him. There is no description on the print other than the words "Custer's Last Fight" in bold across the bottom. And though it is technically a beer advertisement, there is no tagline or motto, no exhortation to drink Budweiser, only the words "Anheuser Busch Brewing Association" in smaller letters under the title. The purpose wasn't to sell beer—it was to sell the idea that Budweiser was distinctly American.

This connection of consumption to nationalism was revolutionary. Busch was betting on the idea that a beer drinker would choose Budweiser

Chromolithograph of *Custer's Last Fight*, 1896. (Courtesy of the Missouri Historical Society.)

over other beers because it made him or her feel more American. His bet paid off and a century of similar marketing followed. The image proved so popular that Adolphus Busch printed 150,000 copies. If an establishment sold Budweiser, it had a print. Likewise, if a customer walked into a bar and saw *Custer's Last Fight*, he knew the place sold Budweiser. By World War II, the company had printed and distributed over a million copies. One hangs in the Smithsonian today.

Advertisements in the early years of the twentieth century connected the beer to national heroes like Thomas Jefferson, Robert Morris, and James Madison, despite these men predating German beer in America. An article in *Smith's Magazine Advertiser* read in part: "Anheuser-Busch have been brewing the kind of honest barley and hop brews which Jefferson hoped in his day to see the National beverage of Americans. The famous BUDWEISER is sold throughout the civilized world—the drink of your forefathers—the drink of the noblest men who ever lived—the drink of the great triumphant nations."

The beer company grew as the city moved into modernity with the turn of the century. Bridges now stood where ferries once crossed the nearby rivers. Street names like Lemay Ferry and Dougherty Ferry still trace the routes St. Louisans once took to utilize them.

The year 1904 was a triumphant one for St. Louis. The city hosted almost 20 million people for the Louisiana Purchase Exposition, known as the St. Louis World's Fair. Originally intended as a centennial celebration of the Louisiana Purchase, building delays forced the city to miss the mark by one year. Visitors from across the world and all forty-five states filled the fifteen hundred buildings on twelve hundred acres of land that now makes up much of Forest Park. So much was there to see and do and eat that it was considered impossible to experience it all in less than a week.

John Philip Sousa provided the fanfare. Geronimo signed autographs for a dime. Forty-one states and forty-three countries presented whatever they wanted to show off. For Pennsylvania, it was the Liberty Bell. Louisiana built a replica of "the Cabildo," the building within which the Louisiana Purchase was signed. Ireland built a Blarney Castle. India built a Taj Mahal. America's newest colony, the Philippines, had a large exhibit on the current Washington University campus. Over a thousand Filipinos of various ethnicities provided a human zoo for visitors to observe, providing the fair's most regrettable activity in retrospect.

Crowds gathered around 140 models of automobiles, some of them steam or electric powered, and looked to the sky in wonder at dirigibles and primitive airplanes. They tried for the first time the waffle cone, invented when a Syrian immigrant combined his wafer dessert with the neighboring ice cream stand. Just don't tell anyone from St. Louis about the New Yorker who patented the waffle cone a year earlier. Other supposed inventions of the 1904 World's Fair, such as the hot dog, iced tea, peanut butter, and cotton candy, are probably myth, but certainly for many attendees this was their first time trying them. Dr. Pepper and Puffed Wheat debuted at the fair.

Perhaps the most impressive exhibit was the Electricity Palace. Architecturally stunning in the Parisian Beaux-Arts style common at the exposition, the building housed the power plant for the fair. Brightly lit, the palace powered the lights along the central canals and bridges at night. Inside, a machine invented by Alexander Graham Bell transmitted music or speech to a wireless receiver outside in the courtyard, the world's first

Chromolithograph of Alphonse Mucha's poster for the 1904 St. Louis World's Fair, 1903. (Courtesy of the Missouri Historical Society.)

Souvenir postcard of the 1904 World's Fair featuring the main lagoon, 1903. (Courtesy of the Missouri Historical Society.)

wireless telephone. Another machine, the telautograph, could recreate drawings from someone on the other end of the device. Harvey Hubble introduced the electrical plug, which would become common in United States homes within ten years. The x-ray machine, infant incubators, the electric streetcar, and the electric typewriter were also among the many products first introduced at the 1904 World's Fair.

A midway of games and concessions down Lindell Boulevard, called Ten Million Dollar Pike, held a 264-foot-high Ferris wheel so huge that each of its thirty-six cars could hold forty people.

Though it was overshadowed by the fair itself, the first Olympics held in the United States took place in the summer of 1904. As it marked the first Olympics outside of Europe, few European athletes traveled to St. Louis, making it more of a US/Canada games. The tradition of awarding a gold, silver, and bronze medal originated here. While many countries were listed as medal winners, it was discovered later that some athletes were recent American immigrants from those countries.

Among the beautiful buildings of the world's fair stood a squatty thumb of a log cabin called Hardscrabble, once the home of Ulysses S. Grant. The stories of the building and of the man weave through that of Anheuser-Busch.

Grant had married St. Louis native Julia Dent, whose family owned the 850-acre White Haven estate, roughly ten miles southwest of downtown.

Photo of the residence of Ulysses S. Grant, 'Hardscrabble," 1891. (Courtesy of the Missouri Historical Society.)

Julia's father gifted the couple 80 acres, an area that would come to be known as Grant's Farm. It was there that Grant built the log cabin that made its way to the world's fair. To Julia's dismay, Grant had a dream of living simply, of making a living off farming. "This little house," Julia Dent Grant wrote in her memoirs, "looked so unattractive that we facetiously decided to call it Hardscrabble."

The Grants lived there only three months before retreating to White Haven. The Civil War pulled Grant back into the army and onto the national stage. Regional victories led to promotions and praise from Abraham Lincoln, who promoted Grant to lieutenant general, a rank previously held only by George Washington. It was Grant who led the Union Army to victory and who accepted Robert E. Lee's unconditional surrender. Four years later, he was president.

National prominence limited the time Ulysses and Julia spent at their farm, and after being swindled out of an investment years later, Grant used the farm and cabin to pay back a loan from William Vanderbilt in 1884. The railroad tycoon had offered to forgive the debt, but Grant was too proud. Grant's Farm was no longer his. The land was sold and resold, and in 1891 Edward and Justin Joy purchased just the cabin, moving it piece by piece to the Old Orchard area of nearby Webster Groves. Twelve years later it was sold and moved again, this time for the whole world to see.

Cyrus F. Blanke was a St. Louis businessman and the director of the world's fair. He was known for using a jet-black horse to advertise his coffee on the St. Louis streets. It was this horse that President Teddy Roosevelt rode when he arrived at the exposition. Blanke wanted to use Grant's log cabin to promote his businesses at the fair, to tie his brand to nationalism the way Busch had. Blanke purchased Hardscrabble and had it moved to the world's fair grounds. Placed prominently next to the Palace of Fine

Arts, now the St. Louis Art Museum, Hardscrabble could be viewed for ten cents. Visitors dined at the adjacent coffee and luncheon tent with the sign "C. F. Blanke Tea and Coffee Co."

After the fair, the process of building removal was made easy by the fact that many of the structures were built with staff, a temporary material much like plaster of Paris. Only the Palace of Fine Arts and the flight cage for birds were made to last. Blanke had assumed that the city would maintain the cabin, but as no maintenance plan had been established, Hardscrabble was slated for demolition. The house that Grant built was going to be destroyed. Enter Anheuser-Busch.

By the time of the 1904 world's fair, Anheuser-Busch had grown to become one of the largest breweries in the country. In 1901 A-B crossed the one-million-barrels-a-year threshold, turning Adolphus Busch into a very rich man. He paid for the naming rights to the Division of Works Palace, called Busch Hall, which displayed the A&Eagle logo over the entrance. Busch commissioned two grand chandeliers for the fair, both emblazoned with golden eagles.

Lemp Brewery still held a prominent position in St. Louis, and even brewed a special "World's Fair Beer," but by most accounts Budweiser was much more ubiquitous. A bottle of beer at the fair cost forty cents. In a tactic that would come to define Anheuser-Busch, they used their relationships to secure prominent real estate in the food and beverage halls of the exposition. Perhaps the most impressive was the massive Tyrolean Alps dining hall. A nine-acre installation featuring fake snow-covered mountains that visitors could climb via tram, it seated five thousand diners and featured costumed singers. Due to the prominence of Anheuser-Busch products, some joked that the space should have been called "Budweiser Alps."

Surviving Budweiser advertisements from that time show men in top hats and women in fine dresses and ornate hats standing among the grandeur of the architecture, with symbols of Anheuser-Busch prominently displayed in the background. This was a time to celebrate St. Louis, and Budweiser was every bit a part of that. It's easy to toast the ascendancy of a local business when that business is beer.

After six months, one hundred thousand visitors watched on the night of December 1, 1904, as the lights went out. Legend has it the fair completely ran out of beer only an hour before. St. Louis was now in the afterglow of its finest hour. The city held on to this moment in the sun long after the

Photo of the Tyrolean Alps on the Pike at the St. Louis World's Fair, 1904. (Courtesy of the Missouri Historical Society.)

generation who witnessed it was gone. For a century after, locals invited tourists to come "Meet me in St. Louis."

As for Hardscrabble, Ulysses S. Grant's log cabin, it was Adolphus Busch's son August who stepped in to save the historic house. August Anheuser Busch felt more at home in the fantasy of the old West than in the dirty, smelly brewery downtown. In 1903 he purchased much of Grant's farm with the dream of turning it into a wildlife paradise. He stocked it with animals imported from all over the world. Hardscrabble was returned to near its original location, the land around the cabin enclosed with a fence made of rifle barrels.

While August's motivations may have been selfish, with some at the time doubting he even wanted to follow in his father's beer-making footsteps, Grant's Farm over time became the Busch family's personal Versailles, complete with a massive French Renaissance chateau, and a powerful connection to the St. Louis community when in 1954 it opened its doors to visitors—for free.

By connecting itself to American—and St. Louis—history, Anheuser-Busch was solidifying its future. The world's fair was an axis point for the company. It was a celebration of American history, the city's glorious present, and its triumphant future all wrapped up in one.

As the company grew, and America surpassed Germany as the number one producer of beer in the world, Anheuser-Busch employed thousands in St. Louis. When Adolphus Busch died in 1913, thirty thousand people viewed his body, and one hundred thousand lined the procession. Stock in the company he had built paid out yearly dividends between three thousand and eight thousand dollars per share—on stock that was originally valued at five hundred dollars per share. St. Louis banks lent borrowers twenty-five thousand dollars against a share.

The company's American-ness took a hit in the lead up to World War I, when the family's German ancestry and ties to German chancellor Otto von Bismarck made them targets of anti-German sentiment. Prohibitionists piggybacked onto this, claiming beer's German origin proved it should be outlawed. New A-B president August Busch countered by removing anything that could pass as German from the brewery. He removed pictures and busts of Bismarck, and use of the German language was discouraged. On the beer label, the double eagle that resembled the Austrian coat of arms was altered to the logo seen today. August wrote checks to the Red Cross, invested heavily in Liberty Bonds, and offered manufacturing assistance for the war effort. Still, beer sales slumped. Across the nation the drinking of alcoholic beverages became vilified. Prohibition was dawning.

In their efforts to distance themselves from hard alcohol and the image of the passed-out drunk at the bar, Anheuser-Busch began to tie their product to healthy endeavors, to the outdoors, and to sport in general. "Budweiser is liquid bread," one advertisement claimed. "Nothing more, nothing less." Other ads read, "After the finish of a nerve-racking race—nothing is more quieting and soothing than a cool bottle of Budweiser" and "After a hard game of golf—Nothing revives the tired body so quickly as a cool bottle of refreshing Budweiser."

Similar ads included fishing, hiking, and, to signal things to come, simply watching a baseball game. "Baseball—The favorite sport of millions. It's hard to find an American who does not declare baseball to be the best of out-door sports." The ads gave A-B a temporary boost in sales.

Baseball fans in St. Louis packed Robison Field to watch the Cardinals or nearby Sportsman's Park to cheer on the Browns, many proudly drinking a beer that baseball fans all over the country were drinking in their home stadiums. The difference was this beer was made just a few miles away. Then beer sales stopped. Anheuser-Busch faced an impossible decision. The Busch family had plenty of money. They could close up shop for the time being, retreat to Grant's Farm, and ride out this new American experiment. But what of the employees and their families?

Imagine the fear that swept through St. Louis on the eve of Prohibition. Not only would the world be drier, but sixty-five hundred people worked for A-B or associated companies. Were they all out of a job? Nearby Lemp Brewery shuttered without notice. Employees showed up but the gates were locked. St. Louis lost forty thousand jobs in 1920 when twelve of the twenty breweries closed. Anheuser-Busch was not one of them. August Busch told his sons, "In my book Prohibition is a challenge and we owe it to our employees to keep going." If Anheuser-Busch hadn't already claimed the hearts and taste buds of St. Louisans before Prohibition, this act sealed the deal.

The company lost millions each year, and August suffered health problems as a result. Anheuser-Busch stayed afloat by selling a nonalcoholic version of Budweiser as well as a malt drink called Bevo. Barley malt syrup and baker's yeast sold well, likely to the growing number of homebrewers trying to skirt the law.

August Busch made it his life's mission to convince the US government to end Prohibition. He lobbied congressmen and wrote to presidents. In 1930 his *Open Letter to the American People* was effective in tying Prohibition's repeal to the economic recovery needed to pull the United States out of the Great Depression. Franklin D. Roosevelt echoed this argument in his campaign for the presidency in 1932, and Prohibition was officially repealed the following year.

To commemorate the occasion, August's sons Adolphus Busch III and Augustus A. "Gussie" Busch Jr.," gifted their father a six-horse Clydesdale hitch, a callback to when beer was delivered by draft horses in Germany. A second hitch was sent to New York for a grand show Gussie had planned in anticipation of Prohibition's repeal.

Two American breweries were ready to distribute on April 8, 1933. Members of the Griesedieck family had purchased the Falstaff name from the

Photo of Adolphus Busch III, August A. Busch, and August "Gussie" Busch Jr. with the first case of post-Prohibition repeal beer and an envelope addressed to the White House, 1933. (Courtesy of the Missouri Historical Society.)

shuttered Lemp Brewery to create Falstaff Brewing. They and Anheuser-Busch brewed their nonalcoholic beers differently from others at the time. Where others stopped the brewing process before the alcohol level surpassed legality, Falstaff and Anheuser-Busch completed their process and then used a special machine to remove the alcohol. This left both breweries with plenty of alcoholic beer ready to go on day one.

At the stroke of midnight, a brass band struck up a celebration tune outside the gates of Anheuser-Busch. All around town car horns honked and church bells sounded. Delivery trucks dropped off cases to relieved restaurateurs. It was Christmas in St. Louis, and Santa Claus was a beer-maker. Gussie Busch referenced a popular song in a radio address that day: "Happy Days Are Here Again!" Over thirty-five hundred barrels worth of beer left The Brewery. By late morning, it was all gone. In their post-Prohibition fervor, St. Louis had drunk the city dry again.

Falstaff sent cases to the governors of Missouri and Illinois. Anheuser-Busch flew cases to Washington, DC, bound for the White House, and to New Jersey, where the second Clydesdale hitch waited. Imagine the celebration as a team of massive horses pulled a wagon full of beer cases out of the Holland Tunnel onto Manhattan streets lined with cheering New Yorkers. The Empire State Building was their final destination, where former governor Al Smith broadcast the festivities live via radio. So popular were the Clydesdales that Anheuser-Busch continued their tour through East Coast cities, eventually reaching Washington, DC, where they reenacted the April 8th beer delivery to the White House. Onlookers and photographers commemorated the trot down the National Mall.

The Clydesdale hitch became an image associated with Anheuser-Busch. They later increased the number of horses from six to eight and added a Dalmatian next to the coachman. The Busch family converted a substantial section of Grant's Farm into stables and paddocks. And no opening day would be complete without the Clydesdales parade at Busch Stadium.

St. Louis was still in the grips of the Great Depression, but the powering up of the breweries meant more than just jobs returning. The success of Anheuser-Busch boosted civic pride. National advertisements conveying strength of company and country featured Budweiser cases on grand wagons pulled by powerful horses in varying places in the United States. There was a national celebration, and St. Louis was at the heart of it.

At the same time, baseball fans cheered on the Gashouse Gang, the name given to the rough-and-tumble St. Louis Cardinals of the '30s. Managed by Branch Rickey and featuring future Hall of Famers Joe "Ducky" Medwick and pitcher Dizzy Dean, the team won five National League pennants and three World Series titles between 1926 and 1934. "Cards" fans could finally celebrate, legally, with beer.

The celebratory spirit didn't reach into the depths of the Busch mansion in Grant's Farm, where August A. Busch suffered from several painful afflictions, including dropsy (edema) and gout. He had seen his company through its darkest days but couldn't endure his own. He shot himself in the abdomen less than a year after the repeal of Prohibition.

It is a grim testament to the pressures Prohibition put on these men that August Busch was the third St. Louis brewer to commit suicide. The owner of Union Brewery, Otto Stifel, and President William J. Lemp Sr. of the Lemp Brewing Company, both shot themselves near the beginning of Prohibition.

Adolphus Busch III, August's eldest son, took over as Anheuser-Busch president. His brother Gussie ran the brewing division. The relationship between the two was contentious at the best of times and downright adversarial at the worst. Gussie was a short-tempered, egotistical man who enjoyed the attention his family name brought him about town. His job during Prohibition was to keep the brewery pumping out nonalcoholic Budweiser and Bevo, both at a loss. Adolphus oversaw the profit centers of the company—namely, the yeast division. But after the repeal, Gussie found himself with the power and he ran the brewery as he saw fit.

Perhaps the most consequential result of Prohibition's repeal was the overhaul of beer distribution, resulting in a system of middlemen between beer makers and sellers. Breweries could no longer sell directly to the consumer and could not own any retail establishments. Many bootleggers at the time took advantage of their illegal networks to transition to legitimate distribution.

In a sign of what was to come from Gussie Busch, he turned what should have been a negative into a powerful tool for the company. He traveled the country to meet these new distributors, training them on how to properly handle his beer and how to sell it. He negotiated commissions that encouraged distributors to sell Budweiser ahead of other beers, rewards that grew to include lavish gifts and trips. Smaller breweries couldn't—and still can't—compete. The distributor system not only gave A-B a new arena to control but also provided an arm's-length separation, a form of deniability, from the street-level skirmishes in the coming beer wars.

Emerging from Prohibition, Anheuser-Busch held the top spot, but Pabst and Schlitz weren't too far behind. Climbing the ranks was St. Louis's Falstaff Brewery, who became the first brewer to have production facilities in multiple states, a practice that A-B soon followed. But despite the excitement of the early to mid-'30s, Americans weren't as quick to return to the taps as A-B would have liked. Whether it was from lingering temperance or from a populace grown accustomed to the sweeter beverages popular during Prohibition, sales of beer fell flat.

Though the economy was improving, fears of another downturn in the late '30s had Americans pinching their pennies again. The company's reaction was to devote their newspaper and magazine advertising efforts to assuaging economic fears, to restore confidence, to "sell America to Americans," as one A-B statement read.

From the days of Adolphus Busch, the men who ran Anheuser-Busch knew that tying their product to the national interest was good for business. A cynic might denounce such maneuvers as disingenuous, but by every account these men had just as much interest in the health of the nation and the city of St. Louis as they did in their own company. A-B's campaign was a success. The beer industry grew by 26 percent in 1938. Anheuser-Busch sales grew by 173 percent. Anheuser-Busch no longer worried about anti-German sentiment in the lead up to World War II. Budweiser was a distinctly American beer now. A half century of marketing had paid off.

With the outbreak of war came new challenges in the beer industry. Supply restrictions forced breweries to seek out substitutes for their brewing materials. Rice and corn shortages led to experiments with alternative adjuncts. America's lend-lease obligations to Great Britain included enough pork to incentivize corn farmers to focus on selling to pig farmers, leaving the brewing industry scraping for corn-ish ingredients, like barley grits, rye, wheat, and cassava.

It was a tough time to be a small brewery. Many chose to either postpone production until the end of the war or shut down completely. Anheuser-Busch, however, had the purchasing power and the government contracts to keep brewing Budweiser as they always had, providing hundreds of thousands of army-green cans to service members around the world. A-B employees purchased almost nine hundred thousand dollars' worth of war bonds, much of which paid for two B-17 Flying Fortresses, named Miss Budweiser and Buschwacker. In an era of wartime austerity, American beer sales increased by two-thirds. Beer ads pushed the idea that the act of drinking beer supported the troops.

The 1944 World Series featured not only two teams from the same city but the same field, Sportsman's Park in St. Louis. The American League St. Louis Browns squared off against the National League St. Louis Cardinals. The Browns had been at or near the bottom of the league for most of the past decade, but in 1944 most able-bodied Americans, including Major League Baseball (MLB) players, were fighting in World War II. Only players who had yet to be drafted or were 4F, unfit for military service, remained to play the game. A good number of the Browns' core players were 4F. On the Cardinals' side, a young Stan Musial, the 1942 Most Valuable Player, had yet to be drafted.

Dizzy Dean, former ace of the Cardinals' Gashouse Gang, called the radio play-by-play. Two previous World Series were played in a single ballpark, Upper Manhattan's Polo Grounds, in 1921 and 1922, when the New York Giants faced the New York Yankees. This didn't happen again until 2020, when the COVID-19 pandemic moved the series to Globe Life

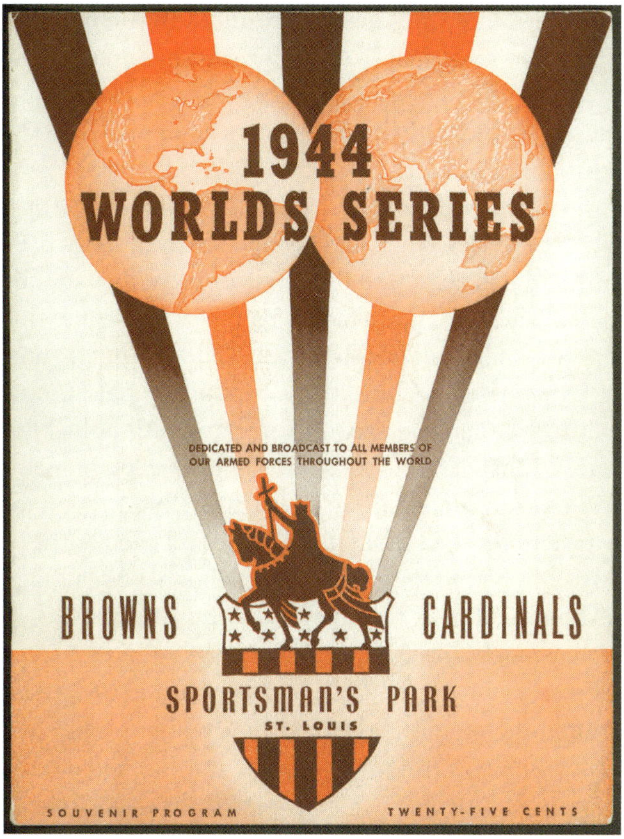


Souvenir program for the 1944 World Series between the St. Louis Cardinals and the St. Louis Browns. (Courtesy of the Missouri Historical Society.)

Field in Arlington, Texas. The Cardinals won the 1944 World Series in six games, and with the end of the war in sight, St. Louis was again celebrating.

Sixteen million Americans served in World War II, and the big three breweries of Anheuser-Busch, Pabst, and Schlitz made sure they had plenty of beer. The GIs who came home had a taste for beer now, and Americans were drinking it more than ever before. After the war, the United States sent several brewers to Europe during the reconstruction period to rebuild the German brewing industry. The group's unspoken purpose was to provide the American, French, and British occupying troops with beer.

One of the effects of the disruptions in the brewing industry from Prohibition to Depression to World War II was a break in the centuries-long chain of brewing masters and apprentices. A 1946 meeting of the Master

Brewers Association of the Americas resulted in the publication of the brewing guide *The Practical Brewer*, written by four St. Louis master brewers.

Gussie Busch served with distinction as a colonel in the US Army Ordnance Department. He returned to St. Louis as popular as ever, with many speculating he would run for mayor. But Gussie's focus was on A-B's ranking among US breweries. They had dropped to number two. Pabst Brewing Company and its Pabst Blue Ribbon beer were now number one. For more than fifty years, the Busch family had taken the "blue ribbon" name as a personal jab. The insult goes back to 1893, when judges at the World's Columbian Exposition in Chicago awarded Pabst beer the best beer in America. Budweiser came in second, infuriating Adolphus Busch. "Captain" Frederick Pabst, a Lake Michigan steamer captain, was so pleased with his win that he renamed his beer Pabst Blue Ribbon and sold his beers with an actual silk blue ribbon tied around each bottle. Eventually, the company switched to the printed blue ribbon we see today.

In 1946 Anheuser-Busch president Adolphus Busch III died of a cerebral hemorrhage, opening the door for Gussie's complete control of the company. His reign would see Anheuser-Busch, and the city of St. Louis, through dramatic changes and earn him the distinction of one of the greatest businessmen in American history. But first he had to return the company to prominence. By 1947, Anheuser-Busch had slipped to number four. Schlitz overtook Pabst as number one. Budweiser wasn't even the number one seller in St. Louis. That title went to Falstaff. It was a shame that Gussie Busch couldn't bear.

As part of Gussie's business plan, he painted a proverbial target on Milwaukee and their two big breweries, Schlitz and Pabst, both of whom had increased profits by cutting costs. Gussie banked on continuing to brew beer at the highest standards, as his family had done for three generations now, even if it cut into their profits. Where Schlitz and Pabst purchased and retrofitted existing brewing facilities on the East Coast, Gussie insisted on building new facilities to his standards.

The end of the war saw a massive jump in unemployment in St. Louis as the country transitioned out of wartime manufacturing. More than 75 percent of the city's manufacturing had been for defense work, including planes from the Curtiss-Wright aircraft company; ammunition from the US Cartridge Company; and TNT, chlorine gas, and sulfa from Monsanto. Emerson Electric was the world's largest manufacturer of airplane armament. St. Louis had connections to the Manhattan Project through several scientists, and uranium for the project was refined in St. Louis by the Mallinckrodt Chemical Company.

Some factories transitioned to peacetime production. Many closed. Over eighty thousand workers lost their jobs, forcing large numbers of transient workers to leave. Soldiers returning home used their money from the GI Bill to purchase houses in growing St. Louis County.

The population in the city in 1950 was 856,000. Not only did that fail to increase, but the number of people living in St. Louis city fell steeply over the next several decades. Americans were moving into suburbia, seeking out bigger, cheaper homes in quieter and cleaner neighborhoods.

Here is where the decision to separate the city from the county came back to haunt St. Louis. As the population began to shift westward, the city's tax income decreased just when that money was needed to transition St. Louis into the postwar economy. Where other cities were starting to feel the boom of the '50s, St. Louis was sliding backward. By now the city had reached the borders imposed by the 1876 separation, stopping any growth. It didn't have the tax money to grow upward.

Contributing to the population's westward flight was a long-troubled relationship between the city's white and Black residents. Earlier in the century, voters who were concerned about the wave of African Americans fleeing the South passed laws that limited the number of nonwhite residents in certain communities. St. Louisans voted overwhelmingly for segregation. When the US Supreme Court overturned the measures, St. Louisans began to add racially restrictive covenants to the deeds of properties, effectively segregating the city on a house-by-house basis.

The Black population before World War II was 13 percent, though that number doesn't include predominantly Black East St. Louis, just across the Mississippi River in Illinois. Due to wartime job demands, more African Americans moved into the city. Those who had served in the war expected better treatment when they returned, and now that they were a growing percentage of the workforce, they could demand better wages. St. Louisans elected their first Black alderman in 1943. In 1944 a Black sailor in uniform was refused service at a lunch counter, sparking a wave of sit-ins and protests. The growing civil rights movement in St. Louis included not just the Black population but white students and Catholic, Jewish, and Protestant leaders as well. St. Louis University enrolled its first Black students in the fall of 1944.

Times were changing, and many white St. Louisans were threatened by the direction of the change. Tensions boiled over in the summer of 1949 when city officials voted to integrate the city's pools and playgrounds. Fairgrounds Park pool was one of the biggest municipal pools in the country, located blocks from Sportsman's Park. In the stifling heat and humidity of the St. Louis summer, Black kids previously had to settle with just watching from outside the pool fence. On June 21 they could finally take the plunge. But an alarming number of white St. Louisans, many of them young men, couldn't stand the thought of Black kids sharing the pool with white children. A mob armed with baseball bats and bricks at first harassed and then attacked the Black swimmers. As word spread, the mob grew larger and more violent, chasing down and beating any Black person they could find. Twelve were hospitalized. The mayor of St. Louis responded by resegregating the city's pools.

One year later, the local chapter of the NAACP filed a suit to desegregate the pools once again based on the argument that anyone who contributes taxes to recreation facilities can use those facilities. They won the suit, and the pools were desegregated for good, a victory that served as a basis for the 1954 *Brown v. Board of Education* decision, which ended school segregation.

Racial equality was too much for many white St. Louisans. The '50s saw a significant demographic shift as the county grew with mostly white transplants. The city became more Black, but its overall numbers began to shrink. To be clear, county residents still considered themselves St. Louisans, and still took advantage of what living near a city had to offer, but no longer held any financial responsibility for it.

By most accounts, Gussie Busch was at least outwardly supportive of the St. Louis Black community. When he brought his new wife, Trudy, from Switzerland to St. Louis, she was reportedly uncomfortable by the number of Black people on the street. But to Gussie these were his people. Many had worked in The Brewery or in the many companies that supplied them. One quote in particular summed up Gussie Busch's worldview: "Hell, we sell beer to everyone."

When he bought the St. Louis Cardinals in 1953, Gussie was surprised to find the team all white. "Where are our Black players?" he said. "How can it be the great American game if Blacks can't play?" The next year, Tom Alston became the Cardinals' first Black player. Anheuser-Busch's foray into baseball may have had more to do with their rivalry with Milwaukee breweries than any love for the sport. Regardless, it was a public relations triumph that cemented the company as perhaps the most beloved in the city.

Neither the Browns nor the Cardinals played well in the early '50s, and the Browns left for Baltimore in 1953 to become the Orioles. Now rumors began to swirl that the Cardinals were up for sale as well. They had become the dominant team in town, with six World Series titles in the past twenty-seven years. Stan "The Man" Musial was not only one of the greatest players of his generation, but his kindness and modesty won over a generation of fans. He was, in the words of MLB commissioner Fred Frick, "baseball's perfect knight" and was a friend of Gussie Busch.

Gussie later admitted to not caring much about baseball at all. Stan Musial and Red Schoendienst may have sparked his interest in buying the club, but it was a rumor that an investment group was interested in moving the team to Milwaukee that convinced him. By purchasing the team, he could both help his city and deny his rivals. Milwaukee may have had the number one beer at this time with Schlitz, "The beer that made Milwaukee famous," but Gussie Busch was going to make sure they didn't have one of the best franchises in baseball as well. "If we do something in the public interest which is at the same time profitable to the company," Gussie once said, "then this is, indeed, very good business."

One move Anheuser-Busch made for the public interest was opening Grant's Farm to the public for free. There visitors could see the Clydesdales, tour an extensive zoo, and drink free beer. Over 24 million visitors have passed through the doors.

Gussie wanted to rename Sportsman's Park Budweiser Stadium, but Major League Baseball didn't take kindly to a stadium named after a beer. They settled on Busch Stadium, and in a move typical of the brash A-B president, Gussie debuted Busch Bavarian Beer, a beer named after a stadium.

The purchase of the Cardinals ushered in a golden age for sports in St. Louis and for Anheuser-Busch. In 1957 they became the top-selling brewery in the country, with over six million barrels produced, 7.1 percent of the industry. They never lost the top spot.

In a move that Gussie must have relished, the Milwaukee Hawks of the National Basketball Association (NBA) came to St. Louis in 1955 and promptly won a championship in 1958. They spent the next decade as a strong playoff team. Local boxer Sonny Liston fought his way up the ranks to multiple world titles. In 1960 the National Football League (NFL) Cardinals moved to St. Louis from Chicago. The '60s were a dominant decade for the baseball Cardinals, with three National League Pennants and two World Series behind Bob Gibson, Lou Brock, and Ken Boyer.

In 1964 Anheuser-Busch crossed the ten-million-barrel threshold. They were muscling smaller brewers out. Of the 700 breweries in America after Prohibition, only 125 made it to 1970. The Busch family was now royalty in St. Louis. To the average St. Louisan, drinking a Budweiser was a pretty easy way to pay the company back for what they had done for the city.

As the marketing of products led to the "golden age of advertising" of the '60s through the '80s, companies began to focus on their brands and a consistent message to consumers that crossed print, radio, and television media. In this way, Anheuser-Busch was ahead of the trends. Their messaging had been consistent for generations: Drinking Budweiser makes you more manly and more American. "Where there is life," one advertising campaign promised, "there is Bud." The ads show men meeting up at a bar to talk sports, among a crowd at the beach, or pouring a beer into the glass of their "best girl."

The advertising trend that A-B now adopted, though slowly, was the targeting of the young demographic through humor. Beer ads had been targeting middle-age men, but Madison Avenue was beginning to recognize the purchasing power of younger men. It was a sticky subject for Anheuser-Busch, as their oldest employees remembered the temperance movement that had led to Prohibition. Anheuser-Busch did not want to be accused of promoting underage drinking.

Over the next several decades, sales of Budweiser—and then Bud Light—skyrocketed due to clever and memorable ad campaigns that became part of the zeitgeist. Once they found their voice with the younger generation, they never lost it. Though Pabst and Miller made a run at Anheuser-Busch's number one spot in the '70s, marketing helped A-B leave the two far behind.

Fewer than one hundred American breweries remained when President Carter legalized home brewing in 1979. The Falstaff plant closed in the early '70s, leaving Anheuser-Busch as the only brewer left in St. Louis. Their domination was complete.

The city took a hit in the early '80s, when it lost forty-four thousand manufacturing jobs. The city population was down to 453,000, almost half its peak, and the county population had stabilized at just short of a million.

Anheuser-Busch was increasingly becoming a source of pride for the city in decline. St. Louis was a mecca for beer lovers in the Midwest and beyond; visits to the city often included a tour of the historic brewery, complete with tastings and souvenirs and Clydesdales, and then on to catch a Cardinals game at Busch Stadium. The Cardinals returned to dominance with a 1982 World Championship and National League Pennants in 1985 and 1987. In 1984 the Cardinals retired the number 85 in honor of Gussie Busch's eighty-fifth birthday. In 1986 Anheuser-Busch produced its billionth barrel. Happy times were here again.

The year 2000 was a high-water mark in St. Louis history. Though the city still felt the sting of Boeing's recent takeover of McDonnell Douglas, from which seven thousand lost their jobs, an announced expansion of the company's St. Louis production facilities breathed some hope. Trans World Airlines operated as many as 515 daily flights out of St. Louis Lambert International Airport. Thirty million travelers passed through the Gateway City, a massive increase since the establishment of St. Louis as a major air hub in the mid-'80s.

Anheuser-Busch wasn't the only local Fortune 500 company. St. Louis also had Monsanto, Ralston Purina, General Dynamics, and the May Department Stores Company. There was reason to be optimistic about the city's future, but it was sport that lifted St. Louis to new heights. The city and county had worked together—a rare thing in St. Louis—to build a stadium and convention center to lure an NFL team back, with the long-term goal of revitalizing downtown. Starting in 1995, fans packed the Trans World Dome to watch the St. Louis Rams, the first professional football team in the city since the football Cardinals had left for Arizona in 1987.

Several mediocre seasons did nothing to dampen the city's enthusiasm for their team, but a season-ending injury of quarterback Trent Green in the 1999 preseason seemingly quashed the hopes of a team that had just acquired star running back Marshall Faulk. In the unlikeliest of sports narratives, Kurt Warner, an unknown quarterback from a secondary football league, led the St. Louis Rams to a Super Bowl championship in one of the most electrifying seasons in NFL history. Throughout the city, fans packed the stadium, bars, and living rooms; drank Budweiser or Bud Light; and savored the fellowship as the world turned its attention to this flyover city, this former fur trading post at the confluence of the Missouri and Mississippi Rivers.

*The Sporting News* declared St. Louis the "Best Sports City" in the country. On the magazine's August 26, 2000, cover, framed by the Gateway Arch, stood Jim Edmonds of the Cardinals, who drew more fans than any other MLB team that year on their way to a National League Central title; Kurt Warner of the Rams, "The Greatest Show on Turf"; and Chris Pronger of the Blues, who won the Central Division title with the most wins of any team in the National Hockey League (NHL). The fact that the national publication was based in St. Louis didn't bother anyone. It was just reaffirming something locals already knew in their hearts: St. Louis was pretty great.

For a long minute this wasn't a city in decline. There was new optimism. In a uniquely St. Louis way, Anheuser-Busch tied it all together through the marriage of beer with sport. The seeds planted by A-B founder Adolphus Busch and his son August A. Busch connecting Budweiser to American nationalism and sport had borne fruit. In nearly every sight line or camera angle there was—behind the quarterback making the impossible throw, or the center fielder laying out for a highlight reel catch, or the goalie snatching a puck out of the air in slow motion—a Budweiser or Bud Light sign prominently displayed. If it were possible, Anheuser-Busch would have hung a Budweiser banner from the Gateway Arch. At the end of every Super Bowl Budweiser commercial—where Clydesdales run along a beach, where an acting dog cries on command at the memory of failing to catch a Budweiser delivery truck, or where friends "watching the game, having a Bud," greet each other with variations of "Whassup!"—are the words "Anheuser Busch, Inc. Budweiser Beer, St. Louis, MO."

There was a unity of message here that led to a unity of feeling among the locals. For St. Louisans, it was all wrapped up together: the greatness of their teams, their beer company, and their city. The first two could not be questioned, at least not in 2000. A-B had spent the previous two decades cementing its dominance, leaving former rivals too far behind to be considered rivals anymore. In 2000 they controlled 47.6 percent of the domestic market, more than double their closest competitor. While Budweiser had been declining in sales, Bud Light was picking up the slack. Two years later Bud Light overtook Budweiser as the top-selling beer in the country. A city's greatness is more difficult to qualify, but if the city itself was no longer at its peak, at least St. Louisans had their teams and their beer. What more do you need?

High points are difficult to recognize without the benefit of time and contrast, but locals had a pretty good idea in 2000 that things couldn't get much better. What they never expected was for things to go wrong so fast. Boeing's takeover of McDonnell Douglas was not an isolated event but rather the first of several corporate dominoes to fall in the city. American Airlines purchased TWA in early 2001, promising to retain Lambert as a reliever hub to Chicago and Dallas/Fort Worth, but the economic and travel disruption after the events of 9/11 caused American to rescind their promise. Twenty million passengers flew out of St. Louis in the following year, a number that continued to decline over the years. Though Southwest Airlines picked up some of the slack, the current number of 13.6 million travelers pales in comparison to the airport's heyday.

International conglomerate Nestlé purchased Ralston Purina. It is difficult to overstate the influence Ralston Purina had on St. Louis over the century of its existence. Similarities between Ralston Purina and Anheuser-Busch—and their founding families—are many. Purina founder William Danforth holds a spot near Adolphus Busch among the pantheon of revered businessmen in the history of St. Louis. Purina Farms, a visitor-friendly research farm west of the city, mirrored Grant's Farm.

The Danforth family provided the quiet and reasoned counterpoint to the at-times brash and showy Busch family. William Danforth had attended St. Louis's Washington University, and his grandson William was a medical faculty member and its thirteenth chancellor. The Danforth Campus is named after him and the Danforth family.

Though Ralston Purina owned the St. Louis Arena for only seven of its seventy years of existence, locals still refer to it as the "Checkerdome" after the company's checkerboard logo. St. Louisans do not let go of things easily.

While Nestlé kept their now renamed Nestlé Purina PetCare headquarters in St. Louis and made minimal changes to Purina Farms, the city did lose jobs. To the average St. Louisan, the merger didn't impact them much, but here was one more local company swallowed up and no longer their own.

May Department Stores Company sold to Federated in 2005. Though Macy's was once a prominent tenant in downtown St. Louis, the company's fortunes seemed to mirror the fortunes of the city itself. It had shrunk to a shadow of its former self. But here was one more company leaving. Even the Rams' days were numbered.

Then in 2008 the unthinkable happened. Even as Anheuser-Busch was outmaneuvered and then taken over by InBev, many in St. Louis were in denial that their brewery could ever be run by anyone not named Busch. For some, anger and resentment grew, leading to a short-lived boycott. Others shrugged and continued drinking Budweiser as they always had. No more did the cases of Bud or Bud Light show up at the family cookout. For those employees who survived the sale, such perks dried up. For those who lost their jobs, well, who wants such reminders?

Over the next several years, the craft beer scene in St. Louis swelled from a handful who predated the sale to over sixty today. Tap handles in bars and restaurants illustrated the slow change in the city. Where once draft beer selection was entirely Anheuser-Busch beer, bars began to offer one or two local craft beers. Over the years, A-B lost more bar top real estate to new and exciting craft offerings until only one or two A-B products remained on tap. In many bars and restaurants today, they are relegated to cans stored in a beer fridge.

All of this is not to say that A-B simply disappeared in the city of St. Louis. To those not paying attention, not much changed at all. The brewery was still there, as was the omnipresence of Anheuser-Busch products throughout the city. Busch Stadium, for now, remains Busch Stadium.

True to its name as the Gateway to the West, the arch acts as a jumping-off point for four highways, radiating like spokes away from the Mississippi River. Heading north and then west, Interstate 70 passes through North St. Louis on its way to Kansas City and beyond. Calvary and Bellefontaine cemeteries house the memories of Tennessee Williams and Kate Chopin, as well as those of the two men who began this story, Eberhard Anheuser and Adolphus Busch.

Interstate 55 passes south under the shadow of The Brewery, a monument to past glories still packed with daily tours, before following the river through Memphis onto New Orleans. Much of Interstate 44 from St. Louis southwest to Oklahoma City follows the original "Mother Road," Route 66. Just outside of the city proper is Grant's Farm, still operating as a combination nature preserve, zoo, and stables. Many of the commercials featuring the Clydesdales were filmed here. When its contract with AB InBev ran out in 2021, five members of the Busch family stepped in to keep the farm running as it always has.

The highway that passes through the city, known to the locals as "Highway Forty" (or, to those with a St. Louis accent, "Farty"), has technically been Interstate 64 for over thirty years. But for much of the city's collective memory, it was US Route 40, and so it remains. How one labels this stretch of road, as well as how one pronounces the various French-named roads and neighborhoods in St. Louis, indicates whether he or she is a local. Here's a hint: not French at all.

Over the years, as the population of St. Louis moved west, 40 became a cultural artery, and much of what defines the city today was built along it. A traveler from the east crosses the Mississippi on the Poplar Street Bridge, with the 630-foot-tall stainless steel Gateway Arch to the right, the tallest structure in the city. Near the base of the arch stands the Old Courthouse, almost two hundred years old, where slaves Dred and Harriet Scott successfully sued for their freedom in 1846.

Continuing on, travelers pass close enough to the newest Busch Stadium to catch a moment of the game. The honking of cars of passing fans adds to the noise of the crowd. Many are the St. Louis baseball fans who still call their team "The Baseball Cardinals" because once, two NFL teams ago, there existed "The Football Cardinals." St. Louisans do not let go of things easily.

At least a dozen railroad tracks run parallel to Highway 40 downtown, some of which cross under the highway to terminate in Union Station, a once-thriving transportation center for the city turned playground for young and old alike, complete with aquarium, soda fountain, bars, and restaurants. A glowing Ferris wheel turns slowly.

Along the south side of Highway 40, a massive illuminated eagle in red and yellow flaps its wings for passers-by. Framed within a giant "A," the eagle is perched above the word "Budweiser." Made of neon tubing and colored bulbs, the A&Eagle sign once graced Wilshire Boulevard in Los Angeles before relocating to downtown St. Louis in 1961. Here is the reminder. It feels like an old flame, this company still here in body, if not in spirit.

Budweiser represented something bigger than beer to locals. St. Louisans took personal pride in the success of their home brewery. If Anheuser-Busch could succeed where all other breweries had failed, if they could hold out against industry consolidation by megacorporations, if they could endure the hardships and come out on the other side unscathed—then maybe St. Louis as a whole could endure.

# SCHLAFLY

A new era of St. Louis brewing began with a party, a glowing oasis within blocks of darkness. December 26, 1991, was warm for St. Louis, but no one was tempted to go outside in this section of a downtown whose heyday had long passed. The streetlights didn't work. Three blocks north and west of Union Station, a crowd huddled within a brick building that had sat vacant for decades. An ornate sign over the arched door told of the building's long-ago occupants:

Photo of John S. Swift Company's building on the southwest corner of Twenty-First and Locust Streets, 1943. (Courtesy of the Missouri Historical Society.)

John S. Swift
Company
Planographers
Printers

Time had not been kind to the building at 2100 Locust Street. Squatters had squatted, graffiti artists had tagged, and entropy had set in. In 1976 the vacant Heyday Shoe Building across the street caught fire. As the building had lost its roof in a previous fire, its current structure acted as what one fire official called a "perfect flue." The resulting firestorm created its own wind, redirecting fire hose spray and blowing helmets off firefighters a block away. The fire chief estimated its power at five hundred times greater than a five-alarm fire. It took over two hundred firefighters and fifty-one trucks to contain the blaze, but the surrounding neighborhood was in ruins.

Photo of firefighters fighting blaze in a vacant warehouse on the corner of Twenty-First and Locust Streets, 1971. (Courtesy of the Missouri Historical Society.)

The Swift Building survived, its soot-stained facade and damaged roof showing the scars of the firestorm's embers. Hollywood found the building and its neighborhood sufficiently apocalyptic to stand in as a bombed-out area of New York in the 1981 Kurt Russell movie *Escape from New York*. For a decade longer, the neighborhood sat ignored, a blight to avoid. And then came a light in the dark.

It could have been a party at the end of the world. But the apocalypse, at least for this part of St. Louis, had already come. This celebration was a rebirth. A new brewery was opening in St. Louis: Schlafly. It was the unlikeliest of settings for a beer revival, among the dark and burned-out buildings of a former time. But these were the ashes from which a new beer culture rose.

It was the day after Christmas. Inside the Swift Building, instead of the scents of traditional spices and roasted chestnuts, the air smelled of pretzels and hops. In place of mulled wine, revelers held glasses of the first new beer brewed in St. Louis since 1934. Packed into a space a fraction of Schlafly's current footprint, the guests were a cross section of the city. Some had played a part in the new brewery's formation. Others would guide its future. There were politicians and lawyers and business leaders, hopefuls and skeptics and the just plain curious. Members of the press were on hand, for what better story than this upstart David appearing in

Goliath's hometown? The crowd could be divided into two groups. One celebrated what Schlafly was doing in the backyard of the biggest brewery in the world. Something new and exciting to drink to, and to drink. The other group thought they were crazy.

Perhaps they remembered that this had been tried before in nearby St. Charles. In 1967 Nicholas Van Dyke opened Van Dyke Brewery and ran it with a tongue-in-cheek humor, advertising that if people wanted two six-packs, they should make the second one Budweiser, as Van Dyke didn't want to run out of beer. A commercial suggested beer drinkers "take a case of VD home to your wife." One of Nicholas Van Dyke's brewing goals was to see his beer served at Busch Stadium, but it wasn't to be. The brewery failed to make a profit and closed after three years.

Was Schlafly another Van Dyke? Would they ever see their beer poured in Busch Stadium? Would they even make it more than three years? "It can't be done," a partygoer said aloud, not bothering to keep his voice down. "A microbrewery can't work in St. Louis."

Who were they kidding? They were going to brew beer in the shadow of the eagle? This was the place where Anheuser-Busch saved the beloved Cardinals. A good chunk of the population profited directly or indirectly from The Brewery. Clydesdales trotted down nearby streets in city parades. A single share of Anheuser-Busch stock was enough to secure a loan. This was momentous. This was madness. The skeptics may have outnumbered the hopefuls. Missouri was, after all, the "show-me" state, where once Missourians were skeptical until proof was presented before them.

Most, if not all, of the guests had been to a brewery before—The Brewery was 142 acres of kettles, mashers, a tasting room, a cannery, and a stable. Could this new little place even be called a brewery? Where were the tanks in the back? Surely there must be more of them. Schlafly was a little candy store. The Brewery was Willy Wonka's Chocolate Factory for adults. The whole endeavor was laughable, looked upon by some with a patronizing smile reserved for children who say they're going to fly a rocket ship to the moon.

Microbreweries had popped up in various regions of the United States. Some of them had found success, like California's Sierra Nevada Brewing Company and Boston Beer Company, but St. Louis, those at the party knew, was a whole different animal. What lunatic would have the audacity to open a brewery here of all places?

Tom Schlafly worked his way through the crowd, looking every bit like someone with his wits about him. If he was putting on an act, he was doing a good job. Born in St. Louis in 1948, Schlafly was a lawyer. Nothing about his life so far predicted his second act. Dressed in a suit with a plaid tie, he shook hands and clinked glasses with friends and strangers. By the end of the night, they were one and the same. They asked him where this idea came from.

"It began in London," he said. "I liked the pub beers they had. It kind of grew from there."

Did he consider himself a beer connoisseur? "Not particularly." What kind of beer did he drink in college? "Whatever was cheapest." The smile under his mustache grew.

Occasionally someone asked the big question: Could a small brewery survive in St. Louis? Tom shared a look with Charles Kopman, fellow lawyer and friend. Years before, Kopman was there when Schlafly had returned from a brief stint at Oxford University eager to talk not about law but about differences in English and American beer. "You should talk to my son, Dan," Kopman had told Schlafly back in 1983.

At the party, Dan Kopman approached the two lawyers. He was young and beaming, dressed in a striped shirt and tie. Perhaps there was a bit of forced confidence, but he had reason to be proud. Look at what they had accomplished in such a short time. Here were the founders, three native St. Louisans.

Beer, to Dan Kopman, was part of the St. Louis psyche. His grandfather was an Anglophile who encouraged Dan to go to Edinburgh for his junior year of college abroad. There, Dan found he was far more interested in beer than scotch and began to learn about the styles of beer that were popular in Great Britain. He caught the bug and brought back some recipes for his senior year at Ohio's Kenyon College, where he and classmate Stephen Hale started a homebrewing club.

Upon graduation in 1983, around the same time Tom Schlafly was learning about what the British called "real ales" at Oxford, Dan returned to England to work for Young's, a century-and-a-half-old brewery and pub in London. He started as a trainee brewer for six months and then interned six months with Scottish brewers in Edinburgh. Returning to Young's, he was offered a position both in production and as a salesman for a new endeavor for a British pub: packaging and selling beer to markets around the world, including the United States.

Light lagers had become so dominant in America that many beer drinkers thirsted for variation. Young's wanted to be that beer, and they sent Dan Kopman to make it happen.

Consider the time frame here and what was happening with the craft beer culture in the United States. By 1983, Sierra Nevada had opened in California but had yet to go national. Boston Beer Company and Bell's were still one and three years from opening. Charlie Papazian and the Association of Brewers (now known as the Brewers Association) had started the Great American Beer Festival only a year before.

Increasing demand for new flavors opened the United States market to British beers. Bass, once the largest brewery in the world in the nineteenth-century height of the British Empire, was perhaps the widest available alternative to light lagers in the early '80s. Guinness had fallen on hard times in the 1970s and began their rebound with a relaunched Guinness Extra Stout in 1981. Their timing proved to be precipitous, as the craft beer movement helped Guinness to regain its footing.

At this time, Coors was the first of the big brewers to recognize the growing craft beer movement when they purchased the Killian's name from Lett's, a shuttered Irish brewery. Their new Killian's Irish Red was both an attempt at breaking into the import market and, as evidenced by its inclusion at the first Great American Beer Festival, the growing craft beer market as well.

In his travels Kopman witnessed the groundswell of the craft beer movement. He made connections with the brewers at Anchor Brewing Company and Sierra Nevada. He knew the distributors. He was part of the nascent craft beer scene as brewpubs began to appear in cities across the country.

St. Louis was not one of those cities. Not even a hint. A microbrewery couldn't work in St. Louis. "A microbrewery can work in St. Louis," Dan Kopman had proclaimed at lunch with his father and Tom Schlafly in the mid-'80s. St. Louis wasn't a particularly successful market for Young's—a fact that surprised no one—but Dan made sure to include his hometown in his US trips to visit his friends and family. It was on these trips that the conversation between the three began, the spark of an idea.

"St. Louis is different from those other markets," Tom Schlafly argued. He didn't dismiss the idea—in fact, he was more than intrigued—but Schlafly was right: St. Louis was a different animal. How could anyone think of opening a new brewery in the beer capital of the world?

Over the course of numerous lunches, Dan convinced Tom that it could work, or perhaps they convinced each other, talking through the idea of what their brewery would become. They wouldn't compete with Anheuser-Busch. Budweiser was a light lager, like most other mass-produced beer. They would limit themselves to the other 99 percent of beer styles. A-B was a massive corporation that sold beer in almost every bar in America. Schlafly and Kopman's brewery would sell beer in one small taproom in downtown St. Louis. Who would ever consider such an operation competition?

"So is this a brewery or a restaurant?" To the partygoers this was something new and a bit confusing. "Yes," Tom Schlafly would say with a smile.

In the early craft beer movement there were two kinds of breweries: those who sold to consumers and those who sold to wholesalers. If brewers wanted to sell their beer anywhere off site, they had to sell to wholesalers, who would then distribute to bars, restaurants, and retail outlets. If they wanted to sell directly to consumers, those people would have to come to them. The best way to attract more people was to offer food. Microbrewery or brewpub? Bottles or burgers? Boulevard Brewing chose bottles. Schlafly chose burgers.

The creation of a pub culture in St. Louis was important to Dan Kopman. There were plenty of bars, but bars were places to go to drink and maybe watch a game. Pubs were comfortable places to sit and have a beer. It wasn't work and it wasn't home. America, Dan thought, needed a third place.

Where would they build their brewery? The obvious answer was to build it where people lived or where businesspeople could stop in for lunch or after work. Instead, they settled on a location where no one lived and few businesses existed. They chose a burned-out neighborhood in a forgotten corner of downtown St. Louis. They weren't just being quixotic. It was their first act of love for their native city, and it set the foundation for a culture of civic responsibility that continues to this day.

Tom Schlafly was forty-three in 1991 and had witnessed the steady decline of downtown St. Louis. Placing the new brewery somewhere it could do good for the city was important to him. The city was built on beer. Could beer play a part in its rebuild? If this experiment was going to work, Schlafly wanted it to help St. Louis along the way. Plus the building was really cheap.

Now that Tom Schlafly and Dan and Charles Kopman had a plan and a building they wanted to buy, it was time to find a bank whose managers believed in this project as much as they did. In St. Louis that proved difficult. Dan Kopman remembers their frustrations: "I wrote the business plan and my dad and Tom told me to go see this guy at Boatmen's Bank. I told him what we're going to do and it took ages. He finally came back and said no, that's the dumbest idea I've ever heard. You want to open a brewery in St. Louis? And buy this building?" Essentially Dan was laughed out of the room.

Tom, Charles, and Dan came back together to figure out their strategy and to discuss possible methods to come up with collateral. "My dad told me to call someone he knew at Commerce Bank," Dan Kopman says, "and if they needed collateral, we'll collateralize the loan with stock that Tom owned. I started with the original pitch: I have this business plan for a new brewery in St. Louis. It's myself and my dad and Tom Schlafly and we're buying this building and here's where it's going to be. This guy says we're not going to do that. So I said what if we collateralize the loan with stock? He said what stock? I tell him and the guy says, 'Give me five minutes.' A few minutes later, we have a three-hundred-thousand-dollar loan."

The stock? Anheuser-Busch. It was one part of the origin story that the three would keep to themselves that opening night.

So now they owned the Swift Building. One can imagine the three founders standing in their new place. The same people who believed that craft beer could succeed in St. Louis also thought this shell of a structure, where parts of the basement were illuminated by sunlight passing through holes three stories above, would be perfect for a brewpub. Time would prove them visionaries.

As work began to rehab the dilapidated building, Schlafly and the Kopmans considered what to name the beer. The vast majority of beers are named after their founders, including the big three of Anheuser-Busch, Miller, and Coors. Lemp, Pabst, Heineken, Guinness, and Yuengling fall into this category as well. Of the top ten producing breweries in 1980, all but one, Olympia Beer, was named after its founder. But craft beer was moving away from this trend. Samuel Adams was named after a historic figure/brewer but not the owner. Anchor Steam was named after the process. Sierra Nevada got its name from the stunning mountain region.

The name on Schlafly brewery's articles of incorporation from August 1989 is "The Saint Louis Brewery, Inc." It's hard not to see a swipe at Anheuser-Busch or hear a playful stress on the first word, like THE Ohio State University. Anheuser-Busch was THE Brewery and had been for many years. Schlafly had barely gotten started, and already they were making wordplay about competing with the world's largest brewery. It was an in-joke, a wink-wink, and a hint at the lighthearted Tom Schlafly.

For years the company's official name and location confused those who didn't know what Schlafly was, with some mistakenly treating Tom Schlafly like a dignitary of the world's largest beer company, as if he owned Anheuser-Busch. The truth was they had not yet decided on the name for the brewery when the articles of incorporation were drafted. Dan Kopman lobbied to name the beer Schlafly, not only to reflect that this was Tom's vision and investment but also to place the brewery within a tradition of St. Louis breweries named after their founders. It signified they put their name behind what they were making—they were proud of it. There was a direct line from Lemp to Anheuser-Busch to Griesedieck to Schlafly. It helped that "Schlafly" sounded somewhat German. The Schlaflys were of Swiss descent. Close enough.

The founders wanted to stay away from the perception that craft beer was designer beer, akin to fancy bottled waters. Instead of naming each beer a funny or clever new name, they simply named it what it was—pale ale or *hefeweizen* or coffee stout. It came across as more grounded, less snooty. In a town like St. Louis, that was important.

However, a more significant problem faced Schlafly: What they were trying to do was illegal in Missouri. As part of Prohibition's repeal, breweries were unable to own the establishment within which their beer was sold and consumed. By 1991 several states had passed or amended laws that allowed for brewpubs of various sizes, but Missouri was not one of them. Kansas City's Boulevard Brewing Company, the state's first craft brewery, had sold only to distributors since their opening in 1988. They did not, and could not, sell beer at their brewery. Nor, for that matter, could Anheuser-Busch.

Both Tom Schlafly's and Charles Kopman's law backgrounds came into play as they found what they thought was a legal workaround: Section 311.070 of the Missouri statute on alcoholic beverages stated, "A brewer . . . may have financial interest in the retail business for sale of intoxicating liquors at entertainment facilities owned by the brewer . . . including, but not limited to, arenas and stadiums used primarily for concerts, shows and sporting events of all kinds."

What if they opened their brewery as part of a concert hall or some other kind of entertainment venue? The Missouri Division of Liquor Control denied them such a license, as it did not fit their interpretation of the statute. In Tom Schlafly's back-and-forth with the division, he found no interpretation of the statute that would allow him, or anyone else, to open a brewery/entertainment venue. The statute seemed to exist to allow for two specific places: the Anheuser-Busch Soccer Park and Busch Stadium. It's hard not to see the fingerprints of the world's largest brewery all over the law—and the Missouri Division of Liquor Control's refusal to allow it to benefit anyone else.

Luckily for Schlafly, a group of Missouri homebrewers was at the same time working with the Missouri General Assembly to pass a bill that would allow for a microbrewery to brew up to twenty-five hundred barrels a year and to sell them on—and only on—its premises. They could not, however, sell to distributors. It was essentially the opposite of the law that Big Beer followed, as breweries like Anheuser-Busch could sell only through distributors.

Soon after Section 311.195 of the Missouri statute was established, The Saint Louis Brewery, Inc. held the first microbrewery license in Missouri. And here they were in the winter of 1991, after years of planning and work, pulling their beer from taps for others to enjoy. On the wall behind the bar was the original crest-shaped Schlafly logo of an ibex standing on a mountain with hops and barley poking out of the top of the crest.

People were drinking their beer. They were drinking a lot of their beer.

Schlafly paper coaster showing original logo, 1990s. (Courtesy of the Missouri Historical Society and The Saint Louis Brewery.)

Schlafly head brewer Dave Miller, between tours of the facilities, kept a keen eye on the reactions of the patrons. This may have been Schlafly beer—and early on it was a collaborative process with Dan Kopman and Stephen Hale—but as head brewer, the taste was ultimately Miller's responsibility. He was one of the homebrewers who had lobbied for the new law. A St. Louis native, the goateed Miller was among the pioneers of the homebrewing movement. He had brewed his first homebrew in 1975. With his "Best of Show" Dutch pilsner he won the title of Home Brewer of the Year by the American Homebrewers Association in 1981, the same year he published his first book, *Home Brewing for Americans*. He published *The Complete Handbook of Home Brewing* in 1988. In 1991 Dave Miller became Schlafly's first brewmaster.

The brewmaster job may have seemed destined to go to Dan Kopman. He was the only co-owner with any brewing experience, and his was extensive. Kopman's time at Young's in London as well as an internship with Scottish brewers in Edinburgh gave him more than enough experience to handle the fledgling Schlafly. But one result of spending time in Scotland in his young twenties was meeting and falling in love with a Scottish lass. Kopman married his girlfriend Sheena in Scotland two weeks after The Saint Louis Brewery purchased the Swift Building in early 1991. Tom Schlafly flew over to attend.

The work that Dan Kopman put into the brewery in the years leading up to the opening would ultimately be for other people to enjoy. By the time of the opening party, Sheena was pregnant, and the health insurance that came with a startup brewery in St. Louis, Missouri, couldn't compete with what they could get in Edinburgh. The young couple were together to celebrate Schlafly's opening, but their days in St. Louis were numbered.

Still, Dan wanted everything perfect for the brewery he would leave behind, so he worked to bring in the right people. Susan Katzman was a friend of the family and a St. Louis foodie and restaurant consultant. Her vision of food extended beyond the Midwest and even the country. The quality of the food you serve, she argued, reflects the quality of the beer you brew.

Katzman recommended Tom Flood to run the food program. Flood had previously worked for Schnucks, the local market chain, but in 1991 was working at a brewpub in California. Kopman convinced him to return to St. Louis.

What all these people at the party hoped, but couldn't tell just yet, was that Schlafly would be as much of a destination for its food as it would be for beer. They needn't have feared. Schlafly's white bean chili, sticky toffee pudding, fish and fries, and ploughman's plate all became St. Louis favorites.

The one person Dan Kopman really wanted for his new brewery was his college friend Stephen Hale. For Dan, all of this had begun with the two of them at Kenyon College in the early '80s. Hale had read Charlie Papazian's pamphlet on homebrewing in New York when he was only nineteen years old. The legal drinking age in New York at the time was eighteen, but in Ohio it was twenty-one. Though they were underage, Hale and Kopman brewed anyway.

Hale moved to New England after college and spent the next decade homebrewing, running a homebrew club called MALT—Maine Ale and Lager Tasters—and working jobs that fit his larger-than-life personality. He was a chimney sweep, complete with top hat and tails, though his Cockney accent left much to be desired. He spent four years jumping off a lobster boat in Maine winters diving for sea urchins for the sushi industry. Perhaps his most daring job was teaching English and Latin to eighth graders.

For much of the '80s, only the Boston Beer Company and the D. L. Geary Brewing Company in Maine represented New England craft beer. Hale worked a stint as a guest brewer at the brewpub Gritty McDuff's, which opened in Maine in the late '80s. Dan Kopman ran into Hale at a beer festival in 1989, where Hale was judging a homebrew competition. They talked of Kopman's plans to open a brewery in St. Louis, a place Hale had never visited.

Initially, Hale agreed to drive his truck to St. Louis for a couple of weeks, staying with Dan and Sheena. Tom Flood took Hale around town and introduced him to what Flood called "the cult of Anheuser-Busch," to "red roadies," or Budweisers and "blue roadies," or Bud Lights. Every bar seemed to have the same beers on tap. Variation was provided by the atmosphere, not the taste.

Stephen Hale wasn't going to stay long. He had a girlfriend back in Maine, so Kopman hired her at Schlafly with the hope of keeping Hale longer. Stephen Hale stayed for nearly thirty years because of a girl, but she was not the one he brought from Maine.

At the opening night party, Hale was pouring pints behind the bar and wishing everyone a happy St. Stephen's Day when a young Sara Choler walked in with her boyfriend and another friend and found seats at the bar. Whether it was the beer or Hale's charm, Sara Choler became a regular at Schlafly and then an employee as the first female brewer in Missouri—and the wife of Stephen Hale.

Behind Sara and her friends, brewmaster Dave Miller led another group around the bar and through the busy kitchen to the beer tanks. The brewhouse consisted of three fermenting tanks and a serving tank. One of the fermenting tanks was for their pale ale, the kind of beer that had hooked Tom Schlafly during his Oxford University stint. It was a balanced ale, lighter on the hops than other popular pale ales of the time. It was the kind of beer you enjoyed at a pub with your mates. Schlafly English Pale Ale was soon the gateway into craft beer for countless St. Louisans.

The second fermenting tank held an oatmeal stout. The third tank, through the magic of brewing, was making two beers. Hefeweizen, when filtered, becomes wheat beer. So they filtered half of the hefeweizen tank into the serving tank. The unfiltered half was kegged. Kegs were stored downstairs in the basement, but because the building had no elevator for them, the kegs had to be brought up by hand.

Any such venture would seem minuscule compared to those of Anheuser-Busch, but there was nothing small about what the Schlafly team had accomplished. They had hurdles behind them and before them, but they would worry about those tomorrow. Tonight was for celebrating.

Anheuser-Busch had a significant presence that night. President August Busch III was unable to attend, but brewmaster Phil Colombatto was unmistakable, sporting a bright red "Budweiser" jacket as he carefully inspected, smelled, and tasted each of Schlafly's beers from small taster glasses. Several other Anheuser-Busch brewers were in attendance as well, signaling the beginning of good relations between the two companies, at least at the brewing level. Brewers, no matter their company, are passionate about beer. Perhaps jealous of the variations of styles available to the craft brewers—and intrigued by their tiny operation—the Anheuser-Busch brewers questioned the Schlafly brewers about their process. Phil Colombatto was known to be encouraging of young brewers, and the future St. Louis craft beer culture would be heavily influenced by his protégés.

Here is where the past and future of the St. Louis beer culture hinged. They wouldn't know it for some time, but the people in that room would shape the next three decades and beyond. And not just the Schlafly people but also their guests, some of whom took inspiration from the endeavors of Tom Schlafly and Charles and Dan Kopman.

Tony and Fran Caradonna were two such people. They were as passionate about beer as anyone there, and Fran's laughter could be heard across the room. The first craft beer wave of the late '70s and early '80s may have passed unnoticed to most St. Louisans, but one South City bar showed what was to come. The Filling Station was perhaps the first "beer bar" in the area, with every beer that was available in St. Louis at that time, which meant Anheuser-Busch variations and deep cuts, like Classic Dark.

The Caradonnas brought the craft beer movement to St. Louis through their Signature Beer distribution company. The presence of a popular new brown ale called Pete's Wicked Ale was 100 percent their doing. The Caradonnas knew beer and knew what people thirsted for. They had an almost prophetic sense of what was coming.

Stores, the Caradonnas found, weren't quick to take on this new premium category of beers. The profits were better—craft beer drinkers had proven a willingness to pay more for craft beer—but there was always the question of loyalty to Anheuser-Busch. If a store freed up shelf space for new beers, would the store owners still receive the same perks from Anheuser-Busch? Would they still get neon signs and ornate displays? Would the distributors find ways to punish them? For someone on that food chain, there were trips on private jets on the line—it would be naive to think moving on to A-B turf in their hometown would be easy.

Here was the potential conflict, and the local press fed off of it: David versus Goliath. But David and Goliath were in a direct battle. In no way could anyone consider Schlafly a threat to Anheuser-Busch. Schlafly's output in their first year, around one thousand barrels, wouldn't come close to what Anheuser-Busch produced in a day. The fledgling brewery never presented itself as a rival to Anheuser-Busch, nor did The Brewery see Schlafly as anything other than a curiosity. Schlafly was a tiny brewery who served different styles of beer than A-B did and at numbers that would look like a rounding error to the beer Goliath.

Tom Schlafly wasn't there to slay Goliath, but he certainly didn't appear afraid of him. Schlafly stood on the bar and gave a speech that included reference to St. Louis native T. S. Eliot and invoked Sumerian gods. Welcome to the Schlafly Tap Room. Schlafly grinned and raised his glass.

His parents were there on opening night, his father clearly among the group who didn't think this would work. Daniel Schlafly had himself worked in the beverage business as president of Mountain Valley Water Company. He looked around at a building that, despite the renovations, was still in a terrible state. Over half of it was unusable. The neighborhood was abandoned. Restaurants, everyone knew, were terribly risky investments, even in crowded areas. And a brewery in St. Louis? "Limit your losses," he had told his son. "Don't throw good money after bad."

One man at the party, Joe Edwards, represented proof that something like the Schlafly brewpub could work. Edwards had been part of the revitalization of the Delmar Loop, a hip, multicultural area of nearby University City that featured food, music, and art. His Blueberry Hill restaurant became legendary with the help of over two hundred concerts by local Chuck Berry. Less than two years later, when distribution of Schlafly beer became legal, Blueberry Hill became the first restaurant in the area with a Schlafly tap.

A mainstay behind the Schlafly bar opening night and the decades to follow was Paul Jensen. Jensen, who worked for the A-B wholesaler in Texas, became a master at steering a craft beer skeptic toward something he or she would enjoy. How many people walked through the Schlafly doors having tasted only Budweiser products? How many fought, and often succumbed to, the baked-in habit of ordering a "Bud"? Paul talked to them about what flavors they liked and disliked, what they should try and what they should avoid. At this time, when Schlafly beer was available only over the bar, Paul was their salesman.

Tom Schlafly and Dan Kopman had turned an idea into a place to drink beer and be with friends. They converted a ruined building into a warm oasis in the dark. With only weeks to spare until their opening, they had begun to brew. There was no room for error; the beer needed to be good. And now here they were, raising glasses to a future that promised to have more variety, more flavor. "*Prost!*"

At the end of this December night in 1991, revelers spilled out into the quiet and dark street. If they could stand on this corner and look into the future, they would see a vibrant business district. To the east the whimsical City Museum would stretch above the revived Washington Avenue. Just a block to the south of the Schlafly Tap Room, the new CITYPARK soccer stadium would breathe life into a quiet downtown.

"We were believers," reflects Dan Kopman more than thirty years later. "And there were enough other believers that Twenty-First and Locust kind of became a magnet for the few people who believed in what we believed in. People might drink non-light lager beer, and people might believe that the city had a future."

It is not hyperbole to say that the decision to build their brewery at this particular spot helped to revitalize a sluggish downtown, just as Tom Schlafly and Dan Kopman hoped it would. A microbrewery *could* work in St. Louis.

Within weeks of their party, Schlafly ran out of beer. The demand was greater than their supply, a faint echo of fifty-eight years prior, when, on the morning of Prohibition's repeal, the city drank through its supply of beer. As Schlafly waited for their tanks to finish fermenting, Tom Schlafly and Stephen Hale picked up one hundred half barrels of beer from fellow Missouri craft brewery Boulevard. It was a good start. People wanted to drink their beer.

Fran Caradonna looks back on the early days as a succession of parties that melded together after thirty years. "Dan and Tom's goal was to make good beer and throw good parties. And if you talk to people who were here in the early days, the party was a way to get people to show up when they didn't know what a taproom was or where it was or what it meant."

"It was a blast," remembers Dan Kopman. Schlafly was figuring out their place in St. Louis. "We closed on Super Bowl Sunday—those were not our days. Those were every other bars' days. Then we started coming up with crazy events that were our events."

A month after their opening celebration, Sheena Kopman's parents visited from Scotland. Dan remembers his mother-in-law complaining about missing her local Burns Night celebration, a tradition celebrating Scottish poet Robert Burns. Dan jumped on the idea: "I thought, 'Here we go! We're going to have our own Burns Night.'" On January 25, 1992, and every January 25th thereafter, Scotland came to St. Louis. "We made Scotch ale, found a piper; Sheena made some sticky toffee pudding," Dan says. "It's still on the menu—it's the only menu item that's at all our locations. And we had a Burns Night. The customers who were there on that 25th of January in 1992 had no idea what was going on, but my mother-in-law was happy. Sheena stood on the bar that first year to read the poems."

After the Kopmans left for Scotland, Tom Schlafly continued the tradition, standing on the bar reading Burns poetry and some of his own. They made haggis, and Stephen Hale took such a liking to the kilts they wore that he often wore them on other nights as well.

Now came the wait, the calm after the storm. Was this experiment going to work? Would people come to the Tap Room on non-party days? The best answer came the following September, when Tom Schlafly threw a party to honor his father's eightieth birthday. Firmly in the skeptic column nine months earlier, Daniel Schlafly put his arm around his son and said, "Tom, this is really marvelous. I want to invest in it."

Early on, there was no reason for Anheuser-Busch higher-ups to act anything but supportive for this upstart brewery. After all, considering where Schlafly was located, and that it was dependent on consumers to go to there, it was reasonable to believe that it wouldn't last the year. But Schlafly did last the year, and it seemed as if the experiment was working—but only just. The restaurant was doing well. The brewery produced a thousand barrels in their first year but didn't see room for growth if they were selling their beer only over the bar. Tom Schlafly set out to change that with an amendment to the Missouri microbrewery law to raise the production limit from twenty-five hundred to sixty thousand barrels and to allow microbreweries to sell to wholesalers. It would be a game changer for Schlafly if they could get it passed.

Around the same time, Anheuser-Busch was pushing for a bill to allow alcohol sales on Sunday in Missouri. As it was, grocery store beer aisles were covered with a chained curtain on Sundays. Several state senators who supported small breweries attached Tom Schlafly's amendment to A-B's bill, a move that was sure to get it passed. The press smelled a story. Here was a bill clearly designed to help Anheuser-Busch, but this microbrewery barely large enough to merit notice wanted to use the bill to grow exponentially. The front page of the *St. Louis Post-Dispatch* featured the headline "Tiny Brewery May Come Up Against A-B."

An Anheuser-Busch lobbyist came out publicly against Schlafly's proposed barrel limit, claiming that 60,000 was an "inordinate" amount of beer. While the number did seem massive compared to Schlafly's then-current yearly production of 1,000, the number was taken from the federal definition of what constitutes a small brewery. To put that into perspective, Anheuser-Busch was producing 87 million barrels of beer a year. What followed was a back-and-forth flexing—both in public and behind closed doors—of Anheuser-Busch muscle. Someone convinced the senator who had introduced the original Sunday bill to attach an amendment to Schlafly's amendment, capping production at ten thousand barrels. As the largest and oldest brewery in St. Louis, Anheuser-Busch seemed to be dictating the operational limits of microbreweries. Publicly, Anheuser-Busch representatives expressed an openness to negotiate the production cap. They were beginning to look like bullies in the press. So Tom Schlafly began a conversation with A-B's liaison of government affairs, culminating in an agreement on a 17,500-barrel production cap.

Schlafly contacted sympathetic senators in Jefferson City to finalize the wording of their amendment to reflect the deal that he and Anheuser-Busch had reached. It wasn't a perfect solution for the small brewery, but as they were a long way away from 17,500 barrels a year, they would worry about what to do next if and when they reached that mark.

The bill allowing beer sales on Sunday passed in May of 1993, including the amendment that capped microbrewery production at ten thousand barrels a year.

Wait. What?

Those within the Schlafly Tap Room, the Anheuser-Busch brewery, and the state capitol in Jefferson City were all confused, or at least they appeared so outwardly. What happened to their deal?

At some point between the introduction of the microbrewery amendment and the passing of the Sunday beer sales bill into law, the production cap changed. The senators who proposed the Sunday beer sales bill said it wasn't them who had made the change. Anheuser-Busch claimed it wasn't them. The government affairs liaison expressed embarrassment over the appearance they had gone back on their deal. He was right; it wasn't a good look for them.

*The Wall Street Journal* ran a story with the headline "Battling a Goliath Remains as Daunting a Task as Ever." Anheuser-Busch executives interviewed in the story distanced themselves from the decision to change the production cap. The nearest to an explanation Schlafly received was that unnamed legislators took it upon themselves to cap production at 10,000, as they felt 17,500 was too much. Since we don't have a public record of why the legislators would do such a thing after a deal had been made, we can only guess at what occurred behind closed doors. Did someone at Anheuser-Busch ask them to do it? Did someone in Jefferson City think they were doing Anheuser-Busch a favor by limiting microbrewery growth?

Schlafly had entered into a feudal system as an outsider, and they were learning what that meant. Anheuser-Busch in St. Louis acted as a monarchy. For most, it was a benevolent king, funding various organizations and sports teams, donating water and supplies in emergencies. At the next level down were the wholesalers, who felt the profits of the company most immediately. They were highly motivated to continue the dominance of Budweiser and Bud Light. Wholesalers separated the company from anyone below: bar and restaurant owners, event organizers, and anyone else who sold their beer. Included at this level was anyone who benefited from the success of the company, including politicians. Some received direct contributions from Anheuser-Busch, while others saw the benefit of having the world's biggest beer company in their district, city, county, or state.

Everyone on the food chain was eligible for the largesse the king could bestow, including dinners, gifts, and lavish trips on jets. How could a microbrewery compete with that? In essence, Anheuser-Busch was several layers removed from the ground-level skirmishes that increased as the city's craft beer scene grew, giving the behemoth deniability, whether they were involved or not. The people at Schlafly couldn't see the amendment change as a loss, though. The production limit was still a long way off, and the most important part was they could now sell to wholesalers. For an operation as small as Schlafly, this was monumental.

For many in St. Louis, this was the first time they saw a beer on tap at a restaurant or bar that was not from Anheuser-Busch. Blueberry Hill in University City was the first, where a hard-to-miss new logo appeared among the A-B taps, with Cardwell's in Clayton and the Trainwreck Saloon in Brentwood close behind.

The craft beer conversation, once limited to the Schlafly Tap Room, was spreading to restaurant tables and bars, where some longtime light lager drinkers could try this newfangled thing and make a face of disgust while pushing it back across the bar with some choice words. But many more found something in the new beers that they liked. Still others weren't sure but were open enough to let the new flavors grow on them over time. That's all Dan Kopman, Dave Miller, and the other brewers at Schlafly were asking for: Just give us a chance.

Stephen Hale remembers a shift in Schlafly's relationship with Anheuser-Busch once Schlafly began distributing to restaurants and bars. From the beginning, Schlafly and Anheuser-Busch brewers had a collaborative relationship. Some Anheuser-Busch brewers had privately expressed jealousy at the freedoms the Schlafly brewers enjoyed.

Budweiser beer has a strict recipe and brewing process that ensures consistency of taste no matter if it is brewed in St. Louis or at any of A-B's other dozen breweries across the country. It is one of their greatest accomplishments and goes back to its founder's dedication to quality along every step of its brewing process. But it doesn't provide for much in the way of variation, and a brewer can feel like a cog in a machine.

Hale felt a kinship with the brewers at A-B: "We shared information. They helped us a lot on a professional level from brewer to brewer. When it came time to have a beer festival, we're picking each other's brains, we're having a great time. It's all about beer."

When Schlafly began distributing, they stepped into a battle they may not have been expecting. "Once we hired sales reps to go sell beer on the market," says Hale, "we heard from them, 'Ease up on the love fest, guys. We're trying to take their tap handles, get some shelf space. It's not as cozy love-y out there in the trenches.'"

The ability to distribute did not launch Schlafly into the stratosphere by any means; they were in no danger of reaching that ten-thousand-barrel limit. They were, however, profitable and were able to purchase a fourth fermenter and rehab the rest of their building at 2100 Locust Street in preparation for eventual expansion.

Head brewer Dave Miller left in 1994 to work for Blackstone Brewery in Nashville. Stephen Hale took over for a time as head brewer, returned to Maine to help open Casco Bay Brewery, and then came back to Schlafly to stay. Hale's kind and playful personality influenced the St. Louis craft beer culture as much as the beer he was brewing.

Now that they could distribute, Schlafly faced some tough questions. If they wanted to get their beer into people's homes, they needed to bottle it. But they faced two hurdles. One, they had no bottling plant, and, two, even if they did, such a production might push them too close to the ten-thousand-barrel limit. The solution was to pay someone else to brew their beer and then slap a Schlafly logo on it.

Contract brewing has a complicated history within the craft beer community. To purists, a beer brewed somewhere other than the original brewery, even if it was made to exact specifications, was not craft beer. But economic and legal realities forced small breweries like Schlafly to turn to contract breweries to expand. The contract brewery Schlafly chose was August Schell Brewing Company in New Ulm, Minnesota, the same brewery that made Pete's Wicked Ale.

The year 1996 became a turning point for craft beer, where the national community came together to answer the question of what did and didn't constitute a craft brewery. In an effort to phase out the term "microbrew," the Association of Brewers renamed their annual meeting that year the National Craft-Brewers Conference. It would take more than a decade for the phrase "craft beer" to overtake "microbrewery" in public discourse. Now the term "microbrewery" is rare.

At the conference, David Geary of Maine's D. L. Geary Brewing Company, spoke counter to prevailing trends in the craft beer culture. First, he gave a speech defending the consistency of Anheuser-Busch beer: "You would kill to have the consistent quality they have. You may not like the style, but it's not a bad beer." The crowd wasn't so sure. Geary followed this up with a defense of the contract brewing of Samuel Adams and Pete's Wicked Ale. The crowd was not with him.

Schlafly's first contract-brewed bottles hit the market later that year. Now that they needed a wholesaler to sell their beer, they turned to Tony and Fran Caradonna's Signature Beer company, but because Signature didn't yet have the manpower necessary for the Schlafly rollout, the Caradonnas recommended someone larger. Over the next year, thanks in part to sales of Pete's Wicked Ale, Signature grew enough to hire several new employees. Schlafly then switched over to them.

In October 1996, an NBC *Dateline* investigation broadcast a shocking truth into eight million homes: Many of the exotic and expensive craft beers aren't being made in a small brewery. They are contract brewed by big breweries far away. Reporter Chris Hansen peppered Boston Beer Company president Jim Koch with gotcha facts like "95 percent of all Sam Adams beer isn't brewed here—or near Boston, for that matter." Though the episode came out long before Hansen garnered fame with his series *To Catch a Predator*, his involvement makes it feel indecent in retrospect.

What followed was a nationwide slump in craft beer sales, known as the "Great Shakeout," lasting several years. From 1996 to 2000, nearly a third of all craft breweries in the United States closed. In 1999, for the first time, more craft breweries closed than opened. Had contract brewing tainted the industry as a whole, or was this an expected burst of the craft beer bubble?

As Schlafly was still a tiny brewery, the company didn't feel the slump as much as others did, but perhaps the "Great Shakeout" accounted for the slow growth of craft beer in general in the St. Louis area. Schlafly's contract-brewed bottles, emblazoned with a new, more streamlined Schlafly logo, were making their way into St. Louis homes. Their presence was growing.

Over the years, Busch Stadium had become an architectural beer ad. Tradition had merged with consumerism so fully that it was hard to tell where baseball ended and Budweiser began. Anheuser-Busch advertisements dotted the stadium at every sight line. Each opening day featured a parade of retired players in convertibles around the warning track, led by a hitch of Budweiser Clydesdales. In addition to the seventh-inning stretch, the Busch Stadium experience includes the eighth inning playing of "Here Comes the King" accompanied by video of Clydesdales pulling wagons with Budweiser crates. Spectators clap along to the polka beat. From the retired numbers mural in left field, Gussie Busch waves to his adoring and loyal Budweiser—I mean Cardinals—fans. Good luck trying to find a beer not made by Anheuser-Busch in Busch Stadium.

By 1997 two things had happened that very slightly opened that door. First, Anheuser-Busch sold the team in 1995 as part of a series of cost-cutting measures. The Cardinals—and MLB in general—had been losing money as a result of fan resentment over the recent baseball strike. Schlafly started a collection at the Tap Room to raise the $150 million to purchase the team, but the jar of coins and small bills on the bar fell short of the mark. The press came along for the fun ride.

The new team owners pulled up the artificial turf and replaced it with grass, hired new manager Tony LaRussa, and signed slugger Mark McGwire. Anheuser-Busch may have been too quick to dump the team; the Cardinals were soon the focus of the baseball world as McGwire battled Sammy Sosa in the chase to break the MLB home run record held by Yankee legend Roger Maris, a spectacle credited with saving baseball, their alleged steroid use notwithstanding.

The second thing that happened was Schlafly's success. By 1997 they were a known and respected local business, whose rise felt even more impressive within the Budweiser capital. If another beer was going to be poured in the stadium named after the world's biggest beer maker, it made sense that it was from St. Louis. It didn't hurt that Schlafly's beer was pretty good.

Tom Schlafly's dog Sparky, unintimidated by the banners of Clydesdales pulling wagons of Budweisers, pulled the first keg of Schlafly beer into Busch Stadium in a red Radio Flyer wagon.

Schlafly beer was now available in the cathedral that Gussie Busch built. Perhaps if you had a map of the stadium, and with some help from friendly ushers, you could find the two Schlafly taps.

Dan Kopman returned to the brewery he helped build in 1997 and as chief operating officer went to work on several projects that launched Schlafly into the next millennium. Kopman and Tom Schlafly worked to raise their barrel limit beyond ten thousand. Schlafly went back to the Missouri General Assembly asking them to consider a new bill. A representative from Anheuser-Busch expressed the company's resistance to the proposed bill, not due to the potential barrel limit but fearing legislators would attach amendments that would affect them. What if Schlafly were to apply for a winery license?

The wine industry, Dan Kopman explains, operates under laws that are different from those of other alcohol producers: "They could do anything. They could make wine, be their own wholesaler, be their own retailer—whatever they wanted. They had a really good setup." Wine fell under a special license that allowed wineries to make a product up to 22 percent alcohol by volume. There was no limit to the amount they could make. With Schlafly making cider, they could qualify. Once Tom Schlafly had assurances that the Division of Liquor Control would approve their new license, he withdrew his bill. Now unencumbered by a barrel limit, Schlafly could continue their growth.

It was finally time to remodel the north building of the Tap Room. Up until that point, they had use of only half of the historic Swift Building. They replaced the windows and repaired the roof. A blade sign went up at Twenty-First and Locust Streets.

The city of St. Louis declared September 17, 1998, the day of the official grand opening of the north building: "The Saint Louis Brewery, Inc. Day." Dignitaries, politicians, and clergy of three different religions attended, blessed the new space, and drank beer. The brewery marked the occasion every year in September with their annual Hop in the City Festival, held outside the Tap Room.

The 2001 Hop in the City showed just how important to St. Louis the brewery had become, as Schlafly played a part in the collective healing of its community. In 2001, in the wake of 9/11, the people at Schlafly made the difficult decision to go on and hold the festival as planned. After days of stunned confusion, it felt right to gather people together, to be a community. The festival wasn't important anymore. Being together was what counted. In this instance, beer was good for the soul.

Two thousand people attended a more subdued Hop in the City. Attendees were quieter and more patient in beer lines, perhaps with renewed awareness of the importance of being with other people again. You didn't have to know your neighbors to love them.

Tom Schlafly took the microphone and made some remarks about gratitude and freedom and then asked for a moment of silence. What followed was a prolonged silence not possible at a beer festival, a stillness that settled over the crowd and then the neighborhood. No whispered voices or clinking glasses. Bystanders walking the nearby sidewalks stopped and observed the silence. And then the cars on the street stopped as well. A bagpiper played "Amazing Grace," after which the cars drove, the pedestrians walked, the taps poured, and the conversations resumed, a return to a normal everyone had craved for the past six days.

Schlafly had become what Tom Schlafly and Dan Kopman had hoped, a place where people would come together and build a community. And the community was growing around it. Nearby Washington Avenue was becoming a downtown hot spot. Between the Tap Room on one end and the newly built dome for the St. Louis Rams on the other were new restaurants, bars, and hotels.

It was a slow process, Kopman recalls. "The Tap Room doesn't appear and Washington Avenue suddenly happens. It's another building this year, and another building the following year."

Something special was happening downtown, and Schlafly was part of it. The neighborhood and the brewery were growing. The next step was to bottle their own beer. They needed a new space.

In 2001 The Saint Louis Brewery Inc. paid off their ten-year note to Commerce Bank; the Anheuser-Busch stock Tom Schlafly had used for collateral was safe. Now full owners of the Swift Building on Twenty-First and Locust, Schlafly used it as collateral for the loan needed to build their next project, Schlafly Bottleworks. They chose an abandoned grocery store in the city of Maplewood, located in St. Louis County at the border of St. Louis city, a convenient location for residents of both. Maplewood at this time had some hip bars but also plenty of empty storefronts. Here was another neighborhood Schlafly could—and did—help revitalize.

Photo of a six-pack of Schlafly Pale Ale Expedition Reserve, commemorating the two-hundred-year anniversary of the Lewis and Clark Expedition, 2004. (Courtesy of the Missouri Historical Society and The Saint Louis Brewery.)

After buying the building and land for $1 million, they spent $6 million on the build-out. They took everything they learned about running a brewery and restaurant and supersized it. The restaurant was bigger and the bar was longer. The brewery space must have felt like heaven to Dan Kopman, Stephen Hale, and the other brewers at Schlafly. Two massive white fermenting tanks outside separated the restaurant from the brewery, with rows of aluminum fermenters and mashers visible through glass. In addition to the all-important bottling plant, the building also hosted a Brewseum, a space highlighting the history of St. Louis brewing. The result was a beautiful space for the growing number of craft beer drinkers in St. Louis to come together, another glowing oasis in a dark neighborhood. It wouldn't be long until Maplewood's main strip filled in with restaurants and retail shops.

For any doubters who still remained, the opening of Schlafly Bottleworks showed that a microbrewery could work in St. Louis. Schlafly was here to stay. Now that it was clear that Anheuser-Busch would have to coexist with this tiny, but growing, brewery, how would that affect their relationship going forward?

Tom Schlafly remembers when the two breweries' interests aligned, Anheuser-Busch could be quite helpful. "When I was preparing to write a letter to the newspaper in opposition to a proposed increase in the beer excise tax," he says, "Anheuser-Busch provided me with the data to make the case." In this and other cases, Schlafly's was the more sympathetic voice.

But not all was rosy between the two breweries. In 2002 Schlafly found themselves shut out of the St. Louis Art Fair after eight years. Held in the city of Clayton in St. Louis County, the art fair was an important event for Schlafly. One year Schlafly had sold sixty-six kegs in a single weekend. Abruptly and without explanation, Schlafly was told that their beer would no longer be sold at the fair. After some pressing, they learned that the fair was consolidating its vendors and reducing wholesalers. In St. Louis this was code for "Anheuser-Busch products only." The decision could not have been a financial one, as the fair profited more from the higher-priced Schlafly beer. Schlafly was getting muscled out.

Similarly, Schlafly was denied inclusion in the St. Louis Strassenfest, a German-style street festival near the Tap Room. Schlafly's German-style beers would seem the perfect pairing for spaetzle and schnitzel, but, alas, it was an Anheuser-Busch event.

For Schlafly, their exclusion from fairs stung. This was a perfect opportunity for them to be out in the community and to support artists or vendors. Craft beer went well with the festival vibe. So they created their own art fair, called Art Outside, held at the Bottleworks. They brought farmers' markets to them. They wanted to feature stouts, so they created the Schlafly Stout and Oyster Festival. "How do you sell more stout?" Dan Kopman asks. "You throw a festival. We had to make our own events to get people to come to us."

"Beer is living proof that God loves us and wants us to be happy." We are complex creatures who can believe Benjamin Franklin's quote is true while at the same time accepting that he never said it. At best it is a misquote, with the first word far more likely "wine." In any event, in 2006 Schlafly and Anheuser-Busch came together to honor Franklin on his three-hundredth birthday. The Anheuser-Busch brewers used the opportunity to act like craft brewers for a short time, as both breweries created their own versions of Poor Richard's Ale, based on Benjamin Franklin's original recipe.

In the Anheuser-Busch tasting room, brewers from both sides lifted their glasses and toasted each other. They agreed that their beers tasted alike. It was a moment of community between a 15-year-old brewery and one that was nearly 150. They were there to honor a founding father born three centuries before and to promote the very idea of beer, together.

# 3

# THE EARLY WAVE

Within the Gateway City, a new gate was opening. The next wave of craft brewers could not have been more diverse: A fourteen-year-old kid. A young man just out of veterinary school who realized he didn't want to be a veterinarian. And a couple who graduated from pouring to distributing to brewing beer.

Marc Gottfried moved to St. Louis from rural Connecticut as a teenager in the late '80s. His mother had taken a position as a microbiologist teaching at the University of Missouri, St. Louis. In getting to know their new town, they attended Cardinals games, visited St. Louis Centre, once the largest urban shopping mall in the country, and, fatefully, toured the Anheuser-Busch brewery.

The smell hits you as soon as you step out of the car, a potent mélange of barley, hops, and yeast. In brewing, malted grain is mixed with water and heated to activate enzymes that convert starch to sugar. The resulting liquid is called wort, which is then boiled. Hops add bitter flavor, and yeast begins the fermentation process of converting sugar to alcohol. Steam from the process spreads the smell from The Brewery throughout the nearby neighborhoods. To some it is off-putting, and many visitors hold their noses as they approach the entrance. To others it is bakery-like, moist and yeasty, like fresh bread on its way.

Young Marc Gottfried loved the smell immediately and found even more to love inside: tanks, fermenters, shavings of beechwood, and knowledgeable brewers excited to answer all his questions, like a movie where the scientists were the heroes.

Gottfried walked out of The Brewery that day with a mission: He wanted to brew beer. He wanted to brew beer with those guys. Perhaps it was his mother's scientific influence on him. Or maybe, at fourteen years old, he just really liked beer.

The first book Gottfried read on brewing was by Dave Miller, Schlafly's future brewmaster. Worm's Way, a homebrew supply shop, became Marc's second home. He could ride his bike to the Westport area and talk to the owner about brewing, after which Marc filled his backpack with his purchases and rode home. Gottfried was there so often, the two began a friendship. He started with ginger beer but quickly turned to the real thing. His first bottled beer is stamped with a "1" and currently sits on the shelf among his many brewing medals and awards. It was the start of something.

His mother tolerated Marc's hobby, as it was evident from the beginning that he was interested less in the creation of alcoholic beverages and more in the science behind it. This kid was producing chemical reactions in his home, turning starches into sugars, and sugars into alcohol. His early testers were either his parents' age or his own of-age friends, and they liked what Marc was brewing. Tolerance turned to support, and through a friend of the family, young Marc was invited in 1991 to take a private tour of the Anheuser-Busch brewery and to speak with the brewers within.

Head brewer Phil Colombatto, who later that year witnessed the advent of the St. Louis craft beer scene at the Schlafly grand opening, saw the potential in this young man and spent hours with Gottfried. He even let Marc sit in August Busch III's chair. "It was crazy stuff," Gottfried says three decades later. "You just don't get that. It really blew my mind."

At the end of the experience, Colombatto gave Gottfried a copy of *The Practical Brewer*, the book that the Master Brewers of St. Louis wrote in 1946, and signed it with the inscription, "Marc I hope your experiences in brewing will be as fulfilling for you as they have been for me." It was—and remains—one of Marc Gottfried's most prized possessions, displayed on the shelf among the medals and his first beer. Marc was now sixteen years old, and he was hooked.

Soon, Marc's knowledge and dedication convinced the owner of Worm's Way to give him a job, and potential homebrewers many years his senior began to pick his brain about techniques. Gottfried handwrote recipes for them. He sold them equipment. He taught classes. It didn't take long for customers to realize that the kid knew what he was talking about.

A homebrewer recruited young Marc to help build a new brewery in nearby Alton, Illinois. The man, Marc soon realized, knew extract brewing, which essentially skips the wort-making process through the use of premade malts, but had no concept of all-grain brewing. Nor did he seem to have any permits. Because Marc was paid under the table to brew in what seemed to be ketchup kettles, he did what was asked, which wouldn't have been a problem if Dan Kopman and Stephen Hale hadn't walked through the door. The Schlafly brewers had heard about a new brewery in the Alton area.

Gottfried remembers his embarrassment: "This brewery would have been the first to follow them. They were '91, this would have been '93 –'94. They heard about this place and came over to check it out." Kopman and Hale were not impressed. "Of course I'm trying to sound cool," Gottfried says. "I knew exactly who they were. I'm sure I looked like an idiot—still totally a kid." Marc drove to the potential brewery five or six times to earn some money brewing. The Alton brewery never opened.

Northwest of St. Louis along I-70 is the town of St. Charles, a growing community nestled between the Mississippi and Missouri Rivers. Considered part of the greater St. Louis metro area, St. Charles distinguishes itself from the other two hundred plus municipalities through its charm. Its quaint historic Main Street feels like much of what downtown St. Louis is not: small, clean, and quiet.

The city's rich history predates the Louisiana Purchase of 1803, which transferred the land from French-owned to American. Its location on the other side of the Missouri River from St. Louis made it a jumping-off point to frontier lands beyond what was considered civilization at the time. American pioneer Daniel Boone spent the last years of his life there. His sons continued to live in the area, and many placenames there call back to the Boone family. Boone's Lick Road, named after a salt spring, connected settlers moving westward to the Santa Fe, California, and Oregon Trails.

Meriwether Lewis and William Clark used St. Charles as a final meeting spot for their expedition to cross the newly acquired western expanse of the growing United States. President Thomas Jefferson had tasked Lewis, already an accomplished hunter and frontiersman, with providing an accurate accounting of the new land. Lewis recruited his good friend William Clark to join him. Their decision to begin in St. Charles was made easy by the westward progress made by Daniel Boone. Indeed, Jefferson knew

Boone personally from their Revolutionary War days. One expedition diary mentions passing the town within which Boone lived at the time, but there is no mention of stopping to meet the man. Perhaps Lewis and Clark thought Boone was too old, in his late sixties, to join them. Still, it feels like a missed opportunity in American history.

Lewis and Clark traveled west and north, encountering Native Americans—friendly and somewhat less friendly. Perhaps most fortuitous was meeting Sacagawea, a teenage member of the Shoshone tribe, who became their guide. Her knowledge of the land and Native American customs, as well as sources for food during the lean times, made the entire expedition possible.

A statue of Lewis and Clark with their dog was erected in St. Charles on the banks of the Missouri River in 2003. Seaman, a Newfoundland whose heavy coat proved perfect for the cold climates of the continental divide, saved the expedition on at least one occasion, when he scared off a threatening bull buffalo.

A diary entry from expedition member Joseph Whitehouse provides a description of St. Charles at the time:

> We shall waite here for Captain Lewis, who is to meet us from Saint Louis. Saint Charles is a Village settled by French Inhabitants. It is a handsome situation, laying on the North side of the River contains about 80 houses, built in the french fashion, and has a small Roman Catholic Chapel. Its Inhabitants are chiefly canadian french; who are chiefly concerned & employed by others Trading with the Indians who reside on the River Mesouri, and other Rivers that empty into it. The land adjoining it appear to be hilly, but the soil is good and fitting for Agriculture.

Those hills gave Saint Charles its first name, Les Petites Cotes, "the little hills." When German immigrants entered the region in the 1800s, the Minges family built a winery from roots carried all the way from the Alsace-Lorraine region to plant atop one of the little hills. They cavern-aged their wine barrels in natural caves carved out of limestone cliffs along the river. A little farther north of the Minges Winery and wine garden on Main Street stood a woolen mill powered by a large wheel. The mill served as a school for German children and as a Civil War prison. The building, as well as a descendant of the Minges family, will soon play a part in our story.

The year 1993 saw the worst flood in the St. Louis area in recent history. Thirty thousand square miles of flooding led to fifty deaths and over $12

Photo of Main Street, Saint Charles, early twentieth century. (Courtesy of the Missouri Historical Society.)

billion in damages. Water overtopped or destroyed levees up and down the Mississippi and Missouri Rivers, destroying houses and businesses and displacing tens of thousands. The fifty-two-foot-high St. Louis flood wall held with only two feet to spare. Communities came together with sandbagging efforts, the National Guard and Red Cross set up outposts, and Anheuser-Busch distributed cases of water. The rivers crested after three months of danger, and while some areas remained flooded for two hundred days, the water in St. Charles receded in three months.

From the banks of the Missouri just off St. Charles's Main Street stretches an old train line, now converted into the crushed limestone Katy Trail, named after MKT, the Missouri-Kansas-Texas Railroad. Today, walkers, bikers, and joggers give life to the trail. The great flood of '93 delayed the opening of the St. Charles section of the trail for several years.

The old woolen mill on Main Street housed a restaurant with the suddenly ironic name of Broadwaters, as three feet of floodwater destroyed much of its first floor. The restaurant never reopened, and soon the building was abandoned. A local man bought the building distressed and discounted and turned to local restaurateur Bob Kirkwood to fill the space after significant remodeling.

Kirkwood ran one of St. Charles's most successful restaurants, Lewis & Clark's. He and his business partners saw what Schlafly was doing in St. Louis and were excited about craft beer coming to the area. Main Street St. Charles seemed to them a perfect location for a new brewpub, and the old woolen mill the perfect building. But none of them knew anything about brewing.

Over in Springfield, Missouri, about two hundred miles away, John Witte was seriously reconsidering his life choices. After eight years of college and veterinary school, he was hired by a company that exploited its vets. Overworked and underpaid, Dr. Witte began to consider other professions. An idea grew that was almost too silly to voice: What if he could turn his homebrewing hobby into a career?

John Witte had started homebrewing around the same time he started veterinary school. His first batch came out of conversations he had at a homebrew shop, but he wasn't happy with the results. Then he read Charlie Papazian's book, *The Joy of Home Brewing*. Witte's confidence, and his knowledge of styles, grew from there. A small brewery in Springfield called the White River Brewing Company became his school, and head brewer Dave Lamb his mentor. It was Lamb who convinced Witte to move beyond extract brewing into all-grain brewing, a more involved process but one that allows for better control of the final result.

With a new start in mind, Witte's thoughts turned to St. Charles. The city was in the process of removing bollards on North Main Street after a failed attempt to turn the road into a pedestrian mall. Instead of increasing traffic to the area, the plan had hurt businesses, as empty storefronts attested. What if, Witte thought, he could turn one of those storefronts into a brewery? In a phone call that echoed Dan Kopman's efforts to finance Schlafly, Witte reached out to an uncle who was president of a St. Charles bank: "I was very naive. I called my uncle and pitched my idea—a little shotgun deal, a bar along one side with a couple bar tables, four tops, a small kitchen in back, a small brewery, just something a couple people could run. And there's crickets on the other end. He eventually said, 'I don't know of any properties; let me keep my ear open.'"

The open ear of John Witte's uncle heard that Bob Kirkwood was building a new brewery on Main Street and needed a brewer. Introductions led to conversations, and soon Witte was driving the three and a half hours from Springfield to St. Charles to talk through their visions. Witte impressed Kirkwood with a homebrewed brown ale but was honest about his lack of brewery training. Kirkwood offered to pay for Witte to attend a brewing program at the Siebel Institute of Technology in Chicago.

It was a generous gesture from someone Witte didn't know well, who had tried only one of Witte's beers. Why would this man take a risk on someone who was walking away from his previous career? "He said to me, 'John, even if you suck as a brewer, I'll find a job for you if you're this passionate about it.'" So Witte walked away from a veterinary career with a mountain of debt and a dream to brew beer.

The Siebel Institute rounded out John Witte's brewing education. He found he already had a strong foundation for brewing. Hygiene and sanitation, both beat into Witte's skull in veterinary medicine, accounted for 95 percent of brewing. He learned from professor emeritus Walter Swistowicz, a St. Louisan who had brewed for Griesedieck Brothers Brewery and was one of the brewers sent to Germany after World War II to rebuild the German beer industry. As Swistowicz only taught every two to three years, John Witte had the good fortune of lining up his time there with him. The man was a treasure trove of old-school brewing knowledge, influencing a new generation of young brewers.

The Siebel course included an internship at a Chicago brewpub, Goose Island Beer Company, opened in 1988. Back in 1994, long before Anheuser-Busch purchased a 49 percent stake in the brewery, Goose Island had one location, on Clybourn Avenue. Brewer Greg Hall, who was vocal about his hatred for A-B, took in four or five aspiring brewers every few months for some free labor. As they went off to brew across America, these brewers had the Siebel Institute and Goose Island Beer Company as shared experiences, a built-in network of peers. Schlafly brewer Stephen Hale had taken the course just before Witte.

Back in St. Charles, construction was under way on the new brewery. Witte worked at Lewis & Clark's during the construction and convinced Bob Kirkwood to offer a couple of craft beers there. If they were going to soon offer the community craft beer, he thought, let's get them used to it. They reached out to the people at Schlafly, and soon Tony and Fran

Caradonna's distributing company, Signature Beer, was bringing them kegs of Schlafly Pale Ale and other styles. Lewis & Clark's became one of Schlafly's biggest accounts.

For over a century, the Master Brewers Association of the Americas (MBAA) had been a place for brewers to meet as a community outside of the business dealings of their respective breweries. Knowledge was shared and bonds were formed. But the domination of Anheuser-Busch had forced all other St. Louis breweries out of business, and for fifteen years the MBAA looked a lot like an A-B brewers meeting. Then Schlafly opened. Dave Miller, Dan Kopman, and Stephen Hale represented the next generation of the MBAA, and John Witte was about to join them.

Trailhead Brewing Company, named for the beginning of the Lewis and Clark expedition, was ambitious from the start. Trailhead was thirteen thousand square feet, including three floors of bars, a brewery, and a restaurant. The main floor featured a large, square bar and two outside patios. It was massive for an upstart brewery, but Kirkwood was doing so well with Lewis & Clark's that he was confident Trailhead would work. He was right. They opened in June 1995, and the restaurant was packed from the beginning.

When Witte's mother came to visit him at the brewery, and they walked down what he called the "nave" of tanks—eight fermenters leading to the brewhouse section, all mirror-polished stainless steel visible from the dining room—she said to him, "Now I get it, it's the chemistry set you always wanted as a kid." There was something poetic about John Witte brewing beer on Main Street St. Charles. Those Germans who over a century before came there to build the Minges Winery were Witte's great-great-great grandparents.

Trailhead started with three beers: a blonde, a red, and a porter. Later, Witte added a brown, a raspberry, and the first pumpkin beer in St. Louis, a town that would come to be known for the style thanks to Trailhead's trailblazing. Also available in bottles were Anheuser-Busch products. To Kirkwood, serving Budweiser and Bud Light was just good business. Before the casino opened down the street, Lewis & Clark's sold more A-B products than anyone else in St. Charles. He couldn't expect everyone who was coming to eat at Trailhead to enjoy craft beer, so he offered both. And they sold a lot of both. The brewery was running at near-full capacity, and distributor deliveries were constant. Trailhead passed Lewis & Clark's in A-B sales.

A year after Trailhead opened, Witte and Kirkwood considered the idea of offering Trailhead beer at Lewis & Clark's. The problem was, due to Missouri's alcohol distribution laws, they couldn't just wheel kegs down the street. So they called up Tony and Fran Caradonna and hired them to "distribute" Trailhead beer eight blocks away. The Caradonnas kept the arrangement on the down low, as Witte and Kirkwood were only interested in the beer being available at the two locations. Out went the Schlafly taps to make room for the Trailhead taps. At the next Master Brewer's meeting, the Schlafly brewers let Witte know how disappointed they were with the change. Lewis & Clark's was a big account for Schlafly to lose.

Anheuser-Busch head August Busch III lived in St. Charles County. His wife, Virginia, ran a law office a block away from Trailhead and visited the restaurant at least once a week. As a favor, Witte occasionally delivered food to her, usually fish and chips, when work kept her in her office late. On the occasion of August III's birthday, Virginia set up a dinner for six in the Trailhead restaurant, and Witte made sure to seat them in the section of the dining room looking into the brewery. Witte, all of twenty-nine years old at the time, was busy brewing when the head of the biggest brewery in the world stood at his doors in khakis and a red polo.

"Can I come in the brewery?" It was probably the first brewery August Busch the Third had to ask permission to enter. Witte introduced himself and invited "The Third" in. "He immediately fired off eight or ten specific questions about production and grain handling," Witte recalls. Witte thought he answered the questions well. "He asked if we distribute, and I said no, we're just focused on this restaurant. He said, 'OK, let's drink some beer,' and then he walked back to his table."

The Third's party ordered flights, which came on preprinted place mats with descriptions of each beer. Witte watched them from the brewery without appearing too obvious. August III looked down the row of taster glasses and immediately pushed the raspberry ale away from him. Then he pulled out a small voice recorder and gave his analysis after each tasting. He and his guests discussed what they tasted, nodding and pointing and otherwise frustrating Witte that he was on the other side of the glass and couldn't overhear what they were saying.

Afterward, Busch returned and gave Witte the thumbs-up. "Really good beer," he said, and Witte could not have been more pleased—that is, until Trailhead received a letter a week later from Anheuser-Busch thanking them for the great meal and asking to discuss the possibility of

Anheuser-Busch purchasing their recipes. John Witte was about to step into the big leagues.

What followed was a collaboration between Trailhead and Anheuser-Busch that opened the doors of both breweries to each other. Witte now had access to not only the best and brightest minds at Anheuser-Busch, people who would become mentors and friends, but also the Anheuser-Busch Research Pilot Brewery and their testing labs, where he could take his own beers in to have them analyzed for their exact alcohol content, bitterness, and bacteria.

The blonde ale that August III tasted at Trailhead became a new Anheuser-Busch offering, Catalina Blonde. For this and Trailhead's other recipes, Anheuser-Busch paid thirty thousand dollars. "If we didn't offer A-B beer, and if we weren't the biggest account in St. Charles County," Witte says, "I don't think these things would have happened. It opened the door to all these new relationships with people at A-B."

One of Witte's new connections was Doug Muhleman, resident brewmaster and eventual vice president of brewing operations. When Witte took on an exchange student from Germany, Muhleman opened the Anheuser-Busch brewery to them, showing off parts of the complex not on the regular tour. Using old catacombs and underground tunnels, they walked from block to block without going aboveground. After the tour, Witte and his guest got a look into an Anheuser-Busch ritual rarely seen by those outside the company: the taste tests. Witte describes what happened:

> They brought in a case of Budweiser from each of the twelve plants—they had been overnighted, just off the packaging line. One-day-old Budweiser. The beers were lettered or numbered. Only the moderator knows which one is which. They get quiet, they taste, they write down their notes, and then discuss one by one. Doug Muhleman was the moderator. I remember the fourth or fifth beer everyone around the table was agreeing that there was some oxidation in it. You and I would not taste any difference. They're so hyperfocused on what it should taste like that when it's off, they can tell. Doug was looking for trends. He looked back at the trends and saw that the Ohio one was showing an oxidation trend. He picks up the phone and says get me so-and-so on the phone. "We're testing right now and we've got oxidation creeping up." Our taste buds are more sensitive than some chemical analysis. We can taste differences in parts per billion that machines can't. I was blown away at how intentional and how serious they were to make sure their product was the best it could be when it leaves the doors—the consistency.

The only room they could not enter was the yeast production facility. All the lager yeast was in the library there, grown from a single cell. Once a week they ship out yeast in a concentrated half barrel to each of the twelve plants. The facility is so important to Anheuser-Busch operations that the door is biometrically sealed, with only a handful of people cleared to enter it.

John Witte brewed beer six days a week for Trailhead until 2003, when his divorce and raising his son, August, forced him to leave brewing altogether to seek out a career with more flexible hours.

Only months after Trailhead became the second craft brewery in the region, Morgan Street Brewery opened in St. Louis on Laclede's Landing, a historic district of brick sidewalks and cobblestone streets overlooking the Mississippi, just north of the Gateway Arch. The architecture of "the Landing" is a snapshot of eighteenth- and nineteenth-century St. Louis. Many of its buildings saw downtown riverfront industry rise and fall over two hundred years, until a city ordinance in the 1960s turned the area into an entertainment destination, complete with restaurants, bars, and the legendary music club Mississippi Nights.

Steve and Vicki Owings teamed up with brothers Dennis and Randy Harper, co-owners of the local favorite Harpo's restaurants, to convert historic buildings into a restaurant and brewery. As it was on the corner of Morgan and North Second Streets, they named it Morgan Street Brewery.

Indulge a bit of street history. Just as steamships began to roll along the river, the city of St. Louis passed a street-naming ordinance in 1826 to name streets that ran east and west after trees. This rapidly growing area of waterfront industry featured Oak, Cherry, Hickory, Pear, and Willow Streets. As the city extended west, so did the streets. Most of the tree streets were renamed over the years, with only Olive, Pine, Chestnut, Walnut, Poplar, Spruce, and Locust surviving to this day.

Oak Street was renamed Morgan Street in 1842 after Revolutionary War hero Daniel Morgan. Unfortunately, due to its position near the water, its high traffic of steamer crews and prostitutes, and a high concentration of saloons, Morgan Street came to be synonymous with lawlessness. Nineteenth-century St. Louisans doubted the local police even had control of the area. The city courts saw more cases from riverfront Morgan Street than from any other area of the city. When the western portion of Morgan Street was widened, no one objected to renaming it Delmar, after two early

Postcard showing the St. Louis riverfront from the perspective of Lucas Place, 1854. (Courtesy of the Missouri Historical Society.)

settlers from Delaware and Maryland living on opposite sides of the road. The name Morgan Street Brewery carried a rich and seedy history that would have given it a cool mystique if those at the turn of the millennium had known its history.

Nineteen-year-old Marc Gottfried, the underage brewer working in the homebrew shop, didn't know any of that. He did know enough about brewing to impress Steve and Vicki Owings. They gave him a part-time job at Morgan Street as an assistant brewer, helping to brew beer he couldn't legally drink.

The design of the space was perhaps more ambitious than Trailhead's but, as it turned out, perfect for that part of downtown St. Louis. Essentially two buildings of brick and wood and creaky floors, Morgan Street featured a restaurant with a chef from the Culinary Institute of America, a banquet center, bars on each floor, and multiple dance floors, including a rooftop patio. It was much too large for a fledgling brewery, but the owners knew Laclede's Landing could get busy on the weekends, and they wanted to be ready for it.

Weekdays were a mostly quiet mix of people stopping by to check out the new local brewery and tourists coming in for a bite. Weekends were completely different. Whatever the founders' original intention for the brewery, it's unlikely they envisioned what it would become: the top nightlife spot in St. Louis. "It was like Dr. Jekyll and Mr. Hyde," Gottfried recalls. "During the day it was business people, tourists, sporting events, conventions. We had the Dome [at America's Center] right there so all the convention-goers. You'd have forty thousand Baptists, then you'd have some tennis association. It was these waves of different groups. When the sun went down, we were a badass nightclub that would serve thousands. It was an effort to get from one side of the building to the other." Marc Gottfried was at the center of the St. Louis party scene.

Local weekly *The Riverfront Times* described the party:

> Morgan Street Brewery isn't so much a dance club as it is a dance compound, with changing vibes, beats and bars around every corner. The lower level's nothing special, but things start to change once you climb the stairs. At the top there's a sparse bar with down-tempo music that seems geared to grown-ups. Cruise through that room and you've hit a lush rooftop patio, open to all the fabulously muggy air and noise that flows near our dirty stretch of the Big Muddy. This patio serves as a connection to yet another building equipped with two levels of dark dance club, complete with gut-bouncing bass and seizure-inducing lights.

With the recent arrival of the Rams, downtown was coming alive for the first time in decades. Schlafly and Morgan Street anchored either end of a growing entertainment corridor.

Two years into Gottfried's time there, Enterprise Rent-a-Car rented out all of Morgan Street for a company party. The brewery ran out of beer early in the night, sending owner Steve Owings scrambling to find out why. As the head brewer was missing that day, Owings cornered Gottfried for an explanation. "I said I was the assistant," Gottfried says. "This other guy just wasn't spending a lot of time at Morgan Street, and I was doing a lot of the stuff. I said, 'Look, all these tanks are empty. I don't know what to tell you.'"

Owings asked him, "Can you run this place?"

"Yes."

"He's fired. You're hired. You're brewmaster."

This kid had convinced his mother to let him brew beer at fourteen, had impressed a homebrew supply store owner enough to hire him at sixteen, and at nineteen knew enough about beer to assist the head brewer at newly opened Morgan Street Brewery. Now twenty-one, he was a brewmaster.

Photo of Morgan Street Brewery owner Steve Owings (standing) and head brewer Marc Gottfried (sitting), late 1990s. (Courtesy of Marc Gottfried.)

Anheuser-Busch head brewer Phil Colombatto had advised Gottfried to go to college to pursue his passion for brewing, to focus on organic chemistry. But Gottfried had proved to be more of a hands-on learner, both at the homebrew shop and Morgan Street. As a new member of the Master Brewers Association, he took advantage of a short course they offered. Now the brewer for one of the three craft breweries in St. Louis, Marc developed friendships with the brewers from Schlafly as well as Trailhead's John Witte.

Morgan Street was unique among the craft breweries in that, in a time when pale ales and IPAs were beginning to dominate the category, Gottfried brewed only lagers. Because of the difference in brewing methods, where ales are brewed with top-fermenting yeast at warm temperatures while lager yeast is bottom-fermenting at colder temperatures, breweries often have to choose which to brew. Ale yeast imparts more flavor into the process, but lager yeast allows for a crisper and cleaner finish. Though Schlafly and Trailhead brewed almost entirely ales and Morgan Street brewed only lagers, they were skilled enough to brew ales that tasted like lagers, and Marc Gottfried at Morgan Street could brew lagers that tasted like ales.

Photo of Morgan Street Brewery head brewer Marc Gottfried (sitting) and assistant brewer Christopher Shea (standing) after winning gold at the 2010 World Beer Cup, 2010. (Courtesy of Marc Gottfried.)

Gottfried became one of the most decorated brewers in St. Louis, winning gold medals at Great American Beer Festivals, US Open Beer Championships, and World Beer Cups. His Golden Pilsner, Honey Wheat Lager, and a *helles* style called When Helles Freezes Over all have earned Gottfried medals.

As Gottfried's involvement with the Master Brewers Association increased over the years, he became president of the St. Louis district. Phil Colombatto came to Gottfried's inauguration and gifted him the same book, *The Practical Brewer*, as he had given him before—this time a first edition. Marc holds that gift in higher regard than any of his medals.

All through his career as brewer, Gottfried maintained a positive relationship with Anheuser-Busch. Like John Witte, Gottfried was invited and encouraged to use the Anheuser-Busch labs and to seek out the advice of A-B brewers. "Those guys and gals supported me," he says, "and at any given point I could pick up the phone and talk to the resident engineer at Anheuser-Busch. I could take beer over there and they could test it for whatever. 'Hey, Marc! What's going on?' And I'd walk right into the Research Pilot Brewery. 'Not much, how's it going? Hey, could you check this out for me?'"

The A-B brewers' fondness for this kid was certainly genuine, but it didn't hurt that Morgan Street had become one of A-B's top accounts. Morgan Street Brewery sold an astronomical amount of beer. Most of it wasn't theirs. They were A-B's number one local account outside of the sports stadiums. They sold so much Bud and Bud Light that Anheuser-Busch created a special twenty-two-ounce bottle just for Morgan Street, which came in handy when its weekend crowds made getting back and forth to the bar difficult.

Those dancing through seizure-inducing lights, for the most part, weren't interested in craft beer. Many didn't even know Morgan Street brewed beer—they figured it had been named for a historic brewery long closed. And that was just fine for Gottfried, who brewed for those on the first floor who wanted to try something different.

For a time, Morgan Street Brewery represented the transitional period from St. Louis as an Anheuser-Busch town to a craft beer town. Both lived in perfect harmony under one roof, and the overwhelming numbers of one didn't detract from the enjoyment of the other.

The fourth brewery in town, O'Fallon, had its roots in a South City bar and a couple who were prophetic in their understanding of what was next in beer drinking trends. Tony and Fran Caradonna were there for Schlafly's opening night and were there with them when distribution forced Schlafly to build their own bottling facility. Fran Caradonna is herself a thread that weaves through the rich story of St. Louis craft beer history, all the way to today.

Tony Caradonna's story is much like Marc Gottfried's. Enamored with beer after tours at the Anheuser-Busch brewery as a teenager, Tony became a tour guide there after graduation. Tony opened a bar on South Kingshighway, The Filling Station, which offered more variety than any other bar in St. Louis. Before the coastal craft beers dared to distribute in St. Louis, the variety came from within Anheuser-Busch. If A-B tried something new, The Filling Station had it. If there was a little-known line of Anheuser-Busch beer, The Filling Station served it. Tony highlighted the differences in the taste of the various beers through blind tasting competitions, with the champions' names on the wall.

Fran's connection to beer began in college in South Carolina. "There was this beer called Natural," she says. "It was 1977 and I was a nature girl—we were kind of the late end of the hippies—and that beer appealed to me for that reason, without really understanding it."

She moved to St. Louis, married Tony, and the two began their beer journey together. There were people like them, they knew—people who were looking for something different. And different was coming—first the imports, then the coastal craft beers of Sierra Nevada and Sam Adams, and then the trend moved inland with New Belgium and Boulevard Brewing companies. Exciting things were happening in beer, and they were there for it.

Tony began to work for Griesedieck Imports, a company descended from Falstaff beer, importing beer and wines. The distributorship was boosted by the arrival of Corona beer in the region, and while the Mexican beer didn't take off as much in St. Louis as it did on the coasts, there were signs that there was a market for new flavors.

By 1990, Tony and Fran's understanding of beer had grown enough for them to start their own distribution company, Signature Beer. Tony worked to bring on small Midwest breweries like Iowa's Millstream, Minnesota's James Page, and Wisconsin's Capital Brewing. As much as they would have loved to distribute Schlafly products, Missouri law denied brewpubs that opportunity. Needing more options to sell, the Caradonnas created their own brand, Spirit of St. Louis Ale, a golden ale contract brewed at Oldenberg Brewery in Fort Mitchell, Kentucky. In those days, Tony drove a box truck the six hours to Oldenberg to pick up batches of Spirit of St. Louis.

Tony's father joined him on occasion, and one particular night at their hotel bar, Tony's gregarious father made his rounds talking to strangers around the horseshoe-shaped bar. "Hey, Tony," he shouted to his son. "Have you ever heard of Pete Slosberg?"

"Uh, yeah, Dad." Who in the industry hadn't heard of Pete Slosberg? Pete's Wicked Ale had recently won "Top Ale" at the Great American Beer Festival and was ranked as one of the top five beers in the United States.

"This is Pete!"

Tony hurried over to talk to the brewer and perhaps convince him to distribute in St. Louis. Slosberg told him they had been trying to get anyone in the St. Louis market to return his calls. The distributorships were, for the most part, loyal to Anheuser-Busch and weren't eager to bring in competition. It had been a dead end for Slosberg before this chance meeting.

Signature Beer began to distribute Pete's Wicked Ale, securing over a hundred tap handles in the city and shelf space in local grocery stores Schnucks, Dierbergs, and Shop'n Save. The demand for craft beer was growing, and the Caradonnas weren't just riding the wave—they were fueling it.

By 1996, St. Louis had grown from one craft brewery to three in five years. Tom Schlafly won his battle to increase production and distribute beer. August Schell Brewing Company in Minnesota soon pumped out more bottled Schlafly beer than the small brewery had ever sold over their counter. Now Tom Schlafly and Dan Kopman needed someone who understood craft beer to distribute it. Who better than the couple they had known for years, who had celebrated Schlafly's opening night with them, and who had brought Pete's Wicked Ale, also brewed at August Schell, to St. Louis? Tony and Fran Caradonna's Signature Beer distribution company would be perfect. "We weren't ready," Fran Caradonna remembers. "I was working full-time, except I was a mom with an infant. Tony was full-time. Ben Bruker, Tony, and I were all the employees. Dan Kopman had big ideas of how big and fast this was going to go, and we knew it was overoptimistic. We politely declined."

The contract went to St. Louis Beer Sales, a precursor to Summit Distributing. Over the course of the next year, Schlafly's launch into distribution came up short of their expectations, while sales of Pete's Wicked Ale grew enough for Signature to hire three more people and buy two more trucks. Dan Kopman came back to Tony and Fran and said things weren't working with St. Louis Beer Sales. Could they handle Schlafly now? This time the Caradonnas said yes. "We did the same thing for them that we did for Pete's," Caradonna says. "We got a few hundred tap handles, we got placements in all the primary stores, and we got it going for them. And we grew our company."

The Caradonnas were a driving force behind Schlafly's growth from a pub to a presence throughout St. Louis. Other distributors began to look at them with envy. Anheuser-Busch products had always and would always sell well, especially in St. Louis, but the only area of true growth was in the craft beer category. With other brands like Boulevard, Sam Adams, and Bass, Signature seemed to have craft beer all to itself. And where other distributors might not understand the appeal of brands like Pete's Wicked Ale, Schlafly was something they could wrap their heads around. It was a local brewery that was growing fast. Griesedieck Imports made an offer to buy Signature Beer. Then other offers started to come in. The Caradonnas had some decisions to make.

There is a sweet spot for small distributorships where the business is all about the individual relationships. They know the brewers personally, and they know the store, restaurant, and bar owners. But Signature was moving beyond that, and while the money was starting to flow in, growth meant they had to continue to increase their volume, which moved them away from individual relationships. Could they use this opportunity to follow their dream of making their own beer? They accepted an offer from distributor Major Brands and began work on starting their own brewery.

The O'Fallon Brewery opened in 2000 in St. Charles County. With sixty-five thousand square feet and brewing four thousand barrels a year, O'Fallon was the fourth craft brewery in the St. Louis metro area, but it was the first that was packaging their beer for distribution only. They were the first without a brewpub, choosing bottles over burgers. This was before Dan Kopman and Tom Schlafly successfully changed the state distribution law that allowed for both bottles and burgers. "At the time, you could get two of the three licenses: manufacturers, wholesalers, and retail," Fran Caradonna remembers. "Because we knew the distribution side, we got the manufacturing and distribution. No one else in the state had that except for Boulevard. We didn't want to be in the restaurant business."

At the start Fran was working in the brewery while Tony delivered the beer and worked to set up new accounts. But because Fran was a beer wholesaler, she didn't have much experience with brewing: "We did not know how to make beer. We would call John Witte or Stephen Hale or Marc Gottfried and ask, 'OK, now what do we do—this is happening and it's not in the book that the manufacturer gave us.' And they walked us through it."

It was on one of Tony's sales calls that he met Brian Owens, a homebrewer who became O'Fallon's head brewer. The brewery took off.

O'Fallon offered four core styles. O'Fallon Gold, a golden ale, was one of their earliest and most successful. To people who were used to Budweiser, O'Fallon Gold was light enough but had a freshness, a fullness of flavor. Fran Caradonna likened it to eating fresh-baked bread. "One of our neighbors was strictly a Budweiser man," she says, "and I watched him slowly adapt to O'Fallon Gold. One day he said, 'If you had told me three months ago I would ever drink anything other than Budweiser, I would have told you you were nuts.' And then I watched this guy over the years reach for the hoppiest beer he could find. It was his gateway." The hoppiest beer he could find was probably O'Fallon 5-Day IPA. Owens created the recipe where the IPA was dry hopped for five days, giving it a powerful aroma. For a time, 5-Day IPA was a runaway success in St. Louis.

A wheat and a smoked porter rounded out O'Fallon's initial offerings. The smoked porter won a gold medal at the 2004 Great American Beer Festival and then won gold again in 2020. The wheat won bronze at the

2005 GABF. These new St. Louis breweries weren't just pumping out beer—it was some of the best beer in the country.

O'Fallon's seasonal styles included Goats Breath Bock Ale, a beer that Tony Caradonna had created when they were distributors and contract brewed out of Minnesota. They had Wheach, a peach wheat beer, and a Cherry Chocolate dark ale. Their pumpkin beer, which became one of their best-selling seasonals, came directly from Trailhead's John Witte. "Brian Owens called me in the summer of 2001 and said they wanted to do a pumpkin as a seasonal," Witte recalls. "'How do you do it?' So I got to walk him through the process." Witte had originally tried adding fresh steamed pumpkin to the mash, which turned it almost to concrete. So he added the pumpkin flesh to the kettle as it was flowing. The trick that Witte came up with was to make his own extract in order to keep the spice flavor and aroma consistent. He essentially made a spiced concentrated tea. According to Witte, "Marc Gottfried once went through the whole process of roasting off the pumpkin himself. He did that once. 'Never again,' he said. 'That was horrible.'"

O'Fallon's Pumpkin Beer launched a taste trend that Schlafly joined in with their Pumpkin Ale, silver medalist at the Great American Beer Festival in 2017. Today, as the flavors of fall creep earlier and earlier, pumpkin beers appear on St. Louis grocery shelves by early September. O'Fallon's motto, emblazoned on their logo, was "We Love Beer!"

Continuing westward thirty miles down the Katy Trail is Augusta, the heart of Missouri's wine country. Founded, depending on whom you ask, either by a member of Daniel Boone's expedition or an early German settler, Augusta lays claim to America's oldest wineries. The Germans who migrated to Missouri found the climate and the soil of the rolling hills perfect for wine making. In 1870 Augusta vintners helped save a French wine industry decimated by insects by sending insect-resistant rootstock that was then grafted onto French cuttings. That decade, the Missouri River cut a new channel near the town, leaving a fertile swath of land behind that became the heart of its current wine country.

A good two-and-a-half-hour bike ride from the Lewis and Clark (and Seaman) statue in St. Charles will take you, tired and thirsty, into the heart of Augusta. In the late '90s, St. Louisan Steve Neukomm figured you would want a glass of beer, not wine, when you got off your bike. Thus began Augusta Brewing Company, a small beer garden in the middle of wine country.

Steve Neukomm owned a historic building in the Lafayette Square neighborhood just south of downtown St. Louis. As with many parts of the city, Lafayette Square had gone through phases of importance, distress, and recovery. Named after Revolutionary War hero the Marquis de Lafayette, who visited the city in 1825, Lafayette Square features Second Empire–style Victorian homes surrounding a thirty-acre park.

Once the home to St. Louis VIPs, including Supreme Court justice Louis Brandeis, Lafayette Square fell into a state of neglect. A return to the neighborhood and its stunning architecture began in the 1970s. By the time Neukomm bought the brick building at 1727 Park Avenue, Lafayette Square was a thriving pocket of St. Louis.

Back when breweries could own taverns, the building at 1727 Park was built in 1883 to be a tied house—that is, a tavern "tied" to a particular brewery. This particular tied house, like many others in St. Louis, was tied to Anheuser-Busch. George Van Der Berg ran the saloon and, judging by the press clippings of the time, was quite unlucky. A newly hired bartender ran off with the contents of the till in 1909, and former major league pitcher Frank Pears wrecked the place when a misunderstanding over his missing watch led to his throwing china, silver, and ketchup bottles into the windows, mirrors, and shelves of liquor bottles. His watch was found in his coat pocket.

An attempted robbery of the saloon in 1916 ended poorly for one of the young criminals, who was shot by St. Louis's Soulard District police. After the advent of Prohibition, the bar, under new ownership now, was raided for serving alcohol. The proprietor claimed to be serving only Bevo, the nonalcoholic beverage made by Anheuser-Busch.

Sometime in the '20s Mary Settich bought the bar and turned it into a club and cabaret, Mary's Dreamland. Appearing as a café in front, the interior turned seedier, sexier, and certainly more illegal the closer one got to the interior courtyard. Girls danced while patrons drank, and neighbors sat in their windows above. A legend in St. Louis was born.

Mary's Dreamland was far enough from the entertainment center of St. Louis, the Grand District, to operate under the radar. Part of the attraction was Hester Kelly, a six-foot-tall, two-hundred-pound singer and comedian who often peppered her stories with in-jokes about her own size. In one interview she was asked why Mary's Dreamland advertised sixteen girls but had only six. She joked that when they realized the girls would have to be on stage with her, they had to let ten of them go. "After all, our stage is none too roomy."

When the St. Louis Cardinals made the 1934 World Series, Hester Kelly arrived at Sportsman's Park days before tickets went on sale. The papers had fun reporting on the "Night Club Mistress" who asked her sister Nedra to hold her spot each night while Hester performed her duties at Mary's Dreamland. "With Frisch's brains, my yelling and Dizzy's arm," Hester said, "we're going to take them in five games." Dizzy Dean and the Gashouse Gang won it in seven. Mary's Dreamland operated into the 1940s with an eclectic and multicultural mix of musicians, singers, dancers, and storytellers.

As Lafayette Square lost its reputation as a nightlife spot and swiftly declined, the building sat vacant. The resurgence of the area led to a series of owners with new restaurant concepts, but a fire in 2004 nearly destroyed the building that once housed Mary's Dreamland. The building's owner, restaurateur Steve Neukomm, tore out what survived the fire down to the floor joists. For his new concept, he was going to start from square one.

Square One Brewery was an homage to Lafayette Square, its history, and the history of 1727 Park Avenue. Before Prohibition, small breweries were equipped to deal with only their immediate market, the nearby neighborhood. Over the years, large brands either forced them out or bought them up. Craft beer, to some extent, is a return to breweries supplying their immediate markets. Square One would do just that. They would not distribute. Their beer would be as fresh as beer could be, brewed just a few feet away from where it was consumed.

Square One needed a brewer. Though Neukomm himself had extensive brewing training from the University of California, Davis, his other projects kept him out of the brewhouse. After asking around, it was Morgan Street's Marc Gottfried who suggested giving former Trailhead brewer John Witte a call. Gottfried suspected that Witte wanted back in the game. Gottfried wasn't wrong, but Witte's interest in a new job had as much to do with the housing market as it did with beer. As now-president of a mortgage company, he saw some strange things happening in the industry, and as he was working 100 percent on commission, the idea of a steady paycheck and being close to his son appealed to him. Witte accepted the job, got out of the mortgage industry before it collapsed, and opened Square One Brewery in February 2006.

Square One was much smaller than Trailhead, but Witte felt closer to his customers. Where saloon owners once dodged ketchup bottles, bartenders now pushed craft beer across the bar. Where Hester Kelly once danced and sang in the inner courtyard, residents of Lafayette Square and visitors now munch on fish and chips and stout-braised pot roast. And John Witte was back where he belonged—among his chemistry set and his nave of tanks.

On a warm weekend in May 2007, the Grand Basin of Forest Park smelled of wood chips, bringing Clydesdales to mind. Ten truckloads were brought in after heavy rain. Within two expansive white tents, one for lagers and one for ales, brewers from seven St. Louis breweries poured their talents into commemorative glasses for fifteen thousand beer lovers. It was the inaugural St. Louis Brewers Heritage Festival, initially conceived by Tom Schlafly and Dan Kopman and financed by Anheuser-Busch as part of their "Here's to Beer" campaign.

Signs above each of the sixty-some taps indicated the styles, not the individual names of the beers. In one section of the lager tent, attendees could taste a dark lager from each of the seven breweries, all from the same recipe, and distinguish flavor differences between them. Food pairings from local chefs were available within a third tent.

Anheuser-Busch flew in members of the growing beer media to visit St. Louis and see the history and future of beer on display. They spent the day before the festival learning what St. Louis beer was all about. Mayor Francis Slay spoke of the city's beer history at the opening reception. Schlafly hosted a lunch at the Tap Room, where Stephen Hale led brewery tours. A tour of the Anheuser-Busch brewery followed, led by head brewer and future craft brewer Florian Kuplent. Schlafly's Dan Kopman kicked off the festivities: "It doesn't matter if you're a small or big brewery," he says, "if you've been around five or 150 years—we all share a common passion for beer. For this weekend, we're thrilled to join arms with Anheuser-Busch and other local brewers."

Pouring beer in Forest Park that weekend were Anheuser-Busch, Schlafly, Morgan Street, O'Fallon, Augusta, Square One, and Alandale, a new brewery from Kirkwood that would change its name twice, first to The Highlands, then to Kirkwood Station Restaurant & Brewing Company. Dan

Kopman and Stephen Hale were there, as were Tony and Fran Caradonna, John Witte, and Marc Gottfried.

As day turned to evening, the brewers toasted how far craft beer had come in St. Louis. It only took looking around the grounds to see the festival was a success. Locals wore pretzel necklaces and drank beers while talking to the brewers who brewed them. Their city was becoming a craft beer town. The festival became a tradition in St. Louis, moving to the grounds of the Gateway Arch. Craft beer was no longer a novelty in the city of St. Louis. It wasn't a flash-in-the-pan trend. The number of craft breweries was doubling—and then doubling again. An emergence was on the horizon. Not all would be successful. Buffalo Brewing Company near Saint Louis University closed soon after opening, and Route 66 Brewery in Union Station didn't last.

They were a handful of people who were passionate about brewing, and their passion came through in their beers. Their knowledge was expanding, their brewing abilities refining. A group whose love of beer brought them together was becoming a community. Their Master Brewers gatherings provided a place for a meeting of the minds, and events like the Heritage Festival built camaraderie. But it was the mutual respect—the phone calls asking, How do you do this or handle this problem?—that proved they were becoming a family.

The Caradonnas had built O'Fallon out in St. Charles, among other reasons, to avoid competing directly with Schlafly. But competition among craft brewers, they found, was not the same as it was between the big brewers. Where a Budweiser drinker may drink Budweiser only, the craft beer drinker was eager to try everything.

Fran Caradonna explains it this way: "Craft beer drinkers are loyal to the category, not the brands. That's been a fact from the beginning. By definition a craft beer drinker wants to buy different beers. They may have their favorites, but it's not the kind of brand loyalty marketers understand. They don't understand the collaboration between breweries. We learned early on in the craft business that if it was good for the segment, it was good for all of us. It's not that we don't compete—we do—but the example I like to use is a baseball game. The ultimate goal is to entertain the fans. Yes, it's competitive, but you watch them play and the batter gets to first base and chats up the first baseman because they know each other."

A rising tide, they found, lifted all pint glasses.

4

# INBEV

At the intersection of a Venn diagram of Greek myth, Shakespearean tragedy, and the HBO television series *Succession* sits the InBev takeover of Anheuser-Busch. It is a story of greatness, of hubris, and of betrayal. At the time of the sale, Anheuser-Busch brewed half of all beer sold in the United States. The company's triumph over rival breweries, and its rise to heights unmatched by few American companies, occurred under the watch of August Busch III. He was a feared and respected mogul, but before this Zeus could rule over Olympus, he had to overthrow Jupiter.

Called "Auggie" by the St. Louis public, August the Third showed little of the harsh focus that would characterize his time as Anheuser-Busch CEO. In this way he was similar to his father, Gussie, and his grandfather, August A. Busch. Wealth and fame turned young men of the Busch family into princes of St. Louis. August III spent his youth at great speed, whether flying his planes or driving his cars. He traveled the world's ski slopes and sandy beaches.

The Third's relationship with his father was strained at best. It didn't help matters that August was one of eleven of Gussie's children from four wives. Whereas Gussie was outgoing and ebullient, August was quiet and serious. Associates considered him cold. But behind the stone facade, August was a planner.

As was tradition for Busch children, August started small at the brewery, shoveling used grain and beechwood chips from the vats. From the company's inception, the Busch family placed value in knowing every facet of its production. In 1960 August flew his plane to Chicago weekly to complete a twelve-week course at the Siebel Institute of Technology. Gussie named August sales manager of Busch Bavarian, their low-price offering. The promotion marked a change in the young prince. He reportedly dedicated himself so fully to the job that he was intimidating and exhausting to those who worked for him. He flew the country to oversee sales reps and wholesalers and to check that no bottle or keg of Busch Bavarian was out of date. Brewery policy dictated that shelf life was capped at 105 days, after which hop flavors and aromas begin to fade. August ran a tight ship, and soon everyone under him knew to meet his expectations or suffer his wrath.

Gussie promoted his son to vice president of marketing in 1963 and made sure he was elected to the board of directors. That same year, August married Californian Susan Hornibrook in Beverly Hills. They welcomed their son, August IV, the following year, feeding the baby a thimble of Budweiser.

The Third's quick rise continued with a promotion in 1965 to vice president and general manager of the brewery. He set out quickly to modernize a company his father had grown to national prominence, producing ten million barrels a year by the mid-'60s. It's not an exaggeration to say Gussie shook hands with nearly every employee and distributor, a personal touch that endeared him to employees at each level of beer production and sales. Further growth would be difficult, but August was determined to take the company to even greater heights. He couldn't do it by shaking everyone's hand.

A point of annoyance for August III was Gussie's insistence that all decisions go through him. It wasn't uncommon for Gussie to hear of a change that he hadn't personally signed off on and loudly countermand the order. Such behavior may have worked for a smaller Anheuser-Busch, but the company, August thought, had long outgrown it. The Third began to surround himself with the best and brightest of the country's business school graduates, from places like the University of Pennsylvania's Wharton School, Harvard, Stanford, Columbia, and Northwestern. While visiting the Wharton School, August sat in on a speech on corporate planning and afterward wooed the professor by promising him a substantial salary to become the new vice president of corporate planning for Anheuser-Busch. Another Wharton professor became a mentor for August, instilling in him a sense of "preactive" corporate management, which helped a corporation deal with inevitable change.

Under August's urging and despite Gussie's objections, Anheuser-Busch endowed the Wharton School with enough money to conduct yearly computer modeling of corporate practices. The results showed that Anheuser-Busch needed to build new plants across the country to meet growing demand and limit freight costs. Again Gussie objected—A-B would be taking on too much risk—but August convinced enough of the board of directors to support the plan. Houston, Columbus, and Jacksonville soon featured their own Anheuser-Busch plants.

The Third's computer models told him that even with the new plants the company was not brewing enough beer to meet demand. He pushed for two more plants, in New Hampshire and Virginia. As a direct result, Anheuser-Busch passed the twenty-million-barrel mark in 1970, doubling production in six years. The models were right.

Beer growth in the 1950s and '60s had been slow but steady. Whereas American breweries produced 82 million barrels in 1950, in 1960 they produced 87 million barrels. Then Madison Avenue got involved. Beer

Photo of Gussie Busch bunging, or stopping with a cork, the twenty millionth barrel of Anheuser-Busch beer. Looking on are August A. Busch III and other executives, 1970. (Courtesy of the Missouri Historical Society.)

advertising began to evolve, to appeal to the common man, injecting more humor and occasional silliness. The ads worked. By 1970, breweries were producing 121 million barrels a year, and it still wasn't enough to meet demand.

America was drinking more beer than ever, and the big breweries began to publicly duke it out over who would supply it. Miller Brewing Company controlled only 4 percent of the market—5 million barrels a year—when Philip Morris purchased them in 1969. The tobacco company injected immense sums of money. By introducing Miller Lite, they changed the trajectory of American brewing.

Light beers had been attempted before. Coors introduced Coors Light in 1941 as a low-alcohol beer to ease drinkers into the post-Prohibition world. But due to the restrictions placed on the industry in World War II, Coors chose to focus on their Banquet beer only, discontinuing Coors Light after just one year.

Miller Lite has its roots in Rheingold Brewery of New York, which brewed Gablinger's Diet Beer in 1964. It was the first beer marketed as a lower-calorie beer. Dr. Joseph L. Owades, a biochemist at Rheingold, removed starch from the brewing process, lowering carbs and calories. The idea of a diet beer didn't appeal to consumers at the time, and Rheingold discontinued the beer. Owades shared his recipe with a friend at Meister Bräu Inc. in Chicago, who created Meister Bräu Lite. Unfortunately, the company went bankrupt in 1972, giving the Philip Morris–controlled Miller Brewing the opportunity to buy up their brands, including the formula for Meister Bräu Lite, which they used for their own light offering. Miller Lite was born, but it was arguably the marketing behind it that made it successful.

Beer drinkers weren't interested in a diet beer. They liked beer and they wanted to drink more of it. Miller focused their marketing on how Miller Lite tasted great and didn't fill you up. And they had plenty of athletes and celebrities saying just that. Business boomed.

Schlitz, a longtime rival of Anheuser-Busch, approached the beer wars in a different way. They cut production costs of their beer substantially by speeding up fermentation and replacing expensive malts and hops with corn syrup and hop extracts and pellets. One side effect of rapid fermentation is a haziness that forms when the proteins don't settle out naturally. Schlitz added silica gel to prevent haze from forming. The short-term results were a manufacturing boom for Schlitz, who could pump out more beer than their rivals. For a short time they were the darlings of the beer industry—they had figured out a way to make a lot of money brewing beer faster. This left Anheuser-Busch with an existential problem: If they had any hope of matching the cheaper production of Schlitz, they would have to turn their back on everything that made Budweiser *Budweiser*. No more beechwood aging. No more imported hops. Less expensive barley and rice. There were plenty of ways to cut costs and increase production, but would the product still be Budweiser?

Despite voices within Anheuser-Busch calling for cost cutting in the brewing process, both Gussie and August the Third stood firm, one of the few times they spoke with one voice. The recipe would not change. Instead, they would find other ways within the company to cut costs: middle management layoffs, fewer company cars, and cutting back on the number of free cases of Budweiser they gave out. The president of the company at the time, Dick Meyer, resigned over the layoffs, opening the door for August the Third to step in.

The counterpunch to Schlitz came in an advertising campaign that reinforced the virtues of Budweiser's brewing process and its natural ingredients, all while referring to the shortcuts and cheap ingredients of their rivals. At the same time, Schlitz beer began to show the effects of its new anti-hazing additive, Chill-Garde. White flakes appeared in the beer, which, while worrisome, weren't nearly as bad as a layer of mucus-like substance that began to form in bottles and cans. Schlitz, drinkers complained, had snot in it.

Gussie and August were vindicated. Schlitz couldn't recover from such a disaster. The cost-cutting decisions may have given Schlitz a temporary boost, but it started them down a death spiral that resulted in their sale to the Stroh Brewery Company in 1982.

Coors was a player in the beer wars but held more of a niche position. There was something cool about Coors. It was sold only in seven western states and had little to no marketing. A mystique surrounding it made drinkers feel like they knew something that other people didn't know, that they could drink something most Americans couldn't drink. You could practically hear John Denver's "Rocky Mountain High" when you opened a bottle. It was so popular in eastern states that the plot of the movie *Smokey and the Bandit* centered on bootlegging Coors, driving it to places where it was illegal to sell.

Coors had the opportunity to cash in on its popularity and expand into those areas where demand was highest, but expansion would cut into the very heart of what made Coors special. Any plant built outside Colorado couldn't boast of the Rocky Mountain water. And would it lose its mystique as a hard-to-get beer? Would it lose what made it cool? In the beer wars, Anheuser-Busch didn't have much to attack Coors for—their commitments to quality ingredients and brewing practices were similar.

Part of the success of Anheuser-Busch was its ubiquity—it was available everywhere; Coors was successful because it wasn't. So, for the most part, Coors stayed out of the fray, growing slowly and introducing Coors Light in 1978. By 1980 they were producing almost double what they were in 1970 but had dropped from fourth to fifth place thanks to the rise of Miller.

So the beer wars of the '70s came down to Anheuser-Busch and Miller. August the Third understood the threat that Philip Morris–owned Miller posed to the company. *The New York Times* wrote in 1977:

> The cigarette giant has twice the cash flow of the largest beer manufacturer ($348 million last year, compared with Anheuser's $155 million), and cigarette profits have furnished much of the $500 million that Philip Morris has spent in revitalizing Miller, including the cost of acquisition. In addition, Miller's own earnings have been poured into advertising budgets which, per barrel, have consistently dwarfed the industry averages. Last year Miller showed an operating income of $76.1 million, nearly triple the previous year and more than enough to compensate for all of Philip Morris's expenditures.

Gussie was so laser-focused on his old rival Schlitz that he didn't see Miller coming, and August feared Anheuser-Busch was unprepared for this fight. In 1975 August III deposed his father as CEO in a carefully orchestrated boardroom coup.

Gussie Busch, the seventy-six-year-old king of St. Louis, was blindsided, betrayed by his own son. Board members whom he considered in his corner voted with his son to remove him. Gussie showed up to work as the third-generation head of Anheuser-Busch and left with a generous severance package. Consider the dilemma board members and company executives faced: The company owed everything to Gussie Busch, but August was the heir apparent, and opposing him might jeopardize their own futures. They were nobles and court advisors of a Shakespeare play unfolding in real time, choosing between the old king and the new. They chose the new.

In his rage Gussie looked for ways to get his company back. His son had usurped him. But Gussie still owned about 30 percent of Anheuser-Busch.

Tobacco company R. J. Reynolds quietly approached him about buying his shares at a premium. They were eager to jump into this arena to battle with longtime rival Philip Morris. With Gussie's shares, R. J. Reynolds could position themselves to control the board of directors and oust August III. But Gussie's revenge would mean Anheuser-Busch would be owned by someone other than a Busch for the first time in its history. Gussie didn't follow through with the deal. He didn't need the money—his personal wealth topped $500 million—so it really came down to revenge. That, it turned out, wasn't enough reason to sell his family company. Gussie accepted his new role as king emeritus and continued as president of the St. Louis Cardinals.

In one year, Miller increased its production by five million barrels, the largest single-year increase in brewery history. Their overall production jumped from only five million in 1970 to eighteen million by mid-decade. They doubled that to thirty-seven million by 1980. Miller Brewing Company was a juggernaut, poised to overtake Anheuser-Busch. Their creative and humorous ads were working, becoming part of public discourse. Miller understood that beer drinking trends were changing: More people were drinking at home. Their customer base was mostly blue-collar. And drinking among college students was rising fast. So they kept the beer light, cool to drink, and cheap.

Even now August III did not believe light beer was the future. No one, he thought, would want a watered-down Budweiser. In this his "preactive" corporate planning was wrong. Where August got it right was marketing, the arena within which this battle was decided. He doubled the company's marketing budget and sought sponsorships for every major sporting event. Most of those events, including the Super Bowl and all other major sports championships, were already bought by other breweries, including Miller. Anheuser-Busch found themselves playing catch-up. They scooped up nearly every other available sponsorship with the goal of tying American sport to Budweiser, just as his grandfather had done more than fifty years earlier.

Anheuser-Busch introduced Natural Light and Michelob Light in 1977, but since The Third didn't really believe in the future of light beers, he didn't give them the marketing push necessary to compete with Miller Lite. Still, Miller sued A-B over using the "light" name, beginning a series of legal squabbles that devolved into pettiness. Michelob Light, Miller alleged, was not a light beer, as it was over one hundred calories. Miller's

Lowenbräu line, A-B alleged, was marketed and sold at the price point of an import beer but was in reality brewed in Texas with corn grits and chemical additives. Miller alleged that the beechwood Anheuser-Busch used had been chemically treated. A-B argued that Miller's slogan "The Champagne of Beers" was confusing and misleading. The two biggest beer companies were acting like toddlers.

When beer sales flattened out, the breweries had to ask themselves if it was the marketing or the beer? It's easy to look back and claim it was all marketing, as the belief now is that most light lagers taste too similar to differentiate. But the beers in the '70s did not taste the way they do now. There was a moderate-to-significant taste difference among the available beers at the time. Should Budweiser change their recipe?

To specifically attack Miller Lite, the A-B marketing department stuck with what had worked against Schlitz: They attacked the process. Ads showed Natural Light, brewed with water, hops, rice, barley, and yeast, next to Miller Lite, brewed with water, corn syrup, hops extract, and three other multisyllabic chemicals of unknown origin. Famous athletes claimed on television that Natural Light was superior in blind taste tests.

A-B's marketing continued beyond sports into a more blue-collar feel. As before, they were behind Miller in this way. Their "For All You Do, This Bud's for You" campaign hit at the right time, resonating with an America that was buying into Ronald Reagan's promises of an American resurgence on the world stage. The ads praised the efforts of the common man, whatever they may be. Without referring to the record unemployment of the '70s, it spoke to a vision where every American had a job.

Schlafly CEO Tom Schlafly describes the effect the ad wars had on beer advertising going forward:

> Way back when, a Budweiser ad would show the beer with fine dining or at a swimming pool. What changed when Philip Morris bought Miller was they brought marketing experts who said the beer drinker doesn't see himself in the ad, so now comes Miller Time. Instead of showing the guy getting out of the limousine, it's the guy getting off work at the steel mill. And Budweiser then woke up to that and said, "This Bud's for You." And it's all manly activities, not a computer programmer. The ads for Busch Bavarian used to show yodeling and the Alps. What they realized is every American identifies with cowboys, so suddenly the mountains are the Rocky Mountains and the men are doing something manly, like fixing a fence or sitting around a fire. They're still selling masculinity.

Anheuser-Busch's marketing push worked. The company celebrated its fifty millionth barrel produced in one year—1980. Miller, meanwhile, failed to make a dent in A-B's market share, despite the influx of cash from Philip Morris. Miller controlled just over 20 percent of the beer market in 1980, a significant jump from low single digits a decade before. But Anheuser-Busch controlled 28 percent, and that number continued to grow.

August III finally gave in to pressure to roll out Budweiser Light in 1982. Because it had the Budweiser name, he felt more pressure on its success than Natural Light or Michelob Light. He worked closely with brewers who tried to reduce calories without reducing taste. They chose to slightly increase the bitterness to make up for the reduced sugar in the mashing process. By 1985, Bud Light, as it was now labeled, was selling well at around 5.4 million barrels. Overall the company produced 72 million barrels that year, increasing its market share to 36 percent. Paradoxically, Americans were actually drinking less beer, but a greater share of that beer was coming from Anheuser-Busch.

A decision in 1987 to target the youngest of their drinkers cemented the company's dominance. The marketing department rolled out Spuds MacKenzie, a "party animal" dog that drank beer surrounded by beautiful women. Young men loved it, and sales of Bud Light jumped 20 percent. Others objected to the dog's appeal to children, as well as the fact Spuds could pretend to be partying while drinking Bud Light, something a human actor couldn't do in television ads.

The Spuds MacKenzie ads marked a new direction for Anheuser-Busch marketing. They wanted their ads to be remembered, to be repeated. They wanted their slogans to be catchphrases, part of the zeitgeist. Budweiser and Bud Light were going to be cool. The rise of the attention-grabbing marketing, a precursor to viral videos, coincided with the beginning of August IV's involvement with Anheuser-Busch. The Third's son hitched his wagon to this new kind of marketing. He—and Bud Light—would soon be number one.

But first the company and the city of St. Louis had to say goodbye to Gussie Busch. Gussie had spent his final years watching over the St. Louis Cardinals, who won three World Series championships on his watch. The number 85 was retired in honor of Gussie, who was eighty-five years old at the time of the ceremony. The relationship between Gussie and his son August III improved enough over the years for them to meet at least weekly, and any hard feelings over the boardroom coup seemed to have faded. In September 1989, at the age of ninety and surrounded by his children, Gussie died in his home on Grant's Farm. He was worth over $1.3 billion in Anheuser-Busch stock alone at the time of his death.

The city of St. Louis mourned their fallen king in a public ceremony that included TV host and Budweiser ad spokesperson Ed McMahon and baseball star Joe DiMaggio. Gussie had been larger than life, and it was difficult to imagine a St. Louis without him in it. He had cast a long shadow.

Attention turned to the up-and-coming Busch, August IV. His youthful indiscretions had exceeded previous Augusts Busch, though perhaps some sympathy could be extended to a young man who grew up under the microscope, whose cold and distant father ousted his grandfather from the family business, and whose mother was accused in the papers of having an affair with Cardinals announcer Harry Caray. But that sympathy dried up after a young woman, his passenger Michelle Frederick, was killed when nineteen-year-old August IV rolled his Corvette in Arizona in 1983. Despite evidence that Busch, who had fled the scene, was driving impaired, no charges were filed. Two years later he led St. Louis police on a high-speed chase through the city, resulting in arrest and one year of probation.

For five years August IV worked to rehab his image in St. Louis, finishing school at Saint Louis University. He worked at the Anheuser-Busch brewhouse while apprenticing in the brewers union. Like most A-B brewers, he earned his Master Brewer certificate in Germany. He came back to work directly with marketing VP Michael Roarty, the man who gave us Spuds MacKenzie. In 1991 The Fourth was promoted to brand director for Budweiser.

Around this time Anheuser-Busch began to dip its toe into international markets, purchasing small stakes in breweries like Grupo Modelo. A-B's international growth plan was extremely conservative in retrospect: They wanted inroads to distribute their beer in other markets, but they didn't want any of the risk that came with owning those breweries. Plus, they trusted no one else to make Budweiser. They passed on opportunities that other breweries didn't. Their inaction proved fatal.

In 1991 Schlafly opened its tiny taproom in downtown St. Louis. Though Schlafly didn't move any needles on Budweiser sales in St. Louis, nationwide Anheuser-Busch was beginning to see the effects of the craft beer movement. Pete's Wicked Ale, Samuel Adams Boston Lager, and Sierra Nevada Pale Ale were expanding their distribution. New Belgium Brewing debuted Fat Tire Amber ale in 1991. More flavors were becoming available, which fed consumer appetite for something new, something different. This helped the import market, as beers like Foster's Lager, Heineken, and, notably, Corona were starting to push into Anheuser-Busch territory. Anheuser-Busch sales dropped 6 percent in 1991. Over the next few years, A-B production grew slightly, but they lost market share, as the country was seeing the ascendancy of small craft breweries.

Anheuser-Busch was not blind to this new sector and sought ways to profit from it. The difficulty lay in the unwritten definition of craft beer: Not mass produced. Not mass marketed. Not Anheuser-Busch.

A-B bought partial shares of Pacific Northwest breweries Redhook Brewing Company in 1995 and Widmer Brothers Brewing in 1997. Miller bought into Celis Brewery and Shipyard Brewing Company. In an effort to sneak into the craft beer world, the big breweries created stealth breweries with no clear connection to their parent entities. Anheuser-Busch released Elk Mountain Amber Ale and then later Red Wolf red ale without any reference on the bottle to Anheuser-Busch. Miller began the Plank Road line with their release of Red Dog beer.

Blue Moon beer was born as a hybrid of the two worlds. A brewer at the Sandlot Brewery in Denver's Coors Field brewed the Belgian-style wheat beer in small batches, but it became so successful that Coors produced it but did not label it as Coors, leaving it in the murky in-between space between craft and macrobeers. Blue Moon became the most popular of the stealth craft beers. In this small skirmish between the big three, Coors was the clear winner.

After limited success with their Elk Mountain and Red Wolf lines, Anheuser-Busch moved their experimental lines to the Michelob brand, with Amber Bock, a pale ale, *Märzen*, pumpkin spice, and honey lager, most of which were sold in holiday sample packs. While Michelob Light fell out of favor over time, their Michelob Ultra line of low-carb, low-calorie beer rode the Atkins Diet wave to prominence in the late '90s and continues to sell as being "keto-friendly." In 2022 it was the second highest selling brand in America behind Bud Light. Miller Lite and Coors Light dropped to fourth and fifth, behind number three Corona Extra.

By 1994, August IV had been promoted to vice president of all Anheuser-Busch brands. It was time for a new marketing campaign to bring the company out of the doldrums. A handful of executives, including August IV, loved a St. Louis marketing firm's quirky pitch that included frogs sitting on lily pads croaking the name Budweiser. It was so absurd it was funny—and definitely memorable. But August III didn't get it. To his credit, he had publicly stated that he didn't understand the motivations of young drinkers anymore, but after some convincing, he gave the campaign the green light. The spot aired in the first commercial slot of the 1995 Super Bowl to immediate acclaim. The frogs increased the brand's awareness among young drinkers, winning the advertising agency several Clio Awards. Subsequent variations on the theme, including a lizard and a ferret, proved just as popular and made Budweiser cool again.

The brewery was making money; the baseball team was not. The Cardinals had been a lifelong passion for Gussie Busch, regardless of the cost. It surprised no one that a Busch could make a lot more money making beer than running a baseball team, but that didn't matter to Gussie. It did matter to August III, who wasn't as crazy about baseball as his father. The recent baseball strike had hurt the team's bottom line, so he decided to sell the Cardinals in 1995. To his credit, he sought assurances from the new buyers that not only would the team remain in St. Louis, but the stadium would continue to carry the Busch name and appear as a giant beer advertisement. To St. Louisans, the sale of the team came with an uneasy realization that echoed twelve years later: A beloved institution could be owned by someone else, someone unknown.

Bud Light passed Miller Lite to become number two. Anheuser-Busch now held the top two selling beers in the world. August IV, now vice president of marketing, deserved some credit for the resurgence. New titles came quickly for the young August. He was being fast-tracked for leadership as August III publicly stated he himself would retire at sixty-five.

When 2002 came around and August III turned sixty-five, he didn't quite follow through on his promise, choosing to remain as chairman of the board of directors. He did step down as CEO, elevating company president Patrick Stokes to that position. During his tenure as president, Stokes saw growth from 80 million barrels a year to just short of 102 million. Thirty-eight-year-old August Busch IV became president of Anheuser-Busch Inc. He now ran the entire brewing division of the company.

Here was the beginning of the end, though it would be some time before anyone could see it. Once the wobble began, the center could not hold. Where were The Third's computer models once consolidation began in earnest? Where was his "preactive" corporate management? It was as if from here on out he was content to be the second guesser in chief to his inexperienced son.

Beer consumption was slowing across the country. The craft beer industry's constriction in the late '90s and early 2000s had slowed its growth considerably. A-B's old rival Miller had fallen far behind Anheuser-Busch, bringing Philip Morris's foray into beer to an ignominious end. Strapped with debt, they sold to growing beverage conglomerate South African Breweries, now called SABMiller, in 2002. While August III could toast to his clear victory over his onetime rival, Miller's sale to SAB should have been a wake-up call: International corporations were coming, and Anheuser-Busch had a giant target on its back.

The 1987 merger of Flemish brewery Brouwerij Artois, brewer of Stella Artois, and Walloon brewery Piedboeuf resulted in the new Dutch company Interbrew. In 1995 Interbrew bought Canadian brewery Labatt, and then UK breweries Bass and Whitbread, which made Boddington's, in 2000. In 2001 they purchased German breweries Bräuerei Diebels and Bräuerei Beck & Company, maker of Beck's Beer. Their rapid expansion led to a merger with Brazilian group AmBev.

AmBev, or Companhia de Bebidas das Américas, formed in 1999 when two Brazilian breweries, Brahma and Antarctica, combined. Anheuser-Busch had an opportunity to buy Antarctica first, but they moved too slowly, offered too little, and generally underestimated the men who ran Brahma, men who would ultimately own Anheuser-Busch.

The quick growth of both Interbrew and Ambev brought them together in a 2004 merger. The new InBev may have been based in Belgium, but its CEO was Brazilian Carlos Brito, the former executive of Brahma and CEO of AmBev. For the first time in two generations, Anheuser-Busch was not the largest beer company in the world. They now sat at number two, sandwiched between InBev and SABMiller, two companies with takeover ambitions. Coors Brewing Company merged with Molson Brewing Company to create Molson Coors in 2005.

*Dethroning the King* by Julie MacIntosh is a must-read on the steps and missteps that culminated in the InBev buyout of Anheuser-Busch. In it, MacIntosh illustrates how A-B's relationship with Grupo Modelo played a vital role in the coming InBev takeover.

A-B's stake in Grupo Modelo had grown over time to a 50 percent stake of the Mexican company, but hard feelings at Grupo Modelo lingered over the perceived arrogance of Anheuser-Busch executives—August III in particular—as well as deals that heavily favored Anheuser-Busch in retrospect. At a cost of only $1.6 billion, Anheuser-Busch gained a stake that was later worth $13 billion.

Growing animosity between the companies led to a fight over distribution rights, which Grupo Modelo sold to non–Anheuser-Busch distributors. Despite its ownership stake, Anheuser-Busch did not have distribution rights for Modelo in the United States, which infuriated August III. MacIntosh quotes an unnamed executive: "He would just get livid. He would threaten, he would cajole, he would do everything he could to try to make them do it. That's not the way you negotiate a deal."

InBev and Anheuser-Busch began to talk about securing a distribution deal that would see Anheuser-Busch handling InBev distribution in the United States. In 2004, InBev CEO Carlos Brito negotiated directly with August IV, who was eager to jump-start A-B out of a stagnant couple of years. What resulted was a deal that gave Anheuser-Busch the distribution rights to InBev products Stella Artois, Beck's, and Hoegaarden, among others. In retrospect, the deal looks more like a Trojan horse, as August IV opened the door to his enemies, so to speak, and allowed them to see the inner workings of Anheuser-Busch.

What Carlos Brito and others from InBev saw was excess. Anheuser-Busch was bloated with unnecessary expenses: multiple corporate jets that required multiple corporate hangars, unlimited budgets for decorating executive offices. The rollout of Bacardi Silver rum alone had a $60 million promotional budget that included a high-speed powerboat and racing team. Everything Anheuser-Busch did was over-the-top expensive, and they weren't seeing much in the way of increased sales. Brito could see profit opportunities everywhere. He went back to InBev HQ and started to plan.

August III told his son the deal with InBev was a mistake but didn't veto it. When August IV gathered investment bankers and Anheuser-Busch executives together in Cancun to talk about how to fend off a takeover attempt, August III reportedly raged at his son that he was putting up a "For Sale" sign and showing the bankers how to seal the deal. Then, continuing his contradictory words and actions, August III elevated August IV to CEO of Anheuser-Busch in September 2006.

Meanwhile, InBev was planning their move. Thanks to August IV, they were already inside. They had bankers who understood the company ready to finance a takeover. But InBev didn't move too fast; they knew they would have only one chance at this. It was a game of chess that August IV didn't realize he was playing.

In 2007, SABMiller merged with Molson Coors and launched their American joint venture as MillerCoors. Anheuser-Busch was increasingly isolated and ganged up on. They were vulnerable. A whisper of a rumor started in St. Louis that was almost too silly to share: Anheuser-Busch might be the target of a takeover. Even worse, the company seeking to buy them was foreign. It was a difficult concept for the average St. Louisan to wrap their head around. The older generation had seen a vibrant downtown replaced by empty storefronts and rising crime. They saw factories close down. The younger generation was witnessing something of a downtown renaissance, isolated in pockets like the corridor from Morgan Street Brewery to the Schlafly Tap Room, but the recent buyouts of TWA and Ralston Purina showed that no local company was safe. "Don't worry," people scoffed, "the Busch family would never sell."

What was St. Louis without Anheuser-Busch? The brewery employed upward of six thousand people, but the true impact came from the company's tax revenue. They provided $32 million in state and local taxes, $21 million of that to St. Louis alone, nearly 5 percent of the city budget. Anheuser-Busch was one of the top givers to philanthropic organizations, with $13 million in charitable giving.

Even outside of St. Louis the idea was preposterous. Anheuser-Busch had so successfully tied themselves to American nationalism that they made everyone forget that they were originally a German family making German beer. They were one of the largest family-run businesses in America, made even larger by the omnipresent advertisements and product placements. Their commercials had been part of the zeitgeist for decades. The image of a Dalmatian sitting on a beer wagon pulled by Clydesdales represented America. The Busch family was larger than life; they were royalty. Kings don't just walk away from their kingdoms.

While takeover rumors swirled, few within Anheuser-Busch believed such a thing was possible. They were so big, and held so much history, that the thought of a buyout seemed ludicrous. A Busch would always run this company. They would block any takeover attempt.

A New York meeting in 2007 between August IV and Brazilian investment banker Jorge Paulo Lemann, one of the original owners of Brahma who had grown the small brewery into InBev, started the ball rolling on

InBev's takeover. As the two spoke of the MillerCoors merger, Lemann suggested an AB–InBev merger. August IV either didn't think Lemann was serious or, as CEO, didn't know what he should do in the moment. He waved off the advance and failed to report the conversation to his board of directors. It was one of a series of missteps that characterized The Fourth's handling of the threat.

Rumors of a potential takeover led to *Wall Street Journal* articles suggesting talks between the two companies were already under way. They were not. Outside of August IV's meeting with Lemann, no one from Anheuser-Busch was talking to anyone at InBev. Still, A-B stock rose slightly, hovering around $50 a share, as investors hoping to profit from a potential merger bought up available shares. In May 2008, reports of an imminent InBev offer of $65 a share, for a total of $46 billion, jumped A-B stock to $56 a share. August IV made public comments that his family's company was not for sale. It was a statement that might have been true if the company had been primarily owned by members of the Busch family. It was not.

The InBev takeover brought to light the surprising fact that the Busch family owned less than 4 percent of Anheuser-Busch stock. Combined, they weren't even the largest shareholder. That title went to Warren Buffett, who owned 5 percent of the company. The sentiment that the Busch family would never sell hinged on the misconception that they owned enough stock to block a buyout. If they controlled more than 50 percent, InBev could offer the moon and the combined Busch family could wave them off. But as it was, even if they somehow convinced Warren Buffett to help them, they couldn't come near 50 percent. They could try to block the sale through a vote of the board of directors, but InBev had ways to work around that and appeal directly to shareholders. And the harsh truth was the board of directors' primary function was to look after shareholders' interests, not the company's, and certainly not the city's. The matter was largely out of Busch family hands.

Since the beginning of the takeover rumors, investors bought as much stock as they could, hoping to cash in on the buyout. By early to mid-2008, most likely a majority of shareholders were already in favor of selling. Warren Buffett made the smart play and sold at around $60 a share, ensuring he profited if the takeover fell through.

August IV began to play defense, first by rolling out a wide-ranging cost-cutting plan that should have been implemented years before. His second move was to purchase the remainder of Grupo Modelo, making

Anheuser-Busch too big and too risky for InBev to buy. It would be a master riposte to InBev's attack if he could make it work. Much of the Anheuser-Busch executive team was tasked with the details and negotiations.

A-B's initial offer to Grupo Modelo was significant: Not only would they be paid handsomely, but Grupo Modelo CEO Carlos Fernández would run the new Anheuser-Busch Modelo as its CEO, moving August IV to a position overseeing all of A-B operations, including the theme parks and non-brewery divisions. The Anheuser-Busch board felt the offer went too far and balked at Fernández running the combined company. They asked how the Grupo Modelo CEO running the beer division was any different than getting bought out? August IV was forced by his board to amend the offer, removing Fernández as potential CEO. Once again the Busches insulted Grupo Modelo.

As negotiations between A-B and Grupo Modelo continued, InBev secured funding for a buyout of Anheuser-Busch in an increasingly volatile financial market. Investment bankers who had once shown great interest in funding InBev found themselves on the wrong side of the subprime mortgage crisis in 2008, which bankrupted Lehmann Brothers and led to the fire sale of Bear Stearns and Merrill Lynch. Investment banks that survived now operated under stricter regulations. It was a terrible time for a buyout, and though InBev thought they had enough for an offer that would win over shareholders, if Anheuser-Busch merged with Modelo, the takeover would fall apart.

The official offer came via fax: InBev offered sixty-five dollars a share with the promises that they would continue the relationships with Anheuser-Busch wholesalers, keep the merged company's headquarters in St. Louis, and operate under the Anheuser-Busch name. August IV knew the Grupo Modelo buyout was their only play at this point, and he smoothed hurt feelings with Carlos Fernández by offering more of their payment in cash rather than stock.

August IV and his army of A-B executives spent the Independence Day weekend scrambling to secure their own independence from InBev. By July 7, when the Anheuser-Busch board was scheduled to meet, the deal with Grupo Modelo was complete. It just needed the board's approval. It would be expensive. It would be risky. But the company would still be theirs.

The architects of the Grupo Modelo merger made their pitch to the board. Concerns had been anticipated and addressed. They were ready for this. What they weren't ready for was the man at the head of the table, August III. The chairman of the board had been uncharacteristically silent during most of the takeover saga, seemingly content to allow his son to call the shots. It was a facade.

At the meeting, August III tore into the Grupo Modelo deal, point by point, objecting to issues that he could have easily addressed at any time prior to this eleventh-hour ambush. August IV and his team were in shock. It became clear that August III was opposed to the merger, and most, if not all, board members would vote with him. Their plan to save the company was dead.

It was starting to look as if August III had accepted the idea of selling the company long before others had. In *Dethroning the King*, members of the board are quoted as saying August III began to ask if they could get $70 a share. The whole Grupo Modelo sideshow began to appear like leverage to pump up the selling price, which would account for the elder August's silence throughout the negotiations. Adding insult to injury, August III and the board sent August IV himself back to InBev to ask for their best and final offer. The offer came back at $70 a share, for a total of $52 billion. It was more than Carlos Brito and InBev wanted to pay, but the King of Beers was worth it. The deal just needed shareholder support to finalize.

St. Louisans who had waved off the possibility of a sale the way they laughed at the possibility of the Chicago Cubs winning the World Series, who just assumed the Busch family would shut down all of this nonsense at some point, were caught off guard. It was all happening again: Some faceless, soulless conglomerate with no concern for their history was swallowing up a piece of what made the city St. Louis.

They took to the streets and protested on Lynch Street outside the brewery. "Hell no, Bud won't go!" Hopefuls signed petitions, collecting tens of thousands of signatures against the deal. A local man set up the website SaveAB.com to help direct opposition efforts. Their comments reflected their frustrations.

"Why not sell the Statue of Liberty too!"

"Boycott all InBev products!"

"If you sell, I have purchased my last Bud."

The arguments against the sale were sound. It wasn't just those employed by Anheuser-Busch who would be affected but the tax revenue and philanthropic giving as well. As InBev was known for cutting costs, layoffs would be extensive. The year 2008 was a terrible time to add to

America's unemployed. InBev's size would lead to antitrust issues: With so much control over the market now, they could unfairly control prices.

The main argument was that InBev was a foreign country. It's an argument that's more visceral than logical, rooted in nationalism. On its surface, the buyout was no different from any other acquisition. American companies buy foreign companies and foreign companies buy American companies. The wheels of business keep turning. This felt different. Over their 150 years of existence, Anheuser-Busch had tied themselves so fully to nationalism that it felt like InBev was buying a piece of America.

InBev CEO Carlos Brito made his appeal to locals in a *St. Louis Post-Dispatch* interview where he promised he would not close breweries and would "protect Budweiser's heritage." Busch Stadium would remain Busch Stadium. Few locals believed his promises or cared much for his opinion at all. Really his words were to give cover to shareholders, if any still existed who opposed the merger.

While some politicians spoke out against the sale, with Missouri governor Matt Blunt labeling the possibility "deeply troubling," the truth was there was little they could do. Senator Claire McCaskill said she was "nervous" and "upset" by the merger, but any actions she and others took behind the scenes came to nothing.

Even now some held out hope that shareholders would vote against the merger, as if the American-ness of a company mattered at all to its investors. Most were eager to sell, if only to see some gains in a 2008 that was mostly losses. Even Warren Buffett expressed regret that he didn't hold out long enough for a bigger payout. The vote was never in doubt.

After over 150 years as a Busch family–run company, Anheuser-Busch was sold to the foreign conglomerate InBev on July 11, 2008. St. Louisans were stunned. In this waiting period between agreement on the deal and its closing, where a team of lawyers pored over every detail, employees feared what it would mean for them. Ancillary businesses from distributors to marketing firms to beechwood chip suppliers waited to see if there was still room for them in the newly formed AB InBev. (Its American subsidiary would still be known as Anheuser-Busch.) Locals wondered if Brito would keep his promises long term, or would this deal echo American Airlines' purchase of TWA? Would the brewery tours and Grant's Farm still be the same? Would they still be free?

The merger was officially finalized the week of Thanksgiving 2008. Those who had stock options made a lot of money, from the executives to the scientists to the brewers. "Everyone is a multimillionaire in the top management," board member Jim Forese said. Tom Schlafly saw Goliath fall and even profited from it with the Anheuser-Busch stock he had used to secure Schlafly's initial loans. Layoffs began almost immediately. To be fair to Carlos Brito and InBev, the layoffs were initially part of August IV's cost-cutting strategy and were already in the works. But it wasn't a good look for the new boss in town.

Anheuser-Busch had been such a marketing powerhouse that Madison Avenue firms were expected to keep satellite offices in St. Louis. InBev didn't need them anymore, and the offices closed down. One of three suppliers of beechwood chips was told the company no longer needed their product. Within a year, only one supplier remained. A-B's growing IT department met in a conference room where they were told that AB InBev was a beer company, not an IT company. Most were let go.

The week of December 8 was particularly rough. On Monday, AB InBev announced the cuts of fourteen hundred salaried workers, most in the St. Louis area. On Wednesday employees gathered in a conference room to learn how the rest of the week would go. Thursday they would receive an email with instructions to come in on Friday to meet with someone from human resources.

On Friday, the offices of Anheuser-Busch were closed so that employees who were let go could gather their belongings in private. Local Trueman's Bar opened at 8 a.m. that day, serving one-dollar beer to those who wanted to commiserate or just drown their sorrows. Scenes of crying employees holding cardboard boxes flanked by security guards repeated throughout the day. "I was at Trueman's that morning," said one former employee. "One by one my coworkers arrived, hung out for a bit, left for their appointment [to see if they still had a job], and came back to start drinking because they lost their job. Nobody was kept. People were angry, crying, in denial. I saw tons of emotions that day. After my coworkers with more-important jobs all lost their jobs, I knew I wasn't going to be kept. So I went to my 3:15 appointment drunk off my ass. The HR lady even asked if I had been drinking. My response was, 'What do you think?'"

Marc Gottfried saw an immediate impact at the Master Brewers Association of the Americas: "I was president of MBAA at that time and we were the biggest district—we had three hundred plus members. A lot were A-B. Overnight we were down to fifty to sixty members. They fired everybody. A-B used to subsidize MBAA membership, and all that stopped overnight.

So we went from being the biggest district to like number six or something. Really lost our way after that. It was very difficult. I didn't know if we would be able to continue. Not only was it A-B but people ancillary in their trades—so many businesses here in St. Louis that are here because A-B is here, like valves, controls, mixers, all kinds of stuff—and all of a sudden all the A-B people weren't there anymore, so all these guys left as well. So I lost the A-B people, then I lost all the tradesmen, and then all that was left was a handful of us who had the drive to keep it going, stuck with trying to entice craft brewers to join."

That all of this occurred right before Christmas during the worst economic crisis since the Great Depression made it seem even more ghoulish. A city should go through this much pain so a beer company can make a little more profit? And that company wasn't even American now? Where once most residents of St. Louis were connected to the brewery either personally or through friends and family, now they were feeling the betrayal for the same reason. St. Louisans were angry. The company that had once built bridges of goodwill throughout the city was now burning them down.

Cost-cutting measures continued. The walls of the executive offices were sledgehammered out to fit more tightly packed tables and desks. No more free beer. No more company Blackberry phones. No more tickets to Busch Stadium or any of the Busch Gardens family of theme parks. InBev offloaded the theme parks. Clydesdale appearances now came with a price tag. The once loose, free-spending Anheuser-Busch was no more. Gone, too, was the family atmosphere, the feeling that A-B employees were all in this together.

As Carlos Brito and the InBev group stepped into the spotlight, August IV stepped back into obscurity. He had fought to keep his family business and had been thwarted by his own father. All anyone in St. Louis could see was The Fourth's failure. He had made over $100 million through the sale and a continuing three-year deal with InBev but had earned from his home city only the enmity of those he was trying to defend. Whatever InBev's expectation of August IV in the next three years, they—and the press—would get only his silence.

Public news of August IV came through media reports, which gradually worsened. He divorced his wife of two years in late 2008, just after the deal was closed. Rumored depression and substance abuse culminated in the 2010 death of his girlfriend, Adrienne Martin, from an overdose of cocaine and Oxycodone in August's bed. This was the second young woman to die in August IV's company and the second time he escaped responsibility.

Craft beer in St. Louis saw the biggest growth, with Schlafly as the primary beneficiary. Dan Kopman and the team at Schlafly couldn't make beer fast enough. They were brewing twenty-five thousand barrels a year, increasing each year. "We were getting calls from people asking where they could buy Schlafly Light in thirty-pack cans," Kopman says. Such a product didn't exist. "We weren't set up to do that. We had built the new brewery to give us the capacity to make more pale ale in twelve-ounce bottles, and that's what we did. We just did more of the same and doubled down on the tactics we did to get there. A lot of ad agencies were telling us we could be the next A-B. We said no, that's not happening. That's not who we are."

Schlafly Bottleworks ran at full capacity as they began to expand distribution into fifteen states, culminating in their biggest growth in the years following the A-B sale. Tom Schlafly received over a thousand resumes from former Anheuser-Busch employees.

What followed the sale of Anheuser-Busch to InBev was a short calm before the explosion of craft beer in St. Louis, a decade of exponential growth. Was it a result of the vacuum created by the Anheuser-Busch sale? Were beer drinkers turning to craft beer after years of loyalty to Budweiser? Or was the wave of craft breweries that began on the coasts two decades earlier finally reaching the middle of the country?

Ask a craft brewer those questions, and you'll get different answers. Some, like Tom Schlafly, give no credit to the sale of A-B: "Complete coincidence. The wave was coming anyway."

Fran Caradonna sees too much distance between the flavors of craft beer and those of Anheuser-Busch. "The explosion of craft was coming," she says. "In St. Louis it gave Schlafly a pop for a minute. The fact that some Belgian company owned A-B did not change the drinking habits of anybody long term. For a minute they said, 'I'm not drinking that beer anymore. Let's try Schlafly. Ugh. No.' It's a flavor thing."

Morgan Street's Marc Gottfried saw drinking habits change but not in the direction of craft beer. "The Budweiser and Bud Light loyalists were like, 'Screw this; this beer is now from a foreign country and I'm not drinking it anymore'—and that lasted for like a year," Gottfried notes. "They may have started to dabble in craft beer, but that didn't drive the growth of these craft breweries. We're talking two completely different demographics. Those dyed-in-the wool Bud and Bud Light drinkers, they switched to maybe Miller. They weren't like, 'I'm going to drink IPA now!'"

Schlafly's Dan Kopman and Stephen Hale see a confluence of events leading to the boom. Kopman likens Anheuser-Busch to a dam keeping craft beer away, and their sale allowed locals to turn to something else: "There was a social contract between A-B and the people of St. Louis. The moment the deal gets done and the aftermath of that—all these people getting laid off—there was a contract that was broken between the brewery and the community that meant it was now OK. Those same bars and distributors who were getting these amazing trips from A-B? All those jets got sold. No one was going to play golf at Pebble Beach."

"Things happen on the third coast later than they do on the left and the right coast," Hale explains. "Things move to the center. But when things get going, they get going. When A-B was sold and people were let go suddenly, there were brains and money out there looking for a new home."

To John Witte at Square One, the proof was in the numbers: "Those next three years after the sale, we entered double-digit growth. It wasn't like Square One was still in the honeymoon phase—it was clearly because of the sale. We haven't seen that kind of growth since then. After those three years you start seeing opening, opening, opening, opening." Urban Chestnut. Perennial. Civil Life. 4 Hands.

A seismic shift in beer was happening in St. Louis. The Gateway City was going back to its roots. Where once a giant brewery represented the city, soon small, independent craft breweries would represent individual neighborhoods and provide new sources of pride for communities grown too used to losing.

5

# 2ND SHIFT'S FIRST ACT

The first new St. Louis brewery after the sale of Anheuser-Busch wasn't a St. Louis brewery at all. It was built sixty miles away in the little town of New Haven, Missouri. But time, influence, and an eventual move proved it to be perhaps the most St. Louis of them all.

Underestimate Steve Crider at your own risk. This self-proclaimed "hillbilly mechanic" is a brewer with a tattoo artist's sensibility, whose irony versus sincerity axis leans heavily toward irony. Somehow, impossibly, his technical versus artistic axis maxes out in both directions. A perfectionist, he claims to have made two good beers in his life. Fearless, tenacious, and often profane, Crider approaches life with just the right amount of snark—which is to say all the snark—and creates beer that is shocking in its elegance.

Steve Crider lovingly refers to his hometown as "Granite Shitty," Illinois, where his only connection to the big brewery in nearby St. Louis was drinking ninety-nine-cent quart bottles of Busch. His father, a machinist at McDonnell Douglas, drank Pabst. Steve himself became a millwright machinist, developing at an early age an understanding of machines much deeper than lifelong brewers ever achieve. Crider's gateway beers were Guinness and Fat Tire: "Shit, beer can have flavor!"

The obsession began Christmas of 1999, when his mother gifted him a homebrewing kit. He said in 2024, "I just recently found the original bucket from my first beer ever. I wrote 'January 7th' on it. My first beer was January 7th, 2000. It was a Bass Pale Ale clone. She got me the kit, but not the beer, so I went to Worm's Way supply shop. By March I had forty-two kegs, three deep freezes, and a ten-gallon system I had made myself. I was obsessed pretty quickly with it."

Most brewers come to the hobby from the science side, learning the mechanics of it along the way. Crider is one of the rare brewers who mastered the mechanics before the science of brewing. It didn't take long for him to master that as well.

Crider's beers had impressed enough of his friends and family for them to push him to turn his hobby into a profession. It was on a road trip with his uncle that Crider was convinced. It didn't take much: "It was Thanksgiving of 2006," he recalls. "I was driving from Salt Lake to St. George, Utah, with Uncle Bob. He said, 'You should start a brewery,' and I said, 'Noooo.' And he said, 'Fuck it, do it!' I said, 'All right.' I didn't know anything about business—still don't—but I went, 'Fuck it, I'll do it. I'll give it a try.'"

He began to collect books on the business end of brewing, which didn't exist in high numbers in 2006. One was written by Dogfish Head founder Sam Calagione, another by Brooklyn Brewery's Steve Hindy. A stint at Chicago's Siebel Institute rounded out his education.

During his time as a millwright machinist, Crider had preferred working the second shift. Working from the afternoon into the night suited him, and he expected the same for his future brewing business: "When I started the brewery, I thought I'd be out hustling beer during the day, going up to bars and saying, 'Hey, will you buy my beer?' And I'd be back brewing in the afternoon. I liked working second shift, and I figured I'd be brewing in the afternoon anyway."

Crider had a plan for the brewery. It would be somewhere in St. Louis, possibly in the Delmar Loop, preferably partnered with a really good restaurant for the food program. Instead, he built his brewery sixty miles away in an old Western town. Steve's wife's family owned a conference center in New Haven. They offered to let him build his brewery there for cheap, as it would work as a draw for the location, which would serve his beer. "There was an old Western town that was built by her grandparents on this property. It was kind of run down. They knew I was going to build this brewery and were like, 'Hey, why don't you put the brewery out here?' Shit, I really didn't want to be out in New Haven; I wanted to be in the Loop. I didn't know any better. So I said screw it and built my building out in New Haven."

Crider ran before he could walk and never slowed down, never let what he didn't know hold him back. He figured things out as he went along, only occasionally running into something he didn't know.

In 2008 there was a worldwide shortage of hops due to a combination of environmental factors in Europe and a large warehouse fire in Yakima, Washington, that destroyed a portion of the state's crop. Hearing that hops would be tougher to come by, Crider went to the West Coast to see for himself, visiting brewery manufacturers and hop growers: "I flew to Salt Lake, then drove down to LA, then all the way up the coast. I was scared because I was already building the brewery. I met with growers and farms, and they said, 'No, we've got hops, don't worry about it.' Screw it, so I went back and finished the building."

With a supply of Simcoe and Columbus hops, Crider brewed his first beer as a professional brewer: Art of Neurosis, an IPA that tasted so new and original in 2009 that it became an instant favorite among beer lovers. The hops were strong and flavorful, with notes of pineapple, but were balanced by the malt. Its name came from Crider's insistence to get his first beer exactly the way he wanted it. "That is the beer I've probably fucked with the most, and still do today," he says. "We've brewed it ten thousand times. Before I put it out into the world, I played with it the most, got neurotic about it."

Now that his IPA was out there, Crider turned to his true passion: mixed fermentation beers. "I wanted to make lambics [a Belgian beer] and that kind of shit," he says. "The first beer I brewed was Art of Neurosis because I needed to get a beer out to get a couple of bucks coming in. The second brew was what became CID, Chaotic Insecure Delusions, a saison. The next beer I brewed was Right in the Wood, and I added Pedio, Lacto, and Brett, and as that was aging for months, I would brew another beer. It was a mixed fermentation beer. That's what I wanted to do initially, and I'm glad I didn't now, but I just wanted to make nothing but saisons and Belgian beers, mixed ferm, funky stuff."

*Brettanomyces*, or "Brett," is a type of wild yeast used in the production of sour beers. Not all Bretts impart the same flavors, so often the resulting flavor is a bit of a surprise. Brett works slowly, requiring time and brewery space, both of which Crider had. *Pediococcus* ("Pedio") is a bacteria that works with *Brettanomyces* to lower the pH of the beer over time and impart funky aromas and flavors. *Lactobacillus* (the "Lacto" in his recipe) is a bacteria that eats sugars and converts them to lactic acid, lowering the pH and imparting a sour, clean taste.

When the time came to brew more Art of Neurosis, Crider found he was short of the necessary hops. His efforts to secure them reads like a "Who's on First" of the beer world.

CRIDER: I need some more Simcoe and Columbus.
HOP DEALER: Do you have a hop contract?
CRIDER: A what?
HOP DEALER: If you don't have a hop contract, best I can get you right now is Citra and Amarillo.
CRIDER: OK, give me that.

So Crider followed the same recipe for Art of Neurosis but this time with Citra and Amarillo hops. He named the new beer El Gato Grande, after his brewery cat. Beer drinkers loved it. He called up the hop dealer.

CRIDER: Give me some more of that Citra and Amarillo.
HOP DEALER: Do you have a hop contract?
CRIDER: Uh, no.
HOP DEALER: Best I can give you is Zythos.

So Crider brewed the same recipe with Zythos hops, this time calling it Ratsalad, after the Black Sabbath song. Black Sabbath music was on regular rotation in the New Haven brewery and influenced the name of several beers over the next decade and a half.

He called up the hop dealer.

CRIDER: Give me more of that Zythos.
HOP DEALER: Do you have a hop contract?
CRIDER: Fuck!

Eventually—after eight different hop combinations of IPAs—Crider wised up to the fact that if he was going to brew the same beers over and over, he would have to secure a steady supply of the right hops. He signed a hop contract, an agreement between breweries and hop growers guaranteeing future purchases and deliveries.

As the IPAs were paying the bills, Crider was using his microscope to pull apart strains of yeast for his newest mixed ferm creations. Bacteria that up until then the craft beer world had avoided, Crider was going to harness. What he came up with were beers that were startlingly unique, like Katy, a wild ale that was definitely named after the nearby Katy Trail and not Crider's soon-to-be ex-wife. He wanted to make a wine-barrel-aged saison with funky notes of *Brettanomyces* without it being too sour, which required a deft hand in its brewing. After the beer spent two weeks in a stainless fermenter, he transferred it into wood barrels with the Brett to develop over the next three to six months.

If Art of Neurosis put Crider's 2nd Shift Brewing on the map for St. Louis beer drinkers, Katy revealed what this little brewery way out west was capable of, and soon so-called beer nerds were lining up to secure 2nd Shift bottles. Crider was experimenting with what only a handful of breweries throughout the country were trying. Up in Chicago future Perennial brewery owner Phil Wymore, Goose Island's cellar manager at the time of 2nd Shift's opening, was creating similar styles with their Sofie and Madame Rose. Jester King Brewery, in Austin, Texas, which specializes in wild yeast beers, opened the year after 2nd Shift.

Crider wasn't just ahead of the curve; he was so far in front of the curve in the late 2000s that it was hard to see. Newspapers and other media didn't know how to describe 2nd Shift, often settling on something as vague as "quirky."

Considering the styles Crider was experimenting with, it is notable that he did not do test runs. He was confident that he was going to make something that tasted pretty damn good. "Since the moment I brewed my first batch of beer, I've never brewed a test batch," he says. "I always tell people it's like a baker who's baking a cake. If he's made a thousand cakes, he knows not to put cinnamon, black licorice, and tree bark into a fucking chocolate cake. That tastes gross. You know what works. That's

Photo of 2nd Shift brewer Steve Crider and dog in his New Haven brewery, late 2010s. (Courtesy of Steve Crider.)

not saying I don't tweak shit. Most of the time it's 90 percent of where I want it to be, if not more. You know what you're doing with these malts and hops, or you hope you do. It usually comes in real close to where you want."

Because 2nd Shift had no tasting room—Crider didn't think anyone would come all the way out to New Haven to taste his beer—100 percent of the profits came through distribution. Early on, Crider did it all himself, just as he had planned when he named the brewery.

While making his rounds of the St. Louis bars and restaurants, Crider talked beer with people like Cory King, who was managing a beer bar called the International Tap House, known to the locals as iTap, in the Soulard neighborhood. "We hung out and bullshitted a lot," Crider says. "I knew he was a craft dork. Right after that he went to work at Lohr Distributing to be their craft beer guy. Every brewery hates distributors, but I knew Cory would take care of me. That's why I signed with them. He quit three months after that and went to work at Perennial." Several years later, Cory King opened one of the top breweries in the world, Side Project Brewing.

Now distributing through Lohr, Crider got to know Cory King's replacement in their craft beer division, Mike Sweeney. Sweeney eventually came over to 2nd Shift as their operations manager.

Though 2nd Shift opened almost immediately after InBev bought Anheuser-Busch, the two events were independent of each other. Crider's beer obsession had nothing to do with the end of the once-great St. Louis brewery—he was sixty miles away, pushing craft beer into the future. According to Crider, "I personally think it was going to happen anyway. I spent three years figuring out how to build a brewery. I don't think anyone said, 'I'm going to start a brewery tomorrow because A-B sold.' It takes more than a year or two to plan your own brewery. A lot of work and time. It may have influenced one or two, like Urban Chestnut, but I don't think it was a big factor."

As for the effect the sale had on craft beer sales at the time, Crider didn't think there was much of a shift in habits as a result of the sale: "I was going out every night to bars. Some people were bitching and moaning about it because we were losing our St. Louis brewery, but [I] don't know anybody who said, 'Screw 'em, I'm not drinking them anymore.'"

Perhaps coincidentally, 2nd Shift began to make the area's most popular pilsner. Crider took a trip to the Czech Republic to drink—and learn how to brew—their style of pilsners. "No craft brewers were making lagers really back then," he says. "I like Czech pils. We went to Pilsner Urquell. We went to Budvar. I listened to these guys talk, and it's a very technical beer to make. I thought, 'This is hard to do right.'"

A reverse osmosis water filter finally allowed Crider to crack the code. Water in New Haven was mostly well water, too hard for something as delicate as a pilsner. After running water through the filter, Crider added brewing salts to build the water to the required specification. "We brewed the beer great the first time and we called it Technical Ecstasy." The title reflected the technical aspect of brewing a Czech pilsner—and also happens to be the title of a Black Sabbath album. That first batch Crider considers the second of the two good beers he has made: "That one was the best in my head, and I'm always trying to reach that."

With 2nd Shift not geographically part of the St. Louis craft beer community, Steve Crider brought the community to him. Starting in 2012, the annual 2nd Shift and Friends festival became a gathering spot for craft beer lovers during the day and brewers, brewery owners, and distributors at night. By this point in his career, Crider was well respected in the beer community, and it didn't take much to convince them to come out to New Haven. His 2012 "2nd Shift and Friends 23rst Annual Beerfest" reads like a who's-who of breweries from all over the state and several from outside Missouri. The class of 2011—Urban Chestnut, Perennial, Civil Life, and 4 Hands—were all there, as were the old guard of Schlafly, Morgan Street, O'Fallon, and Square One. Brand-new Illinois brewery Scratch was there, as was Weeping Radish, North Carolina's first microbrewery.

At the time Crider opened 2nd Shift, the St. Louis craft beer community was small enough that everyone knew everyone. They were collegiate, shared ideas, and discussed trends, mostly while drinking beer together. Schlafly's Stephen Hale kept the tone congenial and convivial. But the growing number of new breweries after the Anheuser-Busch sale threatened the close-knit camaraderie that came with a small community. Steven Crider filled that need as his festivals became an important bonding opportunity for new members and old.

Ferguson Brewing Company owner Joe Lonero credits Crider's beer festivals with introducing him to the greater craft beer community, and their after-festival hangouts by the fire served as almost a retreat for the brewers and brewery owners. Abbey Spencer, future head brewer of Third Wheel Brewing, remembers the festival after-party as the real reason people drove out there. "I went to several overnighters there," Spencer remembers. "So fun. The most fun. The pool, the bonfire—it felt like it was more for us than the people coming to try the beers. It was very much a brewers' festival."

"That's why we do it," Crider says. "It's a party. I invited everyone I could because, fuck it, I wanted to drink beer and hang out with brewers."

Over the years, the number of friends attending 2nd Shift and Friends grew. Still, Crider struggled with the question of whether he was technically a St. Louis brewery. When asked, he would hedge, saying he sold his beer in St. Louis, but was 2nd Shift a St. Louis brewery? Probably not. The matter was settled at a brewer's guild meeting.

Steve Crider remembers the moment: "Stephen Hale from Schlafly jumped up and said, 'I want to start off by asking, Is Crider and 2nd Shift a St. Louis brewery?' And everyone said, 'Yes!' And I said, 'All right, shit.'" Was that a tear in his eye? "There's no better industry," Crider says. "St. Louis has some of the best huggy-feely vibes. I hope it never goes away. Some cities I go to, their breweries are not like that. That's one of the reasons I wanted to come into the city."

Craft beer lovers in the area owe much to Crider. He pushed the category forward at a time when the second wave of breweries in the area had yet to get their footing. He championed wild yeasts and mixed fermented beer, mastering styles that took another decade to break into the mainstream. His motto, "Don't be a dick, and drink beer," sums up St. Louis perfectly.

# 6

# FERGUSON

Few towns in America call to mind images of civil unrest the way Ferguson, Missouri, does. Buildings and cars aflame. Lines of police in SWAT gear and shields facing crowds of protesters. Young men throwing Molotov cocktails. Law enforcement pointing rifles at protesters from atop military vehicles. Tear gas. Looting. Destruction. Ferguson carries the scars of its darkest hour, when long-simmering anger and resentment over the St. Louis area's racial history and the country's growing frustrations over police violence against Black people boiled over into violence during the hot August 2014. For a moment in time, all eyes were on Ferguson.

When in the mid-2000s Joe Lonero bought the building that would become Ferguson Brewing Company, he didn't know that it would bear witness to such turmoil, or that those outside of Ferguson would come to view his town as everything that's wrong with race in America. It's a reputation Ferguson doesn't deserve.

Back when riverboat travelers disembarked onto a lawless Morgan Street, much of the area fifteen miles northwest of St. Louis was farmland. Local farmer William B. Ferguson signed over ten acres of his property in the 1850s to the North Missouri Railroad in exchange for a depot and the rights to name it. Ferguson became a regular stop, and well-to-do St. Louisans found they could live conveniently away from the grime of the city. They built large houses, many still standing today. Farms gave way to a small town that grew quickly. A streetcar connected Ferguson to the town of Kirkwood, providing a loop that facilitated the growth of St. Louis County.

After the Civil War, one of Ferguson's largest landowners, Thomas January, freed his enslaved workers and granted them and other free Blacks drawn to the area land along modern-day Eddy Avenue. There a church was built. By the twentieth century, the neighborhood, called "Little Africa," was an early example of Black residents allowed only tiny areas within which to live. Before schools were desegregated due to *Brown v. Board of Education* in 1954, Black students in St. Louis attended Sumner High School in the St. Louis City neighborhood known as "The Ville," or Vashon High School at the current location of Harris-Stowe University, or Douglass High School in north Webster Groves. A Works Progress Administration grant in 1936 led to the construction of Kinloch High School, a fourth option for the growing Black population.

The Ville was, for Black St. Louisans, a center of culture and community. Located just north of the affluent white Central West End neighborhood, it drew comparisons to Harlem and Tulsa. The Homer G. Phillips Hospital not only was a source of middle-class jobs but also provided a sense of pride as one of the country's only Black teaching hospitals. This small section of land saw a cultural boom that launched the careers of Josephine Baker, Chuck Berry, and Tina Turner.

White flight fragmented the city and county into white neighborhoods in the south and west and Black neighborhoods in the north. "Redlining," a real estate designation intended to keep "desirable" neighborhoods white, funneled Black residents toward declining or hazardous neighborhoods.

Larman and Geraldine Williams, two Black educators, tried to move to Ferguson in 1968, but they found their way blocked by a real estate agent who refused to show them a house for sale and an owner who openly stated that neighbors would object to their moving in. It was the Williamses' white pastor who interceded on their behalf, gathered the owner and neighbors for a prayer meeting, and smoothed the way for them to become two of the early Black residents of Ferguson.

A slow growth in the Black population of Ferguson increased with the closing of the Homer G. Phillips Hospital in The Ville and the demolishing of public housing in St. Louis City in the '70s. The St. Louis Housing Authority gave relocation assistance to displaced families, resulting in a wave of new Black residents in Ferguson. Although Ferguson experienced white flight, it occurred at a lower level than other North County neighborhoods, and those who stayed began to develop an integrated community unique to the St. Louis area.

Emerson Electric provided the Ferguson community with a source of well-paying jobs and a sense of pride in their very own Fortune 500 company. A growing Black middle class took root in the city, and the number of Black college graduates grew. By 1980 Ferguson was 14 percent Black. The Black population expanded with a section of government-subsidized housing in east Ferguson, and by 2000 over half of Ferguson residents were Black. By 2010 that figure had grown to two-thirds.

In essence, Ferguson was split in two. South Florissant Avenue, the central business district, which housed the city hall and police department, was a racially diverse community with white and Black business owners. West Florissant Avenue, which is confusingly east of South Florissant, is predominantly Black and has come to be known as Ferguson's Black business district. Scattered throughout the town are streets of large, century-old houses as well as pockets of high poverty.

The Ferguson Station Depot once acted as the town center, and its whistle signaled noon lunch and supper time. At its height, the depot served forty-two trains a day, but it slowly declined in use until the stop was passed over altogether. Two local families leased the now-defunct Ferguson Station Depot from the city to build Whistle Stop Frozen Custard shop.

Business visionaries started to move the city forward after an economic lull in the '70s and '80s due to the closing of St. Louis area factories. Ferguson was uniquely located in St. Louis—its central location meant it was a maximum of fifteen minutes from anywhere.

Enter Joe Lonero, a restless force of nature whom *St. Louis Magazine* once called a "serial entrepreneur." He was a believer in Ferguson and what it could be. Lonero built two auto body shops in Ferguson starting in the mid-'80s, then opened the Corner Coffee House in 1999. Joe's son Mike Lonero described his father as someone constantly looking for new endeavors, new trends: "My dad was a different guy. He worked 24/7. He worked and he stressed about work. We would go on these trips—'We're going to Seattle to check out this new thing called Starbucks.' One day he says, 'Hey, soup and salads; let's do that.' And then we'd go somewhere else. One year we flew up to Chicago for the day to look at cereal bars."

Joe Lonero wasn't just looking to make money; he wanted transformative businesses in Ferguson, ones that would help improve the city. Says his son, "He's looking at, What can I open up in Ferguson that no one else ever would, and what's going to attract people to this area? His ultimate goal was to own property and to develop an area and make that area better than it was before."

Lonero had his eye on the stretch of South Florissant Avenue that made up the city center, from the old Ferguson Station Depot to Maline Creek, an area that came to be known as the Ferguson Citywalk. The corner of South Florissant Road and Paul Avenue had become run down, with two liquor stores, one of which Lonero believed was attracting drug users to the area with a food stamp fraud operation.

Joe Lonero and several members of the Ferguson community started a farmer's market in 2002 on the southwest corner of South Florissant and Paul that became so popular it attracted people from all over St. Louis. The city transformed the location into Plaza 501, a mixed-use outdoor space for community gatherings. Farther north, Joe and Mike opened Vincenzo's, an Italian restaurant that, like the farmer's market, drew diners from well beyond Ferguson. To facilitate transportation along this stretch of Ferguson, the Loneros operated a trolley with stops at various shops and restaurants.

The corner north of the farmer's market became Joe Lonero's next project. He purchased the property, demolished the run-down buildings, and built lofts and commercial space. He was intentional about who he would lease to, opting for multicultural businesses that might lift a community, such as locally owned restaurants and shops, and rejecting operations like liquor stores and payday lenders.

In 2003, on behalf of the North County Chamber of Commerce, the Missouri House of Representatives honored Joe Lonero as the inaugural Citizen of the Year, recognizing his "lifetime of unselfish assistance to his neighbors and fellow business persons." In addition to his business endeavors, the House recognized his support for the *Ferguson Times* newspaper, the construction of the town's gazebo, and the retrieval of the town clock in time for Independence Day 2001.

The lot across South Florissant from Lonero's development came up for auction in the mid-2000s. Once the home of a liquor store and beauty shop, the building had fallen into disrepair. It was Lonero's understanding that the city was poised to purchase the lot to continue the redevelopment and beautification projects they had begun with the farmer's market and Plaza 501. So sure of that outcome, Joe didn't even go to the auction. But his son Mike did. "I came to the auction with one of Joe's friends, and the city wasn't bidding on it," Mike says. "The guy who was bidding on it wanted to keep it as a liquor store. Joe wasn't in favor of that." Mike called his dad, who rushed across the street and bought the building that became Ferguson Brewing Company. Joe's wife told him if he bought another building, she was going to leave him.

Joe Lonero didn't set out to build a brewery—he didn't even drink. "He was already financially invested in the building on one side of the street," Mike Lonero says. "He wanted good neighbors. He wanted control of what was next to him. He had a whole vision—lofts, restaurants." As someone who had his finger on the pulse of national trends, Joe Lonero knew that not only could a brewery work in Ferguson, but it also could provide a gathering spot for the community. The problem was he knew nothing about brewing beer.

Local entrepreneur Ray Hill heard word of Lonero's plans and approached him about taking over the space to open his own brewery. It would be the first Black-owned brewery in St. Louis, one of just a handful in the United States. No stranger to brewing, Hill had made headlines several years earlier by teaming up with Anheuser-Busch to brew and distribute Ray Hill American Pilsner, the first contract production agreement between the beer giant and an entrepreneur. Anheuser-Busch VP Doug Muhleman said of the project, "We saw this unique partnership with Ray as an opportunity to get ahead of a trend combining a niche urban market with the popularity of craft beer."

Ray Hill American Pilsner took the gold medal at the 2007 St. Louis Microfest, one of the city's craft beer festivals. A year later it earned second-favorite local microbrew and Top Ladies Choice award. The beer was making waves in the St. Louis beer scene, and as more were exposed to Ray Hill American Pilsner—often from Ray Hill himself handing them out bottle by bottle—the beer, for some, even supplanted Budweiser as their regular choice.

Then InBev bought Anheuser-Busch, and Ray Hill's partnership with them was dissolved. To Joe Lonero, Ray Hill seemed like the perfect tenant. Here was an experienced brewer in the industry with ties to the community. The plan was for Hill to gather a group of investors to lease the space from Lonero and open the Ray Hill Brewery. Lonero found he had to purchase the name from Anheuser-Busch, who owned the rights. With an agreement in place, Lonero began to build the brewery, no easy task once he realized just how far gone the building he bought was. Many years of poor maintenance and a walk-in refrigerator condensation tube that drained directly onto the floor left some areas warped and others without floor joists at all.

Lonero's search for brewing equipment took him to Fort Collins, Colorado, where he found a recently closed brewery selling its tanks. He hired a local man off the internet to help disassemble the equipment and load it onto an eighteen-wheeler. Because the new brewhouse in Ferguson had not been completed, they unloaded the equipment onto Joe Lonero's yard, where it sat waiting, much to his wife's consternation. Two months and several tow trucks later, Lonero was faced with the daunting task of remembering how to reassemble these things.

At the same time, Joe's son Mike built a wine bar, CORK, across the street. It was an exciting time for this section of Ferguson. Soon locals and visitors could choose between a brewery on one side and a wine bar on the other.

Joe Lonero pieced the kitchen equipment together through restaurant auctions in Chicago, Kansas, and Iowa. St. Louis Cardinals hero Ozzie Smith's Ozzie's Restaurant closed in Westport Plaza, and Joe Lonero lured as many employees over as he could, including chef Robb Wiesen.

With the brewery nearing completion, Ray Hill's search for financing stalled. Joe Lonero made the decision to move ahead with the brewery plans on his own, essentially starting a business he knew nothing about. He found the St. Louis brewing community welcoming and ready to help, especially Square One brewmaster John Witte.

John Witte had by now established himself as one of the top brewers in St. Louis. Affable and generous with his time, Witte had an open-door policy in his brewhouse at Square One. If an aspiring brewer wanted to come in and learn, they were welcome. One such young homebrewer, Josh Wilson, walked into the Square One brewhouse one day and walked out as John Witte's apprentice. Witte brought Wilson with him up to Ferguson to help set up the new brewery.

It was through the interactions with Witte and Wilson that non–beer drinker Joe Lonero began to take to the brewing process and the taste of craft beer. O'Fallon brewmaster Dave Johnson allowed Lonero to shadow him while brewing and the two became friends. Interactions with Morgan Street brewmaster Marc Gottfried resulted in a similar friendship.

Owning a brewery agreed with Joe Lonero. "You would think the breweries wouldn't get along," Mike Lonero says, fourteen years later. "It was the complete opposite."

Though the original partnership with Ray Hill never materialized, Joe Lonero was forced to open his new business as the Ray Hill Brewery anyway, as they already had signage and merchandise. Lonero needed a head brewer. John Witte pointed to his apprentice, Josh Wilson.

The restaurant and brewery opened in April 2010 to immediate crowds. Word of Josh Wilson's beer and Robb Wiesen's food spread, and soon the Ray Hill Brewing Company was drawing from all over the St. Louis region. Workers from Emerson Electric filled the restaurant during the lunch hours. Evenings were lively and bright. The space had become what Joe Lonero had envisioned: a place for locals to build community over a beer and a bite.

Mike Lonero remembers the excitement of their opening: "Oh, man, this place was packed. It was nuts. It was crazy. Madness. I don't know if it was the beer or the food. Or a mixture of both. The atmosphere. We had Boeing people, a lot of suit and ties around here with Emerson and Express Scripts. As far as the neighborhood, they loved it. At first, they were a little weirded out that we didn't sell A-B products. At the time, you did—nowadays no one thinks twice about it."

After a year Joe Lonero changed the name of the brewery to Ferguson Brewing Company to better reflect the community. It was an arduous process that essentially saw them reincorporate the business from the ground up. He bought new signage and merchandise. In just a decade, this corner of South Florissant had transformed into a model of business and community growth. Ferguson, already a close-knit community, was drawing customers from all over St. Louis.

Joe Lonero's and brewmaster Josh Wilson's relationships with the craft beer community grew with each beer festival. "Every year we'd all get together for a big bonfire at 2nd Shift," Mike Lonero says. "He would have an overnight and they'd love it. They'd go there and do the festival, then stay overnight and have a big bonfire—the brewers, some owners, distribution people. People who just really enjoyed the camaraderie of the people, and I think that's what my dad really liked about owning a brewery. It was a community—people were great."

Joe Lonero suffered a stroke in 2012 that severely limited his ability to communicate. No longer able to run the brewery himself, Joe stepped back into a supporting role while his son took over. The stroke was a wake-up call for Joe, who quit smoking and turned to bicycling to get in shape. He and his bike became a regular sight on the Ferguson streets, and he was even known to travel great distances, showing up one day at Square One in Lafayette Park to visit John Witte.

Ferguson Brewing Company's mascot gorilla came about as a way for Mike Lonero to honor his father after the stroke. Joe Lonero had decorated his property with concrete animals, including four gorillas—one large, one smaller, and two little ones—to represent his family. Mike Lonero bought a similar concrete gorilla and placed it outside the brewery on South Florissant. It has become the company logo.

In a 2012 article on best places to live, *St. Louis Magazine* named Ferguson one of the top communities for "locavores," or people who seek out locally grown food, highlighting Ferguson's farmer's market. Also mentioned were Ferguson's Savoy Theater building and its train depot museum, home of Whistle Stop Frozen Custard. Joe Lonero had done his part and continued to support the community in any way he could, including providing free kegs of beer for local events. It was his hope that others would continue what he started and Ferguson would continue to grow.

A report produced by the BBC in 2012 was the proverbial canary in the coal mine for St. Louis race relations. There was nothing in the video that surprised a native St. Louisan, but the fact that another country was taking note of some glaring inequalities brought to the forefront issues too long ignored. Nowhere was the imbalance more apparent than the Delmar Divide, a stretch of Delmar Boulevard that came to symbolize the city's race problem. The BBC video report drew on a Manhattan Institute study of the disparity between the predominantly white and well-to-do south side of the street and the predominantly Black and impoverished north side. St. Louis was one of the most segregated cities in America. The median home price south of Delmar along one stretch was $335,000. North of the same stretch, the median home price was $73,000. Median household income on the south was $50,000, on the north $18,000. The population with a bachelor's degree on the south was 70 percent, on the north 10 percent.

These are just comparisons of neighboring communities. In other towns in the region, the disparity becomes staggering. One of the wealthiest cities in the country and home to various members of the Busch family, Huntleigh, boasts a median income of $250,000+, with its top 5 percent of residents making over $2.7 million. The average income of the 63106 zip code of North St. Louis City is $20,000. The once-prosperous and dynamic Black neighborhood known as The Ville now has an average income of $24,000.

Wildwood, a quiet, predominantly white city to the far west of the St. Louis region, boasted in 2015 a life expectancy of over ninety-one years. In Kinloch, a Black St. Louis County neighborhood picked apart by the building of St. Louis Lambert International Airport, the life expectancy was fifty-six years.

Forty-four percent of Black children in St. Louis live at or below the poverty line. Statistically, they can't get out. St. Louis ranks near last in probability that a child can climb out of the lowest fifth in income into the highest over the course of their lifetime.

Perhaps the largest factor in the region's segregation is the city's separation from the county. Within St. Louis County are eighty-one different municipal courts and sixty police departments. It is easy to ignore the problems of your neighbors when they live in a different town, under different jurisdictions.

Economists say segregation has held St. Louis back significantly. The gross domestic product for the entire region would be 10 percent higher if not for the racial income gap. The racial divide in St. Louis stems from segregation laws and racial covenants from the early twentieth century. In 1916 the city was the first in the nation to segregate by voter referendum. Black people could not move into a neighborhood that was three-fourths white. The Supreme Court struck down such laws a year later after the NAACP challenged them in Kentucky. Thus began the application of racial covenants, a house-by-house segregation effort that involved riders attached to property deeds that explicitly forbade ownership by non-whites. Over one hundred thousand St. Louis homes held a racial covenant, many of which still exist today. Segregation in St. Louis was carefully orchestrated.

In one instance, a young Black couple purchased a house in North St. Louis in 1948, despite the existence of a racial covenant on the deed. When the sale was challenged by a neighborhood association, the Supreme Court of Missouri ruled against the couple. The NAACP and future US Supreme Court Justice Thurgood Marshall brought the case to the US Supreme Court. Three of the court justices recused themselves because they themselves owned homes whose deeds included racial covenants. *Shelley v.*

*Kraemer* resulted in a win for housing desegregation, but racial covenants weren't banned outright until 1972.

Delving into the legalese of housing deeds in St. Louis today is an archaeological dig into a racist history too recent to dismiss as "a different time." St. Louisans are still living with their consequences. An early twentieth-century map of racial covenants overlaid atop a current demographic map of St. Louis looks similar. Webster Groves High School student Samantha Enlund is working with homeowners to add a clause to their deeds disavowing the racial covenants. Simply removing the covenants didn't seem sufficient to her. They must be renounced.

Unfortunately, the damage had long ago been done. Early segregation efforts funneled Black St. Louisans away from areas of opportunity and growth. By the time the BBC video was aired, places like the Delmar Divide had not only become widespread in St. Louis but were also shrugged off as "that's just the way it is."

The reaction to the BBC piece was mixed, from "how dare they criticize our city" to "we really need to look at what they're saying." Local news ran the story and discussed its merits long enough that the term "BBC Report" became shorthand in conversations—everyone knew what it meant. The Missouri History Museum and Pulitzer Foundation for the Arts began to engage their community in discussions about the disparity. Six months later the BBC produced a follow-up to the video, much of it focused on the mixed reactions to their first. In it, St. Louis alderman Antonio French said, "Conversations about race in general are uncomfortable. And it's been such an issue for so long. I think it's one of the defining issues in St. Louis. People's patience sometimes has just gotten a little thin from dealing with it." Two years later, French's words would look like understatements as riots engulfed Ferguson, where French would be arrested while protesting.

In the second BBC video, French lamented the frustrations of North St. Louis's best and brightest, who didn't see St. Louis as a system they could change. "We're losing so many young, talented people because they don't want to deal with these issues," he said. "They don't want to deal with the racial polarization of this city. So many of the best who come out of North St. Louis are helping make Atlanta a better place, New York a better place, Chicago. If we're really going to turn this city around, we're going to have to keep those folks and change this culture."

In conversations about demographic and economic disparity, Ferguson was not usually mentioned. Located north of Delmar, and surrounded by predominantly Black neighborhoods, Ferguson could boast of Black-owned businesses existing alongside white-owned businesses. All things considered in St. Louis, Ferguson appeared to be less affected by white flight than other areas of the city and county. The problem with that mentality was it pushed real problems into the background and asked residents and visitors to look past them. Look at this stretch of South Florissant pushing Ferguson toward economic prosperity, not the quarter of Ferguson residents living in poverty, many of them concentrated in an area where a young man was about to be killed by a police officer.

On August 9, 2014, Ferguson police officer Darren Wilson came upon Michael Brown and a friend walking in the middle of Canfield Drive around noon. When the two refused to walk on the sidewalk, Wilson noticed that Brown was carrying a box of cigarillos that matched the description from a robbery call. According to Wilson, when questioned about the robbery, Brown attacked, attempting to gain possession of Wilson's weapon. Wilson shot, wounding Brown, who began to flee. After a brief chase, Brown allegedly turned back to attack Wilson. While moving backward away from Brown, Officer Wilson fired at least six shots, killing Brown.

Other members of the Ferguson Police Department arrived within minutes as a crowd began to gather. The arrival of the homicide division of the St. Louis County Police Department was delayed due to their having to attend another crime scene. An hour and a half after the shooting, police put up privacy screens around the area, but sounds of gunfire in the area combined with an increasingly hostile crowd slowed the investigation. An investigator from the medical examiner's office didn't arrive until 2:30. Brown's body wasn't moved from the site until 4:00, an act the crowd viewed as demeaning and disrespectful.

Community anger grew the following day as memorials and candlelight vigils near the location of the shooting turned to violence in other parts of Ferguson. Twelve businesses were looted and vandalized, and a QuikTrip shop was set aflame. Police in riot gear arrested thirty people. Two officers suffered minor injuries.

The vacuum created by law enforcement policy not to talk about cases under investigation was filled by those claiming to be eyewitnesses who said that Michael Brown had his hands up and was surrendering when he

Photo taken by Lawrence Bryant of the unrest in Ferguson, 2014. (Courtesy of the Missouri Historical Society and Lawrence Bryant.)

was shot. As a result, protesters in Ferguson and elsewhere took up the chant "Hands up, don't shoot."

The veracity of this part of the incident became a lightning rod for both sides. The narrative that Brown was surrendering when he was killed resonated because it fit with so many Black citizens' experience of being policed by a predominantly white police force. Fresh in protesters' minds were the deaths of Eric Garner and John Crawford, two Black men killed by police just days before. Garner was choked to death in New York during a confrontation over illegally selling cigarettes. Crawford was shot and killed in an Ohio Walmart as he attempted to purchase a BB gun.

But subsequent police and FBI investigations that found the "hands up" part of the story to be false gave credence to those who opposed the protests, saying they were based on lies from the beginning. Those on opposite sides of the issue pulled even further apart, while the majority of St. Louisans who sought a peaceful way forward felt drowned out by the violence and vitriol.

Over the course of the following week, mostly peaceful protests during the day were followed by violence and arrests at night. Ferguson's boast of being fifteen minutes away from everywhere in St. Louis suddenly had its drawbacks. Locals tried to remove "bad actors" from the protests, insisting the rioting and violence were done by nonresidents. Indeed, of the fifty-one people arrested in one night of violence, only one was a Ferguson resident. Locals knew destruction would only distract from their goals and justify racist attitudes.

Caught between criminals who took advantage of the situation to wreak havoc on Ferguson and law enforcement—who, in their new Homeland Security armored equipment, looked every bit like an occupying force—the vast majority of St. Louisans struggled to see themselves in any of it. Members of the press and community leaders, including Antonio French, were arrested or shot with rubber bullets when their definition of peaceful demonstration did not align with those of the police.

Nine days after Brown's death, a group of several hundred protesters defied an imposed curfew, facing off against a wall of police officers and newly arrived soldiers from the National Guard sixty wide and five deep. Some protesters threw bottles; some riled up the crowd to violence. The crowd surged, rushing at the line of police. Between the two groups, a line of

Photo taken by Lawrence Byrant of protesters facing off against police in front of the Ferguson Police Department, 2014. (Courtesy of the Missouri Historical Society and Lawrence Bryant.)

community leaders and clergy formed, locked arm in arm, and stopped the mob from advancing. Here was where the true spirit of Ferguson emerged: through those who maintained the delicate balance of protest and peace, fighting for the future of their city, not against its present or past.

The people at Ferguson Brewing Company found themselves at the geographic center of the unrest. Two blocks north of the brewery was the Ferguson Police Department and city hall. Mike Lonero's restaurant, Vincenzo's, sat one building south of the police department. The eyes of the world were on Ferguson, and the streets the Loneros had worked to improve were in chaos.

Neither the brewery nor Vincenzo's closed that August—no employee refused to come to work—and both developed a reputation as places where people could step away from the inflamed emotions on the street. They were not places to take sides. What mattered was Ferguson as a community, and community leaders and law enforcement who may have stood opposite each other earlier in the day could be seen at neighboring tables in either restaurant.

Photo taken by Lawrence Bryant of police in riot gear lined up in front of the Ferguson Brewing Company, 2014. (Courtesy of the Missouri Historical Society and Lawrence Bryant.)

The Loneros' efforts to stay above the fray weren't always successful, and Ferguson Brewing Company found itself in the news after a large group of protesters claimed they were denied water there, saying the owner only repeated no while pointing at the door. But as Joe Lonero's stroke had left his speech limited to yes, no, and the occasional obscenity, his repeated nos in that particular situation were a form of diplomacy.

City and business leaders like the Loneros met repeatedly with community leaders, and Mike Lonero realized that many came to the conversations with preconceived notions that just weren't true. There was an underlying belief that Joe Lonero was part of the problem in Ferguson, that he must have been in cahoots with the white city council and police. He must have been getting government kickbacks or, at the very least, sweetheart deals to do all that he had done in that area of Ferguson. The truth was the opposite; Joe Lonero never experienced preferential treatment, and his businesses paid out nearly one hundred thousand dollars a year in property taxes. Communication led to deeper understanding for some and an agreement that they were all in this for the good of Ferguson. "I was raised not to treat people differently," Mike Lonero says. "My dad taught me to stay where you are, support what's around you, and help the people around you."

As the unrest calmed, it was time to examine the causes. Some surprising revelations came out—at least surprising for those unfamiliar with the socioeconomic struggles many in Ferguson faced. In a city that was two-thirds Black, almost the entire police force was white. Of its fifty-three police officers at the time, only three were Black. The mayor was white. Only one city councilperson was Black.

Ferguson residents were being fined at an alarming rate for nonviolent offenses, such as traffic violations. The criminalization of poverty became part of the national conversation. Ferguson's municipal court issued 32,975 arrest warrants for nonviolent offenses the year before the riots. The city's total population was 21,135. Court fines totaling $2.5 million accounted for one-fifth of the city's operating revenue that year, up from $1.4 million two years before. To put that into perspective, Webster Groves, which is 87 percent white, generates only 7 percent of its overall revenue through court fines and fees. Ferguson was squeezing its poorest residents.

When failure to pay led to jail time, nonviolent offenders were removed from their families and their jobs, worsening the problem. As with most of the eighty-one small municipal courts in St. Louis County, the Ferguson court did not meet every day. Those who were jailed and could not post bond had to stay there until the court met next.

Ferguson had been hit hard by the subprime mortgage crisis, which steered lower-income buyers into riskier home loans. Ferguson in 2008 saw foreclosures, a drop of housing values, and a decrease of home ownership from 67 percent to 59 percent. Over half of all homeowners in Ferguson were underwater, owing more than their homes were worth. By 2010 median household income had come down 14 percent from 2000, and the poverty rate doubled from 12 percent to 25 percent. Home ownership, or lack thereof, drove the wealth gap between white families and Black families. A Brandeis University analysis concluded that the wealth gap tripled from 1984 to 2009, from $85,000 to $236,500. The report singled out home ownership as the largest driver of the gap.

Missouri governor Jay Nixon established the Ferguson Commission to study "the social and economic conditions that impede progress, equality, and safety in the St. Louis region." Their 2015 report, titled "Forward Through Ferguson: A Path Toward Racial Equality," is careful not to use the term "racist" to refer to individuals. Rather, the Ferguson Commission Report says, "The data suggests, time and again, that our institutions and existing systems are not equal, and that this has racial repercussions." The report lays out the duality of St. Louis:

> If you live in a safe suburb, and you've got a good job, and you've got health insurance, and you never worry about your kids' schools, and you don't wonder if you might get pulled over because of the color of your skin, then maybe the status quo is working just fine for you.
>
> But for thousands of St. Louisans, the status quo is killing them. The status quo means living in a food desert, with no grocery stores for miles around. The status quo means sending your children to underperforming schools that get fewer resources but dole out more punishments. The status quo means driving in fear of a court system that will put you in jail for failure to pay a traffic ticket . . .
>
> When someone is jailed for failure to pay tickets, the justice system has not removed a dangerous criminal from the streets. In many cases it has simply removed a poor person from the streets.

After laying out the root causes of the Ferguson unrest and the structural inequity in St. Louis, the report concludes that the only way forward is through. To that end, the commission advocated specific goals: Police reform should focus on a decreased use of force and investigations into the use of force free from the perception of bias. Increase community involvement and civilian oversight in police matters. Consolidate the cities of St. Louis County. Consolidate their courts. Consolidate their police departments. Address early education and child hunger, access to affordable health care, job training, housing, and transportation. Nothing that the report suggested was going to be easy, but community leaders felt concerns that had been ignored for decades were in the open, and they had a plan to address them. Ferguson as a city could begin to heal.

Most of St. Louis recognized that the Ferguson that the world had witnessed was not the Ferguson they knew. They sought ways to help, to support the community. Many marched in solidarity, attended community meetings, and volunteered for clean-up efforts and community events. Merchandise flew off the shelves at Ferguson Brewing Company, and sales of gift certificates in store and online surged.

Unfortunately for Ferguson, what locals thought was over kept coming back, and the area in front of the Ferguson police station became the convergence point for further unrest. When a grand jury declined to indict Officer Wilson in November 2014, protests and riots returned even stronger, and a dozen businesses were burned down. The next March, following the resignation of the Ferguson chief of police, two police officers were shot in front of the Ferguson police station.

Along with the one-year anniversary of Michael Brown's death came looting throughout Ferguson, as well as several shootings. Protesters throughout St. Louis shut down area highways. When the traffic obstruction was repeated on the second anniversary, a motorist sped through the protesters, hitting one and throwing him into the air.

Protests returned in 2020 after the murder of George Floyd by officer Derek Chauvin in Minneapolis. Mike Lonero's children, who weren't old enough to understand what had happened in 2014, now rode their bikes to South Florissant to join their neighbors in marching for justice.

Once again daytime protests gave way to nighttime riots. This time Vincenzo's was damaged. Mike Lonero drove to the restaurant that night but found the situation too dangerous to stay. When he returned at 6 a.m., four people were there cleaning up, three of whom Mike had never met. The other was Red Harris, owner of Red's The One and Only BBQ, next door to Vincenzo's. Within an hour, Mike and Red were joined by over a hundred people there to offer what help they could.

The following night, Ferguson Brewing Company was vandalized. It was starting to feel like one step forward, two steps back, and Mike was near his breaking point. It took a young man, a stranger to Lonero, to bring him hope. "It will bring you to tears," Mike says. "This young African American kid shows up, he's seventeen years old—he's a kid—and he says, 'What do you want me to do? I'll do whatever. Give me that shovel.' And he just starts cleaning stuff up."

It's easy to feel discouraged. It's easy to feel as if nothing has changed. On the national level, police reform programs begun under President Obama were abandoned under President Trump, who went so far as to limit what the Department of Justice could require of state and local police departments. But in 2020 Ferguson elected their first Black mayor, Ella Jones, and the police department grew its number of Black officers to twenty-one.

"Progress is small," says Forward Through Ferguson's 2019 report "State of Police Reform," "and can seem excruciatingly slow, and beset by failed and superficial attempts. But it's here. Change is happening, and that means we can learn from it, and try to do better moving forward."

To locals, "Ferguson fatigue" is real. Community posttraumatic stress disorder is real. People are tired. They're tired of the perception that the city is a racist hellhole or a bombed-out wasteland. They're tired of being a political football. They're tired of their home being used as a background for celebrities to post selfies. But, as the Ferguson Commission Report states, "The only way forward is through." There are scars in the community, and sometimes those scars reopen.

Today the crowd at Ferguson Brewing Company is as diverse as the surrounding community. A loud hum of conversation and laughter, mixed with the clinks of plates and pints, give life to the wood-paneled space. A square bar juts out from the kitchen area. Copper fermenters work their brewing magic behind glass windows. A colorful chalkboard across one wall lists the brewery's core beer styles, along with several rotating offerings currently available and those on the way. It is a little touch of hope for the near future, as if the brewery is saying: No one knows what tomorrow will bring, but we'll have a seat here for you with a Pecan Brown or a Raspberry Gose-rilla. Come be part of our community.

Those who visit for the first time and see what the news reports didn't show have a similar reaction: "This place is pretty great."

It always has been.

# 7

# KRÄFTIG

The 1975 boardroom coup that saw August Busch III supplant his father, Gussie, was just one in a series of blows for the extended Busch family. Several months prior, eight-year-old Christina Busch, Gussie's daughter with his third wife, Trudy, died in a car accident on her way home from school. Gussie took it hard, falling into periods of crying that angered Trudy, who argued that their other children needed them right then. Despite the sentiment, Trudy left for Switzerland soon after.

That May, August III convinced the board that his father was no longer fit to run Anheuser-Busch. In the days that followed, The Third's half siblings demanded answers as to why he would treat their father in such a way. They organized a meeting at the fence of adjoining Busch family properties. August III parked his Jeep and walked to the locked fence on one side, his nine-year-old son, August IV, remaining in the car. The Third's twenty-two-year-old half brother, Adolphus IV, drove a Jeep from the other side, bringing along little brothers Peter, Billy, and Andy.

Billy Busch was fifteen years old and had expected to find something between *High Noon* and *West Side Story*. One of the two farms, after all, was nicknamed "The Shooting Grounds." In the lead up to the meeting, Gussie had told Billy, "Sock August III in the puss if you get the chance." But the meeting didn't go as Billy expected. August didn't bring a gun, as Billy feared he might, but calmly laid out the reasons why Gussie was no longer able to run the company, focusing on the recent trauma of losing young Christina. They were reasons Billy couldn't dispute; the boys in the Jeep were all witnesses to Gussie's struggles. August, Billy had to admit, was right. There was no brawl, no socking in the "puss." Adolphus IV had his own future with the company to think about. After the meeting, the boys drove back to the lodge silently, resigned that they would not be able to stop this new era of Anheuser-Busch from beginning.

Over the next thirty years, Billy Busch watched his family company rise to new heights and then saw the ground fall out from under it in 2008. August IV, who had stayed in the Jeep during the fence line meeting all those years ago, was now in charge, and things weren't going well. Billy could only stand on the sidelines and watch his family business sell out to an international conglomerate. For the first time in 150 years, no member of the Busch family was brewing beer in St. Louis.

Billy Busch could fix that. He had kept the Anheuser-Busch stock his father gifted him with every Christmas and now, with the sale, found himself with a significant windfall. What better way to use that money than to build a brewery? After all these years of watching other Busches brew, it was finally Billy's chance. He gathered a team of brewery veterans with over one hundred years of experience. Several former Anheuser-Busch executives signed on. But instead of hiring as brewmaster one of the many local graduates of prestigious German beer schools, Billy Busch chose a local craft brewer.

Marc Gottfried, the brewing savant who had started as a teenager in a homebrew shop, had become the brewmaster of Morgan Street Brewing Company and then the president of the local chapter of Master Brewers, was about to get a call from a Busch. By the time Billy Busch was putting together his new company, Gottfried had stepped away from brewing at Morgan Street to try to make some money in craft brewery equipment installation and brewery consulting. The 2009 phone call was, Gottfried assumed, a prank. His friends were putting him on. The person on the other end couldn't be Billy Busch. But it was, and after embarrassing himself only slightly, Gottfried jumped at the opportunity. Like Busch, Gottfried was disappointed in the sale of Anheuser-Busch. He told National Public Radio in 2012, "To see the changes that took place over the last two years was heart-wrenching for me. And for us to bring that back or just to take a shot at bringing that back is a chance at writing brewing history, and it's an amazing feeling."

Certainly Billy Busch wanted to capitalize on the Anheuser-Busch backlash happening in St. Louis—if there was a vacuum forming, he wanted to fill it. But it wasn't just a business decision, Gottfried explained: "He expressed to me that he didn't like how nobody in his family was brewing beer all of a sudden. I think he saw that opportunity to take that torch and run with it. It was less about this big grand marketing plan and more about tradition."

"It's something that I felt in 2008 was a big loss, a big part of me, a big part of our family," Billy Busch told *The San Antonio Express-News*. "A big part of the industry in America was gone when our company was taken over by InBev. It would have been easy to walk away. But this is my contribution and my family's contribution to our ancestors, to our heritage, to the beer industry and the beer consumer to keep this going in our family. So we're basically writing chapter two of the Busch family history in brewing." He named his new beer Kräftig. Pronounced *kref-tig*, it means "powerful" in German, a reference as much to his family legacy as to the flavor of his new beer.

Years later neither Busch nor Gottfried could recall who recommended the Morgan Street brewer to Busch. Billy Busch was not associated with Anheuser-Busch at all and so would not have known the brewers there. Many of them were looking for a job after the InBev buyout but may have been blocked from competing so directly with A-B in their home market. Most likely, Gottfried's tenure as president of the local chapter of the Master Brewers Associations, as well as his stellar name among the brewing community, earned him the nod.

What Gottfried had going for him that most other prospective brewers didn't was his extensive experience with lagers. Except for some dabbling in ales, Gottfried had brewed only lagers for his entire career. As evidenced by his growing number of awards, he made some of the best lagers in the world. He knew what he was doing and had the hardware to prove it.

Despite a name that sounded a whole lot like "craft," Kräftig belonged in the Premium Lager category, or macrobeers over 4.5 percent alcohol by volume, what most Americans drank. This new beer was going to compete with Budweiser, not Schlafly.

But Busch hired a craft brewer. He recognized the effects of the craft boom: "People are moving to beer with more flavor," Billy Busch told Gottfried in 2011. He wanted to make the best-tasting premium lager available. "I want to attack it like a craft brewer would, from a purely quality standpoint. Let's pilot it, let's brew it, let's figure out if we can do it, and then we'll look at the finances."

Quality was first, business second. Busch wanted his beers to follow Reinheitsgebot, the German beer purity law that limited beer to four ingredients: water, malt, yeast, and hops. They didn't use corn or rice. They didn't use preservatives.

Gottfried tweaked traditional German lager recipes for the modern palate, creating a classic lager and a light. Usually a light beer comes from watering down or removing starch from an original, but Gottfried developed the two beers independently in order to ensure optimal taste. The drawback was they now needed double the production facility. Though Kräftig was initially contract brewed in Wisconsin, one of Busch's goals was to grow the company enough to build a brewery in St. Louis, perhaps on Grant's Farm itself. Next, they tested their beers, bringing in a company run by former Anheuser-Busch executives to run blind taste tests. Just to see what would happen, Gottfried hid some Anheuser-Busch products he had bought at Walmart among his own creations: "They were like, 'Sample 7 is fucked! What in the hell is that?'"

Gottfried turned the can around to show one of the Anheuser-Busch beers. "And they'd groan. They'd say if this was happening while *I* was there, I wouldn't go home at night. August would have me down at Spirit of St. Louis with the clothes on my back flying to that brewery, whatever the brewery the can came out of. They were astonished at the change." The Kräftig beers fared much better in the blind taste tests.

Their next step was to bring in self-proclaimed Bud Light drinkers to try Kräftig and Kräftig Light, talk about them, and indicate if they would choose them over Bud Light. If the percentage was in the high single digits, they could consider the trial a success. Twenty-seven percent of Bud Light drinkers in the test indicated they would choose Kräftig or Kräftig Light over Bud Light. Gottfried, Busch, and others on their team were high-fiving on the other side of the one-way mirror.

Billy Busch believed the excellence of the beer went beyond the taste: "It foamed beautifully; it had perfect lacing. It had the perfect level of carbonation. It had a wonderful hop-and-barley smell. And, yes, it tasted delicious. Our standards were excellent. My dad would have loved it."

The William K. Busch Brewing Company announced the release of Kräftig and Kräftig Light in November 2011. The beers sold well in St. Louis; the company produced ten thousand barrels in their first year. Gottfried entered the beers into national and international competitions. He wanted everybody to know how good these beers were. The medals started flooding in, and soon their marketing reflected their awards. They dominated the category in the US Open Beer Championships, winning gold eight times over the course of the 2010s in the American Premium Lager

Photo of Marc Gottfried, brewer of Kräftig, 2015. (Courtesy of Marc Gottfried.)

and American Light categories. Overall, the company won twenty-nine national industry awards in its first five years, including gold and silver at the Denver International Beer Competition. Gottfried himself won Missouri Lager Brewer of the Year in 2018.

"We dominated. We beat the shit out of those guys," Gottfried says. "And we knew there was indisputable proof that we made better beer. And I have nothing against Anheuser-Busch, but it's not that hard to make better beer. Our beer was all malt, and if you put an all-malt beer up against a beer that has rice or corn syrup, it's going to be better. And our beer was genuinely better."

The problem with Kräftig, and what would ultimately lead to their shuttering in 2019, was never the flavor. They were fighting against forces much bigger than an upstart company—even one owned by a Busch—could overcome. They found themselves up against the three-headed monster of marketing, consumer habits, and a system of street-level distributors who had been fighting back any encroachment onto their territory for decades.

The beer wars that began in the 1970s moved big beer companies into greater reliance on the marketing of their beers than the taste. By the 2010s, even with new owners, Anheuser-Busch pumped an absurd amount of money into making sure their product was in every medium possible. "The blind taste tests said we're better," Gottfried explains. "But the world is not blind. The world is full of expensive marketing. You've got Brad Paisley singing about crushing Bud Light cans, the whole backdrop of the concert has got Anheuser-Busch stuff, the movies, Netflix, baseball stadium, the billboards, TV. At one point we were spending seven digits on advertising per year, which is horrendous for a small company, and Bud, Miller and Coors each spent two billion dollars a year at the brewery level and the distributors collectively another two billion. You just can't get away from this."

Whether we recognize it or not, marketing affects our behavior, and in a city like St. Louis, where beer drinkers have baked-in habits of ordering a Bud, Kräftig faced an uphill climb. Take a television show that has nothing to do with Budweiser: "If you're in the beer industry, the marketing is just gratuitous," Gottfried says. "There will be two people at a bar, both drinking a Budweiser; their labels are out. In the background is a blurry but still readable Budweiser neon; they're shooting pool and it's a Budweiser dome light. If you're in the industry, you see it. If you're not, you're just getting impressions. Commercials on the radio, pass by a billboard, you're just getting these impressions constantly. You can't compete. It's brilliant psychology. You see a logo enough and it's associated with positive, fun things that connect to your lifestyle."

Gottfried realized what they were up against during one particular interaction with a Bud Light drinker. He explains, "I was in a bar where we were having an event and I walked up to a guy drinking at the bar and said, 'Hey, I don't want to bother you. I'd like to buy you a beer. I see you're drinking Bud Light. Would you like to try a Kräftig Light?' He says, 'Oh, yeah, I'd like to try one, thanks a lot.' And he drinks it, and I came back and he said, 'This is awesome! I love this beer. Thank you for introducing it to me. What does it cost?' 'It costs exactly the same [as Bud Light].' And then later in the night I come back and the guy is drinking a Bud Light. I actually went up to him and said, 'I'm not trying to screw with you, but why'd you order a Bud Light? You told me you liked this other one better and I told you it cost the same, so why wouldn't you order one?' The guy looked back at his beer, genuinely confused. 'I don't know,' the guy said. They don't know. It's unconscious."

In the 2009 documentary *Beer Wars*, drinkers of the big three beers who were sure they could pick out their favorite were given blind taste tests of

Bud Light, Miller Lite, and Coors Light. Few could differentiate between the three. A self-proclaimed "Coors Light Guy" failed to pick out his beer but maintained he was still a Coors Light Guy. When asked why, he said, simply, "Habit."

Early in Kräftig's run, the company worked to get their beer sold in Busch Stadium. It was a symbolic victory for them to compete side by side with Budweiser in the stadium named after Billy Busch's family, where an image of Billy's father, Gussie, waves from the retired numbers mural in left field. They went through all the proper channels, completed all the paperwork, found real estate for their neon signs, and set their price to match the Anheuser-Busch products, still pricey at twelve dollars for a twenty-four-ounce can.

On opening day, Gottfried and others from Kräftig entered the stadium with their badges, ready for perhaps the biggest day for the fledgling company, and found their neon signs taken down and their beer prices nearly doubled to twenty-two dollars a can. "We were running around at the beginning of the game, trying to figure it out. What the fuck happened? We had all the paperwork on us. No one could tell us what happened. Someone didn't like it, we got changed to twenty-two bucks, and it never went down. We're talking for baseball seasons. So we were the twenty-two-dollar beer. You have to really care to spend twenty-two dollars for a beer."

Busch Stadium hadn't been owned by Anheuser-Busch for twenty years, and yet forces within it made sure to knock the legs out of the upstart Kräftig. For the rest of the company's existence, Kräftig was never given an explanation. Anheuser-Busch may have been sold, but the old distribution network remained in place, and distributors had used the same tactics when Miller tried to encroach during the beer wars. They had spent their whole careers maintaining Anheuser-Busch's dominance.

Billy Busch explained the hurdles they faced in his book *Family Reins*: "Anheuser-Busch/InBev asked their managers and distributors to do everything they could to disrupt our sales. They would go into restaurants and bars and take down our signage and erase a promotion we may have had with an account. They would bribe owners with tickets to the Super Bowl, World Series, and other prime sporting events. They did this almost everywhere we sold our beer. It was malicious, and they had the money and wherewithal to stop us." The monster the Busch family created had now come back to bite one of their own.

Companies like Kräftig, who couldn't blanket whole regions with promotions like AB InBev could, had to pick and choose which places would give them the most visibility, the most clout. "We got a tap handle into this one restaurant," Gottfried remembers. "We gave them coasters and a neon sign, rail mats, everything. Then we came back three days later and the neon's broken—someone snapped a tube. All the other stuff is gone. It had all been trashed. The tap handle was down and there's a Bud Light where it was. And we asked the owner, 'What happened?' And he's like, 'Oh, man, the Bud Light guy was none too happy about all that Kräftig stuff.' 'And? This is *your* restaurant! He doesn't run this place, *you* do!' 'Oh, I didn't want to make him mad.' This is what people said! . . . I have heard a hundred stories of people's entire families being taken on vacation, exotic hunting trips, paying for draft equipment, fixing decks, building decks. I could go on and on and on. The bottom line is we were held to a standard where we have to play by the rules, but these distributors are doing all this stuff."

Rhonda Kallman cofounded the Boston Beer Company with Jim Koch in 1984. When she set out on her own to brew a caffeinated beer called Moonshot, she ran into the same obstacles Kräftig faced. "You put up a sign one day," she said in the 2009 documentary *Beer Wars*, "and you go back to that store or bar the next day and it's down and there's another banner in place. The big guys have the muscle to muscle us out if they want."

Soon after working bar to bar and restaurant to restaurant to get Moonshot into Boston-area establishments, Kallman learned that Anheuser-Busch was suddenly interested in getting into the caffeinated beer market. "I have seen their handiwork," she says, "particularly when Moonshot launched in Boston. A-B targeted Moonshot accounts specifically, and the managers told me they were coming in offering them five or ten free cases to have the exclusive beer with caffeine. I know some people took the deal, partly because they get tickets to something. You know how that stuff works."

Those who dismiss such accounts as exaggerated need only look at the history of investigations Anheuser-Busch and its distributors have faced and the total millions both have paid in fines over the years for the very actions Busch, Gottfried, and Kallman describe. While the company has faced many such accusations over the course of its existence, here we will limit the examples to those that affect craft beer.

In 1997 the US Justice Department probed Anheuser-Busch after it pressured distributors to drop rival beer brands. A *New York Times* article titled "Anheuser-Busch Queried on Distribution Practices" stated that "competitors, particularly microbrewers, contend that Anheuser-Busch, the industry leader, has been trying to keep their brands off of store shelves." A spokesperson from A-B responded that they were merely offering incentives to prioritize their products.

*Beer Wars* highlighted many of the struggles small breweries face in a market dominated by Anheuser-Busch. Eighty percent of all beer sold is out of a liquor store, convenience store, or supermarket. Walk into any grocery store and you will see Anheuser-Busch hoarding shelf space like a greedy dragon, pushing craft beers to the periphery. It's even more egregious when you realize how many beers fall under AB InBev's umbrella. They claim their sales numbers justify such real estate, as if real estate didn't drive the sales in the first place. The people behind store real estate are called "set captains," and 75 percent of them work directly for Anheuser-Busch. As Boston Beer Company's founder and CEO Jim Koch says, "The big guys control the shelf space."

Anheuser-Busch brought legal action against the Delaware brewery Dogfish Head to stop them from using the terms "chicory" and "punkin'" in their beers. Founder Sam Calagione holds up the paperwork with a confused shake of the head in the *Beer Wars* documentary: "It's a further example of just how oppressive and obnoxious they are. They have the ability and I'm sure they plan to lawyer the bejesus out of us."

Justice Department probes returned in 2015 after Anheuser-Busch inked new deals with distributors in five states. Craft brewers cried foul when they found their representation limited as a result. Oregon-based Ninkasi Brewing Company CEO Nikos Ridge says his volume and growth with one such distributor stalled after A-B came on board. Another executive said, "We're at the mercy of a lot of big players."

Charlie Papazian, godfather of homebrewing, echoed the sentiment: "When that system begins to break down and that middle tier is not as independent as it should be," he says, "that's when craft brewers have challenges in getting their beer to the customers."

Though not in violation of any trade laws, AB InBev bought the beer site RateBeer.com, a beer review community that craft brewers had relied on since its inception in 2000 to build followings. Dogfish Head owner Sam Calagione called out the beer giant publicly: "We believe this is a direct violation of the Society of Professional Journalists Code of Ethics and a blatant conflict of interest."

The year 2016 saw AB InBev fined $150,000 for paying two concert venues in Seattle to exclusively sell Anheuser-Busch products. "These kinds of pay-to-play arrangements," one article said, "aren't necessarily uncommon in the alcohol business, but seem to be coming under increased scrutiny in recent years, partly due to the skyrocketing number of small breweries and the fracturing effect they've had on big companies' monopolies and therefore the industry as a whole."

A 2017 state Alcohol and Beverage Control investigation into California distributors who were linked to Anheuser-Busch found widespread illegal pay-to-play practices, including distributor-financed refrigeration units, draught systems, and TVs for thirty-four retailers throughout one Southern California area. The fine, four hundred thousand dollars, amounted to 3 percent of AB InBev's profits for one day.

Also in 2017, a Massachusetts Anheuser-Busch distributor was fined $2.6 million in a separate pay-to-play scheme. They had given Boston-area bars nearly $1 million worth of equipment, provided, investigators alleged, the equipment was used only for Budweiser products.

In 2018 Colorado fined Anheuser-Busch $500,000 for trade practice violations, a fine that was later increased to $5 million by the Federal Alcohol Trade and Tax Bureau. In their decision, Colorado spelled out almost line by line what Gottfried had experienced in St. Louis. Anheuser-Busch, Colorado found, violated trade laws by:

- Entering into sponsorship agreements with various entities in the sports and entertainment industries requiring concessionaires and other retailers to purchase A-B's malt beverages and prohibiting them from purchasing specific competitor brands;
- Inducing sports industry concessionaires to purchase A-B's malt beverages by furnishing fixtures, equipment, and services;
- Reimbursing, through credit card swipes, retailers for the cost of installing malt beverage draft dispensing systems, thereby inducing them to purchase A-B's malt beverages;
- Requiring retailers to purchase A-B's malt beverages in return for such retailers' use of equipment A-B furnished them free of charge or below market value;
- Using third parties to provide money or things of value to retailers in exchange for placement of A-B's malt beverages; and
- Paying retailers purportedly for items such as consumer samplings, when, in fact, the retailers did not receive the goods or services

> purportedly purchased, and such payments were actually for A-B product placement.

Through the first several years of its existence, Kräftig experienced double-digit growth and was able to expand distribution throughout Missouri, as well as areas of Texas. But starting in 2016 Kräftig began to see a steep dip in their sales. Down to producing seven thousand barrels a year, Billy Busch couldn't continue to operate and closed the company down in 2019. Few will sympathize with a Busch heir falling victim to the dirty tactics his family perfected, but if the path is that difficult for a Busch, imagine the struggles of those who just want to make good beer and get it to people who want to drink it.

The company's failure cannot be entirely blamed on the practices of Anheuser-Busch or its distributors. The area-wide boycott of Anheuser-Busch products that began with the sale to InBev in 2008 was never as big as advertised, and many of the angriest eventually returned. Sales of Anheuser-Busch products nationally may have stagnated following the sale, but old habits die hard. Starting around the same time Kräftig's sales declined, A-B's surged. The number one selling Bud Light in 2016 was doubling the sales of number two Coors Light.

The executives brought over from Anheuser-Busch to Kräftig did more harm than good, as Billy Busch explained in his memoir, *Family Reins*: "The problem I didn't anticipate was that 'executives' (even unemployed ones) didn't want to take start-up pay, work start-up hours, or do things a new and different way. Not only that, but they wanted free equity in the company, which I granted, believing it would motivate them to work harder. Boy, I was wrong." It seemed Anheuser-Busch culture hurt his company both from without and within.

But Billy Busch is not giving up his dream. In 2022 he announced the Busch Family Brewing and Distilling Company, located in the aptly named Defiance, Missouri, in St. Charles County. There he and members of the Busch family brew and distribute Adolphus German Style Pilsner and Gussie Bavarian Lager. In the lead up to the project, both beers were made in limited production by Urban Chestnut Brewing Company and distributed to select area restaurants like Culpepper's, Cafe Napoli, Sam's Steakhouse, and Mike Duffy's Pub. There's still a Busch brewing beer in St. Louis. Craft breweries are helping him do it.

8

# THE CLASS OF 2011

Anheuser-Busch was sold. Budweiser was no longer king—or if it was, its throne was now in Belgium. Craft brewers could sense it. There was a growing anticipation, a convergence of macro- and microbeer history centered on a time and place. Right here. Right now. Something big was coming—a separation from the national craft beer pack, an elevation of the form at a time when the St. Louis market was in a period of transition unseen since Schlafly opened its doors in 1991. In 2011 the city began to shift from its reputation as the beer capital of the world to a craft beer destination. For the first time, beer lovers traveled to St. Louis for breweries not named Anheuser-Busch.

Four craft breweries opened in St. Louis in 2011: Urban Chestnut Brewing Company, Perennial Artisan Ales, Civil Life Brewing Company, and 4 Hands Brewing Company. It seemed like oversaturation, but each was successful in its own way, and the niche each carved out inspired the breweries that followed. Not one of them was a classic brewpub—that is, a restaurant that serves its own beer. But outside of their shared love of beer, each was vastly different.

The people who formed the Class of 2011 were, at the time of InBev's purchase of Anheuser-Busch in 2008, an owner of a wine bar in Lafayette Square, the cellar manager of Chicago's famed Goose Island Beer Company, a wine rep for Gallo wines, and two men from Anheuser-Busch itself. As German immigrants provided the origin story of America's nineteenth-century beer boom, it is fitting that the story of the craft beer explosion in St. Louis also involves a German brewer. He became the city's craft beer ambassador, the bridge from the city's beloved Anheuser-Busch to what was coming.

## Urban Chestnut Brewing Company

Urban Chestnut co-owner Florian Kuplent was born in the world beer capital of Bavaria, where monks in monasteries as early as the sixth century brewed for themselves and thirsty travelers. While they may not have invented beer—archaeological records from China and Egypt date beer back to at least 5000 BC—European monks revolutionized cleaning and sanitation in their practices; discovered the process of lagering, or storing beer at cold temperatures to improve flavor and clarity; and were the first to use hops. Today, Bavaria is home to Oktoberfest, the world's largest beer festival, and pilgrimage destination to over six million people a year.

*Biergartens* in Bavaria began as outdoor spaces above the brewery cellars, where beer lagered for months at cold temperatures. Ice carved out of local lakes and rivers kept the barrels cold. Brewers planted chestnut trees above, perfect for their shade-supplying broad leaves and shallow root systems, cooling the ground above the cellar without risking structural integrity. It didn't take long for brewers to place tables in the shade of the trees and sell their beer fresh. Chestnut-shaded biergartens could soon be found all over Bavaria.

Kuplent spent his late teens working at Munich brewery Bräuerei Erharting. What was initially a summer job started Kuplent down a path that led to a job as brewmaster for Anheuser-Busch and one day a brewery of his own. "I was always more interested in science," Kuplent remembers. "I really had thought about getting a degree in chemistry or biology or something along those lines. I had worked at a local brewery for a few summers just to make extra cash basically, mostly in packaging and distribution, beer delivery, and some of the festivals. Then I kind of enjoyed that atmosphere and work and asked them to take me on as an apprentice."

Though German breweries are steeped in tradition, it had been some time since the brewers at Bräuerei Erharting had taken on a true apprentice. In 1994 Kuplent became their first apprentice in decades while he studied at the nearby Bavarian College of Food and Beverage Science.

Bräuerei Erharting had opened in 1872 and hadn't modernized all that much in its century and a quarter of existence. Kuplent was learning true, old-school, artisan-based brewing near the finest hop farms in the world. The famed Hallertau region of hop gardens traces back to the establishment of the Reinheitsgebot beer purity laws. William IV of Bavaria decreed in 1516 that beer must contain only water, barley, and hops. While the regulation removed potentially harmful additives used in beer making and preservation, the stated purpose was to ensure affordable bread in the region, as the use of wheat and rye in brewing affected supply, increasing prices. As the law also established standard pricing, it made taxation easier.

At the time, yeast was not included in the regulation, as we had not yet come to a full understanding of its role in brewing. Often, yeast was passed from batch to batch the way bakers propagate their yeast. Bakers were even known to add beer to their recipes in order to achieve the same effect.

After the 1516 order, hops became the primary source for beer flavor. The Hallertau hop gardens were only kilometers from Ingolstadt, where William IV issued the decree, and grew into Germany's largest source of hops. It is this region where Bräuerei Erharting sources their hops, promoting their "pleasant bitterness." Kuplent would come full circle to open his own brewery in the Hallertau region thirty years later, but first he had to travel the world of micro- and macrobeer.

Kuplent spent time at the New England Brewing Company in Connecticut, becoming their head brewer. After returning to Munich to study at the Technical University of Munich at Weihenstephan, once a Benedictine abbey and brewery dating back to the eleventh century, Kuplent helped open Meantime Brewing Company in London. He returned to the United States two years later to work for Anheuser-Busch, first as a production manager in New Jersey, then as a brewmaster in product development at the home brewery. His journeys had taken him from one beer capital, Munich, to another, St. Louis.

This was a time in beer history when Anheuser-Busch could no longer ignore the growing craft beer trends. If they were to continue to grow, they had to understand and tap into the craft beer market. Florian Kuplent, with his traditional beer background and experience with craft breweries, could help bridge the divide from macro to micro. Anheuser-Busch gave Kuplent freedom to create new products and to develop prototypes within the Research Pilot Brewery, or RPB, the same brewery within The Brewery that had opened its doors to St. Louis craft brewers Marc Gottfried and John Witte.

While at The Brewery, Kuplent saw what made Anheuser-Busch so consistent, practices he would bring to his own future brewery. "The quality assurance programs we have set up, the processes—there's a lot of stuff you don't see from the brewing perspectives," Kuplent says. "There's in-line systems that check certain parameters; there's a lot of energy recovery."

As to the differences between working at a small craft brewery and the beer giant, Kuplent says, "The process is relatively similar; it's just the scale is obviously different. And the approach from a supply chain, that's focused on fostering relationships with anybody that supplies anything—the maltsters, the hop farmers. That's a big thing that A-B is really good at. And just the overall approach. The professionalism, for a lack of a better term. They just really standardized things. Improved processes. Ran tests to see what parameter changes impact the product, stuff like that."

In a group called New Products and Innovations, Kuplent met David Wolfe, a St. Louis local. Where Kuplent developed new products, Wolfe marketed and sold them. The two could discuss new product possibilities from differing perspectives, and a friendship formed. Each had children around the same age, and their families grew close. Over time, Anheuser-Busch brought the RPB and the New Products and Innovations group under the Michelob umbrella in an effort to equate the Michelob name with craft beer. The original Michelob and Michelob Light existed then, as did Michelob Ultra, A-B's attempt to appeal to low-carb drinkers. Michelob Golden Draft and Michelob Golden Light were available in the upper Midwest to compete with Miller Lite.

Added to these were newer, craftier styles that Anheuser-Busch made available in seasonal packs. They included offerings like Michelob Amber Bock, a porter, as well as more-experimental styles. Here was where Kuplent and Wolfe could test out their new beers, judge the response, and determine which styles would become regular offerings. A pale ale and a Märzen became regulars. Jack's Pumpkin Spice Ale was seasonal. Their Winter's Bourbon Cask Ale predicted the coming barrel-aged trend. Their new orange wheat beer became a sensation. Originally called Spring Heat Spiced Wheat, Kuplent's recipe was soon known nationally as Shock Top. Brewed with citrus peels and Hallertau hops, it was served with an orange wedge on the glass. After its inclusion in the 2006 pack as a seasonal offering, the beer went on to win gold in the Belgian White category at the North American Beer Awards. Shock Top became so popular that it formed its own brand within Anheuser-Busch, spinning off such flavors as Wheat IPA and Twisted Pretzel Wheat.

But the company's efforts to tie their craft-y beers to the Michelob name did more to confuse craft beer drinkers than entice them. Anheuser-Busch was proud of their brands and figured name recognition would help their new beers get noticed. In fact, the opposite was true, as craft beer drinkers considered Anheuser-Busch the antithesis of craft. The success of Shock Top was partly due to the fact that it was not billed as an Anheuser-Busch product but acted more as a stealth craft beer like its rival, Blue Moon. As craft's popularity soared in the coming decade, Moody's named Shock Top the fastest-growing craft brewery. A-B's stealth efforts worked.

In many ways Kuplent was the company's connection to the St. Louis craft beer community. During the inaugural St. Louis Brewers Heritage Festival in 2007, it was Kuplent who hosted St. Louis craft brewers and visiting media on a tour of the Budweiser brewery. He judged at the craft-heavy Great American Beer Festival in 2006, 2008, and 2010, and continued to judge for years after opening Urban Chestnut. Both during and after his time at Anheuser-Busch, he judged for the World Beer Cup, the North American Beer Awards, the European Beer Star, and the International Brewing Awards.

Kuplent had a foot in both worlds. At some point near the end of the decade, conversations with David Wolfe about what they could do on their own grew from idle speculation to concrete planning. The sale to InBev changed the environment at Anheuser-Busch and what Kuplent and Wolfe were used to. "I thought they were going to come in, cut, and then continue business as usual," Kuplent says. "But that's obviously not what happened. Cutting is their MO and that's continued."

When the time came to set out on their own, they looked for possible locations in New Jersey and upstate New York but ultimately decided to stay where they knew the craft beer scene. It didn't hurt that building and living in St. Louis was much more affordable than the East Coast.

David Wolfe told *Feast* magazine in 2011, "The category still is experiencing double-digit dollar growth. We looked at St. Louis compared to other markets in the country and . . . the craft beer share in St. Louis is still less than 4 percent, where the overall general market in the United States is 5-plus and getting closer to 6 percent." He was right. Craft beer's share of the market more than doubled in the next five years.

Photo of Florian Kuplent, cofounder and brewer of Urban Chestnut Brewing Company, 2019. (Courtesy of Florian Kuplent.)

In February 2010, Kuplent and Wolfe closed on a building on Washington Avenue in midtown St. Louis, walking distance from the Fabulous Fox Theatre and Grand Center Arts District. A converted 1920s garage became their tasting room, brick walled and filled with dark wood tables. The expansive biergarten brought a bit of Bavaria to midtown St. Louis: long narrow tables imported from Europe shaded by chestnut trees—Urban Chestnut.

Kuplent and Wolfe's dream became a reality on January 26, 2011, as they poured the first beers of their new brewery. The beers fell into two categories, Reverence and Revolution, a philosophy they called "Beer Divergency." The Reverence series included more traditional beer offerings but often in styles the St. Louis region had yet to taste. Their Zwickel, for instance, a slightly hazy Bavarian lager made with Hallertau hops, quickly became a favorite in the city and won several national awards over the years. Of their early Revolution offerings highlighting modern and experimental styles, STLIPA, or St. Louis IPA, was an early winner, as was Winged Nut, a *Dunkelweizen* brewed with chestnuts. These they packaged in sixteen-ounce bottles with color-coded caps, blue for Reverence and red for Revolution.

Urban Chestnut had an accomplished brewer and an experienced marketer. They weren't the only new brewery to open in 2011, but they already seemed to have a head start.

## Perennial Artisan Ales

Phil Wymore's road to Perennial Artisan Ales seems, in retrospect, paved with good fortune, as if the beer gods were lighting his path at every step. It is hyperbole borne out by the details. The Kansas City native studied anthropology and biology at the University of Missouri, but it was a job as a sushi chef that started him down the path to brewing. There he met St. Louis native Emily Bryant, and the two began their beer journey together.

The owner of Grindstone, a new brewpub in Columbia, Missouri, approached Wymore about designing their food program. He was, as Wymore remembers, a "really colorful dude" who made all manner of alcohol, perhaps not all strictly legal. He had five acres outside of Columbia where he liked to shoot things, or blow them up. "I had never met a brewer before," says Wymore. "I'm trying all these beers, asking questions. I was working on a biology degree, so I was asking about the science behind it. As all that was happening, the lightbulb went off and I realized I wanted to commit myself to becoming a professional brewer. I had to figure this out. I asked the guy so many questions, it was just easier for him to hire me as his assistant."

Wymore started homebrewing but with perhaps a different method than most. Instead of targeting a beer he wanted to drink, he explored ways to understand the science, to ask what would happen if he manipulated the recipe this way, or tried this kind of yeast. Wymore was conducting science experiments in his apartment.

Though Grindstone Brewery lasted only six months, Wymore continued homebrewing, and when he and Emily were ready to move out of Columbia in 2005, he called Goose Island in Chicago looking for a job on the very day a brewer in Goose Island's cellar program quit to take a job at Michigan's Bell's Brewery. When could Wymore start?

Brewers for centuries have aged their beers in wooden barrels, which protect from bacteria while imparting subtle flavors. Anheuser-Busch uses beechwood chips in their stainless-steel fermentation tanks to achieve similar flavors. In 1992 Goose Island brewer Greg Hall filled two barrels that had once held Jim Beam bourbon with an imperial, or high alcohol, stout. The result was a bourbon-flavored sipping beer called Bourbon County Brand Stout.

At the time Wymore joined Goose Island, the brewery had been making Bourbon County Brand Stout for over a decade, but outside of a small minority, it had yet to make a splash in the beer community. People didn't know about it yet, at least not at the level they soon would. "When I first started working there, I think we filled maybe a hundred barrels at most," Wymore says, "and four-pack twelve-ounce bottles of Bourbon County Stout just collected dust everywhere. And then it just exploded. I don't know what the tipping point was for stout, but when it hit, Goose Island was ready to scale."

As part of Goose Island's cellar program, Wymore created Madame Rose, a Belgian-style wild ale aged on cherries in wine barrels. He helped create Sofie, a farmhouse ale aged in wine barrels with orange zest. Wymore was discovering he had a talent for barrel-aged beers.

Wymore and Goose Island were a perfect fit, and soon Bryant came to work at the brewpub. Wymore took classes at the Siebel Institute of Technology as part of the school's partnership with Goose Island.

Wymore's and Bryant's time in Chicago overlapped with Anheuser-Busch's collaboration with Goose Island, which eventually led to the outright purchase of the Chicago brewery by the beer giant in 2011. The infusion of A-B money funded the growth of Goose Island and the rapid expansion of Bourbon County Stout and other cellar offerings. Soon, entertainment venues that had contracts with Anheuser-Busch—nearly all of them—now served Goose Island beers.

After Wymore was promoted to cellar manager, an idea began to form. What if there was a brewery that just did the cellar stuff and didn't have to worry about standards like Goose's Honker's Ale or 312 Wheat? He was beginning to imagine what his own brewery might come to be and started working on a business plan.

Chicago's Half Acre Beer Company was fairly new at the time, contract brewing their beer while they built a physical brewery in the Lincoln Square neighborhood. After their new brewer quit suddenly, leaving them with tanks full of beer, Half Acre reached out to Goose Island for the names of anyone who could come in and take over. After considering Half Acre's needs, Wymore found the perfect candidate: himself.

At first, Wymore came to Half Acre on his off hours to clean up after the former brewer and to brew new beers for them. Very quickly the people at Half Acre wanted Wymore brewing for them full-time while they completed the new space. The timing of Half Acre's offer was fortuitous. Wymore had already made the decision to set out on his own. What if he could learn how to open a brewery with Half Acre, a kind of dry run for his own future brewery? He was open with Half Acre about his plans, and their response was "If you help us, we'll help you." "It was very synergistic," Wymore says, "because when you're trying to start a little brewery and you're working at a place like Goose Island that's expanding and growing like gangbusters, it doesn't really make sense. But Half Acre just started a brewery, and it was at a scale that I could picture. It was the perfect blueprint to get a glimpse of what it was like to open a brewery."

A path was laid before him, both figuratively and, as it turned out, literally: "Half Acre's location was about a mile from where I lived in the north side of Chicago, so I would ride my bike or walk to work every day. And one day I was walking and I see all these ginkgo leaves just scattered all over the sidewalk. I thought they looked so cool just the way they were framed, the way they were oriented, and I thought, 'Somehow I want that to be the mark.' So rather than picking a name and designing a logo around the name, I kind of did it in reverse. I want that mark; how do I come up with a name for it?"

His research into ginkgo revealed that they are living fossils, unchanged in the fossil record for a hundred million years. It is for this reason they are celebrated in Asia as symbols of hope, strength, and resilience. Phil wanted a name that reflected that enduring quality. Perennial.

Wymore had gone from Goose Island, one of the biggest and most respected craft breweries in the country, to Half Acre, an up-and-coming brewery that made a name for itself with their Daisy Cutter Pale Ale and their limited release double IPAs and wild ales. But it was time to move on. Wymore and Bryant celebrated the birth of their first child during the year at Half Acre. They felt the pull of St. Louis, where Bryant's family could help with the baby while they chased their dream of opening their own brewery. Wymore's vision had come into focus: He was going to brew in the style of the cellar program at Goose Island with the scrappiness of Half Acre. "I needed both of those things to merge in order to do something like Perennial," he says.

With Bryant's father the pair looked at about ten properties around St. Louis, including the location that Heavy Riff Brewing Company eventually used in the city's Dogtown area. A mutual friend of the elder Bryant was building a development in the Carondelet neighborhood of South City. The concept was seventy-seven loft units above what they hoped would be cool and interesting businesses on the first floor. What was cooler and more interesting than a brewery? Wymore remembers, "We pulled up to the parking lot and we couldn't believe the size of the building. And it's all brick. This is different. We thought we could have space for manufacturing. We could build out some retail, and if they come, great. If they don't, we thought, we could still make it on manufacturing. So we fell in love with it right away."

*St. Louis Post-Dispatch* food writer Evan Benn, author of *Brew in the Lou*, kept a beer blog called *HipHops*. Tipped off that Wymore was coming down from Chicago with impressive bona fides looking to open a brewery, Benn arranged an interview. Perennial was getting press before it even opened. Benn's writing caught the attention of the manager of the International Tap House, Cory King. Here is where the ascent of two craft beer icons converged. "Cory was our first employee," Wymore remembers. "He was the most passionate and most qualified of everyone who reached out to me. He had a lot of knowledge. I just knew he was going to be great."

The prediction played out over the next decade as King followed Wymore's path of setting out on his own to create Side Project Brewing, one of the world's top breweries. But first he had to learn how to put his ideas into practice. Perennial, with its focus on barrel aging, was the perfect place to start.

Very quickly the St. Louis beer scene was getting crowded. "We were getting Perennial going and we would see these other brewery announcements happening," Wymore says. "We were at first a little disheartened. 2nd Shift started a little before. Urban Chestnut opened a few months before. Civil Life opened the same day as us. 4 Hands opened a few months after. It's really remarkable that all four of us opened within nine months of each other."

As they came to realize, each brewery approached craft beer in a unique way, and instead of competition, they began to view each other as colleagues. According to Wymore, "We were all very differentiated. We at Perennial came out saying we're going to do what we're going to do. It just happened that what we were going to do wasn't the other peoples' plans, which was great. We were working together and involved in all these events, festivals. They and the existing breweries were welcoming. And like a lot of industries, this is very much driven by people, and it's pretty easy to get along with other people who are into beer. We all just kind of got along and liked each other. A lot of times you need something—'Dammit, we're short twenty-two pounds of Cascade [hops] right now.' You go through your Rolodex and start texting your friends. It's like borrowing sugar from your neighbor. We made sure not to schedule anything on the days they were having events or releases.

"Once we all got our doors open, we realized that the craft beer drinker tends not to be the most brand-loyal person; they're just looking for good beer. And if that's the case, if we're all making good beer, I think they're going to visit all of us. Let's work together and try to steal some market share from the big boys."

Wymore and King settled on Perennial's core styles: Saison de Lis, a saison brewed with chamomile flowers; Hommel Bier, a Belgian pale ale; and Southside Blonde, a Belgian blonde ale. They began to experiment,

Photo of Phil Wymore, Jonathan Moxey, Cory King, Emily Wymore, Kerry Bryan, and Andy Hille in the Perennial Artisan Ales cellar, 2013. (Courtesy of Phil Wymore and Jonathan Moxey.)

pushing the envelope of what was possible in brewing, celebrating new flavor combinations, and pouring down the drain those that didn't work. One failure from his Goose Island days, when Wymore tried to add mint to a barrel of Bourbon County Stout, haunted him enough to come back to it at Perennial, where he perfected it. Dried peppermint and cocoa nibs added to a mellow stout base and aged in rye barrels—then hit with mint and cocoa again—resulted in Andes Mint perfection, named 17 after St. Patrick's Day. Within a year of opening, Perennial Artisan Ales won their first medal at the Great American Beer Festival. Their Heart of Gold, a wheatwine-style beer, won silver in its category in 2012.

The beer that made Perennial famous was actually chosen by one of their customers. On social media, Wymore challenged Perennial fans to submit their ideas, and he and King would pick the one they liked the most. The winner could come brew with them. The submission that excited Wymore and King the most was a Mexican chocolate stout. "That style was already being brewed in places like Westbrook and Cigar City, and Cory said, 'Yeah, I'd love to throw our hat in that ring, and try to make the best one we can.' And that's history," Wymore says.

Using King's award-winning homebrew stout as a base, they added ancho chili peppers, cocoa nibs, vanilla beans, and cinnamon sticks. The result was Abraxas, and it created a sensation in the beer community. BeerAdvocate, a popular website for everything you want to know about beer, gave Abraxas a rating of 100. "It was successful from the start," Wymore says. "The drinker was ready for something like that. We debuted it at a magazine event. We brought one keg and people were loving it. They just kept coming back for it and it was gone in no time. We knew we were onto something. Cory says, 'We need to make more of this and we need to get it in barrels ASAP.'"

As craft beer grew in the '90s and 2000s, consumers who loved beer, who began to seek out new varieties of beers becoming available, and who appreciated more and more the skills of those making the beer, formed communities of like-minded people. In person and on websites like BeerAdvocate.com and RateBeer.com, so-called beer nerds developed methods of discovering, reviewing, and trading beer. BeerAdvocate's tagline is "Putting the beer into geeks since 1996."

Another, less kind, term for beer nerd is "beer snob." While some drinkers clearly stick their noses up at anything mass-produced, more often than not people in the beer community are supporters of all kinds of beer and even have their favorites within the mass-produced lagers. What they as a community don't take kindly to is when craft breweries are bought out by the big breweries, like when Goose Island was purchased by AB InBev in 2011. This was a clear encroachment, according to the beer community, into an arena where AB InBev didn't belong. Craft breweries purchased by the big breweries carried a stain among craft enthusiasts. AB InBev purchased 10 Barrel, Blue Point, Elysian, and Breckenridge, to name a few. Heineken purchased Lagunitas. Constellation Brands, one of the largest beer importers, purchased Ballast Point. The average beer drinker may not have known who really owned the craft beer they were drinking, but the beer nerds did, and they complained loudly.

The Craft Brewers Association created the Independent Craft Brewer Seal, a label for craft breweries not owned by the macrobreweries, capped at a maximum annual production of six million barrels or less. Though exceedingly high for craft breweries, the production ceiling meant Sierra Nevada, the Boston Beer Company, and Pennsylvania brewery Yuengling could be considered craft breweries. They produce between one to five million barrels a year, compared to Schlafly's peak of sixty thousand barrels in 2015.

The early belief among craft brewers was it was nice to be rated highly on websites, but there weren't enough of these fans to move the needle on sales. That belief, as Perennial was about to show, was wrong. They were going to harness the beer nerd community.

The Abraxas that King and Wymore had placed into bourbon barrels was ready to bottle, and they set a release date of January 2013 for Barrel-Aged Abraxas. In the days leading up to the release, an excited customer asked King what the bottle limit was going to be. "Limit?" he responded. "Why would there be a limit? You can buy what you want."

Perennial employees who arrived that morning to prepare for a 4 p.m. release found a line had already formed around their parking lot. Those closest to the door had arrived at 6 a.m. The Perennial team was in shock: Should they have a bottle limit? They quickly set one at six, and one person walked down the line to find who wasn't going to buy all six so that he could buy from them.

How had Perennial gone from a brewery that created out-of-the-ordinary styles to a place where people would line up for hours to buy their beer? Word of mouth got them there. Beer nerds got them there. Early on, Wymore had decided to distribute their beer to where it would get some attention, like New York, Chicago, and Washington, DC. And they were sending only a little bit of beer there, so if it was something that people liked, there was built-in scarcity, which made people want it even more. Soon distributors were calling Wymore asking if they could get more of the company's beer. When Perennial decided to sell Barrel-Aged Abraxas, a beer that was already getting drinkers excited, the community was abuzz.

It turned out a lot of the people waiting in line that morning were going to drink some of their beer and sell the rest—for a significant markup. This led to a quandary for Perennial. Were they leaving money on the table? Were other people profiting off their work? "We never let the resale value ever inform our pricing," says Wymore. "It's an interesting thing if people can fetch five times whatever you sold it for. But at the end of the day, we didn't ever want the reputation for being price gougers. We wanted to provide good value. We take a lot of pride in the quality of our beer and we charge what we think is an appropriate price for it, and I don't ever want someone to feel ripped off by Perennial."

BeerAdvocate named Barrel-Aged Abraxas the number five best beer in the world. It won gold in the Experimental Beer category at the 2014 Festival of Wood and Barrel-Aged Beers in Chicago, a triumphant homecoming for the Goose Island and Half Acre alum. The festival named the beer the "Best in Show" runner-up for all categories.

Wymore and King realized they needed to make more barrel-aged stouts right away. The demand was clearly there—now it was time to supply it. Instead of increasing production of Barrel-Aged Abraxas the way Goose Island had increased production of Bourbon County Stout, Perennial created multiple styles of barrel-aged stouts, all with different characteristics and different names. Anyone who was going to line up to get a bottle or six of Barrel-Aged Abraxas was going to line up to get each of those as well. Craft beer drinkers are notorious about wanting to try everything.

Soon they had Barrel-Aged 17; Barrel-Aged Sump coffee stout, a gold medalist at the Great American Beer Festival; and Maman, which won silver. King, Wymore, and the rest of the Perennial team were coming up with new combinations and excelling with each one. Ads began to appear on Craig's List for "beer mules"—that is, people who would wait in Perennial lines for releases for a fee.

The name Perennial Artisan Ales was on the lips of beer lovers across the country. To capitalize on the interest their brewery was generating, and to bring more people into the taproom to try out all their other styles, Wymore and the Perennial team decided to offer a completely new beer on tap every Thursday. Wymore, King, research and development (R&D) brewer Jim Leabig, and brewers Andy Hille and Jonathan Moxey now had to produce a completely new beer every week, even if it was only a small amount—and it had to live up to the standards Perennial had already set for itself. "If we're going to put our hat in the ring for any style," Wymore says, "it needs to have Perennial's reputation for quality behind it. And so we're going to R&D it, and we're not going to release it unless we think it's an outstanding version of something. A great example is Weird Era, which is a spontaneous *gueuze*-style beer. It took us four years to be able to release a couple hundred bottles. That's the most extreme example of us crafting something until we're happy with it to put it out. But every beer was like that."

"We were out there on the edge," Jonathan Moxey says. "There weren't a lot of other breweries doing that stuff. We were taking chances. Some of them worked out fantastically, and then there were some others. We were developing new methods." The result was a pushing of creative boundaries that nudged the brewers beyond the core styles, accelerating their growth. Moxey had very little commercial brewing experience when he started at Perennial. He went on to become one of the city's most decorated brewers and the brewmaster of Rockwell Beer Company.

But in Perennial's first years, Cory King was a star. He was the rare brewer whom beer nerds knew by name; they were paying attention to his career. After two to three years at Perennial, King began to explore the idea of setting out on his own. He had the experience. He had the name. It was time for him to have his own place.

Instead of setting out immediately, Cory approached Phil about brewing his own beer, but within the Perennial brewery on his own time—a kind of side project. As Wymore tells it, "Cory said he was interested in incubating his own little thing that he could release on his own in his spare time, spare capacity, if we would allow it. He's so talented and we work so well together that, hey, if we can figure this out and he can grow a little bit, then we can keep him for a while. Talented people often move on." It was an echo of Wymore's relationship with Half Acre.

So began something of a tradition at Perennial, one that reflects well on its owners. Cory King was the first of several Perennial brewers who left to make their mark elsewhere. Instead of a repeated feeling of loss, it felt like growth, as if Perennial were planting seeds in the community that grew independently: a family tree of brewers in St. Louis—and the Wymores were right there at the top. "We've been very fortunate from the beginning, starting with Cory, Chuck Stockstrom, Jonathan Moxey, Chris Kinast; we've had tons of great brewers come through here," says Wymore. "They're passionate, they're hungry, they're like I used to be when I decided I wanted to be a great career brewer."

Phil Wymore's path to Perennial Artisan Ales is a sequence of improbabilities—a Columbia brewery open for only six months, a phone call to Goose Island on the day a brewer quit, and a knock on the door from Cory King—resulting in a brewery that pushed craft beer forward.

## The Civil Life Brewing Company

Of the four breweries in the Class of 2011, Civil Life Brewing Company may be the most inward-looking. It isn't flashy, nor will its beers punch you in the mouth with the strongest, funkiest flavors. Even its building is a nondescript former newspaper warehouse. But it might as well be decorated Tardis blue, because stepping inside transports you out of time and into a place that is decidedly English, four thousand miles away from London. "It's a little bit of a mind game when you look at the outside and then you walk inside," explains owner Jake Hafner. "'Wait a minute, this is an old-school pub.' There's no better medium than wood to make people feel comfortable, the warmth of it, and that was a deliberate choice. As was the brick wall in the brewery. It's meant to feel like a different place."

Hafner and brewers Dylan Mosley and Mike Bianco have managed to tie the quality of beer to the experience of a space, no easy task. At a time when IPA was the top-selling craft beer style, Civil Life offered lower-alcohol, malt-driven beers. Their goal was balance, where ingredients didn't compete or overpower but rather complemented each other. They created beers that were sessionable, meaning you could settle in for two or three beers without consuming too much alcohol. "When you sit down at Civil Life, a beer like ours isn't going to be the only thing you're talking about that night," Hafner says. "We want the beer to hit on all the notes, but balance can't be achieved by a lot of styles, so we don't do those. We don't want to create a beer where it's all you talk about: 'Man, that beer's so crazy!'"

Of the big four breweries that opened in 2011, no two are alike. Urban Chestnut brought a distinctly German feel, Perennial focused on Belgian

Sketch of the Civil Life logo by St. Louis artist Joseph Allhoff. (Courtesy of Joseph Allhoff.)

styles and barrel-aged beers, and 4 Hands pushed the envelope on big flavor combinations. "You couldn't write a story like that so perfectly," says Hafner. "You had four companies come up—we're all in different neighborhoods and enough apart from each other that we could draw from our own neighborhoods without being on top of each other."

Tied together by a common year, there was a feeling of camaraderie among the new guys. Perennial's Phil Wymore came to Civil Life's grand opening parade, where two hundred people walked from Tower Grove Park to the Civil Life brewery. That Wymore was opening up Perennial Artisan Ales on the very same day made the gesture all the more meaningful.

The four breweries did not see each other as rivals, which Hafner credits to the guidance of St. Louis craft godfathers, the guys at Schlafly: "Dan Kopman and Stephen Hale really set the tone for us in that 2011 group. Schlafly was super welcoming to all of us. They would come to all the events. Businesses can be real territorial. Someone opens next door and you think, 'They're going to take all of my business.' Instead you need to think, 'Actually, if they do well, that's going to bring more people here. If I continue to do a good job, then their success can mean my success.'

"That's where Schlafly were the real leaders in this sense of community among the brewers and among the companies. They didn't have to be like that. They could have said, 'We've been here for a long time,' and not that they would say anything bad, but they didn't have to actively participate in helping us be better companies. I have so much respect for those guys. I would email Dan a question or two and he would always get back to me. We'd email Stephen and Otto Ottolini, and they'd send these detailed emails, and that was information that wasn't really available at the time. That was a company-wide philosophy at Schlafly and a credit to the kind of people who worked there. It meant a lot to me and to all of us what Schlafly did in those early days to create that foundation."

Jake Hafner was a St. Louis South County kid whose neighbor Mr. Miller, despite his name, worked for Anheuser-Busch. Hafner remembers Mr. Miller's den filled with Anheuser-Busch mementos and signage. It was early exposure to The Brewery, and as Jake grew, he met more people who worked either directly or indirectly with Anheuser-Busch. After graduating from De Smet Jesuit High School, Hafner attended Truman State University in the final years that it was known as Northeast Missouri State. A love of food and wine that came from working in food service in high school and then waiting tables in college took him to the French Culinary Institute in New York in 1996. Hafner became a certified sommelier and worked as the assistant cellar manager at Windows on the World in the World Trade Center North Tower under Andrea Immer (now Robinson), the first woman to be named "Best Sommelier in the United States."

Neither Hafner nor Andrea Immer were still in New York on 9/11, but some of their friends lost their lives that day. "There was one man, Jupiter Yambem, who passed away," Hafner says. "He was the restaurant manager. I always try to say his name when this comes up because he was one of the nicest humans. I was twenty-four or twenty-five years old and we sat by each other at the 'somm' wine classes. He was in his mid to late thirties. I was the lowest in rank there and he was genuinely so nice to me."

Andrea Immer connected Hafner with Astor Wines, one of the largest wine retailers in New York, exposing Hafner to the retail side of wine. Hafner realized he wanted to open his own business, but the barriers to entry in New York were just too high. So he moved home.

In a scene that mirrors Dan Kopman's struggles to find a loan to start Schlafly, Hafner remembers his first meeting with a bank: "You learn a lot when you open that first business. I went to the bank and wore a suit. I had a program where I wrote a twenty-page business proposal. But I didn't have any money. The loan officer said, 'We're not going to lend you any money if you don't have any money.' And the loan officer was my soccer coach from grade school! They didn't teach me that in business school. I felt ripped off!"

Eventually, Hafner's father loaned him money, and Jake was able to secure a business loan for a new concept in St. Louis: 33 Wine Bar, located in the Lafayette Square neighborhood. "I had a hybrid concept, which was new at the time, where you could sell wine retail and also have wine there—nobody really did that," Hafner says.

Hafner's 33 Wine Bar had only eight tables. He spoke to every customer, talked through their wine likes and dislikes, and poured multiple samples to try to find just the right wine for each person. The personal attention combined with the comfort of the space made it a place customers returned to over and over. "It started off slow, but I think that's how you grow things organically," says Hafner. "You develop a regular base. It makes it worth it to come into work when you become part of people's lives, and you get to see them and they bring in their friends."

Local press praised 33 Wine Bar, and in 2005 Hafner was voted "Best Bartender in St. Louis" by *The Riverfront Times*. For a city that is known for its bars, it was notable that a local newspaper chose someone who didn't mix any cocktails—he only served wine and beer. From *The Riverfront Times* article:

> Can a person who doesn't mix drinks—who owns a bar that doesn't even stock spirits—be considered St. Louis' "Best Bartender"? Is a wine bar a bar? Yes. Is there a physical "bar" with stools in this wine bar? Yes. Does the man behind it actually "tend" it? Yes. OK then. Jake Hafner, owner of 33 Wine Bar, is, indeed a bartender, and the city's best, because he's got great taste, knows his wine and beer, is the perfect advocate and runs a clean, well-lighted *bar* in Lafayette Square. Along with wonderful wines, 33 stocks one of the city's best beer selections. And despite the fact that Hafner spends 80 hours a week at his place, he manages to smile and chitchat like a pro. As in: like a bartender.

When Hafner hired Dylan Mosley in 2006, he felt like the beer list really shined. 33 Wine Bar didn't carry mass market beers. They catered to people who were looking for something different, brands like Australia's Coopers, Germany's Paulaner, or Belgium's Lindemans or Cantillon beers. They also carried Schlafly, Anchor Liberty Ale, and O'Fallon Wheach. Hafner wrote clever descriptions of each on the menu, removing much of the intimidation over trying something new. "I was trying to curate an experience," he says. "Why come to me if I'm carrying the same thing that everyone else does? We had tons of people who had only had Budweiser and we'd have a conversation. I'd say, 'Why don't you try Bitburger Pilsner?' I had a better shot of turning those guys into craft beer drinkers than those who don't drink beer at all. People who came in were fine that we didn't have A-B on the menu. If we were carrying Coors, now that would be an issue."

Hafner was at 33 during the InBev takeover of Anheuser-Busch and took no joy in the beer giant's downfall: "A-B drinkers were super loyal to it, and rightfully so. A-B pumped millions and millions into this economy. They donated to every single charity. That company is a lot different now than it was then. I had friends who worked there during that time. I would love it if A-B was still locally owned. Every dollar you spend there now, it's going to a faraway place. We had tons of customers at 33 who were upper-level management. Those aren't here nearly as much. Those high-paying jobs pumped tons of money into our economy, into our restaurants and businesses. We saw them on foundations. We saw them on boards." The craft beer wave that hit St. Louis was going to happen anyway, he believes. "But the sale put gas on it."

Hafner, Dylan Mosley, and Mike Bianco were thinking about a future in craft beer long before the sale turned on the gas. It was beer, not wine, that they turned to after a long workday. Mosley had begun to homebrew. What if they opened a brewery?

In 2009 Jake Hafner sold 33 to a friend, Jeff Stettner, and took off for Europe. In the name of research, he visited the beer-producing countries of Europe and drank in as many pubs as he could. He spent eight months in England studying pub culture and saw how some pubs marked the bar with chalk to keep a tab. A tapas bar in Sevilla put check marks on their bar for each dish. A bar in Düsseldorf put check marks on the coaster. Today, Civil Life continues to track purchases at the bar with chalk.

Upon his return, Hafner purchased a former newspaper warehouse in the Tower Grove South neighborhood. Next door was an old body shop with upward of forty cars in varying condition strewn about. "This is such a great neighborhood," says Hafner. "We're so fortunate to be here. There's a mile of people to the north here. Dutchtown and Southampton are a mile away. We don't have a highway here, which is tough. People can walk down the street here. This neighborhood has modest homes, so we try to keep our prices as low as possible. I don't want to price out of the neighborhood."

Hafner, Mosley, and Bianco got to work converting the warehouse into a brewery and pub space, installing 104 solar panels on the roof. Hafner recruited artist Joe Allhoff to design the logo, a mustachioed man in a bowler hat holding up two beer mugs.

What customers found when they walked into Civil Life was a new kind of drinking experience, or at least new to St. Louis. They may not have understood it at first, but this was a place designed to make connections, to build community. Notably, Civil Life had no TVs. "When you put a TV on at a bar, most people don't talk to each other," says Hafner. "Do you know how many people have made friends here? Because they come in at certain times and see the same people. Eventually they come in and say, 'Oh, yeah, I recognize you,' 'Oh, yeah, I sat by you.' That doesn't happen overnight. It's a process. Two months later maybe they sit next to each other. Three months later they come in and wave and choose to sit next to that person. It's not chance."

The beer itself tastes like comfort, no matter the style. "We sit in a unique spot in that we really do have a fair amount of beer that a new drinker could enjoy," says Hafner. "It's by design. My mom doesn't drink a lot of beer. She likes a light wheat beer. I want my mom to come here. I never want someone to come here and feel like this place isn't for them."

Of the early styles that Civil Life offered, one stood out: Civil Life American Brown Ale. It is everything that Hafner, Moseley, and Bianco set out to do: light, malt-forward, balanced, and flavorful.

Abbey Spencer, former head brewer at Third Wheel Brewing, teaches at Saint Louis University's Brewing Science and Operations program. There she uses the American Brown as a model. She told *Sauce* magazine, "It's such a great teaching beer for me, but it's also outstanding and approachable. Even though it's a dark-colored beer, you're not going to get a bunch of roasted coffee—it's going to be caramel and toasty and nutty and easy and approachable, very fall-like flavors. The hop component is interesting. It's citrusy, sometimes a little floral, maybe a little pine-y, but not to an overwhelming point. The malt is complex and interesting, the hops are complex and interesting, but nothing outshines the other." *Sauce* called the American Brown a brewer's beer: "The American Brown's paucity of imitators speaks volumes."

Manny Negron, former general manager of Craft Beer Cellar and current proprietor of the lager-only pub Little Lager, says of the American Brown, "A lot of breweries in the St. Louis area don't have a brown ale because they know Civil Life has got it." Narrow Gauge brewer Jeff Hardesty says, "When brewers come to town, they want to try it."

"Our beers," Hafner says, "get reviewed really well, but there's a balance that we strive for and that really comes from Dylan's philosophy. We can produce a beer that a craft beer drinker or beer writer wants to drink, but so many people have told me that the American Brown was the first craft beer they loved. Those were not craft beer drinkers. To me, that was an extraordinary accomplishment, that one beer could have these really wide-open arms."

Jake Hafner had built a brewery that was more than a place to have a beer. It was a place to connect, to put down your phone, and to talk to a stranger over a pint.

## 4 Hands Brewing Company

Step into a taproom built of brick and whimsy. A bartender pushes a draft across a concrete countertop. Take a moment with it. How does your beer look? Is it hazy, opaque, or clear and crisp? Do tiny bubbles rise up from the etching on the bottom of the glass? Does it swirl in slow suspension, a galaxy of flavor? What is the aroma when you bring the glass to your nose? Can you smell the dry hops the brewer poured into the tank near the end of the brewing process? When you bring it to your lips, and the meter in your brain that registers joy begins to flicker, can you taste the backbone of malt, courtesy of barley and wheat farmers, or notes of citrus from hops grown in Washington? What depths of flavor did time spent in California wine or Kentucky bourbon barrels impart? The barrels themselves have lived multiple lives.

The beer in your hand isn't just the work of the men and women working at the tanks on the other side of the tasting room window. It carries the fingerprints of many. Recognize the moment, what led to it, and your place within it.

Half a mile from Busch Stadium, just downriver from the confluence of the Missouri and Mississippi Rivers, you sit and enjoy the confluence of passions, the work of many hands.

Cheers. *Prost. Slainte. Cin cin.* Whatever your toast is, enjoy.

4 Hands Brewing Company was the last of the Class of 2011 to open its doors. Of the breweries that opened since Schlafly debuted in 1991, 4 Hands would outgrow them all, and then they would surpass Schlafly itself.

Kevin Lemp was studying psychology and marketing at Missouri's Columbia College when he caught the craft beer bug. New Belgium's Fat Tire and the German Franzikaner Weiss acted as his gateway beers. They were, to Lemp, flavors that told a story. He wanted to know those stories, to perhaps tell his own one day. Out of college, Lemp worked for Glazer's, a wine and spirits distributor, specifically with California's Gallo wines, where he came to understand that it was his job to connect the consumer to the product that best fit him or her. Lemp's time at Gallo influenced what 4 Hands would become.

After ten years in the wine industry, he was ready to set out on his own. He considered starting a restaurant but realized he knew nothing about that industry. Craft beer seemed to better fit his personality. Could he tell stories through beer? It was a leap of faith. Lemp and his wife, Maegan, had two young children, and leaving a steady job with Gallo to set out on his own was a huge risk. Lemp credits his wife's support, her strength through that transitional time, for making the leap possible.

Lemp couldn't name the brewery after himself: There is a Lemp family with a rich and storied history in St. Louis beer, but that was not his family. Kevin is not related to those Lemps. Instead, Lemp turned to his immediate family for inspiration. The four hands are his, his wife's, and his kids', stacked atop each other like a huddle. They were all in this together. For the brewery logo, Lemp incorporated the four hands into a single hop.

A year before opening, Lemp brought his family into the new twelve-thousand-square-foot space, a former machine shop just south of Busch

4 Hands Brewing Company logo. (Courtesy of 4 Hands Brewing Company.)

Stadium. It was all white walls and blank space, and all Lemp could see was possibility. Before filling the space with tanks, Lemp and his son enjoyed skateboarding through the empty building. Once the brewing system was in place, the two had less room to skate, but it was still possible. Within five years there was barely space to walk through sideways. The back bar, tables, and chairs in the tasting room are all recycled from the same barn. Recycled glass gives color to the concrete bar. A bench outside is made from beer conveyor belts.

The beer was not going to be subtle. He didn't just want to make an IPA; he wanted an IPA that smacked you in the face with rye and hop flavor. He wanted a brown ale with coffee and chocolate. He wanted a red ale aged in Cabernet barrels. But just when you think it's all explosions of flavor, here comes a subtle saison that reminds you of the skill of the brewer.

That brewer was Will Johnston. Johnston had started at Union Colony Brewery in Greeley, Colorado, before taking a job as a brewer at Goose Island. There he studied at the Siebel Institute of Technology and traveled to Munich to earn a degree from the World Brewing Academy. He served as head brewer at Lucette Brewing Company in Wisconsin before responding to Lemp's job posting. Lemp had hired a good brewer; now he gave Johnston the space to create.

The St. Louis craft community was a small and supportive group. When Lemp said he needed a brewery manager, Schlafly's Stephen Hale brought over Martin Toft, who was interning at Schlafly at the time. Toft had studied at Siebel in Chicago and the Doemens Academy in Munich. "You guys," Hale said, "should know each other." Toft became brewery manager and assistant brewer.

Their brewing philosophy, and 4 Hands' motto, was "Ales Without Borders." They were not worried about brewing true to style. It was more about brewing what they wanted to drink. Happily, it turned out a lot of people wanted to drink what they wanted to drink.

4 Hands launched with taps of Cast Iron Oatmeal Brown, Reprise Centennial Red, Divided Sky Rye IPA, and Single Speed Session blonde ale brewed with jasmine flowers. Their Chocolate Milk Stout—a Martin Toft recipe—became a local favorite, as did their Incarnation IPA, which soon became their top seller. They added barrel-aged specials that drew lines on release days. In 2014 their skill in brewing diverse styles was recognized at the Festival of Wood and Barrel-Aged Beers. Their Volume #2 won a silver medal in the Barleywine category.

Lemp tapped local artist Josh Rowan to design much of the brewery's art, including its growing slate of beer labels. The graphic designer created an eye-catching mix of urban street art and tattoo design. Rowan told *Sauce* in 2014, "To put something like that—that has a little bit of childish whimsical feel about it—on a product that is definitely meant for adults is a fun thing."

Perhaps as a result of Lemp's decade of experience with wines, he added suggestions for food pairings on 4 Hands bottles and cans. These were a sometimes-tongue-in-cheek mix of food choices that gave the drinker an indication of what kind of flavors the beer would complement. A strong, flavorful beer should be paired with something with a strong flavor, while a delicate saison should pair with something that doesn't overpower it. The Divided Sky Rye IPA, a proverbial punch in the mouth, should, according to the packaging, pair with spicy Thai, blue cheese, salami, or blood orange panna cotta. Pairing suggestions for other styles were equally creative. For the St. Louis natives out there, City Wide should be paired with toasted ravioli, pork steaks, slingers, and square pizza.

Lemp and the people at 4 Hands created City Wide American Pale Ale as a way to give back to the community that has given so much to them. Starting in 2016, 4 Hands paired up with a local charity, donating a dollar for every case of City Wide they sold. Early on, they even showed off the charity on the packaging. Some of the many organizations that have partnered with 4 Hands include Mission: St. Louis, Forest Park Forever, and the Ollie Hinkle Heart Foundation. As of 2024, 4 Hands has donated over $400,000 to area charities and they look forward to crossing the $1 million mark.

Lemp's alma mater saw another alum, Judson Ball, open Logboat Brewing Company, one of Missouri's most respected breweries, not too far from the Columbia College campus in 2014. Ball used Lemp's 4 Hands as a model. Lemp echoes the philosophy that started with Schlafly three decades ago: that a rising tide lifts all boats. The goal, according to Lemp, is to grow craft beer's share of the market. Only through working together, by providing great beer and bringing more people into the segment, can true growth occur.

Ball spoke of such collaboration with Columbia College: "We're not fighting against each other. We're fighting to raise education for the people who are still drinking the big beers. We're trying to convert them to craft beer drinkers, let them know that there are other options out there. That's a big part of the job for us: not fighting each other but working with each other."

It's a sentiment that runs counter to the idea that oversaturation would harm St. Louis's craft beer community. As it turned out, the market wasn't saturated. It was, in fact, underrepresented. The demand for craft beer was there, and it was growing quickly.

The year 2011 was a high-water mark in St. Louis history. Though the city still felt the sting of InBev's recent takeover of Anheuser-Busch, this new craft beer enthusiasm breathed some hope.

The St. Louis Cardinals stood ten and a half games out of the final Wild Card spot with only thirty-one games to go in the season. Las Vegas gave them a 1.3 percent chance of making the playoffs. An epic run resulted in a postseason berth. Inspired by a rally squirrel and the heroics of David Freese, the Cardinals completed their impossible comeback with an unforgettable World Series championship.

For a long minute St. Louis wasn't a city in decline. There was new optimism. More and more St. Louisans celebrated in the stadium or at home with a beer not made by Anheuser-Busch. Maybe it was a Schlafly or O'Fallon beer—or one from the Class of 2011. Urban Chestnut, Perennial, and Civil Life had opened by the time the Cardinals shocked the world. Just blocks south of the stadium, 4 Hands opened their doors two weeks later, beginning a new era of Cardinals pregaming. It was an auspicious start for the Class of 2011.

The years that followed were the craft beer decade, and all four breweries grew in their own way. Urban Chestnut built a new production facility and beer hall in the Grove that dwarfed their midtown location. Their Urban Research Brewery, where beer lovers could pair experimental beers with a slice of pizza, echoed Kuplent's time at the Anheuser-Busch RPB. Urban Chestnut even brought American craft beer to Florian Kuplent's native Germany, opening the UCBC Hallertauer Bräuerei not far from where Kuplent was born.

Perennial grew into the adjacent commercial spaces in their building, taking over the entirety of the first floor. Phil Wymore's influence on the St. Louis craft beer scene spread with the brewers who moved on to other places, like Side Project, Rockwell, and Perennial on Lockwood. Civil Life grew modestly, keeping to their identity as a cozy pub. They purchased the auto body shop next door, expanded their patio and their parking, and eventually built a full kitchen.

4 Hands grew into every inch of their beer house, replacing their small system with one much larger. They were named one of the fastest-growing private companies by the *St. Louis Business Journal* in 2017 and soon supplanted all other St. Louis craft breweries in production. City Wide American Pale Ale, available only in cans in the St. Louis metro area, became 4 Hands' number one selling beer in 2018, accounting for 20 percent of their production. They expanded the brand to include City Wide Pils, City Wide Stout, City Wide Light, and State Wide Hazy Pale Ale.

It had been a long time coming—twenty years since Schlafly opened its doors—but 2011 marked the city's final transition from a Bud town to a craft beer town.

9

# SIDE PROJECT

Winemaking, a delicate relationship between the farmer, the earth, and the climate, long ago surpassed brewing as an art form. It is the terroir—the culmination of environmental factors that make up the flavor of a vintage—that makes a particular wine unique. It is an afternoon fog that blankets a block of a vineyard, or smoke from a nearby wildfire, or an extended heatwave on cracking soil.

There is little such influence in brewing. Brewers work indoors with the same ingredients sourced from the same suppliers: malt, hops, and yeast. But with the rising skill of new brewers came practices that approached a kind of beer terroir: the harnessing of wild yeasts on the front end and the blending of barrel-aged beers on the back. The results were unique, elevated, and nearly impossible to replicate.

The 2015 version of Barrel-Aged Abraxas did not taste exactly the same as the 2014. Beer now had vintages. Perennial brewer Cory King was pushing craft into new frontiers, and his work with Phil Wymore resulted in some truly special beers. Lines formed, bottles were traded across the country, and the craft beer community was thirsty for more.

It is fitting that King's background was in wine. After graduating from Southeast Missouri State in 2007, where he met his wife and business partner, Karen Ivers, Cory sold wine for the distributor Southern Glazer's. "I wanted to get into winemaking," he says, "but then to make a great wine you need great grapes, and to have great grapes you have to be close to them. For beer, we all have the same ingredients; we just need to make better beer than the next guy. Honestly, it kind of fit my competitive side."

Karen, whose brother introduced Cory to homebrewing, worked as a sales rep for Goose Island in the St. Louis area. Though neither knew Phil Wymore yet, it was Karen who was instrumental in bringing Wymore's Goose Island beer to the St. Louis area. "When Karen started in St. Louis, she was one of three or four craft brewery reps," King says. "That jumped to about fifty brewery reps. Goose Island was starting to come out with Matilda, Sofie, and other high-end beers. Bourbon County stouts were just taking off, as were their variants."

A community rose out of the rising interest in such beers, and the Kings were part of it. They traded for beers they couldn't get locally and then attempted to make them at home: "I always tried to make beers I couldn't buy. I started making sour beers. I made big stouts at home. My first all-grain recipe was a Belgian *witbier* [white beer], and my second was an imperial stout. My favorite beer at the time was Founders Breakfast Stout, which we couldn't get here in Missouri."

The couple even tracked down beers that may not have been their favorites but were considered the best examples of the style. They studied them, isolated the characteristics that made one better than the other, and implemented them into their homebrewing.

Cory King's beer and wine education advanced in sync. Each Friday, Glazer's employees went through wine tasting and palate education. "When you're picking up nuances in wine," says King, "they're minuscule compared to nuances in beer. When you taste wine, you might pick up a hint of mocha. When you taste mocha in a beer, it's because someone put actual chocolate in it. In wine there are tiny little minuscule compounds; it's really, really subdued. Having palate training every week just taught me what I liked. Doing sales I'd see what other people's palates are like."

Beer, the Kings found, could accompany and even elevate good food, but too often a menu filled with world-class wines featured macro lagers and maybe an IPA. Though beer couldn't hope to achieve the status of wine, there seemed to be a vacuum that skilled brewers could fill. Cory King, his wife argued, could fill that gap.

The International Tap House opened a location in Soulard and recruited King to manage. There, surrounded by more taps and bottles than anyone in St. Louis thought possible, he was at the eye of a storm that was only just forming. Anheuser-Busch had been sold, the beer scene in St. Louis was shifting, and locals were thirsty for variation.

A 2010 food column in the *St. Louis Post-Dispatch* announced that Phil Wymore, the former cellar manager of Goose Island and current head brewer of Half Acre, was planning to start his own brewery called Perennial in St. Louis. King took notice. This was the guy he wanted to work with. When Phil Wymore hired Cory King as Perennial's first employee, the transition from homebrewer to head brewer felt seamless. King says, "It wasn't that big of a difference for me. I have a mechanical mind-set. I grew up building four-wheelers and go-carts. My dad and I built my first car. If you go to a big brewery, the brewmaster isn't a brewer; he's an engineer. It's process oriented. Even the science behind brewmaking is a process."

Wymore brought his extensive experience in Goose Island's barrel aging program to Perennial, and soon Wymore and King were experimenting and expanding their own cellar program. If brewing is a science, barrel aging is a skill, and King's palate training was paying off. "There's finesse on the other side when it comes to barrel aging—more art," King says. "In the very beginning we were just filling barrels blindly. A lot of the finesse in barrel aging isn't what you do; it's your palate in blending after the fact."

After King's Abraxas drew national attention, his skill in blending for Barrel-Aged Abraxas garnered perfect ratings, festival awards, and long lines of craft beer enthusiasts. "I think Phil coming from Goose Island, who were very well regarded for their barrel aging, their stouts and sours, that his name alone brought a lot to it. And then, weirdly enough, Abraxas was my recipe and that just made us a power team. And so everything we were doing at the time really marketed itself. The wave kind of built upon itself. A lot of this story is based on all of us catching the right wave at the right time."

When Karen traveled for her job as a sales rep, first for Goose Island and then Deschutes, Cory found himself getting in to work early and staying late, running through possible recipes and blends. He was brewing Perennial standards but in his head running through combinations he wanted to test out. What if he blended the caramel sweetness this bourbon barrel stout imparted with a touch of the peppery spice this rye barrel offered? "I have the attention span of a four-year-old," King says with a laugh. "I started buying my own oak barrels. That way I didn't have to ask permission to use Perennial's stuff—I could just do whatever I wanted, as long as they didn't mind me storing the beer. And so what happened was I was experimenting with my own money and time—before or after work, because Karen was out of town—and before we knew it, Phil said, 'God, Cory, you've got like twenty barrels' worth of your own stuff here. What are you going to do with it?' I didn't know. They came up with the idea—'Why don't you sell it on the side? More income for yourself.' So I thought of the name Side Project."

King announced the formation of Side Project in February 2013, only a month after Perennial's Barrel-Aged Abraxas release. But excited beer drinkers had to wait for King's beers to age in their barrels, stacked up in the Perennial brewery, branded with the new Side Project logo, a hanging lightbulb. He released his first beers that September: Saison du Fermier, a saison aged in Chardonnay barrels; Brett Project #1, a saison fermented with a brett yeast strain isolated from a bottle of '07 Cantillon Iris; and The Origin, a blend of imperial stout, black oatwine, and Baltic porter aged in in a Rittenhouse Rye barrel with Madagascar vanilla beans. BeerAdvocate gave the Saison du Fermier a score of 100 and named it the "Best Saison in the World."

That November, Side Project's Fuzzy, an American wild ale brewed with Missouri white peaches and aged in Chardonnay barrels, won gold at Chicago's Festival of Barrel Aged Beers. *Draft* magazine named Side Project a brewery to watch. In December, *Draft* named Saison de Blé batch 2 one of the best twenty-five beers in the world. Side Project had debuted to immediate acclaim.

Beers were sold in the Perennial tasting room for the first year and a half of the new company's existence. To Phil and Emily Wymore, the writing was on the wall: King was ready to make his own way in the industry. For Phil it felt like a callback to his time at Half Acre, when he helped them brew and open a new space, and they helped him prepare for his own future. King says of Wymore, "He was an open book—I could ask him anything. He understood what I was doing because Half Acre did that for him. I was a sponge. He helped me learn."

Side Project was among the best one hundred breweries in the world according to RateBeer, and King didn't even have his own brewery. Demand for Side Project at the Perennial taproom was increasing.

Cory and Karen King began to conceive of their own tasting room and found a location in Maplewood, a neighborhood in St. Louis County with incredible craft beer luck. Schlafly built their Bottleworks brewpub on one end of Manchester Road. In November 2014 Side Project set up shop on the other. King describes those early days: "I would start holding back bottles from all our releases at Perennial, and people would come into Maplewood to drink them. That gave an identity to Side Project. We didn't have an identity at first because you'd just go to Perennial. It took years before people realized that we weren't the same company. Obviously, it's confusing for customers—I work at Perennial, of course you'd think it was the same place."

The Kings named the tasting room The Side Project Cellar, and from the beginning it felt special. Side Project beer and a selection of other world-class beers were available by the bottle or on tap, with the draft lines programmed for the proper temperature for each one. Breweries across the world sent Side Project their beers because they knew The Cellar would serve them properly.

Karen's brother Brian Ivers, who had interned at Schlafly before brewing for Goose Island in Chicago, joined the Side Project team. Tommy

Photo of Side Project founder and brewer Cory King in the Side Project Cellar, 2014. (Courtesy of Cory King.)

Manning, another Perennial brewer, joined as well. They were ready to leave Perennial to build their own brewery facility.

In December 2016, the Side Project brewery opened on Manchester Road, around the corner from The Cellar. Lines that had once formed at Perennial now gave life to Maplewood. The early morning arrivals found Maplewood rich in coffee and breakfast food. The annual Maplewood Coffee Crawl featured local coffees and special Side Project coffee stout releases. The transition from Perennial to Side Project came with a slight shift of style. Where Perennial focused on Belgian-inspired and experimental beers, Side Project was mostly oak barrel–aged saisons, sours, and wild ales. Where they crossed over was the imperial stouts, started in King's basement, perfected at Perennial, and reaching new heights at Side Project. At first, all of Side Project beers were barrel aged. They began to make non–barrel aged beers under the Shared name, an employee-owned co-op within Side Project that included all styles. Over time, the Kings found the two names confusing and unnecessary and began to use the Side Project name for everything.

Cory King is something of a magician when it comes to wild yeasts. The harvesting of yeast outside of a lab results in flavors that cannot be repeated or duplicated, as those cultures change and grow. King may go through the same process to make the same wild ale year after year, but no two "vintages" will taste the same. Barrel aging and blending add further depth of variation.

Where the average American is priced out of the highest levels of wine, they are not priced out of the highest levels of beer. Side Project *is* the highest level of beer. Though more expensive than the average craft beer, its prices fall within the range of lower-priced wines.

The cost of craft beer is a touchy subject. The beer wars of the 1970s set the price of beer very low, so consumers have a baseline for comparison. The calculus of beer costs is difficult to solve to everyone's satisfaction. Does this craft beer taste twice as good as a macrobeer? Is it five times as good? Those are really the wrong questions to ask. Outside of how much the whole experience is worth to the consumer, there is the matter of production costs, which are exponentially higher than those of macrobeers. Quality ingredients cost more. A brewery located on a busy street in the city pays much more in rent. Side Project pays higher salaries—and offers better benefits—than most breweries do. But the biggest cost, and perhaps the most difficult to calculate, is time. Most of King's beers are aged. Portions of the brewery are taken up by barrels just sitting there aging, cellaring like wine. Another brewery might use that space to churn out IPAs or kettle sour beers, or beers that achieve sourness through a quick process of adding bacteria, and make more money doing it. As King explains, "These beers take a long time. We have to educate people. They could go to a restaurant and have a kettle sour for four dollars a pint; then they come in here and we have a sour in a 750-milliliter bottle, it's not a kettle sour, and it costs thirty-five dollars. They're like, 'What's the difference between their sour and your sour?' A year and a half. And we can't make it again. It's just different, and hopefully our quality shows that."

Side Project is a part of the St. Louis craft beer community and certainly draws people into the area who try multiple craft breweries. But in many ways it feels like its own ecosystem, fed by a national and international base of beer connoisseurs. It is that rare phenomenon that is better known outside of its own city than within. There is a bit of surprise to a local learning of Side Project's fame. The quiet, unassuming neighbor is world famous.

Pro golfer Rickie Fowler tied the record for the lowest round in US Open history in 2023 with a 62 in his opening round. As he made his way around the course, his sticker-covered water bottle caught the attention of some eagle eyes—What was that lightbulb logo? *Golf Digest* had the answer: "It turns out it's from a brewery that Fowler likes in St. Louis called Side Project."

Side Project has held the top spot in RateBeer's ranking of top Missouri breweries every year since it opened. The site ranked Side Project the number two brewery in the world in 2020, behind Vermont's Hill Farmstead Brewery. The James Beard Foundation honored Side Project as a semifinalist for outstanding bar program. Even the name Side Project Cellar evokes an almost speakeasy type of secret space. Toned-down lights. Refinement, stylishness without stuffiness. Elegance.

The Side Project Cellar is a place that feels like it should exist even if Side Project the brewery didn't—a place to try the world's greatest beers served in their intended glasses at their intended temperatures. And the flavors? Side Project will change your idea of what a beer can taste like. It is like the scene from the Disney film *Ratatouille* when Remy the rat tastes shapes and colors, a synesthesia of flavors. You thought beer tasted like beer until you tried Side Project. Now it tastes like something you can't quite describe, because you've never had anything like it.

# 10

# MODERN

The Forest Park of the 1904 World's Fair glowed with lights strung across buildings and along walking paths. Few wonders on display were more exciting and life-changing than electricity. So profound was the invention of the lightbulb that the image itself became a symbol for great ideas. Those who strolled through the park in a dreamland of illumination couldn't know the future that was in store for them and their children. They had heard of electric streetlamps in New York City, but the idea of a national power grid supplying electricity to every home was too big to imagine. Within the Electrical Palace was Harvey Hubble's electric plug, soon to be common in houses across America. St. Louis was ushering the country into the modern era.

Just south of the fair grew the newly developed neighborhood of King's Oak, named after the corner of Kingshighway Boulevard and Oakland Avenue. Though tiny, the area saw the construction of several St. Louis institutions over the next century. St. Louis University High School (SLUH) moved from Washington Avenue and Ninth Street to its current location on Oakland Avenue. Saint Louis University built Walsh Stadium just west, where the Green Bay Packers played an exhibition game in 1939. Along this stretch stood Falstaff Brewing's corporate office building and Stan Musial & Biggie's restaurant. Construction of US Route 40 in 1937 cut off this little corner from the rest of Forest Park.

Now only SLUH remains. Much of the land that held Falstaff's headquarters and Stan Musial & Biggie's now houses the St. Louis Science Center. The Walsh Stadium footprint now holds Compton/Drew Middle

An aerial view of the south side of Forest Park and surrounding residential neighborhoods, 1930s. (Courtesy of the Missouri Historical Society.)

School; Paraquad, a nonprofit organization assisting those with disabilities; and Modern Brewery and King's Oak restaurant.

When Philip Eisele was born in St. Louis, his older sisters nicknamed him "baby man," which they shortened to "B-Man," then "Beam," then "Beamer." He has been Beamer ever since. Around Beamer's second birthday, a hop breeder in Yakima, Washington, crossed two varieties of hops to create a new experimental variety he called X-114, starting with a single plant.

Before the craft brewery revolution, hops were European varieties, even the ones grown on the hop farms of the Pacific Northwest. As important as flavor was the plants' resistance to mildew and disease. The German Hallertau hops excelled at both. Hop breeder Dr. Stanley Brooks created Cascade, considered the first American hop breed. Compared to other hops at the time, it imparted a strong grapefruit-like taste and proved to be mildew and disease resistant.

A disease known as *Verticillium* wilt destroyed a portion of the German hop farms in the late 1960s, driving up the price of hops for years. Adolph

Coors turned to the new American Cascade hops but found the flavor too strong for lagers. Anchor Brewing Company's Fritz Maytag thought the hop was perfect for his Liberty Ale, the first modern IPA. Cascade so dominated American beer in the decades to follow that by the time of X-114's creation, it accounted for the majority of US hop farm acreage.

As Beamer grew, so did X-114, moving to four plants after a few years and then twenty-one plants a decade later. X-114 was an aroma hop, often added to beer at the end of the boiling process to impart a stronger smell. Because X-114 was more pungent than earlier hops, the breeder wanted to be sure it was just right.

Back in St. Louis, Beamer met Ronnie Fink in middle school, and the two formed a friendship playing football at Lindbergh High School. At thirteen years old, Beamer tried his first beer, a Budweiser from his grandfather's fridge, after mowing the lawn one day. He was too young to know anything about the beer he was drinking, or the ties it had to the St. Louis community. He would learn. "It was huge," he says. "I grew up playing sports. The concession stands at all the sports always sold Bud, Bud Light, and Busch. My dad's cooler always had Busch in it. My dad's refrigerator always had Busch in it. In high school, when we were not drinking beer with our friends, we were not drinking Busch—whatever was the cheapest that was still palatable." He began to understand the role Anheuser-Busch played in St. Louis. "One out of three people probably worked for A-B," Beamer says. "Everybody worked there. There was a good sense of community from that. That's all we knew up until the buyout." Beamer graduated from Lindbergh in 2004, while out in Washington X-114 graduated to commercial testing.

Beamer's football abilities—he was a standout offensive guard—and 4.2 grade point average earned him a spot at Harvard. There, Beamer found two buildings that either made him feel at home or as if he couldn't escape it, Adolphus Busch Hall and the Busch-Reisinger Museum. Unfortunately, Beamer was injured in his first year, ending his football career. Lost and unsure of his future, Beamer spent his sophomore year in Australia as part of a study abroad program. It was there he found his new calling, in the form of a homebrew Beamer considered the world's worst beer. But the fact that some surfer could make it in his dorm room interested Beamer. If this guy could do it, why couldn't he?

Returning to Harvard for his junior year, Beamer worked to incorporate brewing into his studies. Since Harvard had no brewing program, if Beamer wanted to learn about beer, he would have to design the program himself. In all, Beamer created six independent study classes. He worked one-on-one with the heads of the history and chemistry departments. He learned about the mechanics of brewing, about yeasts. He studied the business of brewing with a business school professor. He learned about ancient brewing techniques with an archeology professor.

The Harvard faculty were impressed. Here was a kid who was carving his own path through the country's most prestigious university and providing the professors with something new to study and talk about. They accepted more work to benefit a single student, and they were enjoying it. "I was a kid who obviously wasn't a normal Harvard student in that I got in because I was good at football and had good grades," Beamer says. "It wasn't like I was the smartest kid at my school by any stretch, which almost every other kid there was. They saw I was finding a different way to do something really cool and unique that no one else was even seeing. All these other kids know is they have to be summa cum laude and have two majors. And I wanted to do something cool. I didn't know what that was yet, but I told the faculty this was what I was thinking, so let's explore."

One of Beamer's senior year independent study classes was with a professor of organismic and evolutionary biology. Together they developed a curriculum of food pairings with beer, focusing on the physiological responses to taste. As the professor was English, he enjoyed tying his expertise to beer study.

Beamer's journey echoes that of craft beer pioneer Michael Lewis. A microbiologist and chemist from England, Lewis graduated from Princeton and joined the faculty at the University of California, Davis in the early '60's. There he pieced together existing courses on oenology (the study of wine and winemaking) and food microbiology, chemistry and engineering, and business and marketing to create in 1970 the country's first degree program in brewing sciences. Lewis was directly responsible for the craft beer revolution, as California brewers for New Albion and Sierra Nevada learned from him and sought his advice when building their breweries.

Harvard has a colorful history with beer. John Harvard purportedly learned brewing from William Shakespeare himself—the Harvard House in Stratford upon-Avon, where Harvard grew up, was a short block away from Shakespeare's. The Harvard University brewery supplied daily rations of beer to students, and when one president let beer supplies run short, he was fired.

Over 350 years ago, a "Sister Bradish" ran a tavern near Harvard Yard selling penny beer, bread, and tobacco. By 1654 she had become so popular among Harvard students that parents wrote to the school president complaining that their children were spending too much of their money on her beer. But as their off-campus consumption was easing the strain on Harvard's own campus baking and brewing, President Henry Dunster wrote a letter defending Sister Bradish while praising the quality of her beer.

Harvard alums led the East Coast craft beer revolution. Jim Koch started the Boston Beer Company in 1984. In 1986 three recent graduates started Harpoon Brewery. As Samuel Adams was contract brewed out of state, Harpoon holds the title of first Massachusetts brewery, with license #001. Beamer's new passion led him to an internship there.

The late '80s and early '90s saw the ascent of the India pale ale. California brewer Lagunitas was the first to use the abbreviation "IPA" on their bottles, a designation that stuck in the craft beer community. Lagunitas even tried to sue Sierra Nevada twenty years later over their use of "IPA" on their labels but dropped the suit over consumer outcry.

The origins of the India pale ale are clouded in the myth that high alcohol and hop content were necessary to keep beer from spoiling on long voyages from England to India. While there is certainly truth to that, sailors shipped many styles of beer to India, and pale ales existed before such trips began. Recent scholarship points to one brewery in particular, Hodgson's Brewery, whose proximity to the docks used by the East India Company gave its owner a near-monopoly on beer trade. George Hodgson was known for his pale ales—and his willingness to extend credit to East India Company captains—resulting in the term "India pale ale."

India pale ales were first introduced as a category at the 1989 Great American Beer Festival. Considered one of the more extreme craft beers due to their high International Bitterness Units, or IBUs, they were both a boon and a bane for the category. They resulted in high sales, but their taste turned many people away who, fairly or unfairly, equated the beer with craft beer in general.

Harpoon was far ahead of the IPA trend in the early 1990s when they brewed the East Coast's first IPA. Beamer credits it as his first "good beer." He grins when he talks about his time there. He may not have fully grasped it then, but this was going to be his life. For ten hours a day, three days a week, Beamer worked his way through Harpoon's departments. Their quality control manager, Jaime Schier, told *The Harvard Crimson* in 2008 that Beamer was constantly writing in his notebook: "When I worked with him, he whipped it out at least twenty times to scribble something in it. He kept you on your toes because he is inquisitive about basically everything."

During this time, Harvard alums built a student-run pub called the Cambridge Queen's Head as a gift to the students. It didn't take long for the alums to hear of the student who was designing his own beer courses. Beamer remembers their reactions: "They said, 'Oh, shit, you're that guy? We need some managers to run this place.' It was awesome—the coolest spot on campus."

The pub served Harpoon beers, and as an intern at Harpoon, Beamer was given the opportunity to co-brew a batch specifically for the campus pub. Their honey lager was Beamer's first brewed beer and presented him with the first of many opportunities to pull his own beer from a tap and hand it over the bar to a thirsty customer.

Around the same time that Beamer was getting the Cambridge Queen's Head started, the hop X-114 was ready for its debut. Three breweries invested in X-114, ensuring exclusive rights to its use. Widmer Brothers, Deschutes, and Sierra Nevada had some idea of what this variety could do, and they didn't hesitate to use it. Sierra Nevada brewed their new Torpedo IPA and Hoptimum Imperial IPA, and Deschutes created the instantly popular Fresh Squeezed IPA. Widmer Brothers put it in their pale ale and submitted it to the World Beer Cup in 2008, winning the gold medal. X-114 was something special, and it was time to give it a name. Jason Perrault, the farmer who cultivated it for the past eighteen years, wanted a name for his hop that reflected its mix of citrus and tropical fruit aromas. He named it Citra.

Back in Boston, Beamer's brother-in-law moved into the dorms at Boston University and convinced Beamer to try a homebrew kit with him. "We made four or five batches in the dorm," Beamer says, "which was a huge pain in the ass because you've got to boil it; you've got to sanitize all the bottles and equipment. If I knew how easy kegging was, it would have been easier to just get a kegerator and just keg our own beer. I messed around on some of the extract kits, and I finally got into doing all-grain stuff."

Beamer told *The Harvard Crimson* that he wanted to open his own brewery someday. His own mother expressed surprise at how good her son's beer tasted and showed no qualms about a Harvard degree leading to a career in brewing. "I hope I can come work for him one day," she says. "Maybe I'll be the dishwasher."

The support of his mother, of his friends and family, stood in stark contrast to the response of the parents of his classmates. Beamer says, "I heard it from a lot of parents at Harvard: 'For real? You don't want to go into mergers and acquisitions, or go work for an investment bank?'"

Now a Harvard graduate, Beamer Eisele was ready to venture out into the world of beer. So he did what anyone who just spent four years in Boston would do: He traveled to Hawaii for three months. Let's Go Publications, a travel guide series written by Harvard students, offered to fly him to Hawaii if he would write about his experiences. The book, *Let's Go: Hawaii*, with "Philip Eisele" as contributor, is still available on Amazon.

While in Hawaii, Beamer heard about InBev's buyout of Anheuser-Busch. Perhaps more than anyone there he understood the monumentality of the news. Not only was he from St. Louis, but he had also spent time within the industry, studying it. The more he reflected on it, the less he was surprised at the changes happening in big and craft beer: "There was a movement occurring and we were blind if we didn't see it. It was happening. There were phenomenal beers coming out, different beers. Cocktails were changing. Wine was changing. Beer was changing. Everyone wanted to be more knowledgeable about everything, so we created these subcategories. It was no longer red and white wine. It was no longer ale and lager. It was what subspecies, and then what subspecies of those subspecies. That knowledge created big changes when it came to the market."

As for the explosion of craft breweries that followed the sale, Beamer believed it to be inevitable. "It was going to happen here either way," he says. "All that sale did was expedite it—turned up the heat. It was especially important here because of those one in three people who worked at the brewery. They felt jaded. 'What is going on? Why are you doing this?' There was a fear. A lot of people lost their jobs."

After his Hawaiian summer, Beamer returned to the East Coast. He spent time in New York City and got to know Steve Hindy and Garrett Oliver of Brooklyn Brewery. Beamer had a job offer to work there, but because of his base of people in Boston, he returned to Harpoon to work for eight months and to plan out his own future brewery.

Harvard taught Beamer everything he could possibly know about beer, except how to brew it at the scale he wanted. He applied to the University of California, Davis Master Brewers Certificate Program, the school that Michael Lewis had created four decades earlier. At first, UC Davis wasn't sure what to do with him. Beamer didn't have the usual biology or chemistry background, but what he had done at Harvard impressed them enough to accept him: "I told them I could learn anything if I had enough desire to do it, and this was my desire, so don't hold back on me. You can treat me rough. I'll put the time in."

In the months before the Master Brewers program started, Beamer returned to St. Louis to intern with Schlafly under Dan Kopman, who welcomed Beamer into the St. Louis craft beer community. One weekend, in a buddy's basement, Beamer told his childhood friend Ronnie Fink about his plans to enter the Master Brewers program. Fink, who did have a chemistry background, was unhappy with his current job working for Monsanto in their GMO (genetically modified organism) corn division. He turned to Beamer and said, in all seriousness, "Is it cool if I join you?" Beamer gave his friend the are-we-doing-this look, nodded his head, and said, "Yeah."

Fink contacted the program and was put on the waiting list for the upcoming session. As Beamer headed west to work in the Hudson Vineyards in the months leading up to the program's start, beginning a parallel lifelong love of wine, Fink found out he had gotten one of the last spots. The two childhood friends were going to learn how to brew beer together. The course taught them the minutia and intricacies of each step of the process of making beer. And as they were doing it together, they could bounce thoughts and ideas off of each other and clarify any confusion. After six months, they were ready to brew.

Fink took a job at Freestate Brewing in Lawrence, Kansas, while Beamer returned to St. Louis to find investors for the brewery he was already building in his head. A group of potential investors, acquaintances of his father, wrote him a check for five thousand dollars. It wouldn't help much as far as a brewery was concerned, but he did significantly upgrade his homebrewing equipment and set out to impress with what he could do. Maybe a good beer would convince them to really invest. But the investors passed.

Beamer brought his homebrew to Thanksgiving that year. It was a light Belgian saison—as Beamer described it, "Not funky but interesting enough, easy, clean drinking, almost like a blonde with a little more attitude. It was delicious." Beamer's brother-in-law was impressed enough to invest and get Beamer started. The very first beer Modern Brewery released was a variation of that original saison.

During the time between the completion of the Master Brewers program and the opening of Modern Brewery, the craft beer scene in St. Louis doubled. Beamer watched Perennial, Urban Chestnut, 4 Hands, and Civil Life open in 2011. Instead of discouraging him or convincing him that a window of opportunity was closing, Beamer felt vindicated: "It was more validation that it's not crazy to start a brewery. I can do this. There's room for more."

Beamer's original vision for the brewery was closer to 2nd Shift's model but nearer geographically to St. Louis. No tasting room, just really good beer that he would supply throughout the city. He found a space up against railroad tracks off of Manchester Avenue in a neighborhood no one knew was called King's Oak, where fewer than two hundred people lived. What Beamer saw in King's Oak was a central location. His new brewery would be nestled in the middle of St. Louis neighborhoods known as The Hill, The Grove, and Dogtown. As Beamer planned to seek out accounts and distribute beer himself, proximity was necessary.

An early name for the new company was Clever Brewery, but Beamer decided against it. What he kept was his original idea for a logo, a lightbulb. What, he asked himself, did the lightbulb convey? Modernity, just as the world's fair had intended 110 years before. Modern Brewery. The lightbulb logo featured an "M" as the filament and a "B" as the metal cap.

The brewing system that he had meticulously designed in a notebook began to take shape. It was time for Ronnie Fink to join him. "We got Ronnie back in late 2013, early 2014," Beamer says. "We'd gotten all of our tanks in and in place, doing some of the process piping, and then we needed Ronnie to figure out all the other things we needed."

Together again, the duo split up responsibilities: Ronnie came up with the recipes, often in collaboration with Beamer, and brewed the beer. Beamer's job was to make sure they had someone to sell it to, and, with help from his brother-in-law, he spoke personally with bars and restaurants across the city, developing relationships and delivering kegs in their small truck. For each account, Beamer provided a long, cylindrical tap handle featuring the name of the beer, topped with a lightbulb that actually lit up. In some bars, like Nick's Pub, which boasts 101 draft beers, the lightbulb acted like a bug zapper to craft beer moths: 'I'll take one of those.'

Modern Brewery appeared at their first Microfest, St. Louis's annual beer tasting festival, before their official opening. In the event's program, Modern proclaimed, "We make authentic and unique Belgian and American inspired ales. Our hope is that you enjoy drinking our beers as much as we enjoy making them!"

Beamer was now pouring beer alongside craft pioneers Schlafly and the new crop of breweries. Stephen Hale, the unofficial goodwill ambassador for St. Louis craft beer, welcomed each new brewery into the fold, knowing their success meant the scene was growing. Beamer and 2nd Shift brewer Steve Crider started a friendship there. At the festival, Ronnie Fink told local news station KSDK, "Everyone is pretty welcoming in the beer community. Everyone wants to see everyone do well because the craft market is really a small piece of the beer market. But together we think each year we're going to keep getting bigger and bigger."

Modern did grow bigger and bigger, thanks to good beer and an IPA called Citrapolis. The Citra hop was no longer exclusive to Sierra Nevada, Deschutes, and Widmer Brothers. It was ready for its St. Louis debut. By 2014 the market was top-heavy with IPAs, and Beamer was getting sick of them. But Fink saw the potential for this new hop, and instead of blending it with other hops to give a beer a depth of flavor, which was the norm at the time, he decided to let the hop speak for itself. It was a decision that seems obvious in retrospect, but it was quite revolutionary. "We were the first brewery in the area to do a single-hopped beer—it was all Citra," Beamer says. "This was when Sierra Nevada was the benchmark for pale ale and IPA flavor, so you're thinking old-school IPA—pine, resin, dank. Not a lot of people in 2014 knew what Citra was, outside of the local beer geeks. It's all Citra; it has a cool fucking name—it works. I would argue that there's not a fresher IPA on the market."

Citrapolis. It was a perfect name for a perfect beer. Fink and Beamer had created something truly modern. And since Beamer was the one delivering it from King's Oak to the bar or restaurant, it was as fresh as possible.

It didn't take long for the majority of the illuminated lightbulb taps in the St. Louis area to feature Citrapolis, and in a market dominated by IPAs, Modern's rose to the top. There was something counterintuitive about the groundswell of interest for this new beer. The years 2014 and 2015 were right in the middle of a period of many-hopped—arguably excessively hopped—IPAs. The winners and finalists for the Great American Beer Festivals reflected this. The 2015 gold medal winner, Revolver IPA, from California's BNS Brewing & Distributing, featured six different hops. Runner-up Pernicious IPA, from Wicked Weed Brewing in North Carolina, featured ten! What kind of brewery puts out an IPA with one kind of hop?

"What constitutes the best IPA?" Beamer asks. "Is it the one with the fanciest hops, or the biggest aroma, or the most dank? Or is it the most-drinkable IPA? I would argue we have the most-drinkable IPA. It's got the balance. Is it going to light anyone's pants on fire? If they appreciate balance, then yes. It's a very well-balanced beer."

A year into Modern's existence, Beamer turned a portion of the brewery into a taproom, which really amounted to, as he called it, "a legal college garage party." He and Fink got to drink their beers with their family and friends. And even if you were a stranger showing up on a Friday or Saturday night, you were counted among them.

Modern dipped its toe into canning its beer later in the decade, which meant canning Citrapolis, letting people know via social media that they could pick it up at the taproom, and then almost immediately selling out. It wasn't until COVID that canning really took off.

In 2018 Citra became the most popular American hop variety, overtaking Cascade in acreage. It had grown from 98 acres in 2009, when only three breweries held exclusive rights, to 9,035, accounting for over 15 percent of all hop acreage. As the hazy IPAs took off, so too did the market for more and more aroma hops like Simcoe, Galaxy, and Nelson Sauvin.

Morgan Street Brewery and Kräftig brewer Marc Gottfried explains the shift in hop usage: "No one at the beginning ever foresaw the incredible vast amount of hops they are putting into beer now. A great example is New England IPA. There's no IBUs because there's no bittering hops in there, but there's an incredible amount of aroma hops, so much so that if you actually put that many hops in there, you're going to waste half your fermenter because you've got this salad's worth of vegetative matter. So they've gotten a lot of the vegetative matter out of it and hyper concentrated it."

And brewers across the country are experimenting with a lot more hops now. "What they're doing with hops is insane," Gottfried says. "I don't know if they're cloning or hybridizing, genetically modifying or whatever, but there are hops that taste like grapefruits or onions or dill or melons or pears. We didn't have that." Beamer is even surprised at times at the flavor of his own beers: "The other day I tried a new beer and my face lit up. Oh, yeah, it's Skittles!" As for the hyper-concentrated hops that Gottfried described, Modern used experimental hops that had been frozen and packaged into pellets—what Beamer described as "crushed and sprinkly crystals"—to create Keep Your Heart, an imperial hazy IPA, for the Ollie Hinkle Heart Foundation.

Ronnie Fink left Modern to brew for Six Mile Bridge in 2019, and assistant brewer Brian Harmon stepped into the head brewer role. Harmon harnessed the new aroma hops for a new brewery focus on hazy IPAs. His Party Supplies IPA became an area favorite.

By this point, Modern had outgrown its little warehouse space and was looking for something bigger and more visible. An announced partnership with Webster Groves restaurant Olive + Oak fell through, and Beamer turned his attention back to the little neighborhood of King's Oak.

In the meantime, Modern's full canning line came at just the right time, as COVID took its toll on the beer industry. No longer could people drink their beers at bars and restaurants. But the green cans of Citrapolis, adorned with the St. Louis Arch, were available everywhere now, and a lot of people stuck at home drowned their boredom with it. At one point, Citrapolis accounted for 85 percent of Modern's sales. In a time when other breweries were struggling to stay afloat, Modern was the anomaly. They continued to sell their beer at or above pre-pandemic levels.

Modern opened their new brewery and King's Oak restaurant on Oakland Avenue in 2023. Highly visible from US Route 40/64, Modern acts as a beacon of hope for thirsty commuters stuck in rush-hour traffic. The inside of the new brewery and restaurant is wide open, with long tables for community drinking and dining. Grateful Dead memorabilia line the walls. On the day Modern and the King's Oak opened, it was Beamer's mother who volunteered to do the dishwashing, fulfilling her promise from Beamer's time at Harvard.

The executive chef of the King's Oak is Beamer's longtime friend Charles Hess. He added New Orleans–inspired dishes to the usual brewpub fare of burgers, pizza, and sandwiches. Working with family and friends isn't a kind of security blanket for Beamer; it is a motivation to keep moving forward, to continue to improve. As he says, "You can't stop, because they depend on you, too."

The new space is a success, as lauded as Modern's beer. The brewery that Beamer dreamed up while at Harvard and meticulously planned in his notebook became a St. Louis institution. As Beamer likes to point out, "It's not always rainbows and butterflies." In 2016 Side Project sued Modern Brewery over its use of lightbulbs in its logo and tap handles, claiming Side Project's use of the lightbulb predated Modern's. As a result, Modern changed its logo and lost its iconic tap handles. And in the days leading up to the opening of the new brewery, the retaining wall that held the new patio collapsed from flooding, depriving them of a key feature of their new space. Still, Beamer and Modern pushed forward and let their resilience define them. As beer sales fell flat after COVID, Modern invited those who were turning to cocktails to come check them out.

"What is special about the Modern Brewery?" Beamer asks. "We're small enough that we can be nimble and literally do anything we want. We don't have to make beer anymore. We're going to. But who's to say we can't make Modern cocktails? You think I'm going to alienate anyone who wants to drink a cocktail? You think I'm going to say, 'Cocktails are bad?' What about wine? I fucking love wine. We're working on something with that, too. We were doing draft cocktails that have beer and spirits, made them on site and pumped them out of our draft system. I don't know many people who are pre-batching beer-made cocktails."

Those who meet Beamer at the brewery find him something of a teddy bear, still a kid at heart. Once they find out he's from St. Louis, the next question is inevitable: "Where'd you go to school?" They mean high school—no one in St. Louis seems to care where you went to college.

11

# NARROW GAUGE

Twenty-first-century beer has made it clear: It's time to embrace the haze. In the kind of redemption arc rarely seen in the beer industry, haze journeyed from brewery killer to industry darling in half a century.

In the 1970s haze killed Schlitz beer. Or at least the beer giant's efforts to avoid haze led to white flakes and beer snot, destroying their reputation. The reaction was deserved. Lagers should be clean and crisp, both in flavor and appearance. A foggy haze is anything but clean-looking and could indicate more serious problems. It could mean the batch is infected. The beer may have been stored at freezing temperatures, resulting in what is called "chill haze." Or, more commonly, proteins and polyphenols from hops and malts have bonded to covalent bonds in the beer, creating a suspension—drastically affecting the flavor. It wasn't until 2004 that a brewer in New England harnessed that haze to create flavor and aroma.

John Kimmich moved from Pittsburgh to Vermont in 1994 to apprentice under author and brewing expert Greg Noonan at The Vermont Pub & Brewery. Nine years later Kimmich and his wife opened The Alchemist Pub & Brewery in Waterbury, Vermont. It was there he brewed his first version of Heady Topper IPA and showed the beer world what haze could do to a beer. Beer geeks flocked to Vermont for this new kind of IPA brimming with surprising flavors. Other brewers were intrigued. Something new was coming out of New England, something they weren't quite ready for. Heady Topper was hazy, therefore imperfect.

Kimmich didn't set out to create a hazy IPA. His time as head brewer at The Vermont Pub & Brewery coincided with the emerging dominance of the India pale ale. What we now call West Coast IPA started with those breweries closest to the hop farms on the West Coast. Anchor Brewing created Liberty Ale in 1975, adding dry hops late in the brewing process to improve aroma, a blueprint for IPAs to come. Sierra Nevada Pale Ale proved there was a demand for bitter beer. The 1990s saw Lagunitas and Stone IPAs in California, Bell's Two Hearted Ale in Michigan, Goose Island IPA in Chicago, Brooklyn Brewery's Brooklyn East IPA in New York, and Harpoon Ale in Boston.

The early 2000s started a kind of bitterness race, where breweries pushed the envelope on what was considered too bitter. Russian River Brewing Company led the way with Pliny the Elder, an 8 percent double IPA that tested the limits of the IBU scale. Dogfish Head rolled out the 90 Minute IPA, named after the length of the boil during which hops are added. Bell's brewed Hopslam, a 10 percent double IPA with honey.

It was during this aggressive period that John Kimmich experimented with ways to increase the hop profile of his beers. Quite literally, he threw everything at them. Heady Topper includes six kinds of hops. And instead of adding hops only in the beginning stages of brewing, Kimmich and others at this time added hops in later stages of the process, which boosts the beer's aroma without adding bitterness, often at the cost of increased haze.

Heady Topper was hazy, but it tasted good. It tasted new. Its strong, dank aroma—and the proximity of local band Phish—inspired the weed-y name. Was Heady Topper good despite its haze, as many initially believed? Or was it good because of the haze? It was some time before brewers understood what was happening during the brewing process, that the chemical bonding they had tried to avoid was actually enhancing the beer's flavor.

Morgan Street and Kräftig brewer Marc Gottfried explains how revolutionary the process was: "We've spent our whole lives trying to make beer clear, and here comes somebody who actually made beer as cloudy as humanly possible. Who would ever do that? Of course they hop the crap out of it and accidentally discover that these non–beer soluble hop compounds bond to the haze. And for the first time in the history of beer, you and I are experiencing hop flavors and aromas we've never been able to experience before. That's amazing!"

Heady Topper grew so popular that The Alchemist bought an off-site cannery dedicated to Heady Topper to fill the demand. Why cans, when the craft beer world, outside of Dale's Pale Ale, was almost entirely in bottles? Perhaps it was the haze. Kimmich faced pushback from patrons early on who associated haze with imperfection. The cans themselves even say, “Drink from the can!” Was this a way to remove the haze from the equation altogether? Kimmich maintains that Heady Topper begins to lose its taste and aroma as soon as it’s poured into a glass, that a layer of $CO_2$ in the can preserves the quality of the beer.

The hazy beer trend took a while to get going. Heady Topper was available only in Vermont and took on an almost mythical status for those unable to travel or trade for it. Shaun Hill opened Hill Farmstead in 2010, highlighting the new Citra hop in his hazy IPAs. He described this new, fruitier style of hazy IPA as “juicy.” Vermont now had two beer destinations. As popular as their beers were, Kimmich and Hill were not eager to share their recipes. For a short time the now-ubiquitous hazy IPAs were available at only two spots in Vermont. The floodgates opened with Massachusetts breweries Trillium and Tree House, Maine’s Bissell Brothers, and New York’s Other Half. There was little agreement on naming the style. Was it just another IPA, as Kimmich argued? Was it a hazy IPA, a juicy IPA, or was it specific to the region, a New England IPA?

As the style spread westward, so did the demand. Here was a hop-forward, slightly creamier beer, often with lower bitterness. Hazy beers were perfect for highlighting the flavors and aromas of newly developed hops. The bitterness that defined the style was diminished by the new brewing technique. Aroma hops took center stage.

If you lived in St. Louis in the early 2010s, the only way to get a New England IPA was to travel, trade, or attend a festival where one of the breweries was pouring. A local homebrewer’s love of beer took him to a festival where Trillium Brewing was pouring. Jeff Hardesty was already an accomplished homebrewer by the time he tried his first New England IPA. A native of Bethalto, Illinois, Hardesty had moved to Florissant in north St. Louis County in 2007. His wife bought him a homebrewing kit for his birthday in the pivotal year of 2011. Like many in the community, Hardesty approached brewing as a scientist. “I was intrigued with brewing,” he says. “The homebrew kit kind of started my whole obsession. My first beer was a porter. I honestly wasn’t drinking a lot of craft beer. I was more interested in the science behind it.”

What Hardesty figured out quickly was that he needed empty bottles if he was going to brew and bottle his own beer: “It was pretty much the same price to buy empty bottles as it was to buy bottles full of other people’s beer, so that in turn got me drinking a lot of different kinds of craft beer. That's where I got exposed to a ton of different styles, and it became more and more intriguing the more I drank. 'What's this style I've never heard of?' 'What's an Abbey beer?' 'I'm going to try and see what this is like.' It just kind of made me more aware of the different kinds of styles that were there and the different ingredients that were factors in producing that style of beer."

While working as a mechanical engineer for Winchester Ammunition, Hardesty joined the STL Hops Homebrew Club and dove into brewing and collecting new beer, trading for those unavailable in the Midwest. St. Louis was starting to grow its own reputation for unique and exciting beers. When Perennial's Phil Wymore and Cory King were amazed by the demand their special releases were creating, Jeff Hardesty was one of those waiting in line. The bottles he didn't drink or share with his homebrew club, Hardesty traded in order to try the best of what was available throughout the country.

To be a beer nerd in Florissant in the early 2010s meant drinking at Cugino's, an Italian restaurant famous for their fried softball-size meatballs. Cousins Ben Goldkamp and Dave Beckham bought the restaurant in 2004 and named it after the Italian word for "cousin." They installed fifty-six taps with craft beer from all over the country, one of the biggest selections in the Midwest. Jeff Hardesty was at the bar often enough to form a relationship with the owners as he continued his beer education.

A growing interest in IPAs led Hardesty to some realizations. First, St. Louis had some of the country's best—notably, 2nd Shift's Art of Neurosis and Brew Cocky. And, second, of course, closer, fresher beer tastes much better than beer that has traveled some distance. "2nd Shift was on a different level than a lot of IPAs that were out there," Hardesty says. "It probably helped that it was closer and fresher, so I was getting a fresher version of West Coast–style IPAs. I was very much intrigued by hops; seeing the different expressions of hops just kind of sparked an interest in IPA—what are they doing differently to create this type of beer?" This interest in hops was about to take a turn in the unlikeliest of places: Tampa, Florida.

Tampa Bay brewery Cigar City's Hunahpu's Imperial Stout garnered national attention similar to Perennial's Abraxas, and they capitalized on the excitement in 2010 with Hunahpu's Day, a release party and mini-festival on the brewery grounds. It was a kind of pilgrimage where eager travelers could purchase bottles up to their limit as well as taste variations and rare offerings. A guest tap at the festival changed the future of St. Louis craft beer.

Jeff Hardesty traveled from St. Louis to encounter a beer that had come from New England: Trillium's Congress Street IPA: "I was super intrigued by what the hell I just tasted when I tried it. It was so different than what I was used to."

If Hardesty wasn't hooked yet by this new style, his wife Heather's work assignment in Maine completed his obsession. "I found out about Tree House," he says, "and was able to get some of their stuff when they were just doing growlers. We drove out to Hill Farmstead. We went to Maine Beer Company in Freeport. I was able to try all those styles."

Returning to St. Louis, Hardesty knew hazy IPAs were the beers he wanted to brew because they were the beers he wanted to drink. He was tired of trading away all of his Perennial and 2nd Shift special releases for them. But New England IPAs, Hardesty soon learned, were not easy to brew. According to him, "It was one of the hardest styles of beer to figure out. Part of that was there wasn't a whole lot of information out there, so you're kind of looking at it from the mind-set of brewing the IPAs you know, which is West Coast IPAs. I spent a lot of time messing around with hop timing and scheduling and trying to get that massive hop aroma and flavor. I basically went through a bunch of different elements of the brewing process until I was able to find something that was remotely close to what I was trying to achieve."

At the same time as Hardesty was perfecting his recipe, he was in negotiations with the owners of Cugino's to build a brewery in their basement. A relationship that began over the bar grew as Hardesty impressed them with his homebrewing skills. "Living in Florissant, they were basically the only craft beer spot up there if you wanted to drink draft," he says. "They would do Goose Island Bourbon County tap takeovers. I met Ben at one of those, kind of formed a relationship. I would run into him at beer releases. We just kept running into each other, which in turn led to meeting his business partners at Cugino's. We built a friendship, and they first had one of my homebrews at an STL Hops anniversary party. That kicked off a half-drunken conversation about starting a brewery."

Most, if not all, homebrewers will at some point have this conversation, and it's rarely sober. But the Hardestys had already been working on a business plan, so this wasn't a conversation to be dismissed the next morning. Their original idea was to create a brewery much like 2nd Shift, a mixed fermentation–focused brewery in a rural part of Missouri. But the conversations with Ben at Cugino's eventually shifted their focus, and they all agreed the basement space of the restaurant would be easiest. It was a savvy business decision for the Cugino's guys: If they didn't have to source their fifty-six beers from all over the country, they could save a lot of money. They targeted late 2015 to early 2016 to open the new brewery. Once the decision was made, Jeff Hardesty converted the seventeen-hundred-square-foot basement space into a brewery with two fermenters. It was a challenge to build and to brew, as the ceiling clearance was just over eight feet.

It was important to Hardesty that the brewery name both reflect the community of Florissant and connect to the greater St. Louis region. He chose Narrow Gauge, a reference to the West End Narrow Gauge Railroad, which in the late 1800s ran passengers from Grand Boulevard and Olive Street in the city to Florissant in about an hour for the low price of sixteen cents.

Narrow Gauge opened in 2016 in the basement of Cugino's with offerings of Old Town Porter and Mordecai pale ale. It was initially a one-man operation as Jeff toiled under the unsuspecting diners above. Every ingredient had to be carried down the stairs. Kegs—and, later, cases—had to be carried back up. Fermenters had to be cleaned in the tight space. The location of the brewery may have been ideal; the space itself was not.

The New England IPA that Jeff began to work on after that first taste was coming along, and when the brewery opened, he felt he was 90 percent there. He named his first New England IPA Fallen Flag, a railroad term for a company that has been taken over by another, losing its original name.

Most brewers have a bit of the artist in them. Technique is important, but creativity is what drives innovation. Beer drinkers are constantly looking for what's next, what's new, what's different. Jeff Hardesty is an actual artist. He designed the company logo and, together with Cugino's manager, Jeremy Hegger, drew the designs for the cans. Fallen Flag, drawn by Hegger, depicts the Florissant rail station building as a storage room for hops.

With only two fermenters going, Narrow Gauge didn't make much of a dent in the fifty-six taps Cugino's offered. But word began to spread among the beer community that someone local was making a New England–style IPA. Soon it wasn't just diners at Cugino's ordering a glass of Fallen Flag; people were coming from all over to take a growler of it home. "For half of our first year we were right about two hundred barrels," Hardesty says.

Photo of a can of Narrow Gauge Fallen Flag hazy IPA. (Courtesy of Narrow Gauge.)

"We started selling beer in June and realized real quick that we were going to be out of beer. We bought an additional four fermenters in November. The demand was draft and growler fills all the time."

Narrow Gauge's growlers were smaller than the usual sixty-four-ounce jugs, an intentional choice. The Alchemist's John Kimmich was right—New England IPAs tend to lose their flavor with time—and the last thing Hardesty wanted was someone to judge his brewery from an old growler. Narrow Gauge moved from glass growlers to Crowlers, or thirty-two-ounce-can growlers.

Beer nerds weren't the only ones paying attention. National beer media noticed that the St. Louis craft beer community, already rich with new, exciting breweries, was getting richer. BeerAdvocate listed Narrow Gauge among their Class of 2016, and RateBeer named it "Best New Brewery in Missouri" in 2017. Jeff Hardesty had only gotten started.

Side Project's Cory King gave Hardesty perhaps the biggest endorsement by inviting Narrow Gauge to pour at Zwanze Day 2017, a festival organized by Brasserie-Brouwerij Cantillon to celebrate Belgian lambic beers. The event debuted Hardesty's second New England IPA, OJ Run, inspired by Tree House Brewing's Juice Machine. Attendees of the festival loved it, and the buzz surrounding the new brewery grew louder. OJ Run became Hardesty's best-selling beer.

Those who traded St. Louis beer began to include Narrow Gauge Crowlers with their Perennial or Side Project bottles, spreading Hardesty's beer throughout the country. Narrow Gauge stickers began to appear in far-flung breweries, and more than a few were inspired to brew their own New England IPAs. "It kind of put our beer in front of people to try," says

Hardesty. "Thankfully it was good enough for it to stand out and in turn led us to be able to pour at some of the bigger festivals throughout the country and helped grow the brand even further. I felt like every festival was an opportunity to showcase what we did. From that I met a lot of people within the industry and built relationships, which led to more festival invites, as well as collaborating on beers and so forth."

The Cugino's bartenders began to notice a curious trend: There seemed to be more out-of-towners at the bar than locals. The more of the restaurant's fifty-six taps Narrow Gauge took over, the more people showed up to take Crowlers to go.

The story of Narrow Gauge's success can be told through its signage. Before Hardesty moved in, Cugino's featured a large green, white, and red sign along Lindbergh Boulevard, with a changeable reader board underneath advertising their meatballs or offering buy one, get one free pasta on Sundays. To celebrate the brewery's opening, the owners of Cugino's changed the reader board to "Home of the Narrow Gauge Brewing Co." A year and a half later, they installed a small, more permanent Narrow Gauge logo sign.

People kept coming. This wasn't just a passing fad. It was a true word-of-mouth phenomenon, as Hardesty did zero advertising. "We didn't really put any time or thought into marketing," he says. "It was always word-of-mouth, grow-as-we-could-grow-type thing."

The number of people coming in to take Crowlers to go became a problem for the Cugino's bartenders, whose time filling to-go beer orders took away from their normal duties. The solution was to convert a section of the restaurant into the Narrow Gauge tasting room. Now those who came in could turn right and drink beer at long, wooden tables or fill their Crowlers at the new bar. Those wanting to eat could turn left and enter the restaurant, which still offered all the same Narrow Gauge beer.

The Narrow Gauge sign along Lindbergh grew even larger, now slightly exceeding the size of the Cugino's sign. Hardesty grew his company and hired more brewers, but the cramped space proved difficult, and he struggled to keep brewers longer than a couple of years. A new space, with room to grow outward and upward, soon proved necessary. They debuted their new brewery and taproom next door to Cugino's in late 2024.

The term "New England IPA" has itself become a bit of a fallen flag, as "hazy" has overtaken its use. The Brewer's Association recognized it as a unique style in 2018, choosing "hazy" and "juicy" over "New England." That same year, however, an online poll by beer publication *The Full Pint*, who didn't get the memo about the official style name, resulted in Narrow Gauge being named "Best NEIPA Brewer." Breweries across the country have embraced the style. In 2018, hazy IPAs accounted for 1.5 percent of total craft beer sales. By 2023 that number was up to 8.7 percent, making it one of the most popular styles.

Despite its reputation as a vanguard for the hazy IPA trend, Narrow Gauge isn't a one trick pony. In fact, many of the awards the brewery received came from other styles. In 2019 their Meersalz *gose*-style ale won silver at the Great American Beer Festival, and in 2023 they took gold in the Specialty Berliner-Style Weiss category with Saft, a beer aged with passion fruit, pink guava, and mango, both modern interpretations of classic styles. "I've always been intrigued by classic styles, learning the history behind them. That's why I started homebrewing,"

In some ways, the chill, self-effacing, skater-vibed Jeff Hardesty is a victim of his own success. Narrow Gauge is so good at hazy IPAs, other styles often go unnoticed. It's a good problem to have, and when trends move away from hazy IPAs, Narrow Gauge will no doubt have something beer nerds will be excited about. It will probably be something Hardesty has been brewing for years.

12

# 2ND SHIFT'S SECOND ACT

By the mid-2010s, everything was going well with Steve Crider and 2nd Shift. The brewery he built in New Haven could handle his growth. Steve was eager to live out the rest of his life sixty miles away from where he was selling his beer. Except it wasn't, it couldn't, and he damn sure wasn't: "I got a divorce in 2012. I needed to grow. I was out of room there, and the cows weren't drinking enough beer. I just wanted to be closer to where people are, where the food and drink are. I just wanted to come to the city and live in the city."

Something needed to change. Enter Libby Brown. Originally from Champaign-Urbana, Illinois, Brown moved to St. Louis in 2007. A sommelier, Brown worked at Remy's Kitchen & Wine Bar in Clayton for five years before becoming wine director at 33 Wine Bar in Lafayette Square, the bar Jake Hafner had started and then sold to open the Civil Life.

Steve Crider was something of a staple at 33 Wine Bar over the years, as 2nd Shift had done tap takeovers there and always featured prominently on their beer list. "I loved it there," Crider says. "I still think it's one of the best places to drink in the city. The best wine, the best spirits, amazing beer list."

Libby Brown's first day at 33 Wine Bar was the first day of Craft Beer Week in St. Louis, and the bar was celebrating it with a cask of 2nd Shift Katy. Sean Netzer, who went on to manage Union Loafers Café and Bread Bakery, ran the beer and whiskey program. Brown didn't know much about craft beer at the time and tells the story of their meeting as a comedy of errors on her part. She didn't know how to work the cask and ended up dumping half of it on the floor. And the brewer was right there watching!

But Steve Crider is not a man angered by such things. Rather, he found the humor in it, and realized he kind of liked this woman who was dumping his beer all over the floor. Crider came in often over the next couple of months, but it was Brown, not the wine and beer, that drew him there. After two months, he gathered the courage to ask her out. Now they're married.

By the following summer, Brown had moved out to New Haven to help Crider with 2nd Shift. Her wine background proved invaluable to the company, providing Crider with a partner who could run the business side of things. She even got him thinking the unthinkable: Maybe a brewery should actually make money. "She does everything," Crider says in describing Libby's role. "She doesn't brew, but she helps out in the brewery if we need it. She keeps the shit going. She keeps us all in line and keeps us going. I keep the machines working. I keep the beer-making side going. She's the business runner."

One of their first projects together was a variation of 2nd Shift's farmhouse ale Katy that incorporated fruit. Libby procured 250 pounds each of peaches and blackberries. The next year she bought 260 pounds of organic raspberries. As Katy is a Brett beer, the process of adding fruit involves much more science than simply dumping it in. Brett is a wild yeast that eats sugars from the fruit but also may interact with wild yeasts the fruits bring with them. Needless to say, Steve Crider was up to the task, and the Katy variations sold out quickly.

The Criders spent several years in New Haven planning their move to St. Louis. Once word leaked that New Haven might lose its now-famous brewery, the town offered the Criders a free building in their quaint downtown for a tasting room, along with an old hat factory on fourteen acres out of town for production—for only sixty thousand dollars. But once the Criders had their mind set on a change, they knew their future was in St. Louis.

It may have had something to do with the arrival of Annabelle, their first child. With a little one now roaming the brewery floor, Steve brewed his first batch of Annabelle, a wild ale brewed with *Brettanomyces*. Steve and Libby now had a family to look out for, and that involved growing 2nd Shift for Annabelle. "She's going to take this over," Crider says.

Their search for a location in town echoed Crider's first attempt, back in the late 2000s. The high rents and cramped spaces must have made the New Haven offer even more attractive, but a building on the northern border of The Hill had everything they needed. "We looked at a lot of buildings in the city that were cute, cool brick buildings that would have taken $5 million to get floors and walls and sewers and roofs and everything done," Crider says. "We liked The Hill, and the building was big and kind of new—a big, steel building. It already had everything."

Because the space they were considering was built to dispose of medical sharps, it was already equipped with the floor drains 2nd Shift needed. It had the right electric, gas, and big dock doors. Crider had to put in a bigger water line, but that was the extent of their improvements: "It was just a big, blank space to do what I needed. And not a bad spot. It took me a bit to figure out the water. I think because of the big brewery in town the water is much better, so I use my reverse osmosis now only for when I make lagers, my Italian pils, or my Czech pils."

St. Louisans still hold on to the urban legend that Anheuser-Busch is the reason St. Louis has such good water. The city recently won "Best Tasting Water" by the US Conference of Mayors. At the time of Anheuser-Busch's founding in 1852, however, the water in St. Louis was quite bad. Poet Walt Whitman came to visit his brother, Jeff, a St. Louis water inspector. Whitman wrote, "The water of the west, in some places, is not very good, but they make it up here by plenty of fair wine, and inexhaustible quantities of the best beer in the world." Why Anheuser-Busch never advertised using the quote is a mystery.

While there is little doubt that over the past century and a half Anheuser-Busch championed legislation that would ensure clean local water, the true hero is a little-known chemist and city water department employee named John F. Wixford. In the lead up to the 1904 World's Fair, St. Louis water was still bad, and fair organizers feared the majestic fountains would shoot out brown, sludgy water. Mayor Rolla Wells created a ten-thousand-dollar competition to solve their water problem. Enter John Wixford. Quirky, eccentric, and brilliant, he was an early version of Steve Crider. Wixford had opened his house to boarders who had nowhere else to go. He kept two dismantled buggies in the attic just to tinker with them but rode his bike around St. Louis because he found the motorcars too fast.

With only weeks to go before the opening of the world's fair, Wixford discovered that milk of lime removes the sediment from water. The city had clean water for the fair and for over a century after. But John Wixford did not get his reward, nor did he get much recognition at all. The city claimed they could not reward a city employee, and his name did

Photo of John F. Wixford, St. Louis chemist, circa 1910. (Courtesy of the Missouri Historical Society.)

not appear in histories of the 1904 World's Fair. No one at Anheuser-Busch corrected the record when over the years they were credited with the city's clean water.

Before moving, the Criders convinced Mike Sweeney to come on as operations manager. Sweeney started STL Hops, a homebrewing club that is still going strong today. Sweeney followed Cory King as craft beer manager at Lohr Distributing in 2011 after King left to join Perennial Artisan Ales. In 2014 Sweeney joined the Criders at 2nd Shift. Sweeney's involvement in homebrewing and distribution gave him an insight into beer trends that the Criders did not have. Of course, Steve Crider put his own snarky signature on chasing trends. He named a milkshake IPA Cash Grab.

The transitional period from New Haven to St. Louis proved tough for 2nd Shift. For a brewery that was not making a lot of money to begin with to take on debt for their new space came with risk. And they had nowhere to sell their releases until their space was finished. It turned out a lot of people owed Steve Crider favors. His mechanical wizardry has been a blessing for many St. Louis area craft breweries over the years. If anyone needed help with their machinery, Steve was the guy to call. Now, when the Criders needed it the most, the breweries gave back to them. On more than one occasion, breweries like Exit 6 and Perennial hosted 2nd Shift release parties, finagling the distribution costs so that 2nd Shift earned almost 100 percent of the proceeds.

"We were in transition to moving to the city," Steve Crider says. "It was right about the time Cory was selling Side Project beer at Perennial. I wanted to do a foeder [a large, wooden barrel used for aging beer] Katy, and we had like 100 to 200 cases of it, and no one was going to drive to fucking New Haven for it. So we did it at Perennial. We found a weird way to do it legally. I remember both Cory and us selling about 150 cases a piece in about forty-five minutes. At twelve bucks a bottle back then, I thought, 'This is awesome! I'm going to be rich!' Then we also did it at our place before we were done with construction, out in the parking lot. It was all mixed-ferm stuff, and people would line up for hours outside, winding down the block in July summertime heat for beers."

Indeed, news of 2nd Shift's arrival in 2016 in St. Louis sparked something of a sensation. Although the Blues were in the hockey playoffs, 2nd Shift's move trended ahead of both the Blues and the Cardinals in social media. The city had already seen incredible growth in the number of craft breweries in town, and still it was excited for 2nd Shift's arrival. For many, it was about time.

How would 2nd Shift fit in with all the other breweries in town? What would set them apart? "I get asked that a lot," Crider says. "I never thought I wanted to be different. I talked to one brewery when he was starting, and his goal was to find a niche. I never thought about that—I just wanted to make good beer. I didn't care about what everyone else did. It had no relevance to what I was doing."

What he did want was a tasting room, a way to connect with the people who love his beer in a comfortable and casual setting. Stacked bourbon and wine barrels divide the brewery from a tasting room lined with wooden tables and a comfy corner of couches and board games, disco balls and a Ms. Pac-Man machine.

Sunshine the cat, also known as El Gato Grande, joined them in their move to The Hill. So popular was Sunny among the clientele that when he passed away in 2019 at the age of fifteen, customers celebrated his life with pictures and stories. The instantly popular Sunny Cat New England IPA was named after him. Simon, a black and white cat, now roams where Sunny once did.

2nd Shift has a comfortable, welcoming, everyman feel. There is nothing pretentious about it, like the garage space where you can wait for the other members of your band to show up. It can be quiet and calm or loud and filled with laughter, like the overnighters in New Haven where Steve Crider brought the craft beer community together. As Rockwell brewer Jonathan Moxey told *Sauce* magazine in 2024, "2nd Shift is a place where you really get a brewery's character and what they're all about the moment you get in the door. These lovable weirdos are over there on The Hill and it's like walking into somebody's garage or living room—and I mean that as the highest possible compliment. It's comfortable, fun, and funky."

Steven Crider explains his lack of pretension: "It's because I don't have money to spend on anything hoity-toity. I remember selling bottles of Katy for $6.99 and $7.50. Beer dork buddies were telling me I should raise that to 12 or 13 dollars. No, I know what I want to pay for a bottle of beer. Me and Libby, we still do that now."

The rapid growth of craft beer plateaued around the time 2nd Shift moved to St. Louis, but by all accounts, they bucked the trend. Their own growth may have slowed a bit, but it never went backward, and they have continued to win over fans. "Since 2017 we've been right about 3,000 barrels," Crider says. In his first year in New Haven he brewed 120 barrels. He maxed out that brewery at 750 barrels a year. "This year we might go to 3,700–4,000 if we're lucky."

4 Hands brewery manager Martin Toft told *The Riverfront Times* that Crider was his St. Louis Beer crush. "Not only does he make amazing beer, but he's one of the funniest guys you'll ever meet." Rockwell's Jonathan Moxey has a similar estimation: "I love that man with my whole heart."

Jerid Saffell, brewer of Dogtown brewery Heavy Riff, in 2018 accidentally added way too much lactose sugar to Dear Agony, a Russian imperial stout. Assuming the batch was ruined, he called Steve Crider to see if anything could be done. Crider's advice was to throw the beer in barrels to age, mellowing the sweetness. Not only did the barrel aging work, but the accident launched Heavy Riff into the pantheon of St. Louis breweries who draw lines for their barrel-aged beer releases. They went on to brew multiple variations of Dear Agony, now perhaps their most popular beer.

Collaborations among brewers are fun ways to join forces and spread interest in the participating breweries. For brewers, it's often a break from the monotony of making the same beers over and over. Steven Crider is the type of brewer others want to collaborate with. He is technically precise and funny as hell. As a result, 2nd Shift has collaborated with just about every other St. Louis brewery and has breweries across the country, including some of Chicago's best. 2nd Shift and Hop Butcher for the World collaborated on Gut Feeling, an Imperial IPA. Their collaboration with Pipeworks Brewing Company, an IPA called Unicorn Vs. All Internet Cats, came with a playful game of one-upmanship, as the two breweries added sticky notes, paper clips, and fruits to mailed packages. 2nd Shift glitter-bombed Pipeworks with one return case.

Crider describes his collaboration process using Side Project's Cory King as an example: "We brewed three or four brews together, and I like brewing with him because we talk about everything—water, yeast, beer. Some collaborations are two-to-three-minute conversations. Others we go down a rabbit hole. I really like brewing with someone who I can talk to. Spend three or four days analyzing what we're going to do before we even begin to brew. Our last brew with Cory was the last day before we closed down everything. March 2020. Clusterfuck of a day."

On March 17, 2020, 2nd Shift shut down. Steve and Libby grappled with how to steer the company through COVID. They had moved to St. Louis to be near people, to build a community within their taproom, but now it was looking like the New Haven model fit better with this new social distancing reality. And then on March 22, 2nd Shift sold more beer than they ever had in a single day. Libby organized a drive-through system in the parking lot where customers could support their favorite small business by taking beer to go. Instead of the one or two beers they were accustomed to buying, customers bought several four-packs. "Libby was so good during the beginning of COVID," Crider says. "She pivoted, knew what to do. We had a line of people out front buying beer. People were buying cases of beer, tipping a huge amount. That first six or seven months I didn't know how things were going to go, but Libby was on top of it, way better than I would have ever done."

Communication with other members of the craft beer community, once a forum for hop trades and glitter bombing, now carried messages of support from Libby Crider: "We're going to get through this." Instead of filling kegs bound for local bars, 2nd Shift increased their canning, distributing to more grocery and liquor stores. Where other breweries saw a moderate to significant dip in beer sales during COVID, 2nd Shift remained steady.

A fire at the Criders' home, which sits on the brewery property, destroyed their balcony in 2021. Friends and fans of 2nd Shift, grateful for the community that Steve and Libby built, donated money well in excess of the amount needed to rebuild the balcony. Grateful and humbled, the Criders donated the money to the pediatric burn unit at St. Louis Children's Hospital.

Libby Crider's first decade in the beer industry has been a journey in itself, a transition from wine to beer culture. She has been part of what makes the St. Louis craft beer community great: its supportive community. Brewers and brewery owners have each other's backs. What she may not have expected was her struggle to be taken seriously as a woman in the beer community, an industry that has been dominated by men for a century and a half.

It took her some time to earn the respect of suppliers and salespeople within the industry, and even today she experiences sexism when groups of men size up their options at the bar. "I was working a shift on Saturday night with a male coworker when a group of men came in. I was at one end of the bar. He was at the other. They sized us both up, then moved as a group to the man. My coworker came over after and said, 'I saw that. That's fucked up.' It was a perfect example of assumptions, who you want to go to behind the bar."

Early in her time at 2nd Shift, Libby feared that if she shared some of her experiences as a woman in the industry, she would be seen in an unflattering light, as a complainer or whiner. But with time she has become a pillar of support for other women in the craft beer community.

13

# THE BREWSTERS

The story of women in beer is the story of beer. For much of human history women were the brewers. It is only in recent memory that men have come to dominate. Beer, modern consumers have been led to believe, is a man's drink, and brewing is man's work. Commercials and print ads push the idea that beer is to be enjoyed by groups of men, perhaps surrounded by scantily clad women. It is a construct of the twentieth century, and we have companies like Anheuser-Busch and Miller to thank for it, as they successfully merged beer consumption with masculinity after more than half a century of advertising targeting the male psyche.

Within Anheuser-Busch, the Busch family treated succession like some kind of medieval male primogeniture. The first-born male son inherited the company. While Busch daughters have worked within the company or for distributorships over the years, none got anywhere close to the beer. Beer is manly, or so we have been convinced.

Tom Schlafly says of the connection of beer to masculinity, "I knew someone at A-B when they came up with Michelob Ultra. They knew if you sold it as diet, low-cal beer, guys wouldn't drink it. If it's fitness beer, you're there working out next to a hot girl with spandex, then it's not a girly diet beer. It's about fitness."

As craft beer started to take a noticeable bite out of the market share of big beer, Miller and Anheuser-Busch fought back by appealing to the masculinity of the beer drinker. Big Beer was masculine; craft beer was not. Miller's 2010 Miller Lite ad campaign, "Man Up," points out various actions men engage in that make them less manly, telling them to "man up" and drink Miller Lite. Men tease other men about their skirts, their tramp stamps, or the fact they should be playing from the ladies' tees. In one commercial a man says to another, "Put down your purse and I'll give you a Miller Lite."

While Miller did not specifically call out craft beer in their ads, Anheuser-Busch was more explicit in their 2015 ad showing a man with a curved mustache appreciating a dark beer in a tulip glass. It is an image to be ridiculed, accompanied by the phrase, "Let them drink their pumpkin peach ales. We'll be brewing us some golden suds." An AB InBev spokesperson, in a moment of self-unaware irony, described pumpkin peach ale as "fabricated and ludicrous." There was, however, one brewery at the time brewing such a beer, Seattle's Elysian Brewing Company, a company that had been purchased the previous year by AB InBev.

In a commercial from 2016, a man flicks an orange off of the rim of a beer, with the words "not a fruit cup" across the screen. The message is clear: It's masculine to drink Budweiser. It is unmanly to drink craft beer. Never mind the fact that Shock Top, one of AB InBev's best sellers, is served topped with an orange. The stereotype goes that men who seek out more flavor in their beers are somehow less manly, as if it is the struggle of drinking light lagers that makes a man a man.

Portland's Ninkasi Brewing produced a response ad to AB InBev's campaign. The words "If you aren't drinking a beer for taste, what are you drinking for?" play across the screen as the camera pans past a group of women enjoying a variety of beers to a man drinking from a beer bong and another pouring what looks like a Budweiser onto his head. The ad ends with "Craft is the future of beer," over a US map covered with geographically accurate brewery logos.

Ninkasi was the Sumerian goddess of beer, and a reminder of women's central place in beer history. The current industry's institutional misogyny traces to the formation of guilds in the Middle Ages. Further back, the story of beer is the story of women, of priestesses and alewives.

Humanity's earliest social construct was the division of labor by sexes. While men hunted for food and then began to work the land, we're told, women oversaw everything within the household, including the brewing of beer. Some believe beer led to the earliest farms and that we as a species decided to stop wandering and settle in one place because we just wanted a beer. Botanist Jonathan Sauer hypothesizes that "thirst rather than hunger may have been the stimulus behind the origin of small grain agriculture."

It is a myth that before modern sanitation people preferred beer to water because beer was safer to drink. There were certainly some places where a dodgy water source required the boiling brewing process, but most settlements were built around a clean water source. Historians posit that the myth grew out of frequent mention of beer and wine in early writings; water as a beverage may have been too mundane to include. What beer offered over water was calories, and for those who came in from the hunt or the fields, it pulled double duty—it quenched the thirst and provided much-needed energy. As an intoxicant, it certainly provided a third benefit: relaxation.

Our knowledge of ancient brewing comes from the earliest known civilization of Sumeria. Four-thousand-year-old cuneiform tablets give detailed descriptions of beer making—without hops—while praising the goddess Ninkasi. Her priestesses brewed for religious ceremonies, while women brewed at home for family consumption.

Egyptian records show ration lists according to rank for those who lived in the palace: one quart to one gallon of beer a day. The Pharaoh paid laborers in loaves of bread and jars of beer. Beer paid for the pyramids! So important was beer in Egyptian society that the combination of hieroglyphs of beer and bread together represented "food." While Egypt saw one of the earliest examples of mass production of beer, owned by the Pharaoh, the majority of day-to-day brewing was done by women in their homes. Cleopatra even imposed the world's first known beer tax to raise money to fend off Rome, though she claimed it was to curb drunkenness. She accomplished neither.

Ancient Greeks and Romans, on the whole, spurned beer. It was the drink of their enemies and was believed to cause laziness. Greece and Italy were more suited for growing grapes than barley anyway. Pliny the Elder, a Roman naturalist and philosopher, wondered at the beers brewed by the people of what is now Spain and France, claiming they were preserved for a long time and formed a foam on the surface that could leaven bread. The Gauls had somehow discovered yeast and hops (or a hop-like plant) hundreds of years before anyone else. These early Europeans may not have fully understood the chemical processes, but they had arrived there nonetheless.

The Talmud speaks repeatedly of a beverage called *sheichar*, believed for many years to mean wine. Recent scholarship has shifted its meaning to beer, mainly from the Mesopotamian use of *shikaru* to mean beer. Ancient Israel was rich with barley, one of the seven "'fruits" of the Land of Israel, and beer drinking was commonplace among men, women, and even children.

Over the next millennium, movement from a tribal to a feudal society corresponded with a regression of women's rights. Most brewing was still done at home by women, called "brewsters" from the Latin *brasiatrix* and French *braceresse*, meaning "woman who brews." The term "alewife" first appears in early English and Scottish writings. As beer became a source of profit, men began to take over control of the industry, disparaging brewsters along the way. As Danielle Snowden, brewster of Earthbound Brewing, points out, "Once men realized there was a business to be had, they took over."

In northern Europe, Norse mythology tells of Aegir, god of the seas, who brewed with the help of his nine daughters. Beer was a daily beverage, enjoyed by men and women. But a superstition sprang up across northern Europe that women entering the brewhouse meant sour beer leaving the brewhouse. Here is the beginning of a pattern that would repeat throughout Europe. Slander would be the tool that forcibly removed women from their role as brewsters.

In Belgium and Germany, religious orders contributed to a leap forward in brewing, and though today we think of monks as brewing so-called abbey beer, the practice was done by nuns as well. Monks and nuns brewed beer for daily sustenance, selling their excess. For both groups, a master-and-apprentice system ensured knowledge and methodologies passed down through the centuries. It was a German Benedictine abbess, Hildegard von Bingen, who wrote down the first known description of hops as a preservative in beer in the twelfth century.

It cannot be understated how much hops changed the beer game. Now that beer could be preserved longer, it could be transported farther. No longer was beer confined to a household or to neighbors. Larger-scale breweries run by men grew with distribution size, minimizing the role of women homebrewers. All-male brewing guilds formed and steered the beer industry toward profits and away from the old system of brewsters. The guilds lobbied for the establishment of the Reinheitsgebot purity law in 1516, defining beer as being made with only barley, hops, and water.

Hops were expensive and taxed. No longer could a brewster brew with wheat or botanicals from her garden, and if she wanted to sell her excess beer from home without paying a tax, she now risked arrest.

It wasn't enough for the men of the brewing guilds to take over the role that women had held in brewing for millennia; they had to disparage and discredit them as well. In England and Scotland, the image of a woman brewing at home for her family morphed into the image of a witch stirring her cauldron, an echo of the old northern European fear that women turned beer sour. Brewsters began to appear in writings as argumentative and overbearing, even evil. Let's be clear: Many brewsters were irate at what brewing guilds and tax collectors were doing to their livelihood and made their anger known. Some loudly refused to follow guild instructions, and others poured out the contents of their "cauldrons" in protest. Even women who sold their beer legally in the marketplace were criticized for being argumentative about their prices, qualities admired in men.

Accusations became a form of social control. A fifteenth-century man, in order to destroy the business of one alewife, spread rumors that she had leprosy. A male brewer in 1641 spread false gossip about a woman brewing at Ludlow Castle in the English county of Shropshire in order to move in on her business. Soon, the entire idea of an alewife became synonymous with deceit and immorality. Christian morality plays depicted alewives as deserving of eternal damnation.

Did the image of the witch come from a medieval alewife? Certainly the cauldron is the strongest hint, and brewsters were accused of adding the strangest and grossest of ingredients to their beer as opposed to the clean and pure beer of the brewing guilds. While the pointy witch hat can be argued to reflect hats worn to be noticed in a crowded marketplace, more likely it is an anti-Semitic addition, referencing the *Judenhut*, a conical head covering, that thirteenth-century Jews were forced to wear. Maybe the broom reflects the alestake, a pole used to signal that an alewife had recently brewed beer to sell. In reality, the broom image is far more insidious, as it refers to all women, alewife or not—a man would never use a broom.

Cats, the familiars of the witches, were used by alewives to keep mice away from the grain. Hildegard von Bingen wrote about cats, describing them as unfaithful. Chaucer's description of cats follows that theme, that they would abandon their owners to chase a mouse. At some point those descriptors became religious, and cats were more closely aligned with evil than anything holy. As a whole, the Halloween image of a witch is a relatively recent construct, though the symbolic connection to alewives is not without merit. Honestly, if any modern brewer most resembles a witch, with wild hair, surrounded by cats, and supernatural abilities when it comes to brewing, it would be 2nd Shift's Steve Crider.

In 1620 the *Mayflower* landed earlier and farther north than originally planned because the ship was running out of beer. Really. A lower-alcohol form of beer was used on long voyages to provide the earliest colonists clean drink with some calories. Fearing they would not have enough beer for the return journey, the *Mayflower* captain cut their trip short and disembarked in New England. "We could not now take time for further search," lamented one diary writer, "our victuals being much spent, especially our beer."

As settlements grew out from Plymouth Rock, the brewing patterns matched those of Europe: Women brewed at home for their families and neighbors—and even owned and operated taverns, like Harvard's Sister Bradish—until the potential profits in beer attracted men who pushed them out. The fish native to Harvard's nearby streams had what looked like pot bellies. At some point in the mid-1600s, a snarky nickname for the fish became common use, and now we know the fish as the alewife. Today, the Massachusetts Bay Transportation Authority's Alewife station serves thousands of daily commuters in north Cambridge a couple of miles from Harvard, most of them unaware that women like Sister Bradish played a part in naming it.

As malt and hops initially had to be imported from England, early use of substitutes like corn or molasses led to America's own Reinheitsgebot, an edict that standardized beer production and taxation. A direct line can be traced from the formation of colonial beer taverns, where communities gathered to drink and talk politics, to the US War of Independence.

Thomas Jefferson's daughter Martha earned a reputation as an excellent brewster of wheat beer on the Monticello estate. With the slave Peter Hemings, Martha brewed all-grain beer with locally grown hops and barley. Their beer gained such a reputation among visiting dignitaries that despite Jefferson's own skill at brewing, he had to admit in a letter to James Madison that his daughter was superior.

The growing number of small breweries in America overtook women-dominated household brewing. By the Industrial Revolution, the damage to brewsters was complete. Women in brewing were all but wiped out as quickly advancing technology redefined what was "women's work." Now that steam engines could power cooking and brewing on a large scale, they were no longer seen as feminine occupations. Few women played a part in the growing German brewing industry in St. Louis in the nineteenth century, and Anheuser-Busch spent the next 150 years convincing the country that beer was for men.

The advent of craft beer was a chance to right some historic wrongs, to return women to beer making. But old habits die hard. The names of the women who made the craft boom possible are missing in many of the stories of men building breweries. They are cofounders, managers, brewers. Often they are the money. Their presence is evident in the details, in traces of their work, but rarely in the breweries' official histories. The story of craft beer in America begins with one such glaring omission.

New Albion Brewing Company, the country's first craft brewery, was the vision of Jack McAuliffe. He built the brewery himself, piecing together Coca-Cola syrup drums to use as fermenters and storage tanks. His tiny apartment was accessible by ladder. Assistant brewer Don Barkley lived in a tent up on a mountaintop. But two women, Suzy Stern and Jane Zimmerman, are often left out of the story of the California microbrewery. There from the beginning, the two funded the operation, helped with brewing, finances, and the day-to-day operation of New Albion. Suzy Stern, according to Don Barkley, was the one who made it all work. New Albion was truly a trailblazing endeavor, and Jack McAuliffe deserves the recognition he receives. But ending the story there is a disservice to the women who made McAuliffe's dream possible.

Rhonda Kallman helped launch Boston Beer Company with Jim Koch in 1984. Their Samuel Adams Boston Lager ushered countless beer drinkers into craft beer. Over her fifteen years there, and during her attempt to launch a caffeinated beer, Kallman faced chauvinism and discrimination. Was she a promotional girl? men asked. Was she Jim Koch's wife? When Sam Adams won an award at the Great American Beer Festival, rumors spread that Kallman had exchanged sexual favors for votes.

Kallman was a force in the industry, winning awards while recruiting women into the male-heavy craft beer world. She launched a craft distillery in 2015, predicting the next trend. Kallman told Tara Nurin, author of *A Woman's Place Is in the Brewhouse*, "There was no ladder to climb so I built one."

Boston Beer Company brewster Jodi Andrews was a mentor for new brewsters before they moved on to work for other breweries. In all, she has won eleven Great American Beer Festival medals. After working for several breweries, she left brewing to work in cannabis research, suing her last company for sexual harassment.

Deborah and Dan Carey opened New Glarus Brewing Company in Wisconsin in 1993. Deborah Carey envisioned the brewery, wrote a business plan, and raised money before presenting the idea as a gift to her husband, who already had multiple brewing degrees and awards. Dan Carey had brewed for several breweries and worked as production supervisor for Anheuser-Busch. New Glarus Moon Man and Spotted Cow beers were sensations, turning Wisconsin into a beer destination, especially after they stopped out-of-state distribution, as they couldn't keep up with demand.

In 2009 a New York City bar popular with University of Wisconsin alumni was raided and fined for selling Spotted Cow. Fifty cases were found in the bar, meaning some modern-day bootlegger drove them the thousand miles from Wisconsin. Similarly, a bar owner in Minnesota was caught driving New Glarus kegs illegally across state lines.

As good as Dan Carey's beer is, Deborah Carey's business acumen may be better. She cracked the code on how to make a brewery profitable while keeping it small—if you can call them small. Though New Glarus sells their beer only in Wisconsin, they are within the top twenty of all US breweries by production. Not only has Deborah collected various business awards, but in 2013 President Barack Obama and Vice President Joe Biden recognized her accomplishments at a White House reception.

In 2007 Oregon's Steelhead Brewing's longtime brewmaster Teri Fahrendorf was ready for a change. She put in her notice, packed her signature pair of pink rubber brewing boots in her RV camper, and set out to see the country. It was not her intention to begin an international movement in support of women in the brewing industry. Some things happen organically. An early stop to brew with Laura Ulrich of San Diego's famed Stone Brewing gave Fahrendorf the beginnings of an idea. Women in brewing were rare—what if she sought out other women in the industry during her travels? Conversations led to referrals. Though she couldn't speak with everyone, Fahrendorf began to gather a list to foster connection among the brewsters. It was sixty names long by the time she reached Pennsylvania's Troeg's Brewing. Fahrendorf's trip convinced her there was a need for women in brewing to connect with their peers, to share their experiences, and to seek out other women for advice.

At the Craft Brewers Conference in 2008, Teri Fahrendorf and Laura Ulrich organized a beer brunch for women, where brewers and journalists gathered for what would be the first meeting of the Pink Boots Society, an organization focused on educating and empowering women in the industry and providing that connection they all craved. Over the next several years, Pink Boots grew exponentially, offering scholarships to the Siebel Institute's web-based brewing course. Pink Boots has sent women all over the world to symposiums and conferences. In all, Pink Boots has seventy-two chapters in seven countries. They are, according to Rose Ann Finkel, founder of Pike Place Brewing and cofounder of Pink Boots, giving "women the tools to excel in an industry that was theirs to begin with."

Fran Caradonna has experienced every aspect of the industry, and her contributions shaped the culture of St. Louis craft beer. From her time behind the bar with her husband, to their beer distributorship, to the founding and running of O'Fallon Brewery, Fran Caradonna has been part of St. Louis craft beer in some way. The Caradonnas sold O'Fallon Brewery to former Anheuser-Busch executive Jim Gorczyca in 2011.

In 2019 The Saint Louis Brewery, aka Schlafly, found themselves in need of a new CEO. The previous CEO had resigned after a newsletter circulated in bars and restaurants that insulted rival brewer 4 Hands led back to his office. After a public apology, Schlafly sought out a new CEO who not only understood the culture but also was well regarded in the community. They turned to Fran Caradonna. "I met with them," Caradonna says, "and they said, 'We're really looking for someone who understands the St. Louis craft beer business, who's been doing it for a long time, and who understands the manufacturing side.' I said, 'Well, that's kind of who I am.'"

Her time with Schlafly capped off a storied career. She steered the ship through the COVID years, expanded into St. Charles with the purchase of Trailhead Brewery to create Schlafly Bankside, and partnered with local nonalcoholic beer brewer WellBeing to offer one of the fastest-growing categories in beer.

It is almost poetic how Fran Caradonna has come full circle. If someone had whispered in her ear at the Schlafly opening night party in 1991 that she would one day run this place, she could not fathom what road might take her there: "Isn't it wild? I mean I couldn't have planned this."

Over the past thirty-five years, due to the work of people like Fran Caradonna and organizations like Pink Boots, the number of women in St. Louis craft beer has grown. Schlafly may have had the first woman brewer in Missouri with Sara Choler, future wife of Stephen Hale. Several of Schlafly's beers were her recipes. In talking to *Sauce* magazine in 2014 about creating wedding beers, she gave an etymology lesson on women in brewing: "That's where the term 'bridal' comes from. It's the 'bride's ale.' Women were the brewsters."

Cat Golden and Dave Alley left Tennessee to brew in St. Louis. They apprenticed under Brian Owens of O'Fallon Brewing before buying an old Model T factory in Hannibal to build Mark Twain Brewing Company. Emily and Phil Wymore opened Perennial Artisan Ales, establishing not just a world-renowned brewery but a family culture that launched the careers of multiple award-winning brewers. Karen King opened the Side Project Cellar with her husband, Cory, and over the next decade grew the brewery with the help of a formidable group of women brewers and employees. 2nd Shift's Libby Crider told *Feast* magazine, "Look at Side Project Cellar—that is one powerful force of females there. I'm in awe of them."

But even as opportunities for women in beer grew, the old hurdles remained: gender bias, unequal pay, and sexual harassment. Longtime Anheuser-Busch executive Francine Katz sued the beer giant in 2009 for gender discrimination. Known as the "Queen of Beer," Katz was the first woman appointed to the company's top strategy committee. The sale of A-B to InBev made public the salaries of those she considered equals, and hers fell far short by comparison. She was vice president of corporate communications and was handsomely paid, she thought, until she discovered that her predecessor, John Jacobs, made twice as much as she did. A-B contended that Jacobs had taken on additional responsibilities. In the suit Katz alleged the company fostered a "locker room and frat party atmosphere." She wasn't invited on company trips and wasn't included on the corporate jet. Katz lost the suit.

AB InBev could have used Katz as they fumbled through years of questionable ad campaigns. In 2015 they rolled out the #UpForWhatever campaign, featuring Bud Light bottles with the phrase "The perfect beer for removing 'no' from your vocabulary." So strong was the response from antirape activists that even members of Congress weighed in. American universities at the time were struggling to address a growing rape problem on campuses.

More recently, Salem, Massachusetts, brewster Brienne Allan uncovered widespread sexual harassment and assault within the craft beer industry. She posted to her Instagram account—under the prophetic handle @ratmagnet—about sexism she was experiencing at work. She asked, "What sexist comments have you experienced?" What followed was a deluge of stories ranging from wage discrimination, to inappropriate language and touching, to sexual assault. The courage of the first few emboldened more women to tell their stories, and soon craft beer was in the middle of a sexual harassment and sexual assault crisis. The reality was the crisis had existed long before Brienne Allan brought it to light. In an industry where alcohol is involved, it had become too easy for some to cross lines of appropriate behavior or to take advantage of situations.

2nd Shift's Libby Crider told the *Women Are from Marzen* podcast, "Being a woman in beer, we all have at least one story to tell, our experiences at being patronized and assaulted, verbally or physically, or experiences of friends and colleagues in the industry. How many times have you heard a woman screaming on social media that something is messed up and it just never follows through? 'That was messed up; let's move on.' No one wants to believe that these breweries that we hold in high adoration could foster that type of environment. That got me to reflect on how we dealt with our own misogyny at the brewery, the follow-through, and how we attempted to make ourselves a better, inclusive space. I was crying reading these stories, wanting to hug every single one of these women."

Multiple craft brewery owners, managers, and brewers resigned or were fired as a result of the accounts shared with Allan. While no St. Louis breweries were included in the stories she shared, in the year prior a 4 Hands sales rep was fired after being accused of drugging and assaulting women.

Though many of the stories are horrific, bringing them to light has moved the industry toward more protections for women, more transparency. The Brewers Association put out a statement saying it was working with multiple brewing organizations, including the Pink Boots Society, to form "a coalition to explore how our organizations can collaborate to provide the resources and support that businesses and individuals need to create and maintain a culture of safety, inclusion, and equity."

The Brewers Association partnered with WeVow, a nonprofit for those affected by sexual abuse and assault, and worked to educate its members on sexism, sexual violence, and reporting tools like Red Flag Reporting. "Since then," Abbey Spencer of Third Wheel Brewing says, "you see a lot of celebration around women entering the industry, a ton of scholarship opportunities, a ton of internship opportunities for people of color, women, LGBTQ. So you see the industry is trying."

Organizations that connect and support women have proved vital in the brewing industry. Before Pink Boots established a chapter in St. Louis, it was up to the few women in St. Louis craft beer to make their own connections with each other. A group of women working at the International Tap House and in area breweries, including 2nd Shift's Libby Brown, formed a support group called Femme Ferment to unify and celebrate women in craft beer. At their first meeting they poured homebrews by iTap bartender Troy Bedik and O'Fallon brewster Cat Golden. Both women became key members of the craft beer scene.

Troy Bedik's homebrews so impressed Libby Brown and Steve Crider that 2nd Shift mass produced Bedik's witbier Witty Femme. Only twenty-five years old when she started at iTap, Bedik's talents for brewing were not a secret for long. In 2016 she won a scholarship from the Pink Boots Society for a brewing course through the Siebel Institute of Technology. Soon after, Civil Life hired her to brew and her Kölsch recipe wowed owner Jake Hafner. As part of the scholarship, Pink Boots asked her to pay forward her knowledge, presenting to groups of women. The experience encouraged Bedik to start a local Pink Boots chapter in 2019.

Bedik told *Sauce* magazine, "The craft beer world can be a very intimidating environment for women. It's gotten better, but you have to fight for people to take you seriously, to prove that you know what you're talking about. It's good to have a strong support group. Sometimes if I'm wearing a dress, I wonder if it automatically discredits me because I don't look the part.

"One of my favorite moments while working at Civil Life was one day when I was wearing my big work boots, work shorts, a headlamp and safety glasses, and I walked into the bathroom and saw this little five-year-old girl. She asked me, 'Why are you dressed like that?' And I said, 'I'm a brewer. I work over there.' Her eyes got wide and she said, 'That's so cool!' Then she ran over and told her dad."

Page 209 *Tom Schlafly says of the connection of beer to masculinity*: Tom Schlafly, interview with the author, November 30, 2022.

210 *Anheuser-Busch was more explicit in their 2015 ad*: Jim Vorel, "Analyzing Budweiser's Hypocritical, Anti-Craft Beer Super Bowl Ad," *Paste*, February 2, 2015, https://www.pastemagazine.com/drink/budweiser/valuable-lessons-i-learned-from-budweisers-hypocri.

210 *Portland's Ninkasi Brewing produced a response ad*: Drew Harwell, "How Craft Beer Is Fighting Back Against Budweiser's Belligerent Super Bowl Ad," *Washington Post*, February 4, 2015.

210 *Some believe beer led to the earliest farms*: J. Cohen, "Did Beer Spur the Rise of Agriculture and Politics?" History Channel, August 23, 2018, https://www.history.com/news/did-beer-spur-the-rise-of-agriculture-and-politics#.

210 *Botanist Jonathan Sauer hypothesizes*: Gloria Dawson, "Beer Domesticated Man," Nautilus, December 12, 2013, https://nautil.us/beer-domesticated-man-234697/.

211 *It is a myth that before modern sanitation*: "Dispelling Some Myths: Dirty Water? Drink Beer!" Tastes of History, April 29, 2021, https://www.tastesofhistory.co.uk/post/dispelling-some-myths-dirty-water-drink-beer.

211 *from the earliest known civilization of Sumeria*: Bostwick, *Brewer's Tale*, 8.

211 *Egyptian records show ration lists*: Tara Nurin, *A Woman's Place Is in the Brewhouse* (Chicago Review Press, 2021), 42.

211 *Ancient Greeks and Romans, on the whole, spurned beer*: Kristen Richard, "The Ancient Origins of Beer Geeks and Wine Snobs," *Wine Enthusiast*, May 8, 2023, https://www.wineenthusiast.com/culture/spirits/ancient-rome-history-ancient-greek-history-wine/?srsltid=AfmBOoqVDnxdqaBV2d5qGjEE79u3-vKxVXB_pwuW5RITjNmJvzF2Ral.

211 *Pliny the Elder, a Roman naturalist and philosopher*: Nurin, *Woman's Place*, 84.

212 *Recent scholarship has shifted its meaning to beer*: Nurin, *Woman's Place*, 11.

212 *As Danielle Snowden, brewster of Earthbound Brewing*: Danielle Snowden, interview with the author, May 8, 2024.

212 *In northern Europe, Norse mythology tells of Aegir*: Nurin, *Woman's Place*, 69.

212 *It was a German Benedictine abbess, Hildegard von Bingen*: Nurin, *Woman's Place*, 96.

212 *The guilds lobbied for the establishment of the Reinheitsgebot purity law*: Nurin, *Woman's Place*, 98.

213 *Accusations became a form of social control*: Nurin, *Woman's Place*, 134.

213 *Did the image of the witch come from a medieval alewife?*: Tara Nurin, "No, That Halloween Witch (Probably) Does Not Represent a Persecuted Beer Brewer," *Forbes*, October 30, 2021, https://www.forbes.com/sites/taranurin/2021/10/30/no-that-halloween-witch-probably-does-not-represent-a-persecuted-beer-brewer/.

213 *more likely it is an anti-Semitic addition*: Emma Sachet, "The Antisemitic History of Witches," Heyalma, October 29, 2020, https://www.heyalma.com/the-antisemitic-history-of-witches/.

214 *because the ship was running out of beer*: Lisa Grimm, "Beer Mythbusting: The Truth About Pilgrims, Adjuncts, and Prohibition," Serious Eats, August 9, 2018, https://www.seriouseats.com/beer-myths-corn-pilgrims-first-beer-thanksgiving-lager-prohibition-history.

214 *"We could not now take time for further search"*: Courtney Mifsud, "From Beer to Eternity," *Beer: The Story of the World's Most Celebrated Drink, Time* Magazine Special Edition, 2018.

214 *The fish native to Harvard's nearby streams*: Stephen Paul DeVillo, "What's an Alewife, Anyway?" Bronx River Alliance, April 26, 2010, https://bronxriver.org/post/story/whatsanalewifeanyway.

214 *Thomas Jefferson's daughter Martha*: Nurin, *Woman's Place*, 151.

215 *New Albion Brewing Company*: Acitelli, *Audacity of Hops*, 12.

215 *Suzy Stern and Jane Zimmerman*: Nurin, *Woman's Place*, 1.

215 *Rhonda Kallman helped launch Boston Beer Company*: Nurin, *Woman's Place*, 50.

216 *Boston Beer Company brewer Jodi Andrews*: Nurin, *Woman's Place*, 93.

216 *In 2009 a New York City bar*: Andrew Greiner and Hasani Gittens, "Manhattan Bar in Trouble for Selling Wisconsin Beer," NBC News New York, November 25, 2009, https://www.nbcnewyork.com/news/local/manhattan-bar-in-trouble-for-selling-wisconsin-beer/2121216/.

216 *Similarly, a bar owner in Minnesota*: "Minnesota Bar Owner, Manager Charged in Wisconsin Beer Run," MPR News, February 11, 2016, https://www.mprnews.org/story/2016/02/11/mn-bar-owner-manager-charged-illegally-selling-spotted-cow-beer.

216 *Debrorah Carey's business acumen may be better*: Nurin, *Woman's Place*, 87.

216 *Teri Fahrendorf was ready for a change*: Nurin, *Woman's Place*, 137.

217 *"I met with them," Caradonna said*: Fran Caradonna, interview with the author, December 21, 2022.

218 *In talking with* Sauce *magazine in 2014*: Ligaya Figueras, "What I Do: Stephen and Sara Hale of Schlafly Beer," *Sauce*, February 5, 2014, https://www.saucemagazine.com/people/what-i-do-stephen-and-sara-hale-of-schlafly-beer-17333293.

218 *Cat Golden and Dave Alley left Tennessee*: Daniel Puma, "Mark Twain Brewing Co. Brings Craft Beer to Hannibal," *Feast*, May 27, 2016, https://www.feastmagazine.com/travel/mark-twain-brewing-co-brings-craft-beer-to-hannibal/article_b6bb22c4-22ab-11e6-ad12-93485a8bc665.html.

218 *2nd Shift's Libby Crider told* Feast *magazine*: Liz Miller, "2nd Shift Brewing's Libby Crider Talks Acid Malt, St. Louis Beer and Why This Should Be the Summer of Saisons," *Feast*, July 19, 2022, https://www.feastmagazine.com/restaurants/2nd-shift-brewing-s-libby-crider-talks-acid-malt-st-louis-beer-and-why-this/article_87c8079e-9cc4-11e8-bf1e-13787eebd973.html.

218 *Longtime Anheuser-Busch executive Francine Katz*: Sarah Fenske, "Francine Katz, Anheuser-Busch Exec Alleging Discrimination, Wins Again," *Riverfront Times*, June 14, 2011.

218 *they rolled out the #UpForWhatever campaign*: Bill Chappell, "Bud Light Pulls Label with Message That Sparked Backlash," NPR, April 29, 2015, https://www.npr.org/sections/thetwo-way/2015/04/29/403030019/bud-light-pulls-label-with-message-that-sparked-backlash#:~:text=GhosX9%2FReddit-,Anheuser%2DBusch%20has%20apologized%20for%20a%20message%20on%20bottles%20of,are%20no%20longer%20being%20produced.

219 *Salem, Massachusetts, brewer Brienne Allan*: Kerri Brown, "The Ratmagnet Effect: What We Learned and What Was Left Unsaid," Beer Is For Everyone, June 29, 2021, https://beerisforeveryone.com/the-ratmagnet-effect/.

219 *2nd Shift's Libby Crider told the* Women Are from Marzen *podcast*: "Episode 45: Libby Crider," *Boys Are from Marzen: A Women in Beer Podcast*, June 8, 2021.

220 *The Brewers Association partnered with WeVow*: Jessica Infante, "Brewers Association Launches Initiatives to Combat Sexual Harassment, Receives Second Complaint," Brewbound, May 19, 2021, https://www.brewbound.com/news/brewers-association-launches-initiatives-to-combat-sexual-harassment-receives-second-complaint/.

220 *"Since then," Abbey Spencer of Third Wheel Brewing says*: Abbey Spencer, interview with the author, April 17, 2024.

220 *Bedik told* Sauce *magazine*: Julie Cohen, "Ones to Watch 2017: Troy Bedik of Civil Life Brewing Co.," *Sauce*, January 2, 2017, https://www.saucemagazine.com/people/ones-to-watch-2017-troy-bedik-of-civil-life-brewing-co-17340112.

221 *opened Earthbound Beer*: Danielle Snowden, interview with the author, May 8, 2024.

222 *found themselves the new owners of three caves*: Chris Naffziger, "A Tour of Cherokee Brewery's Old Lagering Cellars with the Earthbound Beer Crew," *St. Louis*, November 18, 2015.

224 *Brad Wheeling told* Feast *magazine in 2016*: Heather Riske, "Third Wheel Brewing to Open in St. Peters in 2017," *Feast*, September 16, 2016.

## Chapter 14. City

Page 232 *Local breweries like Ballast Point*: Tom Acitelli, "Ballast Point Turns 20: A Backroom Brewery's Billion-Dollar Arc," All About Beer, 2014, https://allaboutbeer.com/ballast-point-turns-20/.

233 *prompting the Brewers Association to wonder if they could get to "20 by '20"*: Jason and Todd Alström, "20 Percent in 2020. Can It Happen?" BeerAdvocate, May 2014, https://www.beeradvocate.com/articles/9621/20-percent-in-2020-can-it-happen/#:~:text=And%20based%20on%20this%2C%20the%20Brewers%20Association,the%20US%20beer%20market%20volume%20by%202020.

233 *After just four years, Constellation Brands sold Ballast Point for $100 million*: Peter Rowe, "Ballast Point's Rise, Fall and Sale: Inside Craft Beer's Most Baffling Deal," *Los Angeles Times*, December 12, 2019.

234 *a St. Louis investor purchased the brewery for $2.55 million*: Hannah Wyman, "Local Investor to Buy Urban Chestnut Brewery Following Bankruptcy," *St. Louis Post-Dispatch*, February 12, 2025.

234 *Over their thirty-five years, they have had only five*: Justin Kendall, "People Moves: Great Lakes CEO Exits, Brewmaster Moves at Goose Island, Rogue," Brewbound, May 27, 2019, https://www.brewbound.com/news/people-moves-great-lakes-ceo-exits-brewmaster-moves-at-goose-island-rogue/#:~:text=Keith%20Gabbett%20officially%20became%20the%20fifth%20brewmaster%20at%20Anheuser%2DBusch%2Downed%20Goose%20Island.

235 *a brand-new employee could claim a small role*: Jonathan Moxey, interview with the author, September 17, 2024.

235 *The New York Farm Brewery bill*: "Farm Brewery," New York State Brewers Association, https://newyorkcraftbeer.com/farm-brewery/.

238 *they were sued by the Department of Labor*: Ian Froeb, "Feds Sue St. Louis' Rockwell Beer Co. over Alleged Labor Violations," *St. Louis Post-Dispatch*, November 1, 2022, https://www.stltoday.com/news/local/feds-sue-st-louis-rockwell-beer-co-over-alleged-labor-violations/article_e54001b1-9e2b-566c-b2b6-f9006b6ec18c.html.

238 *Phil and Emily Wymore teamed up*: Phil Wymore, interview with the author, April 15, 2024.

238 *Brewer Chris Kinast is quintessential St. Louis*: Chris Kinast, interview with the author, June 5, 2024.

242 *At around twenty-six thousand barrels a year*: Maddy Simpson, "Largest Breweries," *St. Louis Business Journal*, August 30, 2024.

243 *an anonymously published newsletter titled* Brew IQ in the Lou: Doyle Murphy, "Schlafly Executive Resigns over Anonymous Newsletter Blasting 4 Hands Brewery," *Riverfront Times*, December 7, 2018.

244 *2023 was the first year spirits passed both beer and wine*: "Spirits Surpass Beer for U.S. Market-Share Supremacy, Data Shows," PBS, February 9, 2023, https://www.pbs.org/newshour/economy/spirits-surpass-beer-for-u-s-market-share-supremacy-data-shows.

244 *now kegged cocktails are moving in*: K. Bernot, "As Beer Sales Lag, Draft Cocktails Are Taking Over More Tap Lines, *Washington Post*, March 7, 2024, https://www.washingtonpost.com/food/2024/03/07/draft-cocktails-bars-beer-sales/.

245 *But no one was earlier than Square One*: John Witte, interview with the author, January 6, 2024.

245 *Kirkwood natives Cameron Lund and Grant Lodholz*: Heather Riske, "Bluewood Brewing to Open on Cherokee Street in Early 2019," *Feast*, October 16, 2018, https://www.feastmagazine.com/bars/news/bluewood-brewing-to-open-on-cherokee-street-in-early-2019/article_f4fb0fc8-d162-11e8-9f15-cbf2e5687a57.html.

246 *Older people in particular were not going out as much*: Jessica Finlay, Gabriella Meltzer, Brendan O'Shea, and Lindsay Kobayashi, "Altered Place Engagement Since COVID-19: A Multi-Method Study of Community Participation and Health Among Older Americans," *Wellbeing, Space and Society* 6 (2024).

246 *The timing of Alpha Brewing's move*: Robert Caruso, "Alpha Brewing Company," The Barrel Cellar, May 21, 2019, https://thebarrelcellar.com/2019/05/21/alpha-brewing-company/.

246 *A 2015 survey published by Nielsen showed women*: Fritz Hahn, "Growing Power of Sours," *Providence Journal*, October 25, 2017.

247 *Studies showed that many families maintained family dinners*: Anne Fishel and Melinda I. Morrill, "How COVID-19 Expanded the Family Dinner Table: Greater Frequency Linked with Improved Quality and New Ways of Eating Together," *American Psychological Association*, 2024, https://www.apa.org/pubs/journals/releases/cfp-cfp0000268.pdf.

247 *Chicago's late-night options dropped 10 percent*: Nathaniel Meyersohn, "Looking for a Late-Night Meal? America's Closed," *CNN Business*, April 6, 2024, https://www.cnn.com/2024/04/06/business/covid-crushed-24-hour-diners-theyre-slowly-coming-back/index.html.

247 *Two men from World's Fair Donuts*: Cheryl Baehr, "Review: Up Late Brings Outstanding After-Hours Eats to St. Louis," *Riverfront Times*, May 17, 2023.

247 *Sixty-two percent of those under thirty-five consume alcohol*: Lydia Saad, "Young Adults in U.S. Drinking Less Than in Prior Decades," Gallup, August 22, 2023, https://news.gallup.com/poll/509690/young-adults-drinking-less-prior-decades.aspx.

247 *now many young people find such displays of inebriation boring*: "Millennials and Gen Zers Embrace 'Life Can Take You Higher Than Alcohol,'" National Public Health Information Coalition, March 17, 2022, https://nphic.org/blog/738-millennials-and-gen-zers-embrace-life-can-take-you-higher-than-alcohol.

248 *Dry January*: Yola Robert, "Dry January Is Becoming a Lifestyle," *Forbes*, January 31, 2023, https://www.forbes.com/sites/yolarobert1/2023/01/31/dry-january-is-becoming-a-lifestyle/.

248 *WellBeing Brewing founder Jeff Stevens*: Shannon Weber, "Jeff Stevens Is Crafting More Than Just Superior Nonalcoholic Brews at WellBeing Brewing Co.," *Feast*, December 30, 2024, https://www.feastmagazine.com/bars/classics/wellbeing-brewing-co-jeff-stevens-na-nonalcoholic/article_97247498-c3a0-11ef-af7b-c77586bb2513.html.

249 *WellBeing partnered with Buoy*: "WellBeing Brewing Company Releases Non-Alcoholic Beer with Electrolytes," Brewbound, May 24, 2019, https://www.brewbound.com/news/wellbeing-brewing-company-releases-non-alcoholic-beer-with-electrolytes/.

249 The New York Times *revealed in 2018*: Ben Crair and Andrew Keh, "German Olympians Drink a Lot of (Nonalcoholic) Beer, and Win a Lot of Gold Medals," *New York Times*, February 19, 2018.

249 *"Better for you" alcoholic beverage sales were up 20 percent*: Kathy Kelley, "Alcoholic Beverage Consumption Statistics and Trends 2023," Penn State Extension, February 14, 2023, https://extension.psu.edu/alcoholic-beverage-consumption-statistics-and-trends-2023#:~:text=No%2D%20and%20Low%2Dalcohol%20and,that%20ended%20June%2012%2C%202022.

249 *sales of wheat beers fell 4 percent*: "What's Happening with Wheat Ale Beer in the US?" Nielsen, January 26, 2023, https://nielseniq.com/global/en/insights/education/2023/whats-happening-with-wheat-ale-beer-in-the-us/.

250 *"My true belief is it's about quality"*: Abbey Spencer, interview with the author, April 17, 2024.

250 *The brainchild of Manny Negron*: Emily Standlee, "Little Lager Bolsters St. Louis' Collaborative Spirit and Lager Legacy," *Feast*, June 26, 2024, https://www.feastmagazine.com/bars/first-looks/st-louis-brewery-taproom-little-lager-manny-negron-lager-beer-princeton-heights-collabs/article_dbb0f7d0-2f44-11ef-94e3-7b0c91efff1a.html.

250 *Manny's once-boss at Modern*: Beamer Eisele, interview with the author, May 15, 2024.

250 *It is the culmination of a lifetime in the beer industry*: Tony Rehagen, "Blue Jay Brewing Takes Flight in Midtown St. Louis," *Riverfront Times*, January 26, 2024.

251 *Nicole Thompson told* Sauce *magazine in 2022*: Iain Shaw, "Blue Jay Brewing Co. Will Open at JC Midtown in Midtown St. Louis in Spring 2023," *Sauce*, October 14, 2022, https://www.saucemagazine.com/places/blue-jay-brewing-co-will-open-at-jc-midtown-in-midtown-st-louis-in-spring-2023-17336434.

251 *Whenever Tom Schlafly tries out a new brewery*: Tom Schlafly, interview with the author, November 30, 2022.

251 *Jeff Hardesty of Narrow Gauge*: Jeff Hardesty, interview with the author, April 11, 2024.

252 *To 2nd Shift's Steve Crider*: Steve Crider, interview with the author, April 11, 2024.

252 *To Rockwell brewer Jonathan Moxey*: Jonathan Moxey, interview with the author, September 17, 2024.

253 *To call the St. Louligans a fan club*: "Welcome to the Party. We've Been Waiting," St. Louligans, https://stlouligans.com/archives/2377.

253 *An MLS commentator called the experience a "wall of sound"*: "Wall of Sound," St. Louis City SC, January 13, 2024, https://www.stlcitysc.com/news/wall-of-sound.

253 *Midfielder Eduard Löwen said after the first home game*: Benjamin Simon, "St. Louis Waited Decades for Major League Soccer. It's Finally Here," *Riverfront Times*, March 6, 2023.

253 *Team president and CEO Carolyn Kindle told Fox 2 News*: "City SC Owners, MLS Leadership Already Amazed by Fan Support of Club," Fox 2 News, February 23, 2023, https://fox2now.com/sports/stl-city-sc/city-sc-owners-mls-leadership-already-amazed-by-fan-support-of-club/.

254 *The official MLS website ranked*: J. S. Jones, "Your Friday Kickoff: Ranking Home-Field Advantage for Every MLS Team," MLS Soccer, January 19, 2024, https://www.mlssoccer.com/news/your-friday-kickoff-ranking-home-field-advantage-for-every-mls-team.

254 *Austin FC fan organization The False 9*: Travis McTravel-Face, "The Comprehensive Guide to MLS Stadiums and Support," The False 9, August 22, 2023, https://thefalse9texas.com/the-comprehensive-guide-to-mls-stadiums-and-support/.

254 *A relationship formed between the player and the brewery*: Alli Hebel, "St. Louis CITY SC's Tim Parker, St. Louis–Based Brewing Company Team Up for New Beer," KSDK, August 18, 2023, https://www.ksdk.com/article/sports/soccer/st-louis-city-sc/city-sc-tim-parker-4-hands-brewing-company/63-4ce4c00f-5f83-4294-8812-0f43dbe0fce3.

# INDEX

**JOSH BITTLE** is a freelance writer in St. Louis and a longtime part of the city's craft beer community.

The University of Illinois Press
is a founding member of the
Association of University Presses.

---

Composed in 10.5/14 Mercury Text G1
with Gotham display
by Lisa Connery
at the University of Illinois Press
Manufactured by Versa Press, Inc.

University of Illinois Press
1325 South Oak Street
Champaign, IL 61820-6903
www.press.uillinois.edu

CONTEMPORARY ASIAN
ART AT BIENNIALS

# CONTEMPORARY ASIAN ART AT BIENNIALS

John Clark

With a Foreword by Charles Green

RIDGE BOOKS
SINGAPORE

Published under the Ridge Books imprint by:

NUS Press
National University of Singapore
AS3-01-02
3 Arts Link
Singapore 117569

E-mail: nusbooks@nus.edu.sg
Website: http://nuspress.nus.edu.sg



print ISBN: 978-981-325-175-5 (paper)
ePDF ISBN: 978-981-325-200-4
ePub ISBN: 978-981-325-211-0

**National Library Board, Singapore Cataloguing in Publication Data**
Name(s): Clark, John.
Title: Contemporary Asian art at Biennials / John Clark.
Description: Singapore : Ridge Books imprinted by NUS Press, 2026.
Identifier(s): ISBN 978-981-325-175-5 (paperback) | 978-981-325-200-4 (ePDF) | 978-981-325-211-0 (ePUB)
Subject(s): LCSH: Biennials (Art fairs)--Asia--20th century. | Biennials (Art fairs)--Asia--21st century. | Art and globalization--Asia--20th century. | Art and globalization--Asia--21st century.
Classification: DDC 700.745--dc23

Cover image: Lü Shengzhong, Landscape Study, at exhibition of Chinese works in Beijing which would have gone to Venice in 2003 but for the SARS epidemic. Photograph by John Clark.

Typeset by: Ogma Solutions
Printed by: Markono Print Media Pte Ltd

# Contents

Foreword

# Biennials as a Metonym

## by Charles Green

In 2016, John Clark wrote a long and generous review of a book by Reiko Tomii for the widely read, online bulletin of the College Art Association.[1] In his examination of Tomii's elegant study about 1960s Japanese conceptualism, *Radicalism in the Wilderness: International Contemporaneity and 1960s Art in Japan*, Clark set out a radical and subversive intention that had for decades, in fact, been his own as well: to urgently rethink and write meaningful regional art histories. In his own books and essays, Clark would not only achieve that grand ambition but also describe for the first time the panoramic sweep of global art history from the perspective of Asian art. In that 2016 review, he was not just praising another scholar whose work resonated with his own but painting a self-portrait, laying out his own immensely ambitious mission statement, one that had long since, including with his *Modern Asian Art* (1998), not just systematized the study of modern and contemporary Asian art but eloquently revolutionized it.[2] Clark's approach blended anthropological and sociological theorizing with art historical attention to the specificity of objects and a sometimes-astounding depth of historical research, usually conducted in the specific Asian language required. Clark questioned and recast much accepted wisdom about Asia, both by more traditional-minded Asian scholars and by putatively progressive, ostensibly sophisticated Western scholars. He was able to do so by virtue of careful, often astonishingly comprehensive scholarship and a polymath grasp of theoretical ideas outside art history, especially ideas and theories from social and political theory, which enabled him to go toe to toe with authorities. And so, with his present book, we arrive at the first methodical study of biennials and triennials across the Asian region.

But why a major investigation of Asian biennials, of recurring Asian survey exhibitions of contemporary art? The first answer is that it has been through biennials, above all, that a new aspect of contemporary art, the ascendency of curators, had appeared, together with whole new typologies of exhibition-making. Curators produced landmark exhibitions. In this book, Clark is able to trace how it was through biennials, triennials, and the German exhibition held every five years, documenta, that late modern and then contemporary art migrated from hermetic, avant-garde and experimental origins into the realm of the spectacular, transcending specialist, insider audiences and garnering wide, global, public attention to contemporary art. Biennials may also be leading the reconsideration and reconstruction of art's biased histories towards properly global narratives.

That is the first layer of Clark's book. He goes deeper, exploring the shifts occurring in the discourse and practice of modern and contemporary art and its industries due to the forces of transnationalism, globalism and the new forms they have taken in the postcolonial period. He does this while rethinking the fierce forces of national and transnational identity. Even though art has engaged deeply with postnational forces, traditional configurations of national identity continue as dominant discourses—national art still rules the art museum roost—despite the 40 years since art historians and cultural theorists around the world began interrogating the assumptions of national cultures. There are several problems with national narratives, not least both the limits of nationalist discourses as they were initially framed in the age of imperialism and the default projection of stale canonical ideas of how, where and when art progresses.

So, with a study of Asian biennials, Clark enriches the existing narrative of national art histories across Asia with sharper stories that are inclusive of contemporary art. He neither leaves late modern (pre-1970s) art locked in the past, nor does he lock contemporary art into an ahistorical and unchronological present. In other words, Clark, like the most important art historians working today, writes the 50-year-old contemporary period as proper history.

There is a historiographical background to such methods, one that Clark was aware of. Those living beyond New York or London had often sought to escape the condition of being provincial artists or provincial art historians. This was, of course, the "provincialism problem" that Clark's erstwhile University of Sydney colleague Terry Smith had defined in an essay of the same name in 1974. As a very young artist way back then, I read the article not long after its publication in the New York art magazine, *Artforum*, and I understood quickly how Smith had arrived at his bleak determinism which he summed up in the sentence, "as the situation stands, the provincial artist cannot choose not to be provincial".[3] Smith had used this definition to explain and lament a model that saw the New York art world as the metropolitan centre, with all other art communities, including large, culturally autonomous, rich, confident cities—Chicago, Los Angeles, Sydney, Seoul, Tokyo or Melbourne—all viewed as provincial. And we can all point to supposedly definitive books, such as the notorious *Art Since 1900*, which wilfully ignored, trivialized or dismissed anything beyond canonical North Atlantic avant-gardism.[4] In his second chapter, Clark explains that "international" or "modern" art would be merely North Atlantic art until the mid-1990s, and it did not ever admit parallel notions of non-Western or Asian modern art. There were various tactics by which this exclusionary story was maintained: the several famous bi-national exhibitions during the early 1990s were tools to compartmentalize nations; curators sought Japanese representatives of New York or European art tendencies. This meant usually selecting artists who lived in New York or exhibited in that city.

But in the period since then, Clark then explains, contemporary art has increasingly engaged with extra-national or post-national contingencies. This created the need for biennials surveying contemporary art from around the world. They established, in effect, a map of postnational art that Clark explores in the knowledge that the nation state and its institutions, including its arts funding bodies, are more powerful than ever. Traditional configurations of national identity continued to underwrite state art museums, agencies, biennial boards and committees across Asia and around the world. And Clark highlights a brutally frank statement by Japanese star curator Fumio Nanjô that the role of national artistic selection was now over, for the production of art now resembled just-on-time multinational car corporation design and assembly. Clark shows us these multiple forces in action across successive chapters that map biennales in Venice, Japan, China, Singapore, and Australia. He does this with four panoramic, pan-Asian narratives in mind.

First, biennials are really a metonym for a much wider, all-pervasive, complex international system that he explains as the operation and interaction of the international and the many national art worlds. Therefore, the international art world's premier showcases of contemporary art—the Biennale of Venice above all—superficially still provide opportunities for artists from around the world to show their work on an international stage, but in fact only within predetermined identities: within an atlas of the world in which the North Atlantic is central and everywhere else either marginal or completely absent. This absence would either be imposed from above, based on rendering control invisible, or the provinces might even pride themselves on their insularity, or they might seek to transform their representation in order to conform to supposed international expectations. Clark explains the contortions that Japanese selection teams subjected themselves to over several decades in preparing for the Biennale of Venice. Within this horizon, the award of the Grand Prize at the Venice Biennale in 1964 to US artist Robert Rauschenberg was inevitable rather than an opening, regardless of the furore and complaints made by French critics at the time.

Second, this book is an analysis of how the value of art is politically constructed and controlled. Based on Clark's massive, in-depth research and his encyclopaedic viewing of biennials, he takes account of a field of exchanges that took place beyond financial transactions. The world that Clark describes is, he explains, underpinned by the idea of gifts that has been drawn from modern anthropology. Biennials are, therefore, governed by cycles of both covertly and overtly regulated accumulations of gifts, donations and benefaction. He explains the corollary: that all judgements about the significance of particular artists are relational and contingent. Further—and his emphasis is immensely important—Clark goes on to establish that artists and their works move in extraordinarily predictable and rigid circuits substantially dominated by political and state forces. For politicians in authoritarian states and in liberal democracies alike, cultural activities are a spectacle that ornament other events. Clark proves that the list of artists within the international selections for Biennials has been surprisingly and massively restricted, and argues that this indicates very clearly the cultural authority not merely of curators, but also of those who choose curators. No curator can wield the brute economic power of oligarchs. And biennials and government policies go hand in hand. In both Singapore and China, biennials were directed so that spectacular pleasure would be allowed but direct criticism deflected or deleted. Such exclusions or complicated renegotiations are continuous with pre-20th century periods of art, even though such hard realities run against most artists' and art historians' ideas about themselves and their present-day cultural autonomy.

Third, Clark investigates the role that biennials played in the formation of modern and contemporary Asian art, finding that this can be explored from an Asian perspective with conclusions that may also then be applied to the North Atlantic's centres. The canonical modernity of New York and Paris was always merely relative. This cuts both ways: Asian biennials were sites for the consecration of North Atlantic artists, as well as sites for national self-promotion and local artist canonization. Clark's first example is Japan. He traces how *nihonga* [neo-traditional Japanese painting] was removed and a new idea of senior "representative" artists from Japan sent to Venice, resulting in the marginalization of both neo-traditional and academic Western-style Japanese art. Both were gradually seen as "not of the current moment" or even as reactionary. Clark describes how this self-censorship was repeated across Asia when artists were selected for biennials. The implication of these chapters is, of course, that though the so-called centre of the modern and contemporary art world, New York, was a vastly larger art world province than Tokyo or Beijing, it was supercharged in its pretensions to universalism courtesy of Cold War and then post-1989 economic might. But from the 1960s on, Asian art had become (self-)consciously contemporaneous with American and European art (as did art in parts of Eastern Europe and South America) and would be so with art just as innovative and significant from this point onwards. Revealing this contemporaneity requires Clark's bottom-up, detailed approach to local art histories, defying the tendency of North Atlantic art historians and their regional acolytes to expect to see derivative art and to label local art according to imported ideas of how art would develop. Connections can be obvious, especially since from the mid-1960s on, air travel was increasingly ubiquitous (and the critical demands both in 1960s Japan and then in 2000s China that art be measured against international yardsticks were so insistent) but the resonances that we retroactively find were all too often wilfully dismissed as mere evidence of belated influence by arbiters at the centre or their local apologists, including in the period we are discussing. Instead, Clark obdurately insists on the transnational, lateral nature of contact and resonance between artists and across borders, refusing the blinkers that assume belatedness at the periphery and mimicry of the centre. But he explains—and I would completely agree—that making a simple assertion that a local Asian artist's practice is pioneering, and then arguing that it should be added to a global list of key artists by including her work in an international biennial (or, worse, in a national pavilion in an international biennial), proved inadequate. He points to the exhibitions of Asian art touring to Europe and North America, even in the wake of research and exhibitions that established a "local" Asian artist's historical importance (much as *Global Conceptualism* at the Queens Museum of Art in 1999 did). He describes a succession of putatively cosmopolitan biennials and, worse given its ethical pretensions, of German documentas that went on to ignore any perspective beyond the North Atlantic except in the most token way, as did every documenta after the historic edition of 2002. Each remained stuck in the most obvious telling of globalized history and only reluctantly admitted the wide perspective of Asian history. So, in Australia at the Asia-Pacific Triennial as in Japan at Fukuoka, neither the image nor the reality nor the threat of centre-periphery domination ever disappeared even as at the same time, as we have ourselves shown in our work on biennials, in *Biennials, Triennials and documenta* (2016), curators had consciously been creating Third World and then pan-Asian networks, and then South-to-South networks from 1955 onwards.[5]

Fourth, Clark is highly critical of curators as cultural entrepreneurs and of museum exhibitions as spectacles, acknowledging their agency as well as their limits. As he says, the early 20th century role of dealers who valorized particular artists and placed them in art museums, and of critics who defended or excoriated particular artists as being ahead of or behind the times, had been displaced by star curators or their understudies. He reminds the reader of the relative availability and low cost of international travel from the 1960s onwards, whereas freight charges for long-distance haulage remained staggeringly large, ensuring that it would be expatriate or part-time expatriate Asian artists resident in New York or in nearby Western Europe who would be selected into biennials to represent Asia. Clark's careful examination of biennial artist lists, which were chosen by curatorial selection systems that ranged from Byzantine in consultative complexity to completely subjective, written on the back of an airplane boarding pass, shows that only a narrow and repetitive set of artist choices was ever made and that it did not, quite shockingly, change much in size over time, sustaining an alarmingly small biennial artist cohort.

In sum, this book has the capacity to change our thinking and even revolutionize our perspective. After all, John Clark asks if biennials could subvert the world art system and overturn its hierarchies. His answer is that biennials, their artists, curators, art museums and collectors alike are actors in an international art system inside which any challenge is incorporated, expelled or rendered invisible. Clark shows us that, as far back as the 1950s, it had been through biennials that the artist-to-artist possibilities, problematic political deals and often-tragic compromises in modern and contemporary Asian art had unfolded with the greatest urgency, vivid surprise and lapidary diplomatic intricacy.

**Charles Green** is Professor of Contemporary Art at the University of Melbourne in the Art History department, within the School of Culture and Communication. He has written *Peripheral Vision: Contemporary Australian Art 1970–1994* (Sydney: Craftsman House, 1995), *The Third Hand: Artist Collaborations from Conceptualism to Postmodernism* (Minneapolis: University of Minnesota Press, 2001), and *Biennials, Triennials, and documenta* (Boston: Wiley-Blackwell, 2016) with Anthony Gardner. He was Australian correspondent for *Artforum* for many years. He is also an artist: Lyndell Brown and Charles Green have worked together as one artist since 1989. They were Australia's Official War Artists in Iraq and Afghanistan in 2007–08.

## Notes

1 John Clark, "John Clark. Review of 'Radicalism in the Wilderness: International Contemporaneity and 1960s Art in Japan' by Reiko Tomii", CAA.reviews, 1 March 2016, http://caareviews.org/admin/reviews/3198/preview#.WK9ZlvLnX2Y; Reiko Tomii, Radicalism in the Wilderness: International Contemporaneity and 1960s Art in Japan (Cambridge, MA: MIT Press, 2016).

2 John Clark, *Modern Asian Art* (Sydney: Craftsman House; Honolulu: University of Hawai'i Press, 1998).

3 Terry Smith, "The Provincialism Problem", *Artforum* 12, 1 (September 1974): 54–69; the essay is reprinted in Terry Smith, *Transformations in Australian Art, Volume Two: The Twentieth Century — Modernism and Aboriginality* (Sydney: Craftsman House, 2002), 113–21.

4 See Yve-Alain Bois et al. "Introductions: Poststructuralism and Deconstruction", in *Art Since 1900: Modernism, Antimodernism, Postmodernism* (New York: Thames & Hudson, 2004), 40–8; for critical reviews see Norman Bryson, "Review: Art Since 1900", *frieze*, 92 (June–August 2005); also see Nancy J. Troy et al., "Interventions Reviews", *The Art Bulletin* 88, 2 (2006): 373–89.

5 See Anthony Gardner and Charles Green, *Biennials, Triennials and Documenta: Exhibitions that Created Contemporary Art, 1955–2015* (Boston: Wiley Blackwell, 2016), and in particular our chapters 2, 3, and 4, all of which bear directly on the period under discussion in Clark's book.

# Acknowledgements

I am grateful for a University of Sydney Sesqui Research Grant during 2001 and an Australian Research Council Discovery Grant during 2002–04 which enabled the research on which this book is based.

I am grateful for the opportunity to have presented and discussed the materials in this book in 2009 to postgraduate students of Sothebys Institute, Singapore, and to Dr Eugene Tan; to students of the Kunsthistorisches Institut, Ostasiatische Kunstgeschichte, Freie Universität Berlin and to Dr Juliane Noth and to Univ-Prof. Dr Jeong-Hee Lee Kalisch; and to postgraduate students and curators in the School of Art History and Aesthetics, Jawaharlal Nehru University, New Delhi, with a Getty Visiting Professorship, and to Professor Parul Dave Mukherjee.

I am also grateful to Asian Art Archives in Hong Kong for the opportunity to revise and update conclusion in a keynote lecture for their October 2013 symposium.[1]

For this project in particular I am indebted to the following people for the provision of research materials or interviews (the names are given in alphabetical sequence of surnames Chinese, Japanese, and Korean surnames coming first):

Thomas Berghuis (TB), Lewis Biggs, Tony Bond (reply to questionnaire, August 2004), Renée Block (June 2006), Francesco Bonami (by TB, August 2003), Isabel Carlos (March 2004), Chang Tsong-zung, Choi Jeong-hwa, Jean-Michel Ducrop, David Elliott (June 2004), Fan Di'an, Fei Dawei (28 April 2007), Furuichi Yasuko, Gao Minglu, Simryn Gill, Gu Dexin, Hou Hanru (July 2003), Hasegawa Yuko (by TB, June 2003), Huang Du, Huang Yongping, Li Xianting, Joo Jae-hwan (12 June 2003), Kim Hong-hee (12 June 2003), Kim Bogi, (17 September 2005), Kim Jheon (21 September 2004), Anne Kirker, Koh Kor Wah (February 2004), Martina Köppel-Yang, Kuroda Raiji (18 September 2005), Kwok Kian Chow (December 2003 and Februrary 2004), Francesca dal Lago (12 June 2003), Ray Langenbach (11 February 2004), Isobel Lee of Plastique Kinetic Worms (5 February 2004), Joanna Lee (5 December 2003), Lee Weng Choy (16 June 2005], Iola Lenzi (December 2003–February 2004), Lieu Kongyu (February 2004), Lim Tzay-chuen (December 2003–February 2004), Low Kee Hong (21 June 2006), Sebastian Lopez (by TB, 27 June 2003), Ahmad Mashadi (December 2003–February 2004 and 21 June 2006), Henry Meyrick-Hughes (11 July 2005), Nanjô Fumio (7 November 2005), Josef Ng (2 February 2004), Matthew Ngui (December 2003–February 2004), Hans-Ulrich Obrist (June 2004), Sharmani Pereira, Eugene Tan (21 June 2006), Rawanchaikul Toshiko (19 September 2005), Brett Rogers

(July 2005), T.K. Sabapathy (December 2003–February 2004), Hasnul Jamal Saidon (February 2004), Alain Sayag (July 2003), Shao Dazhen, Shao Yiyang, Amir Siddharta (12 June 2003), Ulli Sigg (July 2005), Singapore Art Museum Library for press cuttings on the 2001 and 2003 Singapore pavilions at Venice, Terry Smith, Eugene Tan (20 June 2006), Ushiroshôji Masahiro (September 2005), Wong Hoy Cheong (February 2004), Wu Hung, Yao Souchou.

I am grateful to Thomas Berghuis for interviews conducted for this project with Francesco Bonami (12 June 2003) and others and for his important work on a database his report on which is included in appendix 3.

I am indebted to Russel Storer, then of the Museum of Contemporary Art, Sydney, now of M+ Hong Kong, for interviews conducted on my behalf with the following;

Tien Woon Wei, Jennifer Teo and Lim Tzay-chuen (1 October 2004); Tien Woon Wei (4 October 2004); Juliana Yasin and Kai Lam Hoi (6 October 2004); Matthew Ngui (5 November 2004); Chua Beng Huat (2 October 2004); Ong Keng Sen (3 October 2004); T.K. Sabapathy (5 October 2004); Ahmad Mashadi (5 October 2004); Lee Weng Choy (7 October 2004); Kwok Kian Chow (7 October 2004); Kim Machan (4 October 2004); Goh Ching Lee, Aun Koh, and Katharyn Peh of Singapore National Arts Council (4 October 2004); Kwok Kian Woon (7 October 2004); Ho Tzu Nyen (31 October 2004).

With the permission of Thomas Berghuis and Russel Storer their interviews were included in other interview transcripts and recordings which I donated to the Asia Art Archive in Hong Kong on my retirement from the University of Sydney in October 2013.

I am in addition greatly indebted to Thomas Berghuis, Gabrielle Ewington, and Russel Storer, who at various times were assistants in the research.

Lastly, having put aside the idea of publishing this work in 2009, in 2012, I was grateful for some good editorial advice from Charles Green, and for the very constructive suggestions of Terry Smith.

It did not prove possible to secure all the basic information on biennials which was desirable. This includes true full-cost accounts, biennial strategy documents, marketing analyses, reports to sponsors, papers relating to curatorial decisions and artist or art work appraisals.[2] These may not be usual to art history but access to them would certainly have helped understand biennials as institutions. Beyond the coruscating carapace of handouts and press conference speeches, it is surprising how many of these materials fall into the legal domain of "commercial-in-confidence". This level of control about the public availability of attributable facts is one more commonly attributed to political campaigns or diplomatic and security bureaucracies.[3] Nonetheless, I remain responsible for all errors of fact, interpretation, or translation.

**John Clark**, Sydney, 2009–17

Some of the original texts on which these chapters were based have previously appeared in part or whole in the publications listed below.

**Chapter 1**
In various forms the text of this chapter has been included as "Contemporary Asian Art and Biennials: the Perpetual Modern?", in *Asian Art History in the Twenty-First Century*, ed. Vishaka Desai (Williamstown: Sterling and Francine Clark Art Institute, 2007), and as "Biennales as Structures for the Writing of Art History: The Asian Perspective", in *The Biennial Reader*, ed. Elena Filipovic, Marieke van Hal, and Solveig Øvstebø (Bergen: Kunsthal; Ostfildern: Hatje Kantz, 2010), 164–83.

**Chapter 2**
The original text for this chapter was given as "Japanese Contemporary Art and Globalization, Largely Seen from Participation in the Venice Biennale" and delivered at the Conference *Globalization, Localization, and Japanese Culture in the Asia Pacific Region* organized by the International Center for Japanese Studies, Kyoto, and the Department of Japanese Studies of the National University of Singapore from 28 to 30 October 2004. It was published as "Japanese Contemporary Art and Globalization Largely Seen from Participation in the Venice Biennale", from *Globalization, Localization and Japanese Studies in the Asia Pacific Region*, 2 (Kyoto: International Research Center for Japanese Studies, 2010), 131–50.

**Chapter 3**
A version of this chapter was published as "Between the Worlds: Chinese Art at Biennials since 1993", *Yishu: A Journal of Chinese Contemporary Art* (2005). A short version was also given at the conference "Displacements: Transcultural Encounters in Contemporary Chinese Art" at the Cantor Arts Center at Stanford University in January 2005 in conjunction with the exhibition *On the Edge: Contemporary Chinese Artists Encounter the West.*

**Chapter 4**
This material is largely unpublished.

**Chapter 5**
This material is largely unpublished.

**Chapter 6**
This material is previously unpublished.

**Chapter 7**
Parts of the typology were presented at the Bergen Biennials' Conference in 2009. The models of circulation are in papers from a workshop with other colleagues in

Sydney in 2005, and most were formerly available at http://www.arts.usyd.edu.au/departs/arthistory/research/workshops.shtml.

Chapter 8

An earlier conclusion was revised, extended, and delivered in October 2013 as a keynote lecture for the symposium "Sites of Construction: Exhibitions and the Making of Recent Art History in Asia" at the Asian Art Archive, Hong Kong.

## Notes

1 See my paper, "Asian Biennials: History, Practices, and Literature", *Yishu: Journal of Contemporary Art* 13, 2 (March/April 2014) which is a version of what is now chapter 8 here.

2 An at that time rare analysis of biennial finances in depth is "The Financing of International Contemporary Art Biennials", Istanbul Foundation for Culture and Arts (IKSV) (February 2013), which is in Ute Meta Bauer and Hou Hanru, ed., *Shifting Gravity, World Biennial Forum no.1* (Gwangju: The Gwangju Biennale Foundation; Ostfildern: Haje Cantz Verlag, 2012), 20–3. The papers from the second symposium in São Paolo, 2014, are Galit Eilat et al., ed, *Making Biennials in Contemporary Times* (Amsterdam: Biennial Foundation; São Paolo: Fundação Beinal de São Paolo and Instituto de Cultura Contemporânea, 2015).

3 With which type of archives I am quite familiar through my University of Sheffield PhD in 1986, published as *Japanese Foreign Policy and the War in Vietnam 1964–1969* (Ann Arbor: University Microfilms International, 1989). In my direct experience and so long as major security issues did not arise, I have found military bureaucracies far more obliging about the factual material required for independent analysis and more interested in my questions than most curators.

# Introduction

Biennials (Biennales) are periodically recurring temporary art exhibitions.[1] They are usually surveys of both local and international contemporary art which are held at the same geographical site, and usually presented by the same organizing institution. As the term indicates they are normally presented every two years such as the Venice Biennale (since 1895), the Biennale of Sydney (since 1973), the Bienal de Habana (since 1984), and the Shanghai Biennale (*Shanghai Shuangnianzhan*, since 1994). For convenience this book will also use the term "biennial" generically for recurrent exhibitions of varying periodicity, to include triennials, such as the India Triennale in New Delhi (in some years after 1968), and for other recurring exhibitions such as the quinquennial Documenta at Kassel in Germany (since 1955). As will be seen from the developmental implications of these sequences, all the new Asian biennials which began in the 1990s were part of a series of exhibitions that had Euramerican precursors which often functioned as their prescriptive models, or from which they may have sought to differentiate themselves.

Many curators and many biennial catalogues have supported the view that each biennial and its site was different in kind and objective in its selection of works. They sometimes have seen biennials as exhibitions the realization of which were to be very differently assessed for each version in the series, or each edition. In most curators' views, recursion at the same site was not repetition of the same exhibition. They have also assessed such realizations from a view of the curators' ability to constitute discursive knowledge by their own activities. Or, they have seen themselves and the biennials they curated, often in post-colonial understandings, as the embodiment of resistance to those forces of globalization which the very existence of international curators and biennials materialized.[2]

I sympathize with some of these views, but my position here is not that of particular curators, or this class of actors. From a perspective which is derived from art historical and institutional analysis, I focus on how biennials constitute themselves as a system into which contemporary Asian art from different countries has situated itself. By extension, biennials in Asia are the Asian extension of a very complicated and dynamic system of international relations in art with multiple levels, units of organization, goals, and types of actors. This book concerns the way biennials have functioned to position artists and their work from particular nation-states in the international art world, or to insert some tangible but not always eluctable 'national presence' into an international art scene.

The position of this book intersects with an inclination to think of biennials as having become a new kind of transnational site, activated by a particular, and sometimes new, set of transnational actors (artists, mediator-curators, audiences). At these sites, all the pressures of globalization seem to dissolve identities constructed around national affiliation. I have examined some of these phenomena quite closely in another text so will not repeat these discussions here.[3] The transnational qualities of this discursive and material space may seem to dissolve the possibility of new and locally-based—but internationally-articulated—trajectories of the modern into a kind of transnational commonality, and often a new type of artistic homogeneity. In contrast, I have concluded that whilst biennials often position themselves as resistant to hegemonies in institutional art discourses, they are also the site where resistance to the biennial institution itself has become latent if not manifest.[4] This resistance can even take the form of a refusal of the idea of the end of national modernities.

Nevertheless, however much biennials generate informal, non-discursive knowledge, they do so inside structures which display and depend on a hierarchy among the actors, and on a relative distribution of hegemony among the institutions.

This work is based on five years' intensive experience of visiting and very closely looking at biennials, chiefly in Asia, but also in Venice, from 2001–07, and later during 2009–12. Chapter 1 serves by way of an initial survey of issues. Some reviews of biennials I have visited are reproduced in appendix materials in the hope they communicate the flavour of the experiences on which more analytical perspectives were arrived at. I should reiterate that the generalizations advanced here are based on very intensive looking at biennials themselves, even when the formulation and presentation of my understanding can be abstract. My basic approach in these reviews was to show biennials as a lived exhibitionary experience where the art works and their producers were positioned for the different kinds of biennial audience via the activities of mediator-curators.

The following chapters are Case Studies. Chapters 2 to 5 for Japan, China, Singapore, and for Australia via a study of the Asia-Pacific Triennale, foreground national or nationally-sited artists and objectives. I then move to a broader and less exhibition-and-object based examination of the difference between art works and art objects in chapter 6, and then analytically classify the biennials in question in chapter 7. Some brief comments on the changing international space for a contemporary Asian art and the functioning of this system will form the discussion in the concluding chapter 8.

In the conclusion I have included some observations on biennials and the burgeoning literature on curation since 2007, roughly up to 2015. The book deals with events in the historical past, not an evolving present, and has no claim of up-to-date-ness. Thinking that the present has no past, and is not formed by one, is an ideological mode common to tyrannical regimes, even those with "liberal" or "progressive" labels. Somewhat at its own peril this book resolutely sets its face against the historical amnesia so characteristic of our time, one which in various ways pervades much of the field of contemporary art. The study is mostly concerned with the rise of new biennials in Asia and with their functions in defining contemporary art. If often only by implication, this defining function is also one for a contemporary *Asian* art.

However much one would like to think that a new, trans-nation state level of interactions in art creation and exhibition came into play through these biennials, thereby creating exhibition sites beyond the level of the nation whose boundaries themselves had become increasingly permeable, in fact, most actors remained at the level of the state. So far as I know *all* artists and curators carried the passports of nation-states, even if, for some, these states were ports-of-call rather than final destinations their arrival at which had been privileged by infinite deferral.

Contemporary Art was internationally circulated within parameters set by a generalized market in a limited number of geographical nation-states (France, Germany, Italy, Japan, Switzerland, United Kingdom, United States); or, through overseas resident communities such as those of China in Taiwan and North America; or, those of South Asia especially India in Europe and North America; or, it was circulated internationally by private and public single nation-state structures of support. Even the much-vaunted international art market was usually constituted by merchant-collectors firmly situated in one nation-state, such as Saatchi in the United Kingdom, Pinault in France, Sigg in Switzerland, Budi Tek in Indonesia and China, amongst others. There was very little sign yet of a specifically "Asian" trans-nationality in contrast with or resistance against or even simply parallel to the Euramerican hegemony. No biennial, even the most radical, such as Havana, was entirely beyond the constraints of the single nation-state which situated it. No biennial acted effectively beyond the constraints of the international art system based on an overlapping series of state hegemonies with which it interacted. Such was the case, however much artists, curators and even national governments may have subscribed to what might be called "a transcendent rhetoric of trans-nationality". This book gives most attention to these structures, orientations and, somewhat reluctantly in its pessimism, to their limitations.

## Notes

1 I repeat my expression of gratitude to many artists, international curators, art historian colleagues, gallerists and collectors for materials and interviews in conducting this research on Biennials whose names are listed in the Acknowledgements. This chapter was originally written for the Asia Society/Clark Institute of Art conference on *Asian Art History in the Twenty-First Century*, April 2006, and an earlier version was published in "Contemporary Asian Art and Biennials: the Perpetual Modern", in *Asian Art History in the Twenty-First Century*, ed. Vishaka Desai (Williamstown: Sterling and Francine Clark Institute, 2007), and as "Biennales as Structures for the Writing of Art History: The Asian Perspective", in *The Biennial Reader*, ed. Elena Filipovic, Marieke van Hal, and Solvig Øvstebø (Bergen: Kunsthal; Ostfildern: Hatje Kantz, 2010).

2 The whole series of tangled references to globalization as a causative element in the rise of biennials and contemporary Asian art is frequently found in Asian biennial catalogue texts. A proper understanding of these locutions would require following globalization theory away from art rather than just seeing, as is often glibly the case, that transnational art somehow represents globalization or its underlying economic forces. This would be an implicit re-run of Marxist development stages analysis - and a long way from the intentions of this book. But we have to note that that the problem of globalization has occupied the minds of many curators of Asian biennials. Their responses to it have served in arguments which support their conceptual and organizational structures.

3 See my book *Asian Modernities: Chinese and Thai Art of the 1980s and 1990s* (Sydney: Power Publications, 2010).

4 For an informative discussion see Oliver Marchart, "The Globalization of Art and the 'Biennials of Resistance': a History of the Biennials from the Periphery", *World Art* 4, 2 (September 2014).

# Chapter 1

# Overall Issues

The increasing participation of Asian artists at international art biennials and the large number of such biennials organized in Asian countries from the 1990s have implications for the construction of modern and contemporary Asian art history. This chapter will summarize some of the issues dating roughly from the 1980s until the mid-2000s, and in part point to some initial conclusions for the whole book.

It was only from the 1990s that work began to appear on modernity in Asian art.[1] The notion of modernity itself permits the formation of a conception of an art which was transnationally applicable across various Asian contexts, and allowed art historians to see Asia as a discursively constructed space which had existed in parallel to, or as a relativizing contrast which reciprocally constructed, a modern Western art. It should be emphasized that this position meant that the very conception of a modern Asian art relativized the notion of modernity itself, and problematized the presumption that modern art originated in modern Western art. Many texts on modern Western art do not acknowledge modern art outside the West, and thus deny this relativization.[2] The economic growth of Japan in the 1980s, of China in the 1990s and 2000s, followed by India in the 2000s and 2010s, has had enormous impact on global, transnational relationships. It may have been the motor for the wider entry of Asian artists into international circuits, or, at the very least, produced the economic context that allowed this movement in art a certain degree of autonomy.

## The Type and Scale of Biennials

Whilst the history of biennial art exhibitions, beginning with the Venice Biennale from 1895 and the Carnegie International in Pittsburgh from 1896, is fairly well known, and subject to research,[3] the recent role of biennial exhibitions in constituting the canonical works of contemporary art has been neither carefully nor fully examined.[4] This is a particularly important area not only because of the increasing number of such exhibitions during the 1980s and 1990s, but also because they would appear to have functioned for contemporary art in as

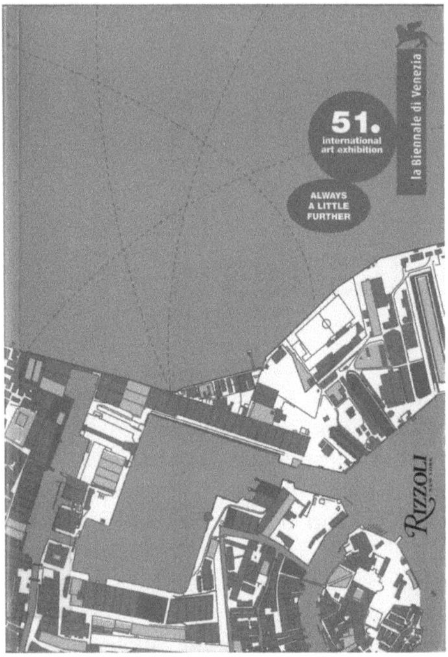


1.1 *Always a Little Further*, volume one of the catalogue for the 51st Venice Biennale.

yet not fully understood ways as arbiters of taste, as consecrators of esteemed practice and works, and as the mediating sites or distributors of artworks, artists, and curators.[5]

Biennial exhibitions were functioning in these ways for a contemporary art from countries in Asia which have in the main found major international circulation only since the 1980s.[6] Indeed biennials, biennales, and triennales—and for brevity's sake I shall refer to all such exhibitions as "biennials" whatever their periodicity, institutional site, or given nomenclature—were increasingly founded in various Asian countries. They have not merely functioned as exhibitors of international art to local audiences, but as exhibition sites for local art deemed worthy of attracting international attention.[7] Biennials have functioned to draw contemporary art from other Asian countries into new interregional circuits of comparison and circulation, although only latently so in most cases. For most official organizers of biennial exhibitions in Asia, and it would seem for most curators and artists, this type of exhibition functioned by transferring exposure of sites, works, artists, and curators, from the national to the international levels. They only began to function in a transnational activity, which may be thought to have transcended the national/international dichotomy, from the late 1990s.[8]

Most biennials had, however, the intention to developmentally tie a city or region to an international constituency. These non-art and often economic and political functions of biennials were not without their art-world side effects, particularly in the flow of knowledge and people between local communities below the national level.[9]

The final chapter of this book (chapter 8) will formulate a detailed typology of biennials, since this facilitates further examination of how and why they function, but here let me make simple observations about general types.[10] Biennials may be simply defined as both prescriptive international and national exhibitions, some with further prescription of regional or local dimensions. "Prescriptive" indicates inclusion by positive selection, or exclusion by non-selection, that is an appraisal was made regarding the importance of a work or an artist as a representative of current contemporary practice, usually in terms of a curatorial concept. By implication this indicates a direction others may, or should, follow.[11]

In the Venice or São Paolo biennials, nationally selected artists were also shown at the international level. The national selection was sometimes intended at the same time to represent the art of a region, such as the regional Korean artists who were shown in a separate exhibition hall at the Gwangju Biennale in 2004. In the case of Documenta, a quinquennial exhibition since 1955, there was claim to a prescriptive role for the art of one nation conceived as a cultural region in the world, in this case for Germany.[12] This locally prescriptive role gradually and latently—if not always manifestly—expanded to become the projection of a prescriptive intention for the whole of an international art world, conceived from that local position. Whilst the function of prescription was thus similar if not identical across different levels, its purported scope and its hegemonic intent could be of a quite different order. For Documenta itself, very few Asian artists were selected for exhibition before 2007.[13]

If we then consider the links between North European and North American critical discourse and the restricted membership of the international curatorium—a selected group of curators whose opinions and subsequent selections have canon-making effects (which one could call a "curatoriate" to indicate its quasi-ruling functions) then the hegemonic effect of Documenta becomes clear.[14] This was a hegemony of position despite Documenta's own anti-hegemonic claims, or even its procedures in 2002, when it appointed as its artistic director a US resident of Nigerian origin, Okwui Enwezor. Documenta XI went on to expand the intellectual positioning away from Kassel itself, and arranged various non-German sites for critical "platforms" as well as critical visits to several Asian sites. However, the platforms were by invitation only, and had the curiously hegemonic effect of privileging only some, but not all, international critical discourses presumed to have a local site where the platform was held.[15]

Indeed, if there are different kinds and levels of prescription in operation at various biennials, these themselves have created a quite clear hierarchy between "international biennials", such as Documenta, Venice or São Paolo; "national biennials", such as Guangzhou, Shanghai, Beijing, Gwangju or Yokohama; and "local biennials", such as Chengdu, or the Triennial of Chinese Art whose second edition in 2005 took place in Nanjing.[16] Alongside these levels of biennale were found what might be loosely but effectively understood as "quasi-biennials", that is exhibitions of nationally selected art shown overseas as a representative selection from current practice. The last type was found very often in national retrospectives selected for symbolic consecration overseas, such as *German Art of the Twentieth Century* in 1985.[17] I am not sure how much this precursor type of international circulation of national exhibitions was known to Chinese colleagues, but there seems to be a distant echo in the first exhibition of Chinese contemporary art overseas sponsored by the Ministry of Culture, *Living in Time*, held in Berlin in 2000.

The prescriptive exhibitions at the international level attempted to define what contemporary art is or could be. The definition was articulated through the selection of sites, works, artists, and curators. Those funding the exhibition could be a municipal body, a regional or national bureaucracy, or a private corporation seeking exposure at a higher and more prestigious international level. We may suppose, somewhat reductively, that those supplying the objects, the artists, often included their own artistic position or personality as a virtual object, and clearly wished their work to be circulated at an international level in order to secure greater prestige and if possible greater prescriptive approval or cultural "consecration".[18] The latter was not in itself an economic reward but might have been the symbolic node of conversion for many artists, from those who contributed to cultural capital to those who derived real economic benefit from their production of objects which they could then sell in various markets.[19]

However, the experience of viewing various biennials together with knowledge of the restricted number of curators who actually curated them, and of the equally restricted number of artists who were selected to exhibit, whether under national or thematic selection, has led me to the conclusion that what was on show at biennials was as much the curatorial selection as any particular works or artists selected.[20]

I will examine the roles of curators much more concretely in chapter 3 on China, but for now let me note that the biennial functions as that site whereby "international" and "national" curators also show themselves to each other through their selections, and the audience is in a very immediate and present sense composed of other curators. The biennial is the site through which curators themselves circulate and try to achieve their own, further circulation.

If the international biennials are, de facto, organized according to an external hierarchy of levels, then so internally did the institutional organization of biennials often follow in the structure of their curatorium, or body of single or multiple curators. These curatoria were often composed from a "master curator", "delegated" or "sub"-curators, and operational supplicants or what I shall call "minion" curators. In Venice in 2003 the master curator was Francesco Bonami, the 11 delegated curators included Hou Hanru for *Zones of Urgency*, Molly Nesbit, Hans-Ulrich Obrist and Rirkrit Tiravanija for *Utopia Station*, amongst other sub-curated exhibitions in the Arsenale. In Venice in 2005 there were two master-

1.2 Cover of the 2005 Fukuoka Triennale catalogue. Author's collection.

curators or directors, Maria de Corral and Rosa Martinez, both acting as their own sub-curators for *The Experience of Art* in the Giardini and *Always a Little Further* in the Arsenale. The supplicant assistants or minion curators cited in the catalogue were Martina Bertaggia, Lorena Martinez de Corral, Paolo Cimarosti, Maria José Balcells, and Marimó Llaràs.

Other biennials such as Fukuoka and Brisbane have had an institutional and quasi-curatorial function based on the institution itself nominally functioning as final master curator. In the case of Fukuoka the Asian Art Museum director and in Brisbane the gallery director also seemed from time to time to play final decision-making roles.[21] But in each of these two cases, instead of a formal single master curator, there were overlapping and themselves hierarchically structured but delegated curatorial committees, each with their own minion curators, in which I would include the various local referees who helped establish an initial artists' list. There was no clear claim for equality between the organizing institution and the advisors or local curators since their views could be set aside, and frequently were so.

Perhaps such a group of master curators was envisaged for the first Yokohama Triennale in 2002, but in effect this became a triennale composed from four separate exhibitions, composed by four separate curators each with their own minion curators. At least one of them, Nanjô Fumio, thought this was inadequate, and that it would run contrary to the international experience of an organization based on artistic director and sub-directors.[22] The organization of such a

| Research Dates | Places of Research | Name of Researchers | Number of Artists Interviewed |
|---|---|---|---|
| **2003** | | | |
| 3.12-3.25 | India(New Delhi, Mumbai), Sri Lanka(Colombo) | Kuroda Raiji, Yamaki Yuko | India 14, Sri Lanka 9 |
| 3.30-4.12 | Malaysia (Kuala Lumpur), Indonesia(Yogyakarta, Bandung, Jakarta) | Matsuura Jin, Nakao Tomomichi | Malaysia 19, Indonesia 35 |
| 10.9-10.17 | China(Shanghai, Hangzhou, Beijing) | Rawanchaikul Toshiko, Horikawa Lisa | China 18 |
| **2004** | | | |
| 1.22-2.1 | Bangladesh(Dakha, Chittagong), Thailand(Bangkok) | Kuroda Raiji, Igarashi Rina | Bangladesh 11, Thailand 12 |
| 3.8-3.21 | Pakistan (Karachi, Lahore), India(Mumbai, Bangalore) | Kuroda Raiji, Yamaki Yuko | Pakistan 38, India 18 |
| 4.18-4.27 | Cambodia (Phnom Penh), Myanmar(Yangon, Mandalay) | Rawanchaikul Toshiko, Oki Ryoichi | Cambodia 10, Myanmar 29 |
| 4.18-4.29 | Singapore, Brunei, Philippines(Manila) | Nakao Tomomichi, Kamachi Masae | Singapore 31, Brunei 9, Philippines 21 |
| 7.15-7.25 | Nepal(Kathmandu), Bhutan(Thimphu, Paro), Thailand(Chiang Mai) | Kuroda Raiji, Yamaki Yuko | Nepal 49, Bhutan 6, Thailand 20 |
| 11.10-11.15 | Korea(Seoul, Gwangju) | Kuroda Raiji, Igarashi Rina | Korea 16 |
| 11.15-11.22 | China(Guangzhou, Beijing, Shanghai) | Rawanchaikul Toshiko, Horikawa Lisa | China 29 |
| **2005** | | | |
| 1.11-1.14 | Taiwan(Taipei, Tainan) | Yamaki Yuko, Horikawa Lisa | Taiwan 13 |

Countries where on-site research were not conducted: Mongolia, Vietnam, Laos

1.3 Curation by committee, with all the tradeoffs that come with attempting to survey a vast region. Author's photograph of a working document from the Fukuoka Triennale, 2005.

"curatoriate", or ruling group of artistic director and sub-curator, may appear to be a minor matter. But it is surely central to the impact and cultural-political dynamics within the organization of biennials, since one can imagine many kinds of sub-negotiation about selection, support for given artists, and discernment of themes. These all significantly vary the range of artists shown as well as the nature and possibility of the exhibition as a representation of art tendencies at any one time, let alone as a specific conceptual position or even as a display of the zeitgeist.[23]

Perhaps the master curator based his or her judgements on a deep working experience of art and of some duration, but to a non-curator at least, there was very little effective difference in knowledge or discrimination when compared with other actors in the field. Sub-curators or even some minion curators had often the same level of knowledge as master curators, and in most cases had been curators in cognate fields such as not-for-profit art centres for some time.

Art history has not supplied much interpretation in this field, save perhaps in the biographical studies of dealers or curators.[24] The everyday banality of curatorial decisions might be deflected by the celebrity of the artists parading fabulist designs, for example, for one curator to decide to display "your" Navin Rawanchaikul as against another curator's decision to show "my" Rirkrit

Tiravanija. Indeed many exhibition works come to the viewer like pre-loved *objets de luxe* with guaranteed pedigree, known high expense and production values, and often the hint of a genealogy of previous consecrations by other curators. Maybe the Morimura could be chosen this time, and not the Sugimoto again, or indeed, vice versa? There are so many cases of such discriminant selection and display at biennials that the field of curatorial choice does indeed appear to function like a high-class shopping mall, only the curator is there to channel the high-class collector.

The curator basically propagandizes a fashionable intangible, the taste on which he or she proposes we should all agree. The *all* refers beyond anyone else, first, to other curators in the field.[25] However, often there are claims to be humble or for the need of humility.[26] I cannot avoid the feeling, sometimes reported by other curators in private, that selection has actually been made with other curators at least half in mind. The key audience is this private or restricted group, notwithstanding the pretended openness or flexibility of the notional *all*.

Biennials also substituted at the international level for survey exhibitions of contemporary or modern art at the national level. Such surveys for a period in the 1990s became a staple of institutional exhibitors of modern and contemporary art within national boundaries but were attenuated or disappeared thereafter.[27]

These art surveys might be categorized as those of periods, of surveys of national art, of surveys of other-cultural specifications within or across national boundaries, and of surveys of regional tendencies between nations.[28] Among non-national surveys are found surveys of conceptual unities, surveys of mental frames informing art or zeitgeist,[29] surveys of art movements with a manifesto or position which may have embraced different concepts, periods, or nations. Or they can be surveys of usually period-specific practice as of "now", the "last decade" or other close-to-present periodization as defined by media or the art practices which approach "newer" notions of the interactions with media so transforming the underlying practice.

Perhaps the most interesting chaste comparators to biennials are the art exhibitions or competitions held to accompany the Olympic Games.[30] They appear to be "chaste" because they often claim to disinterestedly assemble art supposed to be representative of the host nation for a specific period. They are also deployed to officially consecrate by high cultural accompaniment the low cultural sporting events with which they coincide—so the host country can prove that beyond *our* superlative bodies we also have *our* superlative artistic imaginations, and superior collections of *our* treasures.

Unfortunately Olympic art exhibitions are often not well attended or given the publicity they deserve. I think particularly of the magnificent Papunya Tula exhibition held to accompany the Sydney Olympic Games in 2000.[31] It was barely visited on the three occasions I went, and yet included some of the country's most important paintings by indigenous artists, many of which in a differently constituted international art world would have been recognized already as masterpieces of our age. When the vagaries of sectional art world interest are momentarily suspended on such occasions we see what biennials might intend: the consecrated demonstration of a kind of Olympian achievement in the field of art relevant to an age and representative of a contemporary spirit. But, as significantly, they also point to the isolation of even the most achieved contemporary art from popular discourse. They display the competitive nature of national submission to biennials, whether by designated national pavilions or through the consecrated selection of master curators in the thematic displays.

## Biennials and Contemporary Asian Art

How have biennials, as specific institutions for the exhibition and thereby consecration of art, functioned for the contemporary art of various Asian countries? These institutions have had two levels: the international, which was hierarchically conceived as superior or more important, and the national, which was interested and local, therefore less important, even if it wanted to elevate local artists and their works to the international level. Biennials had been organized in Delhi, Dhaka, Gwangju, Guangzhou, Shanghai, Beijing and Yokohama to show local artists at an international level. But they also introduced what were in theory previously unexposed or relatively unknown international artists to the local art-viewing public. There were no explicitly cross-national but regional biennials, although some clearly intended to fulfil that function, such as Dhaka, Gwangju, and, in a slightly different politicized mode, Havana, for the Global South or for Hispanic America.

The last type of biennial which presumed a regional leadership function, appears to be caught up in, if not stand as a distanced representation for, those changing interrelations or processes between nation-states and their cultures which are loosely called globalism or globalization. The habit of taking art world phenomena and reading out from them world views, or states of relationship between econo-political structures and cultural or more specifically art values, has been part and parcel of modern art history since the mid-19th century.[32]

Furthermore, in the opposite Euramerican methodological direction, the longing for metatheory might have been a theological residue from the 18th century European Enlightenment that was mediated by the developing educational and ideological structures of the modern state.[33] It would be premature even facile to attribute all of the phenomena of new international biennials and their relations with local art worlds as having been due to globalism. Or, to link these phenomena to whatever change in inter-state relations, or to the different nature of the state unit itself in order to understand international relations. There are far too many art- and art institution-specific phenomena in play at biennials to make sensible such a theory-down approach.

Before looking at international biennials and their function as sites for the exhibition of contemporary Asian art, and their interaction with its production, one would like to know more about biennials themselves, and particularly biennials of the last 15 or so years. These have not yet been systematically researched. Those who might have had direct knowledge of biennials were tied up directly in their organization, or were doing contemporary art criticism and theory, or were disinclined by their art historical training to do basic institutional analysis.[34] A gap exists between the conceptual base of international curators which was almost entirely constructed around their operational activity, and understanding what biennials are or how they function at a systemic level. There are reasonably extensive series of interviews with and papers by international biennial and other curators thinking aloud about exhibitions, but very few if any of them want to say what the system is in which they are operating.[35] This lack means that in then current research there is no basic description of biennials and, as noted above, scarcely any analysis of their typology.[36]

Biennials have a specific relation to the consecration of contemporary artworks or their practices. As a specific type of exhibition site they are also related to the way certain kinds of noneconomic goods are created and made prominent through the spectacle of exhibition. The noneconomic situation of artworks, and of artists as a kind of art performer, might metamorphosize into economic benefits for the artist via the sale of works, and the work may later transform via secondary sale into a kind of commodity circulation.

If the above simple comments apply to the international level, they do so more strongly at the local or national level. However unsatisfactory from a wider systemic perspective, one can still draw inferences from specific local engagements of the national with the international level. There are the art-world functions of country-specific collections, seen for example in the contemporary Chinese art collected in Europe.[37] This book includes analyses of Japanese contemporary art and globalism with reference to the Venice Biennale in chapter 2,[38] and of Chinese contemporary art and biennials in chapter 3.[39] Basic research established a simple, non-relational database of selected exhibitions between 1989 and 2005, which ranked artists and curators by frequency of appearance in these sites (see appendix 3). The case study of Singapore in chapter 4 observes various activities which led up to the first Singapore Biennale in 2006.

In this book, the questions of central concern to art history, insofar as it concerns itself with contemporary art, may be grouped under four headings: circulation, mediation, units and levels of analysis, the dynamics of art worlds.

## Levels and Types of Circulation

How do artworks, artists, and their curator-mediators circulate? It may seem self-evident that artworks circulate, but in fact the work often seems like the secondary imprint of an artist-producer who is selected to produce a new variant on a known range of work, or replicate one already known. Not merely do works and their producers circulate, information about both does as well. Sometimes an artist achieves prominence by a very small notice in an art magazine by a particular curator.

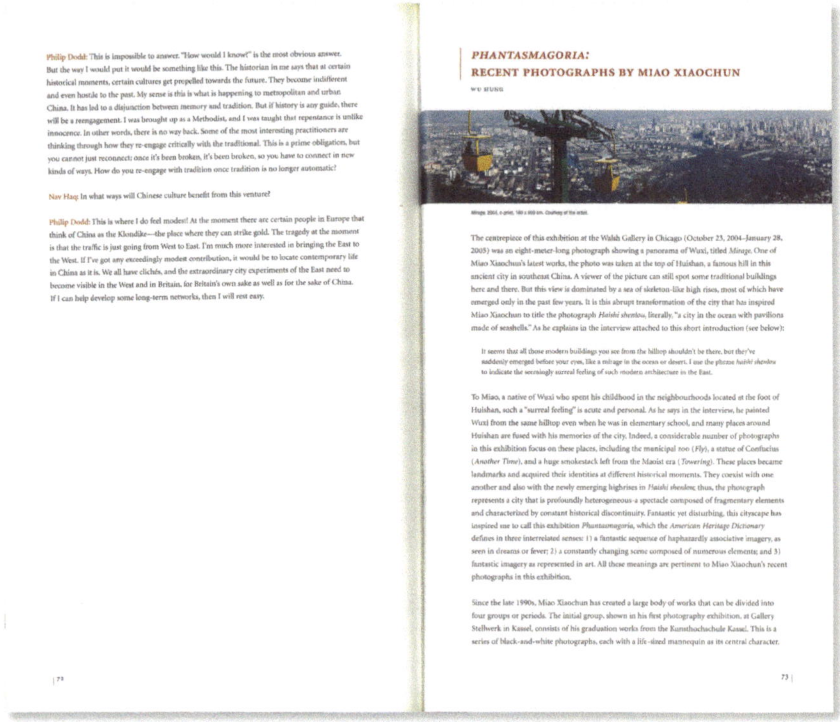

**Philip Dodd:** This is impossible to answer. "How would I know?" is the most obvious answer. But the way I would put it would be something like this. The historian in me says that at certain historical moments, certain cultures get propelled towards the future. They become indifferent and even hostile to the past. My sense is this is what is happening to metropolitan and urban China. It has led to a disjunction between memory and tradition. But if history is any guide, there will be a reengagement. I was brought up as a Methodist, and I was taught that repentance is unlike innocence. In other words, there is no way back. Some of the most interesting practitioners are thinking through how they re-engage critically with the traditional. This is a prime obligation, but you cannot just reconnect; once it's been broken, it's been broken, so you have to connect in new kinds of ways. How do you re-engage with tradition once tradition is no longer automatic?

**Nav Haq:** In what ways will Chinese culture benefit from this venture?

**Philip Dodd:** This is where I do feel modest! At the moment there are certain people in Europe that think of China as the Klondike—the place where they can strike gold. The tragedy at the moment is that the traffic is just going from West to East. I'm much more interested in bringing the East to the West. If I've got any exceedingly modest contribution, it would be to locate contemporary life in China as it is. We all have clichés, and the extraordinary city experiments of the East need to become visible in the West and in Britain, for Britain's own sake as well as for the sake of China. If I can help develop some long-term networks, then I will rest easy.

| 72

*PHANTASMAGORIA:*
**RECENT PHOTOGRAPHS BY MIAO XIAOCHUN**

WU HUNG

The centrepiece of this exhibition at the Walsh Gallery in Chicago (October 23, 2004–January 28, 2005) was an eight-meter-long photograph showing a panorama of Wuxi, titled *Mirage*. One of Miao Xiaochun's latest works, the photo was taken at the top of Huishan, a famous hill in this ancient city in southeast China. A viewer of the picture can still spot some traditional buildings here and there. But this view is dominated by a sea of skeleton-like high rises, most of which have emerged only in the past few years. It is this abrupt transformation of the city that has inspired Miao Xiaochun to title the photograph *Haishi shenlou*, literally, "a city in the ocean with pavilions made of seashells." As he explains in the interview attached to this short introduction (see below):

> It seems that all those modern buildings you see from the hilltop shouldn't be there, but they've suddenly emerged before your eyes, like a mirage in the ocean or desert. I use the phrase *haishi shenlou* to indicate the seemingly surreal feeling of such modern architecture in the East.

To Miao, a native of Wuxi who spent his childhood in the neighbourhoods located at the foot of Huishan, such a "surreal feeling" is acute and personal. As he says in the interview, he painted Wuxi from the same hilltop even when he was in elementary school, and many places around Huishan are fused with his memories of the city. Indeed, a considerable number of photographs in this exhibition focus on these places, including the municipal zoo (*Fly*), a statue of Confucius (*Another Time*), and a huge smokestack left from the Maoist era (*Towering*). These places became landmarks and acquired their identities at different historical moments. They coexist with one another and also with the newly emerging highrises in *Haishi shenlou*; thus, the photograph represents a city that is profoundly heterogeneous-a spectacle composed of fragmentary elements and characterized by constant historical discontinuity. Fantastic yet disturbing, this cityscape has inspired me to call this exhibition *Phantasmagoria*, which the *American Heritage Dictionary* defines in three interrelated senses: 1) a fantastic sequence of haphazardly associative imagery, as seen in dreams or fever; 2) a constantly changing scene composed of numerous elements; and 3) fantastic imagery as represented in art. All these meanings are pertinent to Miao Xiaochun's recent photographs in this exhibition.

Since the late 1990s, Miao Xiaochun has created a large body of works that can be divided into four groups or periods. The initial group, shown in his first photography exhibition, at Gallery Stellwerk in Kassel, consists of his graduation works from the Kunsthochschule Kassel. This is a series of black-and-white photographs, each with a life-sized mannequin as its central character.

73 |

1.4 Scanned pages of interview by Wu Hung, "Phantasmagoria: Recent Photographs by Miao Xiaochun", *Yishu: Journal of Contemporary Chinese Art* 4, 3 (September 2005). Image courtesy of *Yishu: Journal of Contemporary Chinese Art*.

Prior to market consecration, artists appear to achieve prominent circulation simply because their name is taken up in a variety of communication media, printed or electronic. This actual and virtual information media chatter is found in a kind of mirroring process. But this only happens if the signs attached to work or artist are appropriately configured—as perhaps one might see more obviously in the repetitious generation of a style or look in fashion magazines. The cultural background of some curators is an unspoken feature of their presence in an exhibition where they become quasi-artists by virtue of their being art world celebrities. Circulation at the international level of curators and artists, however physical their presence, often appears to be of their persona as a simulacrum. But perhaps more profoundly, if the phenomena of circulation are difficult to empirically describe, it is far more complex to identify what kinds of circulation are in play and what hermeneutic models curatorial operators or art historians could deploy to effectively understand them.

## Mediation

The participation of contemporary Asian art at biennials inside and outside Asia has thrown into relief the crucial role of curator-mediators. Some would wish audiences to think curators are ethically neutral and simply exercise difficult aesthetic judgments which select and position artists. In fact, such judgments are imbricated in a landscape of personal and public institutional self-interest from which curator-mediators are not only never freed, but which they may on the contrary have to more concretely assert simply to function effectively. To understand such functioning, a more precisely articulated typology of functions and units of analysis is required, and will be presented after the case studies. Such a typology ranges from artists themselves, to curators who may have been nominally free of institutional attachment. Other curators who are explicitly involved in institutional goals and may be formally attached to a museum of contemporary art or non-profit arts centre. It is unclear where exactly art critics fit into such a typology, or even what function might be exercised by academics, from art historians to those from other disciplines like anthropology or sociology.[40] These are another kind of mediator who often critically comments on, or analyses the judgements of, curators but who are only responsible to a viewing audience in an indirect sense through their impact on knowledge. The opinions of critics and academics are part of a circulation of ideas and knowledge which itself affects mediation, and academics are increasingly stepping away from mere opinion-forming mediation to mediation through the works they themselves as curators select for exhibitions which they may lead.

## Units and Levels of Analysis

It is doubtful whether there is actually an artwork in circulation anymore at biennials. Artworks are increasingly notional and became actual only for the limited moment of physical or conceptual reference in an exhibition, an actual or virtual site of mediation to a receiver. They are not simply concrete, physical works defined in specific media or site contexts which can be transferred between exhibition or storage sites. If this is the case for works it is even more so for the types of actor involved in artwork circulation.

For if the role of the artist may be absorbed into, if not usurped by, that of the curator, is art simply a peculiar category of perceptual and conceptual life that itself circulates between producer, mediator, and reception functions? In other words, the notion of different kinds of actor defined by their functions may have become transparent, due mostly to a change in the institutional properties of the siting of these actors which makes them inter-penetrable to each other.

If this is true of units in question, levels are equally problematic. What many observers by the 1990s tended loosely but with experiential reason to call the global appears to have dissolved national artistic practice in the same way as

1.5 Exhibition catalogue cover of Lim Tzay-Chuen, *Mike* (2005), exhibited at the Singapore Pavilion of the 51st Venice Biennale, 2005.

the producer or mediator unit associated with a transnational level. This is where circulation functions between like units but no longer at a level defined by a nation-state, and purportedly beyond it.[41] That is, circulation is defined by the distribution of like functions within nation-state entities. This does not allow for the very different cultural functions of different kinds of nation-state entities, certainly in relation to their cultural pretension or spatial aggrandizement beyond the state. Artists have often claimed to me that they just did what they did in order to make art. Curators may state they just operate discrimination in a neutral but personal manner, but that does not alter the fact that the whole context in which they do so alters around them because of their curation.

## Dynamics of Art Worlds

Finally, a range of issues involving the dynamics of art worlds has been brought out by this research. Why were artworks made and circulated? Or, put differently, what caused them to be made, or what processes of causation can we identify in their making? These may look like re-formulations of long-standing issues of concern to art history but they are brought up because these are basically new phenomena, or those which have to be newly conceptualized. They are identified above in terms of the fragility or inter-permeability of the functions assigned to the main actors in this field, as much as the levels and nature of units inside or between which they operate. If these actors and units were not so unstable or redundant we would not have had to think again about the dynamics by which artworks are created, since we could simply aggregate old conceptions into the new ones: the making of works whose aesthetic features (beauty or ugliness or iconograpically coherent representationality) outstrip our social categories for handling them. They may give us a sense of the uncanny or of an unfathomable sublime, they may give a sense of a contested field and of the intervention of art in issues of the quotidian world. Many artworks no longer make the audience secure within the unknown and overthrow the religious or spiritual level with ambivalence and instability.

By the 1990s, because of the interpenetration of what we may call cultural worlds, the discourses in which artworks function and the units and levels between which they flow had lost their internality, their autonomy. As much as all art is potentially "our" art, so the units which structure the relations between the actors in art worlds dissolve, even old guises.

Visual artworks are peculiarly able to slip across cultural boundaries because of their apparent independence from language systems. But when an artwork can be made at one end of the globe and shown at the other, then the audience that receives it and for whom it is mediated by the curator who had been to both ends of the chain, is differently constituted than one which is simply the local variation of some internationally sited set of tastes. Is this new audience the site of a dynamic which is quite different from the production of an artwork for a national art salon, from a dealer exhibition, or from a manifesto or thematic exhibition previously confined to a single art culture? What makes the work for this audience is surely the connection and the connector. I would say the work does not exist without either. And since the connection is supplied by the mediator-curator, it is a function of the mediation and the actor who bore it that claims sovereignty in such a process. Aesthetic sovereignty belongs neither to creation of the work nor to reception of the work at either end of this circuit.

Could aesthetic sovereignty exist at all? I ask this question because there are cases of artists who were passed on from one biennial curator to another, and who produced new work at one end of the world, for exhibiton at the other. When biennial curation can call up an existing producer on the circuit, perhaps aesthetic sovereignty belongs to those whose slippery insertions actually direct or control the circuit itself.

## Biennials and the Formation of a Modern Asian Art History

The principal intention of this book is to show that modernity might be discussed from a specifically Asian perspective with a generality that may also be applied to Euramerican phenomena. Euramerican modernity is thereby relativized because the process of defining or specifying canonical artists and works has spread beyond Euramerica. The consequences of the rise of biennials as the sites for consecration of other-than-Asian artists or works, or as the sites within Asia of national consecration and later canonization, were manifold. Let me name just two here.

The first consequence, if we take Japan as a paradigm case, evident since the removal of *nihonga* (neo-traditional Japanese painting) from Japanese art sent to Venice from the 1960s, was the exclusion and relativization of both neo-traditional and academic Western-style art as "not of the current moment" and deemed retrograde if not explicitly atavist. This phenomenon, widely repeated in selections from Asian countries for Venice by international, usually Euramerican, curators has meant that a historical link with the immediate past of many art cultures became severed from the domain of current, transnationally accepted practice. Neo-traditional and academic Western-style art can be shown at such sites as subordinate to art discourse, as material or technique, but not as the constituent of art discourses themselves. This means that an artist within a neo-traditionalist discourse such as *nihonga* is unlikely to be selected at the international level, unless, like Murakami Takashi or Nara Yoshitomo, they previously assimilated their conceptual position to that of their contemporaries or to some interpretation of a zeitgeist which is clearly not that of simply repositioning art customary to a particular art culture.

The second consequence is that modern art history as the history of modern art comprising the contemporary is continuously being recomposed by the display functions of current exhibition. Artworks which stay in the studio are dead, according to this interpretation, however known to a circle of the artistically well-informed. These display functions are assimilated with ease into intellectual and commercial fashions, shown tellingly by the work of some video artists moving between advertising and artistic cultures. Or, such displays can function analogously to the way some images from popular cultures are massified into grandiose symbolic icons for art biennials. In fact, if in the 1920s and 1930s art deco fashion was a kind of parasite on avant-garde art in Euramerica, since the 1990s, at least, advanced or thought-provoking art almost everywhere became inalienably complicit with the flow of images and information found through the mediascape of commercial culture (merchandising). The positions are now reversed: art becomes dependent on fashion, and this time art is the parasite.

The historical function of consecrating artworks as worthy of regard and then canonizing those of a near-present range of artists as valuable to collect was increasingly performed by the patronage decisions of the small group of mediators. They now situate themselves within cultural markets in the way artists once put themselves in their mind's eye alongside other, largely passed-on masters.

This stratum is increasingly in touch across national boundaries and as it increased in the size and frequency of its activities, the stratum of mediator-curators fragmented into those oriented to the transnational and those oriented towards the projection of the national into the international. From the late 1990s the biennials allowed a further fragmentation—or role-specialization—into mediator-curators who functioned in the transnational arenas opened up by globalization. These new spaces were dependent neither on single cultures, nation-states, nor indeed the nation-states' tenuously constituted inter-national organizations. This fragmentation among mediator-curators is sometimes accompanied by rotation back into the national domain of mediation after work at the international level, followed by the transnational. Indeed if one considers the career path of Asian curators like Nanjô Fumio from the mid-1980s, Hasegawa Yûko from the 1990s, or Hou Hanru from the late 1990s, the tendency is already plain.

The meaning of this fragmentation for art history, insofar as it in part tracks selections made by such mediators, is that art history and its companion art theory themselves start to cycle between these three levels. The integrity of their subject comes from understanding the processes of such cycling, rather than remaining within any one of them. If the Asian modern, and its complement or derivation the Asian contemporary, is to be found by art historical and art theoretical investigations, it is surely located or articulated in this triple set of levels rather than in some putative binary transfer from the Western to the Asian.

## Notes

1 For an introductory outline of the problem of modernity in Asian art see the entry by John Clark, "Asian modern and contemporary art", *Grove Art Online*, Oxford University Press, published online 22 September 2005, https://doi.org/10.1093/gao/9781884446054.article.T097937. For a more academic overall view see my "Modernities in Art: How are They 'Other'?" in *World Art Studies: Exploring Concepts and Approaches*, ed. Wilfried van Damme and Kitty Zijlmans (Amsterdam: Amsterdam University Press, 2008). The first book in this area, to my knowledge, was Japan Cultural Forum, ed., *Modern Art of Asia: New Movements and Old Traditions* (Tokyo: Toto Shuppan, 1961). A conference which systematically brought various parts of modern and contemporary into comparison was *Modernism and Postmodernism in Asian Art*, held at Australian National University, Canberra, in 1991, and most of the papers were published as John Clark, ed., *Modernity in Asian Art* (Broadway, NSW, Australia: Wild Peony Press, 1993). My own overall study was *Modern Asian Art* (Sydney: Craftsman House; Honolulu: University of Hawai'i Press, 1998).

2 Clearly the life histories, intellectual placement, and personal investment of the Western scholars studying modern Western art may account for this refusal. See my review, "A Short Review of a Very, Very Long Book," review of Hal Foster et al., *Art Since 1900: Modernism, Antimodernism, Postmodernism* (London: Thames & Hudson, 2004), in *Yishu: Journal of Contemporary Chinese Art* (December 2005). Unfortunately, the printed version of my review left out the original list of Asian artists mentioned in this book who, except for Gutai, were all largely active in New York. The published review also used the term "Euro-American" not "Euramerican" as I have long argued we should (since 1998, see *Modern Asian Art*, 11–12). Significantly, North American writers seem to find the term "Euramerican" more problematic than Chinese or Japanese writers, for example. This does not remove the need of those

in Asia outside Euramerica trying first of all to understand their own modernities, and secondly to grasp how these may or may not fit into a wider perspective on modernity in art other than the available and Euramerican-centred one.

3 There was a Frick Fine Arts Library bibliography, International Exhibitions (Library Guide Series no. 42), which was available online from www.library.pitt.edu/subject-guides/arthistory/. Of particular relevance here is Jean-Marc Poinsot, "Large Exhibitions: A Sketch of a Typology", in *Thinking about Exhibitions*, ed. Reesa Greenberg, Bruce W. Ferguson, and Sandy Nairne (London: Routledge, 1996). Histories of the Venice Biennale and national participation include Lawrence Alloway, *The Venice Biennale, 1895–1968: from Salon to Goldfish Bowl* (Greenwich, CT: New York Graphical Society; London: Faber & Faber, 1968); Sophie Bowness and Clive Phillpot, *Britain at the Venice Biennale, 1895–1995* (London: The British Council, 1995); Enzo di Martino, *The History of the Venice Biennale, 1895–2005: Visual Arts, Architecture, Cinema, Dance, Music, Theatre* (Venice: Papiro Arte, 2005); Harumi Miwa, ed., *The Venice Biennale: 40 Years of Japanese Participation* (Tokyo: The Japan Foundation; Tokyo: The Mainichi Newspapers, 1995). Among excellent works which have appeared after the period of research for this book is Robert Fleck, *Die Biennale von Venedig. Eine Geschichte des 20. Jahrhunderts* (Hamburg: Philo Fine Arts Verlag, 2009). This includes useful bibliographies including "Chronologien", 228–9, which list various European and North American country representation surveys.

4 A discussion of definitions of "contemporary art" may be found in Terry Smith, *What is Contemporary Art? Contemporary Art, Contemporaneity and Art to Come*, Artspace Critical Issues Series (Sydney: Artspace Visual Art Centre, 2001). Robert Storr, curator of the Venice Biennale for 2007, led a by-invitation-only international symposium, *Where Art Worlds Meet: Multiple Modernities and the Global Salon* in Venice in December 2005. But I am afraid that, contrary to Stephanie Britton, "Biennials of the World: Myths, Facts, and Questions", *Artlink* 25, 3 (September 2005): 34, where she refers to "mountains of ideas, analysis and critiques", after some reading I do not find the literature on current biennials is particularly well-endowed, save for what are mostly practitioner discussions. Among these are the following: Alex Farquarson, "I Curate…You Curate…We Curate…", *Art Monthly* 269 (September 2003); William Furlong et al., *La Biennale di Venezia 1999* (Wimbledon: Wimbledon School of Art, 1999); William Furlong et al., *Venice Biennale 2001* (Wimbledon: Wimbledon School of Art, 2001); William Furlong, et al., *Venice Agendas 2003: a Series of Three Breakfast Meetings* (Wimbledon: Wimbledon School of Art, 2003) (I am grateful to William Furlong and Wimbledon School of Art for copies of these publications); "Global Tendencies: Globalism and the Large-Scale Exhibition", *Art Forum* XLII, 3 (November 2003); Walter Grasskampf, "For Example, Documenta, or, How is Art History Produced", in *Thinking about Exhibitions*, ed. Greenberg, Ferguson, and Nairne; Mari Carmen Ramírez, "Brokering Identities: Art Curators and the Politics of Cultural Representation", in *Thinking About Exhibitions*, ed. Greenberg, Ferguson, and Nairne; Ralph Rugoff and Larry Rinder, "In Conversation", previously available at www.stretcher.org/archives; Ralph Rugoff, "Rules of the Game", *frieze* 44 (January–February 1999); Terry Smith, "Biennials in the Conditions of Contemporaneity", *Art and Australia* 42, 4 (Autumn 2005). Since this book was written largely about eight years ago a first port of call would be the excellent overall work by Anthony Gardner and Charles Green, *Biennials, Triennials, and Documenta: The Exhibitions that Created Contemporary Art* (Chichester: John Wiley & Sons, 2016).

5 This often takes place in a quasi-cultural market, before artworks actually become objects in art markets for purchase. In place of the two-level notion of a primary gallery and secondary investment art market, beloved out of self-interest in the trade talk of gallerists and auction houses, a four-level conception of art markets may be of more interpretive use:

1. artist to artist or artist to client for cultural esteem
2. artist to curator for cultural consecration
3. artist to gallery to client for economic sale
4. gallery to gallery, collector-investor to other collector-investor for monetary sale, or to institution for esteem and sometimes tax benefits

6 "Circulation" may be identified as key concern of current art history insofar as it addresses the link between museum and gallery practices and the definitions of contemporary art. I am grateful to participants in a workshop on "Circulation" held at the University of Sydney, Department of Art History & Film, in 2005. See also my paper "Biennials and the Circulation of Contemporary Asian Art", *Yishu: Journal of Contemporary Chinese Art* 8, 1 (January/February 2009). This a useful issue devoted to "Contemporary Asian Art and the phenomenon of the Biennial". Another reconsideration in Chinese is of exhibitions at Gwangju, Yokohama, Fukuoka, Taipei, in "The Past, Present and Future of Asian Biennials", in *Xiandai Yishu (Modern Art from Taibei Fine Arts Museum)*, 174 (September 2014).

7 This term is not unproblematic and hinges on the nature and level of units between which "internationality" is supposed to take place. For a discussion of the problem of units see John Clark, "An Australian Creative Space: where is Australian-Asian art now?", in *2006 Contemporary Commonwealth*, ed. Charles Green (Melbourne: Council of Trustees for the National Gallery of Victoria, 2006), 26–33. This treatment will also be covered in Chapter 8.

8 Indeed not-for-profit and artist-run spaces are increasingly trying to get around national mediators and international curators by organizing direct exchanges between themselves which bracket both the "national" and the "international" levels. See *The 2nd "In-Between" International Alternative Space Conference—Globalism and Alternative Spaces*, organized by Duksung Women's University, Alternative Space Loop, Yellow Sea Publications (Seoul: Yellow Sea Publications, 2004). There are many examples of artist-to-artist exchanges which exemplify non-institutional exchanges such as the *Womanifesto* exhibitions in Thailand since 1995. See Brian Mertens, "Womanifesto 2001", *Art AsiaPacific*, 36 (2002).

9 Fukuoka Asian Art Triennale has made particular efforts with residential artist programmes which link up with broad sectors of the Fukuoka population. See Matsuura Jin, "Notes on the Artist-in-Residence Programme", in *Arutisto in rejidensu seikaten* (Fukuoka: Asian Art Museum, 2002).

10 See in particular Charlotte Bydler, *The Global Art World Inc.: On the Globalization of Contemporary Art* (Uppsala: Acta Universitatis Upsaliensis, 2004). Henry Meyric-Hughes, "The History and Significance of the Biennale, as an Instrument of Globalization", draft copy provided by author in 2005 and later published in *Art Criticism and Globalisation* (São Paolo: Assoçiao Brasiliera de Crtiticos de Arte, 2006).

11 Alan Quemin in *L'art contemporain international: entre les institutions et le marché: le rapport disparu* (Nîmes: Éditions Jacqueline Chambon/Artprice, 2002) discusses "prescriptive countries" in contemporary art from an assemblage of factors including size of population and GDP per capita, the role of leading institutions and collectors, and the numbers of artists ranked in international comparative indices

such as Kunstcompass. See Linde Rohr-Bongard et al., *Kunst = Kapital: Der Capital Kunstkompass von 1970 bis heute* (Köln: Salon Verlag, 2001).

12 The distance between the early Documenta curated by Arnold Bode and the later exhibitions has not gone unnoticed: "Today, the levity and transience of contemporary art would have driven a man like Bode to despair". See René Block, "Never Play Sorcerer's Apprentice", in *Words of Wisdom: a Curator's Vade Mecum on Contemporary Art*, ed. Carin Kuoni (New York: Independent Curators International, 2001), 28.

13 So far as I am aware, Matthew Ngui from Singapore was the first recent exhibitor in Documenta X in 1997. But before him, Richard Lin (Lin Shouyu, 1933–2011, from Taiwan, where he returned to live in 1982) was selected from Britain in Documenta III of 1964.

14 For other signs of this hegemony see the Asian artists thought worthy of inclusion in *Art Since 1900: Modernism, Antimodernism, Postmodernism*, op. cit., 2004, which mentions only the following: Ay-O, Gutai Group, Hsieh Tehching [Xie Dejing], Kusama Yayoi, Motonaga Sadamasa, Murakami Saburo, Ono Yoko, Paik Nam-jun, Shiomi Mieko, Shiraga Kazuo, Sumi Yasuo, Tanaka Atsuko, Rirkrit Tiravanija, Yoshida Toshio, Yoshihara Jiro and Yoshihara Michio.

15 Okwui Enwezor's visit to China with other Documenta curators in 2000 also involved a discussion in Beijing at the Central Academy of Fine Arts when, local and informal sources report, Enwezor gave very concrete advice on what kinds of art could be included in Documenta from an international perspective. This first meeting was not transcribed in the reports later printed in *Yishu: Journal of Contemporary Chinese Art* 1, 1 (2002).

16 See Pauline Yao, "The Second Triennial of Chinese Art: History in the Making", *Yishu: Journal of Contemporary Chinese Art* 4, 5 (September 2005).

17 See Christos M. Joachimides, Norman Rosenthal, and Wieland Schmied, *German Art in the 20th Century, Painting and Sculpture 1905–1985* (London: Royal Academy of Arts; Munich: Prestel Verlag, 1985).

18 Pierre Bourdieu, *Outline of a Theory of Practice*, trans. Richard Nice (Cambridge, UK: Cambridge University Press, 1977), 195, writes "consecration cycles perform the fundamental operation of social alchemy, the transformation of arbitrary relations into legitimate relations, de facto differences into officially recognized distinctions". And later, "The endless reconversion of economic capital into symbolic capital, at the cost of a wastage of social energy which is the condition for the permanence of domination, cannot succeed without the complicity of the whole group…". Also see Pierre Bourdieu, *La distinction: critique sociale du jugement* (Paris: Les Éditions de Minuit, 1979), 463–5. How this articulates on a global scale may be seen in Quemin, *L'art contemporain international*, 136–72.

19 From my limited and personal observation of gallery purchasing interactions, there would seem to be a profound asymmetry between the volume/level of "sales" of contemporary art and patrons' wish to "purchase". Above a certain price for the artist, even a very low price relative to the work, skills, and materials involved and in production, "selling" characterizes the nature of an exchange, usually from artist to gallery to client, but "buying" hardly characterizes the client's situation. Whether giving money for a work for pleasure or social esteem or investment (and usually all three) the buyer is not choosing between comparable or equivalent goods. The choice is between different goods whose price he or she will pay according to a

desirability market usually given both by private taste and public fashion, and not directly some utilitarian evaluation of satisfaction, quality, or need-fulfilment. There is no equivalent calculus between the artist's need to sell and the client's wish to buy and both are usually articulated in quite different domains, the one economic, the other mostly as a store-symbol of cultural capital which will only be converted to economic capital at a deferred date.

20 A research database has been compiled for this project from names of Asian artists and the curators, including those of Asian origin, at selected Biennials and other art exhibitions from 1989–2004, and included in appendix materials here. The exhibitions where the artist or curator appeared were awarded points which were ranked according to the importance of the exhibition, both for China, and for all Asian countries. In the case of China the total sample was of 157 curators (after November 2005 this number slightly increased), and there were 19 curators with 4 points and above. With the actual points given in brackets, the top 5 curators were Hou Hanru (23), Chang Tsong-zung (13), Huang Du (09), Nanjô Fumio (09) Harald Szeemann (08). In the case of Asia overall, there were a total of 103 curators and 15 curators had 4 points and above. The top 6 curators were Harald Szeemann (10), Nanjô Fumio (10), Kim Hong-hee (07), Apinan Poshyananda (05), Hasegawa Yûko (05), Tatehata Akira (05).

In the artists' database, for China there were 858 artists overall [as of November 2005, this number slightly increased] with 55 artists on 10 points and above. The top 8 artists were Cai Guoqiang (36), Xu Bing (30), Fang Lijun (26), Zhang Peili (25), Geng Jianyi (22), Huang Yongping (22), Yang Fudong (21), Zhang Xiaogang (21). For Asia overall, there were 632 artists and the top 10 artists had 10 points and above. Those artists were Heri Dono (17), Anish Kapoor (14), Kim Soo-ja (14), Miyajima Tatsuo (14), Navin Rawanchaikul (11), Ono Yoko (11), Hatsushiba-Nguyen Jun (11), Yanagi Yukinri (11), Montien Boonma (10), Funakoshi Katsura (10).

21 If one may unsatisfactorily so judge by informal, non-attributable reports. The Queensland Art Gallery director, Mr Doug Hall, refused a request for an interview for this research. In the circumstances I felt unable to continue with a plan to interview Queensland Art Gallery curators since—whatever may be right or wrong about subsequent interpretations—one topic of this research was to model such decision chains where information was available and reliable. For much better transparency in this field see Toshiko Rawanchaikul, "How were the Artists Selected?", in *The 3rd Fukuoka Asian Art Triennale 2005*, ed. Igarashi Rina (Fukuoka: Fukuoka Asian Art Museum, 2005): 030–033.

22 See Nanjô Fumio, "Yokohama Toriennaare 2001 kôki – sono tenmatsu no kojinteki memorandamu", *Aica Japan Newsletter*, 2 (November 2001).

23 For example the Venice Biennale 2003 exhibition included such a *Zeitgeist* survey *Painting in the Twentieth Century* at the Museo Correr.

24 See, inter alia, Meryle Secrest, *Duveen: A Life in Art* (Chicago: University of Chicago Press, 2004); Sybil Gordon Kantor, *Alfred H. Barr Jr. and the Intellectual Origins of the Museum of Modern Art* (Cambridge, MA: MIT Press, 2002); Alice Goldfarb, *Alfred H. Barr, Jr., Missionary for the Modern* (Chicago: Contemporary Books, 1989).

25 There are an increasing number of texts on curating practice including Carolee Thea, *Foci; Interviews with Ten International Curators* (New York: apexart curatorial program, 2001), and Kuoni, *Words of Wisdom* (2001). A very useful collection with a comprehensive analysis of the functions of art in such events is Lewis Biggs, "'Art, Money, Parties' and Liverpool Biennial", in *Art, Money, Parties: New Institutions*

*in the Political Economy of Contemporary Art*, ed. John Harris (Liverpool: Liverpool University Press, 2004). The broader problems of the "celebritization" of artists and curators are examined in John Walker, *Art and Celebrity* (London: Pluto Press, 2003).

26 As for example, the exhortation to "Live Humble" by Marcia Tucker, "Become a great curator in six simple steps!", in Kuoni, *Words of Wisdom*, 170.

27 In the contemporary Asian area there is a discussion by Kamiya Yukie, "A Potential Role of Asian Art in the International Art scene: a Study of Asian Art Exhibitions in the United States and Japan", in *The 2nd "In-Between" International Alternative Space Conference*.

28 As in exhibitions like Ushiroshôji Masahiro, supervising curator, *The Birth of Modern Art in Southeast Asia: Artists and Movement* (Fukuoka: Fukuoka Art Museum, 1997), or Tatehata Akira et al., *Cubism in Asia, Unbounded Dialogues* (Tokyo: The Japan Foundation, 2005).

29 The title of Harald Szeemann's *When Attitudes Become Form* (Bern: Kunsthalle, 1969) was clearly invoked in Philippe Vergne's, *How Latitudes become Forms: Art in a Global Age* (Minneapolis: Walker Art Centre, 2003).

30 These would make an elegant study in their own right. There were art exhibitions at the Tokyo, Seoul, and Sydney Olympics. There is a study by Richard Stanton, *The Forgotten Olympic Art Competitions: the Story of Olympic Art Competitions of the 20th Century* (Victoria, BC: Trafford, 2000). Significantly the Venice Biennale is located on the site of a previous national exhibition of Italian Art and the current building for the British pavilion was once the café for the Italian national exhibition. One is thus led to the question: are Biennials actually a kind of "national" exhibition projected onto the "international" level, and where the "nation" no longer exists as the legitimating site, but only as a source of materials for producers and mediators?

31 The Sydney exhibition was Hetti Perkins and Hannah Fink, *Papunya Tula: Genesis and Genius* (Sydney: Art Gallery of New South Wales in association with Papunya Tula Artists, 2000).

32 The *locus classicus* is Jacob Burkhardt, *The Civilization of the Renaissance in Italy: An Essay*, trans. S.G.C. Middlemore (1860; London: Phaidon, 1951).

33 Art History since the mid-19th century has been the result of an uncomfortable series of positions established between a changing *weltanschauung* and an unstable conception of art. See Hans Belting, *The End of the History of Art*, trans. Christopher S. Wood (Chicago: University of Chicago Press, 1987), 15.

34 Apart from the work of Quemin and Byndler cited above. The place of the Fukuoka Asian Art Triennale in Japanese international cultural flows is analyzed in detail in Kishi Sayaka, "Bijutsukan 'Ajia' to deau toki – Fukuoka Ajia Bijutsukan no setsuritsu to tenkai", in *Sengô nihon no kokusai bunka kôryû*, ed. Hirano Kenichirô (Tokyo: Chikusô Shobô, 2005).

35 See Kuoni, *Words of Wisdom*.

36 The exception is Bydler, *The Global Art World Inc.*

37 Such collections include the Guy & Myriam Ullens Collection in France (see Fei Dawei, ed., *The Monk and the Demon* (Lyon: Musée d'Art Contemporain du Lyon, 2004)); the Sigg Collection in Switzerland, (see Bernard Fibicher and Matthias Frehner, ed., *Mahjong: Contemporary Chinese Art from the Sigg Collection* (Ostfildern-Ruit: Hatje Cantz, 2005)); the Frank Uytterhagen and Pascale Geulleaume collection in Belgium (see Hans Van Dyck, ed., *Modern Chinese Art Foundation* (Gent: Provincie Oost-

Vlanderen, 1999)), and in Holland the collection of Cees Hendrikse (see https://www.beeldenaanzee.nl/).

38 See John Clark, "Japanese Contemporary Art and Globalization, largely seen from participation in the Venice Biennale" (Conference lecture, *Globalization, Localization and Japanese Culture in the Asia Pacific Region: an International Symposium*, Singapore, 28–30 October 2004).

39 See John Clark, "Between the Worlds: Chinese Art at Biennials since 1993" in *Yishu, A journal of Chinese Contemporary Art* (2005). The full version is Chapter 6 here and the original short version was given at the conference *Displacements: Transcultural Encounters in Contemporary Chinese Art* at the Cantor Arts Center at Stanford University in January 2005 in conjunction with the exhibition *On the Edge: Contemporary Chinese Artists Encounter the West.*

40 This is because art criticism in news media is largely life-style oriented mediation to a niche market in order to increase the attractiveness of the newspaper for advertisers, and is often in any case linked to those commercial galleries able to secure such exposure for their artists.

41 See Clark, "An Australian Creative Space".

Chapter 2

# Japanese Art, Largely Seen from Participation in the Venice Biennale

The next four chapters are case studies of national participation in biennials or the organization of biennials from a national base. In this chapter I shall feature Japanese participation at the Venice Biennale, but the study should also be seen to double as a consideration of some of the changes at the Venice Biennale itself.[1]

## Globalization and Globalism

The rise of Asian Biennials in the 1990s has been tied by many biennial organizers to processes of globalization whereby markets and investment flows for goods, production systems, and cultures previously identified by the control of the nation state have increasingly escaped that control. Biennials have constituted a key site for exhibition of art works within but beyond the hegemonic control of nation states. They are a site but also a gap between national discourses where such national kinds of cultural domination were avoided or passed by flows of people, goods, concepts, and values. These move across territorial borders in ways which appear autonomous of the state units, and even the sub-state cultural units, between which the movements take place. Globalism is the ideology which defended and fostered these globalization processes. At least latently, globalism constitutes a system of knowledge about how, why, and in whose interests those processes take place. Understanding of the ideology of globalism implies knowledge of the processes of globalization, and this provides ground for an external critique.

I have examined theories of globalism and globalization elsewhere in the context of Chinese and Thai art of the 1980s and 1990s and will not rehearse those arguments here.[2] But I would like to simply identify certain perspectives based on that study which may also be indicative in looking at this strategy of inserting one national art, that of Japan, into the Venice Biennale, among other nations' art.

With regard to the problematics of globalism/globalization in the cultural domain for Japan in the 1990s and early 2000s, was there a full-blown absorption of contemporary Japanese art into the global "world-system", or was the Japanese art world still bifurcated into domestically oriented and internationally oriented sectors?[3] The last reservation is critical because we can quite easily conceive of the Japanese art world as two-tiered or with two articulations until the 1980s when there was extensive exhibition of Japanese contemporary art abroad for the first time. Thereafter Japanese art of the 1990s assumed a certain importance and automatic inclusion in international art exhibitions curated by non-Japanese. Yet despite absolute dependence of the Japanese economy on world markets, Japanese art in the 1990s also included a latent desire for intervention and resistance to Euramerican modernism, without quite the force of a search for an alternative modernism one might see in China at the same time.

The search for a Japanese modernity had already been realized by the Taishô period (1912–26) when the critical identification of an individualized artistic life had been achieved which was relatively free from broader social goals or national agendas.[4] With 50 years of broad, translated knowledge in Japanese of Euramerican modernism, there was no way Japanese art in the 1980s could be conceived of as apart from this modernism.[5] How was there a domestic space that was already quasi-international, or how was a "nested endogeny" constituted within Japanese art discourses? [6] The relatively small-scale incorporation of post-modernist theories in Japanese art criticism of the 1980s was partly the result of the syncretic tendencies already having been found for a long time in modern Japanese art, at least since the 1870s of early Meiji. [7]

Of more particular interest was the Japanese reaction to theories of multiculturalism or resistance to Eurocentricity (abbreviated from "Euramerican-centricity"). Here one may assume that resistance to Eurocentricity was in part carried by the very translation culture incorporated in Japanese knowledge systems including those for art. There had been a long trend of resistance especially in aesthetics to find in Japanese identity an ethnic specificity for life forms, tied especially to aesthetic discrimination.[8]

The essentializing search for a certain Japanese aesthetic was not countered with the post-World War II consumerist flood of mass images. Much *manga* and later *animé* imagery has been subsequently tied to specifically Japanese image geneaologies and narrative techniques into which other-cultural interpretations can be read *post facto*. Such interpretations of mass cultural images and artifacts depend on the levels of cultural affiliation assumed between Japanese and other international or global material. But in a mass visual culture long exposed to both American cinema conventions and comic books, Japanese material was the inflection of an extant visual domain rather than its reconstitution from an other-culture, that is it was *not* ethnically or culturally specific Japanese discourse.

The structure of the visual domain did not hinder a Japanese culturalist construction found in *nihonjinron* theories and interpretations from representing a cultural conflict between "East" and "West", but it did so as a content rather than a modality of narrative or visual practice. As pointed out by several Japanese scholars, "multiculturalism" in a Japanese context is more a plea for a Japanese uniqueness not actually possessed by "Japanese", either as ethnos or as culturally specific practice.[9] It may be merely supported as another version of an originally exclusionary tactic found since Meiji Japan, and of course earlier in late Edo nativist thought.

Identification with the national has atrophied in Japan with the increasing residence of Japanese overseas, and with the movement of artists and curators. This has increased rapidly since the early 1960s' move of many artists to New York, following on from earlier movements to Paris. But if globalization has increasingly led to a weakened distinction between "Japan" and its others, usually named in the Japanese language as *Seiyôteki* (Western) or *Ôbeiteki* (Euramerican), the end of the Cold War had consequences we are still learning to engage with. For the ideological constraints which associated art with the US' freedom or its system superiority against the former Soviet bloc have been lost as social and cultural systems have been re-constructed. This may have led to a "festivalization" (i.e. spectacularization) of international cultural events with the Olympics in sport or World Fairs as sites for the display of cultural goods taken as a model types.

It is to this context we may link the increasing number of art biennials, and their Japanese participation. To borrow the term of Appadurai, "ideoscape",[10] the creation of ever more spectacles of international cultural exchange focused on art (as well as film, performance, new media, ceramics, to name the fields of those biennials recently founded in Korea alone) meant that a new kind of ideoscape had been established as the consequence of global relativization of the "national". Biennial participation overseas or organization at home also functioned at the same time as a strategy for the re-insertion and re-assertion of the "national" within global discourses, such as art, where the international level denied or denuded the "national".

The following table allows debate over certain relationships:

| | **São Paolo**[1] | **Venice**[2] | **Own Biennial**[3] | **Olympics**[4] | **"Meijification"**[5] **[or "National Development"]** |
|---|---|---|---|---|---|
| Japan | 1951 | 1952 [1955] | 2002, Yokohama | 1964 Tokyo | >1890–1950< |
| Korea | 1963 | 1986 [1988] | 1995, Gwangju | 1988 Seoul | >1945–2005< |
| China | 2000 | 2003 [2005?] | 2003, Beijing | 2008 Beijing | >1949–2009< |

1 Year of first participation, Chinese participation was non-official in 2000.

2 Year of first post-1945 participation, [ ] indicates year of own pavilion. Taiwan and Hong Kong exhibit separately.

3 Japan earlier had the Tokyo Print Biennale and China had biennials in Guangzhou and Shanghai. These years mark the beginning of a full-scale biennale with official, central government support.

4 The years the Olympics are held mark significant changes in economic stability and political advance, and the events themselves were accompanied by major nation-defining cultural events in both Japan and Korea, and in China in 2008.

5 "Meijification" refers to relatively closed, state-centred, national development for notionally 60 years.

If globalization in art may be at least partially defined as an increasing level and intensity of participation in recurring temporary exhibitions at an international level, it has some relationship to the trajectories of national development which art may articulate or represent, with temporal variation between countries. Before the mid-1950s in Japan with the rise of the Gutai group, or before 1970 in Korea with the local development of the Seoul school of monochromists, or before the early 1990s growth of a secure and self-innovating non-official art in China, growth of modern art was broadly linked to economic factors which developmentally facilitated the transfer and adaptation of formal discourse from Euramerica. Many other factors made this transfer more like local counter-appropriation, and the modernity produced was a 'parallel' one subject to local contingencies. One of the principal indices of development was economic because this field also signed the theoretical potential for transfer of capital from economic to cultural fields, although how this actually went on remained to be ascertained in practice.

Such earlier transfer and adaptation from one centre to another, from Euramerica to Japan since the 1890s, Korea since the 1980s, or China in the 1990s, was not the case when globalization marked, or created, an increasing sectoral bifurcation of the economic and cultural (and here) art worlds. This split was part of the processes of role specialization, and separation of the production from the life-worlds, as considered by Habermas.[11] In whatever way the above time-scales differed, they tended to indicate a process where development reached a certain level, and economic capital was accumulated and then re-directed into cultural capital, usually through education and initially by the agency of the territorial state. One expression of the subsequent but often simultaneous transfer of cultural capital onto the plane of a globalized art, if we may so theorize it, was in national participation at exhibitions which transcended the national level. This occured even as significantly national participation was simultaneously constituted by the global: it took place, for example, through exhibition of a designated, single national representative in São Paolo, in the sending of national sections to the Venice Biennale, or in the national organization of biennials themselves.

For Japan, as with different periodizations for Korea and China, the 1990s saw the establishment of trans-territorial discourses of the national.[12] Trans-territoriality was shown internationally by artists identifying as Japanese but living in another country, such as Japanese artists long resident in New York like Kasahara Emiko. Trans-territoriality amounted to a "de-territorialized discourse of Japanese-ness", one already noted for Chinese and Thai artists in similar locations.[13] Artists found themselves having one national origin and often aesthetic affiliation, but were living and working at an interface with other nationally defined or sited art worlds. They began to work at the interstices of cultural contact both in their own practice and in their own institutional location. They became hybrid entities and persons, and operated transnational networks which even bypassed national mediators such as curators. This was clear in the work of Kusama Yayoi in 1960s New York or as later seen in the work of Murakami Takashi. He had originally been a *nihonga* painter, who began to work with pop cultural imagery and icons drawn from Japanese everyday life but which also had a very strong base in US cartoons and the Disney imagination of Mickey Mouse with his plastic toy avatars.

## Japanese Art at Venice[14]

Japanese negotiations with the changing context of international art could be seen by the developing perceptions of Japan's participation at the Venice Biennale. Analysis of the participation at Venice is useful, particularly since the texts on which we can draw are both reliable and indicative of a deepening and developing Japanese understanding of the significance of biennials. The reports on Japanese participation come from a long-standing Japanese bureaucratic habit of reporting on national participation in overseas world expositions and exhibitions, and fastidious noting of the reception and sale of works exhibited.[15] Such reports also show different perceptions of the nature of international artistic flows. In the next section, I will examine how this understanding may change or at least re-contextualize our understanding of Japanese international exhibitions including other Biennials in the 1980s and 1990s.

Shifts in appraisal of Japanese artists internationally were recorded in the commentaries to the various participations at the Venice Biennale. Japan had had sporadic exhibits at the Venice Biennale since the 19th century.[16] In the early 1950s it was clear that sending established Japanese *yôga* artists to Venice was unlikely to meet with international success. Takiguchi Shûzô noted in 1952 that:

> Established Japanese painters have just emerged from an exclusionist, reactionary period, but they need to look back even further in the past and reflect on the path of modernization taken since the Meiji period. That is, they need to undertake a re-examination of modern art. beginning with its fundamentals. What has become as new problem for us is the relevance of Japanese-style painting for the world. A new Japanese art can only be created from Japanese reality, and this reality is not isolated from developments in the rest of the world. If one tries to shut one's eyes and make a unique Japanese art, it will only be treated as a local or regional art. I believe that the *poésie* [poetics] of a global spirit will have the utmost effect on others when it appears in a different form. This is the kind of dialogue that we desire.[17]

This was a frank and immediate postwar declaration that the international level provided a global aesthetic for art which could take Japanese art out of the localism or contingent history in which it had arrived at a 'parallel' modernity by the 1920s. The position was important for having been adopted by the leading Japanese pre-war surrealist poet and critic, but could easily have been countered by the award of prizes to the print-maker Munakata Shikô at São Paolo in 1955 and at Venice in 1956. Although trained as an oil painter, Munakata was in many senses a modern traditionalist whose subject matter was 'Japanese spirit'. Some Japanese informally appointed curators at early post-war Biennials such as Hijikata Teiichi early on noted that:

> As international contacts in art have increased since the war, the inconsistency between domestic and international judgement has become obvious to everyone.[18] ...being different from others, not slavish copying, is an attribute of originality, but penetrating to the source of undiscovered plastic form to achieve self expression is most important. We need to get rid of the bad habit of leaving international valuation up to foreigners. Here too, a contemporary tradition in our own country is badly needed.[19]

Here was a basic contradiction, found later in many discourses elsewhere on global/local comparison and strategies of artistic choice. Hijikata thought that the evaluation of self-expression should be an internalized, domestic contemporary art. He fell back into the domestic evaluation so disliked by Takiguchi who was in favour of international appraisal. In addition, the appraisal of domestic art circles was always likely to prefer artists who were not known internationally. Kamon Yasuo in the summary of his later overall analysis of Japan's participation at Venice posited that the

> basic concept of international exhibitions is to introduce a large number of promising young artists. Perhaps we should reflect on the fact that, in the early days, we only exhibited well-established masters who were nonetheless unknown outside Japan.[20]

Thus the contradiction of domestic evaluation was not merely that it was likely to deal with art which would not find international acceptance, it actively removed the possibility of recognition from younger artists. Kamon was the commissioner of the Japanese exhibit in 1964 when Paris-based Dômoto Hisao won the Arthur Lejwa Prize at Venice. He thought by that time that the wave of new international currents in the 1960s and the concomitant outburst of creative energy meant that the distinction had become even clearer between "domestically-oriented artists who participate in art association exhibitions", and "internationally oriented artists who work and show as individuals and respond to international art trends".

After a hiatus between 1968 and 1974, to which I will return, it became clear in the 1978 Venice Biennale with Nakahara Yûsuke as Commissioner, that some younger artists would see the Biennale as a way of changing Western perceptions of Japan. Suga Kishio, exhibiting at Venice in 1978, wanted to break down the illusory idea of Venice (the West) held by previous Japanese participants as well as the illusions about "Japanese things" held by Westerners and thus changing the structure of these ideas. Suga hoped to introduce an "intrusive feeling" "enabling it to disturb "the typical preconceived ideas of Japan" seen from the West".[21] By the 1980s the view had prevailed that the function of Japanese exhibition at the Venice Biennale, and the Japan Foundation which supported it, was 'how to nurture and develop international artists". 1978 was the year when the old structure of the national pavilions was to be circumvented by the advent of the independently curated *Aperto* sections. From now on these were to be concerned "with effectively presenting the direction of the moment, the dramatic appearance of New Painting or Neo-Expressionism".[22] By 1988 the freshness and langour of the figurative wood sculpture of Funakoshi Katsura was remarked on, "this was probably the first showing in the Japanese pavilion of an artist with a postmodern (or quasi-postmodern) sensibility".[23] By 1993 it was felt by Tatehata Akira that the Japanese Pavilion and *Aperto*,

> have enhanced steadily the international reputation of Japanese art. Quite a few of the artists have been able to go on and exhibit their work in major galleries and museums outside Japan, so generally speaking, the determined efforts of the Japanese officials and participants in the Biennale have been repaid.[24]

Overall participation in Venice, particularly after the *monoha* expansion overseas from the mid-1970s, was felt to be different from earlier locally oriented activities. International exhibitions had become seen as a step to greater opportunities like artist-in-residence programmes and "excessive concern with the impact of the exhibition at Venice had implied quite a change in priorities".[25] The general consensus had always been that the Biennale should provide the opportunity to activate the domestic art scene. Presumably it was to do so by providing a different set of opportunities to younger artists. The next step was a choice between a single-person show or a group show, and there were only two one-person shows, those of Shinoyama Kishin and Kusama Yayoi, in the whole 40 years of post-war participation at Venice,[26] By the time the 40 years' of participation was being re-examined in 1994/95, historical analysis led to the conclusion that "we must be aware that it is time Japan attempted its own international exhibition".[27]

Recognition was beginning to be firmer, although a fact of Japanese artists' residence and work abroad since the 1960s was that for Japanese artists according to Sakai Tadayasu,

> awareness of their native country is not necessarily an imperative. There exists, however, a mechanism which compels them to feel uneasy unless they have something that somehow relates to the heart of Japan, especially when looked at from the outside.[28]

But this position was compromised, according to Nakahara Yûsuke, because

> when Japanese artists are described by non-Japanese as having typically Japanese qualities, they tend to get hurt, thinking that they are associated with a very old-fashioned image of Japan.[29]

Thus, by the mid-1990s Japanese participation was directed at positioning younger artists internationally. But this was still problematic because artists were caught between themselves identifying with Japan and still being over-identified as Japanese by outsiders.

## Structure of Japanese Participation

A few points about the structure of Japanese participation: the method of selection of commissioners and artists is also indicative of changing Japanese official perceptions about the structure of international artistic relations through the medium of Biennale exhibition. In the 1950s, the rather ad hoc appointment of specialists in literary exchanges with Europe such as Takiguchi, or of curators who were specialists in modern European art such as Hijikata, were followed in 1960 by the Japanese decision to formally appoint a commissioner for Venice. The choice of artists was left up to this one individual rather than letting a committee select a broad range of artists which reflected a Japanese domestic range of appraisals, including those of then still influential art groups. This system continued until 1982 when Tani Arata was appointed commissioner; he was the first curator born since World War II. The appointment of a professional to whom choice of artists was left, and one outside the Japanese art association and museum hierarchies, spoke of an increasing self-confidence in the appointment procedure. It indicated a wish to match a younger curator with more contemporary art practices thought to be current internationally. From the 1980s artists were selected from a group of three to five artists born after the war who had been nominated from six different regional recommendations and other information. The final decision was made by Tani, and approval was then sought from those who had made the recommendations. This was clearly a procedure adopted after French antecedents, but there was also study of British Council methods to

> strategically introduce British artists to the world. An intensive effort is made to give the artists international exposure, and an international tour is arranged for the work shown at the Biennale.[30]

In the 1980s, Venice exposition was increasingly seen in Japan as part of a cycle of other international exhibitions in which to further position the Japanese art and the artists selected for Venice. In 1983, there was an exhibition of *Five Contemporary Japanese Artists* at the Düsseldorf Kunsthalle, three of whom had been artists selected for the 1982 Venice Biennale. Kunsthalle exhibitions had since 1968 become the site for a new exhibition type, the theme show curated by an independent curator.[31] In other words, Japanese selection for Venice was increasingly being tied in with perceptions of other international contemporary art and its exhibition sites. When in 1984 Tani Arata, was again appointed Commissioner, the exhibited artists all had prior international exhibition records. The artists were: Itô Kôshô (4th India Triennale, 1978), Takubo Kôji (9th Paris Biennale 1975), and Hori Kôsai (10th Paris Biennale 1977). The need to promote European exposure had been recognized, and a Japan Foundation staff member was assigned as assistant commissioner, the person to occupy this post in 1984 being Nanjô Fumio.[32]

Furthermore, greater sovereignty was given to the curatorial team's decision to select artists who would succeed internationally and the procedure of regional nomination was no longer used, judgment on selection being made by the commissioner alone.

1986 saw the choice of Sakai Tadayasu as Commissioner. The choice of a museum curator from the Museum of Modern Art, Kamakura, probably reflected a greater concern for effective planning of the exhibition "as well as the selection of the artists". At the same time, the importance of thematic selection became increasingly recognized with the creation of *Aperto* as a new site at Venice for curated shows of contemporary practice. The 1988 *Aperto* included Morimura Yasumasa, Ishihara Tomoaki, Endô Toshikatsu, Nishikawa Katsuhiko, and Miyajima Tatsuo. Most importantly, Nanjô Fumio became a member of the international selection committee for *Aperto*. This was due in part to recognition of Japan's economic strength, and in part to the effective intervention of the then British Council official, Henry Meyric-Hughes, who supported Japan's inclusion. It was followed in 1993 when Jeffrey Deitch, an international curator for *Aperto*, selected Yanagi Yukinori's *World Flag Ant Farm*, which won the Swatch Prize, as well as Tsubaki Noboru and Nakahara Kôdai. In the same year *Transactions*, another supplementary exhibition, included Tarô-Chiezô, Morimura Yasumasa, and Yoko-o Tadanori.

By the mid-1990s the increasingly trans-national location of artistic practice was recognized both in the Venice Biennale theme which was "Cardinal Points of Art" and referred to nomadism and "a flexibility transcending national or regional barriers".[33]

Trans-national articulation was shown in the selection of a single artist Kusama Yayoi, only the second one-person show in the Japanese national pavilion, and an artist who had spent much of her creative earlier years in the USA. The selection rather forced the need to consider the notion of an "international artist" in the Japanese context, and 1995 saw the turning point exhibition *Transculture,* the first Japanese-sponsored exhibition outside the national pavilions of the Giardini, and a truly international exhibition where nationality was secondary to curatorial categories and type of artistic practice.[34]

2.1 Yanagi Yukinori, *The World Flag Ant Farm* (1990), as shown at Aperto, Venice, 1993. Ants, colored sand, plastic boxes, plastic tubes, and plastic pipes, 24.0 x 30.0 cm (x179 pieces with 3 monitors). Courtesy of Yanagi Studio.

Nanjô Fumio made several important observations about the structure of the Venice Biennale:[35]

1. The grand prize tended to go to only the most powerful countries. To middle-sized and smaller countries, this appeared to be a reflection of power politics. However, there was a loss of goals for artists once the prize system was abolished.
2. Giardini exhibitions were conservative and there was a need for a place to introduce young talent.
3. There was a lack of unitary theme or overall direction for the Venice Biennale.

But Nanjô made a most frank statement that the role of national artistic selection was over, and in which the production of art was tellingly compared to multi-national car corporation design and assembly techniques:

> My belief that the time is past for simply selling the artist of one's own country to the world. In this postmodern, multicultural period, there are problems with the very idea of categorizing artists according to nationalities. The most important issue is the country where the artist and curators find the source of his or her ideas or where they live. It is like determining the identity of a car which is designed by an American, made in a British factory, and sold under the name of Honda.[36]

## Japanese Perceptions of the Structure of the Venice Biennale

Interacting with the perception of what it meant to exhibit Japanese artists at Venice, and how their selection and curator should be determined, lay the issue of the kind of site Venice was in Japanese perceptions. The clearest perception was that Venice, and indeed most international exhibitions, were about modern art, and by implication "Western" modern art: "an international exhibition of this kind in the West has a single orientation, toward modern art".[37]

What was called "international" or "modern" at least until *Transculture* in 1995 was "Western" and did not involve, or did not yet imply recognition of a separate, parallel, or competitive-conflictual notion of "non-Western" or "Asian" modern art. Japanese reports about Venice were full of shrewd and accurate perceptions about the politics of prize-giving, and its relative significance in appraising the significance of artists. In 1958 it had already been noticed that major prizes in painting and sculpture went to Italians, that Mark Tobey won the Venice Mayor's prize, and that Antoní Tapies won the David E. Bright Foundation Prize. Okada Kenzô won the Astore Meyer Prize and the work was purchased by National Gallery of Modern Art in Rome.

Japanese reports noted that the French were scandalized by the lack of an award to French artists. In 1960, the international jury of the Venice Biennale was kept independent of the national committees. Nonetheless there was conflict over the prize given to the French progenitor of *art informel*, Fautrier (in the Italian pavilion), or to Hans Hartung (in the French pavilion), and there was a telegram intervention by André Malraux on behalf of Fautrier. The most significant shock to French pride came in 1964 when the American Rauschenberg won the Grand Prize for painting, so marking a shift in the perception of the world centre for contemporary art from Paris to New York. This had only partially been deferred in the late 1950s by the international tendency towards *art informel,* typified by the work of Fautrier. In retrospect Malraux's action was clearly observed in Japan as shift towards state intervention in the prize awarding: "what used to be a contest among art dealers for a prize suddenly seemed to have turned into a national competition".[38]

The 1968 Venice Biennale came after the almost year-long student unrest in France and other parts of Europe and there was much media attention on the protests. The Biennale was criticized as a "festival of commercialism and super-powerism",[39] and all artists except Arman closed their exhibitions. The French commissioner Michel Ragon even went to so far as to state "it is an insult to be assigned [to this task] by the De Gaulle regime". The Japanese commissioner in 1968 was Haryû Ichirô, and the "situationist" Takamatsu Jirô won the Carlo Cardazzo prize. Two of the Japanese artists, Takamatsu and Miki, left the decision about opening or closing the Japanese pavilion to Haryû. He decided to keep the Japanese pavilion open because of the request of Sugai Kumi and Yamaguchi Katsuhirô who wanted to exhibit: they had come at their own expense and did not have much chance to show internationally elsewhere.[40] This decision must have been a considerable irony for a well-known leftist art critic like Haryû, but it was greatly to his credit that he supported the artists above all other considerations. His decision to keep the Japanese pavilion open indicated the emergence of a certain Japanese distance from international art fashions.

In 1970 the Biennale Council abolished the prize system. It was observed in Japanese reports that the Biennale authorities sought to put the emphasis on the participation of artists as individuals around a given theme rather than as representatives of countries, despite the costs of their exhibiting still being borne nationally. This position was ignored by national governments. But the problem was more acute because the political problems of Venice were overshadowed by other large openings in the international art scene. Modernist art was being criticized on all sides during the 1970s because of its implication in established or repressive state positions, and there was a real risk of Venice being supplanted by the much better funded Kassel Documenta (Quinquennial) and Paris Biennale for Young Artists (since 1959).[41]

Venice Biennales in the 1970s suffered from the absence of prizes, but this was more a problem of the authority of the Venice Biennale itself. Haryû wrote that "although there has been some modernization in structure and operations, everyone felt that it had lost its authority as an international stage".[42]

Venice was indeed in danger of being superseded from the outside because Szeeman had "successfully presented a representative sampling of the hottest new art movements, including Hyper-Realism, Conceptual Art, and Happenings".[43] Prominent contemporary artists like Estes, Richter, and Dibbets had all been shown in Documenta. At Venice, from the inside, the Japanese commissioner Tôno Yoshiaki noticed that the Italian exhibition of "Works or non-works" challenged the notion of the exhibitable art work. He wrote that this sub-exhibition:

> focused on the opposition between artists who stick to the old forms of "works of art" like painting and sculpture, and the "non-works" which depart from these forms, entering into the space of real life or presenting conceptual situations prior to works of art.[44]

The 1974 Biennale was cancelled, but by 1976 the Biennale had established on a four-year plan, 1974–77 being the first quadriennium. This envisaged a change of emphasis:

1. to make the exhibition more audience-centred.
2. to take an anti-fascist position and cooperate with democratic forces in exile.
3. rather than making a festive, tourist-oriented event, to carry out continuous activities over a four-year period.
4. to expand the exhibition to the entire Veneto region.

Artistic Directors were recruited from outside, like Achille Bonita Oliva, promoter of the concept of "Transavangardia" and Harald Szeeman from Documenta V who was chosen in 1980.

This seismic shift in the positioning of younger curators away from national intervention within the Biennale was followed by other structural changes such as the introduction in 1984 of a substantial catalogue rather than a pamphlet. Post-exhibition documentation was to become a permanent feature of Biennials thereafter and was absorbed, so far as I know, by every other new Biennale in the 1980s and 1990s. In 1986 the prize system was reintroduced, and gradually the policies of participating countries became "more international, politics [as a theme] assumed a prominent place in art".[45]

Official receptions at hotels outside the Biennale became a more prominent part of the social networking among curators and art world people and in 1990 for the first time the Japanese curators and officials held an official party at an hotel. A much more multi-cultural or other-than-exclusively national approach became evident on the part of national pavilions. This had in part been signified earlier by the participation of artists in their country of residence or affiliation rather than natal origin. The Japanese-born artist Kuniyoshi Yasuo had shown in the American pavilion in 1952. In the participation of artists Venice was becoming the site for the manifestation of the "borderless nature of the modern world".[46] Some Japanese curators in retrospect even thought that:

> From now on, in my opinion, it is desirable to work together with curators and artists from other countries to plan Biennale exhibitions, searching together for new directions in art rather than simply showing off Japanese art on a larger scale.[47]

It was the smaller or non-national pavilion exhibitions in *Aperto* at the Arsenale which became the most important markers and certifiers of contemporary practice.

> Participation in these exhibitions has been related to fundamental issues of living in today's world, specifically the issue of contributing to world culture from a global point of view.

However, some Japanese curators like Nakahara Yûsuke presciently warned that if the national system were to be abolished then there would be no need for commissioners. The selection of artists would narrow down and privilege some art world actors: "selection would inevitably concentrate on a number of countries, since there is no one who is perfectly well-informed about contemporary art all over the world".[48]

Nakahara, a curator who was well experienced in international exhibitions in Japan during the 1970s and overseas in the 1980s, recognized that removal of national curators would present problems of evaluation, and also possible concentration or reduction in the choice of selected artists, which is exactly what occurred later.

## International Exposure of Japanese Art in 1980s and 1990s

If we briefly go back to the general sending abroad of art exhibitions from Japan in the 1980s and early 1990s, there was a concerted effort to position Japanese art in the Europe and North America via various modern and contemporary art exhibitions. I have analyzed the selection of artists for these exhibitions elsewhere, and it remains a feature that the cohort of artists selected remained relatively constant and there were only about 30 per cent or fewer new artists introduced to foreign viewers by each successive exhibition.[49] Indeed what was clear about this kind of horizontal, inter-state positioning of Japanese art was that a small cohort was drawn for the purposes of international introduction from a much larger cohort of Japanese artists. This reduced and replicated fraction of national artists became a feature of international circulation of art and artists under the conditions of globalization, almost as if only a numerically restricted list of names were all that could be identified and circulated. But the functionality of this restriction can only be seen, I think, as a feature of curatorial interest on the side of Japanese mediators restricting the outwards flow of Japanese artists.

On the reception side this restriction was reflected in the narrower knowledge-base of non-Japanese, local curators, or in their perception of the reception by a local audience for non-Euramerican and specifically Japanese contemporary art. If the variation in the Japanese artists was too large, the flow would increasingly go beyond the capacity of a limited range of Japanese outward mediators to position them; if the flow was too small, Japanese production would seem monotonous and limited. However, with the movement of Biennale curation into the hands of "independent" artistic directors like Bonito Oliva in 1993 and Harald Szeeman in 1999 and 2001 at Venice, as well as the entry of Nanjô Fumio, a Japanese curator, to selecting for *Aperto* in 1988 and in creating a substitute for it in 1995 with *Transculture*, we might see the level of international Biennials as having been penetrated by another type or level of globalization than just the number and intensity of artists exhibited. The wish to select artists who from several Asian countries together indicated such tranculturality was the artistic component in the ideology of globalism. This was the case whatever particular styles or artists these curators favoured, such as Oliva's selection of Chinese artists in 1993, or Szeeman's showing of many Chinese artists from the Swiss Sigg collection in 1999. Indeed we might from 1995 identify a tension in the selection of artists at biennials between the number of artists and their purported representationality. Maybe international curators began to notice that only a certain number of names and a certain level of national complexity could be recognized at the international level.

If the number of Japanese artists in international circulation was more or less circumscribed at exchange exhibitions between two nation states or metropolitan centres as their surrogate, that is bi-national exhibitions in the early 1990s (e.g. Germany-London, Paris-Berlin, Mexico-Paris), it was also restricted by the advent of new curators at the international level who were seeking representation of art tendencies from Japanese artists in terms of criteria set internationally. That usually meant selection of artists, curators, and gallerists who were active in New York, almost exactly as implied by Nakahara Yûsuke. Thus the exhibitions of Japanese artists in the late 1980s and early 1990s, which almost all involved selection in collaboration with non-Japanese curators, and represented the leading edge of a phenomenon to be much clearer by the end of the 1990s and early 2000s. The artists and art works in circulation at the "international" or "global" level became restricted, rather than their supposed inverse, the increase in the possible range of such circulations under the effects of globalization. This restriction may have been due to the motivated ability of a small number of curators who had access to the information which allowed them to control its flow, as much as to the demand of international curators for a "new" art from "other" cultures. Such demand occurred simultaneously with the restriction on the curators' own absorption and learning capacities due to their status as independent curators with restricted time and budgets for research investment.

Even in 2004, the restriction on flow was quite clear in, for example, a Japanese contemporary art exhibition which I saw in Seoul, "The New Trend of Contemporary Art and Culture of the New Generation". Despite the expansive title this consisted of the works of only two artists and one lecture by a Japanese commentator.[50]

## Japan at Biennials: Yokohama 2001,[51] Gwangju 2004, Busan 2004, and Shanghai 2004[52]

What can be gleaned from Japanese organization and participation at Biennials in the early 2000s for understanding the relation of Japanese art as a national type to trans-national tendencies under globalization? Indeed, did this participation point any further to the nature of globalization processes in art?

The peculiarity of the Yokohama Triennale in 2001 was curation by four different curators, each with their own conceptual position. The Triennale was premised overall on the obsolescence of the scientific approach which would not provide any answers to the problem of "how to relate as individuals to the whole, or how the individual can be singled out from the whole".[53] The exhibition envisaged a flexible approach crossing traditional and professional boundaries with the aim that "we want this exhibition to present a new, more comprehensive vision of the role that art can play in society".[54] The exhibition, as envisaged in the title "Mega-Wave", was seen as "drawing in the accomplishments of all fields of human endeavour".[55] The expression of such grandiose designs was a feature of many other Biennial catalogues. The fact that Japanese curation sought the same kind of scale meant such curation had similarly obvious pretensions as other such declarations. The intention was to meet a perceived international standard, however distanced from achievement the different practical implementations must have made this.

Nakamura Nobuo, one of the four curators at Yokohama Triennale, laid down a progressivist dimension into which this exhibition fitted, from *magiciens de la terre* (1989, Paris) through *Cities on the Move* (1998–2000, Vienna, Bordeaux, New York, Humlebaek [Denmark], Helsinki, and Bangkok) to *Laboratorium* (1999, Antwerp), to *Mutation* (2000, Bordeaux). Albeit this was a progressivist development against the trend of the other major international exhibitions including biennials. Nakamura did not present much substantive argument as to why Yokohama should be on this track save for it having had the intention and willingness to "rethink issues" and address "the creativity of the human race in the 21st century".[56] The modality Nakamura presented was that of "a dialogue that is starting to take place amongst people with heightened sensibilities and new ideas about the future", 30 years after their first appearance in English.[57]

The second curator, Nanjô Fumio included an essay in the catalogue which was basically a compendium of recent ideas from genetics and chaos theory, with citations of the artists Miyajima Tatsuo, Cai Guoqiang, and Mario Merz. He praised ambiguity and concluded after citing Tanizaki Junichirô's 1933 essay *In'ei Raisan* (In Praise of Shadows), that,

> seeing positive value in grey zones is an extremely important attitude for we who are setting sail from desert of chaos for the sea of the post-genom[ic]. The domain of shadows is indeed a fertile source for new life.[58]

I am not quite sure what this mixing of metaphors was intended to achieve save provide intellectual freedom for the curator to select.

The third curator, Tatehata Akira, in a more thought-through piece, positioned the value of nostalgia as a way out from, or for simply handling, the colonial and its residues, and suggested the flexible use of the notion of "Asia as passage" in order to put the "concept of Asia in as broad a perspective as possible". [59] Tatehata was clearly aware too that supposed mutual respect for cultural difference was also a ploy by which chauvinist essentialism was let in by the back door:

> if pluralism means that each regional culture should be maintained in a pure condition, there will be too much emphasis on difference and an unfortunate disdain for eclecticism and mixing. This ultimately leads to the position that it is impossible to translate the meaning of one culture to another.[60]

This was a remarkably supple understanding of the way the globalist acceptance of difference could be a masquerade for the lack of its actual acceptance, and by implication a support for its culturally essentialist rejection, above all in Japan. That this should have been the position of at least one curator in the first Japanese international Triennale meant that some Japanese understandings of globalism in art had gone beyond the national, not as an international compact between nationalities or nation-states, but as a trans-nationality: by implication appeal was made to a trans-cultural and cosmopolitan evaluatory position.

The fourth and last curator, Kômoto Shinji, criticized the application of an "International Standard" for the selection of artists and hoped that the system of four curators had allowed the Yokohama Biennale to step outside this. Moreover, he also considered his own exhibition area, which was in a re-built 19th century brick warehouse separate from the large trade-fair type exposition hall of the other three curators, as in a kind of critical opposition to its chaos. Kômoto, like Nanjô, also resorted to metaphors drawn from recent biological thinking to structure his concepts but in his case used the notion of transmission across cell membranes as a way of understanding how boundaries might be transcended. For him,

> The boundary is not a restrictive barrier that needs to be removed. It is an active intermediary zone that connects the inner and the outer (the self and the other). It can be interpreted as an interface that vitalizes the organism.[61]

In a conclusion which might be an extension of Tatehata's concepts, Kômoto writes,

> We must transmit ourselves in order to know what position we occupy in the world. It thus follows that in order to know our own positions, we must also understand that in a certain sense, we are also forgetting the other.

The language used to position artists so clearly related across these curators to the problem of barrier, the relocation of the knowing subject—be it the curator or the nation-Japan as subject. Indeed, despite all the inter-connectedness of Japanese economy and culture to the world that had increased many times beyond that which followed World War II and US occupation—the notion of incommensurability and barrier was still the implicit tenor of this discourse. Despite the complexity of the process of artist selection across putative cultural boundaries, only in the case of Tatehata were the methods used to understand cultural difference, or to conceptually position artists and works, those germane to this field. In the case of the other three curators, the analytical frame was provided by concepts drawn from anthropology, genetics, and cell biology. It is difficult to judge whether this discursive trope was simply the Japanese avatar of an international tendency to use elaborate metaphors imported from other disciplines, rather than acute and direct social analysis. Certainly light thinking with heavy ideas is a curatorial habit elsewhere and we could simply see its manifestation in this Japanese site as a global tendency within a Japanese context. Alternatively, it was the claim of curators to intellectual status within the Japanese art world which had local and more deep-seated causes.[62]

Nanjô Fumio also wrote a retrospective summary of his experience of the Yokohama Triennale in which he very roundly criticized the system of four curators.[63] He wished to see it replaced by a single overall director who could take responsibility, together with a Non-Profit Company to take charge of organization. This would be rather than the system at Yokohama 2001 where

| YOKOHAMA, 2001, 113 ARTISTS |
|---|
| **Japanese** |
| Aida Makoto, Akasegawa Genpei, Akimoto Kitsune, Akita Masami [Merzbow], Endô Toshikatsu, Fujihata Masaki, Ichihara Hiroko, Ichiyanagi Toshi, Itô Zon, Kasahara Emiko, Kusama Yayoi, Nakagawa Sôchi, Muraoka Saburô, Nakagawa Sôichi [+Laurent Moriceau], Nakazawa Ken, [Nguyen-Hatsushiba Jun], Oda Masanori, Oki Keisuke, Ôno Yôko, Orimoto Tatsumi, Ôzawa Tsuyoshi, Shimabuku, Shinoda Tarô, Shiota Chiharu, Sone Yutaka, Sugimoto Hiroshi, Tabaimo, Tomoita Toshiaki, Tone Yasunao, Tsubaki Noboru [+ Muroi Hisashi], Tsuzuki Kyôichi, Yanagi Miwa [32/113=28.3%] |
| **Korean** |
| Bahc Yiso, Choi Jeong-hwa, Ham Kyung, Koo Jeong-a, Sowon Kwon [5/113=4.2%] |
| **Chinese: [including Overseas, Hong Kong & Taiwan]** |
| Cai Guoqiang, Ding Yi, Huang Yongping, Sun Yuan, Peng Yu, Wu Ershan, Xing Danwen, Yang Fudong, Zhang Huan [9/113=7.9%] |
| **Other Asia-Pacific** |
| Atul Dodiya [India], Destiny Deacon [Australia], Anita Dube [India], Katya Guerrero [Philippines], Heri Dono [Indonesia], Navin Rawanchaikul [Thailand], Stelarc [Australia], Fiona Tan [Indonesia] Rirkrit Tiravanija [Thailand] [9/113=7.9%] |

| GWANGJU, A GRAIN OF DUST, A DROP OF WATER, 2004, 78 ARTISTS |
|---|
| **Japanese** |
| Torimitsu Momoyo, Iijima Kôji [with Daredemo Picasso TV show], Miyajima Tatsuo, Muzucks [Mori Yoshiaki, Mori Masaaki, Horiguchi Kazunori] [4/78=3.1%] |
| **Korean** |
| Jheon Soo-cheon, Park Bul-dong, Jeon Joon-ho, Kim Byung-jon, Kim Seong-young, ECO Artists, Geum Yoong-ki, Buan People, LeeK.H., SAA, Kim Jin-ran, Lim Ok-sang, Lee Jin-yong, Lee Doh-soo, Hwang Ho-sup, Kim Min-jung, Pai Dong-hwan, Koh Hon, Cho Young-nam, Baik Soon-shil, Hong Sin-cha [21/78=26.9%] |
| **Chinese [including Overseas, Hong Kong & Taiwan]** |
| Yue Minjun, Sun Yuan & Peng Yu, Sun Xiaofeng [3/78=3.8%] |
| **Other Asia Pacific** |
| Francis Ng [Singapore], Anish Kapoor [India/UK], Nguyen Minh Thanh [Vietnam], The Kingpins [Australia], Alfredo & Isabel Aquilizan [Philippines], Moelyono [Indonesia], Tisna Sanjaya [Indonesia], Michael Perkowhai [New Zealand] [8/78=10.2%] |
| **Gwangju, Biennale** |
| Amusing footsteps 8 artists<br>Korean / other [6/8=75%] |

| Korea Express 31 Korean artists [100%]<br>And others 50 Korean artists [100%]<br>Ecometro, 2004, 27 artists |
|---|
| **Japanese** |
| Majima Ryôichi, Yamamoto Motoi, Matoba Satami, Tamai Takeshi, Ôishi Hirokazu [5/27=18.5%] |
| **Korean** |
| 14 artists & 5 institutions [19/27=70.3%]<br>Chinese Chinese [including Overseas, Hong Kong & Taiwan]<br>Lin Tianmiao & Wang Gongxin [1/27=3.7%] |
| **BUSAN, CONTEMPORARY ART EXHIBITION, 2004, 137 ARTISTS** |
| **Japanese** |
| Takamine Tadasu, Novaia Liustra [group], Nakamura Masato [3/137=2.1%] |
| **Korean** |
| Bahc Yiso, Choe U-ram, Choi Gene-uk, Han Kye-roon, Park Eun-kuk, Sim Jun-hwan, Yang Haegue, Yoo Young-ho [+Bernhard M. Kinzler], Ahn Chang-hong, Anh Sung-keum, Chang Yong-Chang, Ipgim, Lim Song-ryong, Li Set-byul, Gyon Son-kuk, Song Sang-hee, Yang Man-ki, Hong Sung-min, Im Heung-soon, Jo Seub, Kim Sung-hwan, Lee Yoon-jean [22/137=16%] |
| **Chinese [including Overseas, Hong Kong & Taiwan]** |
| Lu Hao, Shi Qing, Wu Ershan, Yang Fudong [3/137=2.1%] |
| **Other Asia-Pacific** |
| Nindityo Apurnomo [Indonesia], Herman Chong [Singapore], Tran Luong [Vietnam], Tsangaandarin Enkhjargal [Mongolia], Emil Goh [Malaysia/Australia], Rosemary Laing [Australia], Apichatpong Weerasethakul [Thailand], Trinh T. Min-ha [Vietnam/USA] [8/137=5.38%] |
| **BUSAN, SEA ART FESTIVAL, 2004, 46 ARTISTS** |
| **Japanese** |
| Hayakawa Mayu, Kaji Mizuho, Tsubakihara Akiyo [performance] [3/46=6.5%] |
| **Korean** |
| Chung Hyun, Ha Suk-won, Kim In-tae, Kim Yoon-joon, Park Jong-hyun, Choi Hbok, Group [Choi Soon-hwan, Shin Jae-hong, Youn Sung-june], Group [Choi Ji-yeon, Lee Khyung-hou], Chon In-sik, Jang Jun-seok, Jung Dong-myung, Kim Hee-young, Kim Kyoung-ah, Group [Lee Hyun-geol, Kwon Min-gyu, Lee Dong-ju], Sleeping Bird [collective], Yang Hae-chung, Kim Chun-gee [performance], Zo Sung-zin [performance] [18/46=39.1%] |

| **Chinese [including Overseas, Hong Kong & Taiwan]** |
|---|
| Chen Jianhong, Lu Sun [2/46=4.3%] |
| **Other Asia-Pacific** |
| Ajesh S. Kumar [India], Chumpon Apisuk [Thailand, performance] [2/46=4.3%] |
| **BUSAN SCULPTURE PROJECT, 2004, 20 ARTISTS** |
| **Japanese** |
| Saitô Tôru [1/20=5%] |
| **Korean** |
| Kang Yi-soo, Kim Byung-chel, Kim Dong-yeon, Kim Czong-ho, Kim Jin-Soo, Park Eu-seang, Kim Chang-gon, Lee Jong-bin, Kim Jong-gu, Pae Jin-ho, Yi Hwan-kwon [11/20=55%] |
| **Chinese [including Overseas, Hong Kong & Taiwan]** |
| Huo Liang, Sui Jianguo [2/20=10%] |
| **Other Asia-Pacific** |
| Pintor Sirait [Germany/Indonesia] [1/20=5%] |
| **SHANGHAI, 2004, TOTAL ARTISTS 110** |
| **Japanese** |
| Suzuki Ryôko [with Wang Qiang], Nibroll, Ono Yoko [Japan/USA] [2/110=1.8%] |
| **Korean** |
| Choi Jongbum, Park June-bum [2/110=1.8%] |
| **Chinese [including Overseas, Hong Kong & Taiwan]** |
| Big Dipper group, Sun Zhezheng, Wang Kia, Yan Fenglin, Chen Haiyan, Chen Chieh-jen, Chen Shunchu, Chen Xiaouyun, Digital Art Group of Peking University, Zhu Qingsheng, Feng Mengbo, Feng Qianyu, Fu Yu & Jia Haiqing, Gan Zhao & Liang Zi, Geng Jianyi, Gu Xiong, He Jianjun, Hung Tung-lu, Hong Kong Art Centre, Hu Jieming, Hung Keung, Jia Zhangke, Jiang Yue, Ladder to Heaven Group, Cao Fei, Yang Fudong, Leung Meeping, Li Tiangbing, Li Xiao, Li Yang, Liu Shumin, Liu Bingjian, Liu Wei, Liu Zheng, Lü Chunsheng, Ni Haifeng, Ellen Pau, Qiu Shihua, Qiu Zhijie, Qiu Ting, Rongrong & Inri, Shao Yinong & Mu Chen, Su Xia, Sun Liang, Tsai Wen-yin, Tseng Kwong-chi, Tsui Miranda Ngai, Wang Bo, Wang Ningde, Wang Qiang, Wang Xiaoshuai, Wang Youshen, Wei Xing, Wu Ershan, Wu Quan, Xiao Yu, Xu Zhen, Young Hay, Yu Hong, 25000 Cultural Transmission Center & Government of Yanchuan County, Yue Minjun, Zhang Hui, Zhang Peili, Zhang Xiaogang, Zhao Gang, Zhou Hao & Ji Jianzhong, Zhou Tiehai [68/110=61.8%] |

| Other Asia-Pacific |
| --- |
| Tiong Ang [Indonesia], Jun Hatsushiba Nguyen [Vietnam/Japan], Khyentse Norbu [Bhutan], Vong Phaophanit [Laos/UK], Vivan Sundaram [India], Trinh T. Min-ha [Vietnam/USA] [6/110=5.4%] |

the Japan Foundation, Yokohama City, NHK, and Asahi Shinbun were all on the actual organizing committee. Some of the other curators he criticized—although not by name—for only concerning themselves with curation and not taking up the ancillary curatorial tasks: talking to sponsors, operating the appropriate managerial environment, or trying to arrange additional satisfaction for the unpaid volunteers who assisted the Triennale, such as organizing a party for them and the artists. For Nanjô one of the significant features of the Triennale was its ability to attract about 350,000 visitors on a two-day pass, probably around 200,000 individuals, of which he calculates around 180,000 were new to contemporary art. His only observation about criticism was a view that from overseas the exhibition overall seemed to lack a clear direction and from the domestic side that "there were [too] few paintings". Nanjô did not comment on the relationship of works shown to tendencies in art elsewhere and indeed referred to the layout of the four sub-exhibitions by naming them by their curators, such as in "Nanjô's artists", "Tatehata's artists" et cetera. He named neither international connections or significance, although there was considerable attention to how the artists and some works were placed in the various spaces for "exhibition effect". Another critic, Nantô Hiroshi, commented on the absence of a symposium which had meant that even though "there were not very many overseas critics and curators" who came, they could at the next meeting of *aica* (Association Internationale des Critiques d'Art) "make meaningful suggestions to the organizers".[64]

Analysis by Hasegawa Yûko about Istanbul 2000 which she had curated, was far more forthright in situating that biennial. She intended,

> ...a positive proposal on how culture could function as a device for resistance under conditions where there had been much criticism given about the influence on spiritual and cultural matters of the global economy such that it could be called a new colonialism.[65]

Hasegawa clearly situated her Biennale in a globalizing context again using some biological concepts to suggest a theme based on the idea that "whilst recognizing the ego, that there would be a "lithe" [*shinayaka*] escape from it, in which a separation and a distance could be held whose result was that a field of consciousness could be held in common with the other".[66]

> As in the warm acceptance by the people of Istanbul, the success of the first large scale exhibition in our country the Yokohama Triennale showed the present multiplicity of expression just as it is through the high quality of the

works. How each exhibition actually functions differs in each country and city. The most important thing is that the curator first of all creates for the people living there and combined with their own history truly considers what kind of dialogue is possible in that temporal space.[67]

Whilst Hasegawa was full of praise for the "multiplicity of expression" shown at Yokohama, she was more concerned to relate her exhibition conception and selection to the demands of a place or site, and fairly clearly to a quite different and globalized problematic than Nanjô. His position was derived from the pragmatics of his experiences at Venice and other Japanese exhibitions in Europe where the relevance of the nation-state as a constructor of the art expressions of artists no longer seemed valid, either due to the artists' very mobility or to the permeability of the nation-state as a unit. But like three of the curators at Yokohama, including Nanjô, Hasegawa resorted to heavily biological metaphors to interpret the context in which she worked and had established exhibition goals: she did not offer an analysis of the structures of art institutions themselves. This detachment of reflective, conceptual analysis from the avowed practice of a good few curators may be due to the complexity of the interests they must satisfy, and to their own self-interest in cultural brokerage. That they were so enabled in their practice may be seen as one of the most telling effects of globalism. Why, after all, should *national* actors, be seen as making *non-national* aesthetic decisions in selecting artist and works?

## By Way of a Conclusion

It is quite revealing to look at some simple statistics which show the overall structure of Biennials into which Japanese exhibition has fitted. We can see that against the 28.3 per cent of Japanese artists to total artists exhibiting at Yokohama, there were 26.9 per cent Koreans in the main exhibition *A Grain of Dust* at Gwangju, 16 per cent Koreans in the *Contemporary Art Exhibition* at Busan, and 61.8 per cent Chinese artists at Shanghai. However, if we take the total number of Korean artists in all the collected exhibitions at Gwangju the real percentage of Korean artists to total artists exhibited was more like 65.4 per cent.[68] There were thus around twice as many Korean artists at Gwangju and Chinese artists at Shanghai as there were Japanese artists at Yokohama. Around 2–8 per cent of artists at Gwangju and Shanghai were Japanese or Chinese, whereas around 4–7 per cent were Korean or Chinese at Yokohama. We can thus see, perhaps counter to expectations, that the Yokohoma Triennale was far more internationalized than Gwangju and Shanghai—although not as highly as Busan. The Yokohama Triennale as an exhibition event (in 2002) was far more strongly constructed as a world event than the other two Asian Biennials. This was due both to deliberate policy on the part of the exhibition organizers, but also to the far greater openness of the Japanese art world to outside currents.

2.2 Muzucks [Horiguchi Kazuya, Mori Akira] work in smoking booth with director Yi Yoon-wu, Gwangju.

The Japanese experience of exhibiting at Venice, with its careful if bureaucratically directed history, also indicated, if we take the Yokohama Triennale as its result, that globalization of a domestic art world or its contact zone with a putatively international one, was only achieved as the result of a long-drawn out series of contacts from the national to the international level. It was not achieved by the immediate organization of a Biennale or Triennale as such.

## Notes

1 John Clark, "Japanese Contemporary Art and Globalization, largely seen from participation in the Venice Biennale" (Revised version of conference lecture, *Globalization, Localization and Japanese Culture in the Asia Pacific Region: an International Symposium*, Singapore, 28–30 October 2004). I am grateful to Nanjô Fumio's office in 1995 and to Furuichi Yasuko of the Japan Foundation in 2004 for the provision of some catalogue materials.

2 See John Clark, "Chapter 7: The Global", in *Asian Modernities: Chinese and Thai Art Compared, 1980 to 1999* (Sydney: Power Publications, 2010).

3 See the introductory essay by Yaguchi Kunio, "The Venice Biennale and Japan", in Harumi Miwa, ed., *The Venice Biennale: 40 Years of Japanese Participation* (Tokyo: The Japan Foundation; Tokyo: The Mainichi Newspapers, 1995), 11.

4 In English see, for example, Jackie Menzies, ed., *Modern Boy, Modern Girl: Modernity in Japanese Art, 1910–1935*, co-curated by Ajioka et al. (Sydney: Art Gallery of New South Wales, 1998); Elise Tipton and John Clark, ed., *Being Modern*

*in Japan: Culture and Society from the 1910s to the 1930s* (Sydney: Australian Humanities Research Foundation; Honolulu: University of Hawai'i Press, 2000); Gennifer Weisenfeld, *Mavo: Japanese artists and the avant-garde 1905–1931* (Berkeley: University of California Press, 2002); Kaido Kazu and David Elliott, *Reconstructions: Avant-Garde Art in Japan 1945–1965* (Oxford: Museum of Modern Art, 1985); Alexandra Munro et al., *Scream Against the Sky: Japanese Art after 1945* (New York: Harry N. Abrams, 1994).

5 The most telling index of this Japanese knowledge and its thoroughness is in the ten-volume series, *Sekai Bijutsu Zenshû* (Tokyo: Heibonsha, 1928–30).

6 On "nested endogeny" see John Clark, Introduction of *Asian Modernities: Chinese and Thai Art in the 1980s and 1990s* (Sydney: Power Publications, 2010).

7 See for example, John Clark, "The Conditions for Post-Modernity in Japanese Art of the 1980s", in *Japanese Encounters with Postmodernity*, ed. Johann Arnason and Yoshio Sugmimoto (London: Kegan Paul International, 1995), now reprinted in John Clark, *Modernities of Japanese Art* (Leiden: Brill, 2013).

8 See for example the essay by Kishida translated in *Modern Boy, Modern Girl*.

9 This could be seen expressed in September 2004 in a personal conversation with Tatehata Akira in Gwangju, Korea.

10 See Arjun Appadurai, *Modernity at Large: Cultural Dimensions of Globalization* (Minneapolis: University of Minnesota Press, 1996).

11 I cannot follow this in detail here. See Jürgen Habermas, *The Theory of Communicative Action*, 2 volumes, trans. Thomas McCarthy (London: Heinemann, 1984).

12 Bert Winther-Tamaki has indicated that the very word yôga, meaning "Western painting" also has the connotation of "international" almost from its 19th century inception in Japan. See Bert Winther-Tamaki, "Global Consciousness in Yôga Self-Portraiture" in *Crossing Cultures: Conflict, Migration and Convergence*, ed. Jaynie Anderson (Melbourne: Mieygunyah Press, 2009).

13 See Clark, "Chapter 7: The Global", in *Asian Modernities*.

14 Japanese art at Venice is conveniently thoroughly surveyed in Miwa, *The Venice Biennale*. I quote extensively from this work which is unfortunately not widely available because as an important survey touching on many aspects of post-World War II Venice Biennials it deserves to be much better known outside Japan or Japanese Studies circles. It details in both Japanese and English translation the reports of curators about that year's Japan Pavilion exhibits. The reports are full of appraisals, from a Japanese position, of what were perceived to be changes in the kind of work exhibited at Venice that were likely to draw international attention. Thus it also forms an important historical source for understanding changes at Venice overall and of the international art world in the period it covers.

15 In 1995, when the French artistic director Jean Claire cancelled *Aperto*, there was also a major Japanese intervention at Venice in the form of the exhibition funded by the Fukutake Science and Culture Foundation which sought to situate work of artists from a wide range of non-Euramerican cultures. See Nanjô Fumio et al., curators, *TransCulture* (Tokyo: The Japan Foundation & Fukutake Science and Culture Foundation, 1995). Japanese reports about Venice usually appeared in Bijutsu Techô at the time of the Venice Biennale, such as the special issue in September 1995.

16 These reports go back to those for participation in the 1873 Wiener Weltaustellung, and are carefully kept in the archives of the Tokyo Cultural Properties Research Institute. They were also followed in domestic exhibition reports. See for example the illustrations from the 1877 Domestic Manufactures Exhibition in John Clark, *Modernities of Japanese Art* (Leiden: Brill, 2013), 83. The great Japanese scholar of international expositions was Yoshida Mitsukuni who first brought these issues to my attention in about 1975. See, inter alia, Yoshida Mitsukuni, *Bankoku hakurankai no kenkyū* (Kyoto: Sibunkaku Shuppan, 1986); *Bankokuhaku no Nihonkan* (Tokyo: IMAX, 1990); *Zusetsu bankoku hakurankaishi, 1851–1942* (Kyoto: Shibunkaku Shuppan).

17 In 1897 at the 2nd Biennale, a large display of Japanese arts and crafts was sent of 75 works, including 35 *nihonga*, and was organized by Nihon Bijutsu Kyôkai which then had 1,067 members, Naganuma Moriyoshi being sent to handle works. In 1924 the 14th Biennale included a display of 13 paintings and prints, and in the 1928 16th Biennale Léonard Foujita [Fujita Tsuguji, then resident in Paris] was included in special School of Paris section. In the 1930 17th Biennale one work by Terasaki Takeo was shown. He had studied etching in Italy. In 1931 planning of Japanese national pavilion was begun, but was scrapped after outbreak of the war with China. It was also later proposed that Japan take over the pavilion of Austria in 1942. In 1934 at the 9th Biennale, work by Kuniyoshi Yasuo was shown in American pavilion, as also in the 22nd Biennale of 1940. See historical materials in Miwa, ed., *The Venice Biennale.*

18 Takiguchi Shûzô was the surrealist poet and translator of the 1st Surrealist manifesto who forms an important critical bridge between the pre-war avant garde and the post-war art world. Miwa, ed., *The Venice Biennale*, 12.

19 Miwa, ed., *The Venice Biennale*, 12.

20 Hijikata Teiichi was the founding director of the Museum of Modern Art, Kamakura from 1951. Miwa, ed., *The Venice Biennale*, 13.

21 Miwa, ed., *The Venice Biennale*, 216. Suga also thought in a kind of internationalized manifesto of Mono-ha ideas that, from their position seeing means that something must be seen, but in contrast to this, in the content of the "completely Japanese thing" I am seeking, I give positive value to the vague, indistinct realm on the periphery of objects which have definitive presence, things which can be seen but cannot, which exist but are not there.

22 Miwa, ed., *The Venice Biennale*, 33.

23 Miwa, ed., *The Venice Biennale*, 38.

24 Miwa, ed., *The Venice Biennale*, 39.

25 Miwa, ed., *The Venice Biennale*, 15.

26 Miwa, ed., *The Venice Biennale*, 218.

27 Miwa, ed., *The Venice Biennale*, 218.

28 Miwa, ed., *The Venice Biennale*, 218.

29 Miwa, ed., *The Venice Biennale*, 217.

30 Miwa, ed., *The Venice Biennale*, 14.

31 Since that curated by Harald Szeeman, *When Attitudes Become Form* of 1968 at the Bern Kunsthalle.

32 Nanjô mentions there were three jury meetings to plan *Aperto* 1988. The first meeting was for getting to know the other curators to discuss basic issues, the second meeting deliberated artists' selection. Nanjô showed some but not all of his

slides, and at a third meeting eight artists were selected, and guidelines laid down based on key words between curators agreed at the second meeting. Selection was by strong support or majority support, rejection by not particularly strong support or opposition by one of the juries. Nanjô took 15 portfolios to the third meeting, of which 5 were accepted (Miwa, ed. *The Venice Biennale*, 202). One juror said that "since the artists chosen by *Aperto* have increased in value in the art market, we must be very careful", thus indicating a sharp awareness by curators of the economic impacts of their selection judgments (Miwa, ed., *The Venice Biennale*, 200).

33 Miwa, ed. *The Venice Biennale*, 39.

34 The artists exhibited at *TransCulture* were: Gordon Bennett [born and working in Australia], Frédéric Bruly Bouabré [born and working in Ivory Coast], Cai Guoqiang [born in China and working in New York], Ping Chong [born in Canada and working in [USA, New York], Simryn Gill [born in Malaysia, then living and working in Singapore], Joseph Grigely [born and working in USA], Kômura Masao [born and living in Japan], Shani Mootoo [born in Ireland, working in Canada], Murakami Takashi [born in Japan, then working in Japan, also in USA, New York], Shirin Neshat [born in Iran, working in USA, New York], Alwin Reamillo & Juliet Lea [born in Philippines and UK, working in Philippines & Australia], Technocrat [artist group founded in 1990 in Japan by Ameya Norimisu], Adriana Varejão [born and working in Brazil], World Tea Party [artist group born and working in Canada], Rene Yung [born in Hong Kong and working in USA, San Francisco]. For details see Fumio et al., curators, *TransCulture*.

35 Miwa, ed., *The Venice Biennale*, 197–202.

36 Miwa, ed., *The Venice Biennale*, 201.

37 Miwa, ed., *The Venice Biennale*, 11.

38 Miwa, ed., *The Venice Biennale*, 216. See also Fleck, "Robert Rauschenberg: Der Triumph der US-Avantgarde" in *Die Biennale von Venedig* (2009): 144–60.

39 Miwa, ed., *The Venice Biennale*, 24.

40 Miwa, ed., *The Venice Biennale*, 24.

41 Miwa, ed., *The Venice Biennale*, 31.

42 Miwa, ed., *The Venice Biennale*, 31.

43 Miwa, ed., *The Venice Biennale*, 31.

44 Miwa, ed., *The Venice Biennale*, 32.

45 Miwa, ed., *The Venice Biennale*, 38.

46 Miwa, ed., *The Venice Biennale*, 201.

47 Miwa, ed., *The Venice Biennale*, 201.

48 Miwa, ed., *The Venice Biennale*, 217.

49 See chapter 11 of John Clark, *Modern Asian Art* (Sydney: Craftsman House; Honolulu: University of Hawai'i Press, 1998). This text was written in 1995. The exhibitions were:

- Kathy Halbreich, Kômoto Shinji, Nanjô Fumio, and Thomas Sokolowski, *Against Nature: Japanese Art in the 1980s* (New York: New York University Grey Art Gallery, 1989). [Toured USA, 15 June 1989–12 February 1991]
- Nakahara Yûsuke et al., *Europalia 89: Japan in Belgium* (Gent: Museum van Hedenndaagse Kunst, 1989). [Belgium, 28 October 1989–7 January 1990]

- Hara Toshio and Howard T. Fox, *A Primal Spirit* (Tokyo: Hara Museum of Contemporary Art; Los Angeles: Los Angeles County Museum of Art, 1990). [Toured USA, 10 March 1990–22 September 1991]
- Kondô Yukio, Nanjô Fumio, and Peter Weiermaier, *Japansicher Kunst der Achtziger Jahre* (Frankfurt: for the Frankfurter Kunstverein from Edition Stemmle, 1990). [Frankfurter Kunstverein then 15 February–April 1991, Museum moderner Kunst, Wien]
- Namba Hideo and Okada Takahiko, *Japan Art Today* (Tokyo: Sezon Museum of Art, 1990). [Scandinavia, 24 January 1990–25 August 1991]
- Judy Annear and Tatehata Akira, *Zones of Love* (Sydney: Museum of Contemporary Art, 1991). [Australia, May 1991–September 1992]

50 The exhibition was *Saki + Eri: New Stances and Popular Imagination of Contemporary Art in Japan* held from 17 September to 16 November 2004 on the ground floor of the Hungkuk Life Insurance Building and organized by Ilju Art House. The same building houses the Japan Foundation Korea offices as well as those of the British Council. The artists were Yoshimiura Eri and Satomi Saki and the lecture was by Matsui Midori. In addition there was a lecture by Yee Yongro, as well as performances and talks by the artists.

51 The primary information on Yokohama is derived from the catalogue Makabe Kaori, Mikami Yutaka, and the Yokohama Triennale Office, ed., *Yokohama Triennale 2001* (Yokohama: The Organising Committee for Yokohama Triennale, 2001). I have also referred to earlier statements on the website by the curators. There is also a special issue of the *Newsletter*, 2 (November 2001), including articles not only by Nanjô Fumio on 2001 Yokohama, but also by Hasegawa Yûko on the 2000 Istanbul Biennale, and by Shimizu Toshio on the 2000 Shanghai Biennale where both were curators.

52 The Japanese, Korean, Chinese, and other Asia-Pacific artists exhibited at these exhibitions were as follows, with the ratio of each category of artists to total artists given as percentages. Collectives were counted as one artist for this purpose. I have not attempted to derive separate figures for the categories of European, North America, Latin American, African, or Middle Eastern artists who also make up the figure for total artists.

53 Nakamura Nobuo, "Future for Today", in *Yokohama Triennale 2001*, ed. Kaori, Yutaka, and Yokohama Triennale Office, 18.

54 Kaori, Yutaka, and Yokohama Triennale Office, ed., *Yokohama Triennale 2001*, 13.

55 Kaori, Yutaka, and Yokohama Triennale Office, ed., *Yokohama Triennale 2001*, 13.

56 Kaori, Yutaka, and Yokohama Triennale Office, ed., *Yokohama Triennale 2001*, 18.

57 Kaori, Yutaka, and Yokohama Triennale Office, ed., *Yokohama Triennale 2001*, 18. As his sole cited intellectual support Nakamura chooses the 2000 Japanese translation of Gregory Bateson's collection of earlier essays brought together in 1971. Gregory Bateson, *Steps to an Ecology of Mind* (New York: Ballantine Books, 1972). Bateson's earliest and celebrated work was *Naven* published in 1936, six years after the first edition of William Empson's *Seven Types of Ambiguity*.

58 Kaori, Yutaka, and Yokohama Triennale Office, ed., *Yokohama Triennale 2001*, 49.

59 Kaori, Yutaka, and Yokohama Triennale Office, ed., *Yokohama Triennale 2001*, 88.

60 Kaori, Yutaka, and Yokohama Triennale Office, ed., *Yokohama Triennale 2001*, 89.

61 Kaori, Yutaka, and Yokohama Triennale Office, ed., *Yokohama Triennale 2001*, 117.

62 These are too deep to go into here but involve the culture of translation and use of translated terms in intellectually fashionable Japanese discourse, in a kind of institutionalized intellectual snobbism. There is also a prejudice against nonintellectual art which is part of one side of the history of the Japanese avant garde. On the other side is a grandiose and sometimes aggressive expressionism as seen in the work of Okamoto Tarô, amongst others.

63 See Nanjô Fumio, "Yokohama Toriennaare 2001 kôki – sono tenmatsu no kojinteki memorandamu", in *aica Japan Newsletter*, 2 (November 2001).

64 *aica Japan Newsletter*, 2 (November 2001): 8.

65 *aica Japan Newsletter*, 2 (November 2001): 9.

66 *aica Japan Newsletter*, 2 (November 2001): 10.

67 *aica Japan Newsletter*, 2 (November 2001): 11.

68 That is, 127/194 = 65.4% [or ((21+6+31+50+19)/(78+8+31+50+27)) x 100 = 65.4].

Chapter 3

# Biennials as National Art Sites: Between Local and International Artworlds, Chinese Art at Biennials since 1993

The exhibition of Chinese art at biennials since 1993 at Venice is a very complex field with multiple levels of activity that include geographically disparate sites, and multiple, diverse actors.[1] Furthermore from the 1990s, temporary but recurrent exhibitions such as biennials and triennials themselves became a major phenomenon in international art activity into which the exhibition of Chinese contemporary art fitted. Thus, in addition to a very active function in *newly canonizing* domestic contemporary art, biennials had as important a role in mediating to Chinese audiences what for China were previously unseen but *already canonized* international works and artists. This was particularly true of the exhibition for the first time in China of photographic works by Cindy Sherman in 2003 and of video works by Matthew Barney in 2005 at the Shanghai Biennale.

There has been Asian intervention, including in China, by the founding of biennials with a significant international component and direction at Beijing, Busan, Guangdong, Gwangju, Shanghai, and Yokohama. There were other more localized Biennials such as Chengdu, or what might be called "quasi-biennials" such as some exhibitions at Shenzhen. There were many exhibitions which amounted to "state-of-the-field" surveys of modern and contemporary Chinese art which were frequently seen overseas during the 1990s, in which the curatorial line as well as the very curators of the exhibitions cannot be separated from the biennial structure.

Moreover, the content of art practice exhibited at the international level changed during the period of increasing Chinese participation, and this participation in itself was a factor in that change. Whilst Chinese contemporary art was engaged with international structures that it could not direct, those mediating Chinese contemporary art and, in certain measure, the practices adopted by Chinese artists themselves, were agentive with regard to the international field. They were not wholly passive reactors to international trends. That this agency was almost entirely motivated by various and often conflicting domestic agendas, in addition to the sheer exigencies of survival for the particular artists, did not also mean that those Chinese artists and curators active in the international field were unmindful of the international tendencies in art to which they contributed. This was especially the case for those art practices which met with official disapproval in the 1990s such as performance art, installation art, and the first wave of video art. This agency applied to those works with shocking articulations of the human body or dead organic matter, precisely when these works were accused in some official circles of being vapid, imitative or "un-Chinese" following of foreign tendencies. The last accusation was a convenient way of ignoring how much these practices sprang from the realities of everyday Chinese life, and from cultural values which were specifically Chinese in provenance. Such "cadaver" works were also drawn by truculent negation of more, formally conceived fine artworks found in Chinese art academies.[2]

## Types of Exhibitions and Curators

When one looks at where Chinese contemporary art was exhibited and by whom since the 1980s, it seems sensible to identify a typology of sites, exhibitions, and curators. Different types of exhibition usually involved a different kind of institutional site and these employed different sorts of curator.[3] Obviously these categories can be refined and multiplied, but listing them in some way as follows has the merit of allowing us to understand the multiplicity of levels at which questions of Chinese art exhibition in the international environment were articulated. This environment included the international component of domestic exhibitions sited in China, especially the biennials and triennales at Beijing, Guangzhou, and Shanghai.

These categories indicate the plurality of sites, exhibitions, and curators to be considered. They also show that these were not infinite in number, not irregular, and not randomly articulated. Just as importantly, they indicate that the large number of artists shown at these exhibitions does not mean that this cohort was unrestricted. Careful examination of the artists selected, by whatever system, shows that they were relatively narrowly and repetitively chosen. That is, the artists formed a restricted cohort from which selection was made and some artists or groupings of artists were regularly recruited.

| TYPES OF EXHIBITION SITE | |
|---|---|
| Museums of art | Smithsonian Museum Sackler Gallery, National Gallery of Australia, China Art Gallery |
| Museums of Asian art | San Francisco Asian Art Museum, Pacific Asia Museum |
| Museums of contemporary art | Centre Pompidou, Museum of Modern Art Oxford, Chengdu |
| Non-profit but regularly funded museums, galleries, and art centres | |
| • Kunsthalle-type galleries or regional art centres | Wiener Secession, CAPC Musée d'art contemporain de Bordeaux, Shanghe Meishuguan (Upriver Gallery, Chengdu)[4] |
| • Small not-for-profit Institutes of Modern and/or Contemporary Art | Gallery 4A Sydney, Centre A, Vancouver |
| • Commercial galleries with some non-commercial functions | HanartTZ, Sherman Galleries, Ethan Cohen, Shanghart, Redgate, Courtyard |

This regularity or restriction indicates the presence of a structure which, to be unified, must have, in an operational sense, implied a certain definition of contemporary Chinese art. A limited definition of the "contemporary" in China would be that art which emerged in the 15 or so years since 1985, and which usually eschewed academy art practices and definitions of the finished artwork.[5] It was the medium itself, as well as the content to which its deployment ostensibly referred, that defined contemporaneity or more specifically contemporary art practice. Thus, there was present in China from the late 1980s to late 1990s installation, performance, video, certain types of conceptual sculpture, and non-documentary photography. Enwezor wished to add the qualification that, "even if the names are repeated in different places, it's very important to see them [different types of exhibitions including biennials] as completely different events".[6] The professional position of curators inclines them to this view, almost one of professional distinction. But regularity at one level, that of the participating artists, was not overcome on another level, the variety of different works, to constitute different exhibitions. This was a necessary, if professionally required, viewpoint. When both the artists and the mediators/curators provided such regularities, the variety seen from some perspective in the works was merely a currency which linked the other two in a privileged game.

For the Chinese artists the critical issue, or constituting element, of their discourse was non-acceptance by the "official" art world. Artists in most cases were not until around 2000 producing work recognized by the Chinese art academies and other official exhibition institutions. This change in official policy was shown in 2001 by official participation for the first time in an overseas exhibition of contemporary Chinese art at the Hamburger Bahnhof in Berlin, and by official participation in 2002 at the Bienal de São Paulo.

| TYPES OF EXHIBITION | |
|---|---|
| Biennials, Triennales, and other recurrent exhibitions of Contemporary Art | |
| • Chinese artist(s) shown in the national pavilion, or as a single-artist representative | Venice Biennale, São Paolo Bienal |
| • Chinese artist exhibited as part of a whole Biennale thematic | Lyon Biennale 2002 |
| • Chinese artist shown as part of a curated section of a larger Biennale | *Zones of Urgency*, Venice 2003 |
| National Survey exhibitions | "I Don't Want to Play Cards with Cézanne" and Other Works, *China Avant Garde, Inside-Out* |
| Conceptually based, "zeitgeist" or tendency exhibitions | |
| • China included but not central | *Magiciens de la Terre, Zones of Urgency* |
| • China the topic | *China Avant Garde, New Art From China, Alors, La Chine?* |
| One-person exhibitions at various sites beyond commercial galleries | Cai Guoqiang at Iwaki, Xu Bing at Sackler, Washington, Guan Wei at Museum of Contemporary Art Sydney, Chen Zhen at Serpentine, London, Shen Yuan at Arnolfini, Bristol |
| Virtual exhibitions in printed or electronic form | *Fresh Cream* and its successors, the defunct chinese-art.com and the many Chinese domestic art-related websites with a significant international reporting function, like tom.com |

The most noticeable aspects of international exhibition of Chinese contemporary art were early exhibitions of a developing modern painting from 1987 in the US, biennials outside China from 1993 at Venice, and inside China from 1996 at Shanghai. But there were a limited number of curators involved, with above all the prominence of Hou Hanru and Chang Tsong-zung. Also present, especially towards the end of the 1990s, were Wu Hung and Zheng Shengtian, and none of these were mainland China residents (Chang was residing in Hong Kong, Hou Hanru in Paris, Wu Hung in the US, and Zheng Shengtian in Canada). The curators residing in China who became most active internationally, mostly after 2000, were Fan Di'an, Pi Li, and Huang Du.

| CURATORS TYPIFIED BY INSTITUTIONAL AFFILIATION | |
|---|---|
| Employed in public museums | Alain Sayag, Han Ulrich-Obrist, Claire Roberts, Xu Hong, Zhang Qing |
| Independent curators | Fei Dawei (1990–2002), Hou Hanru, Harald Szeemann, Martina Köppel-yang, Zhang Zhaohui, Okwui Enwezor |
| Private museum curators | Fei Dawei (2003–07) |
| Academics or other higher educational teachers or researchers | Fan Di'an, Leng Lin, Jonathan Hay, Wu Hung |
| Art journalists | Huang Du (until 2002), Michel Nuridsany |
| Commercial gallerists | Chang Tsong-zung |
| Non-profit centre directors | Huangfu Binghui, Alice Jim Ming-wai |
| Collectors or patrons with an important curatorial perspective | Jean-Michel Ducrop, Ulli Sigg, Guy Ullens |

It would appear that China first participated as a country at the Venice Biennale in 1980 with an embroidery exhibited in the corner of the Yugoslav pavilion.[7] This was followed by unofficial participation in *Aperto* in 1993,[8] other works shown in 1997, and then by exhibition of large parts of the Ulli Sigg collection in 1999. What would have been the first official participation in a national pavilion funded by the Chinese Ministry of Culture in 2003 was cancelled because of the SARS epidemic. These works were exhibited as a group in September 2003 in Beijing at the time of the first Beijing Biennale (see cover illustration for this book).

Anticipating this official drift were the curatorial activities of Chang Tsong-zung, the Hong Kong art gallerist who in many ways functioned as a cultural mediator and commentator on contemporary Chinese art and had exhibited the first artists from mainland China at São Paulo in 1994 and another group at Venice in 1995. He had also worked as the invited curator at São Paolo for a Chinese mainland artist and one Hong Kong artist in 1996. Chang Tsong-zung was also involved with significant exhibitions in not-for-profit spaces such as the Fruitmarket Gallery, Edinburgh in 1996, or large exhibitions in commercial spaces but which amounted to a contemporary Chinese art survey show such as *Paris-Pékin* in 2002. In retrospect, Chang Tsong-zung's work had an important bridging function which began with his exhibition of many artists from mainly his gallery collection, *China's New Art, Post 1989*, in 1993. This process from time-to-time involved the semi-ostracized mainland critic Li Xianting as a writer or co-curator, and kept up an international exposure for a small group of contemporary Chinese artists, before the seismic shift in overseas exhibition exposure began with the massive display at Venice in 1999.

3.1 Lü Shengzhong, *Landscape Study 2* (2003). Exhibited at *Synthi-Scapes*, Chinese Pavilion of the 50th Venice Biennale 2003, Guangdong. Photograph by John Clark.

Exhibition sites were strongly correlated with the purposes of particular cohorts of China watchers, such as Richard L. Strassberg, and a small number of non-Chinese museum curators and critics in the 1980s to early 1990s, such as Jean-Hubert Martin in France, and Marianne Brouwer in the Netherlands. These sites changed with the rise of new and largely non-China based curators in the 1990s, with a noticeable increase in the range of sites at the end of the 1990s. Thereafter a new willingness emerged by the state to engage in the field of contemporary Chinese art as an aspect of China's repositioning in the world. A new cohort of Chinese curators based in China not only occupied the slots in pre-existing site activities such as at São Paolo and Venice biennials, they actually positioned China as a national unit which was to join in the international process of defining contemporary art, and therefore by implication put China forward as a prescriptor of contemporary art.[9]

Among types of exhibition, biennials must not be regarded as homogenous. They include within them invited national participation in a pavilion as at Venice, or of a single artist as at São Paolo, together with curated thematic exhibitions such as at Venice when a theme is usually announced every other year in January for the following June. Alongside this, aspects of contemporary art practice were surveyed in exhibitions which were loosely conceived of as more openly defining contemporary practice, as at *Aperto* in Venice since 1980. These became very large sub-curated exhibitions, essentially freely delegated to individual curators who both defined their exhibition conception and often were significantly engaged in fund-raising and promotion. Examples at Venice were *Transculture* in 1995, or *Zones of Urgency* and *Utopia Station* in 2003. Indeed *Zones of Urgency* whilst curated by one person, Hou Hanru, actually contained a further sub-exhibition within it, that of artists from Guangdong in *Canton Express*. Incidentally, Hou Hanru was originally from Guangdong, and had his first major participation in a performance event with Yang Jiechang there in 1987. He would appear always to have maintained his links with artists from his home province.

By 1999 Chinese participation had become normal in most sections of the Venice Biennale and at São Paolo, with the national pavilion at Venice being organized from 2003 (as noted above, unrealized in that year). By time of the Gwangju and Busan biennials in 2004, Chinese participation had become standard at international biennials, in both those cases running at around 2 per cent to 4 per cent of the artists selected in the international sections.[10]

3.2 *Zones of Urgency* at the 50th Venice Biennale. Photographer anonymous.

But the almost implacable advance of contemporary Chinese art at major biennials masked a very different series of stories. It should first be recalled that most art at biennials had not been exhibited there first, and there were often cases where the work illustrated in the catalogue was not the work which was actually exhibited at the biennale. Moreover, the art shown at biennials rested on many other different types and levels of exhibition of Chinese contemporary art.

Among these were introductory surveys of private or corporate collections, sometimes with fairly transparent political or business agendas such as the *Beyond the Open Door* exhibition of 1987, with its catalogue introduction by Henry Kissinger. There were public displays of the private taste of some members of the European business elite such as the exhibitions of the Sigg, Ullens, or Uyterhage collections at various times in Europe. These were paralleled by much more inclusive but also modest exhibitions such as the Paris Centre Chine EHESS exhibition in 1987 which showed the very real scale of artistic movement and the range of artists present in one non-Chinese metropolis at a date before the institutional recognition of contemporary Chinese art elsewhere in 1989, 1993, 1999 and 2003. It pointed to the pitiless indifference of curatorial fashion until external events such as the growth of the Chinese economy, or the world political significance of domestic Chinese events like the 4 June 1989 Beijing massacre had forced a different perspective on art institutions.[11]

There were as importantly the small-scale involvements of a number of artists in group exhibitions either focused on Chinese artists, such as *Art Chinois 1990 Demain pour Hier*, or in which Chinese artists were selected as representatives of place such as in *Parisien(ne)s* of 1997 or *Paris pour escale* of 2000.[12] These were above and beyond the very many one-person exhibitions from the 1990s held all over Europe, North America, Japan, and Australia, from commercial galleries to not-for-profit regional art centres, up to major national museums such as the Sackler Gallery exhibition of Xu Bing in 2002.

The most important exhibition type for the consecration or prescription of artistic importance was the major conceptual or thematic exhibition.[13] The latter perforce overlapped with the representative national survey exhibition, with the variation that contemporary Chinese art was implicitly presented as a particular discursive representation of larger social issues, found in many other national and especially Asian contexts from Bombay to Bangkok to Seoul. This was the undercurrent against which *Cities on the Move* appeared in 1997 in which Chinese artists were simply included among many others in this current. China was presented as a national case which typified a new or a more complex relationship between artistic expression and urban change. It was also found at *Zones of Urgency* in 2003.

This implicit motif of "typification" recurred frequently in the curatorial strategies of Hou Hanru, as we shall see below. In a way the motif was a bit like Voltaire's use of Jesuit letters pleading for recognition of ancestor worship as an argument for a secular religion not in the control of the Catholic church in 18th century France.[14] Contemporary Chinese art in exhibitions like *China Avant Garde* of 1993 or *Alors, la Chine?* of 2003 was often presented as an interpretive model for all avant gardes, or for all contemporary art and current social conditions in "modern life of an urban kind now". Because of the appeal required for their own audience, but also in virtue of the curatorial process which usually put final selection power in the hands of non-contemporary Chinese art specialists, conceptual or tendency exhibitions used thematic exhibitions on "China" or "contemporary Chinese art" and how these were displayed as a kind of cross-cultural metonym. They intended to refer to all "contemporary art" and elided specific discursive differences which might have fulfilled an assumed international, discursive continuity.

The functions of the final type of virtual exhibition in printed or electronic form were difficult to qualify. The printed virtual exhibitions always seemed to be "late" in reinforcing existing appraisals of artists long shown by their exhibition record to have been accepted as important.[15] The electronic virtual exhibition could often be seen as 'early' in supplying excessive information of a relatively trivial kind, but also in certain editorial hands showed a capability to supply significant comment and circulate good images on a greater scale than any printed art magazine.[16] The World Wide Web in particular amplified the possibilities of information about artworks coming to substitute for viewing artworks themselves.[17]

What the extension of this virtuality to a world scale meant with an increase in the volume of information and in speed of access, was by no means clear, at least until the late 1990s. Attitudes to the experiential contents of everyday life, the transposition of ritualized corporeal and social time from singular to plural or supposedly transcultural contexts of interpretations were among some of these consequences for art practice. They might have added up to a choice between accentuating the local and conversely of de-toning local experientiality in favour of an emphasis on global commonalities. Many of these tactical choices by artists did not allow anyone outside these processes, such as art historians, to readily access the strategic patterns of interactive timing with curatorial selection. Curators performed as the cultural entrepreneur who positioned or enabled art practice rather than agents who merely redistributed or repositioned exisiting works which were prior results actively produced by artists. The studio was a site which in a sense local to their production at least, was beyond the domain of the global. Some Chinese artists such as Wang Xingwei actively appropriated global discourses but with a rhythm and placement of their pictorial motifs which were locally Chinese.[18] In contrast, the Australian artist Imants Tillers made appropriation not merely the technique of his practice but also the subject of its investigations and explorations.[19]

## The Roles of Curators

### Selectors

Before the late 1980s, one might have believed that the principal function of curators was to select works for exhibition. Of course, they brought to this process prior values and conceptions, including their view of whatever might be thought of as "contemporary Chinese". Since selection involved exclusion as well as inclusion it was sometimes revealing to see where the line of what was to be left out was drawn. Usually the restriction was geographical, but also involved a notion of zone of received or transformed influence and of where the creative energy lay in a particular art culture at any time.

In 1995, Ronte and Smerling saw the goal of their exhibition of contemporary Chinese art and the rationale for their inclusion or exclusion of particular works as follows:

> This publication and the exhibition show pictures of artists that live in the People's Republic of China. This statement would be false if the artists' influences were over-powered by influences gained in New York, Paris, Amsterdam or Berlin. This is not about the overseas Chinese. The works of art are, so to speak, original Chinese, not joint ventures.[20]

And they thought that:

> The alleged Hollywoodisation of painting is refuted by this exhibition. The traditional elements are much more vehement than the so-called imported elements.[21]

The problem of selection from Chinese sources was positioned thus as a discrimination about work which carried *authentic* values, or was representative according to certain criteria of *contemporaneity* introduced from outside. Whatever good intentions European curators had, they could barely escape exoticizing China.[22] According to the viewpoint of Wang Huangshang in 2004, the work selected was trapped in a net of values that were not Chinese. This enmeshing removed or denuded the possibility of having influence on other international discourses by the Chinese artworks so exhibited:

> Chinese contemporary art has not been able to free itself from the cultural net of the Western art system. In the landscape of world culture, the status of Chinese art remains embedded in the transcendental concepts that underlie the frameworks of the exhibitions in which it appears. Western centrism inherently imbues the selection of works of Chinese art with a certain ideology, which results in a serious misunderstanding of the art. This renders the art nothing more than illustrations depicting Chinese social reality, devoid of any real discursive power in the international landscape.[23]

As a critique of Euramerican curatorial practices, the position was straightforward, but it naturally also carried the further problematic notion that there actually was a set of Chinese values which had existed independently of non-Chinese curatorial selection. By implication only certain Chinese persons were suited to make *that* selection.[24]

Such a bracketing-off of Chinese and non-Chinese selection criteria had the twin effect of making selections more subject to the representativeness of the "Chinese" values of Chinese selectors, and of having made the curatorial selection a propaganda effect of the values which this implicitly or explicitly represented. Indeed such bracketing turned the curator into a 'cultural salesman' for the works selected. It would make a fascinating study to compare the language of the internal written defence of curatorial programmes with that of contemporary advertising copy for high-end consumer durables. Sometimes these cross-overs appeared to be noticed by more avant-garde artists. After all, as a work by Gu Dexin implied, the stage of consuming cameras and radios were no longer that of merely drinking more Coca-Cola. Or was it?

## Thinker, Mediator of Thought via Art Works

A more interesting—if for other reasons more fraught—role for the curator was as a major thinker of a period, or at the very least the humble mediator who by the presentation of selected artworks allowed a higher intellectual exchange between cultures conceived of as distant or different. Clearly some curators considered artworks in some way to be the transmitters or the embodiment of a contemporary *zeitgeist*, and their involvement in exhibitions was aimed at facilitating such transmission. Whether curators had enough time and were subject to enough personal and public critical interaction to viably have produced such thought did not appear to be their concern. Repeated interviews with curators over three or more years did not remove the impression, for me, that they were placed to think that if they had situated a work or an artist in a particular way for the exigencies of their exhibition, then this modality of display was what indicated the significance of the work or artist on the level of thought. They were functionally inclined to confuse intellectual or spiritual value with propaganda value. Here the temptation to substitute advertising copy for fully articulated ideas was prevalent.

Wang Huangsheng in 2004 implicitly put himself in this position when he wrote about a major question being set aside which was

> how to truly allow Chinese contemporary art to enter into exchange and communication with global thought, and how to realize and achieve the fundamental prerequisites of openness, creative experimentation, and free exchange.[25]

It was true, to judge from their writings, that Fei Dawei and Wu Hong outside China regarded themselves to be intellectuals or art historians, and among several important critics in China who curated but who were barely known abroad like Yi Ying, Yin Shuangxi, or Wang Lin,[26] the position adopted was as a member of an intellectual class, or more broadly as a thinker on art.

## Cohort Provider, Talent Scout, Theatrical Agent

Among the most important effects of selection was that election provided a concrete definition through exhibited works of a cohort of artists. The curator thus functioned as a kind of talent scout, or, if the pool of talent was already clear to the curator; works and artists were already canonized, the curator served, by analogy, as a kind of theatrical agent for a range of actors who appeared in various spectacular events appropriate to their work and abilities.

Exhibitions were also reciprocally conceived in terms of the qualities of available artists and works, or whose production was to be guaranteed. One of the most obvious features of the field of the exhibition of contemporary Chinese art, whether in exhibitions supposedly representative of "China", or of a field of contemporary practice in China, or in exhibitions representing a particular position in a given non-Chinese art world for which a Chinese representative might be required, was the restricted number of names which appeared repeatedly in these varied types of exhibition from 1993 to 2005. It is interesting, for example, how the works of Zhang Peili and Geng Jianyi, despite the change in their medium from painting to installation and video after 1993, should have been continually seen since 1987 as representative of contemporary Chinese art practice. Or why the very competent and in different ways often interesting paintings by Liu Xiaodong and Yu Hong, in an expressionist-realist manner well-known outside China in Euramerica since the late 1920s, should have so regularly reappeared at many different kinds of exhibition. The institutional consecration of these artists, as well as their market positions, related to a kind of curatorial restriction on other selections, for example, from the unofficial art outside the Chinese art academies.

## High Journalist, Low Journalist

Art catalogues and the explanations found within them have almost always involved explications of recent intellectual currents which justified the curatorial strategy implied in selecting works. This tendency was extended after *Cities on the Move* in 1997 to take the form of a brief reference to a theorist considered relevant to the field in question. This was sometimes via an abbreviated, detached summary, or was given in a "floating" interview which featured snippets of their thought without much contextualization. Contemporary art catalogues were particularly prone to citation of intellectually fashionable ideas, as if this justified their exhibition concept or selection. In *Cities on the Move*, Hou Hanru and Hans Ulrich Obrist cited the emergence of new cities or raised China's "Special Economic Zones" as typical of the shifting phenomena which underlay their exhibition without citing a single statistic, economic report, or data set.[27] This presentational style was a kind of high journalism—*haute vulgarisation*—which dealt with new "facts" or "phenomena" as it they were already self-demonstrated and required no further discussion. Obrist in the catalogue for *Utopia Station* at Venice in 2003, included "floating" interviews with intellectual luminaries such as Wallerstein or Glissant without subjecting their thought to any kind of analysis or introduction, let alone citation as part of an argument.

At least Hou and Obrist were serious and, in an albeit virtually oblique and almost dyslexic manner, put the texts they referred to in a space where their use might be further mobilized by others. Unfortunately another kind of journalist-cum-curator existed in the field of contemporary Chinese art, such as the renowned writer for *Le Figaro*, Michel Nuridsany. His argument usually started by finding a straw doll to attack, such as a non-art specialist Sinophone who had said, "Nowadays there's nothing interesting going on in France. It's all happening in China".[28] This kind of attack was supported by the guise of corroborating realia, usually an artist's interview citation which inveigled the reader into the idea that the text they were reading was well-informed. The reader learned that Huang Yongping called his group Xiamen Dada in 1985–86 because in interview Huang said, "Chinese contemporary art was fifty years behind the times compared to Western art. We believed a reference to Western art was essential if Chinese contemporary art was to exist".[29] The reader was then primed to accept Nuridsany's statements such as the following:

> I should note that when Chinese art historians go to great lengths to point out how original early twentieth-century Chinese oil painting is compared to European works of the same period, or when a critic as on the ball as Shao Dazhen unquestionably accepts Huang Binhong's judgment that "the thought behind Fauvism is close to the power of the line in antique Chinese painting", it is hard to know whether to laugh or cry at such absurd displays of nationalist arrogance.[30]

Unfortunately, Nuridsany did not apparently know that the reason why Shao Dazhen had accepted Huang Binhong's views was likely to have been because Shao knew and admired Huang's late work. Moreover, as Nuridsany could have established via conversation with even a moderately well-versed Sinophone, Huang Binhong was the close intellectual friend in the 1930s of Fu Lei, the Francophone Shanghai translator of Matisse's letters with whom he doubtlessly discussed modern European art. It was via him that we can assume was obtained the profound cross-cultural literary and pictorial understanding—not "nationalist arrogance"—on which Huang Binhong's statement was based.[31]

## Market Maker

Only an outsider to regular curatorial practice who would have naively testified, as very few actual curators did, to functioning as a market maker for contemporary art. Curators almost never publicly acknowledged what was common trade parlance among art world professionals, that curators by their selection consecrated an artist as purchasable. They also made the price for an artist's work by the sum they were willing to offer or recommend to others for the purchase of an artwork. So far as I know only Strassberg in 1991 acknowledged anything like this role by stating:

> In a country still without an independent art market which was now facing international isolation, artists were more than ever anxious for their works to become known abroad, both for psychological as well as pragmatic reasons.[32]

He also acknowledged the interventionary role of an overseas curator by noticing that a handful of artists living independently of the state were small groups within an area and that,

> some maintained strong bonds of friendship growing out of their school days in the art academies... [that curatorial visit could take place was] a sign of hope in what is obviously a depressing situation.[33]

## Cultural Provocateur, Prototype Designer, Entrepreneur

The curator could also conceive of their function as catalyzing social change in the small domain of art, if not the wider society. Sometimes this was because the contemporary Chinese artists had forced a reappraisal of domestic institutional rules, if not also of the institutions themselves, by their mere inclusion in an overseas exhibition. This was certainly the case with the participation of Huang Yongping and his curation by Hou Hanru at the French pavilion at Venice in 1999. The ideal usually advanced in the siting of other-cultural artists at the global centre of the art world was one of equality and enrichment of voice.

> By negotiating with and attacking these dominant institutions artists seek to open up new spaces for a veritable global art in which creations from different cultures and geographic positions can be expressed equally. Huang Yong Ping is also engaged in such a struggle.[34]

In carrying out this transformation of institutions the curator put him or her self forward as cultural radical: "it's necessary to carry out radical strategies to bring the 'foreigner' into the territory of the dominant institutions".[35] But when a curator acted as an agent of social or cultural change, art may only have been a means to this activity's ends:

> I went to art school and became committed to this domain (it's never really a profession) because I wanted to contribute my efforts to change reality, to have more relevance. Maybe visual art is irrelevant to me.[36]

This radicality in the case of Hou Hanru was ambivalent between the culture from which the curator originated and that which they sought to influence.[37] Curators usually admitted to necessarily being co-opted by the institutions against which they reacted,

> I am more anarchist and anti-institution in nature. However, in reality you can never be anti-institution because society itself is already very institutionalized and there is no way for you to get out of this institutionalized space. Therefore the only thing you can do is to use the existent institution and change it from the inside.[38]

Curators, when asked about their deeper purposes, cast around for any idea that would do, as an educator, or a moralist, even though the two positions often converged: "My idea is to transform it [the biennial] into a school, to make the whole process of preparing for the biennial a training school".[39]

## Values of Exhibition and Stance of Curator, Nature of Cultural Difference and Exchange

Art exhibitions often transparently performed a diplomatic function. They showed one society to another, and this official or commercial curiosity was a prominent feature of some exhibitions of contemporary Chinese art abroad in the 1980s and early 1990s. The position was early advanced by none other than Henry Kissinger:

> There is no clearer prism through which to perceive these developments than in the art now being created by the new generation of Chinese artists.[40]

And the notion of cultural openness serving as an antidote to possible narrow diplomatic closure in the past was also evident in 1987: "Channels for international cultural exchange must be kept open".[41]

The most ubiquitous values in multiple exhibitions were that the selection of artists was representative of a current situation including art but extended beyond it, but which was also new: that the selection represented what was contemporary and had left behind some previous value set.

> We wanted to present, however, a representative overview of the actual modern art scene. The motto at the art academies today is still the observation by Mao "Bai hua chi fang", which means "Let a hundred flowers bloom". The young artists left behind this dusty old concept of art behind them long ago.[42]

Perhaps the universal preoccupation of overseas exhibition in the 1990s was also to find that Chinese art had gone beyond old-fashioned Maoist politics. "The exhibition wants to show that China is a country in upheaval, that has a great future ahead of it," and "In China the new art doesn't serve politics anymore".[43]

The belief in transcending politics was a projection of a non-Chinese viewpoint since what the Chinese academic artists fought out in the 1980s was precisely how they could find a new way of connecting with reality, undominated or uncontaminated by party intervention. The underlying value of Chinese curators abroad, typified by by the Francophone scholar and curator Fei Dawei who had been in France since 1986, was to open up a new kind of dialogue which accepted difference, but also a dialogue between contemporaries, not between old views of a China in the past.[44]

The problem was that around 1990 Fei Dawei perceived there to be a radical difference in cultural positioning of contemporary art between China and Euramerica: "Even if formal resemblances apparently exist, the state of mind between China and the West remains radically different".[45] This amounted to the opposition of cultural essences of a kind which, it might have been supposed, exchanges of contemporary art should have overcome. But the trope of self-expression or individual identity was strongly linked to contemporaneity in Chinese art during the 1990s, even if it is stressed that this quest for individuality came from different and specifically Chinese sources.[46]

## Chinese Artists in International Exchange

Just at the time when some non-Chinese curators clung to the notion that art practice in China had been somehow more vital and more representative than that done by Chinese artists abroad, some Chinese curators overseas were beginning to reconfigure the image of the Chinese artist resident abroad away from an exile or an immigrant to that of a traveller or sojourner, who was never quite resident in any overseas metropolis.[47] The selection of Huang Yongping to be one of the two artists in the French pavilion at Venice in 1999 also meant that,

> Instead of promoting a false, or no longer adequate idea of a "national art", this selection serves to emphasize the importance of co-existence and dialogue between different cultures, individuals, as well as the diversity of concerns that are played out in the common spaces of creation.[48]

The conception of international art exchange for China became one of receiving greater recognition for the complexity of Chinese society and the individuality of the artists.[49] Indeed a stress on individual achievement was found evenly through official statements from around 2000.[50] Fei Dawei in writing of a Belgian collection survey of recent Chinese art stated: "the most important thing for the artist to transcend is himself or herself, not the outside world".[51]

Running against this revisited notion of the artistic individual was the notion that China could and needed to absorb other cultural elements in order to resist the globalizing centre. That this "survival strategy" by incorporative tolerance might at some point have comprised a kind of Chinese hegemonizing did not yet surface in Chinese curatorial texts: it was circulating just below the fashionably resisting surface. For example, in 2004, Huang Du mentioned that:

> In order to establish its own position in the age of glocalization, contemporary Chinese art must not only actively absorb the useful elements of other cultures with open mind, but also emphasize its own uniqueness and independence. I want to view Chinese art from the standpoint of glocalization: thinking in terms of a uniquely Chinese modernity.[52]

Speaking of a *Mongolian* (my italics) *yurt* (my use of the term) exhibited by a Chinese artist at São Paolo, he further wrote,

> the work pays tribute to the national heritage of traditional Chinese culture by rediscovering and using the traditional artistic elements that were previously ignored.[53]

Here the laudable aim of rediscovering minority cultural artefacts which had been ignored by both Han chauvinism and the globalizing pressures in the art world, was incorporated into a Sino-centric notion of artistic fusion and tolerance.

## Major Cultural and Ideological Differences

Fei Dawei in 1990 was sure about the differences between Chinese and Western cultures. But his position was by no means rare and was found widely in both China and Euramerica. In 1993 Elliott and Mepham positioned contemporary Chinese art, including specially commissioned in situ work, by means of different views of natural forces.

> We tend to think of reality as an accretion of conflicting forces: man-nature; body-spirit; fire-water; hunger-plenty; life-death. While the Chinese artists recognize the same entities they do not see them as opposites. Such categories are, rather, different states of energy within a greater unity.[54]

Such a bifurcation of the world was also found on the Chinese side. There was an implicit divide where Western events were somehow outside "Chinese" discourse, like the almost complete lack of discussion by the artists themselves in some texts about the first major exposure at Venice Biennale by Fang Lijun and Wang Guangyi and others in 1993.[55] Such an artistic position also carried the understanding that the cultural difference between China and "the West" overlay a deeper ideological conflict. As Wang Guangyi wrote:

> In my view the central point I want to express in "The Great Criticism" series is the ideological antagonism that exists between western culture and socialist ideology, And, true, the significance of this antagonism has more to do with issues in cultural studies than simply art in and of itself.[56]

It is significant that such a motivated set of works as The Great Criticism Series featured the clash between Western commercial values symbolized by their local product avatars with the socialist ideals of the earlier Cultural Revolution period, that it should have been posed as a clash between "western culture and socialist ideology". The artist had not accepted that socialist ideology itself was the very Western product of some hundreds of years of intellectual history. The circularity of his position indicated that the cultural antagonism referred to was part of an internal and projective "Chinese" set of oppositions. Wang Guangyi, like many others in China and outside it who accepted such oppositions, seemed to have very little idea about what the West actually was, or what "China" was, from the opposite position.

## Modes of Exchange between Artist and Curator, Work and Audience/Patron

It was not often acknowledged that "contemporary China"–related events were very useful for the Western art world, fuelling both audience expectations and a sense of being engaged with a powerful centre of contemporary economic and now cultural activity. As early as 1993, the problems of hosting "contemporary China" exhibitions were acknowledged in that competition was deliberately avoided between Western European institutions. An exhibition of contemporary Chinese art had been planned in Berlin for 1989 but had been put off by the Beijing massacre. It was revived in 1993 from the suggestions of Jochen Noth and Andreas Schmid as experts on Chinese art. This "good idea" had also occurred to other European modern and contemporary art museums, and

> we [the curators at Haus der Kulturen der Welt in Berlin] also learned that other institutions in the Netherlands, the United Kingdom, Australia and Hong Kong had independently developed similar plans, and it seemed that the race was on to introduce this hitherto unknown side of Chinese art...we soon agreed that such competition would only damage our common aim and could deeply embarrass the Chinese artists.[57]

The most common mode of exchange was thus a contracted exhibition between several institutions and their different audiences. It was doubtful, aside from issues of convenience or reliability and apart from a kind of ring or market-entry value, whether the particular artist or their works circulated between these exhibitions had any significant impact at all on their circulation.[58] Since exhibitions were likely to circulate, and certainly national retrospective exhibitions tended to do so, the function of the exhibition involved in most cases a contract between local institutions acting internationally. To integrate this field required an ideologically provided coordinating mechanism. There needed to have been either a climate of favourable critical opinion, or some kind of leadership role had to be allocated by common consent among institutional and independent curators to a designated curatorial player in the ring. Unfortunately too little information was available to the research for this book about the contracted exchange between a mediating institution, the designated or consensus curator and the institution and exhibition sponsors. In most cases these relationships also involved a business corporation or a grouping of different economic actors, or a regional, city, or national government. Clearly in the case of the early 1987 *Beyond the Open Door* exhibition in the US, this involved some kind of implicit or explicit compact between a leading diplomatic player, a sinologist, an art museum, and a petroleum company.[59]

What role was there then for the conventional form of exchange, the payment of money for a work between artist and collector or his agent for the transfer of ownership of the work? Some foreign collectors like Ullens collected out of a sense of engagement with the local culture and as a diversion from their more pressing financial or economic duties. This diversion then became a passion, and in some cases a mission.[60] In addition, some domestic Chinese collectors wished to make a spectacle of their collecting, as noted by Qiu Zhijie: "Even when a domestic collector collects, he will inevitably 'event-ify' and publicize his collecting".[61]

But if collectors ultimately could not avoid displaying their collection which was composed of works completed before their exchange through purchase, i.e. before their intervention in the status of the work, what did a curator exchange with an artist in the facilitation of exhibition through their selection? Few curators admitted to having demanded of an artist how to make a work. When an exhibition, like say *Cities on the Move* of 1997, or other exhibitions of "recipe" or "process" art such as *Utopia Station* in 2003, was supposed to constitute an open proposition from works made by artists to which the audience brought their own completion, then would not the selection and display procedures enjoined by the curator have come to replace the aesthetic decisions once in the province of artist alone? Hou Hanru criticized one form of this substitution: "It is the worst of circumstances to use the artist just as an illustration of your ideas".[62] The problem was the relativity implied in the expression "just as", for if the curator had not substituted for the artist, he or she still assumed a mediating if entrepreneurial position between the audience and the artist through the placing of, and sometimes active suggestion about, the work. For Hou:

> The role [of the curator] is to pose a question, and the artist should participate in the formation and answering with different solutions so that the process is a collaboration.[63]

But why should the artist only "participate in the formation and answering with different solutions"? Did this not imply that artistic discourse itself had no sovereignty, no ability to form its own criteria about "solutions"? And was that the purpose of art, or was art in this sense purposeless? The curator might on the one hand have been an entrepreneur of possible solutions, but how far was this from him or her becoming the Leninist "engineer of human souls"? How close was the position of the curator, ostensibly engaged in facilitating plurality and freedom, to the moral identity of the bureaucrat-intellectual offering, and in the narrow operational confines of curating an exhibition, restrictive models of the future? For some Chinese artists like Wang Guangyi, this moralism was also cognate with a notion of Chinese values opposed to those of the West.

The main exchange engaged by the curator was conceivably between objects and their makers being consecrated by their selection with the status of artworks and artist. These consecrations could fall into the hands of officials for, as the curator-historian Wu Hung noted in 2002, the Shanghai Triennale in 2000 had sought to stage itself as an historical event, but the engineer was a state-run institute and

> because many compromises had to be made between these [international] curators and the museum, no clear lines can be drawn between independent decisions and government direction.[64]

He thought he should create an exhibition which consecrated works in a different way, by initiating

> a long-term exhibition and research programme of experimental art in a large public museum ... [and] provide a systematic interpretation of these works in their artistic, cultural, social, and political context.[65]

Wu Hung clearly distanced himself from the working arrangements of the earlier Shanghai Biennale and tried to systematically work through an alternative interaction with an existing and official institution. Curators have commented on how easy or difficult agreement with other curators about the inclusion of a particular artist or work might have been, but they have rarely analysed the functioning of the organizing curatorial group which provided the consecration. A rather deceptively straightforward example comes from Fan Di'an in 2001:

> Everyone [in the curatorial group plus advice from Xu Jiang] exchanged opinions over a broad range, and everyone wished that this exhibition would be an opportunity for an dialogue and equal exchange between Chinese art and the international art world because only if there is this can the prospect of contemporary art obtain its true colouring.[66]

In 2002 he also wrote:

> The Ministry of Culture of the People's Republic of China has extended great support to the participation of Chinese artists at the São Paulo Biennial and the sponsor has made the participation possible.[67]

Here it was very clear two parties were in play: a Chinese curatorial team, in the first case including Xu Jiang, later President of the China Art Academy in Hangzhou, and nephew of the then president of China, Jiang Zemin, and the other of an international art world, vague and unspecified, but by implication also having a curatorial team of its own. Moreover in 2002 acknowledgement was made both of the central government organ, here participating officially in an international Biennale for the first time, and a sponsor. Chinese curation at the international level in contemporary art biennials was thus positioned as the product of a range of official bodies: it was not presented as the choice of one or two curators, or of one or two ideas current in international art circles at the time. Neither, it may need saying, was it a resistance against some habitual institutional position which excluded particular kinds of art practice.

## New Kinds of Circulation in Play

What new kinds of circulation existed between curators, exhibitions, artists, and works active in presenting contemporary Chinese art outside China? The most obvious, but also most indicative, was to suppose that the wave of urbanization in Asia and in China in particular produced new networks for the circulation of goods, ideas, and people, all of which may also have been found in the domain of art. Some curators, like Hou Hanru, felt that these networks peculiarly facilitated reorganizing the power structure in society and the use of the art community as a space of experiment within urban networks.[68] Hou also stated that he had discovered that no urban space was actually planned, but all were a collage of emergency solutions.[69] Hou thought that

> many Asian architects and artists have been thinking about the question of how to adapt to very rapid urban development … how, in the crowded and rapidly developing urban spaces of Asia can we explore the "rifts" and "fissures"? How can we create something out of this "urban void"? … [He also considers that] by joining forces with others, the Asia Pacific region will not only be able to develop economically, but will also become a global cultural centre, one of many world centres. In order to bring this about, Asia needs to have its own artistic set up, critical criteria and media power … I do not think there is any point in Asia following the same model as the West for museums.[70]

This stress on the constituting of Asian cities with new kinds of interstices as a means to the understanding the forces driving contemporary Chinese art was very widely held in China around 1997 to 2004. It could be found very close to official circles in the curatorial frameworks of Fan Di'an amongst others.[71] I have the impression, without much firmer evidence by way of official statements, that the tangible pressures of urbanization all over China may have led cultural bureaucrats to recognize that contemporary art could not be handled with the same perspectives and exhibition policies as had been the case until the mid-1990s, despite their earlier ideological reluctance to engage with international, contemporary art.

The pressure on curators was intense and the people who became curators were temperamentally suited towards adapting to the necessary pressures. A kind of linkage, sometimes intimacy, developed between curators and artists because of the need to trust the artists to provide works which they had not yet produced. Added to which, artists may have produced such incompatible proposals that the skill of the curator lay in knowing how to fit together such disparateness between works. In the pressures which thus arose the works were sometimes an extreme solution to a problem, or indeed as some curators such as Hou thought "the extreme situation in art is beautiful",[72] which may have meant that an extreme situation between a curator and an artist was productive of good art.

Hou became a model if also an active collaborator for curators such as Pi Li, Huang Du, and Zhang Zhaohui who were still in China, and his views may thus have had an importance beyond his particular experiences. Hou referred to the role of good entrepreneurs in anticipating the future, and also in applying management concepts to curating. Rather than seeing himself as a star, he saw himself as part of a system:

> Networking is first of all an economic concept, symbolizing transfer from production to productivity. In post-industrial societies, the key factor is no longer how many products you are able to produce and sell, but how many new ideas you have that you can turn into things people need in everyday life... The arrival of networking directly challenged inherent concepts of our existence... Many people have overlooked the fact that, in reality, you need to become an active part of the network yourself. You need to contribute your own qualities to existing, developing or even as yet non-existent networks.[73]

On the other side from the networking of which the curator became a constitutive if directly active unit, there were the networks which directly linked various biennial and other exhibition sites. These were promoted both in China and internationally as shows which disseminated advanced art and allowed a space for the local. Such exhibitions were propagandized as

> important markers for the expression of the various modernities that unfold within the generative phenomenon of Globalization. They offer the possibility

> for speculations about a modernization recast in favour of local expressions and differences.[74]

The theme of allowing a space for the local or for Chinese expression within the international was often taken up in biennial and representative exhibitions catalogues.[75] Some simple interpretivity between local and global levels was presumed, despite all that Chinese and foreign curators mentioned about different values and historical experiences. Rare but prescient artists remarked on the problems of system absorption: Qiu Zhijie and Lu Jie of the Long March Foundation warned,

> Chinese contemporary art is in the earliest stages of constructing a formal system; yet, it has already begun the game of comparison and competition with the West, buying wholeheartedly into a system based on major museums and biennial exhibitions.[76]

They were aware that participation in the Western biennial system meant the unprepared acceptance of other, external values or art criteria. It was always difficult but necessary for contemporary artists to question the process of canon foundation, that is the selection of a repertory of master works. This process had shifted away from the long historical sifting and re-evaluation that had characterized over time the evaluations of Chinese imperial painting catalogues or the European art market from the 1650s to the 1950s. Curators or collectors may have relied on their love of works, or presumed that what had been collected "includes outstanding examples of the creative minds of this age".[77] Others wished to eliminate the topical popular or sensational.[78]

How was an exhibition to be made representative from a particular curatorial or conceptual position whilst allowing for new positions by which the artist produced and audience interpreted and evaluated the artwork? The contradictions were shown when young artists were presumed to be opposing the academy when in fact they were almost all products of it.

> We wanted to present, however, a representative overview of the actual modern art scene. The motto at the art academies today is still the observation by Mao "Bai hua chi fang", which means "Let a hundred flowers bloom". The young artists left behind this dusty old concept of art behind them long ago.[79]

No doubt just as this problem surfaced in the selection of contemporary Chinese art for exhibition abroad, Chinese artists began to be aware that their work was beginning to satisfy particular curatorial categories. They were caught in various dilemmas about how best to satisfy this demand. Karen Smith noted of Wang Guangyi's work that

> the Great Criticism series connected with the vastly successful brand building process in the western world, and delivered proof for this success…Wang Guangyi combined it with images that even without knowledge of the Chinese context were definable as a Chinese brand type.[80]

But almost as soon as it had arisen some Chinese curators took the opposite approach to branding and wanted to let the audience form the exhibition in their minds whilst they viewed the exhibition.[81] Or they wanted, from Taiwan, to project a complex space of the mind which explored

> a state of flux as a reflection of the frantic transformation taking place throughout the globe. A gulf is constantly, rapidly enlarging between our utopian dreams and reality. The Limbo Zone formed by this disparity hovers in an unstable state of oscillation, expanding continually like a dark void, in a period of transition that seems limitless and nightmarishly murky.[82]

Corresponding to this state of flux in human experience and artistic expression was a new type of institution, an alternative space which was a new paradigm of the institution which was "always moving, flexible, changing and re-inventing itself".[83] New types of artwork would have to be presented more as "part of an art event".[84]

Thus writing from outside the Chinese context but reasonably assimilating it to future trends seen in an Asia-Pacific perspective, self-organized spaces and artist-run-initiatives might be an alternative organizing unit for Biennials themselves. This was what Hou Hanru and Hans Ulrich Obrist attempted in *Cities on the Move* in 1997 and Hou Hanru and Charles Esche did in the Gwangju Biennale of 2002.

## Conclusion

I have deliberately not separated Chinese and other-than-Chinese curators in the above analyses. It might suit essentialist or nationalist constructions of contemporary Chinese art to have separated out these two categories of actors, so that one or other choice could have been deemed "Chinese" or "Western". I would not deny cultural specificity to either selection. But what emerged from the understanding of the list of curators, critics and other actors was that Chinese and other-than-Chinese actors were in such frequent interaction with each other and with the same bodies of artists in China or abroad, that whilst their selections and motivations may have differed due to cultural or interest backgrounds and positions, they could be handled together as one set of actors. To some extent this was due to the increased speed of exchanges via exhibition in the late 1990s, the increasing involvement of official bodies in contemporary art exhibitions, and the increased speed and volume of informational and personnel flows. It is clear that the restriction on the names of artists in the exhibitions given in appendix 4 must indicate some kinds of structural convergence between the bodies which sited those exhibitions and the choice of curators.

It would not be possible to fully describe and satisfactorily analyze all the interactions which took place between these actors and the various exhibition sites. Some issues involving Chinese contemporary art may be pointed to. There was a surprising lack of seriousness by which the prior "Stars" generation artists were regarded by a number of post-*Magiciens de la terre* artists and curators in France when I met them on several occasions between 1999 and 2003. This pointed to unresolved issues between older and newer artists and curatorial cohorts being projected overseas, but also finding their counterparts in generational and regional links among artists and curators in China, some of which went back to the 1980s, even to the late 1970s.

There was also a very large differentiation, not easily mapped but evidently present among artists and curators, between those who handled contemporary art in terms of "China" and the West, whether on the level of an historical cultural or social situational discrimination, and those who saw China as part of a world increasingly defined by multi-ethnicity and hybridity. Euramerican multi-ethnicity and hybridity was not determined as it might be so thought in China by the perceived ability of Sinified culture to absorb cultural and ethnic difference, but by the situational position of immigrants under conditions of a globalized economy which still preserved local cultures fostered by states.

As repeatedly demonstrated by Alain Quemin,[85] until the early 2000s the country or national affiliation of artists still had an enormously determining role in their prominence both in esteem and market sales between national and international levels. The "prescribing countries" of the international art world were overwhelmingly the United States and Germany, followed at a lower level by France, Italy, and the United Kingdom. Even Japan and Korea were barely present among these prescribing countries. In the Chinese case, the state as funder of overseas exhibitions of contemporary art, as a provider of exhibition spaces, and as a facilitator of a contemporary art world, had barely begun to enter before 2000. This was the case, even given that these activities had previously been in the domain of a much older cohort of artists and curators centred on restrictively funded exhibition, educational, and studio institutions. Private patrons had begun to exist in China, but had nothing like the scale, function, and aesthetic range of similar patrons in say Japan or Korea.[86] Thus, Chinese patrons had not yet had an impact on the pattern of practice or the kinds of artwork these artists created.

Many other issues remain to be examined concerning the reception of contemporary Chinese art in China itself during the 1990s, and how this was conditioned by the rise of mass consumerism in the cities. It was particularly so since changes in urban life or in its relation to artistic expression and general aesthetic perception were referred to by artists, or accepted as the basic driving forces behind contemporary art by many curators.[87]

## Notes

1 A list of those active in introducing contemporary Chinese art overseas is given in the appendices. Below many of the texts are in English. Where necessary I remain responsible for other translations from Chinese or French.

2 For the imbrication of the "official" and the "non-official" art worlds see John Clark, "System and Style in the Practice of Chinese Contemporary Art: the Disappearing Exterior?" *Yishu, Journal of Chinese Contemporary Art* 1, 2 (August 2002). Part of this text was translated in "Style et Système au pratique de l'art contemporain en Chine", trans. Jean-Dominique Langlais, *Alors, la Chine?*, ed. Anne Lemonnier (Paris: Centre Pompidou, 2003). The full discussion is found in John Clark, *Asian Modernities: Chinese and Thai Art of the 1980s and 1990s* (Sydney: Power Publications, 2010).

3 A list of exhibitions and texts is given in the overall bibliography.

4 The Upriver Art Gallery was established in October 1998 with the approval of the Chengdu Bureau of Cultural Affairs and with the support of private enterprises and describes itself as a "non-profitable civil academic institute". See *Shanghe Meishuguan / Upriver Gallery* (Tianjin: Tianjin Shehui Kexueyuan Chubanshe, 2000), 13.

5 For the definition of contemporary art see Terry Smith, *What is Contemporary Art? Contemporary Art, Contemporaneity and Art to Come*, Artspace Critical Issues Series (Sydney: Artspace Visual Art Centre, 2001), n.p. Smith broadly distinguishes three aspects to the definition of contemporary art: the "institutionalised network", "art infused with the multiple modes of contemporaneity", and art practice where "artists these days must...work through a particular set of representational problems". In fact, in my analysis his essay includes at least 13 definitions of contemporary art or the notion of the contemporary as it relates to art. See also Alan Quemin, *L'art contemporain international: entre les institutions et le marché: le rapport disparu* (Nîmes: Éditions Jacqueline Chambon/Artprice, 2002), 16–17.

6 See "Curators' Trip to China", *Yishu Journal of Contemporary Chinese Art* 1, 1 (Spring/May 2002): 31, a singular document to be read closely on translating the discourses of the periphery into those now current at the centre and transmitting them back to the periphery. For example there was this aside by Enwezor: "The stories we are telling are *not being told in order for your country* to reconstitute the idea of new identities, new maps, and so on, *but to* reconstitute the idea of modern subjectivity, the idea that we must live not within modernity but within modernities" (my italics).

7 As mentioned in Harumi Miwa, ed., *The Venice Biennale: 40 Years of Japanese Participation* (Tokyo: The Japan Foundation; Tokyo: The Mainichi Newspapers, 1995).

8 The Chinese artists exhibiting at various exhibitions including Biennials at São Paolo, Venice, and other sites from 1987–2004 are given in appendix 3.

9 See Quemin, *L'art contemporain international*, 136–46.

10 The Chinese artists exhibiting at Gwangju and Busan in Korea in 2004 are also given in appendix 3. I have arrived at these figures by comparative analysis elsewhere. See John Clark, "Japanese Art, Largely Seen from Participation in the Venice Biennale" in Chapter 2.

11 Political changes may also have enabling effects. In 1999, when 19 out of 99 participating artists at the Venice Biennale were Chinese, it is reported that Cai

Guoqiang was unable to locate in Albania the copy of The Rent Collection Courtyard sculptures which had originated in Chongqing in 1965 just before the Cultural Revolution. He thus imported an original team member from Sichuan to assist in re-creating the sculptures in Venice as a "work in progress". Harald Szeemann, artistic director at Venice in that year, mentioned that he had wanted to exhibit a latex copy of the same work in 1972 at Documenta 5, still during the epoch of the Cultural Revolution. See Nico Stinga, *Terrecotte Cinesi dalla 48A Biennale di Venezia* (Nove: Antiga Edizioni, 2003), 9. See also the fuller historical discussion in the catalogue, Esther Schlicht and Max Hollein ed., *Art for the Millions: 100 Sculptures of from the Mao Era* (Frankfurt: Schirn Kunsthalle; Munich: Hirmer Verlag, 2009).

12 On the activities of Chinese artists and curators in France see John Clark, "Chinese Artists in France" in *Over Here: International Perspectives on Art and Culture*, ed. Jean Fisher and Gerardo Mosquera (Cambridge, MA: MIT Press, 2004), and the earlier article, John Clark, "Chinese Artists in Paris", *Far Eastern Economic Review* (16 December 1986), of which a Chinese translation was later published in *Meishu Shichao* 4 (1987). Both are collected in my *Modernities of Chinese Art* (Leiden: Brill, 2010).

13 Indeed, we may link the intention to prescribe by such exhibitions which are not ostensibly about a national position, as actually an implicit claim to the right to make prescriptions by the site and its curatorial mediators, as well as by the nation where that site is located.

14 See Voltaire, "Chapter XXXIX: Disputes Concerning Chinese Ceremonies...", in *The Age of Louis XIV*, trans. Martyn Pollack (1751; London: Heron Books, 1961).

15 For example, the Chinese artists appraised by their inclusion in Gilda Williams, ed., *Fresh Cream: Contemporary Art in Culture* (London: Phaidon, 2000), were Cai Guoqiang, Chen Chieh-jen, Qiu Zhijie, and Xu Bing. The other Asian artists were Arahmaiani, Montien Boonma, Choi Jeong-hwa, Heri Dono, Simryn Gill, Murakami Takashi, Navin Rawanchaikul, Shazia Sikander, Sone Yutaka, Takahashi Tomoko, and Yanagi Miwa.

16 This is to the extent that web articles have to be periodically collated in printed form, if also needing to be carefully revised by an outside editor. Otherwise one would lose all touch with the significant opinions and information which had circulated about contemporary Chinese art in a given period and which were no longer accessible on the web. For two such collections from the now defunct chinese-art.com website see John Clark, ed., *Chinese Art at the End of the Millennium* (Hong Kong: New Art Media, 2000), and its successor, Wu Hung, ed., *Chinese Art at the Crossroads: Between Past and Future, between East and West* (Hong Kong: New Art Media, 2001).

17 This should not cause surprise since there is a long modern history in art of circulation of such "substitutes for viewing the work" beginning at least with Diderot. See for example Denis Diderot, "Examen du clair-obscur," in *Essais sur la peinture, Salons de 1759, 1761, 1763* (Paris: Hermann, 1984), 33–8.

18 Szeemann discusses his selection of Wang Xingwei in Wu, ed., *Chinese Art at the Crossroads*, 154.

19 For an accessible reprint of Imants Tillers' 1982 essay "Locality Fails" see Rex Butler, ed., *What is Appropriation: An Anthology of Critical Writings on Australian Art in 1980s and 1990s* (Sydney: Power Publications; Brisbane: Institute of Modern Art, 1996).

20 Dieter Ronte et al., *"Quotation Marks": Chinese Contemporary Paintings* (Singapore: Singapore Art Museum), 27.

21 Ronte et al., "Quotation Marks", 33.

22 See Hou Hanru, *Parisien(ne)s* (London: InIVA & Camden Arts Centre, 1997), where he states, "As was seen with Magiciens de la Terre, in the Parisian context, despite the intention to overcome in-built Eurocentrism, there is great difficulty in discarding a folklorized or exoticized reading of the colonial 'other'" (5).

23 Wang Huangsheng in Fei Dawei, ed., *The Monk and the Demon* (Lyon: Musée d'Art Contemporain du Lyon, 2004), 14.

24 See Zhu Qi, "Why has Art become so Pretty of Late?" in Clark, ed., *Chinese Art at the End of the Millennium*. See also the conversation between Shimizu Toshio and Robert Bernell, "Chinese Contemporary Photography and Video Art", in the same volume, 101.

25 Fei, ed., *The Monk and the Demon*, 14.

26 See for example, Yi Ying, *Xueyuan de Huanghun* (Changsha: Hunan Meishu Chubanshe, 2004); Yin Shuangxi, including *Diaosu 50-nian, 20 shijizhongguo daiosu xueshu lunwenji* (n.d., circa 2000); Wang Lin, *Yin Shuangxi bian Mei shu pi ping jia nian du ti ming zhan, You hua* (Chengdu: Sichuan Mei shu Chubanshe, 1994); Wang Lin, *Dangdai Mieshu Zhuangtai* (Nanjing: Jiangsu Meishu Chubanshe, 1995).

27 See Hou Hanru and Hans-Ulrich Obrist, Section 1 of *Sezession: Cities on the Move* (Ostfildern-Ruit: Verlag Gerd Hatje, 1997), n.p., and Hou Hanru, *On the Mid-Ground*, ed. Yu Hsiao-Hwei (Hong Kong: Timezone 8, 2002).

28 Michel Nuridsany, *China Art Now*, trans. Susan Pickford (Paris: Flammarion, 2004), 8.

29 Nuridsany, *China Art Now*, 8.

30 Nuridsany, *China Art Now*, 9.

31 Huang Binhong's late works were shown in exhibitions at Beijing and Hangzhou in 2004. See Claire Roberts, "The Dark Side of the Mountain: Huang Binhong (1865–1955) and Artistic Continuity in Twentieth Century China", PhD Thesis, Australian National University, 2005. There is no room for academic complacency here since unfortunately this kind of ignorance masquerading as knowledge about art is a danger from which well-intentioned and serious art historical texts dealing with modern and contemporary Chinese art are not immune, including my own.

32 Richard L. Strassberg, *"I Don't Want to Play Cards with Cézanne" and Other Works, Selections from the Chinese "New Wave" and "Avant-Garde" Art of the Eighties* (Pasadena: Pacific Asia Museum, 1991), xi.

33 Strassberg, *"I Don't Want to Play Cards with Cézanne"*, xi.

34 Hou Hanru, *One Man, Nine Animals: Hung Yong Ping's Project for the French Pavilion in Venice Biennale* (Paris: Association Française d'Action Artistique, 1999), 26.

35 Hou, *One Man, Nine Animals*, 26.

36 Hou Hanru, interview by Carolee Thea, *Foci: Interviews with Ten International Curators* (New York: Apexart Curatorial Program, 2001), 30. Hou also said: "For us the first necessity of art is never to return to the enclosure of the self. The second thing is to see how modernity rewrites the process of social transformation in different conditions, and then how it is visualized".

37 Hou Hanru's editor, Yu Hsiao-Hwei, comments in *On the Mid-Ground*, 12, that "Hou Hanru has tried to turn his uncertain and double-edged position into a gateway that opens the possibilities of intervening critically in both cultures, simultaneously. Thus, always seen as a half-outsider, he has been able to critique Chinese (and Asian) contemporary art, as well as Western cultural phenomena".

38 Hou, *On the Mid-Ground*, 15.

39 Hou, *On the Mid-Ground*, 16.

40 Nielsen, Waldemar I. and Richard L. Strassberg, *Beyond the Open Door, Contemporary Paintings from the People's Republic of China* (Pasadena: Pacific Asia Museum, 1987), 7.

41 Nielsen and Strassberg, *Beyond the Open Door*, 22

42 Ronte and Smerling, *"Quotation Marks"*, 9.

43 Ronte and Smerling, *"Quotation Marks"*, 10.

44 Fei Dawei et al., *Art Chinois 1990 Demain pour Hier* (Pourrières: Les Domaines de l'Art; Aix en Provence: Editions Carte Segrete, 1990), n.p. Fei Dawei in interview with Bernard Marcadé said:

> My essential idea has for a long time been to create a new type of dialogue between China and the West. There exists an essentially traditional dialogue between these two cultural entities. The contemporary Western world is most often in dialogue with the ancient Oriental world. It is not really a dialogue between contemporaries. It was before anything else this disequilibrium which led me to conceive of this exhibition.

45 Fei et al., *Art Chinois 1990*, 16.

46 As noticed by Claire Roberts in 1992:

> the desire for individual self-expression and a plea for the artist to be answerable only to his or her own interpretation of, or response to, politics, history and culture....The development of art in China follows a lineage that is distinct from the West, hence my application of the term "Post-Mao".
>
> In Claire Roberts, *New Art From China: Post-Mao Product* (Sydney: Art Gallery of New South Wales, 1992), n.p.

47 In Hou, *Parisien(ne)s*, 7, Hou notices the transformation in the identity of the diasporic artist as follows:

> The contemporary 'Parisien(ne)' is now one who travels between the city and the ends of the earth; the various displacements fill and simultaneously empty the city's spaces, while its boundaries are extended by their journeys and diverse trajectories. The "Parisien(ne)" is being transformed from Walter Benjamin's "flaneur" into a "voyageur".

It is most significant that here Hou is assimilating Chinese artists to patterns of residence shared by many others in the multi-cultural ex-colonial centres, and unlike those who still worked within the terms of a 'China-West' binary, began to see how all artistic identities, and not just Chinese ones would be re-configured. Hou was also affected by debates about the new French immigration law in 1994 and the relationship of immigrants to the culture of their new country. See Hou, *On the Mid-Ground*, 14.

48 See Hou, *One Man, Nine Animals*, 21.

49 See Hou Hanru, Fan Di'an and Gabriele Knapstein, *Living in Time 29 zeitgenössiche Künstler aus China*, Nationalgalerie im Hamburger Bahnhof Museum für Gegenwart in cooperation with the Ministry of Culture of PRC and China International Exhibition Agency (Berlin: Staatliche Museen zu Berlin-Preßischer Kulturbesitz, 2001), 27. Hou Hanru stated that "We should emphasize that China itself is a multidimensional pluralist society, intricate, and complex". He then goes on to stress multiplicity of Chinese cultural identities and the length of China's history and that each Chinese is both an individual and a member of a group: "Those who live in China today, face these challenges together, and also setting out from the position of reality in their own lives make non-identical replies to these issues. Artists increase and manifest this kind of special characteristic while pursing individual expression".

50 See *The 25th São Paulo Biennial: Here and Now: Chinese Art in the Process of Urbanization*, curated by Fan Di'an and assistant Pi Li (Beijing: China International Exhibition Agency, 2002), 29.

51 Actually Fei Dawei puts this position in the context of a re-interpreted maxim *dao gao yi chi, mo gao yi zhang* (As virtue rises one foot, vice rises ten), which was originally Buddhist caution against temptations of outside world, and later used to mean "the greater the success, the even greater the challenges to be faced". The demon (in the exhibition title) hints that "amidst changes in the Chinese environment, the most important thing for the artist to transcend is himself or herself, not the outside world". See Fei, ed., *The Monk and the Demon: Contemporary Chinese Art* (Milan: 5 Continents Editions, 2004), 12.

52 See *The 26th São Paolo Biennial: Chinese Pavilion*, curated by Huang Du with artist Qu Yan (Beijing: China International Exhibition Agency, 2004). As an index of a problem of reception one may go no further than the introduction to this catalogue by the director of the São Paolo Biennial, Alfons Hug, whose paper mentions one artist Shirin Neshat (the Iranian photographer and video artist living in the US), and raises many issues of urbanization in Latin America, but does not once refer to China. He also is more interested in global rather than glocal models of cultural interaction and states that, "The lack of points of contact between different civilizations produces a dangerous vacuum. In this way cultural differences, which could in fact be productive, become fixed and insurmountable. Can Brazil, whose population according to a recent survey embraces 143 different shades of skin colour, serve here as a positive model?" Clearly the issue of incorporative, homogenizing tolerance of cultural difference is not only a Chinese one.

53 Huang, *The 26th São Paolo Biennial.*

54 See David Elliott and Lydie Mephan, *Silent Energy: New Art from China* (Oxford: Museum of Modern Art, 1993), 3.

55 A kind of "cuturalized" indifference to the event privately reinforced by comments to me from observers of their reaction to the Italian environment when they visited the Biennale.

56 See Wang Guangyi's comments in Huang Zhuan and Pi Li, *Tuxiang jiushi liliang/ Image is Power*, at He Xiangning Art Museum (Changsha: Hunan Meishu Chuban she, 2001), 257.

57 See Wolfger Pöhlmann et al., *China Avant-Garde*, English edition (Berlin: Haus der Kulturen der Welt & Editions Braus, 1993), 8. (Berlin: 20 January to 16 May; Oxford: 4 September to 24 October.)

58 Whether artworks are commodities and artists a kind of denotating currency, and what the rates of exchange between them might be for any particular exchange player, whether they are curator or private collector or non-purchasing "public" audience, remains open for significant analysis.

59 It almost goes without saying that this kind of information cannot be treated by insider operators as art historical data because too many quotidian interests are involved. To offer up such data to art historical analysis would probably mean that an insider operator would have to abdicate from this game.

60 See the interview with Guy Ullens in Chang Tsong-zung, *Paris-Pékin* (Paris: Chinese Century, 2002). Chang Tsong-zung says of the Ullens collection, that "this love of the arts of China, old and new, is pivotal to the way the works have been acquired" 15).

61 Feng Boyi and Qiu Zhijie, *The Monk and the Demon: Contemporary Chinese Art* (Milan: 5 Continents Editions, 2004), 122.

62 Thea, *Foci*, 29.

63 Thea, *Foci*, 29.

64 Wu Hung, with Wang Huangshang and Feng Boyi, *1st Guangzhou Triennial: Re-interpretation: a Decade of Experimental Chinese Art (1990–2000)* (Guangzhou: Guangdong Museum of Art, 2002), 18.

65 Wu, *1st Guangzhou Triennial*, 18.

66 Fan Di'an, in *Living in Time 29 zeitgenössische Künstler aus China*, 35.

67 *The 25th São Paulo Biennial*, curated by Fan with assistant Pi.

68 In a lecture by Hou Hanru at the symposium to accompany *Asian Traffic* at University of New South Wales, June 2004.

69 Among theorists who have influenced Hou Hanru are Rem Koolhaas, John Rajchman, and Saskia Sassen, Hou Hanru states in Li Luming, ed., *Guangdong Kuaiche/Canton Express* (Changsha: Hunan Meishu Chubanshe, 2003), a text distributed at the Zones of Crisis at the 2003 Venice Biennale:

> As Rajchman argues, the conceptual and practical changes in the contemporary city and its architecture have rendered traditional geometry, which is based on the linear, stable concepts of space and time, inefficient and incoherent. There is an urgent need to introduce "Other Geometries" which are multi-orientational, multi-dimensional, motional, complex and open to "other elements". These point to a "possible world" by providing us with a new starting point for perception and imagination. The task for cultural restructuring today and in the future is to accept the challenge of adapting to these "Other Geometries". (85)

70 Hou, *On the Mid-Ground*, 17.

71 Fan Di'an wrote in *The 25th São Paulo Biennial* that "For the sensitive artists, the expansion of metropolis is a driving force that stimulates imagination and thinking, a chance for using new media and new languages. It also spurs the artists to have spiritual explorations across the metropolis from his own point".

72 Thea, *Foci*, 38. Earlier in the same interview Hou said: "Sometimes you have to do a show, and you need to view a piece five or six times to understand it, but you decide to use the piece and don't have time to view it. It can be a disaster. It's a kind of curatorial schizophrenia, to deal with this anxiety. I don't think artists are rarified; they're part of our communication system" (Thea, *Foci*, 35).

73 Hou, *On the Mid-Ground*, 20.

74 Fang Zengxian, with curatorial group of Hou Hanru, Shimizu Toshio, Zhang Qing, and Li Xu, *2000 Shanghai Biennale* (Shanghai: Shanghai Shuhua Chubanshe, 2000), from text of Hou Hanru, n.p.

75 As for example, in Hou Hanru, *One Man, Nine Animals*:

> Only when based on the creative wisdom of the logic of local cultural development can the value of oneself be shown in international art exchange; and only when the consciousness and capability of absorbing and integrating contemporary information of the world can the subjectivity of international cultural dialogue be brought into play.

76 In Feng and Qui, *The Monk and the Demon* (Milan: 5 Continents Editions), 128.

77 See Chang, *Paris-Pékin* (Paris: Chinese Century, 2002), 17.

78 As for example Thierry Raspail in Feng and Qui, *The Monk and the Demon* (Milan: 5 Continents Editions), 9, (note that the exhibition does not include Luo Brothers, Fang Lijun, Cai Guoqiang, Xu Bing, Gu Wenda all of whom might qualify for exclusion under Raspail's heads): "Our concern, then, has been to emphasize works of a vertical character, and avoiding those relying on horizontality – on 'fun', the market, the artistic feat, and desperately formal excessiveness or forced individuality – as we believe that these would not outlive their immediate topicality".

79 Ronte and Smerling, *"Quotation Marks"*, 9.

80 In Huang and Pi, *Tuxiang jiushi liliang/Image is Power*, 227. Zhang Xiaogang also skewed this issue in the same volume by relating "branding" to "quality":

> Brands require volume, they are a culture. You want to express a way of thinking and communicate a kind of disposition but they are not some hand-made craft good. Because there are many cases of this, a single work gets a prize in an exhibition but there's no sound of it after that. If you really have a way of thinking, you yourself want to express, it can be a complete one. Thus a good artist doesn't have much variation in quality in his works. (239)

81 See Sung Wan-kyung, with idea and conception by Charles Esche and Hou Hanru, *Project 1 Pause: Conception* (Gwangju: Gwangju Biennale Press, 2002), 27, where the curators claimed that we "don't want to divide the space by theme, we want the viewers to divide the space by their intentions as they go around the exhibition".

82 In Lin Shu-min, *50th Venice Biennale: Limbo Zone* (Taipei: Taipei Fine Arts Museum, 2003), 8.

83 Hou Hanru, "Initiatives, Alternatives: Notes in a Temporary and Raw State", in Philippe Vergne, *How Latitudes Become Forms* (Minneapolis: Walker Art Center, 2003), 39.

84 Vergne, *How Latitudes Become Forms*, 36.

85 See Quemin, *L'art contemporain international*, and elsewhere.

86 Attempts in the early 1990s to have a foundation law established which would allow for art donations and the running of private museums met with failure, coming up against the policy for organization of non-party bodies under Leninist theory, according to my conversation with a leading Chinese art critic in 1999.

87 In this chapter I am particularly grateful at various times to the following colleagues for materials, interviews, or other help: Thomas Berghuis, Chang Tsong-zung, Jean-

Michel Ducrop, Fan Di'an, Fei Dawei, Gao Minglu, Hou Hanru, Huang Du, Huang Yongping, Gu Dexin, Li Xianting, Martina Köppel-Yang, Francesca dal Lago, Shao Dazhen, Shao Yiyang, Terry Smith, and Wu Hung.

Chapter 4

# Beginning a Biennial: The Singapore Biennale 2006

## The Singapore State

This chapter is case study in the structures and intentions which preceded the founding of one Asian art biennial, that of Singapore, which began in 2006. It also looks at the way the resulting biennial actually brought these intentions into practice, and whether or not the underlying intentions were fulfilled.

Organizing the Singapore Biennale was from the beginning a project of the city state to give prominence to its own cultural status rather than an initiative of private individuals, companies, artists, or art agencies. Certainly it sought to bring international art into Singapore, and to expose Singapore art and its cultural sites to an international gaze. But on the other hand, it also was a claim to entry to a certain kind of cultural identity, recognizable by other states and international actors.

According to a study by Yao Souchou,[1] we can see the Singapore state as a multi-faced, 'magical' entity which mobilized various kinds of historical event as traumas from which it had to escape: from geography and ethnos through Singapore's fraught location as a predominantly Chinese city in a Malay world; from the trauma of forced separation of Singapore from Malaysia in 1965 after Federation; from the historical crises mapped ideologically by the personal life of Singapore's first Prime Minister, Lee Kuan Yew, with its conflicts, mental breakdowns, puritan psychopathology and resiliently intelligent pragmatic adjustments; from the breakdown of order at the organic level of the family, by the provision of social housing geared to preserve and reproduce it through regulations binding occupancy to work and distributing housing by marital status and ethnic categorization. To these one may add escape from social disruption in the economic field by strict channelling of workplace pressures through nominated organizations; from the chaos of naked personal desire through effective control of the upwardly mobile ambitious by de facto restriction of higher positions in bureaucracies and government-owned or government-dependent companies to a *nomenklatura* of People's Action Party members whose organization and direction drew from both Leninist and Roman Catholic church models of organizational control; from dangerous political opponents by the selective and periodic application of the Internal Security Act which allowed imprisonment without trial; from loss of "democratic" political power by the ruthlessly efficient gerrymandering of political constituencies and rigorous use of the legal system against extra-parliamentary debate and media, so that chances of gaining any political leverage let alone government by opposition forces—around 2005 thought to be around 30 per cent of the population in those constituencies where opposition candidates were able to stand—were close to zero.[2]

Despite the rhetoric of freedom and democracy, of multi-cultural ethnic tolerance which are facts of street life in Singapore, as much as popular support for the finding of a "Singapore way" through the chaos of desire and freedom found in "Western" democracies, in the early 2000s the overwhelming impression of social and cultural life was of minute, even obsessive state intervention and control. When positively securing its own goals the state allowed the effective privatization of part of its own tax base through the government investment holdings company Temasek; it pursued active importation of foreign capital which changed the Singapore economy from an entrepôt and manufacturing base dependent on its local hinterland into an integral hub within a globalized economy; it carried out active and large-scale state investment in a basically meritocratic education system but one still with significant advantages to the socially and economically privileged; and it selectively supported an arts system which had both educational training, exhibition site, studio and other support components. The general cultural consequence of taking "the past as a lesson for the present;" was "imagining the worst as a way of averting it".[3] It produced the need for a "culture of excess 'that would ceaselessly alert people to real and imaginary dangers and to find means to prevent them",[4] where "worrying to excess—restlessly pondering the uncertain future—is the balm of the 'traumatic mind'".[5]

The "magic" of the Singapore state also lay in "its effort to fill in the 'empty place' of democracy with the wholesomeness of the community, with the ethical force of post-Cold War New Asia".[6] The consequences for art and its institutions were quite complex: disbursements from the public purse that created sites for art and the spectacles for them, allowed, in the main, only for a creativity anaesthetized of the political consequences of lopsided, fraction-oriented distribution of wealth. It was an openness which obviated the creation of a contestatory, splintered, and at least latently anti-establishment cultural elite. Creativity functioned neither for itself, nor for the foundation of any radical or parallel aesthetic which could be consciously and creatively out of synch with establishment values. It was incorporated into the state's pragmatic desire for spectacle and attractiveness without disturbance to social order and thereby to its own legitimacy.[7] Establishment values could be articulated as "Asian" in a purportedly oppositional pair with "Western", the former bound to community, the latter tied to an incompatible ideology of individuality and anarchic, purportedly orderless creation.[8]

Perhaps understanding of how the state intervened with culture, marked within the lineage of Aristotelian theories of tragedy and heroism, was affected by the lack, in Singapore as elsewhere in the super-modern world, of a theory of boredom. Singapore society, despite the bloody excesses of the Japanese occupation in its initial stages,[9] did not experience the actual caesura of war in the mass physical destruction on the European scale of World War II. As professional interpreters, academics, like politicians, lack an ability to understand the imaginary consequences of what happens 'after the revolution', after the end of an economy of real material needs, after the prevention of hunger and cold, even after the material and symbolic satiation of the social field with ever more goods. Could Singapore see a revolt against excess because of a lack of even a marginal escape from the compulsions inculcated and led by the state? This may be the aporia which was embedded within the "opening" to the international domain of an "internal" art world through a Biennale.[10]

## Art Institutions in Singapore

What was the institutional frame into which the biennial fitted, or with which it had at minimum to be socially articulated? Initiated as a kind of social decoration to an International Monetary Fund (IMF) conference, the biennal's frame was provided by Singapore state support for educational institutions, exhibition sites, and in a number of cases by studios for the artists.

On the face of it Singapore was well provided with a cohort of persons with fine arts training to diploma or degree level. They occupied around 1.8 per cent of all University graduates and polytechnic diploma holders, and if diploma students are included, around 318 people with fine arts training per 100,000 population, or about 2 graduates per 100,000 of the population. This last figure put Singapore in Band 3 of fine arts education internationally (see Appendix 6). Two art schools and one teacher training programme produced artists: Nanyang Academy of Fine Arts,[11] La Salle-Singapore Institute of the Arts, and the National Institute of Education at Nanyang Technological University. These were relatively well-funded, Nanyang Academy having a surplus of S$3,370,476 in 2001–02 (hereafter S$ = Singapore dollars, in 2000, S$1.00 = US$0.6) and benefiting from a Ministry of Education Grant of S$39,157,139 in the same period, of which the bulk must have been used for the new campus estimated to cost S$31,001,826 (see Appendix 6).[12]

In the production of artists, or simply those with a Fine Arts training, however, there was considerable dependence on overseas educational institutions and many artists trained to BFA and later MFA level overseas, symbolized by Tang

Da-wu, who went to Birmingham Polytechnic in 1970–74, and later to Goldsmith's College where he graduated with an MA (Fine Art) in 1985. There have been strong and continuing links with Australia, Matthew Ngui, the first Singapore artist to exhibit at Documenta (1997) being one of many to train there.[13] The University of New South Wales was also building a dedicated overseas campus in Singapore with extensive Singapore government financial support and which would have included Fine Arts teaching, but the project was abandoned as loss-making in May 2007.[14]

There was, however, no systematic domestic programme to train art critics, art historians or curators, several of the latter having taken adjunct courses in the Faculty of Architecture or the MA in Cultural Geography at National University of Singapore. Some measures of this unfulfilled demand were that up to seven Singaporean students had by 2007 received their MA. in Curatorship and Modern Art at the University of Sydney, and others received their art historical research training at the University of California, Berkeley (Kevin Chua), University of Manchester (Eugene Tan) and in the more distant past, SOAS, University of London (T.K. Sabapathy).

The heavy dependence on foreign teachers, foreign degree validation agreements such as RMIT with La Salle SIA, and the general dependence on overseas curricula within the existing Singapore art and higher educational institutions, together with the certain movement of Singapore students abroad for MFA or MA certification, *ipso facto*, placed a question-mark over the nature of a "Singapore identity" in art practice, other than the relation of art practice to life in particular Singapore conditions. This situation might have privileged certain kinds of art practice as authentic which particularly sought the relation of art to life, as opposed to those forms such as, say, Chinese landscape painting or Islamic design decoration which might have carried autonomous, culturally legitimating genealogies. Thus an artist such as Tan Swie Hian who engaged in a kind of transnational Chinese eclecticism was in this sense far less authentically a "Singaporean" artist than Lim Tzay Chuen whose work has been engaged with projects to re-name or conceptually shift—and thus demonstrate aesthetic bracketing of if not domination over—figures such as colonial memorial statues and the entirely fictitious Merlion symbol.[15]

In the domain of not-for-profit exhibition spaces, Singapore was by the early 2000s relatively well-provided for with The Substation, Sculpture Square (which held 22 exhibitions between December 1999 and December 2002),[16] and the former artist-run space Plastique Kinetic Worms. These provided accessible exhibition zones for those who had just qualified or not yet established an artistic identity. In addition, numerous community arts centres regularly hosted art association exhibitions of various types. There were also a quite widely distributed number of public art works in various open places and some of the mass transit stations.[17]

In terms of commercial galleries, one art gallery address list in 2004 gave 47 commercial galleries but this must have included some antique shops, and in

2006 the Art Galleries Association listed 21 commercial galleries showing 239 artists of which 72 artists or about 30 per cent of those shown would appear to have been Singaporean artists (including a number based in Malaysia).[18] These rudimentary figures indicate that commercial gallery sales were dominated by works from international, name-value artists, usually Chinese but with two galleries concentrating on India. Thus it was very difficult for a Singaporean artist to be taken up by commercial galleries, so increasing their dependence on not-for-profit spaces, art galleries, arts festival special exhibitions, and some art competitions. Furthermore, anecdotal conversation with some Singaporean artists shown by the commercial galleries indicated they were overwhelmingly dependent on sales by other gallery branches in Hong Kong or New York, or that their work had to be of a superficial and decorative kind to sell in the Singapore market.

There were in addition around 14 artists' groups all of which had intermittent exhibitions and provided a kind of group exposure over time.[19] Anecdotal evidence indicates that they tended to be lead by strong individuals in their initial years and then had a tendency to split or become generational clubs.

Both The Substation and Plastique Kinetic Worms have been associated with art and intellectual journals, *FOCAS* and *Vehicle*,[20] respectively, both of which have received funding from the government's National Arts Council or the private Lee Foundation, but this help to arts publications was intermittent and subject to occasional official displeasure. National Arts Council support for the 5th issue of

4.1 Issue three of *FOCAS, Forum on Contemporary Art & Society* (January 2002), published by The Necessary Stage (and later in association with The Substation).

FOCAS in 2004 was withdrawn at the last minute because it included an article with which the National Arts Council disagreed.[21] Such occasional conflicts, found between dependent arts bodies and government bureaucracies the world over, does not alter the overwhelming impression of a small, closely inter-knitted support structure for the art world. Despite such rumbling conflicts, for example, in 2002–03 The Substation could receive $183,000 and Plastique Kinetic Worms $70,000 from the National Arts Council,[22] when Lee Weng Choy, Artistic Director of The Substation, and Vincent Leow Kong Yam, Artistic Director for Plastique Kinetic Worms, were both listed among its Visual Arts Advisers for 2003–04.[23]

Indeed the fifteen-year period 1990–2005 which led up to the Biennale in 2006 can be seen as one of progressive institutionalization of art practice, marked by the extensive funding of art groups which had begun in 1990, and which would see the opening of the Singapore Art Museum in 1996. The latter followed on from the National Museum Art Gallery rental space which had closed in 1994, but the new Singapore Art Museum began with a "blockbuster and survey show" approach to exhibition making, and this vitiated the concentrated critical exposure of younger or more experimental artists except where they were taken up by various awards and competitions.[24] Despite innovative initial exhibition and collection of Southeast Asian Art this positioning was not followed through by curatorial interventions which enlivened public space. In April 2006, four months before the Biennale, the front of the Museum was painted over with *manga*-like graffiti, and such appeals to the popular on a 19th century neo-classical building could only have been envisaged if the Museum knew the front could be re-painted in preparation for the Biennale in September.

The restricted but superficially active public exhibition space before 1996, and the failure widely mentioned in art circles for the Singapore Art Museum to fully develop the functions of a Museum of Contemporary Art after that for the ten years leading up to the Biennale,[25] meant that artists generally had to stay within their art groups or more temporary associations for exhibitions, or had to exhibit in the increasing number of art competitions which standardized art subjects and practices such as the competititon sponsored by Nokia. Indeed by 1996 the then artistic director of The Substation, S. Sasitharan, saw its activities as "alternative" by default, but not by the content of their practice which he regarded by international comparison as "very mainstream".[26]

Indeed, what had been a genuinely alternative group, the Artist's Village from 1989–90, and which had moved its exhibitions from a rural site taken over by urban development into the city, was actually invited by the then newly-formed National Arts Council in 1992 to organize an exhibition at a refurbished Hong Bee warehouse as a Festival of Arts fringe event.[27] By the early 1990s there had developed a discourse of an art establishment with a permitted and aided counter-establishment. This was occasionally thrown off course by reactions such as the ire with which a performance event was greeted by public officials and politicians. It involved the simulated public tonsure of pubic hair by Joseph Ng in an artists' initiative project by the Fifth Passage (director: Suzann Victor) on 3

January 1994. The performance had addressed the arrest and press exposure of 12 men arrested for illegal allegedly homosexual activities.[28]

## Government Policies

From the late 1980s government policy increasingly moved towards the active support of art either as a community activity in which clearly political and ethnic constituencies were mobilized, or took a role in the spectacular city envisaged by government. In the words of a 1989 report art infrastructure investment was to produce,

> Good facilities and activities held to attract world class performances and exhibitions, thus creating a more congenial environment for investors and professionals to stay and tourists to visit.[29]

Here was a very clear index of how investment towards desired ends was to be directed where spectacular pleasure was somehow allowed in the avoidance of threat. The spectacle might be subject to the same economy of means where the output produced by a given unit of investment was to be the measurement of achievement. It was a direction diametrically opposed to that in which art works, however conceived, had no utilitarian calculus involved, except perhaps their ability to liberate the subject into a new imaginary space or into a new and more authentic relation with life itself. The latter was clearly the aim of some Artists' Village artists.

In the domain of sculpture, too, T.K. Sabapathy already had significantly identified two directions for Singapore sculptural practice *qua* art in 1991: one was in the assumption of a contemplative stance, that is an absorption in spectacle by the audience. The kind of spectacle was related to the policy guidelines sought for exhibitions. The other direction aimed more critically at analyzing the process of making art and systems of language, sometimes with a text or a textural reference incorporated in either the name or the physical substrate of the work.[30] This was the domain of artists, who if not exactly counter-establishment, were not involved in the subtle collusions the former path implied, and would use conceptualism as a way of unpacking ideological brackets which it might have been unproductive to engage with confrontationally, given the nature of the Singapore state.

There is not too much need to outline the government policy in attracting spectacles since this was clear from many sources, although of course there were from time to time significant details about its implementation which became clear. Suffice it to present here a few details.

The aims of the 1989 Report of the Advisory Council on Culture and the Arts, which became the National Arts Council from 1991, had been to establish Singapore as a global arts city and to inculcate an appreciation of Singapore heritage, the founding of the organizations and educational policies to achieve this being carefully assessed ten years later.[31] Among other recommendations, that to upgrade the two art schools of La Salle-SIA and Nanyang Academy of Fine Arts was accepted and resulted in very considerable capital expenditures in the early 2000s.[32] Moreover, very early on in the 1990s an association between sales and spectacular attraction to Singapore with some incidental recognition for artists was clearly in the Singapore government's mind. As Brigadier-General (Res.) George Yeo stated in late 1993,

> We want to make Singapore a centre for the arts partly for its own sake and partly because we need the arts to help make us a centre for brain services [sic]. We want talent from all over the world to meet here. We cannot work the magic without the arts.[33]

A facile link was made between the S$600 million value of art works on sale at *Trésors*, the Singapore International Fine Art & Antiques Fair, and the winners of the Phillip Morris Art competition which were announced at the same fair. The US art critic Lynn Gumpert was funded by the Singapore Tourism and Promotion Board to visit in 1996. She carefully noted the perception of a link between arts spending and general economic activity among bureaucrats.[34] Indeed, by the time of the ten-year re-appraisal, the emphasis was little changed except for a keener awareness of international links with vibrant cultures of Singaporean affinity, as well as a move into programmes to encourage collaboration with these, for which sums were carefully directed for promotional purposes. This investment also extended to,

> ...activities and programmes that will add to the excitement and attraction of our cultural scene, and do this in a way that positions Singapore as an international hub city in the arts.[35]

The weight of the term *hub* in 2000 here was firmly akin to *magic* in Yeo's 1993 statement, bound up with the application of an information and management science model of creative flows going through certain centres and being directed and "multiplied" there, rather like airline routes (without the invention of concepts of flight, aerodynamics, manufacture of aeroplanes...).[36] It closely paralleled the trajectory of spectacular absorption in Sabapathy's 1990 binary above, where it was considered as in opposition to conceptual resistance. By 2003 the National Arts Council clearly saw one of its tasks to put Singapore art into international circulation, and a series of quotations in its annual report indicate the notion of "placement", such as one from Iskandar Jalil:

> Marketing an artist is not a matter of selling art works in a gallery—it takes a concerted effort on the part of the artist and the supporting infrastructure to put a talented artist on the map.[37]

But the question of which map or whose map was not frequently asked. This mapping presumably implied in modern and contemporary art some New York MoMA-derived topology, with one or two cultural affinities—Chinese, Malay, Indian—also to be drawn in. Indeed in some of these government pronouncements a subdued sense of hysteria surfaced, as if the trauma of being a Chinese city-state in a Malay sea was not enough, as if the enormous economic advances for the security and welfare of its citizenry had something missing—dare one call it a spiritual or an aesthetic dimension?

There was a positive side to this apparent anxiety. It was seen in the Arts Education programmes of the National Arts Councils (of S$436,618)[38] in 2002 and its support for a very broad range of community organizations.[39] With various programme and housing support grants to art groups this added up to around S$6 million in the 2002 financial year. It was seen in the intention to spend not inconsiderable sums for a 3.4 million Singaporean citizen population of around S$10 million on a three-year Creative Community Singapore project from 2005.[40]

It had a negative side in the sense of a missing element in "advancement". As we have seen above, there were claims that advance was to be secured for its own sake, but also because it further enhanced the attractiveness of Singapore in providing a cultured environment of the level appropriate to attracting international business and its employees. Aesthetic values, once allowed their own space, were immediately overridden by the pragmatic or utilitarian ones mapped by the production of spectacle.

The argument that art in Singapore may have been funded for its own sake was unpersuasive because of the scale of expenditure to spectacular sites, and the clear embeddedness of the Singapore government and economic elites in their management and control. No clearer case of such provision was to be found than the Esplanade – Theatres on the Bay concert hall, theatre, and shopping complex sited next to various other hotel and shopping mall developments in the Marina area. An impressive building which opened in October 2002, it was locally christened the "Durian" for its shape but without apparently any vernacular connotation of the fruit's pungent and intoxicating smell. It was built with a grant of S$600 million—massive by even Euramerican standards—from Singapore Pools (Private) Limited and Singapore Totalisator Board based on a recommendation from the Advisory Council on Culture and the Arts chaired by the then Deputy Prime Minister Ong Teng Cheong, and built between 1996 and 2002.[41] The Esplanade, it was clearly thought, was a stage in cultural development that boosted demand for talent, and which would be followed by a stage of development of talent itself and audiences.[42]

The Esplanade was made a registered charity and public company limited by guarantee to whose directors the Ministry of Information, Communication and the Arts appointed four members including the chairman (who was also chair of its nominating committee which by 2003 had not met since establishment),[43] and the directors were appointed by the Ministry too. In the financial year 2002–03 it ran with a deficit before grants of S$31.1 million. After grants of S$27.5 million this produced an operating deficit of S$3.6 million.

In capital and cash-flow terms these were extraordinarily high figures, the operating deficit of one performance site which we must presume provided spectacles close to the elite's hearts was thus eight times the arts education budget on the National Arts Council (this did not include support through Ministry of Education outlays under a very different budget head), or half the total amount spent on arts support. Speculatory comparisons are facile, and capital and income expenditures were notoriously subject to the vagaries of political assessment, for The Esplanade itself clearly had many broader cultural creation and artist formation effects. But when it is realized that the Chairman of the National Arts Council, Liu Thai Ker, who was in charge of the latter's budget, was also one of the four members of The Esplanade nominated by the Ministry of Information, Communication and the Arts,[44] one has to conclude that the provision of sites for spectacle was a more important Singapore elite priority than arts education. It was more important than the concomitant production of artists or the raising of educated appreciation of the arts by the wider community, however much they were to be provided for by National Arts Council or Education budgets.

## Precursor Exhibitions

Similar background considerations in the run-up to organizing a biennial for the first time could be provided for each country that hosts one, and also for the many kinds of targeted participation in international arts flows which are supported by national governments. In the Singapore case, perhaps of greater significance were two kinds of investment in exhibitions: at the national level by the Nokia and Seni exhibitions, and at the international level by national participation at the Venice Biennale.

The immediate precursor exhibitions for the *2006 Singapore Biennale* were *Seni-Singapore 2004* and *Singapore Art 2005*, co-organized by the National Arts Council and the National Heritage Board to which Singapore Art Museum reports. In fact the organization of *Seni* (a Malay word translated to mean "Arts", *Bahasa Melayu* still being the official language of Singapore) brought together the two bodies which have been responsible for most government arts policies. The news release for *Seni-Singapore 2004* and *Singapore Art 2005* which reprised the sentiments of Minister George Yeo we saw above of 12 years earlier, gave the following precursor exhibitions:[45]

1969 *National Day Art Exhibition* and on until 1986
1986 *Singapore Art Fair*
1993 *Trésors d'Art* (an art fair with a curated section)
1995 *Singapore Art '95*
1997 *Singapore Art '97*

1999 *Nokia Singapore: Art, City/Community: Singapore art today*
2001 *Nokia Singapore Art: Histories/Identity/Technologies/Space* with a new cyber art component.
2001 *The President's Young Talents Exhibition* inaugurated at Singapore Art Museum.
2003 *The President's Young Talents Exhibition*
2004 *Seni-Singapore 2004–Art and the Contemporary*
2005 *Singapore Art 2005*
2006 *Singapore Biennale*

(Other art competitions have been run by Phillip Morris, Toshiba, and United Overseas Bank).

We have seen above the importance of the art fair in setting part of the government's agenda for artistic creation. At some point, possibly due to meetings with the then Paris-based curator of Chinese origin Hou Hanru who came to Singapore in 1997 in preparations for *Cities on the Move*, possibly due to increased professionalization of the arts exhibition field brought on by movement of Singapore Art Museum curators whose perceptions of accepted practice in international exhibitions developed, it was decided to join international curators to the Nokia exhibitions, and Hou Hanru wrote a catalogue essay for this in 2001.[46] One future priority of Biennale organization was for such exhibitions to function in international networks in order to expose bodies like the Singapore Art Museum to other international curatorial players. It was followed by the invitation to Okwui Enwezor, then about to curate Documenta XI, to come as a symposium speaker for *Nokia 2001*. Enwezor went on to select the Singapore new media collective Tsunamii.net for Documenta XI in 2002. One of its members, Charles Lim Yi Yong had only just graduated, but from the metropolitan centre of St. Martin's College in London. Here again one may question that even if some of the international selections were non-canonical by local criteria, international curators may have had a different notion of what was sufficiently 'in the wave' to be canonized through their selection.

Notwithstanding the "pre-set" nature of "advanced" international taste, these exhibitions did present an opportunity to send local, non-internationally canonical views of Singapore art to an international audience, especially in essays and selections by Ahmad Mashadi,[47] Huangfu Binghui,[48] and Suzie Wong.[49] The main difference between *Nokia 1999* and *Nokia 2001* would appear to have been the shift in quality, the former having had Open and Awardee sections, the latter having a single Main Exhibition over several sites. But the whole was then curated, so providing the "great advantage: evenly high quality works sharing a common theme".[50] Lim Chee Onn, Chairman of the National Heritage Board, also noted a group of younger artists from the 1999 exhibition who had become prominent internationally or had been selected as national representatives for Venice in 2001. These he assessed as having "made good progress in establishing their credentials internationally. This augurs well for the development of Singapore's visual arts scene".[51] Senior members of the Singapore art world clearly thought development would necessarily result in qualities in art which could be internationally recognized.

*The President's Young Talents Exhibition* in March 2003 definitely showed a shift in curatorial recognition and far sharper knowledge of what international curators might want towards younger artists who could receive more notice internationally.[52] Thus *Seni 2004* must be conceived of as part of a long learning curve in deliberate government funding allocations over a wide range of activities, the provision of local organizational structures and an increased understanding of the gap between local and international appraisal which could at some point penetrate the decision-making process and the narrowly-recruited members of the Singapore elite who constituted its participants. The very structure of this decision-making is probably beyond full understanding but to an outsider the concrete case of *Seni* constituted five levels, if we leave out those linkages above them to other politicians and civil service ministries such as Finance:

1. Political I: the Minister of Information, Communication and the Arts
2. Administrative I: the civil servants who advise him or her
3. Political II: the Chairs and Chief Executive officers of the National Arts Council and the National Heritage Board, and the other members of *Seni Singapore 2004*, Steering Committee.[53]
4. Administrative II: The Artistic Director of *Seni* (Professor Chua Beng Huat)
5. Administrative III: seconded officers from other Departments working on this project

The Artistic Director of *Seni 2004*, Chua Beng Huat, who was a sociologist working for the Asia Research Institute of the National University of Singapore, was not formally a member of the Steering Committee. The appointment of Artistic Director had been declined by the art historian and frequent commentator on contemporary art, T.K. Sabapathy, because he thought he would not be properly appointed and paid.[54] Chua was clearly selected because he understood quite a lot about art, had the flexibility from his research position to do the job, and also knew how to present issues to decision-makers with an appropriate political sensitivity.[55] It is not easy to deduce the flow of information and decisions in the Singapore bureaucracy, but it was most often described to me that there was a perpetual tendency for bureaucratic decisions to be sent from an efficient, executive level up to a higher dignified, political level where there would be interventions of preference by those well placed to represent an implicit climate of political opinion to the executive level beneath.

One evident example was in the selection of Tan Swie Hian for the Venice Biennale to be discussed below, but there are other sides to this arms length policy seen in the *Seni 2004* exhibition. In the event this included an extensive review of art collectives and some quite acerbically critical Indonesian political art from the Taring Padi Group (which I saw) and which one might have thought would not have been welcomed if it had come from Singapore sources, or had treated Singapore material. The cartoon-banning incident in 1998 might have served as a learning experience for the Singapore elite. The 2004 exhibition also included a retrospective view on The Artists' Village which tended to indicate a sense of historical objectivity was beginning to be applied in public exhibitions for at least the recent past of Singapore contemporary art.

As various observers indicated about *Seni 2004*, this exhibition was so clearly being promoted as a preparation for the 2006 Biennale that the very obvious contribution of another and subsidiary exhibition of new media art, *Moving Pictures* by Media Art Asia Pacific (MAAP), was downplayed. This subsidiary exhibition had been in preparation for three years in Australia and several Singapore art world figures noticed that it had booked out most of the Singapore Art Museum in advance of the decision on and organization for *Seni 2004*.[56] MAAP's exhibition may have served as an implicit model for the type of organization and length of preparation required for a Biennale. But it did involve problems of more long-standing biennials which were prone to include work from other biennials, or brought in pre-packaged sub-exhibitions by other curators or groups.

## Singapore at the São Paolo and Venice Biennials

By 2006 Singapore had experienced a very wide range of exposure to international art with exhibitions at the Singapore Art Museum since 1996, and to the situating of Singapore artists in international milieu. The opportunities for the latter chiefly came through international biennale exhibitions.[57] Matthew Ngui was selected for the 1997 *Documenta X* because his work had been seen at São Paolo in 1996 by the *Documenta X* artistic director Catherine David.[58] Likewise the media collective Tsunamii.net was chosen for *Documenta XI* because Okwui Enwezor, who as we noted above, had seen their work at *Nokia Singapore Art 2001* where he had been invited to speak at a symposium.[59] Whatever the actual decision chain and the coincidence of these selections with the circulation of international curators, they must have made the Singapore Art Museum aware that international curators could privilege Singapore artists by such selection.

The 2001, 2003, and 2005 Singapore Pavilions at the Venice Biennale varied in their intentions and procedures. In 2001, the intention seemed very simply to privilege Singapore by showing off four young and internationally recognized contemporary artists with a collection of texts by several younger curators.[60] In 2003, it was to privilege Singapore practice and the organizing institution, the Singapore Art Museum, in the international and domestic circuits by the coupling of a senior artist with two quite different younger ones.[61] In the third in 2005, the intention was to privilege Singapore as the producer of one young, 'cutting-edge' and inventive artist who was able to display a kind of artistic maturity for his country by the conceptual irony he was able to display towards a national icon, the Merlion statue.

For the artists the impact was seen more in a change of terms in which contemporary art was regarded in Singapore than as a reflection of the state of art in Singapore. Matthew Ngui encapsulated it thus: "I do not see this so much as a maturation of the art scene but as a small political gain in the profile of contemporary art in Singapore".[62] But there is no doubt that exhibition at Venice gave the artists greater self-confidence, and took away the edge of diffidence they may have felt before. Salleh Japar noted the greater responsibility of the artist which came with the more prestigious arena for the art, and added, "But I am convinced of our ability to engage in art practice at this level". [63]

Like all exhibitions, minor details also point to a deeper set of intentions via their subtexts. The Singapore pavilion moved from the Scola di Santa Apollonia in 2001, to the Fondazione Levi, Palazzo Giustianian fronting the Canal Grande in 2003, and in 2005 to the Calle della Tana, the single exhibition space opposite the entrance to the Arsenale. By 2005, the exhibition was thus intended to be seen by all those who considered the curatorial concept-driven exhibition in the Arsenale of main significance, as opposed to the other national pavilions in the Giardini. This indicated a shift in the official appreciation in Singapore of how the Venice Biennale functioned in circulating artists and countries as their producers.

Exhibition documentation also revealed another shift in self-confidence of the Singapore organizers in the minor entries by the Vice-Commissioner Paolo de Grandis, whose associated company ran many exhibition spaces in Venice for those countries without a Giardini pavilion (and who pay for this service). His statements showed a movement from a grandiose set of hints about discovery of the Asian future in 2001, "Singapore sparkles like a diamond, being the most perfect, beautiful and modern metropolis in the world",[64] followed in 2003 by curatorial-like interventions, "Their sense of awareness...is not coloured by an inevitable absurdity, or metaphysical anguish. It is not passive and indeterminate, but social and political",[65] to in 2005 a conceptual "profundity", "Art: *mise en abyme* effect. No Judgement! Let's accept the admonishment and play with the artist!".[66] It is followed on a whole page with no other text but a quotation from Samuel Beckett's *Endgame:* "This is what we call making an exit". The 2005 Singapore exhibition at Venice was a very definite move away from the slightly diffident approach mediated by a local art expert in 2001, towards a standard international exhibition for recognition format with a single artist, curator Eugene Tan, and essays by a poet Alfian Sa'at and an architectural critic-publisher, Peter Schoppert. But it really did not indicate much of a change in the overseas representation of Singapore which since Matthew Ngui at Documenta in 1997 has been mostly of conceptual artists recognizable in Euramerica, and even theoretically positioned in 2005 by a curator who had a PhD from Manchester University in art history.

What happened in 2003? The selection of the neo-traditional Tan Swie Hian alongside rising younger conceptual artists was surprising. The Giustianian Palace setting was magnificent. I observed that the opening ceremony was extraordinarily lavish and crowded out by visiting dignitaries from the Singapore political and arts worlds. Tan Swie Hian's gushingly eclectic work presented a case of the difference between national and international contemporary art appraisals.[67] His work was that of a locally respected senior artist.[68]

In short the 2001, 2003, and 2005 Singapore selections for the Venice Biennale show an indexical link between the knowledge about international art circulation and the kinds of operational insertion of artists likely to achieve this. But above and beyond there was a circulation of perceptions between a various international and domestic levels mapped by international political-managerial culture at Davos on the one hand and transnational curatorial judgements at Documenta and Venice on the other. In play were a series of notions about what it meant for Singapore to have a contemporary art of a kind which was recognized by that circulation. We shall see now how the actual Singapore Biennale in 2006 manifested these linkages.

## Singapore Biennale 2006, an Analytical Review

The Singapore Biennale was intended to be "global and cosmopolitan yet with distinctly Singaporean characteristics" (Lee Boon Yang).[69] It could be seen as the last stage in a line of state-funded institutions and spectacles which reflected the "prestige anxiety" of the Singapore government, tied to deeper structures of self-perceived lack more broadly seated in the Singapore community.[70] If not on a world scale, then certainly on an Asian regional stage, the first Singapore Biennale in 2006 hoped to make Singapore more prominent, even though the notion of "Asia" to be deployed was in flux.[71] Singapore itself, a first-world country operating inside a linguistic ecumene provided by English, but located in Southeast Asia, was an identity subject to much ambivalence of its own and its situation's making. If it was not an overwhelmingly Overseas Chinese, secular city-state island in a Malay/Indonesian and largely Muslim sea, perhaps Singapore would not have had to prove its accession to an international level which went beyond the limitations of its geographical and cultural placement.

But Singapore *was* so located. It tried through the policies of state organizations to go beyond these regional limitations through biennial goals articulated on the international and domestic levels. One of the goals of such large-scale events was to "reach out to international audiences and register a critical endorsement", but it also "aims to bring current international art practices closer to the people of Singapore and to nourish their enthusiasm for it".[72] The aim of at least the officials running the Biennale was that it should continue, be firmly implanted in Singaporean art discourses, and not be "a spaceship landing in Singapore for two months and then flying away".[73] For politicians, cultural activities were the spectacle of ornament for other events, and, according to the opening speech by Dr Lee Boon Yang, Minister of Information,

Communications and the Arts, in the IMF and World Bank meetings which were to be held two weeks after the opening of the Biennale, the Biennale would function as "an interesting cultural backdrop" and "will show our guests how the arts have become an integral part of Singapore's development and in the life of our people, making our city global and cosmopolitan yet with distinctly Singaporean characteristics".[74] The Biennale was held on some scale over three large sites, the former City Hall and law court complex, Singapore's National Museum, Tanglin Camp, and many smaller sites in places of religious worship.

The Biennale opened at a massive party with rock groups, fashion show, and "young" crowd, dedicated marquee on the *padang* (public open field), and opening by the Prime Minister, all of which marked a cross-generational self-confidence behind these assertions.

For Dr Lee, the theme of the Biennale was "Belief" because of interconnected nature of the contemporary world with its porous borders and torrents of information which made it difficult for some to know what they believed in. Therefore, the recognition of diversity of beliefs would contribute to the improvement of our humanity. The pro-government news media *Channel NewsAsia* chose, however, to highlight another aspect of Dr Lee's speech where he had said,

> Not all arts are intuitively ennobling, inspiring, educational or entertaining. Some are thought-provoking. Some are instantly persuasive. Others are deliberately controversial, but controversy *per se* does not necessarily mean higher quality. This means we need to be discerning in our appreciation and mature in the manner in which we debate and embrace the arts.[75]

This excerpt can be read as having a sub-text, "we have allowed this kind of art to be shown, and do not want our population/officials to get too upset about works they and the government might previously have abhorred". It is known from public statements at the opening press conference by the artistic director Nanjô Fumio that the Minister (presumably Dr Lee Boon Yang) was informally consulted about certain works which might have caused the authorities difficulties, but it would appear in the end none were asked to be changed or toned down. A certain measure of cosmopolitan tolerance, presumably subject to test and revision from time to time, was thus established.

Certainly some works by local Singaporean artists could be construed as politically edgy if artistically not totally successful. The video installation work of Jason Wee's *1987* in a City Hall courtroom linked the memories held in common with his grandmother to the public event of an Internal Security Department operation against a purported Marxist group.[76] This was certainly controversial in Singaporean political-cultural terms. Brian Gothong Tan's installation *We Live in a Dangerous World* offered a walkway with its plugged-in "Singapore citizen" ghouls and a sort of satirical video at the back of the installation in which the face of Senior Minister Mentor Lee Kuan Yew and father of the then Prime Minister was

4.2 Amanda Heng, *Worthy Tour Co (S) Pte* (2006). Mixed media installation at the Singapore Biennale, 2006. Photograph by John Clark.

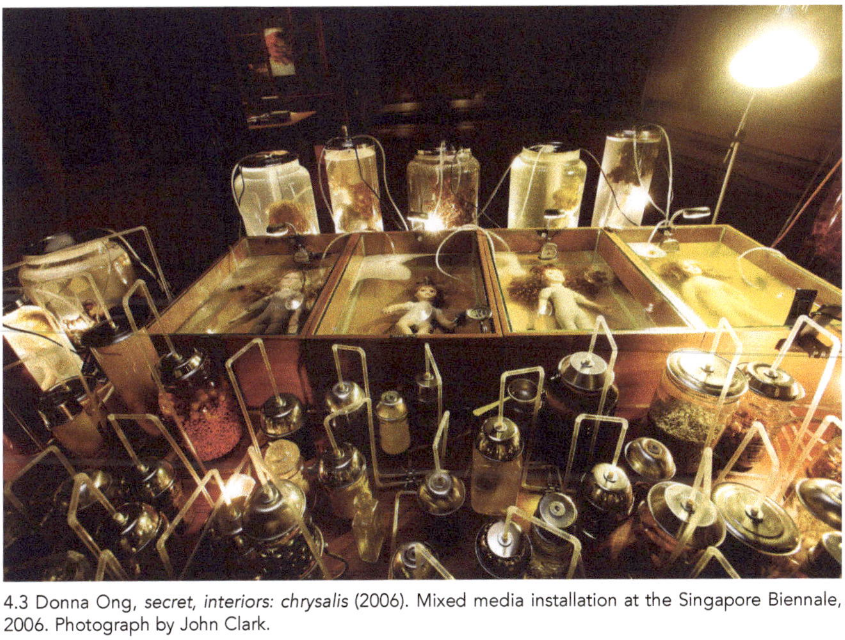

4.3 Donna Ong, *secret, interiors: chrysalis* (2006). Mixed media installation at the Singapore Biennale, 2006. Photograph by John Clark.

visible for a micro-second along with other Asian political leaders. It was all too much to expect a Singapore Gothic in achieved political-cultural critique mode to have been found in one piece, but the hints of a direction were plain among the other Singapore artists.

Ho Tzu-Nyen showed a video, *Bohemian Rhapsody*, including burlesque of a trial, but given that many of the luxuriously wood-paneled, former courtroom sites in the Town Hall, exuded a hegemony which the artist could confront or subvert, this work could have been politically problematic. Amanda Heng's *Worthy Tour Co (S) Pte* was a polite, ironic spoof on a travel agency plus pseudo-official tourism propaganda. Her work "playfully questions the idea of an 'official culture' and explores how diverse cultural memories and identities can form a space for discussion and revelation".[77] Donna Ong's more metaphysical *secret, interiors: chrysalis* series through its glass jars, dead infants, and early 19th century air of unspeakable biological experimentation, realized a more achieved direction towards showing how horrors were imagined, a kind of worm of doubt flying in the night of rosy Singapore control and prosperity.[78] As Lam Yishan asked, "What makes people continue to believe, without the assurance that these beliefs will be rewarded?"[79]

The ultimate subversion lay in the conceptual track, away from the spectacle of a well-made fine art object, as seen in Singapore via the trajectory from Tang Dawu's work of the early 1990s which was not exhibited, but photographs of which were on show at the Singapore Art Museum, to Lim Tzay Chuen. The underlying conception was of a work or an act which took an existing meaning from the environment and relativized or overturned it. The work asked the viewer to question the status of the act, location of objects, or their complex inter-relation. The Biennale saw an elegantly invisible case of this in Lim Tzay Chuen's *The Opposite is True #2* when the artist entered the City Hall site on 9 July 2006 and sprayed the inside of the building with a fog of synthesized human pheromones, chemicals produced by a living organism which transmit the messages that trigger communication signals of a sexual nature that attract or repel beings to one another. The only trace of his action at the time of the opening was in the photograph of the artist from the back in the Exhibition Short Guide, and in presumably the different relations between visitors to the building due to the traces of the pheromones. To limit his own attraction to the building the artist had worn protective clothing whilst fogging.[80] Nihilist superiority might be thought cognate with terrorist anti-values to distinguish such an invisible insertion of the attractors of art into the discourses of site and the hegemonic state's enabling of the event. But I think Lim's action was in the line of humanist absurdism rather than destructive nihilism, since he wanted a sympathetic attraction to take place even through its invisibility: the action situated art as a political joke, and, protected by its subtlety, this may have been more subversive of political hegemony than any other kind of de-valuing, and almost certainly was so in the Singapore context.

The position advanced in the catalogue and in several press conference statements—that Singapore was a multi-cultural society with a tolerance for different religious expressions—was belied by the overwhelming ethnic dominance of the Chinese population who constitute about 75 per cent of the total population.[81] The notion that Singaporean society was particularly devoted to religious beliefs as a prop to its understanding of life—despite the evident freedom of worship for Buddhists, Christians, Hindus, and Muslims—was quite strange, even weird. Singapore society is marked by the daily obsessive belief of its elites in political power, its masses in consumer economic power, and its thinkers and administrators in techno-managerial power.[82] The belief in an economically unconstrained, even empowered multi-culturalism was referred to by Hossein Golba's work which exhibited a gold bar in a museum-like perspex case at the head of the City Hall stairs, with the words "The Diversity is Value [sic]" molded into the bar, suggesting universal value and commercialism.[83] Here lay a most peculiar and magically fantasmal correlation: the Biennale took place alongside the World Bank/IMF conference but every direct connection with it was obfuscated at the opening press conference and in the catalogue despite the fact of its coming to Singapore being the rationale for the original Biennale budget allocations.[84] Even so, in parallel and almost as an aside, the connection to self-perceptions of Singapore's accession to an international economic order was noted with surprising clarity at the ending of the opening press conference. The Chairman of the Steering Committee situated the Biennale within a trajectory of pragmatic Singapore adjustment to its environment, one where "the arts" were delegated a particular function in creative learning:

> We did not start the Biennale with the economic imperatives in mind, although the economic outcomes are not insignificant. Singapore is moving from an industrial economy to an innovation-driven economy. In this phase of development the economy is being driven by innovation and imagination will be very important. We believe that arts is a very important trainer of imagination. So we believe that arts can be an important catalyst for the economy .... At the same time arts is [sic] also an important contributor to the economy as a business ... So I would say at this stage of development that this Biennale can contribute in both tangible and intangible ways.[85]

There was a kind of discrete Buñuel-like charm in the Singaporean claim that the Biennale was about belief when it was actually both a symbol and a manifestation of accession to a different level of the international economic order. The indirect, almost diffident, care of Singaporean artists in treating this situation varied, as we have seen, from conceptual humour to gothic horror: it was better to implicate rather than accuse.

Such a pellucid strategy appeared in the work of Simryn Gill, a Malaysian artist of Indian background who lives in Australia but who has spent periods of her life in and out of Singapore. She chose to do photographic work and contributed deceptively simple texts to a guide/commentary on the Murals at Tanjong Pagar railway station. As part of the work, the artist's guide was on sale at the station newsstand. This station had been built in a late art-deco manner by a Serbian architect in 1932 and included six large murals in a "vast almost cavernous, central hall".[86] Gill's "Guide" was to introduce these ignored works by deliberately understated reference to their colonial origins, and their juxtaposition with casual, *almost* haphazard photographs of travelers on their way through it.

The station, it transpired, was still Malaysian territory due to a 999-year colonial lease and the railway company was still Malaysian. Since it was the major transport entry point into Singapore until the 1980s and also the site of a now vacated and apparently abandoned hotel where many travelers had stayed, the station and the representation of the then Malaya, Singapore being a separate crown colony, was like a congealed historical portal between the adjacent countries, state systems, and cultures. Gill's work was an eloquent testament to the "pointing" function of art, not letting memory slip into a kind of historical and ideologically-driven amnesia. It also indicated that a culture did not need to have a gone through a physically violent historical trauma to facilitate such intentional oblivion.

History may provide a little impediment to the trite conceptualization of Biennale displays. Contemporary societies, even contemporary art are the product of their historical precursors. For some reason the Steering Committee sidetracked what was an important and rare exhibition of Southeast Asian art of the 1970s at the Singapore Art Museum. It was also one curated by the only Bahasa Indonesia-speaking Singaporean in the original curatorial team, Ahmad Mashadi.[87] Billed in the Biennale short guide—the full catalogue was expected to come as a Special Programme, on visiting the exhibition it turned out to be a major, carefully curated and documented survey where much of the practice was an important precursor for the works done at least by some of the Southeast Asian artists in the Biennale. But it was left for the Biennale without a catalogue (although one was later produced) or even a detailed checklist. Perhaps in the reputedly Singapore S$8 million dollar budget for the Biennale there was not enough slack at the time to set aside S$20,000 for its printing. Either the immediate pre-history of regional art was too denuding of authentic originality for the contemporary, or this history, which included the early pop-art, conceptualism, and expressions of popular solidarity in opposition to the political situation in many Southeast Asian countries, was the kind of specific, regional history the Biennale organizers preferred not to foreground.

The Exhibition Short Guide listed 99 named artists and groups and omitted the special programmes and satellite events. However, the fact sheet distributed in the media pack indicated 118 artists, including collectives, of whom 29 or about 25 per cent were given as Southeast Asian. If we include 17 from East Asia, 10 from South Asia, 2 from Australasia, and 3 from Central Asia, 61 artists or about 52 per cent were living and working in Asia. 12 artists or about 10 per cent were Singaporean or worked largely in Singapore. This compared with the around 2+ per cent of Japanese artists exhibiting at the Yokohama Triennale in

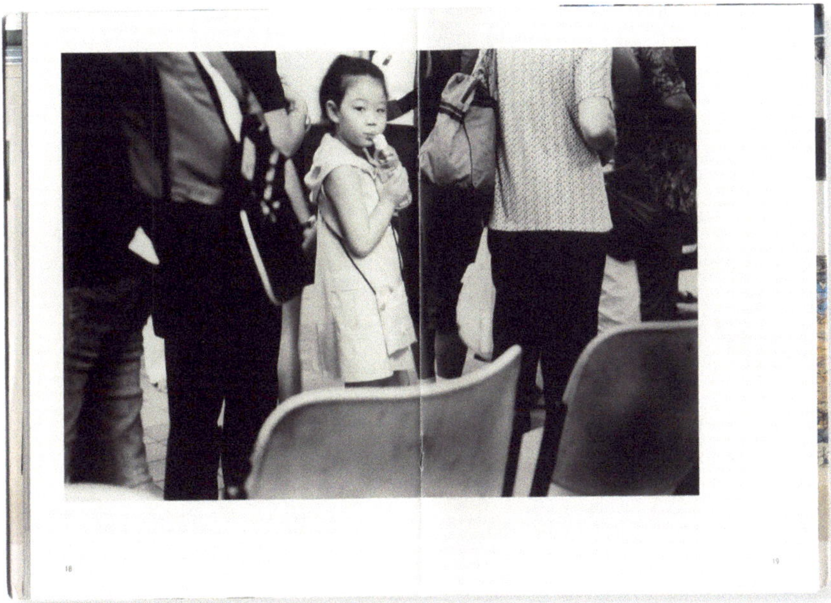

4.4 Doublespread from pamphlet, displayed and sold at the KTM Singapore Railway Station. Simryn Gill, 2006.

2005, or the about 60 per cent artists of Korean and Chinese origin exhibiting at Gwangju and Shanghai Biennials respectively in 2004. This simple proportion indicates how overwhelmingly international was the selection of artists. These proportions might have been due to a perceived dearth of Singaporean artists of the requisite level, but this was surely a discrimination of the Artistic Director or the other curators, since even a non-specialist in Singapore art like myself could rapidly assemble a list of around to 10 or so others who might have been shown. This number would also have rapidly risen if we also included 'Malaysian' artists within the penumbra, more than the single artist selected who might have been so identified.[88]

The resulting biennial was mostly of works form a zone designated "The World" (under many other caveats) and "Asia". Half of the latter came from "Singapore". There was a curatorial pretension evident to have represented works at the regional level of "Southeast Asian regional art" to those of a vaguely understood level of "international art". To have established this distinction more strongly would have required about half the artists to be from Southeast Asia. This would have required a far larger selection from the Philippines and Indonesia, compared with which the Singapore contingent might not have stood out. There was some refreshing originality in the selection of relatively unknown artists from China, India and Sri Lanka, but rather obvious, tired and even some tedious works from Japan which I will examine below.

4.5 Installation view of Vladimir Kupriyanov, *Medirussian Antiquity* (2006). Mixed media, video, and sound. Exhibited at the Singapore Biennale, 2006. Photograph by John Clark.

The European art was of high quality even if the artists were well-known. It included Carsten Nicolai—an expensive, super-high tech acoustic installation. The work by Bigert and Bergström was a confronting video about the last supper given to convicts about to undergo capital punishment. The artists told me that Singapore had the highest per capita capital punishment rate in the world.[89]

But if political eyebrows had been raised this was not in evidence. Mark Wallinger had a procession of 16 flags on the pattern of the Union Jack but in the colours of the Indian Tricolour, 2007 being 60 years from Indian Independence in 1947, and 150 years since the Great Indian Revolt of 1857, or as Erica Tan's very politically correct essay called it the "first Indian War of Independence".[90] This was an expensively funded project art circulated between various biennial or other festival sites. The level of finish and display showed that the biennale and thereby Singapore had truly reached an "international" level, and that the new spaces in the Singapore National Museum were on the grandest and most technically impressive scale.

Among other European artists, Vladimir Kupriyanov demonstrated once more, after works by Olga Chernysheva shown at the Sydney Biennale, and work at other exhibitions in 2006 at the Kunstverein in Kassel by Petersburg artists—how significant and broadly-based Russian video art has become. Kupriyanov intelligently combined photographic memorabilia, photographic replica panels of old, peeling mural paintings (life-size) and video of social rituals with carefully adjusted music that took the viewer into a kinaesthetic space moving between sound and photographic image, sound and moving image, even as their own body moved through the work.

4.6 Installation view of Agus Suwage and Titarubi, *Crossroad* (2006). Mixed media installation exhibited at the Singapore Biennale, 2006. Photograph by John Clark.

Among the Asians, Xu Bing made his honorary entrance with his Europeanized Chinese character writing applied to a carpet, but to little obvious or immediate aesthetic effect. Indeed it later became clear his work had been intended for a temple site but was rejected because the words woven into a carpet were from a religious text on which it would have been inauspicious to walk. The work was re-located to a landing area in the Singapore National Museum but this slip was not noted for the general public. The Taiwanese artist Tsai Char-wei made a far more intelligent and innovatory use of script forms in calligraphy written on Lotus leaves and in a Buddhist sutra copied onto a block of fresh *tôfu/douhu*, fully manifesting the Buddhist notions of transcience through the flower which rises from the mud (of worldly karma) and is not polluted, and the stink of which would arise around the wreck of the decaying *tôfu*, replete with its inscribed transcendental truths. A Philippine artist working in Puerto Rico, Charles Juhász-Alvarado, showed a pinball game, life-size but made from plywood and cardboard. Perhaps coincidentally this reprised the exhibition of a similarly super-sized actual table-top football game by the Japanese artist Kosugei in the 2005 Yokohama Triennale. Agus Suwage reminded the visitor that not only European soldiers died on the Burmese railways: hundreds of thousands of forced Southeast Asian labourers did so too, particularly those from Indonesia.

Some visitors learned that Tanglin Camp, the third major exhibition site, had been a British military base since the 1870s which had developed after the military vulnerability demonstrated during the Indian Revolt of 1857 and which became a Singapore Military hospital later.[91] What happened there between 1942 and 1945?[92] Were the viewers surrounded by the ghosts of those the Japanese executed too, as local rumour had it? Perhaps the opening of the camp and the art would have the prophylactic effect of placating the ghosts or just shooing them away, and then the disused camp, depleted of its supernatural terrors, could become a site for real estate development.

What indeed was the viewer to make of the Japanese art shown, in an exhibition whose artistic director, as well as one of the four "junior" curators, was from Japan.[93] Kusama Yayoi, who might have been the most internationally famous living Japanese contemporary artist, showed a winding installation on the trees of Orchard Road, the main shopping precinct, and a *Ladder to Heaven* installation of a ladder wound with Light Emitting Diode (LED) cables between two mirrors on the top floor of the Sri Krishna Temple. This produced the artist's characteristic mesmerization through image-replication of the ladder to infinity. Perhaps this was based on the religious belief implied in the title, but it would need a religious ritual to enshrine it, and that was absent even though the site was clearly a temple.

The high-tech computer-modulated, massive glass LED by Mori Mariko, international New York resident, with her quaint and quirky new age religious beliefs in cosmology and our human ability to seek order, it was interesting and certainly related to the conceptual theme. But this work, like another of hers in similar vein shown at Venice in 2005, had a kind of a-literal non-narrative opacity, a bit like *2001* without the script of Arthur C. Clarke or the visual genius of Stanley Kubrick. Such a refusal to provide meaning other than a cute fairground joke was seen in the installation of Kuribayashi Takashi where the viewer could see the head of another visitor emerge within an aquarium at floor level. Beneath the floor one could see a strange decapitated penguin, and by going up a quite different ladder emerge inside the pool of a tropical garden visible to no-one else. Clever, well-made, it was a little conceptually challenging unlike Mori Mariko, but after all just an art circus trick. Aida Makoto, one of the domestic superstars of revived "popist" Japanese-style painting, and marginally assimilated to super-flat,[94] distinguished himself by allowing a super-manga of onanistic self-disembowelment by teenage girls to be shown at the Singapore National Museum,[95] even as he presented himself as a punk jungle king at Tanglin Camp. There was no doubt Aida Makoto has attitude, and has tried to turn this into a theory by means of a manifesto. But despite the efforts of his curator to present Aida's work by its devotion to Japanese subject matter as denouncing "the vainglorious antics of professional tasters such as chefs who rework a dull hybridity",[96] his interventions in the mediated everyday as works, whatever his intention, only manifest a kind of impotent puerility, a flaunted distance from

4.7 Mori Mariko, *Tom Na H'iu I* (2006). Mixed media installation, glass, stainless steel, LED, real time control system, 327.4 x 115.3 x 39.6 cm. Installed at the National Museum of Singapore for the Singapore Biennale, 2006. © Mariko Mori. Photo by Richard Learoyd. Image courtesy of SCAI THE BATHHOUSE and Sean Kelly, New York.

4.8 Aida Makoto, the artist posing before his work. Photograph by John Clark.

realities or profound beliefs, where all Aida's technical skills and media-savviness merely served as a screen for a kind of culturally sanctioned narcissism.

Africa appeared in the guise of the political uncanny found by Jane Alexander's strange semi-human beasts inhabiting a court-room where there was no judge, and providing a sense of the uncanny which left me shivering with fear: those recently escaped from totalitarian systems can really show that horror is still around us. This was reputedly the only work to which the Singaporean Minister of Culture had objections, mollified by an explanation by the artistic director, Nanjô Fumio.

Africa/India also appeared in the amazingly fecund but ultimately zany video-like installation of an expatriate Indian, Sheba Chhachhi, who had lived in the Ethiopian capital Addis Ababa, where her father was the Indian military attaché. Her work turned out to be an illusionary loop of cartoon figures moving across a kind of aquarium background via a painted mechanical loop. The artist moved home to work in New Delhi.

For me, the most moving work was the most simple: a video by Jennifer Wen Ma, who was born in China and now lives in the United States, of a hand slowly filling with glass balls and then releasing them to the combined sound-track of the prayers of three different religions. The work was located in three different religious sites, the Masjid Sultan, Saint Joseph's Church, and Maghain Aboth Synagogue, and although I only visited the first, Jennifer Ma informed me that the soundtrack was slightly different between each site. The work's rigorous beauty, its engagement with time, the fated frailty of our grasp of it, the entering and leaving the hands of the glass beads, were a metaphor for our lives, so conscious of but so little able in the end to alter our existence.[97] If the viewer was to be allowed access to the aesthetic of resignation and prayer, even if not a co-religionist, this was a very vivid enactment of the conceptual frame of the Biennale.

Meaning of another than artistic kind is regularly found at biennials, and Singapore was no exception: city-spruiking, political posturing, international art network glitzing, ridiculous curatorial puffing, decoration of mass or elite spectacle, and the institutionalization of contemporary art where it has mostly been transitory or absent. Like Gill's work at Tanjong Pagar, or Alexander's sculptures in the Town Hall, Ma showed that this biennial could be a site where genuine exploration within a given conceptual frame was possible, one which was open for realization by a sincere artist.

The artistic significance of a biennial lies in this discrete, quiet and different space for art beyond the telegrams and anger that may have allowed it to become possible, or through which it is usually self-propagandized.

## Acknowledgements

I am grateful for a Visiting Fellowship at the Asia Research Institute, National University of Singapore from December 2003 to February 2004 when I was there to prepare the conference *Our Modernities, Positioning Asian Art Now*. I was also enabled to do research for this chapter. Some of these conference papers are included in John Clark, Maurizio Peleggi, and T.K. Sabapathy, ed., *Eye of the Beholder* (Sydney: Wild Peony, 2006).

I would like to thank the following for their kind assistance with interviews and materials in connection with this research: Yao Souchou, Kwok Kian Chow [12.2003–2.2004, and the library of the Singapore Art Museum for press cuttings on the 2001 and 2003 Singapore pavilions at Venice], Ray Langenbach [11.2.2004], Isobel Lee of Plastique Kinetic Worms [5.2.2004], Joanna Lee [5.12.2003], Lee Weng Choy [16.6.2005], Iola Lenzi [12.2003-2.2004], Lim Tzay-chuen [12.2003–2.204], Low Kee Hong [21.6.2006], Ahmad Mashadi [12.2003–2.2004 & 21.6.2006], Josef Ng [2.2.2004], Matthew Ngui [12.2003–2.2004], T.K. Sabapathy [12.2003–2.2004], Eugene Tan [21.6.2006].

I am also grateful to Russel Storer then of the Museum of Contemporary Art, Sydney, for further interviews conducted on my behalf with Tien Woon Wei & Jennifer Teo & Lim Tzay-chuen [1.10.2004], Tien Woon Wei [4.10.2004], Juliana Yasin & Kai Lam Hoi [6.10.2004], Matthew Ngui [5.11.2004]; Chua Beng Huat [2.10.2004], Ong Keng Sun [3.10.2004], T. K. Sabapathy [5.10.2004], Ahmad Mashadi [5.10.2004], Lee Weng Choy [7.10.2004], Kwok Kian Chow [7.10.2004, Kim Machan 4.10.2004, Goh Ching Lee & Aun Koh & Katharyn Peh of National Arts Council [4.10.2004], Kwok Kian Woon [7.10.2004] Ho Tzu Nyen [31.10.2004].

## Notes

1 Yao Souchou, *Singapore: the State and the Culture of Excess* (London & New York: Routledge, 2007). At the time of writing the original paper for the work here I had read four draft chapters of Yao's book.

2 In 2006 the percent of vote by party was PAP 66.6%, WP 16.3%, SDA 13%, SDP 4.1%; seats by party—PAP 82, WP 1, SDA 1. That is the government party won 97.6% of the seats with 66.6% of the vote. See https://www.cia.gov/cia/publications/factbook/geos/sn.html (page is no longer available).

3 Yao, chapter 2 draft, *Singapore*, 39.

4 Yao, chapter 2 draft, 39.

5 Yao, chapter 2 draft, 47. He goes on: "like the experience of the 'traumatic', the 'culture of excess' traps people in a history that eludes them; but it also 'incites' them to prompt actions as a way of avoiding similar, often imaginary disasters."

6 Yao, chapter 2 draft, 54.

7 On public state spectacle in Singapore see the chapter by Ray Langenbach, "Garlands of Love: Socialist Realist Aesthetics in Singapore", in *Eye of the Beholder*, ed. John Clark, Maurizio Peleggi and T.K. Sabapathy (Sydney: Wild Peony, 2006).

8 Yao, chapter 3 draft, 25, for analysis of the contradictory counterpoise between "Confucian capitalist" and "Western market" values. On Beethoven's Third Symphony, see the entry for Beethoven 1803–08 in Grove Music Online, "The

symphony was originally entitled simply 'Bonaparte', in tribute to the young hero of revolutionary France, who was almost exactly Beethoven's age. But this idealization of Napoleon as a heroic leader gave way to disillusionment when the First Consul proclaimed himself Emperor in May 1804. The story of Beethoven's rage when the news of this reached Vienna is well known: he went to the table where the completed score lay, took hold of the title-page and tore it in two. On its publication in 1806 the symphony was given its present title of 'heroic symphony', and was described as having been 'composed to celebrate the memory of a great man'. The 'great man' may well have been Prince Louis Ferdinand of Prussia, who was an esteemed friend of the symphony's dedicatee, Prince Lobkowitz, and who in fact died a hero's death in 1806". See also Édouard Herriot, *La Vie de Beethoven* (Paris: Gallimard, 1929), 120.

9 In massacres which followed the Fall of Singapore, from 18 February to 4 March 1942 between 50,000–100,000 Chinese men were executed by the invading Japanese. See "Sook Ching", *Wikipedia: The Free Encyclopedia.*

10 Kevin Chua thinks this contradiction is also a conundrum of the relationship between the forced desire to represent and representation itself: "the compulsion to see representation as such will (already) be something close to a defeat, an inauthentic imitation of what must be the Truth of Singapore". See Kevin Chua, "Singapore in the 49th Venice Biennale", *FOCAS*, 3 (January 2002): 274.

11 Nanyang means "Southern Seas" and became an art discourse with specific practitioners educated in modern Chinese "national realism". See Kevin Chua, "Painting the Nanyang's 'Public': Notes toward a Reassessment", in *Eye of the Beholder*, ed. Clark, Peleggi, and Sabapathy. On pre-war Chinese painting in Singapore see Yao Mengtong, *Xinjiapo zhanqian huaren meishushi lun ji* (Singapore; Xinjiapo Yazhou Yanjiuhui, 1992), and for Singapore art in general see Kwok Kian Chow, *Channels and Confluences: A History of Singapore Art* (Singapore: Singapore Art Museum, 1995). See the Singapore section in Bibliography of Modern and Contemporary Asian Art at http://sydney.edu.au/arts/art_history/documents/Clark_Bibliography.pdf (page is no longer available).

12 Dollar amounts given here are Singapore dollars. See *NAFA Auditor's Report* (April 2001–March 2002), 4, 10, 11.

13 In 2002/2003 the National Arts Council awarded 10 overseas bursaries for fine arts students, 7 of which were for study at Australian tertiary fine arts institutions. See *Challenges: Annual Report FY 2002/2003* (Singapore: National Arts Council, 2003), 115–16. The second artistic unit, actually a new media collective, to go to Documenta was tsunamii.net in 2002 which received $28,000 for this participation and an exhibition in London from the National Arts Council. See *Challenges*, 123.

14 See the press release at http://www.unsw.edu.au/news/pad/media/2004/apr/Singapore.html (page is no longer available). The UNSW Asia campus was intended to be the first foreign university to be sited in Singapore and would have eventually had 15,000 students: "It is envisaged that half of the student load will be in the science/engineering areas, where the initial focus will be on technology, IT, electrical engineering, telecommunications and possibly chemical engineering. In the humanities and social sciences, the initial focus will be on commerce, languages, Asian studies, Australian studies, media and communications and fine arts". On the closure in May 2007 see news.com.au for 24 May 2007, and *The Australian Higher Education Supplement* for 25 June 2007.

15 See Ray Langenbach, *Hidden Things*, on the occasion of the exhibition *A work by Lim Tzay Chuen* (Singapore: LaSalle-SIA, 2005).

16 According to materials kindly supplied by Sculpture Square.

17 On public art in general see Peter Schoppert, "More trouble than it is Worth: What Can We Expect from Public Art in Singapore?", in *Eye of the Beholder*, ed. Clark, Pelegggi, and Sabapathy, and his valuable website with many images of Singapore public art www.nusantara.com (page is no longer available). On the art in the public space of transit line stations see *Art in Transit* (Singapore, Land Transport Authority, 2003), and the reprinted catalogue essay Kwok Kian Chow, "Spaces and Places", *Vehicle*, 10 (2003).

18 See Art Galleries Association of Singapore, ed., *Leading Galleries of Singapore* (Singapore: Art Galleries Association of Singapore, 2006).

19 There is also a considerable programme of government support for housing arts groups and providing artists' studios, see *Challenges*, 125–6.

20 *Vehicle* appears to have run out of money as part of Plastique Kinetic Worms' overall budgetary crisis by its 10th issue in 2003/04.

21 See Lucy Davis, "State of Censorship: Singapore Post-CRC 3", in *FOCAS: Forum on Contemporary Art & Society*, 5 (January 2003): 295–309. It remains that this issue was not itself censored, but that the National Arts Council funding support was withdrawn, effectively amounting to censorship.

22 See *Challenges*, 95.

23 See *Challenges*, 91.

24 See the section on "Precursor Exhibitions" beginning on page 96.

25 In several interviews with curators and artists which I shall leave unattributed.

26 See Joanna Lee, "The Artists' Village: Alterity Examined", unpublished Master's thesis, University of Sydney, 1997, 33.

27 Lee, "The Artists' Village", 19.

28 Onerous pre-event compliance conditions were thereafter placed on performance art which effectively made it impossible to present until it was re-constituted in December 2003 in *The Future of Imagination: Live Art Meeting*, organized by the performance artist Lee Wen at The Substation. Even in this case a performance license had to be applied for and National Arts Council observers were thought to have been present at the event. For a summary of the earlier incidents involving Leow and Ng see Ray Langenbach, "Annotated Singapore Diary", *Art & Asia Pacific* 1, 4 (1994), and in general on this epoch see Lynne Gumpert, "A Global City for the Arts?", *Art in America* (December 1997). Censorship of offending art works or events, however, remained an ever-present feature of the Singapore art scene, in the 1990s particularly when works referred to current politicians. The Hong Kong cartoonist Zunzi's works which included a 2.5 metre caricature of elder statesman Lee Kuan Yew, were removed from the October 1998 Singapore exhibition of ARX (Artists' Regional Exchange), an act which the director of the Singapore Art Museum Kwok Kian Chow did not reportedly characterize as censorship but "sensitivity". This position was later denounced by participating artists (web reports from the Hong Kong Standard and Hong Kong Star). However, the Ministry for Information, Communication and the Arts appointed a Censorship Review Committee on 13 April 2002 to look into censorship guidelines. See *Challenges*, 14.

29 Lee, "The Artists' Village", 40, citing the report by the Advisory Council on Culture and the Arts of 1989.

30 See T.K. Sabapathy, "Sculptors and Sculptors in Singapore: an introduction", in *Sculpture in Singapore* (National Museum, Singapore, 1991). Sabapathy traces this distinction between object for consumption and object for the expression of a concept to an interview with Tang Dawu where he said,

> Here in Singapore the insistence is on art as commodity. But there are other interests. What of concepts, and showing concepts? These concepts are unpolished, non-free standing objects; yet they are still very important as art works or as statements which are important and can be collected. In this way the artist is questioning what is art, what is craft and what it is to look at and understand things; the concept, thinking as art is all within that process. But you can't look at things as objects, as every day objects but in terms of concepts. I think in the West this is not a problem anymore, but I think that whoever collects art here should pay more attention to the kind of art I am talking about. (Sabapathy, *Sculpture in Singapore*, 16.)

This position is also discussed in Lee, "The Artists' Village", 29.

31 The Report recommended improvements to organizations, education, cultural facilities and promotional efforts, and the results were carefully assessed in 2000. See Annex A to Ministry of Information and the Arts, *Renaissance City Report: Culture and the Arts in Renaissance Singapore* (Singapore: Ministry of Information and the Arts, 2000). For an insightful dialogue on the nature of associating the Singapore state with distinguished, earlier polities, in this case Athens, see Lee Weng Choy and Ray Langenbach, "Athens, Singapore" (a dialogue), in *Kunst aus Megastädten Asiens – Art from Asia Pacific Megacities*, ed. Claus Friede and Ludwig Seyfarth (Hamburg: Kunsthaus Hamburg, 2000). For an analysis of the Renassiance City concept see T.C. Chang, "Renaissance Revisited: Singapore as a 'Global City for the Arts'", *International Journal of Urban and Regional Research* 24, 4 (December 2000).

32 There is a general but slightly critical view from Malaysia in an article by the editor of *Art Corridor*, Ming Chua, "Singapore: an Asian Renaissance?", *Art Corridor*, 8 (2002).

33 *Singapore Bulletin* (Canberra: High Commission of Singapore, November 1993). Yeo is also cited in similar in vein four years later in the government's interim document *Singapore: Global City for the Arts* published by the Ministry for Information and the Arts, see Gumpert, "A Global City for the Arts?": 45, 47.

34 Gumpert, "A Global City for the Arts?": 45.

35 Ministry of Information and the Arts, *Renaissance City Report*, 56–7.

36 The French anthropologist Augé has found airports to be the "non-places" most characteristic of what he calls "supermodernity". This is characterized by three figures of excess: overabundance of events, spatial overabundance, and excess individualization without reference to community. See Marc Augé, *Non-places: Introduction to an Anthropology* of Supermodernity, trans. John Howe (1992; London: Verso, 1994), 24–37.

37 *Challenges*, 54.

38 *Challenges*, 69

39 *Challenges*, 25–9.

40 *Channel News Asia* online story downloaded on 9 March 2005.

41 According to the chronology given inside the cover of The Esplanade, *Esplanade Co Ltd. Annual Report, 02/02* (Singapore: The Esplanade, 2003).

42 Interview with Koh Kor Wah of the National Arts Council on 5 February 2004.

43 The Esplanade, *Esplanade Co Ltd. Annual Report, 02/02*, 516. (Pagination is unclear.)

44 Like in Australia and many other countries, the tight social inter-penetration between arts and other elite sectors is astonishing when one examines it. See Annette van den Bosch, *The Australian Art World: Aesthetics in a Global Market* (Sydney: Allen and Unwin, 2005), e.g. chapter 3. I understand that the main architect of the Singapore Marina area was the husband of the chief urban planner, and that their daughter was a section chief in the National Arts Council.

45 "New Platforms to Develop Visual Arts Hub", News Release of National Arts Council and National Heritage Board, 27 January 2004.

46 See Hou Hanru, "Transparency, Complexity, Void and Action", in *City Community: Singapore Art Today; Nokia Singapore Art 1999*, ed. T. K. Sabapathy (Singapore: National Arts Council & National Heritage Board, 1999). This essay could charitably be described as a slight extension of his ideas for *Cities on the Move*, and contrasts with another much more interesting essay in the same catalogue by Ahmad Mashadi, "Cultural Sinkholes: Landscape and Ethnic Representation in Singapore".

47 See his essay in "Brief Notes on the Display and Presentation of History" in *Histories/Identity/Technologies/Space: Singapore Art Today, Nokia Singapore Art 2001*, ed. Kwok Kian Chow (Singapore: National Arts Council & National Heritage Board, 2001).

48 See Huangfu Binghui, "Homegrown—Installation/Conceptual Artists in Singapore" in Sabapathy, *Nokia Singapore Art 1999*.

49 See Suzie Wong, "Deciphering Decoding in Art by Women Artists", in Kwok, *Histories/Identity/Technologies/Space*.

50 Liu Thai Ker (chairman, National Arts Council), in Kwok, *Histories/Identity/Technologies/Space*, 04.

51 Kwok, *Histories/Identity/Technologies/Space*, 05.

52 Heman Chong was selected as national representative for the Fukuoka Asian Art Festival in 2000, the India Triennale in 2001, an exhibition at Centre Pompidou in 2002, and at Haus der Kulturen der Welt in 2003 and the São Paolo Bienal in 2004. At this point Lim Tzay Chuen had been selected in Nokia Singapore Art 1999, Polypolis in Hamburg in 2001, and the Gwangju Biennale in 2002. See biographies in Joyce Fan, ed. and chair of cultural committee, *The President's Young Talents Exhibition, 2003* (Singapore: Singapore Art Museum, 2003).

53 Their names are given Annex 1 to "New Platforms to Develop Visual Arts Hub", News Release of National Arts Council and National Heritage Board, 27 January 2004.

54 Interviews with T. K. Sabapthy and others.

55 Interviews with Chua Beng Huat.

56 In off-the-record interviews conducted in 2004.

57 These include Documenta [Matthew Ngui, in 1997; Tsunamii.net (Charles Lim, Woon Tien Wei, Melvin Phua Yang Chien, Tan Kok Yam) in 2002], São Paolo [ Matthew Ngui in 1996, Heman Chong in 2004] and the Venice Biennale [Chen Kezhan, Salleh Jaspar, Matthew Ngui, and Suzann Victor in 2001; Tan Swie Hian, Francis Ng, and Herman Chong in 2003; Lim Tzay-chuen in 2005].

58 See Ngui's re-presentation of his Documenta work "'You Can Order and Eat Delicious Poh-piah' Amongst Other Things" (Singapore: Goethe Institute, 1998) (which I saw).

59 It is widely believed Okwui Enwezor was asked to speak precisely with the intention of getting him to invite a Singapore artist to Documenta XI.

60 Kwok Kian Chow is reported as saying Singapore Art Museum would then *go international* in ways such as organizing traveling exhibitions of Southeast Asian and Singaporean art, sending Singaporean artists to shows abroad and participating in international visual arts events (my italics; *The Business Times*, 20 January 2001). The same report noted that the eventual goal in sending the video art of Heman Chong to the 10th Indian Triennial was "for Singapore to position itself as a *global arts destination* in Asia" (my italics). Such phraseology, in the tightly integrated public relations atmosphere of Singapore must be regarded as the true statement of intentions, rather than making Singapore a global centre of arts creativity.

61 The total budget from the National Arts Council and National Heritage Board in 2003 was $600,000. It gained local publicity such as the headlines "World Class Art" in *The Straits Times* (13 June 2003). "Singapore Art Captures Venice' was the headline the next day when Liu Thai Ker, chairman of the National Arts Council, was reported as saying "It's necessary for us to be here, partly to tell the world who we are, and partly to find out what the rest of the world is doing" in *The Straits Times* (17 June 2003).

62 *The Straits Times* (25 May 2001).

63 *The Straits Times* (25 May 2001).

64 "Vice-Commissioner's Preface", in *Singapore* (Singapore: Singapore Art Museum, National Heritage Board, 2001).

65 "Vice Commissioner's Preface". At Venice in 2003, Tan Swie Hian painted a calligraphic work on 11.6m by 1.8m white canvas with 143 characters in just under five minutes in 40°C heat, according to *The Straits Times* (13 June 2003). It is also informally reported that a very high charge was made by the Venetian authorities for him to do this work on the square of San Marco, and that the work could not subsequently be exhibited there. Other reports indicate that the work was at least four storeys high and took ten minutes to complete, in *Channel NewsAsia* report on 14 June 2003. The Italian co-commissioner, Paolo de Grandis, perhaps summed up the artistic significance of this work the same source reported, apparently without irony that

> When you see him doing his work, you see him like he has a vibration in his brain and he's completely alone in his moment. This piece of work gives me the energy that the artist wants to make to the people.

The gap between actual artistic achievement and bureaucratic puffing came with a statement also in the same source from Lim Siam Kim, National Heritage Board CEO,

> In order to be part of world art, we have to participate in Biennials like this, *so that the world takes us seriously* that we have also our own art forms to contribute to the world of art. (My italics)

Kevin Chua had already the previous year summarized the contradictions of this position in a review which discussed the Singapore pavilion at Venice when he wrote: "for Chen [Kezhan, an abstract ink painter] , 'Chineseness' occurs not in the move into but out of the contemporary. Painting becomes a regressive cultivation of an endurable panacea for one's authentic origins". See Kevin Chua, "Singapore in the 49th Venice Biennale", *FOCAS*, 3 (January 2002): 277.

66 Khor Koh Wah, commissioner, *Mike (Lim Tzay Chuen)* (Singapore: National Arts Council & Singapore Art Museum, 2005), see "Vice Commissioner's Preface", 11.

67 This difference was discovered very early on in the 1950s by the Japanese pavilion selectors and its perception might be thought to be part of a more generalized Biennale learning process. See Yaguchi Kunio, "The Venice Biennale and Japan", in *The Venice Biennale: 40 Years of Japanese Participation*, ed. Harumi Miwa (Tokyo: The Japan Foundation; Tokyo: The Mainichi Newspapers, 1995).

68 See my review, "Venice Biennale", *Asian Art News* 13, 5 (September 2003), which was written before I knew about the status of Tan Swie Hian in Singapore.

69 See note 79 below.

70 Before the Biennale took place, the Singapore critic Lee Weng Choy noticed this in the preposterous claim that La Salle-SIA was "Asia Pacific's leading arts institution", and saw Singapore participation in the Venice Biennale, the production of the precursor event Seni in 2004, and the Biennale itself in 2006, as part of a series of events which manifested such symptoms. See Lee Weng Choy, "The public remainder: Singapore goes to Venice, the Biennale comes to Singapore", *Broadsheet* 32, 2 (June–August 2005): 88.

71 The then-Singapore Art Museum curator Ahmad Mashadi noted,

> "Asia" itself is a continually shifting term, whether as a conceptual or geographical entity. We could even look at the Asian diaspora, the number of Asian artists working in Australia for instance, or at the transformation of "Asia" in different environments. (*The Business Times*, 20 January 2001)

72 Low Kee Hong, General Manager of Singapore Biennale, in an interview with G. Haupt and Binder, downloaded from http:// universes-in-universe.de/car/singapore/2006eng/txt/low/index.htm on 7 February 2006, 1.

73 Low, interview with G. Haupt and Binder, 2.

74 Singapore Government media release, http://ap sprinter.gov.sg/data/pr/20060901985.htm, accessed on 4 October 2006.

75 The citation is found in Dr Lee's text, but this is the part which was excerpted in *Weekend Today*, September 2–3, 2006, the only very small news item following the opening of the Biennale.

76 As specifically pointed to in the opening press conference by one curator from Japan, Roger Macdonald. I have been reliably informed that the Senior Minister Lee Kuan Yew refused to visit the old law courts site because it included this work.

77 According to Eliza Tan's essay in *belief: Exhibition Short Guide*, ed. Ben Slater (Singapore: National Arts Council, 2006), 82.

78 Compare "The Sick Rose" by William Blake (from *Songs of Innocence and Experience*, etched 1789–94),

> O Rose, thou art sick;
> The invisible worm,
> That flies in the night,
> In the howling storm,
> Hath found out thy bed
> Of crimson joy;
> And her dark secret love
> Does thy life destroy.

See Geoffrey Keynes, ed., *Blake: Complete Writings* (London: Oxford University Press, 1966), 175, 213.

79 See the notes for Ong's work in Slater, ed., *belief*, 100.

80 Some notes to assist interpretation were kindly supplied in a press release by the artist. The subtext given [in capitals in the original] by the artist for the photographs of his action was:

> ON SUNDAY 9 JULY
> HE ENTERED THE
> CITY HALL BUILDING
> HE FILLED ITS INTERIOR
> WITH PHEROMONES

81 The press conference was on 2 September 2006, at which I was present and which I recorded. One can even argue that their dominance has been much accentuated by deliberate Singapore government policies to privilege the use of standard Mandarin, *Putonghua*, and de-privilege dialect, dress and other signs of regional or communal origin within the Chinese population. Significantly this drive to cultural hegemony within the Chinese communities did not choose to privilege the most locally adjusted and regionally assimilated culture, that of the loosely termed *Peranakan* Straits Chinese.

82 The artistic director Nanjô Fumio said in an interview with *Broadsheet* magazine which was widely distributed at the Biennale opening day,

> The theme "Belief" is not only about the religious belief as you have noted. It sounds narrow but it is also very wide open. In this multicultural and postmodern society, it is quite reasonable to question and think about the basis of life. Yet it is linked to the expressions of art of the time, reflecting and commenting the present situation of the world in which we live.
>
> See *Broadsheet: Contemporary Visual Arts + Culture* 35, 3 (September–November 2006), 137.

One presumes someone as sophisticated as Nanjô will have noticed the convenience to the Singapore state of a position which allows art to treat the everyday without directly tackling the political.

83 Nanjô Fumio mentioned this in the opening press conference, and in his catalogue essay for the Iranian artist who lives and works in Tokyo, indicated that he plans to make gold bars in a series and devote the income to charities.

84 According to my interview with Low Kee Hong of 21 June 2006.

85 Lee Suan Hiang, Chief Executive Officer, National Arts Council and Chairman of Singapore Biennale 2006 Steering Committee, from my transcription from a recording of the opening Press conference on 2 September 2006. This citation approved as accurate by Mr Lee via an email from his press officer, Kok Tse-wei.

86 Simryn Gill, *Guide to the Murals at Tanjong Pagar Railway Station, Singapore* (Singapore: Simryn Gill & Singapore Biennale 2006, 2006), 10.

87 There was a slight 14-page gallery guide *Telah Terbit (Out Now), Southeast Asian Contemporary Art Practices during the 1970s* (Singapore: Singapore Art Museum, 2006). It did not list the works shown, nor print the copious documentation provided by the curator as wall or cabinet explanations in the exhibition itself. After the Biennale a more substantial catalogue was produced, Ahmad Mashadi et al., *Telah*

*Terbit (Out Now): Southeast Asian Contemporary Art Practices during the 1960s to 1980s* (Singapore: National Heritage Board, Singapore Art Museum, 2007).

88 Other regional representation from Indonesia [3], Thailand [3], and the Philippines [3] was not very broad so I am not sure how the total of 29 Southeast Asian artists was arrived at.

89 In an informal conversation during the Biennale.

90 Slater, ed., *belief*, 136.

91 There is no mention of its Japanese wartime use in Low Wye Mun (Dr Major), "A History of Tanglin Barracks: The Early Years", *Journal of the Singapore Armed Forces* 25, 4 (October–December 1999).

92 According to one even-handed description which summarizes much other research, probably between 25,000 and 50,000 Chinese citizens of Singapore were massacred during the Japanese occupation, some estimates being much higher, with a deliberate extermination policy by defined category applied between 15 February and 3 March 1942. See "Sook Ching", *Wikipedia: The Free Encyclopedia*, http://en.wikipedia.org.wiki/Sook_Ching_Massacre. For a considered historical account see Christopher Bayly and Tim Harper, *Forgotten Armies: Britain's Asian Empire and the War with Japan* (London: Penguin, 2004), 210–17.

93 The curatorium was composed from Nanjô Fumio [Japan], Artistic Director, and the curators Roger McDonald [Japan], Sharmini Pereira [Sri Lanka/UK], Eugene Tan [Singapore]. The Media Release notes were also unusually forthcoming in providing a list of 41 other "Networking Curators" [local advisors and catalogue essay writers] in Annex 4. Informal advice indicates that Nanjô mostly just sanctioned the pre-existing choices of the younger curators and negotiated with the Arts Ministry about the inclusion of works he thought sensitive, as he mentioned in the opening press conference. Unmentioned there was the issue of the attendance of Senior Minister Lee Kuan Yew, who as internal curatorium discussion explicitly mentioned—I understand from internal sources who prefer not to be quoted—refused to visit the Old Supreme Court site of the exhibition because of the work there by Jason Lee which referred to a notorious anti-left wing case in 1987.

94 On the super-flat see, inter alia in English, Murakami Takashi, ed., *Little Boy: The Arts of Japan's Exploding Subculture* (New York: Japan Society; New Haven: Yale University Press, 2005).

95 Following in the work of Maro Akaji and Maruo Suehiro, quite well known outside Japan for some time. See Yomota Inuhiko, "On the Grotesque Trend in Japanese Post-modern Art", in *Modernity in Asian Art*, ed. John Clark (Sydney: Wild Peony, 1993).

96 See the catalogue entry by Roger McDonald in *belief*, ed. Slater, 122.

97 It made me involuntarily recall these lines in Fitzgerald's translation of Omar Khayyám:

> The Moving Finger writes; and, having writ,
> Moves on: nor all thy Piety nor Wit
> Shall lure it back to cancel half a Line,
> Nor all thy Tears wash out a word of it.

*The Rubáiyát of Omar Khayyám*, First Edition, trans. Edward Fitzgerald, ed. George F. Maine (1946; Glasgow and London: Collins, 1988), 79.

# Chapter 5

# The Asia Pacific Triennial of Contemporary Art

I now want to move to looking at the relationship between curatorial statements of intent and the functions of biennials for artists, curators and art worlds, both domestically and transnationally. Here I will mostly look at the various statements in one group of catalogues, those of the Asia Pacific Triennial of Contemporary Art at the Queensland Art Gallery in Brisbane, hereafter denoted as APT I (1993), APT II (1996), APT III (1999), APT IV (2002).[1] They were followed by APT V (2006), APT VI (2009), and APT VII (2012), all of which I saw but which lay outside my original research period. To these can be added some comparisons with the Fukuoka Asian Art Triennale and the Gwangju Biennale. I will examine the catalogue statements for motivations, curatorial positions, and roles as policy documents. The results of this analysis come into contrast with my own experience of these triennials, all of which I visited.[2]

## The 1993 First Asia Pacific Triennial of Contemporary Art

Since it may not have received the attention it should in the light of different curatorial strategies adopted for later APTs, I will now examine in detail the 1993 APT.[3]

Brisbane, where the Asia Pacific Triennial was held,[4] is a river port from which you can see out to the sea. The recent Australian engagement with Asia, and in particular with what was geographically defined as Asia-Pacific art, was not by this token perhaps going to be one of rivalry between gunboats, but would be presented as one of mutual country trade between small ships. There was to be a good deal of play in the barter, but without too much working through of the real and intractable problems of cultural difference. Perhaps art was precisely that human cultural product which could ignore difference even as it so particularly manifested it.

THE FIRST ASIA-PACIFIC TRIENNIAL OF CONTEMPORARY ART BRISBANE AUSTRALIA 1993

5.1 Logotype of the first Asia Pacific Triennial of Contemporary Art.

The discovery of the Asia-Pacific by Australians in the 1990s ran parallel to their rediscovery of Australia's first inhabitants, ones whom the first navigators recognized as living here, but those whose rights subsequent settlers had erased from their identity until recently.[5] Indeed the discovery of Asia, just as the internal rediscovery took place, was only the last of a long series of reinventions of the inside of Australian cultural space which happened just as the outside was repositioned.[6]

This might have been inherent to a culture of mostly immigrants, but Australia was more accurately a culture of later migrants into an exisiting culture of settlers, of people who brought other-cultural references including language with them to re-form the culture between themselves and the others. All cultures homogenize, but certainly Australia in its slow drift towards a republic without a myth of manifest destiny, war of independence or revolution, and without the cruel conformism of some republican systems, had been allowed room for the virtue of retaining and constructing openness to cultural difference. In 1993, before the great myopia of the Howard government from 1996–2007,[7] Australia had for the moment sensibly chosen to preserve this virtue of openness.

The very enterprise of the Asia Pacific Triennial together with the extensive publication activity connected to, or contemporary with it, was both an indicator of these cultural developments and a site where their problems and possibilities could be observed.

## Goals of APT I

In its initial conception there were five explicit goals for the Triennial:

> **One:** To educate the general Australian public further about Asia, and to change the priorities of a good part of its artistic community for future self-identification and exchanges via an art-related activity. According to the then-Foreign Minister Gareth Evans, "such contacts can only serve to strengthen the Government's wider objectives to broaden Australia's image in the region and to foster a better understanding of Asia in Australia".[8]

**Two:** To change the subculture of Australian Museums and Art Galleries away from stereotyped views of Asian cultures. By implication this thereby meant to obtain a particular international position and status for Australian museums and galleries. The Triennial would address Museum reinforcement of perception of exotic Pacific cultures "by static display of material culture".[9] It was "logical that given the Australian world view that it was no longer a Euro-Americentric society, for an Australian museum to take up the challenge".[10]

**Three:** To position Australia as one participant in multilateral debates between different countries in the Asian region, on an horizontal basis of equality and reciprocation rather than unilaterally from one centre to a periphery.

The Triennial would function as "not an Asian/Australian dialogue but facilitator of a number of debates".[11] It would "initiate dialogue on the art of this increasingly important geo-political region".[12] This would be on a "basis of intellectual equality to disclose knowledge and experience [not comfortable cohesion], regardless of cultural, social, or spiritual differences".[13]

**Four:** To explore ideas and art world dynamics in a de-centred manner which recognized contemporary Asian art as relevant to Australian art discourses and having a dynamic and intellectual density worthy of consideration in their own right.

The Triennial would "be an examination of the dynamics of concepts of tradition, identity, and change".[14] It would "undoubtedly show the arts of Asia as dynamic, relevant and powerful".[15] The Triennial would involve "new ways of looking at art on the basis of equality without a 'centre' or 'centres'".[16] One of its functions would be the "highlighting the dynamics of change, identities, and even twentieth-century cultural dislocation".[17]

**Five:** To see art as the mirror of cultural and other social changes, and (therefore) to accept the national unit without yet placing artists in cross-national curatorial categories. It was assumed "cultures will mirror other dynamic changes".[18] The approach would be "through national contexts".[19] The issue of themes had been raised, but the curatorial decision was made to represent diversity, and artists would be chosen who reflected a range of experiences.[20]

The only goals in conflict seem to be goals three and five, since the nation already and in essence constituted a centre, although it was not, for the region, a Euramerican centre. Goals four and five could be seen disinterestedly as linked to the learning curves of goals one and two, as a kind of adjustment strategy to a changed international environment and not to do with any deep-seated drives generated within the culture. Such goals represented a belatedly mature appreciation of the geographical realities of Australia's place which had been kept in the immature stage of "kidult" (kid-adult, arrested adolescent, in the novelist

5.2 Asia Pacific as mapped in the catalogue of the first Asia Pacific Triennial of Contemporary Art.

Patrick White's memorable phrase)[21] by the infantile delusions of a still-colonized mind. This recognition would have ignored the fact that in a sense all geography is cultural geography, the projection of knowledge on physical topology, and that cultures tend to consciously recognize only what is in their self-interest to do so. This review will have to let the deeper causation for setting them pass.

## Types of Works Exhibited

The works in APT I and most contemporary publications avoided any explicit category except the "national", although the national committee had discussed the possibility of choosing a theme, and relinquished it, possibly for a future occasion.

Within the category of "national" there were quite clearly a range of implicit categories for works, which were most broad in the Indonesian selection. These began with medium, even if there was some reluctance in the lay-out of the Triennial to recognize this. Maybe the gallery floor plan did not just allow it.

### Painting: Senior Contemporary Masters

Perhaps for reasons of art world politics, perhaps from the wish to indicate a little of the historical depth of an art world, this category was used to show types of inspiration and subject matter which younger artists were aware of, and perhaps reacted against. This seems clear in the inclusion of a work by A.D. Pirous with its direct Islamic references to the Holy Koran. I find the early work by Pirous on his return from the US and his dynamic use of holy text and Arabic calligraphy then to have been perhaps the most exciting and, for a non-Muslim, some of the most moving modern Indonesian religious imagery. But APT I showed the very much slicker later and up-market decorative version of Pirous' trajectory for the Indonesian élite. Their taste for "expansive sonority" often ended up in the flat, added-value vacuity of Srihadi, in the same way as their memories of the privations of a hard-fought struggle with the Dutch found their rather too pretty traces in the almost professional angst of the expressionist Kerton. The inclusion of senior masters would only have made sense in the context of a parallel discussion about the local or originating élite's good or bad taste in modernizing what they thought were their traditions.

### Younger Contemporaries

In works which displayed types of imaginary ranging from the straight surreal to the magical decoration, style was subordinate to fantasied subjects. These included the dreamed presents of Ivan Sagito and the fantasies of a displaced or replaced past such as in the mixed media work of Nyoman Erawan. Sometimes this had a melancholic affirmation for lost craft skills in a religious metaphysic, as was also seen in the finely worked painted woven canvases of the Malaysian artist Sulaiman Esa. Or it struck an affirmative note in the recentring of the present in feminist aesthetic with Mastura Abdul Rahman. Clearly the category typified by the work of Nyoman Erawan and Sulaiman Esa, whatever their own particular artistic achievements, was precisely that liked by the Indonesian and Malaysian élites to decorate their homes, offices, and hotels, appealing as it easily did to a kind of superficial and high-consumption nostalgia. Perhaps this superficiality had not inspired Nyoman or Esa, but I wonder why they did not make it more difficult for their work to be absorbed into such a consciousness. Among younger artists at APT I and particularly from Indonesia, there was a type of painting of revolt, which may be called "the tribal", this was clear in the work of Heri Dono, whose two-dimensional work like many artists practising in this domain, constituted a parallel commentary to his performances.

The domain of the tribal moved towards a kind of mystical affirmation of autochthonous value seen most clearly in Australian aboriginal painting by the Petyarre sisters. Their transcendence in a sense disavowed the simplicities of the tribal category, for they came from and represented their people, they did not represent anything about them.

Many Asian cities and their abused rural hinterlands were riven with social conflicts, the scale and dynamic of whose forces was almost beyond the control of the very power structures which had generated them. There was much use of painting for social comment, like the surreal absurdity of exploitation in the work of Dede Eri Supria, or the grand, cruel but liberating sacrament of revolt in the work of Nunelucio Alvarado. Whatever these artists' personal political sympathies, in APT I, I was awestruck at the power their work had for its not being in the sway of sterile party art doctrine, as had been the case in Cultural Revolution China. Sometimes the wish to identify with the people did approach political or religious doctrine. The artist could intend the work to constitute a new mythopoeic history that legitimized the people, as in the work of Edgar Fernandez and his collaborators. The female figure represents their spirits which embody, but also in a generous transcendence overcome, their struggles.

## Installation/Environments

Installations have become a widespread form of social comment art since they can be assembled from temporary realia whose meaning lies in the structure of their collagist effects, often played into life by a performance. Installation could act as an iconic embodiment of current lifestyles and values in the work of Liew Kung-yu. But installations can also function as an almost implacably obscure meta-discourse such as those on power as seen in the work of Zulkifli Yusoff, or on the sacred in the work of Montien Boonma. Their playing of an environment into life was often as a site for ritual. This could be a multimedia presentation of the modern, perhaps manifested as political terror with FX Harsono, or it could be a site for ritual of the tribal, a mute, chlothonic existence, where man communed in agony with the ancient gods who tormented him, as can be seen in the work of Dadang Christanto.

### Performance

Significantly many of the Triennial performance pieces, for example those by Dadang Christanto and Heri Dono, were given in contexts that brought to life a sculptural environment. Or they were given physical context by a medium beyond the performances as such, such as Heri Dono's use of *wayang kulit* (shadow puppet) devices.

### Sculpture

There were not many conventional figurative sculptures at the Triennial. One of the exceptions was the symbolic human types of Julie Lluch, which carried a feminist credo about suffering within the baroque mannerism so beloved of the counter-reformation.

Other conventional redeployments of familiar stylistics were the fantastic objects of Neil Dawson, who presented a kind of aerial *trompe l'oeil*, whose circus big-top placement seemed a bit like an ironic comment on Calder. The by now well-engrained categories of sculptural practice were found in the pure modernist exploration of the pleasurable beauty in form by the late Bronwyn Oliver and the almost scatalogically re-sited totems of decorated fish by Lee Bul.

### Photography

For all of post-modernism's play with the simulacra of being, little photographic consciousness was deployed in most works, an absence which distanced them from many current kinds of Australian practice. We were shown the wistfully traditional and un-staged beauty of the transformed everyday in the retouched photographs of Ismail Hashim, and the fashionably slashed and re-stapled gelatin silver prints of Koo Bohn-chang. Perhaps there was a whiff of the traduced referent in Satô Tokihiro's play with dotted ruins, the translated text for which produced one of the Triennial catalogue's more breathtaking gems of critical opacity: "The space, frozen in the photograph, may be barely breathing after its life force has been violently changed".[22]

## Categorizing Works by More Formal Categories

There were quite a lot of works which fitted into the implicit categories listed above. The unwillingness to place works into critical rather than "natural" categories like those implied above under the "national" was a sign of political ambivalence. It indicated too a certain lack of courage and a testing of the waters.

The following critical categories handled the works actually shown—a different set could have been used for a different choice of works.

Some works tried to be easily emblematic of religious references, sometimes for ease of elite consumption, as the work of Apichai Piromrak. Transformations of transnational styles for individual, cause-oriented, or more broadly cultural purposes were found. The individual transformation was powerfully shown in the private histories and tragedies mobilized through the work of Araya Rasdjarmrearnsook. Other practice used a variety of techniques to situate contemporary issue-oriented concerns. Whatever the intentions of the artist this work fell within the scope of permitted or socially unexceptional practice which was easily ignored by those to whom it appears to have been directed.

The work of Kamol Phaosavasdi, continuously since the late 1980s directed at representing issues of environmental pollution, was most accomplished formally but was conveniently unthreatening or ignorable by those who had caused the environmental problems it referred to.

Political struggles could be identified with via the shock tactics of simply representing them, as in the translation to an urban massacre in the rural fabulist manner of Prasong Luemang.

Vasan Sitthiket also worked in a position close to this by using sacred icons and then showing how others profaned them. His work displayed cynicism about the religious beliefs of those who were profaned and may have accounted for the sloppy technique and punk anger of his practice. Without Prasong's care, Vasan's imagery, like the advertising of which it was the moral adversary, would be soon forgotten because it was neither based on a true belief, nor on a deeply enough tabooed sin.

A few works showed political concern which was situationist in trying to recreate, by a complex constitution of multiple cross-references, the contexts and events which have made revolt desirable or tragic. This was found in the installation of Prawat Laucharoen, a Thai who has long been resident in New York. His work deliberately displayed a formal coolness because of its references to the Thai Royal institutions, the Constitution and Buddhism. This may have been out of trepidation for the work's future exhibitability in Bangkok, or due to personal distance from the belief systems played with, after long residence abroad.

Most artists manipulated or included parts of other artworks, but postmodernist irony lay in an open and conscious game of art discursive references, such as by Fukuda Miran. This game-playing was be extended to quite obscure cultural or philosphical references, much of which was evident late 1980s work from China. But the works of Xu Jiang and Zhou Changjiang did not have the formal directedness to make their game really entrancing.

Only if such a game entranced could it surprise, and the viewer then experience an aesthetic shock, at least conceptually, on the level of ideas through the play of forms of the work. The inclusion of some Chinese pieces that were scarcely on the level of an Australian art school graduation show looked like a cynical Chinese art bureaucrat's apology for the idea of abstract art he may have thought Australian audiences and their Asian visitors would wish to see.

Some works appealed to what may be called presentiment, haptic in the case of Akioka Miho, tactile in the case of Ôtake Shinro. This presentiment was of a sensation the viewer already thought they had about a kind of image which appeared to be recognizable, but for which the artists' manipulation pushed away or left deferred from simple confirmation. What that sense was might be understood indirectly, through the blurring of a photograph and the worked surface of a very large expanse of white Japanese paper with Akioka. Or it could be sensed indirectly by the unheard sound of money falling in the punched-out, coin-like elements of Ôtake's prefabricated ship's stern, as if the monetary holes which filled the keel of modern economic existence would always disappear to leave the keel's structure intact as the ship sank. There was a double play with the material used here since the keel was made of light fibreglass, and not metal.

There could also be critically distinguished certain attempts at capturing subliminal grandeur. Sometimes this resulted in the aggressive vacuity of Yanai Tsuguo, rather in the manner of a 1980s equivalent to 19th century monumental sculpture, all competent display of quality but no lived meaning. APT I also included a realization of subtly co-present transcendence in Toya Shigeo's *Woods III,* the scale of whose remarkable achievement was manifest in the echoes aroused of works by Giacometti, Ernst, Moore, of a gothic cathedral and a Japanese village in a clearing. It was wonderful that this work was purchased by the Queensland Art Gallery.

Art has often sacralized pain, but it can do so by reconstitution of its once religious aura. It serves the empowerment of deferred or repressed discourses. Work from minority peoples or groups so effectively re-mobilized symbols from their past as a token of present authenticity. Art practice of this type could simultaneously appeal to two minority positions at once with Robyn Kahukiwa, both feminist and Maori, or with Selwyn Muru, speak with dignity of a lost sacral grandeur in the re-made treasure-relics which re-empowered those who now bore them.

In parallel to totemic restitution were the expressions of mythological narrative now re-embodied or re-sited in new technical expression. These functioned for the rural group as in the work of Joe Nalo, or Kathleen Petyarre, and in a different urban context can be the individualist expression of lonely, modernist artist-shamans such as Gareth Sansom.

## New Asia-Pacific Modalities

At APT I it was possible to distinguish certain aesthetic modalities within which parallel or common concerns and types of expression were found in Asia-Pacific art. It should have been unsurprising that these modalities were cross-cultural.

Even if cultures discriminate themselves by difference and debate this, I think humanity is not all that different, despite what every governing culture from the tribal to the transnational cosmopolitan would have its bearers believe. The formulations below are created from mostly works exhibited at APT I. Some are single categories, some binary pairs, some clustered in groups.

## The Urban, the Rural

In many different levels and in many different stylistic directions several artists at APT I problematized the experience of urban life. Some in contradistinction were aware how severe the city's abusive use of its rural hinterland was. In it were pockets of minorities who eked a precarious co-existence with the cities, and also with the city's rural dependencies. Sometimes these modalities were distinct, as in the movie-bred infatuation with the guise of the city. These were sometimes in a dialectical relationship, as posing a separate ethic of pure forms or participatory rituals, both affirmative of rural life, and resistant to their absorption into the spectacles of urban consumption.

## The Feminine, the Gay, the Familial

These three modalities were inextricably inter-linked although they frequently appeared to be discrete. Women have never been allowed prominence as creators of fine art in many areas of the Asia-Pacific, although they have frequently subverted this position by their prominence in crafts, particularly textiles and ceramics. To give them their due now as a specific type of high art creator with an aesthetic concern drawn from women's life or objects of daily use, was to claim a particular relation between creators and their aesthetics. This position was also hinted at in what appeared as art from a homo-erotic position, although this was not explicit in some art cultures. Finally, co-harmony—or co-repression in some cases—was given reference in many works which either imaged the family or re-situated the domestic environment, occasionally through installation work.

## The Tragic, the Comic

Many artists positioned their work in terms of basic life attitudes. Two of these concerned an existential stance towards mortality. The fact of human transcience was encountered via blunt acceptance, a mourning at grotesque loss which with sentimental attachment could go over into melancholia, or a more humorous, comic distance. Interesting kinds of cross-cultural comparison and contrast could be found within these modalities between monotheistic, animist, nihilist, and atheist humanist positions.

5.3 Vincent Leow, *Friends* (1991), Oil and enamel on canvas, 77 x 110 cm. Courtesy of the artist.

### The Despotic, The Libertarian

Many regimes in the Asia-Pacific region were less than tolerant of dissidence, let alone recognized the sovereign claims of the oppressed, on whose behalf such rulers mendaciously may have claimed to speak. Several artists used the symbolic truth-telling function of art to countervail official self-images and propaganda. Some used the potentiality of cult objects and everyday materials from the market to legitimate the lives and autonomous beliefs of those who claimed rights to their own liberty, freedom from fear, and freedom from want. In its various functions and styles, political art was very much alive in parts of this region.

## Conclusions Drawn from APT I

APT I was important because a new area of work and artistic inter-national relations in a hitherto unseen geographical zone were being taken up by a major institution for the first time. It was also significant because the exhibition by its very exploratory nature in many ways escaped the controls of the institutional and national cultural positions from which it set out. That these institutional and conflicted cultural agendas became more evident and imposed over time with later APTs, particularly APTs IV and V, meant that APT I was a significant if only momentary opening in artistic and exhibition discourse.

If the exhibition was enmeshed with still unresolved contradictions about Australian cultural perceptions of itself, of cultural others, and a certain naïve clumsiness in understanding how cultural others could relate to Australians, nevertheless this was a liberatory gesture which responded to a far deeper and longer term re-envisagement of Australian culture than is normally credited to Australians in Asia. That some of these contradictions, particularly the place and status of those of Asian-Australian hybrid identity within Australia, became clear through the structure of the exhibition and the public statements of some of the curatorial actors did not mean the effort was unworthwhile. Their resolution will await future re-articulation but this was a genuine and it would appear for many artists, curators, and viewers alike, refreshing opening up of artistic and broader cultural discourses on many levels.

## Types of Implementation Strategies

The goals of APT I were implemented by a five-member national committee who determined what would be the curatorial philosophy and the selection process. The latter took the form of something close to the Parisian/Third World model deployed in 1989 for *Magiciens de la terre*. Local experts would serve as analysts and information providers whose preselections would be narrowed down by an Australian selector dispatched *en mission*, who in some cases could be a member of the national committee. The final choice was legitimated by this committee, and since its membership was all Australian, of whose five members only two of whom had extensive Asian experience and any Asian linguistic ability, this really amounted to a fairly strict decision tree. The whole process may well have been operated collegially with Australian notions of openness, frankness, and equality, but this hardly constituted the decentred multilaterality proposed in Triennial goals three and four. The organizers may have stated that

> it was central to the Triennial's curatorial philosophy that the selection would also reflect what experts in those countries believed were important issues within the art of each country.[23]

This statement was premised on their having first selected which experts would advise them. In some cases, which the organizers were not free to publicly admit, they had to accept the local advisers and their recommendations in a complex local situation, particularly for Indonesia. But ultimately it was "Australian" values and procedures by which the goals would be implemented, and measured against the products of this process: an exhibition, a catalogue, a book, an international conference and a program of artists talks and lectures during the exhibition.

## Explicit and Implicit Attitudes

Some of the Triennial and other publications revealed a particular set of attitudes.

### The Contemporary without a Tradition

The explicit focus of the Triennial was on contemporary rather than traditional art.[24] The basis for this discrimination was nowhere made explicit. It was related to recent debates about Australian identity which had included what the then director of the Queensland Art Gallery, Doug Hall, thought were "spurious claims that it might aspire to be Asian",[25] and by implication that it was the Asian notion of the traditional which would render such claims spurious. Such an approach to cultural difference was opportunistic. It was based on the supposition that "we" would accept difference in the contemporary since some of its form-languages might have been cognate and thus allowed "us" to communicate, however different "we" thought the meaning of the message was. If cultural difference was taken to be founded on the traditional, not only would the substance of difference remain intractable but non-cognate forms would make discourse between us problematic and probably impossible. Some such attitude lay behind the statement that,

> focus on contemporary art has been especially applauded as an opportunity to put aside pre-existing stereotypes and initiate discussion based on the realities of current developments.[26]

This position worked as a tactic of artistic exchange for a given, limited period. Many modern artists elsewhere situated themselves at precisely this cross-cultural node of *bricolage*, from Mark Tobey to Paik Nam Jun. Smith thinks it was a temporary strategy of escape, so long as the artists could get away with it, from the obligations of not only the traditional culture but from the constraints of a relatively recent modernization.[27] But it remained opportunistic because "we" were always trying to use the haphazard confluence of cognate forms to deflect the culturally different purposes for which "you" had deployed them.

Deep cultural learning is not opportunistic. It has very great rewards but is costly, personally and culturally risky, and time-consuming. It involves changing how those forms operate for "us" because "we" have found how they authentically operate for "you". That requires knowing how "you" have reconstructed and transformed "your" tradition by operating those forms. It is a profound vulgarity—and not a *haute vulgarisation*—of modern museum consumer culture to imagine that the contemporary can be separated from the traditional, however that is to be conceived. They are front and back.

## The Artist as Mediator

Artists became seen as shaman figures who bodied forth a complete nexus of values which the analytical processes of modern commercial society inexorably drove apart. Some saw the artist as an "intermediary between the object and a range of experiences and values, cultural, political, or spiritual which are relevant to each of the countries in which those artists work".[28]

This attitude forced the bringing together of artists and works, particularly when their work became a performance or an installation piece that was performed. Not all artists or all works had to function in this way. Because of the different kinds of demand made on the audience there were very strong arguments for separating painting, sculpture, installation, and performance, rather than having them placed together in a kind of aircraft-hangar-*cum*-supermarket which was the Queensland Art Museum water mall and its linked spaces. It is not mere hindsight to see that different kinds of works and different kinds of artists—be they bearers of so many intersecting values or not—required different kinds of space or placement, otherwise the experience of the modern museum became something of a three-dimensional analogue to TV channel-hopping, as was certainly the case in the APT I displays.

## Exoticism and Closure

Sometimes the attitudes found in relation to APT I art which were supposed to resolve each other seemed to fight in the same space or on the same page. One writer confessed an "addiction to the culture of South East Asia",[29] but on the same page another thought "the shutters have been down too long".[30] If exoticism is the yearning for the other which sees in "them" only what flatters "your" self-esteem, then closure to the other would lie in not admitting "they" are even out there. But exoticism is, even thus, a yearning for the other in the first stage of a learning process. Without deep learning, wide exposure to information could simply lead to a further kind of shut-out by presumed mastery, one without even the benefit of an exoticism which yearned.

## Against Euramerica

The long-held and warranted Australian frustration at Euramerican ignorance of its colonial offshoots' cultural products, some of which were every bit as or even more developed than those at the "centre", was the resonating keynote of the Triennial and other texts. "Euro-Americentric perspectives are no longer valid as a formula for evaluating the art of this region".[31] There was a global move away from "dependence on international critical approaches that was evident two and three decades ago".[32]

Finding common ground with Asian art cultures who suffered the same fate may have been a genuine and effective way of re-positioning both Australian art discourse and the history of modern art itself.

## Regional Diversity and Globalization

On two levels regional diversity and globalization were not incompatible. They could have been discrete processes which occured in parallel, or they were different analytical positions from which to explain heterogenous aspects of the same artworks. This breadth of understanding was found in the Triennial catalogue.

> new approaches to art have been developed, some rejecting Western imperatives, and we are also now seeing other artists confident in their synthesising of Western art approaches in the recognition that both Western and non-Western artists have been, and continue to be, inspired by each other's cultures. There was "no sense of a homogenous regional identity, yet there are common themes which emerge from the art".[33]

Fortunately dialogue in this region had gone beyond earlier clichés of Cold War interpretation which often degenerated into arguments about the "comprador bourgeoisie" versus "international cosmopolitan élite", explaining nothing and empathizing with no one.

## Direct Communication

A naive faith underlay some APT-related statements which believed that what "you" said in "our" language (English) somehow constituted direct communication. The same may be said when "we" see "your" works in "our" museum.

> I note with some satisfaction that the articles are not written solely by Australians and that many Asian artists and writers can tell us about their work in their own words.[34]

Apart from the fact that "we" should have already known that what "you" said was not the same when "you" said it in "your" language, or looked at "your" artwork with "your" culture's eyes, even when with translation "we" knew that "you" were speaking to "us", were showing "us" "your" work. The quotation marks here indicate there can be in no sense direct communication, or direct vision across cultures, an issue which the APT I catalogues largely ignored. This does not mean that communication cannot take place, just that it is more indirect and serpentine, and wily.

To understand what did communicate across cultures we would have to examine many complex questions of how culture constructs others, what domain there was for the transcultural, and the a-cultural within communication. Even translated words or seen works were still communication, and "we" could still have eyes to see "your" work. The test of whether this has made sense was when what we said or showed to you was referred to when you spoke to another "we".

In that sense the attitude of opening up what was naively considered to be direct communication, nevertheless indirectly carried with it the radical unmaking of the "we", and the reconstitution of the "us". This was the fresh energy and genuine strength of the opening up of Australian art discourses to Asia, most prominently in the Triennial, an opening simultaneous with the opening to the inside through "Aboriginal" art, and this was what Asian friends may have found of constructive reference as their own art worlds opened (or unfortunately closed) to other art discourses in the region.

## APT Motivations over the Longer Term

In terms of motivations revealed through professed aims, by APT IV in 2002 it was clear the APT was intended to achieve explicitly institutional and political goals. This had already been made absolutely clear by the Queensland Government in a statement by the then minister for the Arts in 1999, when APT expenditures by the government of A$2.6 million over nine years were seen as benefiting the performance of business and the Queensland economy.

> Those who do business in Asia and the Pacific know the face-to face cultural encounters are the necessary and often decisive preliminaries to any corporate deal making. To do business in these cultures, you must speak their language, see yourself through their eyes, understand their vision of themselves and share their aspirations for the future. An event such as the Asia-Pacific Triennial brings Queensland face to face with her economic partners in a way no mere balance sheet ever can....The Asia Pacific Triennial plays a vital role in promoting these economic ties. It boosts our profile and strengthens friendships in a region where when markets get tougher, cultural ties attract a special premium.[35]

The preface of the 2002 catalogue went on to explain that "the Triennials have now become an enduring part of the Gallery's profile", "with the institution committed to a lasting engagement with the Asia-Pacific region through collecting, researching, exhibiting, interpreting the recent and current art of the region".[36] The Chairman, former state premier, Wayne Goss, and the director, Doug Hall, had firmly shifted the aims of the APT towards those of the institution which had supported it. But this trajectory was never very far away from earlier APT statements. In APT I in 1993, the claim was made that the APT

> is a landmark exhibition and the first of its kind of this scale in the world to focus on the contemporary art of Asia and the Pacific, including Australia and New Zealand. In undertaking the Asia-Pacific Triennial the Queensland Art Gallery recognizes the need for an ongoing series of exhibitions and forums which would initiate dialogue on the art of this increasingly important geo-political region.[37]

This was an historical simplification since the trajectory had already been marked in the early biennials of Sydney after 1973, as may be seen from appendix 1. The claims were continued with APT II which was of "unparalleled interest", the APT having "created a cross-Asian dialogue of a kind not experienced previously which involved Australia as one amongst equals". But institutional self-promotion was given a different skew in APT III 1996 when the APT both claimed to bridge centuries *and also* to need to evade the clutches of current euphoria and rhetorical cliché.

> The presentation of the Third Asia-Pacific Triennial will bridge the twentieth and twenty-first centuries, but, It is self-evident to suggest that the Triennials have played an important role not only in expanding a contemporary cross-Asian and Pacific cultural dialogue, but also in giving such diverse artistic practice a greater critical profile beyond the region.[38]

This has the ring of historical positioning from a narrow base, and at several other places APT catalogues betrayed a distrust of art history or made a convoluted critique of what they thought were its mistaken arguments.

> Some have argued that an art so radically different from that associated with the familiar Western sense of Asian history is less about post-colonialism than about representing a new colonialism, as the art draws on current tenets of Western curatorial, intellectual and artistic representation. Such observations have, of course, come from outside the Asia-Pacific region [*sic*, un-sourced] and represent not so much an intellectual or cultural dilemma as the peculiarities of Western mind-sets. This emphasizes the value of the Triennial in presenting such a substantial exhibition and supporting symposium, which disclose and articulate the dynamism of the art itself as well as the shifting perceptions in response to it.[39]

It was very clear that a history-making role was envisioned for the APT, probably from the prior planning stage, about which the organizers were content not just to make what some might think were normally hyperbolic art gallery claims for the importance of its own activities, but beyond that proclaim a true or more engaged grasping with historical issues themselves. They claimed to be "presenting such a substantial exhibition and supporting symposium, which discloses and articulates the dynamics of the art itself as well as the shifting perceptions in response to it".[40] By APT III in 1999 the disenchantment with whatever APT organizers thought of art history had become almost total. This was stated in the *Crossing Borders* section whose avowed inclusion in the APT was to find artists who

> not only cross geographical borders in terms of where they choose to practice, but also *use media and subjects in ways which fracture any sense we might have of a recent art historical continuity*. This is less concerned with traditional

> views of expatriation and diaspora, and more to do with artists finding linkages which enable their cultural specific experience to be relevant beyond their country of origin.[41]

Perhaps the continuities were simply beyond, not the future, as the APT III slogan claimed, but the conceptual or cultural historical grasp of the APT organizers? In such a de-conceptualized, a-historical ambiance, it was of little wonder that APT I had presented itself as "a landmark exhibition",[42] and claimed a peculiar chemistry for its curatorial procedures, that the organizers saw APT II as having "a *unique* curatorial profile",[43] or that the APT III stood out for providing a "*unique* curatorial model".[44] The APT II was also "*uniquely* placed to provide a natural and a suitable site for a forum on issues related to art in our rapidly changing region"[45] (my italics).

The concepts of "unique" and the "equal" run through the APT catalogues without any acknowledged contradiction, but the notion of equal or at least exchange relations is also found in the Fukuoka catalogues, and it may have been a simple contradiction which arose from the notion of curatorial choice. What was chosen was still privileged even if the inequality between the chooser and the chosen had various elements of reciprocality and exchange built in. At Fukuoka, Kuroda Raiji noted,

> what is necessary for us is a courageous attempt to actively communicate, without depending on economic and political power, or without sticking to ideology or fundamentalism with various kinds of "the others".[46]

One may further identify from APT II a sense of objectivism and moral correctness in curatorial statements which spoke of the basis of intellectual equality to disclose knowledge and experience,[47] and of a "commitment to building a contemporary Asia-Pacific collection".[48] It received further emphasis in the APT catalogues in a trope which objectified what were evidently quite specific decisions or approaches, adopting a messianistic tone which saw a special role for Australia. This country was "*uniquely* placed to provide a natural and acceptable site for a forum on issues related to art in our rapidly changing region", and admitted "our belief that Australia is an *equal* participant, not an arbitrator in this process" (my italics).[49]

The notion that artists were selected individually in APT III,[50] tried to historicize what was obviously a highly motivated a-historical choice in Queensland, and as well in effect a national Australian choice. It could be sincerely doubted that Queensland Art Gallery had the historical knowledge to transcend historical, national, and curatorial categories in the ways it pretended.

> Many of the artists represented in the three Triennials have an international reputation and, for some at least, the Triennial has played a part in bringing their work to attention. The Triennial has never been a government-to-

> government project about official exchanges, and nor have artists been chosen to "represent" a country. Rather, invitations have been extended to them to participate as individuals, and this has meant that they can express at times their ideas in ways that are not possible in official exhibitions.[51]

As policy documents, the APT texts' main goal was dialogue with and a re-perception of Australia's region: one policy goal was to reposition Australia's own art culture, a goal incidentally also adopted from time-to-time at Fukuoka for Japan.

> In the context of Australia's geopolitical proximity and developing relations with countries of Asia and the Pacific, it seems logical and appropriate, given that Australia in its world view is no longer solely a Euro-Americentric country, that an Australian art museum would take up the challenge of a major series of exhibitions and forums concentrating on the vitality and diversity of the region's contemporary art at the beginning of what is undoubtedly a new era for both Australia and the region.[52]

The success of the APT was an index of the adjustment of the Australian art world because of the APT itself, among other changes.[53] One of the evaluators of this adjustment was to be international opinion, a revised evaluation of Australia's status, one which was by implication not Euramerican-centred and hegemonic.

> Our concept of the Triennial as an artistic endeavour, not a political one, has been justified by the international reaction to the first Triennial, as has our belief that Australia is an equal participant, not an arbitrator in this process.[54]

## Curatorial Positions in Comparative Perspective

The curatorial positions of the various APTs were even more complex to analyze. They began with the aim of grasping a region, the contemporary art of Asia and the Pacific, including Australia and New Zealand. There are many good reasons for thinking of the Pacific as a special region adjunct to Asia not Euramerica, and for the Anglophone cultures of the Western Pacific, Australia and New Zealand, as having both an Asian geographical location and in some sense cultural placement.

I am prepared to think of this location as "Asian South Pacific". The exclusion of Australia and New Zealand and Oceania from the Fukuoka Asian Triennials was never argued in Fukuoka catalogues which established "Asianess" as an otherness to "Japaneseness", in what may be argued was a direct continuation of World War II Greater East Asia Co-Prosperity Sphere categorizations. For the Fukuoka Asian Art Museum, "Asia" meant East Asia, Southeast Asia, and Southwest Asia. It did not include The Pacific, Oceania, the Middle East or Central Asia. It did include artists from the area active outside it, and European and American artists active within Asia who had an influence on the art scene. Seen more positiviely, this position was part of a attempt to integrate Japanese art into an Asian perspective and to look for a kind of parallel Asian modernity no longer constructed by a binary relation between the West and "Japan".[55]

These problems of location were not argued in any systematic way in any of the APT catalogues. The double marginality of Asian South Pacific cultures to both Asia and Euramerica was not mobilized as a position even though this might have been the strength from which to speak.[56] Certainly the intended function of the APTs was to show the "dynamism and diversity of art practice within the region",[57] and it was always clear this had both inner, Australia-directed, and outer, Asia-directed trajectories.

Whilst relatively similar to that which developed at Fukuoka, the APT curatorial position was in direct contrast to the intent at Gwangju which from the outset was concerned with process. Rather than treating the Biennale as the site of display for achieved works at least the early organizers of Gwangju thought of the Biennale as a site for artistic process, certainly in its first incarnation in 1995 and in its 2002 and 2004 exhibitions. In 1995, Lee Yongwoo, the director general of visual arts for Gwangju, as he was also in 2004, wrote,

> The objective of the Kwangju International Biennale is to encourage independent cultural behaviour. In other words, it is to provide not rhetorics, but a site for artistic creation, and to concentrate on the functions and essence of the arts rather than the importance of art forms...Biennale is a place for discussing various possibilities, not a place for exhibiting or assessing the arts.[58]

This idea was taken up or taken further by Hou Hanru and Hans-Ulrich Obrist in *Cities on the Move* in 1997, and Hou Hanru and Charles Esche in *PAUSE* at Gwangju in 2002.

The selection structure at the first three APTs of beginning with local experts as advisors whose final selections were confirmed by Australian "specialist" curators, and then beyond that level by a five-person national committee, could hardly be regarded as an open structure, even though its closure was not that of the organization around a single artistic director selected for his or her exhibition concept. This was a position that the APT resolutely refused. It meant both the over-privileging of foreign experts as informants, and then the under privileging of their subsequent advice, because the triple structure of the curatorial hierarchy produced decisions highly biased towards particular mindsets in selection.[59]

This was noticeably in contrast with the attitude at Fukuoka where there was a continuous effort to develop curatorial concepts which would grasp new realities of art practice. In one conception in 1999, there was an early move towards relating art to social communication networks, and a courageous attempt to actively communicate a shift towards art as a collaborative process.

> The arts would not be such ones as created from nothing by hands of an isolated individual, not the illustration of values monopolized by the majority or the privileged, not solid, finished objects for sale and consumption, not objects disseminating in limited culture. It would be the arts that artists create that through collaboration with viewers, community, residents, and experts of other disciplines....Such arts might not be called "arts" anymore by conventional and western definition.[60]

The APT avoided taking a responsibility for its evaluative role in selections which were a form of cultural capital appraisal. The subsequent rise in prices and international exposure of some of its artists, Lee Bul in 1993, was one spectacularly clear if well-merited example. It appeared as natural phenomenon of the art world rather than an artificial human-made one engineered by this choice. Such appraisals were also an intervention in a local art world based on a position that external appraisal was of a different kind, and usually on a different level, than local ones. This contradiction ran through all biennials, not just those that took place in Asia, including the APT, since one could hardly claim equality with those selected when the selection had unequal results for those selected and those not selected, and was from a position already unequal. Fukuoka curators were acutely aware of this issue but again placed it in the context of communication, in this case of a cross-cultural context:

> The present Asia is full of problems such as communication gaps, misunderstanding, exclusion, oppression, and ignorance which are recognized among individuals, between an individual and the community to which the individual belongs, as among communities with different cultural backgrounds. These factors lead to oppositions between the western and the non-western world, economical disparity, or religious and ethnic conflicts.
>
> In such a situation, what is necessary for us is an courageous attempt to actively communicate, without depending on economic and political power, and without sticking to ideology or fundamentalism with various kinds of "the others".[61]

The APT, despite its continued and justified pride in its educational and knowledge-enhancing roles, adopted the position that it should not grasp an understanding independent of the local advisors from the art worlds where artists were selected, and which required the provision of the linguistic tools for each major culture concerned. There are almost no texts quoted directly from Asian languages by any of the Australian curators in any of the catalogues, a situation which one would not imagine possible for an exhibition of Matisse or German Expressionism. This meant that the knowledge base of the APTs has been short-term and never based on fully independent appraisals: many of the artist entries and commentaries in the catalogues are transpositions of material already available or regenerated in English, in some cases by non-specialists even when local Australian specialists were available. This knowledge-base was quite unlike that produced by the regular visits of curators to many of the same artists by curators from Fukuoka. They were for the most part conversant fully with the local languages and art literature on each artist visited.[62] Some of these artists have even remarked that Fukuoka curators were even more conversant with their previous work than they were themselves. But APT curators came to see their work as if they were just filling in a category of practice which they had already established, such as performance art by a woman.

The triplicate organizational structure for APT I–III, and the binary structure for APT IV and V, also meant questionable expenses in sending abroad members of the national or curatorial committee to make choices which other experts, even in Australia, could have advised on.[63] It can be argued that the APT was a local initiative by a state gallery which was largely financed at that level. It was also in part financed by purchases of works brought for the exhibition via its support foundation or other pre-arranged donors. The national committee membership for APTs I–III did not indicate such. With membership of important art bureaucrats, an art school head, and a former cultural relations diplomat the whole ambiance of the APT has been of the local articulation of a nationally motivated effort. This was also explained by the very large financial support which the APT received from the Australia Council for the Arts, given in appendix 2. The central government support was accompanied by the continuous and intense collaboration of Australian diplomats overseas, frequently acknowledged in the catalogues.

As we have seen above, if APT I may have tried to take up a missing regional agenda, later APTs were funded for national or state gallery institutional ends. Some unattributable reports indicate that support of the Queensland Art Gallery director and administration for APT I which was originally devised and planned by the Dr Caroline Turner, a cultural historian who was Deputy Director of Queensland Art Gallery, actually came later. She had based her planning on earlier experience of exchange exhibitions with Japan in 1987 and 1989, for which Queensland Art Gallery support was not as high as it subsequently became in APT II and III.[64] Then the audience success and the institutional prominence for the Queensland Art Gallery both nationally and internationally were secured. As an attendee I can testify to the increasing scale but increasing inflexibility of the APT symposia in APT II and III, a fact which was remarked on by many foreign visitors who were disgruntled that their questions were not answered or that the issues they raised were not engaged with.[65] I can only presume this rigidity was in some way a function of increased gallery administration concern with claiming and maintaining this success.

That the APT was a flagship exhibition which focused cultural events in Brisbane must have been a determining factor in persuading the state government to finance the building of a new Museum of Modern Art for the APT V in 2006.[66] It is not hard to see the APT as a unique institutional vehicle of opportunity for the realization of policy goals at national, state, and institutional levels which all the involved political, bureaucratic, and curatorial figures had an interest in pursuing.

The principal curatorial position adopted by APT I–III was the avoidance of a single curatorial or conceptual vision, and increasingly the separation from selection by national representation.[67] This cumbersome, conceptually problematic but broad and mostly representative structure was replaced by in-house selection from Queensland Art Gallery curators in 2004. Thus from 2004 The Queensland Art Gallery must have considered that its curators had mastered their various international art fields well enough for the gallery to make its own direct selections.

Earlier, the trajectory of separation from national representation was flawed by the support of some national governments for their artists' participation. This support meant that a certain locally star status for the artist had become a prerequisite of selection in 1993 and 1996.[68] Such prominence often by implication involved a conceptual programme to do with a particular group or generation of artists. Indeed the claim in APT II that the concern was with "issues of the present",[69] and was not based on "national representation",[70] but with "cultural pluralities",[71] begged the question of within what terms the *now* was to be constructed and where it was to be sited.

In contrast, Gwangju was in continuous search for a new curatorial concept against which the curators were supposed to react in their selections, from "Beyond the Borders" in 1995, to "Unmapping the Earth" in 1997, to *PAUSE* in 2002 when the artistic director Sung Wan-kyung explained:

> The theme of Gwangju Biennale 2002 is P_A_U_S_E, [*zhi*, Chinese character]. Why P_A_U_S_E? The answer is found in the expression, "We get lost in order to find the road." No phrase better explains the reasoning behind this theme. P_A_U_S_E, [*zhi*] was selected to encourage critical reflection on pervasive inertia and to evoke the need of alternatives, whether the inertia is in our lives and civilizations or in international exhibitions such as biennials.

By APT III curatorial choice was being made through a curatorial brief to five different teams (of 13 Queensland Art Gallery staff and 13 external curators with 27 international curators) laid down for them in Curatorial Forums. The brief specified,

> preparatory information including the suggested number of artists, the estimated space allocations for each artwork, and curatorial guidelines for the selection of artists summarized as follows:
> – Artists must be engaged in some way with contemporary visual art practice and discourse
> – Artists of all ages may be considered
> – Artworks in any media and across media may be considered
> – Artworks associated with "indigenous" art practice may be considered

> – Artworks associated with "indigenous" craft practice may be considered
> – Artists located in urban, regional, and rural locations may be considered
> – Wherever possible, artworks should have been produced in three years prior to 1999
> – Every effort should be made to include women artists
> – Artists included in previous APTs may be considered for inclusion in exceptional circumstances, most probably through the Crossing Borders avenue or as part of collaborations.[72]

Despite the wish to be transparent about how decisions were arrived at, this specification raised more problems that it solved, unless there was some quintessential broadness of Australian view and omniscience of information which allowed the Queensland Art Gallery process for APT III to accommodate all kinds of possible contrary opinions. But beyond that, the phrase above that "artists must be engaged in some way with contemporary visual art practice and discourse" begged so many questions about how contemporary art was to be defined, that could ultimately only have been a position defined by curators. It could be defined neither by practitioners, nor situated within general or critical debates about what was the "contemporary". The declaration of curatorial categories then became what Queensland Art Gallery curators considered the contemporary to be, despite all the claims to equality and dialogue. This was to be applied to a region from Hokkaidô to Tasmania, from the Indus to Edo-gawa, and so was a very large, fantastic claim. It may also have been a culturally specific, Australian *braggadocio*.

It was in sharp contrast to the position in Fukuoka where as we have seen from 1999 the definition of art was not in the curator's hands alone, but inhered in a kind of social network which defined the communicative participation in making or defining art. It held that contemporaneity or its relation to tradition was a secondary question or was simply a given.

The other policy orientation running through the APT catalogues was that Australia could, and by implication somehow should, serve as a mediator of art flows or as an honest broker for a debate within that region with which it had only recently and in much of the population and most of the political class only reluctantly identified itself. It would so by somehow forgetting its own cultural past as much as that of the region, without making a contemporary knowledge of those pasts the basis from which to envisage the future. Such arguments about the role or placement of the APT constituted a concrete embodiment of what might be called the post-modernist fallacy that the future may be known proleptically without dependence on a construction out of a relativized past.

> Australia, with its multicultural population and situated, as it is, geographically and increasingly culturally between two worlds, is uniquely placed to provide a natural and acceptable site for a forum on issues related to art in our rapidly

> changing region. Our challenge is to provide a forum which is not a mirror of the past but one open to the future.[73]

Fukuoka has been much more frank in revealing the actual process of its curatorial decision-making.[74]

Gwangju also sought to do so in 2002, but in the event only revealed that ultimate choice lay with the artistic directors.

> The third and perhaps the most original aspect of the biennale will be the invitations to 26 so-called alternative groups or independent organizations mainly from Europe and Asia. Here we want to make a pause in the constant search for new individual artists and make tangible the huge contribution of these initiatives, usually run by artists or their close collaborators… These groups of artists have emerged as the key force in art making as artists developed alternative strategies to negotiate a different basis for making institutions, organization, the relationship between art and society and the reflecting the position of art in relation to globalism…
>
> What we propose for Gwangju is to reproduce on simple terms the floor plan of each space in the Biennale hall. Each space will then auto-curate its own presentation for the Biennale.[75]

This procedure shifted the level of curatorial selection to the level of the invited alternative spaces or groups, so securing a quasi-complicit voluntarism. In fact, as several reports indicated, when the catalogue was initially only provided to groups and not to individual artists, the level of participation by those artists inside groups was downgraded to that of being mere representatives.[76]

Hou Hanru and Charles Esche also wanted the curation process to be transparent and part of the exhibition. They forecast:

> Our first action will be to move our office into the Biennale galleries as the first pavilion. This is not only a formal exercise but also a very important mental step that shows the process of working and collaboration during the Biennale itself. The office will be designed by Chang Yong Ho and the Taiwanese artist Michael Lin, who will make a floor painting on a raised floor of the office of the pavilion. By doing so, we reveal parts of the hidden process of a biennale and create a real atmosphere of work in progress that will continue through the exhibition while it is open to the public.[77]

But architectural placement, like all exhibition layouts, is a notoriously rehearsed kind of staging so that even an open possibility devoid of formal hierarchy, when controlled, ends up like any other kind of aesthetic pre-positioning determined by rules, even though its intent was to overcome previously implicit or naturalized ones. The problem was that the tyranny of pre-positioning by naturalized rules was replaced by that of the curator who pretended to the function of an artist.

Issues of audience-artist-curator communication and compliance were also raised in Gwangju 2004, which I saw. It devised and implemented, "a Viewer-Participant system (see chapter 7), which consisted of inviting viewers to participate as producers of art rather than as traditional consumers of art."[78] This was basically a kind of empanelling of persons by profession worldwide and their pairing with particular artists, but the results of the art and how either artist or viewer-participant actually determined the art produced was never clear from the works alone.

We have seen that curatorial policy weighs heavily on biennial selection, as it professionally should. But here is such a range of positions from prior choices by the gallery administration into whose strategies biennial exhibitions are supposed to fit, to the almost neutral positioning of audiences or artist groups to take part in selection, of single institutions to intense interactions with a plethora of agents, that the local or national political context of a biennial is more significant than the selections of any one curator or their surrogate. This complexity is not easy to see, or see through, because of the enormous investment made in the biennial and the motivated intensity of biennial propaganda from out of which, only with great difficulty, does a space emerge for critical understanding. APT manifested all these issues, and in its move from a sort of monitored local selection in APT I to a locally curated and ordained selection of spectacles by APT IV, a tendency which continued right through to APT VIII, we can see the institutional closure of a space which might have opened up to a new kind of artistic freedom.

## Notes

1 APT V in 2006 and later editions fall outside the corpus considered here, although I will occasionally refer to catalogues and conference papers. The list of catalogues and texts referred to is as follows:

**APT I**

APT I: Janet Hogan, ed., *The First Asia-Pacific Triennial of Contemporary Art* (Brisbane: Queensland Art Gallery, 1993).

Caroline Turner, ed., *Tradition and Change, Contemporary Art of Asia and the Pacific* (Brisbane, University of Queensland Press, 1993).

**APT II**

APT II: Caroline Turner and Rhana Devenport, *The Second Asia-Pacific Triennial of Contemporary Art*, catalogue (Brisbane, Queensland Art Gallery, 1996).

Caroline Turner and Rhana Devenport, ed., *Present Encounters: Papers from the Conference of the Second Asia-Pacific Triennial of Contemporary Art* (Brisbane: Queensland Art Gallery & Griffith University, 1996).

**APT III**

APT III: Caroline Turner and Rhana Devenport, *Beyond the Future: The Third Asia-Pacific Triennial of Contemporary Art*, catalogue (Brisbane: Queensland Art Gallery, 1999).

Caroline Turner and Morris Low, ed., *Beyond the Future: Papers from the Conference of the Third Asia-Pacific Triennial of Contemporary Art* (Brisbane: Queensland Art Gallery & Griffith University, 1999).

**APT IV**

APT IV: Lynne Seear, ed., *Asia-Pacific Triennial of Contemporary Art* (Brisbane: Queensland Art Gallery, 2002).

**APT V**

APT V: Lynne Seear, Lynne & Suhanya Raffel, ed., *The 5th Asia Pacific Triennial of Contemporary Art* (Brisbane: Queensland Art Gallery Publishing, 2006).

2 I spoke briefly at the APT I symposium and had a small article in the book which accompanied it, "Aspects of Taibei modernism in the 1980s" in Turner, ed., *Tradition and Change*. I also was a session chair in the conference of the Third Triennial, see Turner and Low, *Beyond the Future: Papers from the Conference*, 141–2. My own earlier criticisms of the APT had been briefly set out in Pamela Gutman and John Clark, "APT: a Conversation", *Eyeline* 32 (Summer 1996): 21–3. Parts of what I now write cannot avoid the influence of that critical position, but my arguments are open to critique. A review of APT IV in 2004 which was circulated privately with my permission, incurred the direct ire of the then director of the Queensland Art Gallery, Doug Hall, in an email reply of 29 March 2005, when he refused my request for an interview. A more open discourse can be found about APT VI in 2009 in the email interviews with the APT curatorial team and other email dialogues in *Contemporary Art + Visual Culture Broadsheet* 38, 4 (December 2009).

3 This is a version of a lecture given at the Faculty of Fine and Applied Arts, Chulalongkorn University, Bangkok, on 9 February 1994, and is not previously published.

4 The Asia-Pacific Triennial was held at the Queensland Art Gallery, Brisbane, Australia from 15 September to 17 December 1993. Exhibition publications included the catalogue, *The First Asia-Pacific Triennial of Contemporary Art*, ed. Janet Hogan (Brisbane, Queensland Art Gallery, 1993), and a book, *Tradition and Change: Contemporary Art of Asia and the Pacific*, ed. Caroline Turner (Brisbane: University of Queensland Press, 1993). The period leading up to the exhibition saw several related publications appear. A new journal called *Art & Asia Pacific* was brought out as the supplement to *Art & Australia*, and became a regular independent quarterly from December 1991. When its publisher folded for other reasons in 1998 it was bought by a Chinese artist in New York and subsequently re-sold to Simon Winchester and Elaine Ng. There was a special issue of the quarterly journal *Artlink* 13, 3 & 4 (November 1993–March 1994), on "Contemporary Arts of the Region: South East Asia and Australia". The edited version of papers presented at a conference in Canberra in 1991 had by then appeared, in John Clark, ed., *Modernity in Asian Art* (Sydney: Wild Peony Press, 1993).

5 For a recent view of this erasure see J. Hoorn, "Exposing the Lie of Terra Nullius: Joseph Lycett's Awakabal Album", *Art & Australia* 31, 1 (Spring 1993).

6 Several of these issues were rehearsed in John Clark, *Australian Art and Asia — Then and Now*, Occasional Paper No.19, (Sydney: Research Institute for Asia and the Pacific, University of Sydney, 1992); John Clark, "The Notion of Modernity: Discourse [Open and Closed]", in *Modernity in Asian Art*, ed. Clark; John Clark and Christina Davidson, "Transcultural Irony", in the catalogue *Transcultural Painting* (Melbourne: University of Melbourne Art Gallery, 1994).

7 Australia has a fairly high level of incisive critique of the manipulative relationship with the outside world by its politicians. See Robert Manne, *The Way we Live Now: the Controversies of the Nineties* (Melbourne: Text Publishing, 1998); Robert Manne, *The Barren Years: John Howard and Australian Political Culture* (Melbourne: Text Publishing, 2001). The toxic political abuse of this myopia, if the abuse and the myopia are separable, is discussed carefully in two critical collections of journalism, David Marr and Marian Wilkinson, *Dark Victory* (Sydney: Allen & Unwin, 2003), and David Marr, *Panic: Terror! Invasion! Disorder! Drugs! Kids! Blacks! Boats!* (Collingwood: Black Inc, 2011). Marr has more recently iterated the grim myopia of genocide. See his, *Killing for Country: A Family Story* (Collingwood/Wurundjeri Country: Schwarz Books, 2023).

8 Evans in *Artlink* 13, 3 & 4: 3.

9 Hall, in APT I, 6.

10 Turner, in APT I, 8.

11 Hall, in *Tradition and Change*, xi.

12 Hall, in APT I, 6.

13 Hall, in APT I.

14 Hall, in *Tradition and Change*, xii.

15 Hall, in *Tradition and Change*, xii.

16 Turner, in APT I, 9.

17 Hall, in APT I, 6.

18 Turner, APT I, 8.

19 Turner, APT I, 8.

20 Turner, APT I, 8.

21 See Patrick White "A Sense of Integrity" (1988) in *Patrick White Speaks* (Sydney: Primavera Books, 1989; London: Penguin Books, 1992).

22 APT I, 76.

23 Turner, in APT I, 8.

24 Turner, in APT I, 8.

25 Hall, in *Tradition and Change*, xi.

26 Turner, in APT I, 8.

27 Terry Smith in a useful comment on the manuscript, personal communication, 2013. However, when it is recalled that 80% of the population of Edo was literate by the mid-18th century, and primary school attendance in rural Japan was above 90% in the late 1890s, the notion that all Asian modernizations were "recent" requires some qualification, even from the viewpoint of habitual indices used to map Euramerican modernity.

28 Hall, in *Tradition and Change*, xii.

29 Darling in *Artlink* 13, 3 & 4: 4.

30 Britton in *Artlink* 13, 3 & 4: 4.

31 Turner, in APT I, 9.

32 Turner, in APT I, 9.

33 Turner, in APT I, 9.

34 Evans, *Artlink* 13, 3 & 4: 3.

35 Government statement by Hon. M.J. Foley, Attorney-General and Minister for Justice and Minister for the Arts, reported in the *Queensland Parliamentary Hansard* for 26 August 1999, 3578–9.

36 Unless otherwise indicated the references here are to the catalogues of APT. Preface, APT IV, 6.

37 Doug Hall, in APT I, 6.

38 APT III, 19.

39 APT II, 9.

40 APT II, 9.

41 APT III, 19.

42 APT II, 11

43 APT II, 9

44 APT III, 19

45 APT II, 11.

46 Kuroda Raiji, *The First Fukuoka Asian Art Triennial* (Fukuoka: Fukuoka Asian Art Museum, 1999), 14–15.

47 APT I, 6.

48 APT II, 9. Clearly the ability to rely on the Queensland Art Gallery Foundation to purchase works which were to be exhibited in the APT created more flexibility for planning than if the funding requested from supporters and foreign governments had also included return shippage fees and curatorial courier visits.

49 APT II, 11.

50 APT III, 21

51 APT III, 21.

52 APT I, 8.

53 The scope of the Australian political opening up in the Asia-Pacific which to some extent under-pinned the APT, and of which the APT was itself one kind of catalyst, is found in Paul Keating, *Engagement: Australia Faces the Asia-Pacific* (Sydney: Pan Macmillan, 2000).

54 APT II, 11.

55 See Ushiroshôji Masahiro, "Fukuoka Ajia Bijutsukan ni tsuite", in Ushiroshôji Masahiro, Kuroda Raiji, Rawanchaikul Toshiko, *Ajia no Bijutsu, Fukuoka Ajia Bijutsukan no korekushon to sono katsudô* (Tokyo: Bijutsu Shuppansha, 1999), 006–8. However, the excision of Australasia and Oceania from Asia has been abandoned by the Japanese Ministry of Foreign Affairs and mostly side-stepped by The Japan Foundation in their operational organization.

56 As noted by Geeta Kapur in "The Centre-Periphery Model or how are we placed? Contemporary Cultural Practice in India", *Third Text* (Autumn/Winter 1991): 11, "Precisely because of the anthropological bias of the regionalist argument and the dangers thereof, the Third World may be a valid, self-definitional superimposition. It can make for a political realignment of forces. Anthropology must heed the politics of interpretation; regional ethics, Indian, Cuban, or Australian, is not a self-evident political guarantee for any form of liberation." See also the chapters

"Globalization: Navigating the Void" and "Dismantled Norms: Apropos of an Indian/ Asian Avantgarde", in Geeta Kapur, *When was Modernism: Essays on Contemporary Cultural Practice in India* (New Delhi: Tulika, 2000).

57 APT I, 8.

58 Lee Yongwoo, "Remapping the Borders" in *The First Kwangju International Biennale. Volume 1: International Exhibition of Contemporary Art: Beyond the Borders*, ed. Jin Young-sun and Chung Joon-mo (Seoul: Life & Dream Publishing Co., 1995), 17.

59 The first foreign curator allowed to select Australian artists, Apinan Poshyananda in 1996, even had his text removed from the final catalogue for editorial reasons which remain publicly unclarified to this day, a fact all the more astonishing for it neither being announced by the Queensland Art Gallery, nor to my knowledge being remarked on by the Australian art press.

60 Kuroda, *The First Fukuoka Asian Art Triennial*, 14–15.

61 Kuroda, *The First Fukuoka Asian Art Triennial*, 14–15.

62 The contrast has more than once been noted to me by contemporary Asian artists I have visited.

63 Notoriously, in my memory, the selection of Wu Tianzhang from Taiwan for APT II in 1996, but I am sure there were other cases.

64 The retrospective appraisal of the APTs may be found in Caroline Turner, "Cultural Transformations in the Asia-Pacific: The Asia-Pacific Triennial and the Fukuoka Triennial Compared", 221–43, and Francis Maravillas, "Cartographies of the Future: The Asia-Pacific Triennials and the Curatorial Imaginary", 244–70, in *Eye of the Beholder*, ed. John Clark, Maurizio Peleggi and T.K. Sabapathy (Sydney: Wild Peony, 2006).

65 This was clear from the APT II symposium when the Singaporean art historian T.K. Sabapathy complained about the absence of new concepts, and was not answered, and the late Santiago Bose asked what the high-tech art of Murakami Takashi had in common with artists like himself from poor, Third World countries. These views were known to the APT organizers since the art magazine they were published in was from Brisbane. See Pamela Gutman and John Clark, "APT: A Conversation", *Eyeline*, 32 (Summer 1996): 21–3.

66 The museum cost A$100 million as part of a larger cultural precinct which had cost A$300 million. At its opening both the Arts Minister Rod Welford and the Queensland State Premier, Peter Beattie "claimed the new building was among the world's top 10 modern art galleries", according to *The Age*, 6 December 2006. The analysis of gallery attendance and actual funding figures is a recondite art. For an attempt see the discussion in *The Courier-Mail* [Brisbane] of 2–3 December 2006. Another article in the same newspaper described the architectural style as "a bit like a Noosa beach house on steroids", but quite why the extension of a local building vernacular required a grandiose five stories of light well, when, for example, one ideal of modernist gallery architecture, the Gemeente Museum in Den Haag manages with two, was never quite clarified. Other curators indicated that in order to avoid potential damage if there was flooding from the adjoining river, the storage areas had to be on the top floor. This was proved necessary in the massive 2011 floods.

67 This was disavowed in APT II, 11–12.

68 Or in early years the opposition such as that of Indonesia in 1993 for the exhibition of the work of Dadang Christanto, and if I recall correctly Djoko Pecik, which did

not eventuate. In general the same exhibition suffered from the opposition of the Chinese authorities for the work selected which was only overcome by the direct cooperation of Australian diplomats in China.

69 APT II, 11.

70 APT II, 11–12.

71 APT II, 12.

72 Rhana Devenport, in APT III, 26.

73 APT II, 11.

74 On the Fukuoka method of selection which also indicates the systematic depth of curatorial research see Rawanchaikul Toshiko, "How Were the Artists Selected?", in *The 3rd Fukuoka Asian Art Triennial 2005*, ed. Igarashi Rina (Fukuoka: Fukuoka Asian Art Museum, 2005).

75 Curators' Statements, *Gwangju Biennale 2002 Project 1 PAUSE* (Gwangju: Gwangju Biennale Press, 2002), 24–31.

76 Including that of Ray Langenbach in an interview with me 2 November 2004. He said that the decision was communicated via Hou Hanru not to give a catalogue to everyone since there was a need to keep them for VIPs and thus only one would be given to each group and not to each group member. Langenbach got all the artists' groups to come to a meeting and the group then started clipping open the piles of catalogues which were lying in a storage area. They were asked to wait until negotiations could be made with the Korean administrators, then Charles Esche (Hou's co-curator) came in and aligned himself with the artists. There was an agreement to hand out the catalogues and this was done by Charles Esche. Langenbach asked Hou "What do you think about this? Do you think you have organized this properly? Can you really do this if you organize six exhibitions a year?" Hou, enraged, said according to Langenbach, "You're only here because you're invited. Take your performance [away]".

77 Curators' Statements, *Gwangju Biennale 2002 Project 1 PAUSE.*

78 Statement of Chairman of Gwangju Biennale Foundation Kim Po-chun, in Gwangju Biennale 2004, A Grain of Dust, A Drop of Water (Gwangju: Gwangju Biennale Press, 2004). See also *Gwangju Biennale 2004 Viewer-Participants Discussion Papers: The Audience, Who Are They?* (Gwangju: Gwangju Biennale Foundation, 2004).

Chapter 6

# Markets, Biennials, and Contemporary Asian Art

Hitherto in this book I have analyzed largely empirical material based on my own experience of viewing biennials and from other existing viewpoints. Now I now want to turn to look in further depth at two sets of systemic issues, and somewhat more theoretically. This chapter more generally concerns what distinguishes artworks for aesthetic evaluation from art objects for trade, and how art markets have interacted with biennials. Its intent is more theoretical than other parts of this book, but it does also offer certain concrete examples.

## Artworks and Art Objects

This chapter seeks to place biennials within the system of multi-level art distribution systems, from inter-artist exchanges and gifts, to primary market sales from galleries, and secondary markets composed of inter-dealer and inter-collector sales. I will return to the examination of types of circulation and the typology of biennials in chapter 7.

At all levels these distribution systems are linked to a wide range of formal art exhibition institutions from artist-run and non-profit art centres to Museums of Contemporary Art. Beyond these institutions are temporary exhibitions which began with conceptually formulated, "of this generation" shows of contemporary work in the late 1960s. They became an important segment within, and in some cases the organizational principle for, biennials in the 1980s and 1990s.[1] I generally prefer to think in terms of distribution systems, because the underlying and economistic concept of markets carries the misleading notion that the movement of art objects is chiefly to be explained by the dynamics of economic phenomena, both physically and in evaluation.

I will keep the term art for the situation of aesthetic engagement found in the studio or the exhibition, and this chapter will also concern where and how an *artwork* becomes an *art object*. Many values which were not exclusively economic were carried by distribution through the sale of art objects. These values could in various contexts be converted into economic ones which were then be re-circulated as goods. Furthermore, such distribution systems were not just denoted by exchanges where goods such as art objects or artists' reputation appraisals were traded directly for money, but by the circulation of many non-economic values within circuits or networks of more broadly defined cultural values.

Major limitations should be pointed out. As the bibliography and some notes for this chapter reveal there was from around 2005 in Euramerica and more recently in Japan, a broadening set of materials on curatorial practice, the histories of art dealers, and the analysis of art markets. There was some material which increasingly regarded the "Biennale" as worthy of institutional analysis, or designation as a field of curatorial practice, or as an institution in a series of art worlds restructuring into a kind of new international art society. Such restructuring happened under the conditions of globalization, web-mediated networking, and the loss of Cold War ideological conflicts—although new conflicts have arisen in the different areas of economic hegemony over the former "Third World", and in the wars of religious fundamentalisms. But there was until then very little research or overall discourse on what Biennials constituted within or between these variegated local, national, and transnational structures and tendencies.[2]

This position was very unsatisfactory because research on Asian biennials looked at a burgeoning regional phenomenon conceived of in response to this new international "order" which understood the rise of new biennials in Asia, and the articulation of contemporary Asian art into older and mostly Euramerican biennials. It was very difficult to accomplish these latter tasks without arriving at some idea of the structures and tendencies concomitant with the former and still largely Euramerican-dominated art international art world. This had not produced a series of articulated positions about these structures, despite the arrival of some retrospective views on biennials.[3] This book thus makes some excursions into the first area, picking up some ideas and descriptive analysis of phenomena from the existing literature in order to formulate propositions on what that new international "order" was. It will then look at how Asian biennials and Asian contemporary art were enmeshed within.

## Constructions of Value

How are values constructed for art objects? When these circulate in the art world or beyond that of one nation-state through the networks composed from other units including the international, they also do so as items with economic value. There is a nexus of interchange between artistic and economic values, and the economic values may often be used an index of artistic ones. How may switching or exchange between artistic/cultural values and economic ones be understood?

Bourdieu distinguished between *symbolic capital* which is the "degree of accumulated prestige, celebrity, consecration or honour and was founded on a dialectic of knowledge and recognition" and *cultural capital* which "concerns forms of cultural knowledge, competences, or dispositions".[4] The appraisal or consecration of symbolic and cultural capital in art produced the need for a mediatory function which was usually performed by the figure of an actor/agent who mediated between symbolic, cultural and economic fields. This figure concealed their self-interest in the advantages which derived from doing so. Bourdieu, thought that art business was a vestige of a pre-capitalist economy, also surviving in inter-generational gift-giving, and that symbolic capital was disavowed as a "credit" which produced "economic profits" because,

> producers and vendors of cultural goods who "go commercial" condemn themselves, and not only from an ethical or aesthetic point of view, because they deprive themselves of the opportunities open to those who can *recognize* the specific demands of this universe and who, by concealing from themselves and others the interests at stake in their practice, obtain the means of deriving profits from their disinterestedness.[5]

Bourdieu saw the field of cultural production as based on two oppositions: between restricted and large scale production, and between the licensed avant garde and newcomers, that is the field of conflict between cultural orthodoxy and heresy.[6] Value was thus produced by a series of differential oppositions all of which relied on self-denial by "makers and marketers [artists and dealers/ curator-mediators]" who necessarily colluded in the "repressions of the direct manifestations of personal interest".[7] The truth of these repressed interests cannot be claimed by artistic acts, as a limit case of the generation of the value of art,

> because in refusing to play the game, to challenge in accordance with the rules, i.e. artistically, their authors call into question not a way of playing the game, but the game itself and the belief which supports it. This is the one unforgivable transgression.[8]

I think we have to see the value of art as being translatable between symbolic, cultural, and economic fields, and that the value of all art objects is constructed differentially. The problem will arise as to how, and at what marginal rates of exchange, these rules of translation are to be set, and who is to fix these, or act as the efficient agent in such translations. These issues will come up later, but they concern the hierarchy of relation between fields and relative dominance in terms of specific social and economic structures. At the initial stage of analysis we must just posit that all values which are produced are inserted into a system of appraisals. These values are produced probabilistically by the system itself, rather than some categorically or psychologically separate or transcendent level of aesthetic appraisal.

But if *value,* however denotated, is a marker of a demand, then following Baudrillard,

> Needs… are better defined as a *function* induced (in the individual) by the internal logic of the system,
>
> [and that],
>
> everything, even artistic, intellectual and scientific production, even innovation and transgression, is immediately produced as a sign and exchange value (relational value of the sign) [and not as use value].[9]

The implication is that all values are interchangeable, are equivalently inter-valuational, and that the one-way relationship from cultural to economic value is reversible both in semiotic principle and as a social fact. Baudrillard argued that,

> It is not the quantity of money that takes on value, as in the economic logic of equivalence, but rather spent, sacrificed, eaten up according to a logic of difference and challenge. Every act of purchase is thus simultaneously an economic act and a trans-economic act of production of differential sign value.[10]

Baudrillard thought that as long as art made use of the disappearance of itself and its object, it would keep its importance, its value. Art's problem was that it went on trying to capture reality. In 1995, in an article originally published in *Le Monde,* he thought contemporary art claimed to transcend its own mediocrity in "raising originality, banality, and nullity to the level of values or even to perverse aesthetic pleasure" by transcending itself onto a second and ironical level.[11]

Some eight years later in a lecture given at the Venice Biennale in 2003, Baudrillard noticed the reciprocal relations between art and the real whose entire realm it aestheticized.[12] The general exchange between reality and the aesthetic had begun the other way around with Duchamp's automaticist transfer of the objects of the banal world into the domain of art, and in this "action" art and the work itself were transformed "into an object, without illusion or transcendence, a purely conceptual *acting out,* generating deconstructed objects that deconstruct us in turn".[13] Here, following Eagleton, the contradictory nature of the aesthetic emancipates the aesthetic work as much as it is produced from quotidian systems of domination in the real. But such domination also institutes an insertion of real social power into the aesthetic, an internalization of repression due to the actual nature of social relations.[14]

The above considerations indicate that the artworks seen at biennials were not some kind of culturally free good circulating beyond the usual domains of formal control by art discourse, even if the sense of "usual" heavily normalizes field-specific practice in Euramerica. Nor were they free of material control by art markets seated inside the unit of the nation-state. "Artworks" were enmeshed in a web of relations where their values were switchable into other fields when they became "art objects", bearing and distributing value measured in a modern economic world by monetary values given as prices.[15] These considerations also point to the likelihood of very particular relations between the producers of art objects, their mediators and the structures of mediation deployed or engaged by the latter. Whether biennials were not merely linked to the art market but "are the market", as Boris Groys casually remarked of the Venice Biennale,[16] hung on how the complicities between producer and mediator were understood.

All art production and mediation which took place inside relations defined by the hegemony of a nation-state, and with an outside defined by relations between nation-states, immensely privileged both the site and agent of mediation. These sites and agents, because they were relatively free from dominance by the "internal" hegemonies, had in some degree to be established for each transaction. They were also able to be free from hegemonies which might operate at the inter-state level. Certainly it would be empirically tenable to suppose that these agents also became free to deploy the hitherto "structural" qualities of their position into new types of relations in the 1980s and early 1990s.

These redeployments were facilitated by the arrival of new contemporary artists from Asian countries within the international biennials, by the relative availability and low cost of international travel to artists and curator-mediators (as much as they already had been relatively cheap since the 1960s to commercial gallerists). They were transformed by the speed and network-privileging capabilities for transnational communication in message flows unleashed by the internet, mobile telephony, email, and information diffusion via the world-wide web. These networks operated with their own technical kinds of closure determined by access to the internet and by the information skewed for easy loading and display on the world wide web. Even if they were still to be technically discriminated from the hierarchical hegemonies between states, or those between ruling and ruled classes within a state, these networks were and still largely are maintained by physical control over the unequal distribution of resources, including barely tangible financial resources, and material goods.

## Cultural and Economic Values

There are many treatments of the relationship between artistic and economic value, most of which provide insights to the linkage between local or national artists and art worlds and the international and transnational ones.

Throsby thought cultural and economic values were incommensurable,[17] and underpinned this with a review of older theories of use value and exchange value. He included the Ruskinian view that the value of a commodity expressed in monetarized terms and determined by market processes was antithetical to the principles of the intrinsic value of objects, especially art objects.[18] One consequence of separating cultural and economic value was that the valuation of the former was assigned to non-market functions such as canon-formation by particular institutions or mediators like curators, gallerists, and usually indirectly by collectors. If the Biennale was by the early 1990s the appraiser of first inclusion for contemporary art, it was empowered by separation from the market as that body which certified artists or works as worthy of further appraisal and circulation, included in which was economic valuation. But as Throsby later noted, "canonical classification of certain artworks and genius status on certain artists is simply a manifestation of the exercise of power of the artistic and intellectual establishment".[19]

If canonization constrained what was selected by socially empowered institutions and individuals functioning within them as valuable, what were the feedback processes which reinforced tendencies within artistic production which were confirmed by these selections? What kind of institution was the Biennial, or what were the functions of the mediators within it? These questions were not uniquely constrained within one particular culture, even though they may have had a culture of "origin", and a notion of "belonging" to a new kind of transnational intermediate and empowering space between cultures. Transnational intermediacy was sited on but still transcendent beyond nation-states. For the maximization of artistic value, "the utility of the artist is seen as a function of the cultural value of the work, and this utility is the quantity to be maximised".[20] This cultural maximization could be modified by minimizing a certain level of income by the artist as an economic constraint found in most cases for the artist by multiple job-holding.[21] Throsby ultimately proposed "a physical market for artworks and a parallel marketplace for the ideas"[22] where "the idea is a pure public good, the aggregation of individual valuations can be thought of as comprising the total cultural valuation of the idea within the sphere of its circulation".[23]

The last qualification is highly significant because the "sphere of its circulation" was restricted and much of the non-economic cultural competition to secure places in the selection of curators for biennials was routed through a notional international or transnational circuit closed to all but the few having access to it. The repeatability and restriction of artists within the international selections for biennials indicated very clearly the cultural authority of not merely the curators, but also of those who chose the curators. If cultural values are heritage values there may be disagreement but in the end—despite art critics and art historians occasionally subverting the content and order of canonization[24]—the overall set of those artists and works to be included among those culturally valued may be arrived at, even by historical attrition over several generations. The issue of, and for, biennials was that those longer-term historical processes were telescoped into the privileged—and often self-privileging—simultaneous selections of one selector or groups of selectors on a time-scale of usually not more than three years.[25] Whereas biennials dealt with assets which were renewable over short timescales—that is replaceable, in some cases discardable, or circulable—Throsby's cultural values dealt with assets which were barely renewable in long time-scales.[26]

Underlying much of the discussion of the value of art in either cultural or economic fields lay a debate about what created that value. This arose because of a quandary expressed by Abbing as, "Why are so many artists engaged in innovation, if it is, in fact, an unprofitable endeavour?".[27] Throsby later analyzed and tested propositions about creative output and commercial artistic output. To model these he proposed various equations which identify creativity as a special feature of artistic production, whatever the problems there may have been in measuring quality.[28] This approach had much to be said for it as against the statistical ranking exercises applied by Galenson to the prior canonizations of specialists which were found in art historical books, and in tables of art sales, among other measurably qualitative outputs. Galenson came to the rather banal conclusion that some artists who are "conceptual" early in their career are the major innovators in art, and the others who are "experimenters" over the length of their career present a different notion of creativity.[29] Among Galenson's critics, Ginsburgh and Weyers drove a very firm dent into his method of statistically ranking established opinions, by their carefully having showed how the dichotomy between the conceptual and the experimental evoked the earlier debates that "reason…dominates and precedes the senses". They reasserted that creativity was a function of the quality of production over an artist's life-time, not of production at any given age range.[30] This was indeed a position antithetical to most biennials, many of which did not include artists of certain ages, or practices which had come to be conventionally associated with artists of a certain age.

Indeed the problem with all emphases on value, whether cultural or economic, was that they handled as simply extraneous variables the external changes of historical events, social and economic structures, or changes in wider cultural discourses beyond art, they did not see them as intrinsic or determinative conditions for creation at any given period.[31] Evaluative discussions tended to stress supply analyses and equilibria or disequilibria in various social or economic distribution processes that were markets for goods and ideas, they did not foreground the demand of new patrons or historical situations for new or reformulated expressions. These demands, and the contemporary art curators' claim to a prescience about capturing them for as yet unexplored, or unarticulated, or repressed, or subordinated audiences, were their source of authority. It was thus *ipso facto* a rhetorical device for claiming authority for those who curated biennials. Whether this claim represented what curators actually did, or showed what they actually achieved in practice, is another matter.

## Non-Economic Exchanges

Another set of perspectives should also be briefly looked at before we move to see how the notion of markets articulated with the actual functions of biennials. These views posited a field of exchanges which took place outside economic valuation, and one would suppose beyond cultural valuation and outside the domain of exchanges of goods and ideas. The view stemmed from the idea of gifts, and of the cycle of socially constrained accumulation of gifts or their forced giving up, along the lines of *prestation* as discussed by Mauss and later anthropologists.[32] This position made all exchanges the subject of evaluation within a given cultural constellation, so that all judgements of taste—all evaluations—were dependent on their particular situation within a given discourse or the group who upheld it. According to this view there was no "master trope or discourse of value".[33]

Artists or art historians and aestheticians may have proposed the non-universality of value, that all values were relational, and that artworks moved in non-economic, non-culturally dominated circuits, even though all values and notions of circulation could have been seen simultaneously as intrinsically "cultural" formulations. They might even discuss, Duchamp-like, that some "zero degree of value" or of "non-value" was a kind of qualitative limit point which only then allowed the establishment of categories of value which could be evaluated. If one wanted to select art from within a given culture and show it in another, or display it at however nominally and complicatedly an inter-cultural level as was the case with biennials, one had to deny the non-universality of value, yet at the same time needed to claim that all artworks were in some way inter-culturally evaluable. This was through the viewing conditions and through the collateral textural and curatorial positioning. Biennials became the site of a selected display which grounded the terms of that denial and promoted those evaluations. A measure of the complexity of interests involved in biennials was that the competitive nature of the denial of categories of work for selection, and the tendentiousness of the evaluation of those actually selected mostly went unacknowledged, at least in public, by curators.

## Types of Market

I will now look at some of the literature on art markets to see where biennials might fit into an overall structure of artwork evaluations and art object distributions. This is crucial because the selectors for biennials often made non-economic evaluations which, over time, had important, even immediate economic consequences for the price of works by some artists, and thus for their ability to independently fund their future production. This question arose before "art stars" were created, but was intrinsic to the conditions for their appearance.

Artworks became art objects for sale through the working of a quasi-cultural market for ideas or aesthetic pleasures. Artworks were first evaluated by a long series of appraisers—beginning with the artist and then developed a parallel existence as, or were wholly converted to, art objects with a price for sale. One may see this not as a categorical leap from artworks into art objects, but as a multi-stage process where further distribution and circulation then occured through a series of economic markets, before artworks gradually became objects in art markets for purchase. In place of the two-level notion of a primary gallery market and secondary, speculatory investment market which was habitual to studies of art markets, and reinforced by beloved self-interest heard through the trade talk of gallerists and auction houses, a four-level conception of art markets appeared to be of more interpretive use.[34] Each of these four levels may be split into two parallel markets, those of cultural and those of economic valuation, but with economic market functionality being weakest at levels 1 and 2 where the feedback or conversion which secures economic benefit was likely to be time constrained, and operated in the long-term.

Artwork and art object distribution systems were characterized by equivalences or symmetries between cultural market appraisals—despite no denotating unit being readily seen, and economic denotation through monetary prices, all were appraisals assumed to be unified in value unit across very different scales of prices.[35] In fact artworks, art objects and their distribution systems are marked by asymmetries between the ability of the artist to culturally appraise their own work and to secure that appraisal from others. Short of becoming an "art star" who could write cheques with their own works, there was a very strong asymmetry between the volume/level of "sales" of contemporary art as income to the artists, and the patrons' wish to "purchase". Above a certain price for the artist, even a very low price relative to the work, skills, and materials involved in production, "selling" characterized the nature of an exchange, usually from artist to gallery to client, but "buying" hardly characterized the client's situation.

| TYPES OF ART MARKETS | |
|---|---|
| 1. | artist to artist, or artist to client, or artist to other peer in a different field, for cultural esteem [may later be convertible into economic benefits]. |
| 2. | artist to curator for cultural consecration [often convertible into economic benefits]. |
| 3. | the so-called *primary* market: artist to gallery to client for economic sale. |
| 4. | the so-called *secondary* market: gallery to gallery and collector-investor, or from collector-investor to other collector-investor for monetary sale, or to donation to an art institution to gain public esteem [often convertible into economic benefits through peer esteem and collection, in some countries convertible into tax benefits for the collector-donor]. |

Whether giving a work for pleasure or social esteem or investment (and usually all three) the buyer was not choosing between comparable or *equivalent* goods. The choice was between *different* goods whose price he or she would pay according to a desirability market, or *hedonic distribution*, usually governed by cross-cutting cultural and economic evaluations manifested both as private taste and public fashion. There was no equivalence in the calculus between the artist's *utilitarian* need to sell and the client's *hedonic* ability to buy. Both were usually articulated in quite different domains, the latter economic, the former mostly as a symbolic store of cultural capital which would only be converted to economic capital at a deferred date. Artists made calculations, necessarily imprecise and qualitative, about the marginal discount between sales or prestige now, when major works not selling immediately might allow artists to receive later favourable evaluations which increased the economic value of all their works.

Singer tantalizingly conceded that art "trading obeys two separate regimes in interrelated markets, the market for consumer services (client-specific hedonic utility) and the market for financial services (a quasi-monetary resource which appreciates over time)".[36] He raised the prospect that art which he defined as "Museum Art", such as artworks in a museum, could be defined as a cultural asset. However in his impressive equations he defined the primary attributes of these objects as decorativeness, with a subset which he summated as intellectual appeal. He thought the former could be perfectly known but not the latter. This was despite the latter being the only element in an artwork which might be relatively independent of the physical substrate in the art object, barring perfect unities of taste across all populations in the former. Singer considered the inefficiency of primary markets to be because "information is incomplete, exclusive and expensive", where buyers often engage in counter speculation or overbidding—hoping to uncover new genius—on the presumption that the market has excessively discounted the available information".[37] It is compensated for in the secondary market where the art object becomes a kind of monetized commodity with the market transacting business *as if* there were a near perfect accord, at least in the short run, concerning the ranking of most characteristics".[38] In the world inhabited by curators and dealers who mediated to both cultural and economic markets, this perfect knowledge was controlled or constrained. Knowledge about price, however perfect, did not equal knowledge about cultural value, however assessed. The small number of artists handled by leading commercial galleries, the highly restricted list of artists given one-person exhibitions at museums of contemporary art or their equivalent in state galleries (who might have circulated through from either commercial galleries or from not-for-profit art spaces), and the restricted number of artists who appeared in biennials, all indicated a principle of quantitative limitation which operated on the number of artists in each site or cultural market so constituted. This principle controlled the supply of artists and works, or controlled the sales of those already on the market. The limitation was not there because there was only a sufficient supply of works or artists to meet the demands of the system. In short, the principle of a supply-demand feedback did not apply in the short term of, say, four or five years.

The question is, why? The answer could lie in the feedback of economic appraisals from the secondary to primary markets (markets 3 and 4 in the scheme above) which disconfirmed some and confirmed other appraisals made in the primary market. If this economic feedback is thought of as "vertical", then the confirmation and disconfirmation processes between cultural and economic markets at both levels may be thought of as "horizontal". In addition, there were undoubtedly complex "diagonal" feedback processes between cultural primary and economic secondary markets. There was enormous self-interest in dealers or mediator-curators to skew or render imperfect knowledge between cultural and economic markets, and between primary and secondary markets, of most levels. It was in the self-interest of the dealers to increase the marketability of the artists sold in either primary or secondary markets.[39] It was in the interest of the curator-mediator to uniquely privilege the artists and works appraised in any of the four markets because this enhanced their own position and, if successful, would improve their own status as a chooser by making a restrictive appraisal which came to be held by others. In many cases this status converted into direct economic benefit via further exhibition organization opportunities within institutions, or one may suppose, brought them "independent" curatorial opportunities including fees.

Biennials could be considered to function as a further set of cultural markets at levels 2 and 3 and to have performed important evaluatory functions in the short term which have economic consequences later. How much later? If the implications of the position that "Biennials *are* the market" seems unclear, let me cite two personal anecdotes which provide surprising confirmation.

At the Venice Biennale in 2001, I saw the works of Richard Serra in a clearly independently funded area of the Arsenale, judging by the size of the work and the surface plan of the exhibition space. I also saw the work of Yinka Shonibare in the African art special exhibition.[40] Two years later in 2003, I went to the Basel Art Fair immediately after visiting the next Venice Biennale, and saw the same two pieces by Serra and Shonibare in that part of the Basel Art Fair devoted to the display of large art objects for sale to very rich collectors or to museums.

In 2003, I also visited the Australian Pavilion where the work of Patricia Piccinini was on show. At the moment I was asking for a catalogue, someone loudly introduced himself to the assistant as "a major collector of contemporary art". He asked how he might buy one of the works on show. The assistant introduced the collector to the artist who was present. Journalistic rumour in Australia later figured the exhibition as a major sales point for the work of the artist. Thus biennials perform cultural consecration functions, but with very short lead-times of usually not more than two years before the artwork becomes an art object for sale. Meanwhile the biennial itself may often simultaneously function as a sales outlet for the same artist.

## Consecrating

Information or informed opinions which amount to cultural consecration affect how an artwork becomes an art object.[41] This has been analyzed by McCain and others as the "lemon" problem where the sale of art objects points to a broader issue in market formation where "the quality of goods is known to sellers but not to buyers".[42] Used cars are quite likely to be bad cars unless the seller is completely honest and is trusted by the buyer. Dishonesty by the former incurs costs to the latter whose trust is useful only if the information (knowledge about the goods traded) is based on the seller's honesty. There is also an economic effect between goods which are derivative and goods which are genuine and fine, where "dishonesty and misrepresentation cause suppression of the market for fine goods, and the loss of potential profit".[43] Thus the guarantee, or in Bourdieu's terms consecration, of artworks as fine and not merely derivative has provided a cultural evaluation with severe consequences for economic markets, since a "poor" work can in a situation of imperfect knowledge misleadingly or disingenuously substitute for a "fine" one. There are complex ways of analyzing the quantitative relations between the production of "poor" and "fine" goods, and it remains the case that many artists choose to generate a "psychic income" (or cultural value) more often than they obtain the immediate economic returns that an artwork which has become an art object may generate for them.[44]

If the producers (artists) are able to judge quality better than the buyers (dealers, collectors), then any mediating actor (critic, gallery curator, independent curator) who can justify the marketing of any particular art object,[45] particularly in the area of contemporary art where unknowns are greatest and knowledge by buyers most imperfect, will have a much greater role to play than merely the title of "opinion former" might indicate. This is the classic domain of aristocratic patronage, government or other public funding intervention in art to promote the production of "fine goods" by subsidies to artist-producers or to receiver-galleries. Where the object may be to move between quasi-local discourses to a pan-regionalist or international one, the role of the mediating actor will be all the more significant. Such actors in consecrating a work or flow of works, (a movement) act like a catalyst to their becoming transactable cultural objects, and with the intervention of acquisitive desire and concentrations of economic resources these can then become art objects on an art market. The mediating agents do not make the price, but they sanction market entrance, and in terms of opinions held collectively across a cohort of such mediators, their *cultural* evaluations may also sanction *economic* evaluations marked by price gradations.[46]

The leading agents in this transformation used to be galleries who would patent a style by monopolizing certain artists, such as the Sydney Janis Gallery in the 1950s with the American abstract expressionists. Galleries like Janis then distributed this stylistically marked practice (or "consumer technology") to a quasi-syndicate of other dealers who all agreed to bid for the same artists. The tendency to include cliques of artists in the transformation from cultural to economic evaluation (or, if one must be neo-classical, "price setting") and just as significantly exclude others, was reinforced by official mediators such as art museums by their exhibition and purchasing decisions. Collectors also wanted to be first into the primary market and by over-paying against the notional economic value of an artist, to shut out other later purchasers. They thus secured a temporary, collector monopoly over a contemporary artist's output for a particular period. But the period from gestation (or recognition) of an art tendency to monetization was almost regular for early 20th century Cubism, as for the early American pop artists, at around eight years.[47]

Writing about the 1970s in the USA, Singer concluded that:

> The rate of turnover [in styles or consumer technologies] clearly depends on the speed of dissemination of information. The curator, critic, trustee, consultant has a vested interest in episodic art and in spawning new consumer technologies: if this were not so, there would be no need for the pre-eminence of the critic. He is the magician, the priest, the medicine man who "knows the secret language and penetrates the mysteries".[48]

The functions of the "critic" have largely been absorbed into those of the independent mediator-curator of contemporary art because of the inability of many dealers to mediate contemporary art before it was swayed by the market intervention of collectors.[49] Collector-tycoons like the Saatchi bought out exhibitions by artists such as Julian Schnabel or Damien Hirst and effectively obtained a short-term monopoly purchaser position over their output.[50]

Moreover, many independent mediator-curators have appeared since the 1970s from the opportunities presented to mount "critical" exhibitions in the not-for-profit art centres run by local governments, artists or foundations. They provided exhibitions which in themselves served as a critical appraisal of a practice or a movement style, and implicitly a critical negation of those parts of contemporary art practice they left out, chiefly associated with older visual technologies such as painting, sculpture, or prints.[51]

Indeed the association of such movements, once they obtained acceptance, with higher prices meant that artworks became just another marketable commodity, at a certain low-mid level of price. But the translation back into cultural value was blocked because economic values had totally become cultural values.[52] The art object as economic commodity had also increasingly lost its identifiable, parallel and originating cultural value, and at high prices may be thought no longer to have any identifiable existence even as an economic object in some supply/demand relationship, or as forward speculatory investment. The artwork became simply a marker in a flow within a new, networked economy "in which the 'culturpreneur' forges alliances inside and outside the art world and realizes projects in the form of creative joint ventures".[53]

## Dealers and Galleries

A feature of some literature on art dealers and galleries in the early 2000s was that it made hardly any mention at all of biennials, except for the much earlier winning of the Grand Prize at the Venice Biennale in 1964 by Robert Rauschenberg in relation to the dealer Leo Castelli.[54] Those texts which examined art markets and their dealer/gallery operators either considered them to be autonomous of non-market and non-mediated selections and value allocations, or to be actually dominant over all non-monetary or non-economic value-based systems of certification, selection and distribution. The intellectual dearth of studies linking these different domains of the art world does not mean art historians should abandon consideration of their relevance. In this short section, I will tangentially examine the implications of certain dealer histories and activities for understanding where contemporary art in the Biennials' sector may have fitted into the markets they operated, or at least suggest how the one interacted with or articulated the other. I do so aware of the lack of hard data and of the dangers of damages' litigation.

The relation of biennials to other kinds of art exhibition and even market systems was unclear because it was located within transitional and on-going processes of globalization, with consequences for both the nature and level of inter-national units.[55] It might have heuristic value to compare them with the well-demarcated change between the academy and the dealer art market system which took place in 19th century France. White and White noted that four features were imbricated in links between changes in art system and broader society:

1. Concentration of dealers with an international clientele.
2. International scope in recruitment of art students.
3. Higher prices of contemporary French painting, as compared to the contemporary painting of other countries.
4. Dominance of France in forming the language and criteria of art journalism.[56]

Many of these features only need slight adjustment here to see their relevance to the contemporary art world.

As in feature 1 above, many dealers in contemporary art were marked by the quality of their inter-national linkages: in 1990 Akira Ikeda Gallery in Tokyo was selling works in Japan from the world-wide network of galleries linked to Leo Castelli in New York;[57] at Basel Art Fair in 2003 the Australian Roslyn Oxley Gallery was selling some works by the Japanese artist Kusama Yayoi.[58]

As in feature 2, there was recruitment to all of the Biennale exhibitions of a very wide range of largely art school-trained producers, many of whom studied in second countries, particularly North America, or went to Europe for post-graduate or artist-in-residence opportunities. The supply of producers was thus well beyond the ability of a single Academy to control, and this was the case in the developing dealer market in 19th century France.

As in feature 3, but at an international not national level, the price of art was higher for those who were included in this circuit than in their countries of origin, and by the fact that they had been admitted to this level via overseas gallery exhibition. For example, there was an increase in the sales and price of work by Lee Ufan in Japan after its exhibition in Germany 1970 or Biennale selection.[59] Or there was an increase in the sales and prices of work by Lee Bul after exhibition in the 1st APT at Brisbane in 1993.[60]

As in feature 4, but via a discourse which was largely conducted between actors at an international level in non-native English rather than, as it had been in late 19th century Paris, in French within one country, France, the criteria of information circulation, of academic discourse in catalogues and art journals were set at an international level which was increasingly dominant over domestic or base-country discourses. One might say that the international level, although articulated between nation-states, was a domain at a supra-national or transnational level which interstitially penetrated those national discourses which in the late 19th century privileged one nation-state as a centre. This had been the case for France and its capital, Paris, in the field of art.

## Differences and Similarities with Previous Art Worlds

Many features of the contemporary art world in the early 2000s were different from the late 19th century, like the "objective" marketization of art prices and artistic reputations via international art auctions for very recent contemporary art. In the case of recent Chinese artists, these were artists who had only entered international circulation in 1990s chiefly via exhibition at the Venice Biennale.

There were also phenomena of information circulation which were dissimilar to the art world of *fin de siècle* France. These were evident in the contemporary German-American standardization of market values and ranking of reputations in the *Kunstkompass* tables published by the German magazine *Capital*.[61] The units of the international system itself were now quite different and permeable in ways unlike the situation before World War I, but it is interesting how inter-linked had been the art worlds of France, Germany and the USA even then.[62]

Earlier studies may have "undervalued the instruments of the Academy and the Salons to control public opinion and to serve those new audiences".[63] In like manner in the late 20th century, biennials constrained the development of a free market for art goods, in the same way as the sheer world-wide volume of works and producers would have predicated the movement of art goods in 19th century terms. Moreover, insofar as biennials, at least those conceptually or programmatically produced by their curators, may have been intended to serve as a marker of a set of aesthetic responses to a time, they resembled the situation around the Vienna exhibition *Entwicklung des Impressionismus in Malerei und Plastik*, 1903, which served,

> as a point of rupture, where the Secessionists' pluralist, contiguous, and continuous model of international Impressionism would be cast aside in favour of an exclusionary, disjunctive model of modernism in which "movements" succeed and cancel out their immediate predecessors in a linear march to an ever more perfect, more modern art.[64]

We have to consider the transitional role of the biennials within the permeable units of the international system from the mid-1990s to the mid-2000s. Biennials either reduced selection volume through the application of ideological constraints and thus secured a "group" or quasi-"movement" status like that sought by the Secession for Impressionism. Or, they functioned as the harbinger of a system where the quasi-salon functions were about to be overthrown in favour of a new kind of splitting up and isolation of artistic careers. Biennials additionally indicated the advent of new kinds of group structure founded on non-art purposes but represented by art-situations like "process art".[65]

The early 20th century role of dealers to isolate artists and thematize their careers, and of critics to ideologically defend or excoriate particular art or artists as being ahead of or behind the times, seems, by the late 1990s, to have been assimilated by the curator, particular the so-called "independent" curator or the "curator of contemporary art" within Museums of Modern Art. The role of the biennale must have been different in the earlier 20th century because comments on biennials were almost entirely absent from standard surveys of the work of particular dealers. This absence could cause us to overlook certain curious analogies between the position of a curator and a dealer, or the analogues in their behaviour within the art world and art market.

These types of behaviour are indirectly evident from the material on the dealer in Renaissance art, Joseph Duveen. They showed habits such as the monopolization of particular clients,[66] and intervention in a client's buying patterns to secure loyalty to the dealer.[67] In the late 20th century attention shifted to the level of exhibition by a curator at particular kinds of art events. This as a patronage situation could be seen as taking place in lieu of, or which may have led up to, purchasing decisions by a collector or institution. The repeated prominence of a small group of curators over successive biennial or biennial-related events resembled in some ways the occupation of the dealer space, or more accurately the cartel or guild of dealers, by the purchasing horizon of one collector, but then collectivized by the cohort of curators to the level of all those who decided who should be the curator at such events.

A closely related issue was that of the value of attribution decisions by experts, to which may be compared the consecrating opinion by curatorial selection decisions on contemporary art, or by the public offering of judgements of value of an artist or a work to other curators, above and beyond their offering to an interested contemporary art public. The paradigm case here was of Bernard Berenson who, as revealed in the Hahn "slander of goods" action that reached judgement in 1929, had been contracted to give authentifications to the dealer Joseph Duveen for the previous 27 years, and from whom he was to receive a share of the profits on any sale.[68] In 1929 Berenson could no longer maintain the fiction of being independent of the market and to have functioned as the disinterested scholar whose image he had assiduously cultivated for the previous 30 years. He was also notoriously prone to reversals of opinion, and it has been widely suspected that shifts from appraisal of the work "in the manner of", to "studio of", to "by". These sorts of shifts in judgement were almost directly comparable in contemporary art dealer talk that shifted from the description of a work as "representative", to "good", to "important". Both Berenson's and contemporary art dealer's shifts in opinion increased the saleability of works and thus income from sales.

Some so-called "independent" curators of contemporary art appear to have been receiving financial benefits or some fraction of subsequent dealer profits from works exhibited at biennials and later sold by other means.[69] Curators were not be able to impose their views on the collective opinion of collectors because of the scale of artistic activity and the flows of artworks and information not in their control: they were in a situation like that of the gallerist Janis who concluded after various unsuccessful experiences in trying to shift clients' taste that, "no longer do I impose esthetic judgments gratuitously".[70] In addition to other similarities in their roles, the behaviour of contemporary art curators resembled that of some contemporary art dealers in the 1950s and 1960s like Emmerich, himself from the third generation of a family of art dealers:

> What we are is leaders of the pack. Why? Because we experience early what others seem to experience a little later on. The whole game lies in being to identify and experience trends in advance, by the seat of your pants, by feeling and enthusiasm. Art dealers are like surfboard riders. You can't make a wave. If there aren't any waves out there, you are dead. But the good surfboard rider can sense which of the waves coming in will be the good ones, the ones which will last. Successful art dealers have a feeling for hitting the right wave.[71]

Whether (or not) curators were capable of "hitting the wave", and whether biennials represented tendencies or movements of art "before" or "behind" the wave, there can be little doubt the residue of the *Secession*-type mentality from 1903 in identifying movements to be anticipated or followed was found among the conceptual frames of some biennials. This was especially the case at Gwangju, Korea, in 2002, which tried to capture the mood of a time and the movements of art which might accompany it. Like gallerists, curators and particularly independent curators on the international biennial circuit tended to be:

- highly mobile;
- to have worked between several sites;
- they had a reputation which carried between several centres from their previous curatorial activities;
- they may also have been a collector;
- they may have intervened with other curators;
- they knew artists for a long time and placed them in a stable, the members of which became increasingly intimate and with whom they moved towards use of first names;
- they were be able to watch such artists for a long time and intervened with support for their careers from their first exhibition until their entry into a public collection and then on to Biennale or other national representation at the international level;
- they regarded their current exhibition or event space as a surrogate for a museum, where despite highly able and committed staff their presence was required at all times of the event.

The above features of curatorial behaviour were written by me from observations of many different curatorial strategies for Asian biennials, but were formally derived by analogy from an interview biography of the New York gallerist Leo Castelli.[72]

Three other phenomena deserve mention. The first has already been pointed out by some authorities and symbolized at a media level by the buying habits of mycenae such as Charles Saatchi, that of unmediated direct interaction with the artist by the collector which made a market.[73] The purchase and later sale by Saatchi of the work of Julian Schnabel indicated that collectors often functioned directly as dealers, they made and, where they wished, broke the prices of certain artworks or artists. Curators did not operate in the same way, but the inclusion or exclusion, or the relatively considerate or inconsiderate placement of the work of artists in Biennial selections indicated that the curator had an analogous power to collectors' market interventions with the reputation of artists when they "made" exhibitions, that is their cultural capital.[74]

But no curator had the economic power of the super-rich which only they could choose to convert into cultural power, despite some curators having managed to appear on the lists of the most influential persons in the art world.[75] The world of the super-rich was very different from that of merely well-off collectors: the income alone of the super-rich allowed them to have multiple homes, and some of which were only half the price of the most expensive auction paintings.[76] All that some media reports of contemporary art events like *Frieze Art Fair* actually mention was the dependence of the event on the rich collectors who had gathered there.[77]

Collectors sometimes bought in cartels through cumulated funds, and sometimes they bought individually with a curator in their advisory team and where the national tax regime allowed this (as in the USA) promised the work to the curator's institution after a specified period, or after the lifetime of the collector.[78] In these cases the curator was playing a "Berensonian" game with the marginal risk with the danger that their independent reputation would not be enhanced when they no longer advised the collector. There even was a peculiar and evident tension, analogous to that between the current and anticipated future price of an artwork for a collector, between curators who put themselves forward as adopting a radical position and their evident need to persuade the institution they were dealing with to allow them the freedom to transform it.

## Certification and Curatorial Practice

If the actual operations of curators were difficult to grasp externally, their functions within or between the various art systems where they took part were equally slippery. Moreover, the concept of "independent curator" needs some attention. This could be seen as a kind of free-lance mediator or cultural entrepreneur moving between institutional sites provided for on a temporary, or at least intermittent, basis by different patron cartels, usually headed by city or state cultural authorities. Curators tended to move from temporary institutional identities towards fixed ones.[79] This motility leads one to consider their independence to be a kind of fictional passport rather than it indicates any independence of the art worlds within which, or between whose different levels and types of unit, they moved. Curators invested and generated their own cultural capital which was deployable between these sites, so the investment was not merely on the side of the body funding the biennale nor indeed did the benefit accrue solely to the biennale authorities. If the cultural capital of the curators was not further generated, they lost out in the increasingly competitive and globalized game of allocating those "culturepreneurial" sites.

Biennial curators, perhaps because of the very opportunity to increase cultural capital and the risk of its loss, were of necessity highly competitive individuals. They often proffered highly contestable positions for their exhibitions as if, however ideologically constructed, they were indubitably correct.[80] This was because in the selection and circulation of artists and artworks which were in many cases yet to have independent market demand, or where the work was highly vulnerable to exigencies of its display, what curators particularly biennale curators offered was that consecration which deemed the work worthy of placing in this exhibition site or that circulation flow. Competition was for legitimation by consecration, and for the roles which had the authority to accord legitimacy. Consecration was a function, first of all of the self-definition, or autonomization, of the field of art itself, as Bourdieu concluded:

> The more the field is capable of functioning as a field of competition for cultural legitimacy, the more individual production must be oriented towards the search for culturally pertinent features endowed with value within the field's own economy.[81]

The problem for curators, and especially Biennale curators who claimed to inherit the mantle of the avant garde, was that they were thereby forced to multiply their roles, taking over the celebritization of artists which used to be performed by art critics or writers sympathetic to the artist.[82] As Bourdieu again noted:

> Competition for consecration, which assumes and confers the power to consecrate, condemns those agents whose province is most limited to a state of perpetual emergency. Avant garde critics fall into this category, haunted by the fear of compromising their prestige as discoverers by overlooking some discovery, and thus obliged to enter into mutual attestations of charisma, making them spokespersons and theoreticians, and sometimes even publicists and impresarios, for artists and their art.[83]

If cultural capital was formed for the artist by their reputation that had been consecrated by curators, Abbing noted that this had both an individual and a collective component. The former was a personal trademark whereas the latter rested on similarities within a group of related artists.[84]

These individual and group reputations were not some naturally occurring index of genius. They were constructed, and formed largely by which artists were to be allowed circulation. This operation was largely performed by curators, sometimes in reflection of a collective opinion among other curators. It was curators who served as gatekeepers, those who decided on which artists or works to let in (to attain a certain reputation) and on which were to be kept out. In fact, participants in a discourse occasionally let artists in by granting them a favourable reputation, while others were rejected or stripped of their favourable reputations.[85]

The collective reputation was like an investment decision by a caste in a fashion style, with both its *haute couture* and its *prêt-à-porter* brands. The decision maintained their own cultural capital and also sought reinforcement by other consecrators, such as museums. These marked the artwork as a long-term sign-medium of exchange for those fitted to choose. As Baudrillard has also noted, the collective of curators in their various independent or institutional incarnations, sometimes slipping into the class of collectors, sometimes directly in their service, functioned like a caste:

> For caste members the only real values are those produced and exchanged within the caste...the perpetuation of the dominant class "in its essence," is enacted in the aristocratic manipulation of the works as the material of sign exchange.[86]

A final related set of phenomena concerned other aspects of globalization which cannot be considered here in too much detail but which may have marked the way the curator was to fit into the art world in future. Globalization was a process within the very institutions which in the past had provided the sites from which "independent" curators were thought to display their independence, the contemporary art museum. These museums had begun to move outside their original sites in hitherto un-thought of ways as seen in the globalization of the Guggenheim Museum to Bilbao and elsewhere overseas, or of the Boston Museum of Fine Arts to Nagoya.[87] Or, modern and contemporary art museums have seen fit to circulate significant parts of their collections to assist the funding of their rebuilding, so making their exclusive criteria of the modern or the contemporary the standards by which artworks were to be judged in very different societies, often with their own complex and deep histories of modernity in art. A classic exmple of this was the 2004 exhibition of art from the Museum of Modern Art in New York at the Mori Art Museum in Tokyo which included not one modern or contemporary artwork by an Asian artist, let alone a Japanese artist.[88]

Ever since Rauschenberg won the Grand prize at the Venice Biennale in 1964 art prizes have begun to move away from the European centre. Sometimes their judges have also been more broadly recruited. Nanjô Fumio was on the jury for both the Hugo Boss Prize, 1996 and the Turner Prize in 1996,[89] and in 1995 he had been the first Asian curator to sit on the jury of the Venice Biennale. The Hugo Boss Prize also included significant numbers of Asian contemporary artists and was awarded to the artist of Thai origin, Rirkrit Tiravanija in 2004.[90]

## Curatorial Functions

If the number of biennials increased from around 14 in 1989–90 to around 35 in 1991–2001,[91] then, we may suppose, the number of curators operating in the system of biennials will have increased at the same time. There is no firm way of saying by how much. I am not sure this situation can be understood in market terms of under- or over-supply. It is more likely to have made the curators compete via the quality and nature of their proposals, or by the adherence or antipathy of their curatorial practice to the positions of others currently in the field. In short, some kind of competitive hierarchy was almost certain to have developed by the early 2000s although it was by no means clear from curatorial statements what was the character, extent, and means of application of curatorial competition. Certainly some curators admitted to their positions being competitive and ideological. Esche thought the idea of curators being the facilitators of artists should be put away and that there were "competitive and creative and even ideological positions which curators and artists have".[92] Esche thought there could be a productively agonistic relation between curator and artist, and not one which simply facilitated the other's vision. For him there was a similarly agonistic relation for biennials with capital, a relationship which "has to be something which is not affirmative and is not trying to get through the interstices of capitalism".[93]

The strategy of claiming that a biennial was a kind of experimental laboratory which was continuous between various consecutively defined sites, could have been a strategy of resistance to the very globalism biennials instantiated. It was also a way of distinguishing one set of curatorial positions from another, that is this "radical" notion of biennials competed for attention by its very difference. The strongest conflation of these issues was made by Hans Ulrich Obrist in Guangzhou, China, in 2006:

> What are the temporal and spatial strategies we can propose in order to resist an increasingly homogenized reality? In terms of the unique locality of the Pearl River Delta (PRD), the discrepancies between a sustainable culture and its temporal lapse could contribute a different understanding of the overall process of globalization. Under such conditions, we will invite international and Chinese artists to generate projects that are diverse and alternative in nature but also strong with regional interest as tools for confronting and negotiating globalization. Through this process, we can hopefully trigger another exhibition model.[94]

However, some Asian curators like Kim Hong-hee, at Gwangju, Korea in 2006, questioned the idea of an exhibition as a kind of experimental laboratory, one which reproduced the processes of the outside word as a kind of representation. For art practice itself was a form of representation. Kim foreshadowed a return to the artwork, and which saw "artworks themselves producing new forms of relationality that Biennials can stage". Laboratories that proposed to represent what they already had represented were sealed, hermetic ones.

The proposition of the curator floated between the curator's intentions and the instrumentality of the biennial for the purposes of its organizing structure. Did the curator propose and the biennale organizational structure dispose? It was the biennial in the person of its guiding artistic director and curatorial team who validated the local instrumentality by its prestige success in bringing artists and a kind of international esteem to the local site. Biennials legitimated the local to the outside in "a way which few local cultures anywhere" were capable of.[95] But there was a functional reciprocation between the local and now validated community, and the curator as the figure who inserted the international esteem into the local.

> International and transnational communities are not only pressured into focusing attention on the local but they are also given evidence of their own authority by recognizing the power of their legitimizing authority in the local's eyes. In this astonishingly complex and frequently collusive game that demands as much self-consciousness as possible, the local, the regional, and the international can legitimate one another.[96]

The complicating factor in this exchange of legitimacy was the proposition of the biennial exhibition itself. Those which presented both the clarity and diversity of such propositions were likely to be the most interesting.[97] In the sense that curators were marked by the biennials they curated, the proposition became the creative package which the curator presented to the biennial organizations whose various and sometimes conflicting instrumentalities this package must have satisfied. But if these propositions were generated by single curators or a hermetic group of them, a hierarchy through the deployment of curators with a "star" system was likely to develop.

This issue was forced into the open when the architect serving as artistic director Isozaki sought at Yokohama in 2004 to break away from the predictable circulation of curatorial figures with their chosen artists. He was going to choose six "icons", for each of which a conceptualizer would be found who was neither a curator nor an artist, such as Paul Virilio or Asada Akira. These would have been paired with an exhibition designer who might be an architect. The biennial would be organized as an event and production would have been by TV channels. This design, engineered by someone like Isozaki who was himself a "star", although not from the biennial circuit, was aimed at one of its serious organizational issues, but could not be brought off. The failure was ostensibly for budget reasons, but the autonomous organizations who were supposed to select artists under these various concepts could not do so within the time scale or the budgets intended.[98]

The proposition of the curator-selectors could oppose the celebritization of artists at the cost of selecting from an even narrower group of artists with whom curators were in close sympathy and usually ideological agreement. The biennial could thereby claim the mantle of an anti-hegemonic intent. Many curators, as Brenson noted,[99] adopted the rhetoric of the hero and professed faith in the ability of the biennial to insert alternatives, resist, or serve as a transformative agent in social processes beyond the exhibition itself.

But the issues of the institutionalization of the biennial site, the regularity, i.e. the recursivity of its supposedly intermittent space, and the hierarchicization of its supposedly "free" curators remained. Biennials were seen by many curators as a space of resistance not merely to global hegemony, but to the museums which were institutionally imbricated within it. Some thinkers such as Osborne considered that the topological space of the art museum itself, including the Museum of Contemporary art, meant that

> it is now *only outside* these spaces (allegedly dedicated to it) that contemporary art can "live" critically in its own terms...paradoxically art can only "live" there, outside the gallery, by recreating the ontological character of gallery space (art-space) in various ways, transfiguring the social character of the space it occupies.[100]

Biennial curators could legitimize the local, and broker one culturalized identity to another through the mediating figure—salesman/shaman—of the curator.[101] They could construct their own alternative networks to other layers of the biennial circuit already in the hands of globalizing forces or old state hegemonies.[102] But they could not break their own in-built institutionalization. This was produced by the biennial itself becoming an institution with recurrent regularities—the same office, the same office staff, and mostly the use of the same sites. Or, it was found in whether the biennial could be turned into an extended embodiment of the dream of a migratory museum, the regularities of its practice and the accessibility of its codes being prerequisites for artistic understanding, let alone for participation in the receivers' construction of the artwork.[103] With the figure of the curator now seen as the necessary mediator between art markets and biennials, I will turn in chapter 7 to look at some features of biennials as institutions in themselves.

## Notes

1 They were chiefly indicated by the career trajectory of Harald Szeemann from the Bern Kunsthalle exhibition *When Attitudes become Forms: Works, Concepts, Processes, Situations, Information* of 1969, to his incarnations as artistic director of *documenta 5* in 1972, and the artistic director of both Venice Biennale number 48 *dAPERTutto* in 1999, and number 49 *Platea dell'umanità* in 2001. This trajectory may be followed in Hans Joachim Müller, *Harald Szeemann: Exhibition-Maker*, trans. Leila Kais (Ostfildern-Ruit: Hatje Cantz Verlag, 2006). Poinsot notes the various contributions of Szeemann to the establishment of the curator-artist-audience relation such that, "The work of art as object was gradually erased by the increasing use of the convention of the exhibition as a form of aesthetic experience". See Jean-Marc Poinsot, "Large Exhibitions: a Sketch of a Typology", in *Thinking about Exhibitions*, ed. R. Greenberg, Bruce W. Ferguson, and Sandy Nairne (London: Routledge, 1996), 47.

2 The only major, systematic study by mid-2007 was Charlotte Bydler, *The Global Art World Inc.: on the Globalization of Contemporary Art* (Upsala: Acta Universitatis Upsaliensis, 2004). Some curators have from time to time made useful polemical statements with implications for future systemic understanding such as Okwui Enwezor, "Mega Exhibitions and the Antinomies of a Transnational Global Form", *Manifesta Journal* 2 (Winter 2003/Spring 2004), as well as his "The Politics of Spectacle", in *Annual Report: the 7th Gwangju Biennale* (Gwangju: Gwangju Biennale Foundation, 2008); Carlos Basualdo, "The Unstable Institution" in *What Makes a Great Exhibition?*, ed. Paula Marincola (Philadelphia: Philadelphia Exhibitions Initiative, 2006), originally published in *Manifesta Journal* 2 (Winter 2003/Spring 2004).

3 See René Block and Martin Glaser et al., *Das Lied von der Erde / The Song of the Earth* (Kassel: Museum Fridericianum, 2000) [a survey with texts on these Biennials: Havana, Istanbul, Johannesburg, Kwangju/Gwangju, Lyon, Pittsburgh, São Paulo, and Sydney]; Michael Glasmeier & Karin Stengel, ed., *50 Jahre / Years documenta, Archive in Motion* (Göttingen: Steidi Verlag, 2005) [bilingual retrospective catalogue & texts]; Henry Meyric-Hughes, "The History and Significance of the Biennale, as an Instrument of Globalization", 2005 [draft copy courtesy of the author], published in *Art Criticism and Globalisation* (São Paolo: Assoçiao Brasiliera de Criticos de Arte, 2006); Barbara Vanderlinden and Elena Filipovic, *The Manifesta Decade: Debates on Contemporary Art Exhibitions and Biennials in Post-wall Europe* (Cambridge, MA: MIT Press, 2005); "Biennials", Special Issue, *Manifesta Journal* 2 (Winter 2003/ Spring 2004).

4 Pierre Bourdieu, introduction to *The Field of Cultural Production*, ed. and trans. Randal Johnson (Cambridge: Polity Press, 1993, 2000), 7.

5 Bourdieu, *The Field of Cultural Production*, 75.

6 Bourdieu, *The Field of Cultural Production*, 53. Bourdieu's notion of field and habitus (equivalent to hexis) is intended to reintroduce "a relationship of ontological complicity with the world" (14), and that understanding the "social genesis of a field" is to "wrest the producers' actions and the works they produce from the absurdity of arbitrariness and of motivelessness, rather than, as one ordinarily believes, to reduce or to destroy" (20). See Pierre Bourdieu, "The Genesis of the Concepts of Habitus and of Field", trans. Channa Newman, *Sociocriticism* 2 (December 1985).

7 Bourdieu, *The Field of Cultural Production*, 79–80.

8 Bourdieu, *The Field of Cultural Production*, 80–1.

9 Jean Baudrillard, *For a Critique of the Political Economy of the Sign* [texts of 1968–72], trans. Charles Levin (New York: Telos Press, 1981), 82, 87.

10 Baudrillard, *For a Critique of the Political Economy of the Sign*, 113.

11 Jean Baudrillard, "The Conspiracy of Art" (1996) in *The Conspiracy of Art*, trans. Anne Hodges (New York: Semiotext(e), 2005), 27.

12 Baudrillard, "The Conspiracy of Art", 90

13 Baudrillard, "The Conspiracy of Art", 92.

14 The aesthetic:

> figures as a genuinely emancipatory force – as a community of subjects now linked by sensuous impulse and fellow-feeling rather than by heteronomous law, each safeguarded in its unique particularity while bound at the same time into social harmony… On the other hand, the aesthetic signifies what Max Horkheimer has called a kind of internalized repression, inserting social power more deeply into the very bodies it subjugates, and so operating as a supremely effective mode of political hegemony.

See Terry Eagleton, *The Ideology of the Aesthetic* (Oxford: Blackwell, 1990, 2000), 28.

15 Some well-founded scholarship concludes that art is, or becomes, money. See Marc Shell, *Art & Money* (Chicago: University of Chicago Press, 1995), 134:

> In defining the relation between art and money in terms of the epigrammatic interaction between the spiritual intellectus and the material res, I have shown how it comes to seems that money becomes, or is, art and that art is, or becomes money; and I have also suggested how, in the theological terms that masquerade as "secular," the iconology of money and the economic of visual art converge.

16 In a short conversation at the Sydney Biennale in 2006. Mr Groys appeared to consider my questioning about the relationship between art markets and Biennials naïve.

17 Hans Abbing, *Why are Artists Poor? The Exceptional Economy of the Arts* (Amsterdam: Amsterdam University Press, 2002, 2004), 56, 62, is more suggestive, seeing the

> "proposition that market value does not reflect quality" as being supported by three interpretations: 1 That aesthetic value and economic value belong to independent spheres; 2 aesthetic value and economic value belong to non-reciprocal spheres, aesthetic value being independent of economic

> value, but economic value being dependent on aesthetic value; 3 aesthetic value and economic value belong to hostile spheres where market value reduces aesthetic value. These we may call the independent, non-reciprocal, and hostile interpretations. It also becomes clear that there is a type of categorical disjunction between artists and markets where producers are 'relatively unimportant when it comes to directly influencing the market value of art-products, and if they do only usually through experts as co-producers. (62)

18 See David Throsby, *Economics and Culture* (Cambridge: Cambridge University Press, 2001), 20–3, 32. See also the review by Paul Dimaggio Paul in *Journal of Cultural Economics* 27 (2003). Throsby further examines the determination of cultural value in David Throsby, "Determining the value of cultural goods: how much (or how little) does contingent value tell us?", *Journal of Cultural Economics* 27 (2003), concluding that:

> economic value—which is not synonymous with financial or commercial value, although it is ultimately expressible in terms of either a numéraire good or (preferably) money—comprises any direct use values of the cultural good or service in question, plus whatever non-market values it my give rise to (which may perhaps be amenable to CVM {Contingent valuation methods}). Cultural value on the other hand is multi-dimensional, unstable, contested, lacks a common unit of account, and may contain elements that cannot be easily expressed according to any quantitative or qualitative scale. (280)

Subsequent to my drafting this chapter in 2004, the following reference work with many relevant papers has appeared: Victor A. Ginsburgh and David Throsby, ed., *Handbook of the Economics of Art and Culture* (Amsterdam & Boston: Elsevier North-Holland, 2006).

19 Throsby, *Economics and Culture*, 95

20 Throsby, *Economics and Culture*, 96.

21 Throsby, *Economics and Culture*, 100–2.

22 Throsby, *Economics and Culture*, 103.

23 Throsby, *Economics and Culture*, 103.

24 This is incidentally why modern art historians and contemporary art curators may find themselves in conflict because the former know and can demonstrate how much has been left out in the process of canonizing by selection—this often points to a different notion of art—and the latter are situationally and institutionally privileged to make canonizations by limiting selection and restricting their notion of art thought to be "contemporary". It is often curators' own personal quotidian interests and the short-term need to produce exhibitions which requires them to do so, whereas art historians may be in a different career and remuneration path which is subject to different qualitative performance and longer-term temporal constraints.

25 See the analysis of the inclusions elsewhere presented here in the reviews of Chapter 5 for the Taipei Biennial in 2006.

26 See the review by Paul Dimaggio in *Journal of Cultural Economics* 27 (2003): 75.

27 Abbing, *Why are Artists Poor?*, 273.

28 David Throsby, "An Artistic Production Function: Theory and an Application to Australian Visual Artists", *Journal of Cultural Economics* 30 (2006): 11.

29 David W. Galenson, *Artistic Capital* (New York & London: Routledge, 2006), the main elements of his methods being given on pages 3–23 and 95–104.

30 Victor Ginsburg and Sheila Weyers, "Creativity and the Life Cycles of Artists", *Journal of Cultural Economics* 30 (2006): 93.

31 But values are unstable and subject to shock: "even in its own domain, value cannot prevent the possibility that in many cases it is designed to forestall: unpredictable and destabilizing changes in evaluation". D. Ruccio, J. Graham, and J. Amariglio, "'The Good, the Bad and the Different': Reflections on Economic and Aesthetic Value", in *The Value of Culture: On the Relationship between Economics and Arts*, ed. Ario Klamer (Amsterdam: Amsterdam University Press, 1997), 66.

32 See Marcel Mauss, *The Gift: Forms and Functions of Exchange in Archaic Societies* [1924] (London: Routledge, 1990).

33 Ruccio, Graham, and Amariglio, "'The Good, the Bad, the Different'", 60.

34 Some artists have pessimistically concluded that "the market" [undistinguished by levels as in this paper] has come to dominate production of art objects itself. See Ian Burn, "The Art Market: Affluence and Degradation", *Artforum* (April 1975), reprinted in Charles Harrison and Paul Wood, *Art in Theory, 1900–1990: an Anthology of Changing Ideas* (Oxford: Blackwell, 1992):

> What we have seen more recently is the power of market values to distort all other values, even the concept of what is and is not acceptable as "work" is defined first and fundamentally by the market and only secondly by "creative urges" (etc.). This has been the price of internalizing an intensely capitalistic mode of production. (908)

35 Olav Velthuis, *Talking Prices: Symbolic Meanings of Prices on the Market for Contemporary Art* (Princeton: Princeton University Press, 2005), 24, considers that,

> the art market is a site where human action is informed by two contradictory logics: a logic of art, and a logic of capitalist markets. The logic of the first is understood to be a qualitative logic; it centers around the uncompromising creation of symbolic, imaginative, or meaningful goods, whose value cannot be measured, let alone in the monetary metric of the market. The logic of capitalist markets, by contrast, would be a quantitative logic that centers around commodification and commensuration of human activity.

36 Leslie Singer, "Microeconomics of the Art Market", *Journal of Cultural Economics* II, 2 (1978): 21.

37 Singer, "Microeconomics of the Art Market", 25.

38 Singer, "Microeconomics of the Art Market", 22.

39 Richard E. Caves, *Creative Industries: Contracts between Art and Commerce* (Cambridge: Harvard University Press, 2000), 194, comments on the search for interpretability as a criterion of a work's marketability:

> When innovations occur, however, the market for interpretation opens up, and critics get their shot Noticeable in the twentieth century is the positive correlation between critical enthusiasm for a new school or movement and the room that it offers for interpretation.

40 It has also been pointed out by curators to me that the reason why certain works are selected for biennials, whatever their artistic merits, is that funding can be more easily found for them from a patron, a dealer, or a foundation than for works unconnected to these sorts of support, however well they fit the curatorial concept.

41 Moulin and Quemin distinguish "la critique d'information" from "la critique de célébration". The latter is most often expressed in the register of art theory. See Raymonde Moulin and Alain Quemin, "La certification de la valeur de l'art, Experts et expertises", *Annales* 48, 6 (November/December 1993): 1435.

42 Roger A. McCain, "Markets for Works of Art and Markets for Lemons", in William S. Hendon, James L. Shanahan, and Alice J. McDonald, *Economic Policy for the Arts* (Cambridge, MA: Abt Books, 1980), 123.

43 McCain, "Markets for Works of Art", 125.

44 See McCain, "Markets for Works of Art", 132–3.

45 Mel Ramsden, in *The Fox* (April 1975), reprinted in *Art in Theory, 1900–1990: an Anthology of Changing Ideas* (1992), notes that "the administrators, dealers, critics, pundits etc. who once seemed the neutral servants of art are now, especially in New York, becoming its master" and also observes "the astonishing increase in art-world assessors: entrepreneurs, critics, curators, gallery staff, etc. In other words, bureaucrats" (906).

I prefer the term "mediators" since these actors appear because of their mediating function, not because of their employment in an official, salaried, organizational sanctioned hierarchy of roles.

46 This sanction is elsewhere described in a neo-classical methodology as a mapping function or 'a consumer technology capable of translating "characteristics" into the more traditional "demand function". See Leslie Singer, "Rivalry and externalities in secondary art markets", *Journal of Cultural Economics* V, 2 (June 1981): 39. These evaluations can also be re-evaluations, that is the re-insertion of an art historically neglected artist or moment into a market of art objects now. But in the market for contemporary art there is a subtle confluence which amounts to a complicity of views between art dealers and the curator.

> L'effort publicitaire du marchand et l'activité du conservateur agissant en tant qu'historien de l'art et expert institutionnel se conjuguent pour produire les signaux qui font monter les prix. L'efficacité du signal est d'autant plus grande que le conservateur, commissaire de l'exposition, occupe une position du leader. (Moulin and Quemin, "La certification", 1444)

See also Alain Quemin, *L'art contemporain international: entre les institutions et le marché (Le rapport disparu)* (Nîmes: Éditions Jacqueline Chambon/Artprice, 2002), 123:

> Les valeurs s'instaurent selon un double mode: le marché révèle les préférences du moment et vient ratifier les palmarès en vigueur; pour sa part, le monde institutionnel de l'art – essentiellement composé des musées et autres lieux d'exposition tels que les centres d'art (c'est-à-dire les espaces dépourvus de collections permanents) et les Biennials – élabore des classements qui vont distinguer les artistes dignes d'attention. En fait, les deux systèmes précédents apparaissent étroitement dépendent l'un de l'autre, la valorisation financière et la certification de la valeur esthétique prenant appui l'une sur l'autre.

47 Singer, "Rivalry and externalities in secondary art markets", 42.

48 Singer, "Rivalry and externalities", 55.

49 Raymonde Moulin, *L'artiste, l'institution et le marché* (Paris: Flammarion, 1997), 64, notes that,

> Au cours des trente dernières années [i.e. since the 1960s], les musées d'art contemporain ont été saisis par la fièvre de l'immédiateté. Sur le front avancé de l'art, les conservateurs sont présents, de concert avec les artistes, les critiques et els marchands.

50 "Les grand collectionneurs sont capables d'assumer les rôles de tous autres acteurs du monde et du marché de l'art, à l'exception de celui de l'artiste"(Moulin, *L'artiste, l'institution et le marché*, 56).

51 Leslie Singer, "Phenomenology and economics of art markets: an art historical perspective", *Journal of Cultural Economics* XII, 1 (June 1988): 38, concluded that,

> Traditional oligopolistic dealer markets (where the secondary market protects the primary market against infringement by substitute products) appears to have been more conducive to at historical continuity. They also tended to produce a more representative menu of contemporary art for public viewing and buying.

This older structure was broken by the intervention of collector-tycoons like Saatchi in the United Kingdom, and by the compulsion of curators to enter art markets when the price had already been revised upward, the entry of curators itself raising prices. (Singer, "Phenomenology and economics of art markets", 37–8)

52 Olav Velthuis, *Imaginary Economics: Contemporary Artists and the World of Big Money* (Rotterdam: NAi Publishers, 2005), 26, notes that a "relevant development is the 'economization' of the arts: especially during the 1980s, the arts were increasingly transformed into a sector of the economy. This meant that artworks came to be seen as investment products, art buyers as speculators and artists as superstars whose reputation is reflected in the price of their work".

53 Velthuis, *Imaginary Economics*, 100–1, citing from the art magazine *Metropolis M2* "nieuwe economie van de kunst" (special issue) from April–May 2000. Ownership of and the ability to pay huge prices for art objects seems to be an economic-cultural domain where the ability to buy experience, and the older economy of owning goods which denoted one's experiences, intersects. Jeremy Rifkin, *The Age of Access: The New Culture of Hypercapitalism where all of Life is a Paid-For Experience* (New York: Tarcher/Putnam, 2000), 134, consider that in the networked economy "securing access to one's own lived experiences becomes as important as being propertied was in an era dominated by the production of industrial goods".

54 See Malcom Goldstein, *Landscape with Figures: a History of Art Dealing in the United States* (Oxford: Oxford University Press, 2000), 289–90; Alice Goldfarb Marquis, *The Art Biz : the Covert World of Collectors, Dealers, Auction Houses, Museums, and Critics* (Chicago: Contemporary Books, 1991), 228; Laura De Coppet and Alan Jones, *The Art Dealers: the Powers behind the Scene Talk About the Business of Art* (New York: Clarkson N. Potter, 1984), 91.

55 Counter-valuational or unstable elements in a given system mark transitions to a new one as suggested clearly with regard to the role of the avant garde within the late 19th century dealer system: "what appears to be non-structured is really only a new and unfamiliar social framework", Harrison C. White and Cynthia A. White, *Canvases*

*and Careers: Institutional Change in the French Painting World* (New York: John Wiley & Sons, 1965), 95. There is clearly something highly unstable or transitional in the present system which outdoes both the operational capabilities of players to control and their intellectual abilities to comprehend it. See the group discussion in "Money on the Wall", *Vanity Fair* (December 2006): 196–9, 202. This has what I shall call a high-school project lay-out, "The Art Universe", on ibid., pages 230–1, which conceives of the art world as an outer and inner solar system with Larry Gagosian as the "Center of the Universe". The inclusions and exclusions are a mini-mapping of how the largely Euramerican art world sees itself and significantly include only one "Asian" curator, Eugene Tsai [out of 22], and one non-Euramerican "Place to Visit" the Istanbul Biennale. The only non-Euramerican and overseas commercial galleries worth visiting were "Tomio Koyama, Koyanagi, Hiromi Yoshii" in Tokyo. Obviously astronomical observation is not the same science as nuclear physics. Of the 67 artists who make it to the "inner solar system" only 4, or about 6%, are identifiably "Asian".

56 White and White, *Canvases and Careers*, 76.

57 The Castelli network expanded from the early 1960s and in the end included more than 50 other galleries taking works and sharing profits. These included Gallery Akira Ikeda in Tokyo & Nagoya, of which Castelli is reported in 1990 as saying to a journalist, "Everything I sell to Ikeda, he sells. Nothing ever comes back", see Goldstein, *Landscape with Figures*, 294.

58 I saw these works on sale there in 2003.

59 My interviews with Lee U-fan, at Kamakura, 1 June 1991 and with Yamagishi Nobuo in Tokyo, 1987.

60 Interview with Lee Bul in Seoul, 16 September 2004.

61 See their formulation in Linde Rohr-Bongard, ed., with contributions by Margaret Baumann, Linde Rohr-Bongard and Wieland Schmied, *Kunst=Kapital: der Capital Kunstkompass von 1970 bis heute* (Köln: Salon, 2001).

62 See John Clark, "An Australian Creative Space: where is Australian-Asian art now?", *2006/Contemporary Commonwealth/*, ed. Dianne Waite and curated by Charles Green and Mike Stubbs (Melbourne: Australian Centre for the Moving Image and National Gallery of Victoria, 2006), 26–33.

63 Robert Jensen, *Marketing Modernism in Fin-de-Siècle Europe* (Princeton: Princeton University Press, 1994), 50.

64 Jensen, *Marketing Modernism*, 6.

65 See Baudrillard, op. cit.

66 For example of the collector Carl Hamilton by Joseph Duveen, see Meryle Secrest, *Duveen: A Life in Art* (Chicago: University of Chicago Press, 2004), 182–3.

67 Goldstein, *Landscape with Figures*, 160.

68 See Secrest, *Duveen*, 116, 226–43; Goldstein, *Landscape with Figures*, 157–8. In fact the association with Duveen began in 1909 three years earlier than the 1912 contract.

69 If the lateness of the access to the Duveen archives granted to Secrest is anything to go by, it is unlikely that any such information about contemporary art curators will be public within the lifetime of contemporary art historians. We simply have rumour to go on, though reliable rumour in many cases.

70 De Coppet and Jones, *The Art Dealers*, 41.

71 De Coppet and Jones, *The Art Dealers*, 57.

72 De Coppet and Jones, *The Art Dealers*, 80–109.

73 "Les grand collectionneurs sont capables d'assumer les rôles de tous autres acteurs du monde et du marché de l'art, à l'exception de celui de l'artiste" (Moulin, *L'artiste, l'institution et le marché*, 56).

74 The work of Yan Peiming in *Zones of Urgency* at Venice in 2005 was poorly displayed in a partially occluded space against a back wall and Zhang Peili's video installation was still in its boxes at the time the artist had to return home so he could not supervise its installation.

75 The list of "The Top Ten" given in *The Telegraph* report filed on 12 February 2002 gives the following names [I have deleted marginal notes]: 1. Charles Saatchi, 2. François Pinault, 3. Ronald Lauder, 4. Gerhard Richter, 5. Lucy Mitchell-Innes/ David Nash, 6. Sir Nicolas Serota, 7. Francesco Bonami, 8. Helly Nahmad, 9. Alfred Taubman, 10. Patricia Barbizet.

76 Lakshmi Mittal paid £57 million for a home in 2004, see Jonathan Meek, "Super Rich", *The Guardian* (17 April 2006), when in the same year Picasso's *Boy with a Pipe* was auctioned for $104 million by Sotheby's, New York, see *Vanity Fair* (December 2006): 196.

77 Such as the report, by Harry Bellet and Marc Roche, "Les milliardaires font de Londres le grand magasin de l'art actuel" in *Le Monde* of 15 October 2006, writing of the *Frieze Art Fair* in London.

78 According to an off-the-record conversation with a gallery curator in New York, in April 2006. There is a local case in the under-reported purchase interventions by the "Mycenas Group" in contemporary artwork in Sydney during the late 1990s when the art market appeared to contract. Sometimes the market itself functions as a kind of cartel because "it is common for several dealers to be watching an artist's work as it crystallizes, raising the question of who ultimately commits first." See Richard E. Caves, *Creative Industries: Contracts between Art and Commerce* (Cambridge, MA: Harvard University Press, 2000), 28–9.

79 Such as movement of René Block from a peripatetic curator to Director of the Fredericianium in Kassel, or Okwui Enwezor from the Documenta and Visiting Professor at University of Pittsburg to the Dean of Academic Affairs and Vice-President, San Francisco Art Institute, or of Hou Hanru from a freelance curator active internationally to Graduate Faculty of the same institution.

80 For this reason their behaviour resembles that of car salesmen or Hollywood actor's agents trying to diffenrentiate cars or actors whose functional performance is not all that different, save charismatically.

81 Bourdieu, *The Field of Cultural Production*, 117. Baudrillard thinks that it is the circulation of signs itself which produces a sort of surplus value and which does not create profit but legitimacy. See Baudrillard, *For a Critique of the Political Economy of the Sign*, 121.

82 The reverse position is of artists powerful enough to significantly influence if not directly control their own mediation. This becomes perfectly clear from the claims made by some artists that they seek to be both avant garde and acceptable to conventional art markets and curatorial consecrations. See the chapter "Art Stars" in John Walker, *Art and Celebrity* (London: Pluto Press, 2003).

83 Pierre Bourdieu, The Field of Cultural Production, (ed. and trans. Randal Johnson), Cambridge: Polity Press, 1993, 2000, 123.

84 Abbing, *Why Are Artists Poor?*, 271.

85 Abbing, *Why Are Artists Poor?*, 272.

86 Baudrillard, *For a Critique of the Political Economy of the Sign*, 121, where on the same page he also notes that "Museums act as a double guarantee of aristocratic exchange by returning works from a private parallel market to a sort of collective ownership".

87 See Wu Chin-tao, *Privatising Culture: Corporate Art Intervention Since the 1980s* (London: Verso, 2002), 283–92, or in 2007 the "return" of the Ullens collection from Paris to a contemporary art museum at the 798 complex in Dashanzi, Beijing.

88 See my critique, John Clark, "What Modern and Contemporary Asian Art Is (or Is Not): the View from MOMA and the View from Asia", in *Eye of the Beholder*, ed. John Clark, Maurizio Pelleggi, T.K. Sabapathy (Sydney: Wild Peony, 2006), 297–319.

89 Wu, *Privatising Culture*, 173.

90 Other Asian artists who though unawarded made the short-list were Cai Guoqiang and Morimura Yasumasa 1996, Huang Yongping and Lee Bul 1998, Hachiya Kazuhiko and Koo Jeong-a 2002, and Yang Fudong 2004. See Wu, *Privatising Culture*, 173.

91 See Joe Hill, "Festival Mania – Dramatic Growth of a Cultural Typology", *The Platform* 2 (October 2001): 6.

92 Charles Esche in the Gwangju Biennale 2006, transcript of discussion, 5, who has kindly supplied the transcript.

93 Esche in the Gwangju Biennale 2006, transcript of discussion, 5.

94 *D-Lab/The Second Guangzhou Triennial BEYOND: an Extraordinary Space of Experimentation for Modernization*, curated by Hou Hanru, Hans Ulrich, and Guo Xiaoyan (Guangzhou: Lingnan Chubanshe, 2006), 62.

95 See Michael Brenson, "The Curator's Moment – Trends in the Field of Contemporary Art Exhibitions", *Art Journal* (Winter 1998). This article is a report on an August 1997 Rockefeller Foundation Conference at Bellagio at which 15 curators were present. The conference was organized by Noreen Tomassi and Tomas Ybarra-Frausto, and those present included Brenson, Margaret Archuleta, René Block, Germano Celant, Kinshasha Holman Conwill, Vishaka N. Desai, N. Fulya Erdemci, Lillian Lanes Godoy, Madeleine Grynsztejn, Paualo Herkenhoff, Virginia Perez-Ratton, Apinan Poshyananda, Mari Carmen Ramirez, Remi Sagna, and Caroline Turner.

96 Brenson, "The Curator's Moment".

97 See Charles Esche, presentation at the Symposium for the Gwangju Biennale 2006, 12, for the transcript of which I am grateful to Charles Esche.

98 See Tama Bijutsudaigaku Geijutsugakuka Tatehatazemi Shimpojiumu kikaku, Isozaki Akira, Okabe Aomi, Kitagawa Furamu, Nanjô Fumio, Hasegawa Yûko, *Yokohama Kaigi 2004: Naze Kokusaiten ka?* (Yokohama: BankART1929, 2005), 65–72, and 111–13.

99 Brenson, "The Curator's Moment".

100 Peter Osborne, from the text of his address at the Biennale of Sydney Symposium, 2006.

101 See Mari Carmen Ramírez, "Constellations: Toward a Radical Questioning of Dominant Curatorial Models", *Art Journal* (Spring 2000), and also her "Brokering

Identities" (1994), reprinted in *Thinking about Exhibitions,* ed. Greenberg, Ferguson, and Nairne.

102 See Thomas McEvilley, "Arrivederci Venice, the 'Third World' Biennials", *Artforum International* 32, 3, (November 1993).

103 Outlined by Hans-Ulrich Obrist in his palimpsest of quotations "Museum on the Move", a catalogue text for the Johannesburg Biennale 1997.

# Chapter 7

# Biennials, Institutions, and Circulation

Looking from the side of biennials which accept their institutional existence we may ask what museum functions did biennials perform, among their other roles? Biennials may be seen as the continuation of art spectacles and also as an event-industry which began with international expositions in the 19th century, but which had profound differences from the world exposition model and origins.[1] Some curators like Okwui Enwezor thought that the global ideal evidenced in "Biennial Fever" was based

> on a reconceptualization of a nineteenth-century model for displaying cultural heterogeneity [and that there has been] an expansion and extension of the world exhibition model through its proliferation...[now] re-adapted in the form of the mega-exhibition, of which biennials are a prime example.[2]

But Enwezor also made the caveat that not all biennials "function according to the logic of spectacles" and many are low-budget with works of modest scale.[3] This may have been true for biennials such as Havana, but having seen many Asian biennials between 1993 and 2007, I can say that exactly the opposite applied in most cases. They had large budgets and many big, even grandiose works, interspersed only sometimes with the modest and intimate pieces to which Enwezor referred.

These differences arose not merely because the art of the exhibition compensated for the loss of the art object independent of its exhibition and of stylistic change. The myth of stylistic change was

> relying on its artistic and symbolic realities to make the cult of contemporary art into an activity of substitution, [it has become] a means of conjuring the crisis, and resolving on a symbolic level, what cannot be resolved on the political and economic level.[4]

In short, there was a crisis in the world which art attempted to relieve by appealing to a mythological status, as opposed to an independent aesthetic status, for each art object. The crisis sought refuge in appeal to the means (aesthetic categories) or context (exhibition practice) for appreciating the art object. According to Poinsot, since the early 1980s there were three alternative relationships between the exhibition and non-aesthetic systems of value:

1. mythological beliefs were embodied in artworks which had become an object of knowledge;
2. a process was enacted of active mythification which ran the risk of occulting the work's meaning as an artwork;
3. there existed [since the mid-1980s] a mechanism of multiple readings governing aesthetic specificity.[5]

Such changed status for the way in which art objects functioned, or exhibitions that had come to function as constitutive of art objects, underlay the openness of the exhibition and its practices of display as a space of resistance to the non-aesthetic world found outside the exhibition.

The rhetoric of openness, generosity, or resistance was sincerely articulated by many curators and artists and fostered a genuine "biennial culture" which differentiated itself from the normal functioning of art institutions and the art market. Meyric Hughes noted,

> the biennale format has shown that it is capable of deploying a support system for artists, a platform for debate, training opportunities for young people and new audiences which no longer depend on the traditional validation system of critic, gallerist or collector. After all, it has demonstrated the capacity enormously to expand the language of art and its geographical and demographic parameters.[6]

However laudable the possibilities of biennials were as exhibition formats, or how admired for the types of art they allowed, they remained a *system* which needed to be understood. The curator Esche thought the categorization of biennials would be a "tragedy" seen from the perspective that such classifications would narrow in effect and as intellectual structures the possibilities of open curatorial practice.[7]

This position may very well be true for a curator. But for those seeking to understand biennials as a system, some form of descriptive classification is necessary as a basic requirement of further understanding. There are at least four of these schema already available which it would form a separate exercise to analyze in detail, and that is not my purpose. But I should list these as attempts to form typologies of biennials in general before moving on to specifically examine Asian biennials. The first Typology A has been assembled by Bydler, one which I have slightly added to as follows:

| TYPOLOGY A: BIENNIALS DIFFERENTIATED BY HISTORICAL POSITION AND CURATORIAL INTENTION (BYDLER 2004, REVISED BY CLARK, 2005) | |
|---|---|
| 1. | Regional development for a backward region by focusing international attention through other-national representation: Venice Biennale (1895). |
| 2. | Capitalist philanthropy: Carnegie International at Pittsburgh (1896). |
| 3. | Assertion of a power position within a local or regionalized: Whitney Biennial (1932), Melbourne (1999), Echigo-Tsumari (2000), Chengdu (2001), Auckland (2001), and many smaller-scale biennials. |
| 4. | Reaction to previous pasts, strengthening of ties between the European and US art worlds: *Documenta* (1957) vs *Entartete Kunst*, (1937). |
| 5. | Insertion of a regional or peripheral art world into international mainstream sometimes by selection only: São Paolo (1951), Sydney (1973), sometimes by selection and purchase, Brisbane (1993), Fukuoka (1989/1999). |
| 6. | Biennials of the Third World as a channel overcoming the Cold War bifurcation of the First and the Second Worlds, demonstrating cultural status of organizers: Ljubljana (1955), India Triennale at New Delhi (1968). |
| 7. | Later Third World biennials, aimed to promote art from more marginalized Third World nations and at challenging US and European art centres: Havana (1984) Dakar (1994) Johannesburg (1995). |
| 8. | Re-self-definition of a state from an impoverished or Third World to burgeoning rich nation, also involving re-assertion of region or city within national art scene: Gwangju (1995), Guangzhou (2002), Shanghai (1996). |
| 9. | *Retardaire,* late re-assertion of status lost from competition by other art worlds: Yokohama (2001), Beijing (2003), Moscow (2005). |
| 10. | Vehicle for competition between peers in avant garde art world. Selection of up-and-coming curators rather than mega-stars, from different geographical regions with ambition to connect different art world environments: *Aperto* and subsequent curated events in the Arsenale at Venice (1980), Istanbul (1989). |
| 11. | Vehicle for discovery of new non-biennalized talent of a different age cohort than the previously successful, sometimes with pedagogic intent: Manifesta (1996).[8] |

A second Typology B was earlier assembled by the curator René Block from four models which he thought typified biennale practice. It may represent a usable condensation of the variety found in the 11 types of Typology A above. However, when we come shortly to look at Asia the variety of types in Typology A has more descriptive value than Block's condensation.

| TYPOLOGY B. BIENNIALS DIFFERENTIATED BY ORGANIZATIONAL AND SELECTION STRUCTURE (BLOCK, 2000) | |
|---|---|
| 1. | Venice model: grand world exposition with national representation. |
| 2. | Sydney model: smaller scale biennale organized around a curatorial theme, invited artists depend on external financial support. |
| 3. | Kwangju model: artists selected independently from represented countries. |
| 4. | Manifesta model: shifting location, shifting curatorial team, other aims: educational and raising younger or non-circuit artists.[9] |

Bydler next in Typology C categorized biennials more simply by the kind of socio-economic base for the societies which gave biennials exhibition functions specific to their eras.

| TYPOLOGY C. BIENNIALS AS EXHIBITION FUNCTIONS BASED IN POLITICAL AND ECONOMIC STRUCTURES (BYDLER, 2004) | |
|---|---|
| 1. | Exercises in capitalist philanthropy from the late 19th century, some with strong-headed patrons. |
| 2. | Events that originated in the post-World War II period, and were marked by bloc politics or reactions to them. |
| 3. | Exhibitions which arose in the flexible production and event-oriented society of the 1990s and 2000s.[10] |

Typology D was proposed by Okabe in terms of a mapping on vertical and horizontal dimensions.

| TYPOLOGY D. BIENNIALS AS THE INTERSECTION OF FORCES CONSTRUCTING AND DECONSTRUCTING CURATION (OKABE, 2001)[11] | | |
|---|---|---|
| **Vertical Axis** The establishment vs dissolution of the myth of curation | | |
| **the Glocal:** to select globally including local artists whilst focusing on art of regions with high social poten tial leaving matters to the prescient capability of a deified curator (Harald Szeemann type) | **Process:** on a base of collaborative work with objectives set by debate and research, to present documents as the developmental spatio-temporal form of joint work (Catherine David type) | **Network:** to constitute a curation network with open membership re-constituted with each region, and to move towards a network construction which is continuously being renewed (Hans Ulrich Obrist type) |

| **Horizontal Axis** Pan-curation to deconstruction of curation. | | |
|---|---|---|
| **Museology:** a methodology which promotes the reconsideration of the relationality between audience and exhibit, and the participation of the audience to renew museology itself (Gwangju Biennale type) | **Renovation:** as a project for the re-birth of a region, international artists reside locally and in producing work including permanent exhibitions, introduce a sightline from the exterior (Münster Sculpture Project, Echigo-Tsumari, Liverpool type) | **Anonymous:** in the organic contingency of developmental joint curation, to naturally manifest form and themes (Fukuoka Asian Art Triennale, Yokohama Triennale type) |

The relation of these biennials to the creation and circulation of contemporary art is not explained by the above typologies. These assume that under various curatorial organizational or institutional structures (Okabe's horizontal axis) and through quite variegated actual practices (Okabe's vertical axis) the selection of art took place which in some ways reflected, represented, or stood for social, economic, and other cultural forces beyond the biennial exhibition. These were usually beyond the sway of even the artists themselves (Typology C). This approach tended to leave out of consideration the way "biennial art" flowed in a circuit of its own, and greatly under-estimated the inter-functionality of biennials with Euramerican art markets.[12]

Despite the market hysteria about contemporary Chinese art in the early 2000s,[13] it was clear that many non-European artists were largely excluded from these markets, at least until around 2005. Of those that did get into both the market circuits and circuits of prestige appraisal by their receipt of prizes and awards, visiting artist fellowships and commissions, and artist-to-artist mutual esteem, none reached the mainstream of Euramerican art dominance. The phenomenon is visible from examination of art world maps, in elite journalism,[14] or more specialist art magazines.[15] Most of the artists from periphery countries, including Asian ones, who were exhibited at biennials require the intermediary of a foreign gallery.[16] Even those recognized by circuits of prestige appraisal have usually been educated in and/or resided in the US in particular,[17] with several European confrères and some con-soeurs in Amsterdam, Berlin, London or Paris.

Thus I consider Okabe's model should be enriched by a third axis, that of *types of market and esteem appraisal*. But this would be very complex to graphically articulate. The observer seeking a simple clarity should stay with Typology B of Block, or Typology C of Bydler.

## Biennials in Asia, Their Special Features

If we now turn towards an attempt to generate a typology of the Asian biennials, various kinds of data given in the online appendices to this chapter allowed, somewhat arbitrarily but revealingly in terms of Typology A above, a first grouping of these as follows:

3 Osaka, Melbourne, Echigo-Tsumari, Auckland, Chengdu, Kyoto, CPB Jakarta.
5 Sydney, Brisbane APT, Fukuoka AAT, Singapore.
6 Triennale India, Asian Art Biennale Bangladesh.
8 Tokyo, Taipei, Gwangju, Shanghai, Guangzhou.
9 Yokohama, Beijing.

These might be now re-shuffled to generate an even more indicative Typology E.

| TYPOLOGY E: ASIAN BIENNIALS | |
|---|---|
| A | Triennale India, Asian Art Biennale Bangladesh<br>**A biennial of the poor Third World, aspiring for international recognition and artistic equality.** |
| B | Osaka, Busan, Melbourne, Echigo-Tsumari, Chengdu, Kyoto, CPB Jakarta<br>**A biennial giving prominence to one city against another centre** [Tokyo, Gwangju (& Seoul), Sydney, Tokyo, Shanghai (& Beijing), Tokyo, Yogyakarta respectively] Noticeably Osaka, Melbourne, and Kyoto have closed, and CPB Jakarta may not survive. |
| C | Tokyo, Taipei, Gwangju, Shanghai, Guangzhou<br>**A biennial signifying accession of a city and/or a nation to a higher international rank**, usually associated with a move out of a deleterious post-conflict or post-poverty situation [*machiokoshi*, (Japanese) both seeking and marking the rise the city to a higher level of prosperity]. |
| D | Sydney, Brisbane APT, Fukuoka AAT, Auckland, Singapore<br>**A biennial broadly re-configuring perceptions of international art** through a regional and specifically Asian or Asia-Pacific selection held in a rich nation. |
| E | Yokohama, Beijing,<br>**A biennial both claiming a new authority and re-asserting a formerly lost national or international status** in defining a field. |

These biennial trajectories were oriented by instrumental, purposive movements *outwards* from poverty and economic insecurity, lack of political authority, dearth of international prestige for art as much as nation-state,[18] and *inwards* to richness and economic well-being, a symbolic use of artistic accumulation to mark state or city authority, and a critical plenitude or temporally restricted but decent level of recognition.

Asian biennials did not function in an Asian world. They were allowed to develop as an adjunct circuit to the Euramerican biennials which had clearly been organized by and had given priority to the Western world.[19] Just as obviously an increase in the number of biennials within Asia and also world-wide meant that increasing differentiation between biennials would be required if any particular one was to appear distinctive, and to perform local or international leadership functions. It was likely biennials would have regional and global rankings, and would begin to structure a hierarchy in which various kinds of sharing arrangements as well as hegemonies could have tacitly operated. The agreement of three Asian biennials in 2006 to hold their opening ceremonies within a week time span and in sequence—Singapore, Shanghai, and Gwangju—was one example of explicit coordination, but these biennials did not apear to be mobilizing themselves as a network, or network chain, in competition with the large Euramerican biennials.

However, the 2008 announcement that the Biennale of Sydney would join a coordinated *Art Compass 2008* with the Yokohama Triennale and the Shanghai, Singapore and Gwangju biennials indicated precisely that an alternative axis to the Euramerican biennials was coming into existence.[20] Competition took place by occupying circuits of prestige appraisal, as well as providing a linkage of some Biennials to local markets which may have increased in size between competing groups of local and international patrons.

## Forces Affecting Biennials and International Art Worlds: Globalization, Euramerican Hegemonies and Anti-hegemonies

Much of the literature about biennials and many of the texts of biennial catalogues themselves positioned these temporary but recurrent sites as those of resistance to globalization. They did this very directly in an intentional way by the kind of art they selected and by the conceptual line taken by curators, sometimes by the very materials and their deportment in installations. But it was doubtful that work which featured the urban environment like Song Dong's house at Gwangju Biennale in 2006 were in any direct sense *representations* of globalizing forces. What artists did was notice the aesthetic appeal or confusion of urban or industrial forms and made them their subject matter, such as Weng Feng's egg cities at Guangzhou in 2006.

The issue that art served as a poor direct reflection of issues in other domains, such as the economic, stemmed from the fact that the art world-system functioned, according to Bydler, like an additional layer on the inter-state system. The art world also partially overlapped that system.

> Thus, culture does not work as an ideological or discursive support for nation states. Quite the contrary, as it instead forms a separate hierarchy, one which is anchored to nation-states through funding, and therefore available to political nation states as self-promotion.[21]

The art system not only overlapped the system of nation-states, those units themselves were unstable and increasingly interpenetrated each other. There was often confusion between five levels. The large cultural ecumene such as China or The West; the smaller ecumene including cultural alliances; the level of traditional states in apparently hegemonic control over their own cultures such as the post-World War II alliances over many fields between France and Germany; and the small states and quasi-state cultural enclaves within wider units; the level of non-state units and actors which have international activities, like here, artists and curators.[22]

The processes of globalization intersected with biennials on at least three levels: the city itself, the changed structures of feeling of their inhabitants, and the new role for mediators in a culture of spectacles of which biennials clearly were one. The global city was a special kind of mega-city where biennials were enacted in which "Global cities form a network in which the nodes are cities with the most highly developed telecommunications network".[23] The problem for any understanding of the relation of cities to globalization was that cities were no longer the same as they were in pre-globalized conditions, and the huge, massified urban audience of megacities created a kind of hunger for spectacles which seemed to have lost any organic basis as a cumulation of the desires of particular individuals or their articulating groups. The architect Rem Koolhaas who writing for the 2006 Guangzhou Triennale, thought that,

> Cities used to be complex organisms growing over a long time according to predetermined plans, but now cities are simple and immediate accumulations of needs and desires... We no longer have specific memories of individual cities, but we now have a kind of abstract, generic memory of all cities which dictates this fabrication. [24]

He also thought architecture could responsibly repeat itself and become a brand, or that it could "look at the specific differences that exist within globalization".[25] This latter comment made in the context of an architect's involvement with one biennial or in this case triennial, looked like a dilemma for the curatorial conception of biennials as such. But it was made by those mediating biennials from outside in towards the mass audience of one megacity.

However, major collections of research dealing with world cities in the late 2000s hardly mentioned art, let alone art biennials at all. Such exhibitions have done more than just promote megacities. There was no necessary dependence of biennials on megacities such as Shanghai or Beijing, since some like Busan or Gwangju though large were not themselves megacities. Some biennials occured in the peripheral zones of megacities, such as Yokohama in the shadow of greater Tokyo, or Fukuoka at the edge of the virtually linear conurbation in Japan all the way along from the Inland Sea through Kansai to Tokyo. The relation of biennials to globalization was thus not one of a singular institutional type but of one of a modality of function, that of how biennials related to, accepted, or exposed and resisted globalizations, or fostered an art which did so.

> Some cities thus become global places and other do not, and cities exploited or ignored by global forces are peripheralized… This uneven penetration is not simply a matter of *which* institutions, industries, people, and places are affected but *how* they are affected. They might be overwhelmed, exploited, or enhanced.[26]

The interesting comments in biennial catalogues were often made by those negotiating with this external legitimation to produce the biennial for local or national agendas. In the catalogue of the 2006 Guangzhou Triennial the Chinese co-curator Guo Xiaoyan wrote:

> In avoiding the placement of limits on Chinese contemporary art development through [application of] superficial Western methods, the artist will have to change the narrative of a Western-style modernity, and form a new understanding… Identity awakening is needed in response to such a contemporary condition and different methods [need to be found], not just the broad covering-over of non-Western contemporary existence, and its marginalization to pre-artistic historical records. [Such a position needs to] open up a perspective entirely new to art history so as to clear away the present centralization of power in the discourse [of international art]. [Translation adjusted] [27]

Here a possible gap emerged between the international curatorium who sought to derive the local from the gaps in globalization or its specially local modes (such as the curator conceived them), and the demands and desires of the local curator/mediator who may have had quite separate demands of the biennial and the international collaboration.

Who was to speak for such disarticulated masses and the kinds of spectacle they may have required, or, desired?

Okabe had attributed the rise of biennials to the following tendencies:

1. city development projects;
2. resistance to globalism;
3. the tendency towards realization of a "tangible utopia", even though Biennials are temporally restricted temporary institutions;
4. longing by the people of the world for a site of visual communication which opens an experimental breakthrough to the future.[28]

She thought that this desire for utopias, even spectacular ones, was due to a social change.

> Through the transition from a role specialized to a multi-dimensionalized society, [for] artists, designers, curators, producers, critics and editors a borderless site is created which transcends divided, ascribed roles.[29]

From Okabe's perspective, curators in this process were simply the avatars of a popular will, or the bearers of a special and useful technical facility. They were important because they could identify the spaces in between social structures at many local, national, and transnational levels. They could discern the causes of resistance to globalism, and were technically empowered to identify special modes of representation and types of background in radical museum practice which made this feasible. To some extent they were so enabled because they were also the personal avatars of dissent.[30] Perhaps here we may see biennials as having constituted a gap, a disturbance, from which a kind of transnational critical discourse could have emerged.[31]

Could biennials subvert the world art system and overturn its hierarchies? Artists have to work from their inner voice, and their discourse is not system-dependent even though artists may articulate their consciousness through understanding their body as inhabiting a social space. But from the viewpoint of biennials in a world-art system, I would rather concur with Quemin's somewhat pessimistic conclusions about the agency of the nation-state. He saw artists, curators, and collectors alike, as actors in the inter-national system of art of which Biennials were a functional subsystem which took account of past successes and reproduced a hierarchy between countries which counteracted any policies seeking to correct the hierarchy.[32] The idea was scarcely credible that curators based in one zone, Euramerica, and largely living in or dependent on the art markets of one nation-state, the USA, could somehow have made themselves independent of the constraints of the very system of which they were a part. The notion that they could have "reverse engineered" a global system against itself to allow for hybridity, and then deployed this as a counter-system strategy, could only have been a wish-fulfilling aspiration or an empty self-delusion.[33]

## Biennials and the Circulation of Contemporary Asian Art

What kinds of circulation of contemporary Asian artworks, artists, and curator-mediators take place because of the biennial system? This question firstly applied to contemporary art within the existing system from around 1993, and secondly, and in some ways dependently, it applied to the new biennials which had largely been set up in Asia. These began at Delhi (from 1968), were marked by the broad inclusion of contemporary Asian art at the first biennale of Sydney in 1973, and grew with developments at Dhaka (1981), Fukuoka (4 Asian Art Shows since 1989, 5 Asian Art Triennales since 1999), Taipei (1992), Brisbane (1993), Gwangju (1995), Shanghai (1996), Busan (1998), Echigo-Tsumari (2000), Yokohama (2001), Auckland (2001), Guangzhou (1992, 2002), Beijing (1993, 2003), Jakarta (2003), and Singapore (2006). One should also note there were many regional exhibitions in the ASEAN group of nations after 1968, as there were many bilateral exhibitions between different parts of Asia, especially China, Japan, and Korea.

I have written "in some ways dependently" above, because the incorporation of contemporary Asian art at biennials is a complex phenomenon, sited at the intersections of many different currents within world modern and contemporary art, or its other avatar, transnational art. There been three main issues.

Firstly, the broad historical question is of different *kinds* of art modernities in non-Euramerican parts of the world which also include Central and South America as well as Africa. Since Asian developments have been as easily noticed by those in Asia as they were ignored in Euramerica, these Asian modernities might best be understood as parallel or "other" modernities. In large part their advent was before the great integrations of economic markets and cultural representations in the 1990s created a level of the increasingly permeable inter-state system for transnational art discourses, mostly articulated through and by biennials, under the processes called globalization. That art representations are transnationally articulated or integrated does not mean the same for all Asian cultures. For many such cultures there is also a simultaneous localization of global or transnational art tendencies. This is counter-posed with formal analogies and close homologies of taste which can be found between, say, the propaganda use of leadership portraits in China and those of the kings of Thailand or Cambodia, or between Thai and Korean TV game shows.

A second issue is that because those modernities were differently articulated by, but still partly appropriated from the cultural and specifically artistic forms of Euramerica, their presence as *parallel* modernities in the Asian or immigrant settler cultures was ignored as derivative of Euramerica. Or they were seen as still dependent on a colonial pattern of cultural hegemony. Colonial art had already ceased to be simplyor exclusively colonial when its forms were used for purposes other than those of the colonial ruler, and also when colonial hegemony declined or came to an end. This decline took different forms in different conditions.

For example, counter-appropriation could be found in the visualizing of an Indian nation within the academic codes and forms of Victorian realism by Ravi Varma in India during the 1890s, in Australian settler nationalist representations of landscape in the Heidelberg school of the 1890s. Or, even much later in the exploration of non-duality through the rhetoric of the minimalist mark in many types of modern installation and painting by the Korean artist Lee U-fan in the Japan of the 1990s.

A third general issue is not simply that the institutional pattern of biennial exhibition was taken in Asia from its predecessors at Venice, São Paolo, and Documenta. The Asian biennials were integrated into a Euramerican system which *already* existed, and so works and artists were circulated between the new Asian biennials and these predecessors, although the modalities and causal links for these circulations were not transparent. This systemic interlinkage from their outset characterized a type of Asian modernity in the 1990s that was different in both degree and kind from the relatively less dependent and parallel modernities in Asia earlier, even as late as the 1970s.

## Some Models for Understanding Circulation

We should look at some models for explaining circulation from art history and beyond to see what types of tools might be applied to the material which follows. An initial survey of some models was made at a Sydney workshop held in 2005.[34] It is significant how directly some features of these models exemplify Asian contemporary art appearing at biennials.

Some models derived from studies of European art in the 18th century include those of restricted circulation because of guild structures, alongside which may be noted international circulation of journeymen and court artists moving between different centres. In these a figure arose which was seen much earlier, and most vividly in the European Renaissance, of the artist who moved between courts as a kind of cultural currency for aristocratic recognition of prestige and cultural prominence. This also occurred with the advent of Asian "superstar" artists such as Xu Bing and Cai Guoqiang in the 1990s,[35] or in the patronage of the French collector Pinault of Subdoh Gupta, whose skull composed from Indian culinary utensils dominated the Grand Canal in Venice at the time of the 2007 Biennale.

Artists have acted as well as purchasing agents for princes since at least the 18th century. Europe provides many examples of artworks being circulated as part of a gift economy to signal personal ties, where the ability to secure the movement of artworks was a sign of wealth, and sometimes through gift-giving or conspicuously disinterested patronage, functioned as a kind of philanthropy. But the European 18th century also provided different models of anonymous consumption of art through the rise of impersonal collectors who bought from a market by the currency of prestige associated with artworks or artists, but with whom they had no personal acquaintance. In some ways in the late 1990s the very large prints in multiples by contemporary artists like Fang Lijun who had become famous earlier may have had this function to cement the prestige of the collector via the artists' fame.

Circulation of artworks was not dependent on a personal, direct relation presumed between the members of the audience and the makers of the art. A kind of time-lapse circulation took place between sites where art was found which had no temporal relation to the finder, and where it was preserved in collectors' stores or in museums. This happened too in the display of war booty, the preservation of archaeological discoveries, and the forced shift of private collections into a public arena. It could also be seen in art fairs. In March 2008 there was even the illusion of immediate contact at a remote site provided by the Asian Contemporary Art week in New York, which was not able to conceal its function as an expensive street market de-localized from the site of production.

Circulation functioned not merely as a market transfer but also as a preservation of valued art objects themselves. It was sometimes allied to national claims to represent the ancient glories of other civilizations, such as the British acquisition of the Parthenon friezes in the early 19th century, or to the restoration of a "lost" national consciousness found through the collection prominence given to one artist, such as Rembrandt in Amsterdam in the late 19th century. The turning point for this kind of evaluation in 20th century China was the 1935 exhibition of masterpieces of Chinese Art sent from Shanghai to the Royal Academy in London. As Guo Hui's research has indicated, the display criteria, that is the aesthetic categories within which works were grouped for display was subtly different between Shanghai and London, indicating a kind of assertion of national categories.[36]

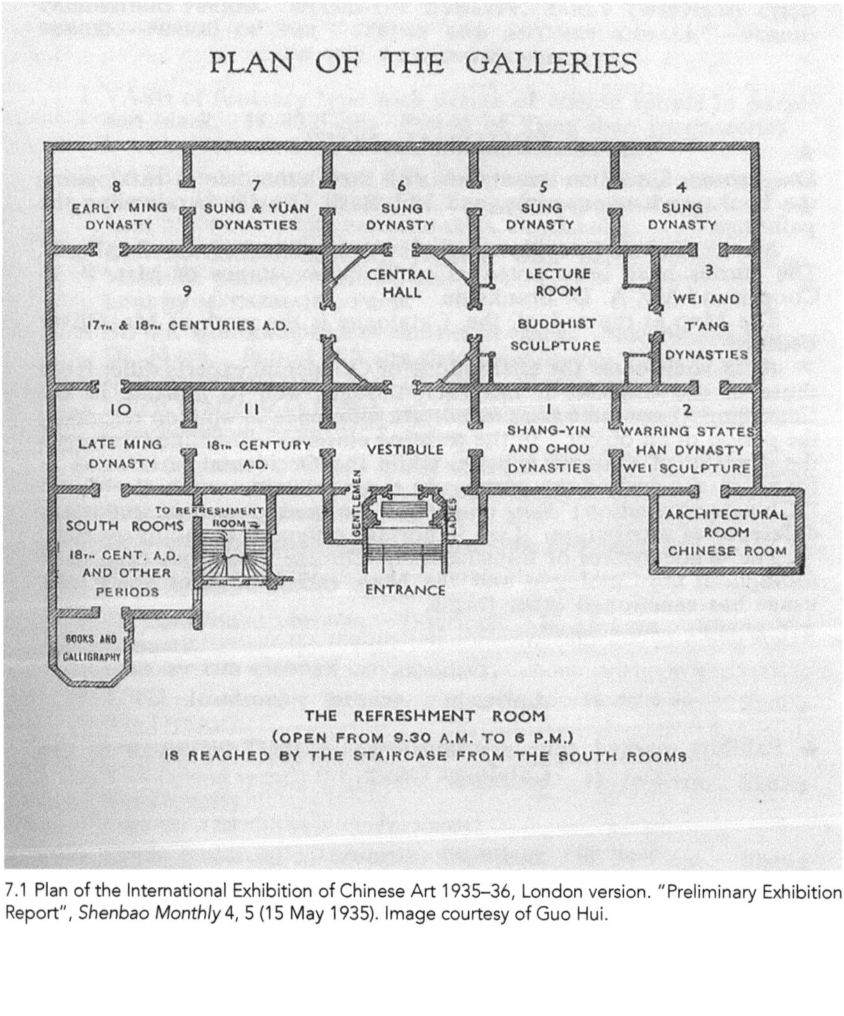


7.1 Plan of the International Exhibition of Chinese Art 1935–36, London version. "Preliminary Exhibition Report", *Shenbao Monthly* 4, 5 (15 May 1935). Image courtesy of Guo Hui.

Further refinements in understanding circulation can be found in studies of 15th through 17th century art in China.[37] These foreground the ancient Chinese practice of collecting and providing coterie encyclopedic connoisseurship guides as means to establish the authenticity of particular classes of objects, including paintings and calligraphy. Genuineness was in part guaranteed by the skills of the scholar-artist whose moral character was an index for many other types of humanistic attainment, including those in literature. By the late 15th century

倫敦中國藝展之預展

參加本年十一月間倫敦中國藝術展覽之我國選品皆歷代古物名畫，近在上海外灘中國銀行舊址舉行預展。此頁所載僅其一斑。

↑預展會中之書畫陳列室

↓瓜耳鼎兩耳作鳥形亦戰國時銅器

7.2 Plan of the International Exhibition of Chinese Art 1935–36, Shanghai version. "Preliminary Exhibition report", *Shenbao Monthly* 4, 5 (15 May 1935). Image courtesy of Guo Hui.

some Chinese scholar-artists also functioned as professionals selling their work on commission for recompense in cash or goods, the circulation of many of which, such as rice and silk, also had a monetary function since they were easily cashed. The commodification of art objects through a system of exchanges, the level of whose complexity drove this process, often bound reciprocal relations between artist and patron over long time scales. Whether all biennial curators act entirely like patrons in selecting artists can be argued. But this sort of relation is indicated among contemporary Asian art at biennials in particular cases such the curator Apinan Poshyananda and the Korean artist Choi Jeong-hwa.

If circulation involved description of transactional processes and of the sites where these processes took place, then art history may simply have had to observe the flow of art objects in one direction and money or other circulatable non-art assets in another. Some reciprocality or inter-dependence was assumed between the directions of these flows, but what was circulated was often not art. It included economic goods, physical objects, money, ideas, signs, people and images of art. We could even speculate that Chinese contemporary art which could in the late 2000s be sold for bewildering amounts of money, may also have been exchanged as a simulacrum of the economic power of China the work denoted, and in this exchange for those who came to own the works, money was a kind of quotidien lubricant, a currency of esteem, rather than just a store of value.

The flow of artists, artworks, and curators in one direction were reciprocated, perhaps with a time lag, by flow of money, esteem or cultural capital, and goods, in the other direction, with many elaborated mechanisms of translation or setting of equivalences between art and non-art flows. The sites where these took place may have been the art-specific ones of workshops, educational structures, collections, and various exhibiting institutions such as Biennials, but these also more abstractly included structures of taste or aesthetic preference, or discursive sites such as ideological and curatorial programmes. What linked transaction processes and sites of circulation under neo-liberal economic models was the transfer of value between immediate and deferred consumption, or on a different level, by the change of circulating into fixed capital, so providing art history with a notion of circulation as a material replenishment of the past by the present. This replenishment was all the more effective if the artwork appeared to carry a stock of valued images of the past or even of recent revolutionary presents.

In Marxian models, the notion of a caesura in commodity relations in the abstract state between purchase and sale, was one which pointed to a model of circulation where art history could account for gaps between the aesthetic value of art objects and their economic value as goods, through recurrent crises of evaluation. Some artists seized on this and used photographic replicas as the means of guaranteeing economic value, whereas the actual artwork was inalienably non-exchangeable. This was seen in photographic records of performance art which were often sold as multiples.

Finally, Keynesian models of the feedback between the marginal propensity to consume and the marginal output efficacy of capital, point to art historical models where the larger the number of artworks produced the smaller the relative effect is on the audience. Monetary theories may lead art historians to think artworks and artists are used as a form of money whereby value is transferred from one site to another, sometimes in an exchange not just for more money, but also for esteem, favours, and life-opportunities, and chiefly of the possibility of continuing to produce art. From the mid-1990s how many more shockingly gaudy testaments in artworks to recent Chinese consumption vulgarity could the international art market absorb? Or was there some absolute point reached back from which no artist could fall, like the numbing replicas of their earlier works which began to appear in Asian biennials by, among several others, Yue Minjun at the Gwangju Biennale in 2006?

7.3 Zhang Huan, *65 kg* (1994). C-print, 152.4 x 101.6 cm. Image courtesy of the artist.

Some semantic theories posit that in any given speech community, meaning in words has long been thought to transfer ideas which are assumed to stay the same between speakers and hearers, even when these reverse roles in a conversation. For art history this pointed to artworks requiring extensive collateral interpretation when they flowed outside any original visual community which understood them as art. This was critically true for religious and political iconography, but Biennale audiences were not constant and may have required more explanation than any presumed transnational "sophistication" allowed. This community of biennale viewers could include audiences stratified by various degrees of art education, and also those able to make their own extensions of meaning when the artwork moved into other culturally defined communities of visual reception. Semantic models also suggested that only a small part of meaning came from the artwork itself. Meaning included the ability to question visual metaphors applied from one field to another, such as a perspectival metaphor used in the composition of a photographic image. But a Wittgensteinian view of languages as lacking fixed or determinate meanings and of all meaning being specific to a transaction series, could lead art historians to think all meaning in art is wholly dependent on semantic negotiations in context, that interpreting the artwork was a complex of visually and culturally specific transactions between the viewer and the work.

A similar notion of insertion was found in Simmel's sociological understanding of money, crucial for interpreting circulation, for money intervenes between desire and fulfillment; ownership can change beyond simpler methods such as theft and gift. The isolation of individual specificities was punctured as money introduced calculable equivalences between goods, and did so publicly. This suggests that art can be interpreted as in a high-level and complex series of exchanges of artworks that constitute circulation, and that the aesthetic incommensurability of artworks is both the inverse of, and is discontinuous with, its highly ordered equivalences in that very monetary order which allows art objects to circulate. The increase in the impersonality of economic ownership, this position suggests, was accompanied by a distancing of relation to the aesthetic states which were embodied in artworks. Thus the increasing market value of some contemporary Chinese art like the works of Zhang Xiaogang at the Shanghai Biennale in 2004, should have been seen as in inverse relation to any artistic value the works may have had. The interdependence of personality and material relationships typical of barter relations was freed up by money in exchange relations. This impersonal distance also allowed for an aesthetic of transient objects where the "flow of things" began to resemble the circulations which were the flow of objects in the money economy.

Commodity spectacles arose where biennials produced competition between "tempting exteriors" and relativized styles by bringing their multiplicity together at one point in time and space for a new kind of detached viewer. This figure was both detached from "home styles" as a cosmopolitan, and minimally engaged with the object at the moment of consumption, so that responses to diverse experiences and objects were similar. One might extend this view to international Biennials and surmise that similarity in response could be one that had already been educated earlier and which was now reinforced by the kinds of artworks shown. There seemed to be a kind of transnational reinforcing feedback on the level of images between the work of Patricia Piccinini in the Australian pavilion at Venice in 2005 and that of Zhu Yu's *Eating Babies* in 1999, part of the exhibition *Bu hezuo fangshi/Fuck Off* a counter exhibition to the Shanghai Biennale.

Curatorial practice has produced landmark exhibitions which as in the 1989 *Magiciens de la terre* found concepts such as the "spirit of place" to allow the juxtaposition of tribal and sacred art alongside that of the Western avant-garde. In this curatorial mode, no context-specific negotiation of meanings and their supporting semantic communities was allowed for. Exhibitions were, in this approach, a kind of concrete thinking through material concepts by which more abstract ideas were to be allowed presentation, or were creatively elided. This was why many curatorial projects which sought to relativize "Western" art discourses did so through the means of site-specific installations. These ritualized for public and trans-cultural engagement what otherwise would have been highly bound and culturally dense meaning systems.

Curators in the Asian Biennials presented aesthetic propositions by means of their exhibition strategy, their selection and then juxtaposition of works. In doing so these curators adopted many guises which were subject to prestidigitative shifts between operant roles.

The often bewildering range of these roles included grand intellectuals or *maîtres à penser*, fairground barkers, automobile salesmen (sometimes of "luxury", sometimes of "second-hand" vehicles, sometimes of "custom" cars), shamans, hack doctors, grand cuisiniers, humble home chefs, playwrights, Hollywood stars, raucous theatrical agents, and, even, artists.

Whatever the curator's position or theoretical justification, the effect of their mediation was to disturb some presumed paradigm of "normal" viewing or monolithic interpretation (not infrequently against the very wishes of the artists shown).[38] The aim was to force on the viewer the necessity of active participation in creating the meaning of the work, to question modernistically the type of representation, and as often to give exposure to an "alternative" and "authentic" national presentation which had been traduced by other local artists and works mimicking external misperceptions.

## Relations between Artists and Curators: "China" and "Asia"

We now have an array of conceptual models for interpreting circulation, for describing its phenomena. What kinds of empirical observations do we need to further assess which of these phenomena exist in the field of contemporary Asian art? Do they allow us to see if new kinds of circulation are taking place within this field due to the advent of increasing exhibition in, and presence of, a large number of biennials?

In order to answer these questions the chief material available to observe is the movement of artists, works, and curators between biennials and other recurrent exhibition sites. I planned for this analysis to be provided in part by empirical materials generated from a database which I designed and supervised, but which in the end due to resource constraints was not able to bring to full completion. The analysis of some results now follows and more details are given in the report in appendix 3 (see QR code on next page) but I do not propose here to re-iterate the data series found in the database itself since this would take up too much space, and in any case would just indicate rankings.

But some published data about biennials themselves are also found in appendix 1. We can also assemble particular details from gallery and government funding bodies' reports (where they are readily available and transparent) that indicate the extent of official support, such as we have for the Australia Council support to the Asia Pacific Triennial given in appendix 2. Another way of assessing these types and patterns of circulation is to interpret the statements of exhibition aims made in published biennial catalogues. We have seen above in the case-study analyses of this empirical material intentions may be matched to outcomes in Japan, China, and Singapore, and in the Asia Pacific Triennial.

Circulation of works and artists through exhibition spaces themselves, particularly biennials, is shown through the artists and curators who were included in a designated series of exhibitions between 1989 and 2004 shown in appendix 3 (see QR code on this page).[39]

The artists are defined in fields of "China" and "Asia" in two separate data series: the former include Chinese artists from Hong Kong and Macao, Taiwan, and Overseas Chinese as well as those from mainland China, the latter include artists from all Asian countries apart from China.[40] The data listed are the exhibition (by a unique number) the exhibition title, the curator, or exhibition concept in collective curation cases, and the artists' names. Each exhibition is weighted for its importance as follows.

**Link to Appendix 3.**

One point is given to an artist for exhibition at a "marker exhibition" which defines a field. Curators are given the same points as artists in each case. There are several marker exhibitions in the "Chinese" field which amount in some cases to extended group shows held internationally, and one major exhibition which overlapps into the "Asian" field, *Cities on the Move*, in 1997.

7.4 Number of artists and curators involved in biennials between 2000–05, as recorded in database. Divided into fields of "China" (including Hong Kong and Taiwan) and "Asia". See Appendix 3, online (QR code above).

Two points are given to an artist for an exhibition at a "regional recurrent exhibition" such as a biennale or triennale like the Asia-Pacific Triennial in Brisbane or the Fukuoka Asian Art Triennale.

Three points are given to an artist for exhibition at a "major recurrent exhibition" of which there were only three, the Venice Biennale, the São Paolo Bienal, and Documenta.

In addition, the late 1990s saw the advent of major book publications like *Cream* and *Fresh Cream* which were presented and written like a virtual Biennale. Inclusion in each of these publications was given 3 points because inclusion there was of the same or greater importance for the artist as being in a Biennial. These books were more likely to be seen by many other art-world actors. One can envisage future movement up or down between the exhibitions given these weightings, but for the period in question the ranking is intuitively clear and unproblematic.

## Rankings of Artists

There were a total of 882 artists in the China field, 160 of whom received more than 5 points, and 13 of whom received more than 20 points, the highest receiving 41 points. In comparison there were a total of 1,089 artists in the Asia field, 69 of whom received more than 5 points, and four of whom received more than 20 points, the highest receiving 27. In other words, the highest-ranked China artist was twice as highly ranked as the highest artist in the Asia field, and about four times as many China artists were found in the upper echelons of the points rankings than in the Asia field.

The figures indicate that in the more broadly cast Asia field only a small number of artists have relatively high selections, and that the Asia field has a smaller number of artists who are not on the same level. Thus in terms of selections there is a first pyramid, at the top of which is a second, even more sharply pointed pyramid. This is more marked for China than for Asia.

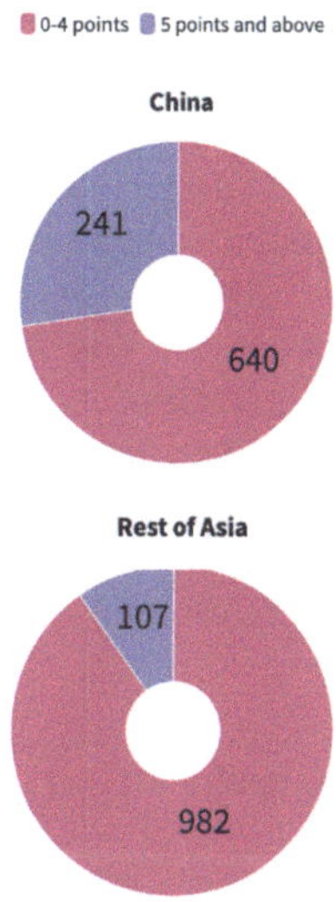


7.5 More Chinese artists with higher rankings.

## Rankings of Curators

In the case of curators, there were a total of 208 curators in the China field, 23 of whom received more than 5 points, and one of whom received more than 20 points, the highest at 27 points. In comparison, there are a total of 199 curators in the Asia field which also includes the curators who selected in the China field, 21

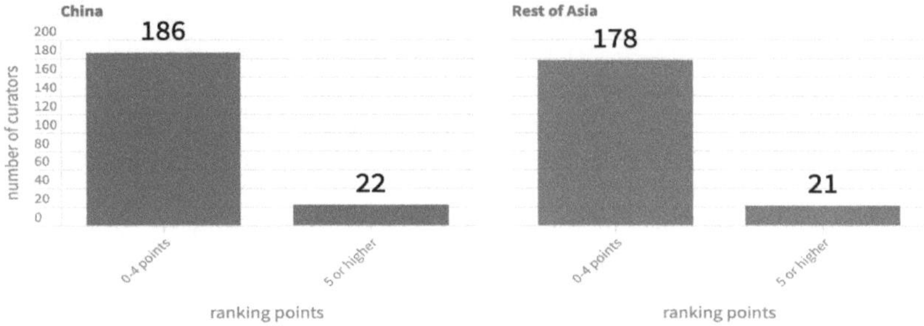


7.6 Rankings of curators, "China" vs "Asia".

of whom received more than 5 points, and none of whom received more than 20 points, the highest receiving 16 points.

Other comparative observations were possible. The total number of Asian artists, that is, non-Chinese artists, considered by biennials were about 20 per cent larger than the number of Chinese, and the number of curators working on China were about the same, given that the Asian curators also included those working on China. These figures point to some predominance in both fields of the curators working on China, despite the fact that the number of Asian artists globally included in these data is larger.[41]

The chance of any Chinese artist being selected overall in biennials against an Asian one was about 20 per cent higher (1.8/2.2=0.81).[42]

Chinese curators overall selected about one artist in four, and those selecting for Asia were choosing one artist in five or so. This again indicates that, for this cohort of artists selected by data from these exhibitions, there is a marginally higher chance of being selected if the artist is Chinese as against otherwise.[43]

## Longevity in Field

One also notices differences in the frequency of appearance and in the longevity within the fields. The number of curators with three or more entries in the China field is about three times that for Asia. When we recall that the Asia field includes several curators who also work on China, we can see how steep and hierarchically organized both these fields are. Most curators (78.9–83 per cent) enter the lists only once. Therefore we can also say this system is stratified by systemic life-chances, and most curators do not re-appear. Despite the smaller number of artists within the China field, it is clear that this field for artists is stratified like that for those in the Asia field with about one seventh, or 16–18 per cent, at the top.

However, the China field is again shown to be less chancy for artists who made some success, or are simply more prevalent in the overall field of biennials from which this data was assembled, with around 46 per cent of artists appearing in more than one exhibition. Whereas only 18 per cent of the artists in the Asian field do so.

## Characteristics of Curators

Observations may be made about particular artists and curators in these series which have significance for the overall understanding. With regard to curators, 13 of the top 30 curators were from the China field (including overseas Chinese), and for Asia, 15 of the top 30 curators were from Asia. Rather unsurprisingly of the top 30 curators in the Asia field, 17 also appeared in the China field. In other words, for biennial curators the China field is a dominant interest, or at least is one they could not ignore. But for the top curators, Asia was an extension or an alternative compartment of that field. Indeed all of the 12 most highly ranked curators in the Asian field also curate for China. This indicates the transnationality of the upper hierarchy of Biennale curation. Conversely the absence in the Asia field of four from the five curators of Chinese origin in the China field, points to the lack of transnationality in their curating interests. The presence of Hou Hanru at the top of both lists indicates that this difference is at least partially due to selection by the biennial system which presumably meshes with particular choices or interests on the part of the curators.

7.7 Artists by number of entries in the database, "China" vs "Asia".

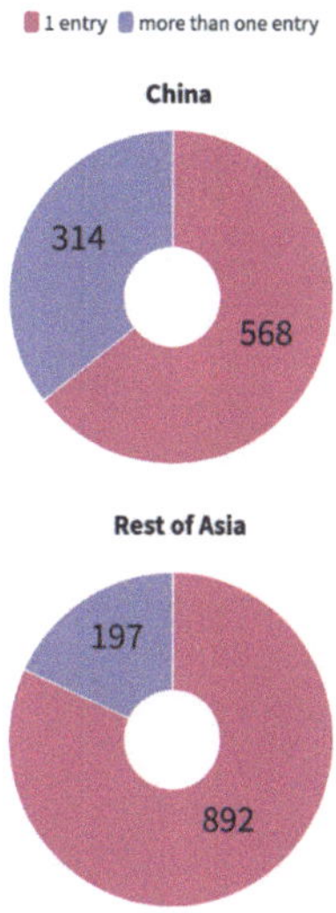


In addition, if we look carefully at the movement of curators between biennials there is clearly a tendency to maintain a cohort from which the choice for overall artistic director, as opposed to sub-curators, was made over a number of years. Although there were different organizational structures for each biennial, many of the committees which appoint directors are highly conscious of the need to mediate international art inwards to their own societies as much as domestic art outwards. They frequently secure the advice and sometimes the membership on their boards of previous biennial directors. René Block became a member of the board appointing the Istanbul Biennale artistic director.[44] The exact timings and statuses of these appointments as well as the nature of advice given is not in the public domain. Sometimes curators regard information about operational decisions at the same level of security only elsewhere found in foreign or defence ministries. But we can intelligently speculate that the opinions of Block were influential in the appointment of Hasegawa Yûko to the curatorship of the Istanbul Biennale in 2001. Again, the appointment of Hou Hanru to Istanbul for 2007 seemed to have been made by the agreement of a cohort of curators present at Moscow in 2005.[45] Charles Esche was the artistic co-director at Istanbul in 2005 (with Vasif Kortun) but had been the artistic co-director at Gwangju in

2002 with Hou Hanru. The idea that curation is an open field selected by merit totally ignores the fact that all the selectors and all the possible artistic directors are closely inter-linked by career and other social relations. If, as we saw earlier, Merrick-Hughes lent his strong voice to the selection of Nanjô Fumio as a jury member for *Aperto* in 1985, it takes very little imagination to see other gate-keeping functions on the entrance of new curators as having been performed by Harald Szeemann, René Block and others in the 1990s and early 2000s.

7.8 Cai Guo-Qiang preparing for *Blue Dragon* (1999), exhibited at the 3rd Asia Pacific Triennial of Contemporary Art (APT3) (1999), Queensland. Image courtesy of Cai Studio.

## Characteristics of Artists

The artists points rankings also display interesting characteristics. Only the 4 top artists in the Asia field receive 20 or above points, whereas 14 did so in the China field. The top-ranked Asia field artist, Heri Dono received 27 points, whereas the top-ranked figure in the China field, Cai Guoqiang received 41 points. These figures indicate the marked dominance of China and especially of the top-ranked China artists in the biennials covered here. But if we take Heri Dono as an example, his frequency of appearance begins in 1993 and resulted in 13 appearances, whereas Cai Guoqiang began to appear in 1990 and had 20 appearances overall. At the top of the rankings therefore frequency of appearance was a very important index of prominence as much as points gained. Indeed the intervention in these rankings of market factors cannot be ignored. Artists like Heri Dono maintained an "Indonesian" trace whilst living less than a month each year in Indonesia. But when one considers that an artist such as Eddie Hara, to pick one example, with very similar kinds of visualization and practice, does not appear in these rankings at all, and had been thought to lose his "Indonesian-ness" by residence abroad in Switzerland, one can see that factors outside these rankings must have accounted for these selections or discriminations. However much a simple deduction this intervention remains, the restriction and concentration of a few figures in the top 30 in both the China and Asia fields is surely be due to deliberate efforts to preserve their exposure and status by those who had invested in them, and this process of conversion of cultural capital (artistic merit) into economic capital (sales of works due to marking among the top artists) cannot ever be ascribed to simple artistic merit alone.

Some features of the China field were particularly interesting. Artists like Zhang Peili may have been selected and appeared in the system for a long time, since 1987. He is ranked four overall. But they were followed by younger artists like Yang Fudong, ranked fifth overall, who only entered it in 2001. In other words, there is evidence for a faster move up the rankings by some of the later entrants, depending no doubt on the recognition given in the field as a whole by much more long-standing entrants, the mobility of some curators seeking newer entrants, and the ability of the art market to diversify its choices.

The top-ranked artists in the China field included those who have become prominent commercially, such as Fang Lijun, who was ranked third with 18 appearances and 28 points. But interestingly some commercially highly successful artists did not figure so highly, Zhou Tiehai being ranked 61 with 9 appearances and 13 points. Neither was avant gardism as a stance, nor significant commercial gallery and Biennale appearance, any guarantee of prominence in this system. Ai Weiwei, who had a reputation among curators and commercial galleries for avant gardism, with 8 appearances and 11 points was ranked 61, and Xiao Yu, who was a radical presenter of "cadaver art", was ranked 81.

The obsessive, even myopic interest of this system with only one kind of art, self-defined as contemporary, needs at least one reinforcement. We can see this easily in the example of an innovatory *guohua* (national painting) artist Chen Ping only having reached a ranking of 173.

The artists in the field of Asia displayed some of the same tendencies, and there was evidence of inter-artist linkage, Montien Boonma who was ranked second, having been the teacher of Navin Rawanchaikul, who was ranked eighth. But there were also curious anomalies since artists like Rirkrit Tiravanija, who had considerable international prominence as an artist and was a co-curator of part of the Venice Biennale in 2003, was only ranked 64th overall as an artist. This indicates that the prominence of artists who cross over into curation may not be easily caught by database categories of this kind. In the Asia field among the top-ranked 30 artists there was no easily observed pattern of national dominance beyond some prominence for Japanese artists. This was to be expected since Japan had been prominent in the biennial system represented by Venice and São Paolo since the mid-1950s. Among the top 30 artists of the Asian field denoted there were nine Japanese, five Thai, five Korean, three Indonesian, one Indian, one Indian-British, two Singaporean, one Malaysian, one Vietnamese-Japanese, one Bangladeshi-British, and one Philippine artist.

## National Affiliations

Other distributional phenomena become clearer if we look at the proportional national affiliation of artists in both the China and Asia fields combined.

The figures again show the preponderance of China in the whole field, and the further significance up to 2005 of Japan and Korea. The Korean figures are inflated because the Gwangju Biennale includes a higher proportion of local artists than other Biennials, and in some years Gwangju has had a pavilion dedicated to local contemporary art. Given the number and quality of their artists, it is interesting that Indonesia and India should be represented in these figures on a level less than Thailand and the Philippines. This is surely an index, at that time and for this body of artists, of how relatively under-represented Indonesia and India are more generally in biennials, and also in some measure how un-integrated into international art circuits their art worlds were in that period (1987–2005).

The prominence of Thailand may have been related to the transnational linkages of one curator, Apinan Poshyananda, and one Thai artist based largely in the US and Europe, Rirkit Thiravanija, who has also performed curatorial functions such as at Venice in 2003. In national terms, disproportionate representation for the artists may be obtained if a country has a nationally-based curator and international artist with these sorts of connections. These figures do not capture radical shifts in selection of artists from one country, such as the large change in Chinese participation after the 1999 Venice Biennale, and the burgeoning strength of India after 2005, which takes place outside the period analyzed and still largely without official support.

## Relationality between Curators and Artists

It was not feasible for technical and resource reasons to complete a proper relational database which linked curators definitively with a cohort of artists in whom they are interested shown by their own frequency of selection. To discuss relationality we must unsatisfactorily rely on anecdotal construction, even though a relational data base might be feasible in future. There is no doubt that the exhibitions of Hou Hanru have included many of the same artists, but the regularity and restricted nature of his cohort could be argued is not significant in itself. This is because it includes only the best, or most prominent artists. "Best" and "prominent" are not the same thing and the two concepts are frequently confused, often blatantly, in biennial promotional material. The Thai artists have almost all been given prominence by Apinan Poshyananda, perhaps because he

| Country | Number of Artists |
|---|---|
| China | 881 |
| Korea | 397 |
| Japan | 276 |
| Thailand | 42 |
| Philippines | 37 |
| Indonesia | 34 |
| India | 30 |
| Malaysia | 28 |
| Singapore | 28 |
| Vietnam | 20 |
| Pakistan | 14 |
| Others | 211 |

7.9 Nationality of artists in Asian biennials 2000–05.

was until the early 2000s the major Thai curator who could make selections for biennials which were thought internationally reliable (the others being Somporn Rodboon and Gridthiya Gaweewong). Perhaps this was due to his professional function as a national curator active in a transnational field being to give prominence to a limited cohort of his co-nationals. But the attention of French officials like the former cultural attaché in Bangkok in Francine Méoule,[46] and other curators who were then Paris-based such as Hans-Ulrich Obrist, has meant that a few Thai artists' international exposure has been significantly improved, such as that of Surasi Kulsowong, Manit Sriwanichpoom, and Pinaree Sanpitak, particularly because these were linked with the major private collector strongly positioned in Parisian art circles through his family antique dealing buisness, Jean-Michel Beurdeley.

Those new to this art historical subject matter may not find most of the names familiar enough to identify regularities, but if one takes the Asia Field alone it is absolutely clear that the top 30 artists had a minimum of 3 and mostly 4–6 selections over the 16-year corpus of exhibitions examined. This meant their work would predictably turn up on average of every two years at biennials, and with greater concentration in some periods than others. Jun Nguyen-Hatsushiba, for example, had been present in this system annually from 2000–05 and was well known for the interest in him of the curator Nanjô Fumio, then deputy director, later director of the Mori Art Museum. The Korean artist Choi Jeong-hwa was regularly selected by Nanjô Fumio and then followed by Apinan Poshynanada. However, Choi denied in an interview with me that he was acting rather like a local, Korean subcontractor to a succession of multinational corporate organizers.[47]

Indeed one existential problem the art historian confronts in understanding curatorial choice in the biennial system is the disjunction between the apparently clear and restricted regularity of choice of the works seen, and the frequent proclamation in biennials' promotional literature of their being conceptually driven, or at least as always presenting the "new" or the "contemporary". The regularities in the materials examined warrant the conclusion that each curator must have been maintaining a list of artists and was occasionally referring to other curators' choices, or discussing this list with others who then replicated previous choices in their own selections. This was obviously evidence for a process of canon formation in a short cycle or thin time-slice. One could see this regularity of selection in the fact that in any given biennial, around 60 per cent of the artists and around 40 per cent of the works were already familiar to those regularly visiting biennials. There was significant movement of artists between the recognition gained at one admission point, such as Lee Bul in the 1993 APT at Brisbane, and their subsequent and maintained circulation in the Biennale system.[48]

## Conclusion

There is a wide variety of anecdotal material available from field observations about particular works in biennials and the movements in and out of circles of evaluation by given artists or specific works. I have mentioned some of this for the artists Jun Nguyen-Hatsushiba, Yi Bul (Lee Bul) and Choi Jeon-hwa. Here I want to synthesize some of the links between the models of circulation and the relations between artist and curators advanced above.

Artists, works, and curators move between biennial sites. They are like three wheels of decreasing size turning in and out of synchronization with each other, that of the curators being the smallest and most determinative for movements in the other two. The most important features of this system, the complexity of the algorithms for how it actually operates being scarcely imaginable, are the relational switching between two planes of value for the work, the artistic and the economic. A second feature is the function of work corpus or artist cohort restriction being simultaneously to allow, and also to be a product of, the intervention of the mediator-curators. This is not a new system, but for the Asian biennials it is an old one over which were articulated, or into which were inserted, a large number of new positions.

One model of circulation which changed from earlier periods is the switch from personal relations between the artist and an aristocratic patron into a market of impersonal relations without a direct producer-client link. In the enlarged biennial system with, in Asia, its own regional specificities, the biennial becomes an institution of quasi-aristocratic patronage through the artist-curator relation which often produces for a selected slot in the curator's gift of a biennial selection on the opposite side of the world. This modality of selection for exhibition at a distance doubled with the very impersonality of a broad and unseen foreign public, and with a very small but more significantly constrained côterie of other biennial curators who could produce the same artist and often the same works into a biennial site which had not yet seen either.

The works and producers circulated in a market of esteem at biennials which precedes, and sometimes anticipates, the marketing of the same works and producers into a commercial market. Its players and motions are unseen by the artist, but have very significant implications for their economic livelihood and continued functioning. A cohort of artists who were in the China and Asia fields have subsequently advanced in sales with every year since 2005, outside the main period covered by this research. The market function of the biennials is to increase the sales of those already identified by it, particularly to some new Asian institutions within the Asian zone such as the Fukuoka Asian Art Museum, the Queensland Art Gallery, and the Singapore Art Museum or from 2015 the National Gallery of Singapore. This purchasing has two future functions: it reinforces the price by canonization of works by artists already in it, and it increases inter-institutional competition to secure for exhibition or purchase marker artists and their works across the region. This was clearly seen in 2014/2015 in international museum rivalry to purchase the works of the Thai abstractionist Chang Saetang.

The critical area for crisis or breakdown in this system is when the artistic value of an artwork does not find equivalence or recognition in its economic value as an art object. It is not clear even with work of commonly accepted artistic significance and economic value beyond particular national boundaries—such as Xu Bing's *Book of Heaven*—how or in what way this work contributes to the replenishment of values. How does it function in a feedback process back from economic values into cultural values? Whether such feedbacks worked for all art objects back into artworks or only did so for canonized monuments is unclear too. But it is unlikely that works not already canonized could function in this way and thus the negative, tyrannous effects of not being an entrant into the biennial system remain high.

But since the Asian biennials are a new extension of an old system, by around 2005 it was yet to be seen whether they could have fully generated their own relative autonomy. One cannot securely say whether any particular localized set of values and their operators in artists, curators, and some collectors, can function to impose these on the regional or even the more generalized biennial systems hitherto dominated by states and art markets in Euramerica. One can also envisage future and hypothetically geographical identification into at least Northeast Asian, Southeast Asian and loosely South Asia-Pacific subsystems, and in some small measure see that regional art markets may arise which are linked to biennial consecration of particular artists.

## Notes

1 See Charlotte Bydler, *The Global Art World Inc.: On the Globalization of Contemporary Art* (Upsala: Acta Universitatis Upsaliensis, 2004), 95–6.

2 Okwui Enwezor, "Mega Exhibitions and the Antinomies of a Transnational Global Form", *Manifesta Journal* 2 (Winter 2003/Spring 2004): 8.

3 Okwui, "Mega Exhibitions", 19.

4 See Jean-Marc Poinsot, "Large Exhibitions; a Sketch of a Typology", in *Thinking about Exhibitions*, ed. in Reesa Greenberg, Bruce W. Ferguson and Sandy Nairne (London: Routledge, 1996), 59–60.

5 See Poinsot, "Large Exhibitions", translating his earlier work of 1986 which appeared in Jean-Marc Poinsot, *L'Atelier sans mur* (Villeurbanne: Art édition, 1991).

6 Henry Meyric Hughes, "The History and Significance of the Biennale as an Instrument of Globalization" in *Art Criticism and Globalisation* (São Paolo: Assoçiao Brasiliera de Criticos de Arte, 2006). I am grateful to Henry Meyric Hughes for a 2004 draft of this paper, this citation from 13. Hughes earlier commented, "if we were cynical, we might merely suggest that they [biennials] offer a kind of ante-chamber to acceptance into the marketplace or the museum (a quick route to Salonfähigkeit [salonisability])".

7 Esche voiced his opposition to typologizing biennials as "a kind of tragedy", because he thinks, "One thing that Biennials have so far it seems to have avoided and need to continue to avoid is a process of institutionalization" (transcript adjusted). He made this statement during the general introductions to the 2006 Gwangju Biennale, at which I was present but for which my notes proved an inadequate record. I am grateful to Charles Esche for a copy of the transcription.

8 After Bydler, *The Global Art World Inc.*, 98, but much adjusted by John Clark.

9 Bydler, *The Global Art World Inc.*, 150. Block made this distinction in the Biennials in Dialogue conference in August 2000 which accompanied the exhibition whose catalogue was René Block and Martin Glaser et al., *Das Lied von der Erde / The Song of the Earth* (Kassel: Museum Fridericianum, 2000).

10 Bydler, *The Global Art World Inc.*, 151.

11 Okabe Aomi, "Gendaibijutsu no hen'yô to Bijutsuten", in *Kansha, Tenji, Kanshô, sono juyô no bijutsushi* (Heisei 14 nendo-16 nendokagaku kenkyûhi hojokin, Kenkyûhôkokusho no. 1430029), ed. Omuka Toshiharu (Tsukuba: Tsukuba Daigaku Geijutsugakkei, 2001), 44–5.

12 See Bydler, *The Global Art World Inc.*, 151.

13 See the discussion between Richard Vine, Christopher Phillips and Barbara Pollack, "Money talks Mandarin", *Art in America* (March 2007) and Andrea Bellini, "This is Not Enough: Contemporary Art in China or Chinese Contemporary Art?", at www.flashartonline.com, accessed on 5 January 2007.

14 "The Art Universe", *Vanity Fair* (December 2006): 230–1.

15 *Art Review* (October 2006).

16 Alain Quemin, *L'art contemporain international: entre les institutions et le marché (Le rapport disparu)* (Nîmes : Éditions Jacqueline Chambon/Artprice, 2002), 227 states:

> Les artistes issus des pays périphériques peuvent accéder aux expositions dans le cadre des Biennials, du moins certaines d'entre elles, mais que le marché leur reste très souvent fermé (du moins tant qu'ils ne passent pas par l'intermédiaire d'une grande galeries occidentale et/ou ne viennent s'établir dans le monde occidental).

17 Quemin, *L'art contemporain international*, 226–7, states:

> Car ailleurs, si nous avons pu observer que, de plus en plus, des artistes originaires de pays périphériques parviennent à se faire reconnaître au niveau international, nous avons pourtant jugé nécessaire de signaler dès la première partie de cette étude qu'il s'agit presque toujours d'artistes originaires de pays périphériques qui, sans être de nationalité américaine, ont souvent connu la consécration internationale en rejoignant les États-Unis où ils résident en créent généralement.

18 See Okwui, "Mega Exhibitions", 24. On the Triennale India see the special issue of *Lalit Kala Contemporary*, no. 36 (1990). "Indian artists had to be provided with a forum to view their works in the perspective of contemporary world art". The then Chairman of the Lalit Kala Akademi, Mulk Raj Anand, also noted "many Asian, African, and Socialist countries" had "not been able to establish a platform where the desired images of the oldest and youngest continents (youngest in the sense of secular achievements in the arts) may be seen together with the achievements of the dynamic west", ibid., 7.

19 See Quemin, *L'art contemporain international*, 226:

> Si les pays les plus riches ont laissé se développer des Biennials dans les pays périphériques, celles-ci ne concurrencent pas vraiment les manifestations les plus consacrées en ce domaine qui, pour leur part, restent clairement celles organisées par le monde occidental.

20 2008 Biennale of Sydney, Press Release of 7 June 2007. The website was www.artcompass2008.com.

21 Bydler, *The Global Art World Inc.*, 35–6.

22 John Clark, "An Australian Creative Space: Where is Australian-Asian Art Now?", in *2006/ Contemporary Commonwealth*, ed. Dianne Waite and curated by Charles Green and Mike Stubbs (Melbourne: Australian Centre for the Moving Image and National Gallery of Victoria, 2006), 26–33, discriminates the following types of culture and "state" units or their agglomerations in "inter-national" relations:

> 1. Large cultural ecumenes, often associated with a single language or dominant language, based on a very large single state or group of states which transfer their cultural products and the discourses which generate them far beyond any geographically restricted domain:
> a. Euramerica, formerly called "The West" and now largely sub-discriminated into 1b and 2a.
> b. America, comprising many domains of political, military, and economic activity enjoined with the multi-national capitalist economic system and with cultural flows now called "global", centred on the United States of America.
> c. The Sinicized world centred on and largely dominated by the People's Republic of China.

d. The South Indian world centred on the Republic of India.
2. Smaller cultural continua, mini-ecumenes, surrounding inter-state alliances, sometimes with an active cultural discourse and solidarity uniting them:
a. The states of the European Community.
b. The states of the Islamic world [potentially in Type 1, but without a single, large, dominating state].
c. The states of ASEAN.
d. Several layers of inter-relation between Latin American states.
e. Several layers of inter-relation between African states.
f. Historically speaking, colonial systems of various kinds with cultural phenomena which follow metropolitan models, eg. Fine Arts Societies on the British model in India, state-organized salons on the Japanese model in colonial Korea, Taiwan and Manchuria. Loose post-imperial associations such as the later Commonwealth, or La Francophonie, or the Commonwealth of Independent States based on the former Soviet Union, despite some common legal systems and a range of politico-social ideals, do not have the potential to constitute an ecumene based on a single large state.
3. Nation-states acting in hegemonic control over their own culture but which are in practice penetrated by global cultural phenomena yet also, and often in contradiction, structured by various kinds of assertion against the "outside" on the model of 19th century European states:
a. Korea, Japan, most ASEAN states when not acting through ASEAN, Australia, Canada, New Zealand.
b. European community states when acting as autonomous units.
c. Smaller states of Eastern Europe and Central Asia which have not yet prioritized inter-unit solidarity of the types found in 2.
d. Relatively more stable states in Latin America like Brazil or in Africa like Ghana.
4. Small states, non-state cultural enclaves within larger states, and diasporas in multi-state communities, which are not in hegemony over their own cultural customs, capital and products, but which have relative and interstitial freedom to assimilate or reject aspects of other cultures:
a. Island states scarcely culturally viable in isolation but capable of incorporating many aspects of inter-island culture, often of extraordinary generative richness e.g. the Antilles/Caribbean, where St Lucia, population 166,312, area 616 sq km, has produced two Nobel prizewinners, Sir W. Arthur Lewis (Economics, 1979); Derek Walcott (Literature, 1992).
b. Fragmented quasi-states, often the result of colonial division, in many parts of Africa and some parts of Latin America.
c. The semi-autonomous but culturally highly productive domains of Third World intellectuals in the Euramerican metropolises, including contemporary Asian artists who live overseas.
d. The communal domains of economic migrants in various groupings and strata.
e. Communities of political and cultural refugees, including religious cults suppressed in their homelands eg. Falonggong overseas.
5. Various further categories of non-state units which have an international activity and which are sometimes in a hegemonic relation to their own intraorganizational culture, sometimes not: international organizations and

> nongovernmental aid agencies; business companies with a multi- or trans-state identity; quasi-cartels among international art curators; some state intelligence agencies semi-autonomously functioning in a non-state mode; interstate terrorist groups and criminal gang cartels.

23 Bydler, *The Global Art World Inc.*, 43.

24 Rem Koolhaas in *D-Lab/The Second Guangzhou Triennial BEYOND: an Extraordinary Space of Experimentation for Modernization*, with artistic director Hou Hanru and curators Hou Hanru, Hans Ulrich Obrist, and Guo Xiaoyan (Guangzhou: Lingnan Chubanshe, 2006), 122.

25 Koolhaas, *D-Lab/The Second Guangzhou Triennial BEYOND*, 127. Interestingly among recent texts which handle the notion of "national brands", no mention is made of biennials in raising awareness of "other" cities. The major cultural events mentioned are Carnival (Rio de Janeiro), fashion shows (Milan), fringe festival (Edinburgh), the Academy Awards (Los Angeles), the Nobel awards (Stockholm), bull fighting (Madrid), pride day (San Francisco), fashion shows (Paris). See Simon Anholt, *Competitive Identity, the New Brand Management for Nations, Cities and Regions* (Houndmills: Palgrave Macmillan, 2007), 110.

26 Robert A. Beauregard, "Theorising the Global-Local Connection", in Paul L. Knox and Peter J. Taylor, *World Cities in a World-System* (Cambridge: Cambridge University Press, 1995), 235. Many other articles in this excellent collection are relevant to understanding how Biennials might function in a globalized economy focused on mega-cities, but few of them take up matters of culture, or specifically art.

27 Guo Xiaoyan in *The Second Guangzhou Triennial BEYOND: an Extraordinary Space of Experimentation for Modernization*, Exhibition Catalogue (Guangzhou: Lingnan Chubanshe, 2006, 59).

28 Okabe, "Gendaibijutsu no hen'yô to Bijutsuten", 33.

29 Okabe, "Gendaibijutsu no hen'yô to Bijutsuten", 33.

30 Okwui thought that

> the periphery does not simplistically absorb and internalize what it does not need. Nor does it vitiate its own critical power by becoming subservient to the rules of the center. In the wake of the globalization of culture and art, what the postcolonial response to it has produced is a new kind of space, a discourse of open contestations that spring not merely from resistance but are built rather on an ethics of dissent...postcolonial theory transforms the dissent into an enabling agent of historical transformation and is thus able to expose certain Western epistemological limits and contradictions. (Okwui, "Mega Exhibitions", 25)

31 Okwui also mentioned that "new relations of spectatorship" which disturb and resist "the nation-state's imperial claim to...territorial autonomy, self-determination, a view of economic totality and the ability to regulate economic and cultural life" rework the notion of spectacle and construct it "as the site of new relations of power and cultural translation" ("Mega Exhibitions", 31).

32 See Quemin, "L'art contemporain international", 179:

> Par ailleurs, nous avons pu montrer que la nationalité des artistes fait partie des critères qui sont pris en compte dans les anticipations effectuées par les acteurs qui, pour minimiser l'incertitude liée à la creation contemporaine, tiennent généralement compte des succès passés, contribuant ainsi à

reproduire la hiérarchie entre pays. Cela contribue donc encore à stabiliser les positions et limite les effets de toute politique "correctrice".

33 See Quemin, "L'art contemporain international", 226:

> Nous avons par ailleurs pu montrer toutes les limites de phénomènes aussi à la mode que ceux de la "globalisation", du métissage et du relativisme culturel, de la formidable ouverture aux différents culture du monde que met en avant le monde de l'art contemporain depuis plusieurs années, qui relèvent en réalité largement de l'illusion.

34 Most were available at http://www.arts.usyd.edu.au/departs/arthistory/research/workshops.html and I have freely adapted and summarized them here. I am grateful for the papers of Jennifer Milam (Art History), Russel Storer (late Ming China), Nick Reimer (Semantics), Michael Carter (Simmel's sociology), Julian Pefanis (Bataille, Clastres) and Tony Bond (Curatorship). My own short paper (Economics) is also used for the summary of models of circulation in this chapter.

35 On the recent behaviour of the Chinese art market see Joe Hill, "Taking Stock", *Yishu: Journal of Contemporary Chinese Art* (Winter 2007): 44–50, and other papers in this Special Issue on the Chinese Contemporary Art Market.

36 See Guo Hui, "New Categories, New History: The Preliminary Exhibition of Chinese Art in Shanghai, 1935", in *Crossing Cultures: Proceedings of the 32nd Congress of the International Committee of the History of Art (CIHA)*, ed. Jaynie Anderson (Melbourne: Melbourne University Press, 2009).

37 Particularly in the work of Craig Clunas, summarized in a paper given outside the Circulation Workshop above by Russel Storer but included on the workshop website.

38 A most stimulating recent overview of the roles of curators and their necessity is Boris Groys, "On the Curatorship", in *Art Power* (Cambridge, MA: MIT Press, 2008).

39 The research was designed and supervised by me and carried out by Thomas Berghuis whose own work greatly improved the outcomes.

40 With the exception of the statistically barely significant inclusion of two artists from Hong Kong and one from Taiwan in the Asia field.

Number of artists with more than 20 points:
China: 14
Asia: 5

41 *Cohort Size Comparisons:*

Sizes of cohorts
Asian to China artists
1089/ 881 = 123.4%
Asian to China curators
199/208 = 96%

42 *Chances of artist selection over both populations*

(Asia+China)/Asia
(1089+881)/1089 = 1.8
(Asia+China)/China
(1089+881)/882 = 2.2

43 *Chances of curatorial choice*

China: Artists/Curators
881/208 = 4.24/1

Asia: Artists/Curators
1089/199 = 5.4/1

44 My interview with René Block of 10 June 2006.

45 I owe this inference to the observations of Thomas Berghuis.

46 Francine Méoule according to our discussion of November 2007 in Amsterdam was planning a Thai art exhibition for the Enrico Navarra Galerie in Paris, along the lines of earlier activities by that gallery in the China field.

47 In a recorded interview with me in Japanese at Seoul on 24 September 2004.

48 For evidence of such movements see, for example, the exhibitions list in Lee Bul, *On Every New Shadow* (Paris: Fondation Cartier pour l'art contemporain, 2007).

# Chapter 8

# Conclusion

This conclusion will somewhat extend the earlier view of Asian biennials to the period between 2006 and 2012. It will also refer to a small part of the copious literature on curatorial studies which has recently appeared.[1]

## Art History and Asian Biennales

Why look at biennials in Asia?[2] These have usually been understood as part of a worldwide phenomenon of growth in large, regular, but temporary exhibitions. We can define biennials as periodically recurring temporary art exhibitions and usually surveys of both local and international contemporary art which are held at the same geographical site and usually presented by the same organizing institution. As the term indicates they are normally presented every two years such as the Venice Biennale (since 1895), the Biennale of Sydney (since 1973), the Bienal de Habana (since 1984), and the Shanghai Biennale (*Shanghai Shuangnianzhan*, since 1994) or Guangzhou Triennale (*Guangzhou Sannianzhan*, since 2002).

8.1 Catalogue cover of 7th Biennale of Sydney (1988).

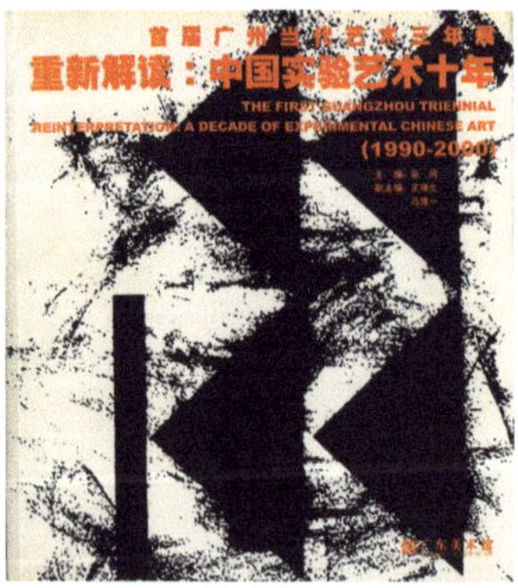


8.2 Catalogue cover of 1st Guangzhou Triennale (2002).

The new Asian biennials which began in the 1990s had Euramerican precursors that often functioned as prescriptive models, or from which, by reaction, they may have sought to differentiate themselves.

One basic perspective for understanding Asian biennials could be the comparative one: how like or unlike their precursors are they, or how basically derived from Euramerican predecessors are they? But that approach carries the art historical premise that in modern and contemporary art it is the Euramerican series of works and institutions and actors which is prior, not the local Asian ones. It leaves aside precisely the local adaption and transformation in changed historical contingencies that should be accepted has accompanied modern Asian art since the 1850s.[3] The very difference in types of adaption, transformation, and local development produces a notion of modernity which may not merely be beyond Euramerican categories, it forces the very re-definition of those Euramerican categories. This means the inclusion of Euramerican historical experiences and notions of modernity within a broader set, not as originator, but as one type within a hierarchy of modernities.[4] One of the art historical reasons for focussing on Asian biennials is that they constitute a site for such modernities to become manifest.

It is often thought that biennials function as an international publicity site or sales point for those who would otherwise have neither advertising hoarding nor shop. On the one hand biennials manifest the hidden hand of a local cultural bureaucracy and local taste. On the other hand, because biennials' entrepreneur-managers are drawn almost entirely from those who have become prominent in Euramerican curating, the advent of particular artists could show the hidden hand of the art market as it operates through the preferences of curators who by inclusion of an artwork determine its cultural value. Sometimes they serve as the cultural capital acquisitions' managers for the art objects bought by collectors and public museums.

Another focus on Asian biennials concerns definitions of the "contemporary". Beyond any simple notion of contemporary art being simply what is done now, the "contemporary" is a trope allowing a separation from the hegemonic discourse of the "modern".[5] However defined, the "contemporary" posits that at some time in the recent past, say in the shift from pop to conceptual art in the late 1960s, there was a broad and multi-causal change in Euramerican art discourses.

Terry Smith identifies postmodernist thought freed from the constraints of singular narratives, a retro-sensationalism trending into the spectacular, and re-modernism, or a conceptualist re-formulation and conscious display of modernist devices, as the three bounding elements in contemporary art. These are articulated alongside three transnational transitions of decolonization and nationalism, globalization and internationalism, and for cosmopolitanism and inter-communal translation.

Smith also identifies concerns and strategies such as world-making and temporal discontinuities. It is part of the attractiveness of Smith's analyses and the generality with which they can be applied outside his originating set found in, but not always derived from Euramerica, that Asian examples appear without too much difficulty. Or, once designated, do so without much much feeling of inappropriateness. By setting aside the notion of the rest of the world as "Third World", associated with a long chain of principally left thinkers allied to the journals like *Third Text* or *October*,[6] or from another capitalist liberalist perspective as "Newly Industrialized Economies", or again as another avatar of the singularity of the Euramerican modern,[7] the grasp of Smith's Euramerican frame has enormously widened. However, that this frame yet allows evidence for a global cosmopolitanism is sincerely to be doubted, even if one believes, as I do, that this is possible.[8]

8.3 Phaptawan Suwannakudt's *Home (away from home)* (2011), seems more an effort at inter-communal translation, mixing Thai cloths, Australian house-shapes and photographs of the doorway of a destroyed Palestinian home. Exhibited at *Edge of Elsewhere* (2012), Campbelltown Art Gallery, Sydney. Photograph by John Clark.

The art historical grasp of movements which give sovereignty to all the domains between which transfer take place, not just the Euramerican one, requires relativizing the contemporary as temporally—and in many cases culturally—specific. Thus we encounter another important reason for looking at Asian biennials: they are another site which tells us—if "we" still need telling—where the West is no longer the West anymore. This is because the historical viewpoint capable of grasping work found at the Asian biennial site must be beyond both the temporality of the Euramerican—read "global contemporary"—and the cultural limitation of the West. In addition, in any constellation which includes the Asian "contemporary", the range and distributions of elements which define it as

"Asian" will be counterposed to those which are "Euramerican", as indeed also in some selections of works, put alongside those which are "South American", "African" or "Near Eastern / West Asian". How this counter-position allows a differential mapping of a broader generic series of "modernities" requires some effort to understand, but it can be seen as both theoretically necessary and empirically feasible.[9]

## Markets for Transnational Art Selection

In looking at biennials as part of the structure and operations of an international art system, it becomes clear that the notion of art flows which are governed by the hidden hand of the art market requires much qualification. In the 1990s and early 2000s, art markets were many-levelled and provided multiple switching points between artworks which had cultural value and art objects which had economic value, as discussed earlier.[10] Many local markets separated in quasi-autonomy from international markets, like that of *pleinairiste* oil painting in Japan. But despite the barely disguised tendency in the early 2000s of some Chinese contemporary artists and, since around 2005, of Indian artists, to sell directly via auction houses, the secondary market in near-contemporary artworks was largely a market of historical objects. These objects may even indirectly have been those of the near past, for which time or cultural distance had sufficiently elapsed for some kind of *market* appraisal as art objects independent of their original *cultural*

8.4 Installation view of Huang Yong Ping, *Ressort* [from French, springiness, resilience] (2012). Exhibited at the 7th Asia Pacific Triennial of Contemporary Art (2012), Watermall, Queensland. Photograph by John Clark.

consecration as artworks to have taken place. Of course, cultural consecration can come before the economic, especially for some national agendas. In addition, many artworks found at biennials are not saleable, being temporary or project installations. Indeed where the biennial is held in an art museum, some works can be purchased by commission, such as a series of works over a number of APTs at Brisbane. In a few cases too, parts of works can be re-assembled as series from which units can be sold via dealers. The biennial may thus serve as an archive of works assembled from recordings or re-mediations of works at other sites. These are now offered for consecration or re-consecration at the biennial before sending on to other museums, to collectors, or to commercial galleries.

## Curators and their Professional Institutionalization

Work at Asian biennials is also highly mediated, necessarily so because the mediators were not fixed in institutional positions up until the 2000s, being frequently employed for one-off appointments *in this system*. However, that they mostly appeared at a given biennial only once did not mean mediator-curators appeared only once at biennials. A principal motivation for their operations was necessarily to remain as operators *in this system*: The overall network of biennials and other "independent" curatorial activities itself *functioned institutionally* as the series of sites within which curators worked, rather than a single, relatively isolated, city or state-based institution. This means that the curators' rhetoric of "independence" and "free selection" has to be taken sceptically, even if such conventional meanings should be accepted in some contexts, for some curators.

This rhetoric has several severe consequences for art history where the notion of canon, the diachronically delimited set of important and sometimes turning-point works, holds a sway for which the comparative knowledge of art historians was authorizing.[11] But curators at many Asian biennials did not feel they had to await such judgements. They authorized their own selections of work by their relevance to what they considered were the significant contemporary issues in aesthetic or political values.[12] By eliding the criteria for long-term judgements or by escaping from history to perform the function of both art critic and, in the disposition of artworks, something of the functions of an artist arranging the structure of an aesthetic experience, curators came to see their own practice as self-authorizing.[13]

Bryszki has told us early on in her studies that canons are both hierarchically ordering, have generative functions, and that:

> The canon is simply a function of the thinking in terms of traditions and historic narratives.[14]

In art historical constructions, like evaluating Manet against Bouguereau,[15] canons can often be proleptic, self-valuing and validating moves by thinkers to create evaluatory paradigms against an historical template such as Modernism, and contemporary artists also try to control canon formation in their own favour.

In antithesis Smith considers that we have to look at what a canon could be if the "inspirational ground" of an artist's practice is the breaking of previous canons.[16] Smith concludes that, given his view of contemporaneity as a space of co-existent but incommensurably multiple meanings, canons as "paradigms that take hold" are "fundamentally antithetical to the very possibility of this kind of universalizing canon formation."[17] He thinks that "the failure of a canon...is not that a selection has been made, but that the particular selection is held to be general, to be of universal significance, and too often, to be binding on future practitioners".[18]

If we turn back now to the questions of how art curating varies in different countries of Asia, and to what the role of the curator might be when an infrastructure for art does not yet exist, we can see from the concept of establishing a canon or a non-canon that the curator's role is determined by whether curators hermeneutically oppose tradition to a non-tradition. Whereas, and often in a mode incompatible with curators' assessment, art historical interpreters can simply be arguing about two different time perceptions of the same set of phenomena and may fail to distinguish the artists' canon, the curators' canon, the art historians' canon, the collector's canon, the museum canon. The artist and the curator in some ways have a compact—against the art historian—to admit the artist's works to the canon, to give them an impossible historical weight even as they are buoyed up on the indeterminate multiplicities indicated by Smith. Here art historical interpreters may fail to discriminate canons by the functionality of the hierarchy imposed in the interests of the figure making the selection, the curator. This is more a matter of artists becoming curators, not of curators becoming artists. Our contemporary obsessions with celebrity, one which is fuelled by the very swirling catalysts of the present, have led us to confuse makers and mediators, as if the known equals known-ness. But let us concede to Baudrillard that this critique, *pace* simulacra, is only possible in cultural domains where there are at least physical traces of the work. Thinking of these functions and the necessary self-interest in those performing them, the art historical canon-making effect necessitates a temporal distancing of different appraisals. It involves not merely a horizontal separation, but with the passage of time a vertical separation as well. Such canons seem to function cyclically or spirally by the rotation of similar appraisals through different works and the curator stands magus-like as the controller of the algorithms at the centre of these forces. Appraisals may exclude or include in any selection, that is, formulators of the canon can either acknowledge or refuse admission of an artwork to the canonical set.[19]

The ground of inclusion/exclusion may vary from notions of profundity and superficiality, genuineness and in-authenticity, exemplary status from outstanding to minor, or range of cultural transmissibility from the transnational to the ethnic. In Thailand I know of curators who have excluded artists from exhibition because they were considered "ethnic" and not "transnational".

8.5 Installation view of Pinaree Sanpitak, *Breast Stupa Cookery* (2005). Mixed media installation as part of the Soi Project at the Yokohama Triennale, 2005. Image by John Clark, courtesy of Pinaree Sanpitak.

And on the contrary, in China I know of an outer-directed, even at times culturally aggressive, push to have some artists recognized who do "ethnic" transformations of "traditions" in order to give prominence to a neo-traditional art as "modern" or "contemporary".

There is clearly no hard and fast rule about such selections between Asian art cultures. In one instance the "ethnic" selection might end up looking as and sometimes more "transnational" than the usual selections, and in another "the ethnic modern" can look like about as far away from the "transnational contemporary" as is possible.

These cycles can be both short-term for contemporary art curators and long-term for museum directors, with leads and lags between the establishment of exhibition goals, selection of works, and the success or failure of exhibition outcomes. Both in the short-term and the long-term the match of goals to outcomes may be determined by the particular functions of artists' public discourse and by the way individual responses are articulated into côterie or larger collective opinions.[20]

The problem of mutual regard and formation of taste or of selection patterns, that is of regularities of aesthetic viewpoint and regularities of consecration, within the mediator-curator group has been shown in principle and in fact by my research on biennials. That the group of mediator-curators who move between biennials is a restricted, small, and not an open or unlimited group, with several levels of interior hierarchy and competition, was also found. It was highly significant that this group although largely Euramerican had major members from Latin America, one or two from Africa, and several from different parts of Asia. In this sense they constituted a group of actors within a transnational institutional system which was formed from a network of temporally recurrent and internationally interlinked sites. This system perhaps more flexibly allows for the representation of cultural difference than one based on relations between nation-state units. Within this system, the curatorial group has governance, control principles, and underlying ideologies which are more heterogenous and probably more easily subject to personal careerism. A national and long-term institutional system formed of established museums and galleries all have, art historically speaking, relatively controlled agendas for genealogies of the modern and how to gain these prominence internationally.

There are now quite a few books which analyse the roles and status of the curator so that these may be more clearly understood during curating courses, and facilitate the practice of curating to become the subject of academic study.[21] Many of these developments have affected Asian biennials, particularly the notion of curator as exhibition author. Everyone who has been to an Asian biennial launch will know the phenomena of the curator as master operator, sometimes as international messiah, sometimes as compromised servant-in-charge of the city or of the national cultural authorities.

But some of these curatorial analyses do not apply in Asia. They seem to be based on the most progressivist interpretation of Euramerican situations, such as the notion that the role of curator has been de-mystified.[22] Through the history of the Gwangju Biennale, for example, two of which I have visited and most of whose catalogues I have studied, whether instituted collaboratively or via an über-curator, or whether with reference panels of ordinary citizens checking on curatorial decisions, the curatorial function has been continuously articulated in terms of power over artists, art groups, and audiences. As one authority, O' Neill, elsewhere acknowledges,[23] biennials serve to canonize works

8.6 Singapore Biennale 2006 opening press conference, featuring artistic director Nanjô Fumio (extreme left). Photograph by John Clark.

and rank artists, curators, and biennial organizing institutions and countries. For not a few countries—and it is national political agendas indubitably which set the funding levels and sources for Asian biennials—if such exhibitions did not have such a ranking function and did not distribute "our" artworks or artists into the international art world, as well as into other kinds of markets for symbolically high-value consumer goods, I believe there would be no political or economic support for them.

## The Quandary of Curatorial Selection

Again within such a transnational system, the domains of choice of curator and of curatorial choice of artworks were highly problematic when so much of the surface propaganda of artists, curators, and biennials, involved the rhetoric of the new, emerging, discovered, or profound. Curatorial rhetoric also mobilized terms like open, generous, process-centred, and experimental, to characterize a presumed homology between the exhibition structure, its selections, and the kinds of work and artists exhibited. How curation can be open and generous when the whole aesthetic imperative and technical necessity of curatorial practice requires curators to exclude a very large number of currently active artists and their works, escapes my imagination. The regularities identified in this research on the part of both artworks and art mediators meant that they were strongly subject to previously arrived-at positions. Large collector interventions via the purchase of particular artists or their subsequent sale, such as the purchase of works of by Sandro Chia and Julian Schnabel and then their subsequent sale by Charles Saatchi, indicated that there could still be a taste-setting effect from outside the existing system by merchant-collectors. But their collectors' intervention in other nationally demarcated art fields such as Saatchi's entry into the China market, including purchase of works by Zhang Dali, indicate that such collectors' behaviour is regularized, and that their choices have predictable directions. Here also operated the intermediate or secondary mediation of artist-advisors such as Shen Shaomin for the gallerist and now foundation director Gene Sherman in Sydney, and Wang Zhiyuan for White Rabbit Gallery collection in Sydney.

## An "Asian" Set of Biennial Structures

Parallel to difficulties in understanding how the market in art objects—artworks considered as economic goods—actually operates, perhaps the greatest operational difficulty in understanding the international biennials' system as much as new biennials in Asia is the lack of transparency about their own economic structure. I can think of no biennial which has a fully clear costing system: all the Asian biennials examined have large and undeclared system costs because the institutions where they were based did not charge the biennial budget for their services.

Or the relevant local, regional, or national governments did not charge for rental or use of buildings or staff. Neither did they charge the cost of capital construction, nor factor in the training costs of curators working in new areas. Even if there are reasonably reliable figures in the public domain such as for the Singapore Biennale, these do not usually include a notional rent for buildings and properties used for exhibitions. More importantly there are many indirect benefits for financial sponsors or contra-exchanges with sponsors or other institutions such as that declared by Queensland Art Gallery in its 2005 report, as cited in chapter 5. In addition indirect benefits flowed to those galleries or patrons supporting the making of large artworks which were shown at biennials for which the financial benefits were recouped later at sale via a commercial gallery. For example, the works shown in a Venice Biennale may appear one or two years later in the Basel Art Fair, Basel-Miami and now also Basel-Hong Kong. With some artists or artworks who are highly prominent on the biennial circuit there is a kind of venture or speculative capital investment by individual curatorial entrepreneurs able to mobilize these funds from dealers or collectors to subsidize exhibition at Venice which is recouped by later sales.[24]

Even despite variation in the structure of curation, one might call it fiddling, at say Gwangju, biennials still by and large function as national art sites. They do so either through national representation as at São Paolo or Venice, or by the dedicated subvention to an artist such as the official funding for French, German, and Japanese artists to Sydney. This amounts to financial support for those Biennials. Indeed the former artistic director of the Biennale of Sydney, René Block, has suggested that there are three biennial models:

- Venice: Pavilions and national autonomy; completely financed by participating countries, followed by the early São Paolo Biennials.
- Sydney: Smaller exhibitions curated by an artistic director, but dependent on the financial participation of other countries, a model followed by most biennials in the 1980s and 90s.
- Gwangju: independent of foreign support, sometimes determines themes then invites curators. Other examples of such independence are the Berlin Biennale and Sharjah Biennale.[25]

Biennial participation and organization are intrinsically operations within international cultural relations, almost all with political motivation. These political aims, whether of a regional kind as in Gwangju or Brisbane, whether of national dimension such as in Yokohama and Beijing, are much clearer in newer biennials. These tend to have been founded with an explicit claim to a local, governmental funding body, a claim which requires a statement of intent and a formal perception and evaluation of political outcomes for the funds invested.[26] Ridiculous curatorial

8.7 The opening audience of the First Beijing Biennale (2003) mingling. Photograph by John Clark.

8.8 First Beijing Biennale (2003) opening event, with a performance gate-crasher being escorted away by security officials. Photograph by John Clark.

claims have been made about the political independence of the biennial or its artistic director when these were intrinsically operated for political aims, and often with explicitly political goals, and in most cases impossible without the direct support of the nation-state and complicity with its goals.

Perhaps the external goals too often cast into shade the internal goals of the exhibiting organization, whether a "temporary" biennial office or an institutionally founded extant gallery. The biennial has an agentive function for its organizers which allows them, with time and politicians' perception of their success, to secure broader support for contemporary art and the funding for a new National Art Gallery (Singapore), Gallery of Modern Art (Brisbane), or to establish the biennial as an exhibitionary compensation for the lack of such an institution (Jakarta). The biennial even functions as a switching mechanism to give contemporary art a place it had not properly found in existing well-founded institutions which were perceived as in the hands of cultural conservatives (New Delhi, unrealized).

However, at the national level, despite their political goals and particularly in Asia, biennials have highly contradictory identities as a unit. They operate on behalf of a nation but they function with other units which are international, be they other states or their cultural organizations. The context is not one of permanently isolated or relatively closed bodies, but of those which open to their exterior under certain conditions. Biennials deal with producers and mediators who increasingly have multiple geographical identities, travelling between states for education, exhibition or information access. Even though many artists and mediators place themselves as belonging to, or as having originated in, one nation-state, they of necessity move, are mobile, or know they can move. These potentialities are part of the interlocked trajectories which form their art or the criteria used to select works for exhibition. They thus constitute a transnational personnel cohort, and insofar as these cohorts produce interpersonal relations, a transnational cultural space. That they do so is in part due to the opportunities of the new global economic and political systems.

But this cosmopolitanism is rooted in one national situation or another, and is not independent of them. The biennial manifests the different stages and strategies of becoming for a nation and the national art world phenomena articulated through it. At the same time, it makes real a new trajectory away from the nation which is not necessarily towards a hybrid inter-nation, but allows for the display of tendencies found across all national sites. The biennial thus proclaims that interspace and denies the small units—the nations—which need to have been gone beyond for that interspace to be composed. This is an intrinsic contradiction which mitigates in favour of a new trans-nation. Even as it strengthens the possibility of national emphasis as identity or origination within a new order, it also mitigates *against* the nation as a unit with which to constitute the system. In this ambiguity lies the system's dynamic, but also its possibility of abuse.

The policies of biennials as an institution which provides services to a patron, usually a local or national government, and of servicing clients who are artists and viewers of art, again reinforces the possibilities of the mediator-curator. This figure stands between guaranteeing the satisfactory provision of the service to a certain perceived standard, and of satisfying the need for artists to be recognized and of audiences to see art which they recognize as such. In certain cases such as Gwangju and Chengdu, because the notion of its contemporaneity in art might have been unfamiliar for much of the local audience, biennials often have a pedagogical role for audiences which remain to be educated in the unfamiliar concept of art, and its problematic contemporary overthrow. Much of the audience in the start-up years of a biennale at least may have no idea that these concepts were involved in their receiving or enjoying it. Indeed some of the events may have been the subject of random interventions by the eccentric exhibitionists or the politically inept, a bit like sports final "streaking" in Europe. The convenient relation to an untutored audience or an as yet unconventionalized "contemporary" display code, is highly suitable to the unquestioned propagation of claims by curators about their exhibition's concepts or significance: the site they are occupying on the audience side is not a critical or an educated one. This is despite the fact that curators themselves may think that their own position with regard to art and even to Biennials is critical.

## Evacuation of Art Historical Meaning

In this context of relations, the biennial catalogue performs an important role as a symbolic embodiment of the exhibition which has a permanent status in the secondary after-life of the event. Unfortunately, many of these catalogues are simply textual domains for the second-hand regurgitation of intellectual debates about art in a popularly accessible and journalistic form. Much of the artist or work information in them is a mere transposition from another catalogue or from the CV supplied by the artists or their gallery.

It is also barely possible to offer critical interpretation of artworks from the catalogues after the biennial, even where the catalogue was designed to allow for this, because the work or artist selected was paradigmatically deemed to have been important by the fact of selection. Many biennial catalogues include images of works by artists which are simply not those in the exhibition. Similarly, many biennial catalogue texts are not about the exhibition but take up some political or cultural atmosphere which is inferred by the curator or curatorial team to surround or contextualize current art practice, that is to problematize it. I have no difficulty with expressions of belief in art, political or otherwise, but I do have difficulty if these are allied to a mystification of the curatorial role, and the presumption of unproblematic acceptance of views which may or may not be those of the catalogue reader. A later viewer would retrospectively get a very strange idea about the biennale or exhibited works from the catalogue which is often not a record of an exhibition that took place but a kind of preliminary, notional album. Curators are frequently insincere in not saying why they had excluded a whole range of contemporary practice or works, let alone other distinguished works, representative of given art worlds, which did not meet the criteria of "contemporary" or a more specific curatorial concept. Some exhibitions, such as Documenta in 2007, perhaps in recognition of this problem, even had a separate photo-album with barely recognizable works which were inconsistently or opaquely credited, and it needed an exhibition visit and some specialist knowledge to identify them.[27]

I have problematized issues of circulation via reference to biennial typologies and to data dealing with artists and curators. There is in addition a wide variety of anecdotal material available from field observations about particular works in biennials and the movements in and out of circles of evaluation by given artists. I will here recapitulate parts of this third range of materials.

Since many artists only enter the biennial circuit once and do not re-appear or are selectively left out thereafter, we may get further hints about the structure of Biennials from brief examination of such cases. Akioka Miho and Xu Jiang were exhibited in APT I in 1993 but were not noticeably active in exhibition at Asian Biennials after that.[28] Akioka's work was characterized by an ink painting aesthetic with a certain type of sensibility we may call "feminine" applied to Japanese media through the relatively high-tech device of high-definition advertising printing on absorbent Japanese paper. This is an attractive and sensitive approach produces works of quite transforming affectiveness. But it is neither a self-proclaimedly contemporary position, nor indeed a particularly conceptually articulate one.

8.9 Performance documentation of Jun Nguyen-Hatsushiba, *Fever Variation* (2006), curated by Binghui Huangfu, 6th Gwangju Biennale (2006), South Korea. According to some oral reports, the bottles were gradually filled up with his own urine. See the blog post by Rosemary Heather, https://rosemheather.com/2011/10/21/the-2006-gwangju-and-singapore-biennales-by-rosemary-heather/. The work is *Story of the Stars*. Photograph by John Clark.

Xu Jiang engaged in a kind of clumsy conceptualism whose statement was momentary, but not particularly extended, and could seem like a simpler Chinese academic trial of previous work by, say, Rauschenberg or Johns. It did not hide the trace of its own imitativeness. Once national selection is removed as a criterion of selection, or the unspoken need to acknowledge an artist of some administrative power within the Chinese art world is no longer required, this selection was unnecessary. Similar comments can be made about some senior Indonesian artists included in the APT I.

Tsubaki Noboru is another artist who had appeared in international Japanese art exhibitions in the 1980s especially *Against Nature* in 1989. He was left out of biennials until selection for the first Yokohama Triennale in 2001 in a work jointly conceived with the media theorist Muroi Hisashi. Why was this exceptionally talented artist not part of the wave of Asian selections at Venice in the 1990s?[29] Why did he have to wait until he was selected for national prominence? Clearly the receptivity of the Euramerican-centred art critical discourse and the marketability of his work were one set of issues in the 1990s. Another must have been that he was (wrongly) perceived as an artist who merely engaged in sensationalist spectacles behind which there was not much conceptual articulation. The danger to circulation of the artist or work transnationally must therefore be that either or both of these are perceived as aesthetically insignificant or trivial according to criteria fixed at a given time, and that these restricted, de-selectioning views are only with difficulty later overcome when assisted by local (re-)selection.

Some artists appear to be well aware of these dangers. After an initial "dream run" of international biennial selections, Jun Nguyen-Hatsushiba in 2007 moved away sharply from his underwater video work which had stereotyped him.[30] At Gwangju 2006 he exhibited an engaging conceptual piece involving water bottles which had to be filled up and moved aside to allow the artist passage.

Other artists are carefully aware of the danger of over-domination by one curatorial interpretation, or demand for, one type of their work. Yi Bul (Lee Bul), who became internationally renowned for her be-sequinned, decorated raw fish that had to be displayed in a refrigerator at the first APT in 1993, soon moved to flying cybernauts, formed in reinforced resin plastic like a Star Wars warrior, and by 2006–07 to artificial playground machines.[31] Some of her work was so successful it appeared to have been the stimulus to other artists across the Asian region including Lee Hyung-koo in Korea and Shen Shaomin in China.

## Curatorial Selection and De-selection

What accounted for this movement of artist and their work in or out of biennial circulation? In some cases like that of some large pieces by Ai Weiwei, this circulation can be of essentially the same massive piece in different edition-guises between biennial and museum of contemporary art sites.

8.10 Interviewing Lu Jie, director of Long March Group at the *Shanghai Biennale 2004: Techniques of the Visible*. The circulations of artworks through media or online are now crucial. Photograph by John Clark.

At a first level, the cause was a fairly marked set of differences between the actual circulation of the artist or works and the virtual circulation by what we might think of as mediatized personalities or objects as information. Sometimes this information is itself already mediatized. The information is not ostensibly about actual or real artists and artworks which have some quotidian existence in the physical world apart, from their presence in the chiefly photographic or electronic media. But this second issue is too large and diffuse to handle here, even if satisfactory empirical evidence were available.

At the first level it could be that after the initial selection, some kind of system-stabilizing function was performed by the opinions arrived at and circulated between curators. These views then became a convention of the circuit cementing in, or in most cases cementing out, future selection of the same artist or works. This process is all the more effective for the negative power of these judgements which could only be so effective because there is an implicit need to maintain the restrictiveness of the selection and therefore the relative closure of the system. This exclusion increases the apparent regularity and order of the system as well as reinforces the status of those privileged to maintain it, the mediator-curators.

## Types of Functioning of the Global(ized) Art World

If borrowing between artists, the existence of common discourses or at least related positions in art practices are basic features of the transnational art world, similarities of technical parameters in video, use of resins, modelling techniques borrowed from architectural displays, are more ways of extending but not necessarily productively moving away from earlier positions. Biennials faced not just the problems of common practices and techniques which have faced most art worlds, but with creating the ability to find art which moves between cultures. This is in some sense a counter-systemic capability, one which can still be inflected culturally with benefit to its inter-referentiality. This potential of biennials as exhibitionary spaces or sites still retains the disjunction between those exhibitors or selectors or audiences who see work elsewhere and those who do not. Information might flow across old boundaries but many of the practitioners and most of the audiences still do not.

Would it be valuable or feasible to have a continually floating, relatively elastic transnational art world? I think not. The limitations of political censorship may maintain walls, but so do value impediments based in one set of cultural values at a particular site, be it New York, Paris, Dhaka, or Dakar. These limitations or constraints are needed to create a potential space for change rather than an eternal fluidity. Many artists still have their eyes either on Euramerica or on home wherever they locate it. Nonetheless, some convivial and co-discursive relations do emerge for individual artists by their participation in non-Euramerican biennials.[32] The transnational art world, because it in general vertically relies on Euramerican art media for information circulation and on Euramerican art markets for the circulation of works, still lacks a critical press and a distribution system of its own which would have achieved the horizontal circulation of ideas and works between non-Euramerican sites. This can be seen through the elevation of a very limited number of Asian artists to international art star status, and the restriction of the rest to the role of interesting but minor players.

One might think that the Asian biennials are intended to achieve this horizontal circulation for Asian contemporary art. They have done this to some extent, and may increasingly do so in future, if Asian inter-linkages become more stable and developed beyond so many sets of binary national exchanges. But the latter step will only be possible if this biennial sub-system were to develop a regionally specific type of transnationality, and did not think it must forever be defined in Euramerican terms.

## Re-definitions of Modernity and the Asian Modern

Many biennial curators consider themselves to be working in domains which permit them to engineer the escape of contemporary art discourses from previous control hegemonies based on resisting hitherto Euramerican modernist genealogies:

colonial, class-based, and gender-demeaning.[33] Their considered task is to make the artwork more visible and their own work in sighting it more transparent. Some think the artist and the curator have merged.[34] It is not self-evident why such an embedded set of choices in highly organized if recurrently temporary sites, whose space is as institutional as the curators' place in it is circumscribed, should be regarded as radical unfoldings of the new. These phenomena look more like a Euramerican transfer to independent Asian curators of the functions of Western intellectuals under early Bolshevism as "engineers of human souls".[35] This could be a sign of an older hegemony re-establishing itself.

The aims and some of the operations of such curators are understandable and, from some political positions, laudable in their own way. But they do not help us with two persistent sets of questions because of ideological hostility to the artwork conceived of as a hang-over from high bourgeois salon practice which needs to be de-mystified. And many curators also repeatedly conceive of art *making* as art *production* which is materialist and communal. This impedes understanding of the role of imagination in art-making which is idealist and based in individual needs and skills. Indeed the "curatorial turn" towards privileging the site, mode, and operator of the site of exhibition, is a denudation of the function of artworks as imaginative extensions of an other-than-quotidian space, as a way of knowing the world which does not depend on reason or planning, and as the work of a making agent, the artist, who is the exhibitor of first resort, not the last.

De-mystification systemically de-privileges other kinds or culturally distant but potentially still cognate types of mystification. We cannot assume modern and

8.11 Marc Boucherot, reproduction of *Mobile Cinema Projection* (2005), in situ at the Second Guangzhou Triennale, 2005. Image courtesy of the artist.

contemporary Asian artworks are all compromised by the Euramerican genealogy of modernism, or in the same ways. Understanding the discursive field of Asian modernism and its classificatory possibilities as well as its transformations of Euramerican modernism must begin from this recognition.

Taking the second and more important set of questions a bit further, everyday space is not the same everywhere, although it might misleadingly appear so in the "airport lounge" spaces of high or post-modernity. There are so many culturally framed ways of knowing the world other than by "universal" reason that any such knowings via artworks will always be larger than the paradigmatic Euramerican set. Thus the curator will also appear as an authorial position denuded by the complex interplay of cultural, social, and economic forces, let alone embedded aesthetic preferences in artworks, as would any artwork produced as an art object. These specific forces have been ignored in the spectacularization of the site in multiplying Asian biennials and in the restricted list of operators who constitute the curatorial field or the limited number of artists who constitute its producers.

But the most critical question concerns modernity itself. If our understanding of Asian biennials is framed by an inquiry into Asian modernity and contemporaneity in art, we will see the biennials as manifestations of a quite discrete if not entirely independent series of frames into which some, but not all, of Euramerican engagements fit. It is the "some but not all" which is the critical lever here. Unfortunately only recently have Asian biennials themselves, together with some linkages through the networks of artist-run spaces, made the inter-regional comparability of Asian art worlds and the functioning of artworks, artists, and curators much more feasible, and in cases of linkages to the wider world, pressing.

Transnationality can be seen to function as a site beyond national constructions, and trans-globality can be regarded as a supranational distributional phenomenon of significant forces in art. Both can overlap and, in their resistance to other-imposed hegemonies, also be in conflict. They are as important phenomena as they are bewitching. I think they have diverted attention from the varieties of modernity and contemporaneity, and occluded understanding types of modernity other than the Euramerican. There is every sign that the linkage between biennials and market appraisal via regional art fairs, of which the linkage of Art Basel Hong Kong to art markets in China and Japan is only the most prominent, has almost in the last hour vitiated understanding Asia as having its own modernities.

Beyond these phenomena, as operating sites of art world forces Asian biennials have significantly globalized what was a burgeoning local Asian set of markets for Asian contemporary art. The plethora of biennials in Asia as *de facto* canon-makers transnationally intervenes with and alters what are judgements about the contemporary in Asian art in its different cultural locales. These judgements are conventionalized by shifting evaluatory criteria to a top-down transnational level. Transnational processes thus evacuate the Asian modern of its global meaning as a reflexive re-positioning of the *modern* in art.

## Notes

1 I am not going to re-cite here other works on curating cited earlier. More recent texts include Paul O'Neill and Mick Wilson, ed., *Curating and the Educational Turn* (London: Open Editions; Amsterdam: De Appel, 2010); Paul O'Neill, *The Culture of Curating and the Curating of Culture(s)* (Cambridge, MA: MIT Press, 2012); the Biennales Foundation; *Yishu: Journal of Chinese Contemporary Art* 12, 2 (May/June 2013), which included some of the papers from the World Biennale Forum no.1 held in Gwangju in October 2012. Its proceedings are published as Ute Meta Bauer and Hou Hanru, ed., *Shifting Gravity, World Biennial Forum No.1* (Gwangju: The Gwangju Biennale Foundation; Ostfildern: Haje Cantz Verlag, 2012). As noted ealier, this has been followed by the papers from the second symposium in São Paolo, 2014, by Galit Eilat et al., eds., *Making Biennials in Contemporary Times* (Amsterdam: Biennial Foundation; São Paolo: Fundação Bienal de São Paolo; Instituto de Cultura Contemporânea, 2015).

2 I have been nudged by friendly colleagues to bind myself by the Anglophone conventions which now prefer the standard "biennial" form except for those exhibitions actually named as "biennales" or "triennales".

3 See John Clark, *Modern Asian Art* (Sydney: Craftsman House; Honolulu: University of Hawai'i Press, 1998), 49–70.

4 I have done this for a Chinese-Thai comparison. See John Clark, *Asian Modernities: Chinese and Thai Art of the 1980s and 1990s* (Sydney, Power Publications, 2010), 26–7.

5 See in particular Terry Smith, *What is Contemporary Art? Contemporary Art, Contemporaneity and Art to Come* (Sydney: Artspace Visual Art Centre, 2001); Terry Smith, *What is Contemporary Art?* (Chicago: University of Chicago Press, 2009); Terry Smith, "The State of Art History: Contemporary Art", *The Art Bulletin* 92, 4: 366–83; and his examination of artworks seen worldwide, Terry Smith, *Contemporary Arts: World Currents* (London: Laurence King Publishing, 2011). These and other related books are sensibly reviewed by Robert Slifkin, *Oxford Art Journal* 35 (January 2012): 111–14; Nikos Papastergiadis, "Can There be a History of Contemporary Art?", *Discipline*, 2 (Autumn 2012); Andrew McNamara in *Australian & New Zealand Journal of Art* 12, open issue (2012): 259–261; an anonymous and unsympathetic review is "NEO RAUCH – 2011", CAP'S CRITS (blog), 6 December 2011, https://capscrits.blogspot.com/2011/.

6 See Hal Foster, Rosalind Kraus, Yves-Alain Bois, and Benjamin H.D. Buchloh, *Art Since 1900: Modernism, Anti-Modernism, Postmodernism* (London: Thames & Hudson, 2004), and my review, "A Short Review of a Very, Very Long book", *Yishu: Journal of Contemporary Chinese Art* 4, 4 (Winter 2005): 107.

7 Jameson, among other thinkers, consigns all the difficult cases of pre-modernity to a reactionary past defined against positions in Euramerican intellectual and other histories. See Fredric Jameson, *A Singular Modernity: Essay on the Ontology of the Present* (London: Verso, 2002), 53. Whatever its grand intellectual qualities, perhaps it still needs reinforcing in some quarters that this theorization is a paradigm case of Euramerican centrism.

8 Recent books from a sociological viewpoint on cosmopolitanism include Gerard Delanty, *The Cosmopolitan Imagination: the Renewal of Critical Social Theory* (Cambridge: Cambridge University Press, 2009), and Nikos Papastergiadis,

*Cosmopolitanism and Culture* (Cambridge: Polity, 2012). Major discussions include Charles Taylor, *Multiculturalism and the Politics of Recognition* (Princeton: Princeton University Press, 1992); Anthony Appiah, *Cosmopolitanism* (New York: Norton, 2006.)

9 See Clark, *Asian Modernities*, 23–47.

10 A summary view of capital transfer to the art market, for those with such capital to transfer, is Christoph Pauly, "Rich Move Assets from Banks to Warehouses", *Spiegel Online*, 24 July 2013, http://www.spiegel.de/international/business/art-as-alternativeinvestment-creates-storage-business-tax-haven-a-912798.html.

11 See Anna Brzyski, "Introduction: Canons and Art History" in *Partisan Canons*, ed. Anna Brzyski (Durham, NC: Duke University Press, 2007), and her essay therein, "Making Art in the Age of Art History, or How to Become a Canonical Artist".

12 For a survey of such issues see Roger M. Buergel, the frame of whose later artistic directorship of 2007 *Documenta 12* is foreshadowed in his essay, see Dorothea Richter and Eva Schmidt, ed., *Curating Degree Zero* (Nürnberg: Verlag für moderne Kunst Nürnberg, 1998), 45–51.

13 O'Neill, *The Culture of Curating and the Curating of Culture(s)*, 12:

> Despite numerous claims to the contrary, from Hoffmann to Obrist, prioritization of the contemporary and the curatorial gesture has created a particular model of discourse that remains self-referential, curator-centred, and curator-led, with unstable historical foundations.

14 See Brzyski, "Introduction: Canons and Art History", 5. Here I adapt some paragraphs from another paper, "Canon-Making and Curating in recent Asian art", which was given at the conference "Curating in Asia" at Zentrum für Kunst und Medientechnologie, Karlsruhe, in December 2011.

15 Anna Brzyski, "Making Art in the Age of Art History, or How to become a Canonical Artist" in Brzyski, ed., *Partison Canons*, 256.

16 As in Rauschenberg's *Erased de Kooning Drawing*, 1953, which generates, in Rauschenberg's own description, a "monochrome no-image". See Terry Smith, "Coda: Canons and Contemporaneity", in *Partisan Canons*, 310–11.

17 Smith in Brzyski, ed., *Partisan Canons*, 313.

18 Smith in Brzyski, ed., *Partisan Canons*, 315.

19 This is an art historical position: perhaps curators are more concerned as entrepreneur-managers with the very many stakeholders between whose demands they have to negotiate, and have a power of selection which is far less independent than some of the external public relations materials for their appointment may suggest, or their subsequent catalogue essays claim.

20 Space only allows for a bare statement of these issues, but I am thinking more empirically of the way artist statements have both functioned to break canons and reform them in the propagation of Young British Art, such as the function of statements by Damien Hirst in catalogues. See chapter 2, "Famous for being Famous" in Julian Stallabrass, *High Art Lite: British Art in the 1990s* (London: Verso, 1999), and chapter 5, "Art Stars" in John A. Walker, *Art and Celebrity* (London: Pluto Press, 2003).

21 Chief among which is O' Neill, *The Culture of Curating and the Curating of Culture(s)*, whose second chapter is on Biennales.

22 O' Neill, *The Culture of Curating and the Curating of Culture(s)*, 9.

23 For example in O' Neill, *The Culture of Curating and the Curating of Culture(s)*:

> The biennial has become a ratifying device for the upper echelons of the contemporary art world, for artists and curators alike, which is characteristic of a more general trend toward establishing rankings within the art world. (75)

24 I am indebted to Joe Hill, in an unrecorded conversation in Shanghai in September, 2006, for this insight.

25 In René Block, "We hop on, we hop off: the ever-faster spinning carousel of Biennials", *Yishu: Journal of Chinese Contemporary Art* 12, 2 (May/June 2013): 33–4. This is basically the same view he has advanced elsewhere including in an interview with me of June 2006.

26 Doug Hall, "It seemed like a good idea at the time", *Art AsiaPacific*, 83 (May/June 2013): 80, states,

> More than anything else, APT provided the raison d'être for the new GOMA, an idea supported regardless of which political party was in office, an idea that was to provide the largest space for Australians to engage with the art of their time, and that includes all cultures – not just Asian, of course.

27 The tendency to provide an unlabeled photo-album in which figures can only be identified by those knowledgeable about who are the principal actors in the field is widespread at biennials. There was even one included for the symposium of the 2012 Gwangju Biennials' Symposium. Such albums manifest the property of "being seen" which many commentators have noticed is a requirement of current art world membership.

28 The Indonesian senior Islamist painter, A.D. Pirous, who although included in APT I in 1993 was left out of other biennial selections. There is also a documented case of a form of modernist expressionism regarded as important locally, such as surrealist and neo-realist painting in Indonesia, being explicitly excluded from exhibition by Dutch curators, because it was regarded as out of date. See Sue Ingham, *POWERLINES: Alternative Art and Infrastructure in Indonesia in the 1990s*, PhD thesis (University of New South Wales, August 2007), 348. The reference was to Martinus Dwi Marianto, "Surrealist Painting in Yogyakarta", unpublished PhD thesis (University of Wollongong, 1995), 11-13, published in Bahasa Indonesia as *Surealisme Yogyakarta* (Yogyakarta: Rumah Penerbitan Merapi, 2001).

29 My opinion is based on an interview with the artist in Japanese on 12 July 1991 in Kôbe. A distinguished international curator who shall remain un-named, said this exclusion was because Tsubaki had no ideas, i.e. he did not meet with this particular curator's need for an artist adding to contemporary art as a critical practice.

30 It was said, by another artist who I will also leave un-named, to have been because of Nguyen-Hatsushiba's over-dependence on particular curatorial advice and demand. This statement has the evidentiary status of gossip, as is frequently the case with the more significant statements from the art world, but insightful gossip nonetheless.

31 It may be this was in part due to her having the capable critical advice of the art writer James B. Lee as a partner. This was clear from a conversation with them both in English on 25 September 2004 in Seoul.

32 This was widely mentioned in my interviews with artists during the main period of research, and most recently in December 2009 by Nilima Sheikh about APT II in 1996, and in December 2009 with Sheba Chhachhi about Havana in 2000.

33 See O' Neill, *The Culture of Curating and the Curating of Culture(s)*, 85. Okwui Enwezor in his lead essay for *The Unhomely: Phantom scenes in global society* (Seville: BIACS Foundation, 2006), 13–16, interrogates the intersection between art and politics thus:

> The question, then is this: how might art become integral rather than peripheral to the widespread challenge that affects not only the production of art but its reception as well, particularly in the light of the deleterious effects of reactionary, conservative and fundamentalist politics on all world social formations today? (13)
>
> ... At a minimum, any art aiming to engage itself in social praxis today must begin with a critique of the romantic illusion of pure distance and total autonomy of art from world events. (13)

His exhibition proposes, among other approaches, to engage these issues by examining:

> The ways in which artistic practice seeks to mediate the distinctions between civil society, civic space, and social reciprocity through community and collective activities. These activities are often configured as gestures of generosity, exchanges devoted to breaking the forms of enclosure, isolation, limits, and retreat that have recently become the dominant mechanism of political power. (14, emphasis in original)

Under these criteria, clearly the curator's allocation of values will be authoritative about what is generous and "breaks the forms of enclosure", and artists who do not engage these issues and methods will be excluded.

34 See Boris Groys, "On the Curatorship", in *Art Power* (Cambridge, MA: The MIT Press, 2008):

> The independent curator is a radically secularized artist. He is an artist because he does everything artists do. But he is an artist who has lost the artist's aura, who no longer has magical transformative powers at his disposal, who cannot endow objects with artistic status. He doesn't use objects – art objects included – for art's sake, but rather abuses them, makes them profane... The contemporary curator is the heir apparent to the modern artist, although he doesn't suffer from his predecessor's magical abnormalities. He is an artist but he is atheistic and "normal" through and through. The curator is the agent of art's profanation, it's secularization. It's abuse. (51)

35 Many curators in addition to Enwezor advance a left nostalgia which motivates their contemporary progressivist curatorship. They long for a revolution which did not take place, and seek an art-world means to re-manifest a utopian position, or route to political utopia. See Charles Esche and de Appel CP, "Stand I don't", in *Curating and the Educational Turn*, ed. Paul O'Neill and Mick Wilson (London: Open Editions; Amsterdam: De Appel, 2010), 299–300.

# List of Illustrations

# Appendix 1

# Indicators for Some Asian Biennials

| A | B year(s) | C period | D emphasis | Ea artists L/NLa/NL non-a/ total | Eb countries | Ec works | F audience | G (US$) direct budget | H (US$) indirect budget | I type |
|---|---|---|---|---|---|---|---|---|---|---|
| Tokyo Biennale | 1952–1990 | 2 | L/G | | | | | | | 8 |
| Triennale-India | | 3 | L/G | | | | | | | 6 |
| | 1968 | | | | 31 | 649 | | | | |
| | 1971 | | | | 47 | 803 | | | | |
| | 1975 | | | | 22 | 606 | | | | |
| | 1978 | | | | 36 | 994 | | | | |
| | 1982 | | | | 45 | 940 | | | | |
| | 1986 | | | | | | | | | |
| | 1991 | | | | | | | | | |
| | 1994 | | | | | | | | | |
| | 1997 | | | 6/38a | 38 | | | | | |
| | 2001 | | | 35/31a | 30 | | | | | |

| A | B year(s) | C period | D emphasis | Ea artists L/NLa/NL non-a/ total | Eb countries | Ec works | F audience | G (US$) direct budget | H (US$) indirect budget | I type |
|---|---|---|---|---|---|---|---|---|---|---|
| | 2005 | | | 43/20a/101/164 | 33 | | | | | |
| **Biennale of Sydney**** | 1973 | 2 | L/G | | | | | | | 5 |
| Anthony Wintherbotham | 1973 | | | ?/7a/?/37 | | | | | | |
| William Wright | 1976 | | | ?/17a/?/80 | 10 | | | | | |
| Nick Waterlow | 1979 | | | ?/0/?/131 | 19 | | | | | |
| William Wright | 1982 | | | ?/19a/?/209 | 17 | | | | | |
| Leon Paroissien | 1984 | | | ?/3a/?/66 | 20 | | | | | |
| Nick Waterlow | 1986 | | | ?/ 7a/?/123 | 21 | | | | | |
| Nick Waterlow | 1988 | | | ?/4a/?/127 | 15 | | | | | |
| René Block | 1990 | | | ?/?/?/148 | 28 | | | | | |
| Tony Bond | 1992/3 | | | ?/6a/?/126 | 33 | | | | | |
| Lynne Cooke | 1996 | | | ?/5a/?/48 | 24 | | | | | |
| Jonathan Watkins | 1998 | | | ?/ 21a/?/101 | 28 | | | | | |
| Nick Waterlow | 2000 | | | ?/7a/?/48 | 23 | | 250,000+ | | | |
| Richard Grayson | 2002 | | | ?/6a/?/56 | 22 | | 245,393 | | $21140 (A$41,140) | |
| Isobel Carlos | 2004 | | | ?/5a/?/51 | 29 | | 281,351 | | $42,188 (A$75,000) | |

| A | B year(s) | C period | D emphasis | Ea artists L/NLa/NL non-a/ total | Eb countries | Ec works | F audience | G (US$) direct budget | H (US$) indirect budget | I type |
|---|---|---|---|---|---|---|---|---|---|---|
| Charles Merewether | 2006 | | | ?/26a/?/85 | 44 | | 316,811 | | $388,500 (A$525,000) | |
| **Asian Art Biennale of Bangladesh** | 1981 | 2 | L/R | | | | | | | 6 |
| | 1981 | | | | 14 | | | | | |
| | 1983 | | | | 13 | | | | | |
| | 1986 | | | ?/?/?/316 | 15 | 490 | | | | |
| | 1989 | | | | 14 | 484 | | | | |
| | 1991 | | | | 13 | 447 | | | | |
| | 1993 | | | | 27 | | | | | |
| | 1995 | | | | 33 | | | | | |
| | 1997 | | | | 35 | | | | | |
| | 1999 | | | ?/?/?/323 | 36 | 604 | | | | |
| | 2001 | | | ?/?/?/392 | 43 | 574 | | | | |
| | 2004 | | | 184/93a/33?/300+ | 44 | | | | | |
| | 2006 | | | 168/78a/100/348 | 31 | 532 | | | | |
| **Osaka Triennale** | 1990-2001 | 3 | L/G | | | | | | | 3 |
| | 2001 | 3 | | 44/30a/41?/115 | 60 | 146 | | | | |

| A | B year(s) | C period | D emphasis | Ea artists L/NLa/NL non-a/ total | Eb countries | Ec works | F audience | G (US$) direct budget | H (US$) indirect budget | I type |
|---|---|---|---|---|---|---|---|---|---|---|
| **Taipei Biennale** | 1992 | 2 | L/G | | | | | | | 8 |
| | 1992 | | | | | | | | | |
| | 1994 | | | | | | | | | |
| | 1996 | | | | | | | | | |
| Nanjô Fumio | 1998 | | | 12/23a/?/36 | 4 | | 128,000 | $600,000 | | |
| Jerôme Sans, Hsu Manray | 2000 | | | 6/9/ 16?/31 | | | 130,049 | $618,620–$773,276 | | |
| Bartomeu Mari, Wang Chiachi (Jason) | 2002 | | | 6/5a/20?/31 | | | 108,622 | $618,620–$773,276 | | |
| Cheng Hueihua (Amy), Barbara Vanderlinden | 2004 | | | 6/13a/13?/32 | | | 106,583 | $618,620–$773,276 | | |
| Dan Cameron, Wang Junjieh | 2006 | | | 6/11a/19?/36 | | Ca 200 | | $618,620–$773,276 | | |
| **Asia-Pacific Triennale of Contemporary Art, Brisbane**** | | 3 | L/R | | | | | | | 5 |
| 10 Aus+12 non-Aus | 1993 | | | 18?/58a/0/76 | 13 | >200 | 60,445 | $196,819**** [A$289,000,Qld Govt] | $165,900 [A$210,000 Australia Council] | |

| A | B year(s) | C period | D emphasis | Ea artists L/NLa/NL non-a/ total | Eb countries | Ec works | F audience | G (US$) direct budget | H (US$) indirect budget | I type |
|---|---|---|---|---|---|---|---|---|---|---|
| 28(7+21) Aus +16 non-Aus | 1996 | | | 30?/50a/0/80 | 17 | | 120,000 | $215,305**** [Qld Govt} | $39,500 [A$50,000 Australia Council] | |
| 27 Aus + 23 non-Aus | 1999 | | | 14/63a/0/77 | 20 | | 155,000 | $176,290**** [Qld Govt} | $66,400 [A$100,000 Australia Council] | |
| 7 Aus | 2002 | | | 6?/10a/0/16 | 11 | 91 | 220,000 | [Qld Govt]? | | |
| (Doug Hall; Lynne Sear, Andrew Clark, Suhanya Raffel, Julie Ewington, Maud Page, Kathryn Weir, Sarah Tiffin) 8 Aus | 2006 | | | 13?/25a/0/39 | 19 | 270 | ? | [Qld Govt]? | $975,000 [A$1,300,000 Cash & contra sponsorship via QAG Foundation] | |
| **Gwangju (Kwangju) Biennale** | | 2 | L/G | | | | | | | 8 |
| Lee Yongwoo | 1995 | | | 7/20a/?/87 | | | 1,640,000 | | | |
| Lee Youngchul | 1997 | | | 8/9a/?/98 | | | | | | |
| Oh Kangsu | 2000 | | | 12/24a/?/84 | | | | | | |

| A | B year(s) | C period | D emphasis | Ea artists L/NLa/NL non-a/ total | Eb countries | Ec works | F audience | G (US$) direct budget | H (US$) indirect budget | I type |
|---|---|---|---|---|---|---|---|---|---|---|
| Sung Wankyung Charles Esche, Hou Hanru | 2002 | | | 18/40a/?/89 | | 325 | 556,000 | $ 6,300,000 | | |
| Kerry Brougher, Chang Sukwon, Lee Yongwoo +3 asst. cur. | 2004 | | | 17/13a/?/90 | 41 | | 542,000 | $ 7,087,000 | | |
| Kim Hongyee, 7 non-Korean, 1 Korean asst. cur. | 2006 | | | 19/22a/?/87 | | | | $10,000,000 | | |
| **Shanghai Biennale** | | | L/G | | | | | | | 8 |
| | 1996 | | | | | | | | | |
| | 1998 | | | | | | | | | |
| Fang Zengxian, Zhang Qing, Li Xu, Hou Hanru, Shimizu Toshio | 2000 | | | 37/18a/12?/67 | 15 | | | $240,000 (Ca2,000,000rmb) | | |
| Xu Jiang, Fan Di'an, Alanna Heiss, Klaus Biesenbach, Hasegawa Yûko | 2002 | | | 32/11a/15?/68 | | | | $360,000 (Ca3,000,000rmb) | | |

| A | B year(s) | C period | D emphasis | Ea artists L/NLa/NL non-a/ total | Eb countries | Ec works | F audience | G (US$) direct budget | H (US$) indirect budget | I type |
|---|---|---|---|---|---|---|---|---|---|---|
| Zhang Qing Zheng Shengtian, Sebastian Lopez, Xu Jiang | 2004 | | | 55/23a/30?/108 | 35 | | | | | |
| Huang Du, Gianfranco Maraniello, Jonathan Watkins, Zhang Qing, Lin Shumin, RheeWonil, Xiao Xiaolan | 2006 | | | 33/20a/30?/93 | 23 | | | | | |
| **Busan Biennale** | | 2 | J/G | | | | | | | |
| | 1998 | | | 12/9a/79?/100 | | | | | | 3 |
| Lee Youngchul, Rosa Martinez, Hou Hanru, Tom van Bleat | 2000 | | | 14/10a/16?/50 | | | | | | |
| Kim Levin, Catherine Francblin, Tatehata Akira | 2002 | | | 16/6/44?/69 | 36 | 67 | | | | |

| A | B year(s) | C period | D emphasis | Ea artists L/NLa/NL non-a/ total | Eb countries | Ec works | F audience | G (US$) direct budget | H (US$) indirect budget | I type |
|---|---|---|---|---|---|---|---|---|---|---|
| Choi Taeman, Park Manwoo [Manu D.?], Lee Taeho | 2004 | | | 56/25a/9?/90 | | | | | | |
| Park Manu D. | 2006 | | | 32/12a/92?/136 | 40 | 140 | | | | |
| **Fukuoka Asian Art Triennale*** | | 3 | L/R | | | | | | | 5 |
| | 1999 | | | 3/52a/0/55 | 21 | 120 | 57,630 | $1,290,000 | | |
| | 2002 | | | 2/36a/0/38 | 21 | 122 | 13,000 | $ 710,500 | | |
| | 2005 | | | 4/44a/0/50 | 21 | 120 | 17,262 | $ 900,000 | | |
| **Melbourne International Biennial**** | 1999 only | | L/G | | | | | | | 3 |
| **Echigo-Tsumari Triennial** | | 3 | L/G | | | | | | | 3 |
| Kitagawa Fram | 2000 | | | ?/12a/?/148 | 32 | | | | | |
| Kitagawa Fram | 2003 | | | ?/11a/?157/ | 23 | 200 | | | | |
| Kitagawa Fram | 2006 | | | ?/10a/?/200 | 40 | | | | | |
| **Yokohama Triennale** | | 3 | L/G | | | | | | | 9 |

| A | B year(s) | C period | D emphasis | Ea artists L/NLa/NL non-a/ total | Eb countries | Ec works | F audience | G (US$) direct budget | H (US$) indirect budget | I type |
|---|---|---|---|---|---|---|---|---|---|---|
| Kômoto Shinji, Nakamura Nobuo, Nanjô Fumio, Tatehata Akira | 2001 | | | 33/21a/55?/109 | 38 | | 349,179 | $6,500,000 | | |
| Kawamata Tadashi with Yamano Shingo, Serizawa Takashi, Amano Tarô | 2005 | | | 34/13a/39?/86 | | 71 | 189,568 | | | |
| Mizusawa Tsutomu with Daniel Birnbaum, Hu Fang, Hans-Ulrich Obrist | 2008 | | | | | | | | | |
| **Auckland Triennial**** | | 3 | L/G | | | | | | | 3 |
| Allan Smith | 2001 | | | ?/?/?/32 | | | | | | |
| Ngahiraka Mason, Ewen Mcdonald | 2004 | | | ?/4a/?/39 | 12 | | | | | |
| Victoria Lynn | 2007 | | | ?/1/?/37 | | | | | | |

| A | B year(s) | C period | D emphasis | Ea artists L/NLa/NL non-a/ total | Eb countries | Ec works | F audience | G (US$) direct budget | H (US$) indirect budget | I type |
|---|---|---|---|---|---|---|---|---|---|---|
| **Chengdu Biennale** | 2001 | 2 | R | | | | | $360,000 (Ca3,000,000rmb) | | 3 |
| | 2007 | | | | | | | | | |
| **Guangzhou Triennial** | | 2 | L/G | | | | | | | 8 |
| (1st Guangzhou 1990s Art Biennale [oil painting]) | 1992 | | | | | | | $153,000 (Ca850,000rmb) | | |
| Wu Hung with Wang Huangsheng, Huang Zhan, Feng Boyi | 2002 | | | 55/0a/0/55 | 1 | 58 | | $600,000 (Ca5,000,000rmb) | | |
| Hou Hanru, Hans Ulrich Obrist, Guo Xiaoyan | 2005 | | | 41/13a/3?/57 | 20 | | 52,000 + 30,000 = 82,000 | $1,260,000 | | |
| **Beijing International Art Biennale** | | 2 | L/G | | | | | | | 9 |
| (China Oil Painting Biennale) | 1993 | | | | | | | $450,000 (Ca2,500,000rmb) | | |

| A | B year(s) | C period | D emphasis | Ea artists L/NLa/NL non-a/ total | Eb countries | Ec works | F audience | G (US$) direct budget | H (US$) indirect budget | I type |
|---|---|---|---|---|---|---|---|---|---|---|
| Liu Dawei, Jin Shangyi, Feng Yuan | 2003 | | | 143?/45a/112?/300 | 45 | 577 | 20,000 | $1,120,000 | | |
| Liu Dawei, Jin Shangyi, Feng Yuan | 2005 | | | 156/78a/268?/500 | 69 | 600 | | $1,860,000 | | |
| **Kyoto Biennale** | 2003 only | 2 | L | | | | | | | 3 |
| **CP Biennale, Jakarta** | 3 | 2 | L/G | 8 | | | | | | 3 |
| Jim Supangkat, Rizki A. Zaelani | 2003 | | | 78/10a?/28?/128 | | 167 | | | | |
| Jim Supangkat, Marco Kusmawijaya, Asmujo Jono Irianto, Rizki A. Zaelani | 2005 | | | 56?/13a?/18?/70 | | | | | | |
| **Singapore Biennale** | 2006 | 2 | L/G | | | | | | | 5 |

| A | B year(s) | C period | D emphasis | Ea artists L/NLa/NL non-a/ total | Eb countries | Ec works | F audience | G (US$) direct budget | H (US$) indirect budget | I type |
|---|---|---|---|---|---|---|---|---|---|---|
| Nanjô Fumio with Roger Mcdonald; Sharmini Pereira, Eugene Tan [originally included Ahmad Mashadi] | 2006 | | R/G | 14/54a/27?/95 | | | [883,300]*** | $4,025,157 | $1,006,289 | 9 |

**Key to columns:**

A: name of Biennale and name of curator(s), B: year in question, C: periodicity, D: emphasis of selection. (L)ocal, (R)egional, (G)lobal;

Ea: Number of artists [including some artist groups]

L: Number of Local artists

NLa: Number of Non-Local Asian artists

NL non-a: Number of Non-local Non-Asian artists

Total: Total number of artists exhibited

L/Total and NLa/Total allows calculation of composition ratios showing the relative importance of other-Asian art in the Biennale;

NLnon-a/Total allows calculation of a composition ratio showing the relative importance of other-than-Asian or international art in the Biennale. Gender ratios could also be so calculated.

?: Indicates figure is unknown or is a deduction;

Eb: Number of countries;

Ec: Number of works;

F: Attendances;

G: Direct budget $US;

H: Indirect budget, $US; usually comprised of the extra funds from sponsors including other national governments, cultural foundations and councils etc.

I: Type in revised Bydler schema above.

Some artists of overseas origin are not counted as 'Asian' if they reside in the country of exhibition.

Currencies have been converted into US$ values *of the time* by http://www.x-rates.com/cgi-bin/hlookup.cgi. Statistics have been inserted in this table to the extent they have been made available by biennial authorities or have been recorded in published reports. If I have been unable to find or receive data I have left a blank since other colleagues may be able to correct or supply them in future.
G is extremely difficult to calculate reliably because of various uncharged allocations of staff time in kind from hosting institutions, separate and often underestimated budgets for new capital infrastructure, and nominal or zero rental charges on existing infrastructure.
H is difficult to calculate because of effective regular subsidy by overseas governments through their direct cultural agencies for funding artist visits or work shipment and loan costs, hidden subsidies by commercial patrons in effect contracting exhibition space to service advertising or their goods' and services' promotion, use of foundation funds to purchase works exhibited, and many other factors including in some cases, one suspects, the real costs of obtaining political support.

**Sources:**

the *invaluable* Asian Art Archive: https://www.aaa.org.hk,
Interview with Low Kee Hong, Singapore, June 21, 2006,
Okabe, Aomi. "Gendaibijutsu no hen'yô to Bijutsuten". In Omuka Toshiharu, kenkyû daihyôsha, Kansha, Tenji, Kanshô, sono juyô no bijutsushi, Heisei 14-nendo – 16 nendo kagaku kenkyûhi hojokin, Kenkyûhôkokusho no. 1430029., 47–8. Tsukuba: Tsukuba Daigaku Geijutsugakkei, 2001.
Some figures for China are in Yin Shuangxi, "Shuangnianzhan zhidu yu fei-yingli wenhua shiye". In *Huiyu yu Chenshu - guanyu 1949 nianhou de zhongguo yishu yu yishu shi*, ed. Lu Peng and Kong Lingwei. Changsha: Hunan Meishu Chubanshe, 2007.
Non-attributable statements by curators or managers in private interview.
Relevant catalogues of the Biennales in question where available.

* Fukuoka *Asian Art Triennale* was preceded by several related *Asian Art Shows* from 1989.
**The four Australasian Biennales, and some minor, short-lived ones I have not mentioned, belong to the Asian art region in virtue of their geographic location, the early exhibition of Asian contemporary art [at Sydney from 1973, 20 years before Venice, 16 years before the first Fukuoka Asian Art Show], the continued incorporation of Asian contemporary art in many mainstream exhibitions, and the increasing size of their Asian immigrant populations [Asian first and second generation populations are about 20-25% of the total population in Sydney whereas Fukuoka, for example, has about 1% non-Japanese Asian population][1]
*** The Biennale "attracted 883,300 people and received rave reviews", according to Lee Suan Hiang, "Firing on All Fronts," in *State of the Arts, National Arts Council, Annual Report FY 2006/07* (Singapore: National Arts Council, 2007), 3. Mr Lee was then the Chief Executive Officer of the National Arts Council. How about 25% of the total Singaporean citizen population can be thought of as visiting the Biennale is unjustified, unless this includes an estimate for those passing works exhibited in public shopping sites such as Orchard Road. This figure is, for example, 3–4 times the number of visitors to the Biennale of Sydney whose visitor figures are known to be quite conservative. Internal and unattributable sources indicate there were two sets of figures arrived at, one for indoor visits which were quite accurate, and one for outdoor visitors to public sites who were assessed as a percentage of those passing but who appear to have been interested in the art works. The 883,000 appears to be a conflation of these two figures.

1 See Clark, 2006, for some sources on population statistics. It is expected the proportions of Asian populations in overall Australian population will increase when the results of the late 2006 census become clear.

****According a government statement by Hon. M.J. Foley, Attorney-General and Minister for Justice and Minister for the Arts, reported in the *Queensland Parliamentary Hansard* for 26 August 1999, pp. 3578–79, the Queensland Government spent A$2.6 million on the APT over nine years, or A$289,000 per annum, so these figures adjusted for annual exchange rates at the time were the *minimum* expenditure of the Queensland Government on the APT in those years. How the fixed costs of the Queensland Art Gallery Building and the salaries budgets for curators and shipping expenditures and other non-fixed operating costs of the Queensland Art Gallery allocated to the APT were factored into this A$2.6 million, or were in addition but then were set aside, is not clear. Further details are excerpted from this speech in Chapter Six.

# Appendix 2

# Funding of APT and Queensland Art Gallery

Richard W.L. Austin was chairman of Trustees of the Queensland Art Gallery from 1988–1995 as crucial decisions were made about setting up the Asia-Pacific Triennial of Contemporary Art. His speeches are collected as *View from the Chair*. He made his first speech in 1988 when there were Queensland exhibitions at the Expo 1988 in Brisbane, and he retired in 1995.

He gave a vote of thanks at the opening of *Japanese Ways, Western Means*, 19 September 1989, which indicated that A$350,000 had been received from four Japanese companies, Nikko Securities, Nomura Securities, Meiji Life Insurance, and Japan Travel Bureau, to purchase works of art. These sums were matched by the Queensland Government to presumably to make a capital fund for purchase of about A$700,000 (Austin 1997: 25). With the addition of a new donor, Hitachi, and later the forming of the Queensland Exhibitions Development Fund in 1990, the fund had reached A$555,000 (Austin 1997: 27, 34). If matched by the Queensland Government, this could have given a capital fund for purchases of about A$1,110,000. Depending on capital replenishment rules, this may have meant a possible annual buying expenditure of around A$100,000 per annum. As seen above in Appendix One, the Queensland government itself calculated nine-year expenditure of around A$289,000 per annum on the APT, but whether this included matching the capital for the exhibitions' fund or was above and beyond that matching is not clear.

The APT project was launched in 1992, and on the death of Kenneth and Yasuko Myer, a donation was made in 1993 from Mr and Mrs Michael Myer of A$50,000 for the purchase of art works.

The Queensland Cultural Centre Trust, which includes the Queensland Art Gallery complex, does not charge rent on premises administered by the Gallery, see *Queensland Art Gallery Annual Report*, 1992, p.57.

As indicated above in Appendix One, the Queensland Government thought itself as having invested $A289,000 in the APT per annum for the nine years 1990–99, or A$2.6 million in total.

**From Queensland Art Gallery Annual Reports, to 1st June each year, in A$ (APT was usually held in September)**

| | 1993 | 1994 | 1995 |
|---|---|---|---|
| Operating expenses | 9,607,412 | 9,914,425 | 9,111,965 |
| Operating income independent sources | 2,307,976 | 1,766,678 | 1,859,301 |
| Net cost of services | 7,299,436 | 8,148,747 | 7,252,664 |
| Government revenue | 7,671,000 | 8,024,400 | 9,326,050 |
| International programmes | 497,343 | 359,806 | 597,070 |
| Acquisitions | 660,891 | 900,578 | 75,993 |

Depending on when costs were charged to budget lines, these figures indicate there was an A$239,687 increase in acquisitions between 1993 and 1994. Since APT I fell within the 1994 reporting period, this indicates that the minimum expenditure on APT I might have been in the region of A$1,088,798.

**Australia Council Grants to Queensland Art Gallery**
(source: annual reports of *Australia Council for the Arts*, A$)

| | | |
|---|---|---|
| 2004–05 | $80,000 | |
| 2003–04 | $50,000 | |
| 2002–03 | $108,000 | |
| 2001–02 | $94,130 | |
| 2000–01 | Nil | |
| 1999–2000 | $62,000 | |
| 1998–99 | $97,539 | |
| 1997–98 | $119,000 | [APT $100,000] |
| 1996–97 | Nil | |
| 1995–96 | $50,000 | [APT $50,000] |
| 1994–95 | $80,000 | |
| 1993–94 | Nil | |
| 1992–93 | $150,000 | [APT $150,000] |
| 1991–92 | $60,000 | [APT $60,000] |
| 1990–91 | Nil | |
| 1989–90 | $55,000 | |

In the case of the APT, other kinds of government, indirect, case-by-case support have been considerable. The catalog for APT I lists sponsorship by various Australian quasi-governmental and diplomatic organizations including the Australia-China Council, Australia-Indonesia Institute, Australian High Commission in Malaysia, Australia-New Zealand Foundation, Australia High Commission in Papua New Guinea, Australian Embassy in The Philippines, Australian High Commission in Singapore, Australia-Korea Foundation, Australian Embassy in Thailand, and the Australian Embassy in the Socialist Republic of Vietnam. Two Australian overseas legal firms and two foreign cultural bodies are listed as sponsors. Six Japanese companies are listed as supporting the Queensland Art Gallery Exhibitions Development Fund.

Many of the same names recur for APT II and APT III, with the addition of the Australia-India Council and the Australian Film Commission for APT III.

Although the Commonwealth Government sources were disparate and funded through many different agencies, this indicates that at least APT I–III can only be considered a major and substantive foreign cultural relations' activity at national level.

## Note

Austin, Richard W.L. *View from the Chair: Speeches of Richard W.L. Austin*. South Brisbane: Queensland Art Gallery, 1997.

# Bibliography

**Asian Art at Biennales and Triennales: An Initial Bibliography**

In addition to references in the notes, this bibliography is grateful for some inclusions from work by Thomas Berghuis, Emma Duffy, Helen Grace, and Francis Maravillas. It is not comprehensive and mostly contains works the author has consulted, with addition of some he otherwise considers relevant.

## Museum & Exhibition Practice


Allwood, John. *The Great Exhibition*. London: Studio Vista, 1977.

Aoki Shigeru and Kitazawa Noriaki. "Bankoku Hakurankai no Jidai". In *Nihon Yôga Shôshi*. Revised edition. Tokyo: Bijutsu Shuansha, 1994.

Barker, Emma, ed. *Contemporary Cultures of Display*. London: Yale University Press, 1999.

Bennett, Tony. *Pasts Beyond Memory: Evolution, Museums, Colonialism*. London: Routledge, 2004.

de Cauter, Lieven. "The Panoramic Ecstasy: On World Exhibitions and the Disintegration of Experience". *Theory, Culture and Society* 10 (1993): 1–23.

Findling, John E., ed. *Historical Dictionary of World's Fairs and Expositions 1851–1988*. New York: Greenwood Press, 1990.

Greenberg, Reesa, Bruce Ferguson and Sandy Nairne. "Introduction". In *Thinking About Exhibitions*, ed. Reesa Greenberg, Bruce Ferguson, and Sandy Nairne. London: Routledge, 1996.

Greenhalgh, Paul. "Education, Entertainment and Politics: Lessons from the Great International Exhibitions". In *The New Museology*, ed. Peter Vergo, 74–98. London: Reaktion Books, 1991.

________. *Ephemeral Vistas: The Expositions Universelles, Great Exhibitions and World Fairs, 1851–1939*. Manchester: Manchester University Press, 1988.

Grynstejn, Madeleine. "The Pittsburgh biennial — The Carnegie International: a history in brief". In *Das Lied von der Erde / The Song of the Earth. Catalogue*, ed. B. Henrich. Kassel: Museum Fridericianum, 2000.

Hotta-Lister, Ayako. "Japan's Participation in Exhibitions". Appendices A and B to *The Japan British Exhibition of 1910*. Richmond: Curzon Press, 1999.

Karp, Ivan. "Culture and Representation". In *Exhibiting Cultures: The Poetics and Politics of Museum Display*, ed. Ivan Karp and S. Lavine. Washington, DC: Smithsonian Institution Press, 1991.

Kreps, Christine K. *Liberating Culture: Cross-cultural Perspectives on Museums, Curation, and Heritage Preservation*. London & New York: Routledge, 2003.

Mitchell, Timothy. "Orientalism and the Exhibitionary Order". In *The Visual Culture Reader*, ed. Nicholas Mirzoeff. Second edition. London & New York: Routledge, 2002.

________. "The World as Exhibition". *Comparative Studies in Society and History* 31, 2 (1989).

Pastor Roces, Marion. "Crystal Palace Exhibitions". In *Over Here: International Perspectives on Art and Culture*, ed. Mosquera Gerard and Jean Fisher. Boston: MIT Press, 2005.

Preziosi, Donald. *Brain of the Earth's Body: Art, Museums, and the Phantasms of Modernity*. Minneapolis: University of Minnesota Press, 2003.

Preziosi, Donald and Claire Farago, ed. *Grasping the World: The Idea of the Museum*. Burlington: Ashgate Publishers, 2004.

Sherman, Daniel and Irit Rogoff, ed. *Museum Culture: Histories, Discourses, Spectacles*. Minneapolis: University of Minnesota Press, 1994.

Šola, Tomislav. *Essays on Museums and Their Theory: Towards the Cybernetic Museum*. Helsinki: Finnish Museums Association, 1997.

## Asian Art, Modern and Contemporary

Akbar, Shireen, curator. *Rickshaw Painting: Traffic Art in Bangladesh*. Fukuoka: Fukuoka Asian Art Museum, 1994.

Clark, John. *The Asian Modern*. Singapore: National Gallery of Singapore, 2021.

________. "Modernities in Art: How are they 'other'?". In *World Art Studies: Exploring Concepts and Approaches*, ed. Wilfried van Damme and Kitty Zijlmans. Amsterdam: Amsterdam University Press, 2006.

________. "What Modern and Contemporary Asian Art is [or is not]: the view from MOMA and the view from Asia". In *Eye of the Beholder*, ed. John Clark, Maurizio Pelleggi, and Kanaga Sabapathy, 297–319. Sydney: Wild Peony Press, 2006.

________. "A Spectacle of Questions". *Asian Art News* 16, 1 (January/February 2006): 68–72.

________. "Between the Worlds: Chinese Art at Biennales since 1993". *Yishu: A Journal of Chinese Contemporary Art* (2005). [Extended version reprinted as Chapter Three here.]

________. "Modern and Contemporary Asian Art". In *Grove Art Online / The Dictionary of Art*. New York: Oxford University Press, September 2005.

________. "Japanese Contemporary Art and Globalization". Paper presented at "Globalization, Localization, and Japanese Culture in the Asia Pacific Region" conference, National University of Singapore, Singapore, 28–30 October 2004. [Reprinted as Chapter Two here.]

________. Essay for www.anthology-of-art.net: "What in the context of contemporary art, is your vision of a future art?", February 2002.

________. "Asian Modernisms". *Humanities Research* 2 (1999) and *Marg* (March 2002).

________. "Modern Asian Art: Its Construction and Reception". In *Asian Contemporary Art Reconsidered*. Tokyo: Japan Foundation Asian Center, 1998.

________. *Modern Asian Art*. Sydney: Craftsman House; Honolulu: University of Hawai'i Press, 1998.

________. "The Conditions for Post-Modernity in Japanese Art of the 1980s". In *The Postmodernity Debate and the Japanese Experience*, ed. Y. Sugimoto. London: Kegan Paul International, 1994.

Clark, John, ed. and contributor. *Chinese Art at the End of the Millenium*. Hong Kong: New Art Media, 2000.

________. *Modernity in Asian Art*. Sydney: Wild Peony Press, 1993.

Clarke, David. "Contemporary Asian Art and its Western Reception". *Third Text* 16, 3 (2002): 237–42.

Flores, Patrick. "Place and Presence: Conditions of Possibilities in Contemporary Asian Art". Unpublished Power Lecture. Sydney: Museum of Contemporary Art, 2002.

Friede, Claus and Ludwig Seyfarth, ed. *Kunst aus Megastädten Asiens — Art from Asia Pacific Megacities*. Hamburg: Kunsthaus Hamburg, 2000.

Kishi Sayaka. "Bijutsukan 'Ajia' to deau toki — Fukuoka Ajia Bijutsukan no setsuritsu to tenkai". In *Sengô nihon no kokusai bunka kôryû*, ed. Hirano Kenichirô. Tokyo: Chikusô Shobô.

Lee, Weng-Choy. "Just What is it that Makes the Term Global-Local so Widely Cited, Yet so Annoying?". In *Flight Patterns*, exhibition catalogue. Los Angeles: The Museum of Contemporary Art, 2000.

McEvilley, Thomas. "Towards a World-class City". *Art in America* 83, 9 (September 1995): 45.

Mertens, Brian. "Womanifesto 2001". *Art AsiaPacific* 36 (2002).

Napack, Jonathan. "Alternative visions". *Art In America* 90, 11 (November 2002): 94–9.

Nuridsany, Michel. *China Art Now*. Trans. Susan Pickford. Paris: Flammarion, 2004.

Poshyananda, Apinan, ed. and curator. *Traditions/Tensions*. New York: Asia Society, 1995.

*Sekai Bijutsu Zenshû*. Tokyo: Heibonsha, 1928–30.

Tipton, Elise and John Clark, ed. *Being Modern in Japan: Culture and Society from the 1910s to the 1930s*. Sydney: Australian Humanities Research Foundation; Honolulu: University of Hawai'i Press, 2000.

Turner, Caroline, ed. *Art and Social Change: Contemporary Art in Asia and the Pacific*. Canberra: Pandanus Books, 2005.

Vine, Richard. "The Wild, Wild East". *Art in America* 91, 9 (2003): 40–9.

________. "Asian Futures". *Art in America* 86, 7 (1998): 34–43.

Wee, C.J. W.-L. "Creating High Culture in the Globalized 'Cultural Desert' of Singapore". *The Drama Review* 47, 4 (Winter 2003).

Weisenfield, G. *Mavo: Japanese artists and the avant-garde of 1905–1931*. Berkeley: University of California Press, 2002.

## Australia, Art and Asia

Australian Academy of the Humanities. *Knowing Ourselves and Others: The Humanities in Australia into the 21st Century*. Three-volume collection. Canberra: Australian Government Publishing Service, 1998.

"Australian Perceptions of Asia". *Australian Culture History* 9, special issue (1990).

Barnes, Carolyn and William Wright. *John Young*. Fisherman's Bend: Craftsman House, 2005.

Birrell, Bob and Virginia Rapson. "Two Australias: Migrant settlement at the end of the 21st century". *People and Place* 10, 1 (2002).

Broiwnowski, Alison. "Asianization and its Discontents". *Meanjin* 57, 3 (1998).

________. *The Yellow Lady: Australian Impressions of Asia*. Melbourne: Oxford University Press, 1992.

Butler, Roger, ed. *The Europeans: Emigré artists in Australia, 1930–1960*. Canberra: National Gallery of Australia, 1997.

Chiu, Melissa. "Rough Trade: Curating Cultural Exchange in Australia". In *Alter/Asians: Asian-Australian Identities in Art, Media and Popular Culture*, ed. Ang et al. Sydney: Pluto Press, 2000.

Clark, John. "An Australian Creative Space: where is Australian-Asian art now?". In *2006/ Contemporary Commonwealth/*, ed. Waite Dianne, curated by Charles Green and Mike Stubbs, 26–33. Melbourne: Australian Centre for the Moving Image & National Gallery of Victoria, 2006.

________. "Art and its 'others' — recent Australian-Asian visual exchanges". In *Australia and Asia: Cultural Transactions*, ed. Maryanne Dever. Surrey: Curzon Press, 1997.

________. *Australian Art and Asia — Then and Now*. Occasional Paper No. 19. Sydney: Research Institute for Asia and the Pacific, University of Sydney, 1992.

Curnow, Wynstan. *Imants Tillers and the 'Book of Power'*. Sydney: Craftsman House, 1998.

Dixson, Miriam. *The Imaginary Australian: Anglo-Celts and Identity — 1788 to the present*. Sydney: University of New South Wales Press, 1999.

Dysart, Dinah, Natalie King, and Hou Hanru. *Guan Wei*. Sydney: Craftsman House, 2006.

Facey, A.B. *A Fortunate Life*. Ringwood: Viking, 1985.

Foss, Paul, ed. *Island in the Stream: Myths of Place in Australian Culture*. Sydney: Pluto Press, 1988.

Gibson, Ross. *South of the West: Postcolonialism and the Narrative Construction of Australia*. Bloomington & Indianapolis: Indiana University Press, 1992.

Grenville, Kate. *The Secret River*. Melbourne: Text Publishing, 2005.

Hage, Ghassan. *Against Paranoid Nationalism: Searching for Hope in a Shrinking Society*. Sydney: Pluto Press, 2003.

________. *White Nation: Fantasies of White Supremacy in a Multi-cultural Society*. Sydney: Pluto Press, 1998.

Hage, Ghassan and Rowena Couch, ed. *The Future of Australian Multiculturalism*. Sydney: The University of Sydney, 1999.

Keating, Paul. *Engagement: Australia faces the Asia-Pacific*. Sydney: Pan-Macmillan, 2000.

Khoo, Siew-Ean. "Inter-marriage in Australia: Patterns by ancestry, gender, and generation". *People and Place* 12, 2 (2004): 35–44.

Manne, Robert. *The Barren Years: John Howard and Australian Political Culture*. Melbourne: Text Publishing, 2001.

________. *The Way We Live Now: The Controversies of the Nineties*. Melbourne: Text Publishing: 1998.

Manton, Neil. *Cultural Relations: The Other Side of the Diplomatic Coin*. Phillip, ACT: Homosapien Books, 2003.

McCulloch, Alan and Susan McCulloch. *Encyclopedia of Australian Art*. St. Leonards: Allen & Unwin, 1994.

Reynolds, Henry. *Frontier: Reports from the Edge of White Settlement*. Sydney: Allen & Unwin, 1987.

________. *The Other Side of the Frontier: Aboriginal Resistance to the European Invasion of Australia*. Ringwood: Penguin Books, 1981.

Rolls, Eric. *Sojourners: The Epic Story of China's Centuries-old Relationship with Australia*. St. Lucia: University of Queensland Press, 1992.

Smith, Bernard. *Place, Taste, and Tradition: A Study of Australian Art since 1788*. Melbourne: Oxford University Press, 1979.

Smith, Bernard and Terry Smith. *Australian Painting, 1788–1990*, p. 312. Melbourne: Oxford University Press, 1991.

Stuart, Francis. "Nineteen Forty-One: Reminiscences of a British/Australian diplomat in Bangkok and Canberra in the Prelude to War". *Journal of the Oriental Society of Australia* 31, supplement (1999).

________. *Towards Coming-of-Age: A Foreign Service Odyssey*. Nathan: Centre for the Study of Australian-Asian Relations, Griffith University (1989).

Walker, David. *Anxious Nation: Australia and the Rise of Asia, 1850–1939*. St. Lucia: University of Queensland Press, 1999.

## Modern & Contemporary Exhibition Systems

"A New Cure for Asian Art Curators". *Asian Art News* 9, 4 (1999).

"Asia and Modernity". *Humanities Research* 2, special issue (1999). With articles by Clark, Lilley, Low, Labrador, and Sang.

"Asian Art: Prospects for the Future". *International Symposium 1999*. Tokyo: Japan Foundation, 1999. With articles by Elliott, Davenport, Mashadi, Nakamura, Poshyananda, Rajah, Tatehata.

"Avant-garde: a parallax view". *A journal of contemporary art and culture / Kanazawa 21 seiki Bijutsukan Kensetsujimukyoku*, Kenkyû Kiyô, 2 (2003).

Basualdo, Carlos. "The Unstable Institution". *Manifesta Journal* 2 (Winter 2003/Spring 2004).

Baudrillard, Jean. "The Beaubourg Effect: Implosion and Deterrence". Trans. Rosalind Krauss and Annette Michelson. *October* 20 (Spring 1982): 3–13.

"Biennials". *Manifesta Journal* 2, special issue (Winter 2003/Spring 2004).

Crimp, Douglas. *On the Museum's Ruins*. Cambridge, MA: MIT Press, 1993.

Davis, A.R., ed. *Search for Identity: Modern Literature and the Creative Arts in Asia*. Sydney: Angus and Robertson, 1974.

Enwezor, Okwui. "Mega Exhibitions and the Antinomies of a Transnational Global Form". *Manifesta Journal* 2 (Winter 2003/Spring 2004).

________. "Between Worlds: Postmodernism and African Artists in the Western Metropolis". In *Reading the Contemporary: African Art from Theory to the Marketplace*, ed. Olu Oguibe and Okwui Enwezor. London: MIT Press, 1999.

Evans, Graeme. "Hard-branding the Cultural City—from Prado to Prada". *International Journal of Urban and Regional Research* 27, 2 (2003): 229–55.

Ferguson, Bruce et al. "Making International Exhibitions" in *Curating: The Contemporary Museum and Beyond (Art & Design Profile)*, ed. Anna Harding. New York: Wiley, 1997.

Griffin, Tim et al. "Global Tendencies: Globalism and the large-scale exhibition". *Art Forum* XLII, 3 (November 2003).

Hall, Stuart. "Museums of Modern Art and the End of History". In *Annotations 6: Stuart Hall and Sarat Maharaj, Modernity and Difference*. London: Institute of International Visual Arts, 2001.

Hansen, David and Jean-Hubert Martin. "A View from the Centre". *Art Monthly Australia*, 48 and 51 (April/July 1992).

Hassan, Salah M. and Olu Oguibe, ed. *Authentic Ex-Centric*. Ithaca: Forum for African Arts, 2001.

Holubizky, Ihor. "Here and Now: Ihor Holubizky looks at Brisbane's millennium-bridging triennial". *International Contemporary Art* 64 (November 1999 – January 2000): 11–14.

Hou Hanru and Hans-Ulrich Obrist. *Cities on the Move*. Ostfildren-ruit: Verlag Gerg Hatje, 1997.

Manton, Neil. "The Arts of Diplomacy". *Artlink* 20, 2 (July 2000) and *Art Asia Pacific* 3, 4 (1996).

McEvilley, Thomas. "Arrivederci Venice, the Third World' Biennials". *Artforum International* 32, 3 (November 1993).

Möntmann, Nina, ed. *Art & Institutions: Current Conflicts, Critique, and Collaborations*. London: Black Dog Publishing, 2006.

Mosquera, Gerardo. "Alien-Own/Own Alien: Notes on Globalization and Cultural Difference". In *Complex Entanglements: Art Globalization and Cultural Difference*, ed. Nikos Papastergiadis. London: Rivers Oram Press, 2003.

Mosquera, Gerardo, ed. *Beyond the Fantastic: Contemporary Art Criticism from Latin America*. London: inIVA, 1995.

Oguibe, Olu and Okwui Enwezor. *Reading the Contemporary: African Art from Theory to Marketplace*. London: inIVA, 1999.

Osborne, Peter. "The Power of Assembly—Art, World, Industry". In *2006 Biennale of Sydney: Zones of Contact*, ed. Ewan Macdonald and Luke Parker. Sydney: Biennale of Sydney, 2006.

Owen, Michael. "Contemporary Art in Asia: Traditions/Tensions." *Third Text* 41 (Winter 1997–98).

Poshyananda, Apinan. "A new cure for Asian art curators". *Asian Art News* 9, 4 (1999).

Poshyananda, Apinan et al. *Traditions/Tensions: Contemporary Art in Asia*. New York: Asia Society Galleries; Sydney: The Fine Arts Press, 1996. [Reports: *Art Asia Pacific* 3, 4 (1996); Mehta in *Eyeline: Contemporary Visual Arts*, 32 (Summer 1996); *Art in America* (February 1997); Ewington, Yang, Munroe in *ART AsiaPacific*, 15 (1997).]

*Seminar on Fine Arts of Southeast Asia*. Bangkok: Association of Southeast Asian Institutions of Higher Learning, 1964.

Sirefman, Susanna. "Formed and Forming: Contemporary Museum Architecture". *Daedalus* 128, 3 (Summer 1999).

Skinner, Sarah J. "Estimating the real growth effects of blockbuster art exhibits: a time series approach". *Journal of Cultural Economics* 30 (2006).

Smith, Dina. "The Narrative Limits of the Global Guggenheim". *Mosaic (Winnipeg)* 35, 4 (December 2002): 85–103.

Stanton, Richard. *The Forgotten Olympic Art Competitions: The Story of Olympic Art Competitions of the 20th Century*. Victoria, BC: Trafford, 2000.

Turner, C. "Getting the Message". Review of Adelaide Festival Sculpture Installations. *Art and Australia* 32, 1 (Spring 1994).

Van Hal, Marieke, transcriber. "The International Dimension". *Manifesta Journal* 2 (Winter 2003/Spring 2004).

Vanderlinden, Barbara and Elena Filipovic. *The Manifesta Decade: Debates on Contemporary Art Exhibitions and Biennials in Post-wall Europe*. Cambridge, MA: MIT Press, 2005.

Walker, John. *Art and Celebrity*. London: Pluto Press, 2003.

Ward, Martha. "What's Important about the History of Modern Art Exhibitions?". In Thinking About Exhibitions, ed. Reesa Greenberg, Bruce Ferguson, and Sandy Nairne. London: Routledge, 1996.

Weiss, Rachel. "Some Notes on the Agency of Exhibitions". *Visual Arts and Culture* 2 (2000): 117–27.

Williams, Gilda, ed. *Fresh Cream*. London: Phaidon, 2000.

Wu Hung, ed. and contributor. *Chinese Art at the Crossroads: Between Past and Future, Between East and West*. Hong Kong: New Art Media, 2001.

Yao, Pauline. "The Second Triennial of Chinese Art: History in the Making". *Yishu: Journal of Contemporary Chinese Art* 4, 5 (September 2005).

Zabel, Igor and Francesco Bonami. "The power of proposing things, of taking risks". *Manifesta Journal* 2 (Winter 2003/Spring 2004).

Žerovc Beti. "'Making things possible' a conversation with Harald Szeeman". *Manifesta Journal* 1 (Spring/Summer 2003).

## Museums, Art Centres and other Art Institutions 2000+

Asai Toshihiro et al., ed. *Promenade in Asia: Cute*. Tokyo: Shiseidô; Mito: Art Tower Mito, 2001.

"Asian Art Now: 21 Curators and Critics Profile 63 Contemporary Asian Artists". *ART AsiaPacific* 37, special issue (2003).

Barucha, Rustom. "Beyond the Box: Problematising the New Asian Museum". *FOCAS: Forum on Contemporary Art and Society* 2 (July 2001).

_________. "The New Asian Museum Beyond the Box: Problematising the New Asian Museum". In *FOCAS: Forum on Contemporary Art and Society* 2 (July 2001): 223–37.

Benett, Tony. "The Rules of Culture: Exhibition and the Politics of Knowledge". In *Asia in Transition: Representation and Identity*, ed. Yasuko Furuichi. Tokyo: The Japan Foundation Asia Center, 2003.

Caroll, Alison. "A Floating World". *Art AsiaPacific* 28 (2001).

Chang, Alexandra. "The Control of Fear: Art and the Epidemic as Excess". *Art AsiaPacific* 38 (Fall 2003): 54–7.

Clarke, David. "Contemporary Asian Art and its Western Reception". In *Site+Sight: Translating Cultures*, ed. Huangfu Binghui. Singapore: Lasalle-SIA, 2002.

"Colonialism or Collaboration?: Intercultural Arts Practice and International Arts Organizations". Forum Transcript, *FOCAS: Forum on Contemporary Art and Society* 2 (July 2001).

Eley, Geoff. "Politics, Culture, and the Public Schere". *positions east asia cultures critique* 10, 1 (Spring 2002).

Enwezor, Okwui and Apinan Poshyananda. "Looking Ahead: Dialogues in Asian Contemporary Art, November 8–9, 2002." *Yishu: Journal of Contemporary Chinese Art* 2, 2 (June 2003): 112–121.

Findlay, Ian. "Looking for a New Vision". *Asian Art News* 13, 1 (January/February 2003).

Furuichi Yasuko, ed. *Asia in Transition: Representation and Identity.* Tokyo: The Japan Foundation Asia Center, 2003.

________. *International Symposium 2002 Report — Asia in Transition: Representation and Identity.* Tokyo: Japan Foundation Asia Center, 2002.

Gao Shiming. "Symposium: Edges of the Earth, Hangzhou; The Syndrome of Asia: Experience and Representation". *Yishu: Journal of Contemporary Chinese Art* 3, 1 (March 2004): 83–8.

Gaweewong, Gridthiya. "On Under Construction and Localization". In *Under Construction: New Dimensions of Asian Art*, ed. Mami Katakoa. Tokyo: The Japan Foundation Center, 2002.

Hoskote, Ranjit. "India Ink, Manila Envelope: Three Mediations on Art and the Global Media". In *Under Construction: New Dimensions of Asian Art*, ed. Mami Katakoa. Tokyo: The Japan Foundation Center, 2002.

Hou Hanru and Hans-Ulrich Obrist. "Cities on the Move". *Art AsiaPacific* 25 (2000).

Kataoka Mami. "Beyond a Progressive Asia: Under Construction Collective Exhibition". In *Under Construction: New Dimensions of Asian Art*, ed. Kataoka Mami. Tokyo: The Japan Foundation Asia Center, 2002.

Kember, Pamela. "A Report on the Asian Art Archive". *FOCAS: Forum on Contemporary Art & Society* 5 (January 2003): 372–377.

Lacayo, Richard. "The Rise and Rise of Asian Art". *Time Magazine* (March 31, 2003).

Lee Weng Choy. "Tomorrow's Local Library: The Asia Art Archive in Context". *Yishu: Journal of Contemporary Chinese Art* 4, 4 (December 2005).

Lee Yong Woo. "Globalism and the Vanity of its System". In *Asia in Transition: Representation and Identity*, ed. Furuichi Yasuko. Tokyo: The Japan Foundation Asia Center, 2003.

Mania, Astrid. "Curation on the Move". *Art AsiaPacific* 47 (2006).

McNeill, David. "Planet Art: Aesthetics and Labour in the Era of Globalisation". In *Site+Sight: Translating Cultures*, ed. Huangfu Binghui. Singapore: Lasalle-SIA, 2002.

Munroe, Alexandra. "Contemporary Art in Asia". *Artforum International* 35, 8 (April 1997).

Pi Li. "Fantasia: an Imagination Towards the Daily Life". In *Under Construction: New Dimensions of Asian Art*, ed. Kataoka Mami. Tokyo: The Japan Foundation Asia Center, 2002.

Robinson, Joel D. "The Construction Sites of Asian Art" [The Exhibition of *Under Construction: New Dimensions of Asian Art* by the Japan Foundation Forum at the Opera City Art Gallery, Tokyo, 2003]. *Asian Art News* 14, 1 (January/February 2004): 52–57.

Shinkawa Takashi. "Promenade in Asia: A Collaborative Exhibition". *Art AsiaPacific* 34 (2002).

Tatehata Akira. "A Trojan Horse?: Multiculturalism in International Art Exhibitions". In *Asia in Transition: Representation and Identity*, ed. Furuichi Yasuko. Tokyo: The Japan Foundation Asia Center, 2003.

Tavassoli, Babak A. "A Fresh Figure of Paradise". In *Yishu: A Journal of Contemporary Chinese Art* 3, 1 (March 2004): 95–103.

Thompson, Jonathan. "Without Borders" [Sovereign Art Prize for Asia]. *Asian Art News* 16, 4 (2006).

Wang Hui. "The Geneology of Asian Imaginaries". In *Asia in Transition: Representation and Identity*, ed. Furuichi Yasuko. Tokyo: The Japan Foundation Asia Center, 2003.

Xu Jiang. "Earth Link and Cosmic Time". *Yishu: Journal of Contemporary Chinese Art* 3, 1 (March 2004): 89–94.

Yamamoto Atsuo. "From Dualism to Oneness". In *Under Construction: New Dimensions of Asian Art*, ed. Kataoka Mami. Tokyo: The Japan Foundation Asian Center, 2002.

## Curatorial Practice

Aiha, Catherine, ed. *Unfolding Perspectives: Three Days of Lectures and Discussions at the ARS 01 Exhibition*. Helsinki: KIASMA [Museum of Contemporary Art] & NIFCA [Nordic Institute for Contemporary Art], 2002.

Biggs, Lewis. "'Art, Money, Parties' and Liverpool Biennial". In *Art, Money, Parties: New Institutions in the Political Economy of Contemporary Art*, ed. Jonathan Harris. Volume VII of the Tate Liverpool Critical Forum. Liverpool: Liverpool University Press, 2004.

"Curators' Trip to China". *Yishu: Journal of Contemporary Chinese Art* (May 2002). [Curators who attended in 2000 were Okwui Enwezor, Suzanne Ghez, Lynne Cooke, Sebastian Lopez, Chris Dercon, Jessica Bradley, Sarat Maharaj. They were accompanied by Annie Wong, Ken Lum, Zheng Shengtian, Richard Yiu, interpreter, Chaos Chen.]

Farqhuarson, Alex. "I Curate... You Curate... We Curate...". *Art Monthly (UK)*, 269 (September 2003).

Flores, Patrick. *Past Periphery: Curation in Southeast Asia*. Tokyo: privately printed with the support of the Nippon Foundation, 2006. Copy kindly provided by the author.

Harris, Jonathan, ed. *Art, Money, Parties: New Institutions in the Political Economy of Contemporary Art*. Volume VII of the Tate Liverpool Critical Forum. Liverpool: Liverpool University Press, 2004.

Heinich, Nathalie and Michael Pollak. "From museum curator to exhibition *auteur*: inventing a singular position". In *Thinking About Exhibitions*, ed. Rebecca Greenberg, Bruce Ferguson and Sandy Nairne. London: Routledge, 1996.

Hiller, Susan and Sarah Martin. *The Producers: Contemporary Curators in Conversation*. Newcastle: BALTIC, 2000.

Hou Hanru. "Interview with Hou Hanru". Interview by Alice Ming Wai Jim. *Yishu: Journal of Contemporary Chinese Art* 5, 1 (March 2006): 71.

________. Lecture in Symposium to accompany *Asian Traffic* at University of New South Wales. June 2004.

________. "Beyond the Chinese". In *Chinese Art at the End of the Millennium*, ed. John Clark. Hong Kong: New Art Media, 2000.

________. *On the Mid-Ground*, ed. Yu Hsiao-Hwei. Hong Kong: Timezone 8, 2002.

________. "'We've become true individuals'". Interview by Zhu Qi, translated by R. Bernell (November 2000). In *Chinese Art at the Crossroads: Between Past and Future*, ed. Wu Hung. Hong Kong: New Art Media, 2001.

Kamiya Yukie. "A Potential Role of Asian Art in the International Art Scene: A Study of Asian Art Exhibitions in the United States and Japan". In *The Second 'In-Between' International Alternative Space Conference — Globalism and Alternative Spaces*. Seoul: Yellow Sea Publications, 2004.

Kantor, Sybil Gordon. *Alfred H. Barr Jr. and the Intellectual Origins of the Museum of Modern Art*. Cambridge, MA: MIT Press, 2002.

Kuoni, Carin, ed. *Words of Wisdom: A Curator's Vade Mecum on Contemporary Art*. New York: Independent Curators International, 2001.

Linde, Rohr-Bongrad, et al. *Kunst = Kapital: Der Capital Kunstkompass von 1970 bis heute*. Köln: Salon Verlag, 2001.

Marquis, Alice Goldfarb. *Alfred H. Barr, Jr.: Missionary for the Modern*. Chicago: Contemporary Books, 1989.

Misiano, Viktor. "'Zones of Contact': from 'Confidential Zones' to 'Operational Zones'". In *2006 Biennale of Sydney: Zones of Contact*, ed. Ewan Macdonald and Luke Parker. Sydney: Biennale of Sydney, 2006.

Mosquera, Gerardo. "On art, politics, and the millenium in Latin America". In *Strategies for Survival — now!*, ed. C. Chambert. Paris: AICA Press, 1995.

Müller, Hans Joachim. *Harald Szeeman: Exhibition-Maker*. Translated by Leila Kais. Ostfildern-Ruit: Hatje Cantz Verlag, 2006.

O'Doherty, Brian. *Inside the White Cube: the Ideology of the Gallery Space*. Expanded edition. Berkeley: University of California Press, 1986.

Ramírez, Mari Carmen. "Constellations: Toward a Radical Questioning of Dominant Curatorial Models". *Art Journal* (Spring 2000).

________. "Brokering Identities". In *Thinking About Exhibitions*, ed. R. Greenberg, B.W. Ferguson, and S. Nairne. London: Routledge, 1996.

Rojek, Chris. *Celebrity*. London: Reaktion Books, 2001.

Schöllhammer, Georg. "documenta 12 magazines". *Ctrl+Pdf: Journal of Contemporary Art* 3 (November 2006).

Sibaya, Judy Freya. "A Note from the Editor". *Ctrl+PDF: Journal of Contemporary Art* 3 (November 2006): 19–20.

Suh Jin-suk, Yun Chea-gap, Moon Hee-chae, Lee Juhi, and Lee Hee-young. *Second 'In-Between' International Alternative Space Conference — Globalism and Alternative Space*. Seoul: Alternative Space Loop & Yellow Sea Publications, 2004.

Thea, Carolee. *foci: interviews with ten international curators*. New York: ApexArt curatorial program, 2001.

Tucker, Marcia. "Become a great curator in six simple steps!". In *Words of Wisdom: A Curator's Vade Mecum on Contemporary Art*, ed. Carin Kuoni. *New York: Independent Curators International*, 2001.

Walker, John. *Art and Celebrity*. London: Pluto Press, 2003.

## Biennales in Art Exhibition Systems:

Birnbaum, Daniel. "String Theory". On Documenta 12. *ArtForum* (October 2007).

Block, René and Martin Glaser et al. *Das Lied von der Erde / The Song of the Earth*. Kassel: Museum Fridericianum, 2000. [A Survey with texts on these Biennales: Havana, Istanbul, Johannesburg, Kwangju/Gwangju, Lyon, Pittsburgh, São Paulo, Sydney.]

Brenson, Michael. "The Curator's Moment — Trends in the Field of Contemporary Art Exhibitions". *Art Journal* (Winter 1998).

Britton, Stephanie. "Biennials of the World — Myths, Facts, and Questions". *Artlink* 25, 3 (September 2005).

Bydler, Charlotte. *The Global Art World Inc.: On the Globalization of Contemporary Art.* Upsala: Acta Universitatis Upsaliensis, 2004.

Clark, John. "Contemporary Asian Art and Biennales: The Perpetual Modern?". Contribution to a Clark Art Institute conference on new approaches to Asian art history, April 2007.

Enwezor, Okwui. "History Lessons". *Artforum* (October 2007). [On Documenta 12 and other large-scale exhibitions in 2007.]

Fleck, Robert. *Die Biennale von Venedig: Eine Geschichte des 20. Jahrhunderts.* Hamburg: Philo Fine Arts, 2009.

Grasskamp, Martin. "For example, Documenta, or, how is art history produced?". In *Thinking About Exhibitions*, ed. Rebecca Greenberg, Bruce W. Ferguson, and Sandy Nairne. London: Routledge, 1996.

McEvilley, Thomas. "Arrividerci Vencie: the Third World Biennials — reviews of Third World international survey exhibitions". *ArtForum* (November 1993).

Meyric Hughes, Henry. "The History and Significance of the Biennale as an Instrument of Globalization". In *Art Criticism and Globalisation.* São Paolo: Assoçiao Brasiliera de Criticos de Arte, 2006.

Okabe Aomi. "Gendaibijutsu no hen'yô to Bijutsuten". In *Kansha, Tenji, Kanshô sono juyô no bijutsushi* [Heisei 14 nendo – 16 nendo Kagaku kenkyûhi hojokin, Kenkûhôkokusho no. 1430029], ed. Omuka Toshiharu. Tsukuba: Tsukuba Daigaku Geijutsugakkei, 2001.

Osborne, Peter. "The Power of Assembly — Art, World, Industry". In *2006 Biennale of Sydney: Zones of Contact*, ed. Ewan Macdonald and Luke Parker. Sydney: Biennale of Sydney, 2006.

Poinsot, Jean-Marc. "Large Exhibitions: A Sketch of Typology". In *Thinking About Exhibitions*, ed. Rebecca Greenberg, Bruce W. Ferguson, and Sandy Nairne. London: Routledge, 1996.

Rugoff, Ralph. "Rules of the Game". *frieze* 44 (January–February, 1999).

Stallabrass, Julian. *Art Incorporated: The Story of Contemporary Art.* Oxford: Oxford University Press, 2004.

Smith, Terry. "Biennales in the Conditions of Contemporaneity". *Art and Australia* 42, 4 (Autumn 2005).

________. *What is Contemporary Art? Contemporary Art, Contemporaneity, and Art to Come.* Sydney: Artspace Visual Art Centre, 2001.

Tama Bijutsudaigaku Geijutsugakuka Tatehatazemi Shimpojiumu kikaku, Isozaki Akira, Okabe Aomi, Kitagawa Furamu, Nanjô Fumio, Hasegawa Yûko. *Yokohama Kaigi 2004: Naze Kokusaiten ka?.* Yokohama: BankART1929, 2005.

Zabel, Igor. "What our village needs now... Biennial localisation factors". Presented at the "Biennials in Dialogue Conference", Kassel, Documenta Halle, August 2000.

## Art, Markets, and the Economy

Abbing, Hans. *Why Are Artists Poor? The Exceptional Economy of the Arts.* Amsterdam: Amsterdam University Press, 2002 and 2004.

Baudrillard, Jean. *For a Critique of the Political Economy of the Sign*. Translated by Charles Levin. New York: Telos Press, 1981. [See the chapter: "The Art Auction: Sign Exchange and Sumptuary Value".]

Burn, Ian. "The Art Market: Affluence and Degradation". *Artforum* (April 1975).

Caves, Richard E. *Creative Industries: Contracts Between Art and Commerce*. Cambridge, MA: Harvard University Press, 2000.

"China is the world's second largest exporter of art". *The Art Newspaper* XX, 66 (February 2006).

"Christie's Going, Going to China to hold Auctions". *New York Times* (October 20, 2005).

De Monthoux, Piere Guillet. *The Art Firm: Aesthetic Management and Metaphysical Marketing*. Stanford: Stanford Business Books, 2004.

Galenson, David W. *Artistic Capital*. London: Routledge, 2006.

Harrison, Charles and Paul Wood, ed. *Art in Theory, 1900–1990: An Anthology of Changing Ideas*. Oxford: Blackwell, 1992.

Ginsburg, Victor and Sheila Weyers. "Creativity and the Life Cycles of Artists". *Journal of Cultural Economics* 30 (2006).

Greffe, Xavier. *Arts and Artists from an Economic Perspective*. Paris: Economica/UNESCO, 2002. [Review published by Walter Snatagata. *Journal of Cultural Economics* 28, 3 (August 2004).]

Linde, Rohr-Bongrad et al. *Kunst = Kapital: Der* Capital *Kunstkompass von 1970 bis heute*. Köln: Salon Verlag, 2001.

McCain, Roger A. "Markets for Works of Art and "Markets for Lemons'". In *Economic Policy for the Arts*, ed. William Scott Hendon, James L. Shanahan, and Alice J. McDonald. Cambridge, MA: Abt Books, 1980.

Moulin, Raymonde and Alain Quemin. *Le Marché de l'art: mondialisation et Nouvelles technologies*. Paris: Flammarion, 2000.

________. *L'artiste, l'institution et le marché*. Paris: Flammarion, 1997.

Napack, Jonathan. "An Art Market with Chinese Characteristics". *Asian Art Archive newsletter* (May 2006).

Quemin, Alain. "Globalization and mixing in the visual arts". *International Sociology* 21, 4 (July 2006).

________. *L'art contemporain international: entre les institutions et le marché (Le rapport disparu)*. Nîmes: Éditions Jacqueline Chambon/Artprice, 2002.

________. "L'art contemporain international à l'heure de la «globalisation». La place de la France dans le concert des nations". *Pratiques: Réflexions sur l'art* 12, 2002.

________. *Le rôle des pays prescripteurs sur le marché et dans le monde de l'art contemporain*. Paris: Ministère des Affaires Étrangères, 2001.

Rifkin, Jeremy. *The Age of Access: The New Culture of Hypercapitalism Where All of Life is a Paid-For Experience*. New York: Jeremy P. Tarcher/Putnam, 2000.

Ruccio, David, Julle Graham, and Jack Amariglio. "'The Good, the Bad, and the Different': Reflections on Economic and Aesthetic Value". In *The Value of Culture: On the Relationship between Economics and Arts*, ed. Arjo Klamer. Amsterdam: Amsterdam University Press, 1997.

Schuster, J. Mark. Review of Wu Chin-Tao, *Privatising Culture: Corporate Art Intervention Since the 1980s*, London: Verso, 2002. *Journal of Cultural Economics* 7 (2003).

Shell, Marc. *Art & Money*. Chicago: University of Chicago Press, 1995.

Simmel, Georg. "On Money and Commodity Culture" in *Simmel on Culture*, ed. David Frisby and Mike Featherstone. London: Sage Publications, 1997.

Singer, Leslie P. "Phenomenology and Economics of Art Markets: an Art Historical Perspective". *Journal of Cultural Economics* XII, 1 (June 1988).

________. "Microeconomics of the Art Market". *Journal of Cultural Economics* II, 2 (1978).

________. "Rivalry and Externalities in Secondary Art Markets". *Journal of Cultural Economics* V, 2 (June 1981).

Skinner, Sarah J. "Estimating the Real Growth Effects of Blockbuster Art Exhibits: A Time Series Approach". *Journal of Cultural Economics* 30 (2006): 109–25.

Swedburg, Richard. "The Cultural Entrepreneur and the Creative Industries". *Journal of Cultural Economics* (October 13, 2006). [Sociological additions to Caves 2000, above.]

Throsby, David. "An Artistic Production Function: Theory and an Application to Australian Visual Artists". *Journal of Cultural Economics* 30 (2006).

________. "Determining the Value of Cultural Goods: How Much (or How Little) Does Contingent Value Tell Us?". *Journal of Cultural Economics* 27 (2003).

________. *Economics and Culture*. Cambridge, MA: Cambridge University Press, 2001. [Review by Paul Dimaggio in *Journal of Cultural Economics* 27 (2003).]

________. "Economic and Cultural Value in the Work of Creative Artists". In *Values and Heritage Conservation*, ed. Erica Avrami, Randall Mason, and Marta de la Torre. Los Angeles: The Getty Conservation Institute, 2000.

Van den Bosch, Annette. *The Australian Art World: Aesthetics in a Global Market*. Sydney: Allen & Unwin, 2005.

Velthuis, Olav. *Imaginary Economics: Contemporary Artists in the World of Big Money*. Rotterdam: Nai Publishers, 2005.

________. *Talking Prices: Symbolic Meanings of Prices on the Market for Contemporary Art*. Princeton: Princeton University Press, 2005. [Review by Valsan, Calin, *The Journal of Cultural Economics* 30 (2006).]

Wijnberg, Nachoem M. Review of James F. English, *The Economy of Prestige: Prizes, Awards, and the Circulation of Cultural Value*, Cambridge, MA: Harvard University Press. *Journal of Cultural Economics* 30 (2006).

Wu Chin-tao. *Privatising Culture: Corporate Art Intervention Since the 1980s*. London: Verso, 2002.

## Art Dealers

Beckmann, Michael. "Art Auctions and Bidding Rings: Empirical Evidence from German Auction Data". *Journal of Cultural Economics* 28 (2004): 125–41.

De Coppet, Laura and Alan Jones. *The Art Dealers: The Powers Behind the Scene Talk About the Business of Art*. New York: Clarkson N. Potter, 1984.

Goldstein, Malcolm. *Landscape with Figures: A History of Art Dealing in the United States*. Oxford: Oxford University Press, 2000.

Jensen, Robert. *Marketing Modernism in Fin-de-Siècle Europe*. Princeton: Princeton University Press, 1994.

Marquis, Alice Goldfarb. *The Art Biz: The Covert World of Collectors, Dealers, Auction Houses, Museums, and Critics*. Chicago: Contemporary Books, 1991.

Moulin, Raymonde and Alain Quemin. "La Certification de la valeur de l'art: experts et expertises". *Annales ESC*, 6 (November/December 1993).

Secrest, Meryle. *Duveen: A Life in Art.* Chicago: University of Chicago Press, 2004.

Simpson, Colin. *Artful Partners, the Partnership: The Secret Association of Bernard Berenson and Joseph Duveen.* London: Bodley Head, 1987.

Paas, Martha White. Review of Malcolm Goldstein, *Landscape with Figures: A History of Art Dealing in the United States*, Oxford: Oxford University Press, 2000. *Journal of Cultural Economics* 26, 3 (August 2002).

White, Harrison C. and Cynthia A. *Canvases and Careers: Institutional Change in the French Painting World.* New York: John Wiley & Sons, 1965.

## Cultures and Commodities:

Clunas, Craig. "Modernity Global and Local: Consumption and the Rise of the West". *American Historical Review* (December 1999).

De Marchi, Neil. Review of Ruth B. Phillips and Christopher B. Steiner, ed., *Unpacking Culture: Art and Commodity in Colonial and Post-Colonial Worlds*, Berkeley: University of California Press, 1999. *The Journal of Cultural Economics* 26, 3 (August 2002).

Mitchell, W.J.T. "Gombrich and the Rise of Landscape". In *The Consumption of Culture 1600–1800: Image, Object, Text*, ed. Ann Bermingham and John Brewer. London: Routledge, 1995.

## Hybridity, Post-coloniality and Globalization [Selected]

Appadurai, Arjun. "Introduction: Commodities and the Politics of Value". In *The Social Life of Things: Commodities in Cultural Perspective.* Cambridge, MA: Cambridge University Press, 1986.

________. *Modernity at Large: Cultural Dimensions of Globalization.* Minneapolis: University of Minnesota Press, 1996.

Bhabha, Homi K. *The Location of Culture.* London: Routledge, 1994.

Canclini, Néstor García. "Remaking Passports: Visual Thought in the Debate on Multiculturalism". *Grasping the World: The Idea of the Museum*, ed. Donald Prezioso and Claire Farago. Farnham: Ashgate Publishers, 2004.

________. "Contradictory modernities and globalization in Latin America". In *Through the Kaleidoscope: The Experience of Modernity in Latin America*, ed. Vivian Schelling, 37–52. London: Verso, 2000.

________. *Hybrid Cultures: Strategies for entering and leaving modernity.* Minneapolis: University of Minnesota Press, 1995.

________. "The state of war and the state of hybridization". In *Without Guarantees: In Honour of Stuart Hall*, ed. Paul Gilroy, Lawrence Grossberg, and Angela McRobbie, 38–51. London: Verso, 2000.

Chakravarty, Dipesh. *Provincializing Europe: Postcolonial Thought and Historical Difference.* Princeton: Princeton University Press, 2000.

Dirlik, Arif. *The Postcolonial Aura: Third World Criticism in the Age of Global Capitalism.* Boulder: Westview Press, 1997.

Erjavec, Aleš. *Aesthetics and/as Globalization: International Yearbook of Aesthetics*. Volume 8. Ljubljana: Zalozba ZRC Publishing, 2004.

Enwezor, Okwui. "Between worlds: postmodernism and African artists in the Western Metropolis". In *Reading the contemporary: African Art from Theory to Marketplace*, ed. Olu Oguibe and Okwui Enwezor. London: inIVA, 1999.

Enwezor, Okwui et al. *Créolité and Creolization: Documenta 11_Platform 3*. Kassel: documenta and Museum Fridericianum-Veranstaltungs Gmbh, 2003.

Glissant, Édouard. *Le Discours Antillais*. Paris: Éditions du Seuil, 1981.

Grewal, Inderpal, Akhil Gupta, and Aihwa Ong, guest ed. "Special Issue: Asian Transnationalities". *positions: east asia cultures critique* 7, 3 (Winter 1999).

Hall, Stuart. "The West and the Rest: discourse and power". In *Formations of Modernity*, ed. Stuart Hall and Bram Gieben. Cambridge, UK: Polity Press, 1992.

Hannerz, Ulf. *Cultural complexity: studies in the social organization of meaning*. New York: Columbia University Press, 1992.

Hoffmann, Frank. "Monoculture and Its Discontents". *Art in America* 88, 11 (November 2000).

King, Anthony D., ed. *Culture, Globalization and the World-System*. Basingstoke: Macmillan, 1991.

Lavrijsen, Ria. *Global Encounters in the World of Art: Collisions of Tradition and Modernity*. Amsterdam: Royal Tropical Institute, 1998.

Miyoshi Masao. "A Borderless World? From Colonialism to Transnationalism Over the Decline of the Nation-State". Critical Inquiry, 19 (Summer 1993). Reprinted in Catherine David and Jean-François, ed. *Documenta X – The Book*. Ostfildern-Ruit: Hatje Cantz Verlag, 1997.

Ong, Aihwa. *Flexible Citizenship: The Cultural Logics of Transnationality*. Durham: Duke University Press, 1999.

Parry, Benita. "Overlapping Territories and Intertwined Histories: Edward Said's Postcolonial Cosmopolitanism". In *Edward Said: A Critical Reader*, ed. M. Sprinkler. Oxford: Blackwell Press, 1992.

Poi, Cesare. "From the Suburbs to the Global Village: Afterthoughts on Magiciens de la Terre". *Third Text* 14 (Spring 1991).

Rogoff, Irit. *Terra Infirma: Geography's Visual Culture*. London: Routledge, 2000.

Said, Edward. "Secular Interpretation, the Geographical Element, and the Methodology of Imperialism". In *After Colonialism: Imperial Histories and Postcolonial Displacements*, ed. Gyan Prakash. Princeton: Princeton University Press, 1995.

________. *Culture and Imperialism*. London: Chatto and Windus, 1994.

Sassen, Saskia. "The Topoi of E-Space: Global Cities and Global Value Chains". In *Politics, Poetics — Documenta X: The Book*, ed. Catherine David and Jean François Chevrier. Ostfildern-Ruit: Hatje Cantz Verlag, 1997.

Thomas, Nicholas. *Possessions: Indigenous Art/Colonial Culture*. London: Thames and Hudson, 1999.

Walcott, Derek, "Exasperating Theory", "More than Criticism", and "The Length of the Breath". In *Créolité and Creolization: Documenta 11_Platform 3*, ed. Okwui Enwezor et al. Kassel: documenta and Museum Fridericianum-Veranstaltungs Gmbh, 2003.

________. *Tiepolo's Hound*. New York: Farrar, Straus and Giroux, 2000.

________. "The Muse of History". In *What the Twilight Says: Essays.* London: Faber & Faber, 1998.

________. *Omeros.* London: Faber & Faber, 1990.

Weibel, Peter. *Inklusion/Exklusion: Kunst im Zeitalter von Postkolonialismus und Globaler Migration.* Graz: Neue Galerie 1996.

Wilson, Rob. *Reimagining the American Pacific: From South Pacific to Bamboo Ridge and Beyond.* Durham, NC: Duke University Press, 2000.

## Other Theories and Histories:

Augé, Marc. *Non-places: Introduction to an Anthropology of Supermodernity.* Trans. John Howe. London: Verso, 1994.

Bal, Mieke. *Double Exposures: The Subject of Cultural Analysis.* New York: Routledge, 1996.

Bateson, Gregory. *Steps to an Ecology of Mind.* New York: Ballantine Books, 1972.

Baudrillard, Jean. *The Conspiracy of Art.* Trans. Anne Hodges. New York: Semiotext(e), 2005.

________. "*The Precession of Simulacra*". In *Simulations.* New York: Semiotext(e) & Columbia University Press, 1983.

Belting, Hans. *The End of the History of Art.* Trans. Christopher S. Wood. Chicago: University of Chicago Press, 1987.

Bourdieu, Pierre. *The Field of Cultural Production.* Ed. and trans. Randall Johnson. Cambridge, UK: Polity Press, 1993, 2000.

________. *La distinction: critique sociale du jugement.* Paris: Les Éditions de Minuit, 1979.

________. *Outline of a Theory of Practice.* Trans. Richard Nice. Cambridge, UK: Cambridge University Press, 1977.

Bourriaud, Nicolas. *Postproduction.* Second edition. New York: Lukas & Sternberg, 2005.

________. *Relational Aesthetics.* Trans. Simon Pleasance, Fronza Woods, and Mathieu Copeland. Dijon: Les Presses du Réel, 2002.

Burkhardt, Jacob. *The Civilization of the Renaissance in Italy.* Trans. S.G.C. Middlemore. 1860; Translation, London: Phaidon, 1951.

Castells, Manuel, "Informationalism, networks, and the network society: a theoretical blueprint". In *The Network Society: a Cross-Cultural Perspective*, ed. Manuel Castells. Cheltenham: Edward Elgar, 2004.

Eagleton, Terry. *The Ideology of the Aesthetic.* Oxford: Blackwell, 1990, 2000.

Foster, Hal et al. *Art Since 1900: Modernism, Antimodernism, Postmodernism.* London: Thames & Hudson, 2004. [See reviews by John Clark and David McNeil in *Yishu: Journal of Contemporary Chinese Art* 15 (December 2005).]

Groys, Boris. *Art Power.* Cambridge, MA: MIT Press, 2008.

Guillory, John. "Canon". *In Critical Terms for Literary Study.* Ed. Frank Lentricchia and Thomas McLaughlin. Chicago: University of Chicago Press, 1990.

Habermas, Jürgen. *The Theory of Communicative Action.* Volume 1 and 2. Trans. Thomas McCarthy. London: Heinemann, 1984.

Heidegger, Martin. "The Age of the World Picture". In *The Question Concerning Technology and Other Essays*, trans. William Lovitt. New York: Harper, 1977.

Heinich, Nathalie. *Le triple jeu de l'art contemporain*. Paris: Les Éditions de Minuit, 1998. [A summary is available in Jean-Marie Schaeffer. *Think Art*. Rotterdam: Witte de With, 1998.]

Sakai, Naoki. "'You Asians': On the Historical Role of the West and Asia Binary". *The South Atlantic Quarterly* 99, 4 (2001): 789–817.

_______. "Modernity and Its Critique: The Problem of Universalism and Particularism". In *Postmodernism and Japan*, ed. M. Miyoshi and H.D. Harootunian. Durham & London: Duke University Press, 1989.

## Biennales and Triennales by Site

[This only lists material available to John Clark, terminus is usually 2006.]

### Beijing:

#### 2003

The First Beijing International Art Biennale, China 2003. Promotional Brochure. Beijing International Art Biennale Office.

The Conference of the First Beijing International Art Biennale, China 2003 – Originality: Contemporaneity and Locality, Handbook, Beijing International Art Biennale Office, 2003.

#### 2005

The Second Beijing International Art Biennale, China 2005. Promotional Booklet. Beijing International Art Biennale Office, 2005.

### Brisbane: Asia-Pacific Triennial of Contemporary Art (APT)

#### Overall

Maravillas, Francis. "Cartographies of the Future: The Asia-Pacific Triennials and the Curatorial Imaginary". Paper presented at the "Our Modernities: Positioning Asian Art Now Conference", Asia Research Institute, National University of Singapore, Singapore, 19–22 February 2004. Revised version in John Clark, Maurizio Peleggi and T.K. Sabapathy, ed., *Eye of the Beholder*. Sydney: Wild Peony, 2006.

Turner, Caroline. "Cross-Cultural Engagements in Asian Art: The Fukuoka Triennale and the Asia-Pacific Triennial". Paper presented at the "Our Modernities: Positioning Asian Art Now Conference", Asia Research Institute, National University of Singapore, Singapore, 19–22 February 2004. Revised version in John Clark, Maurizio Peleggi and T.K. Sabapathy, eds. *Eye of the Beholder*. Sydney: Wild Peony, 2006.

#### APT I 1993

*Artlink* 13, 3&4 (November 1993–March 1994).

*Art Monthly Australia* 65 (November 1993).

*Asian Art News* 3, 6 (November–December 1993).

Britton, Stephanie. "Review of the Conference Identity Tradition and Change: Contemporary Art of the Asia Pacific Region". *Artlink* 13, 3&4 (November 1993–March 1994).

Correspondence: *Art Monthly Australia*, 67 (March 1994) and 68 (April 1994).

Ewington, J. "Identity, Tradition & Change: Photography at the Asia-Pacific Triennale". *Photofile* 40 (1994).

Ewington, J., Quan Nguyen and E. Torres. *Art & Asia Pacific* 1, 2 (1994).

Gallagher, Jane. "An analysis of critical categories operant in the Asia-Pacific Triennale". Unpublished undergraduate honours thesis. Power Institute of Fine Arts, University of Sydney, 1994.

Hall, Doug. *Queensland Asia Pacific Triennial Bulletin* 1, 2 (1992).

Hoffie, P. "1993 Asia Pacific Triennial". Supplement to Art & Australia. *Art & Asia Pacific* (September 1993).

Hogan, J., ed. *The First Asia-Pacific Triennal of Contemporary Art*. Brisbane: Queensland Art Gallery, 1993.

Mendelssohn, Joanna. "Review: First Asia-Pacific Triennial of Contemporary Art, Queeensland Art Gallery". *Artlink* 13, 3&4 (November 1993–March 1994).

Roces, Marion Pastor. "A certain critical mass". *Art Monthly Australia*, 63 (November 1993).

Turner, Caroline. "Introduction — From Extraregionalism to Intraregionalism". In *The First Asia Pacific Triennial of Contemporary Art*. Exhibition catalogue. Brisbane: Queensland Art Gallery, 1993.

Turner, Caroline, ed. *Tradition and Change: Contemporary Art of Asia and the Pacific*. Brisbane: University of Queensland Press, 1993.

Wallace, Linda. "The Asia-Pacific Triennial of Contemporary Art". Review. *Art & Text* 47 (January 1994).

Williamson, Claire. "Remapping the Asia-Pacific". *Art Monthly Australia* 65 (November 1993).

APT II 1996

Clark, J. and P. Gutman. "The Second Asia-Pacific Triennial of Contemporary Art: A Conversation". *Eyeline: Contemporary Visual Arts* 32 (1996): 21–3.

Ewington, Lee and Losche Ushiroshoji. *ART AsiaPacific* 15 (1997).

Flores, Mehta, Kent. *Eyeline: Contemporary Visual Arts* 32 (1996).

Gibson. *Flash Art* (January–February 1997).

McDonald, J. *Sydney Morning Herald* (5 October 1996).

Mendelsohn, Hall, Thomas McCulloch, and Howard Turner. *Asian Art News* 7, 1 (January/ February 1997).

Stein. *Art in America* (June 1997).

Turner, C. and Rhana Devenport. Explanatory pull-out. *ART AsiaPacific* 13, 1997.

________. *The Second Asia-Pacific Triennale of Contemporary Art*. Exhibition catalogue. Brisbane: Queensland Art Gallery, 1996.

Turner, C. and Rhana Devenport, ed. *Present Encounters: Papers from the Conference of the Second Asia-Pacific Triennale of Contemporary Art*. Brisbane: Queensland Art Gallery & Griffith University, 1996.

**APT III 1999**

"The Long Stare: Seeing Contemporary Asian Art Now". Special issue. *Artlink* 20, 2 (July 2000).

Carroli, Linda. "A virtual region". *Art AsiaPacific* 27 (2000).

Chiu, Melissa. "Duplicitous Dialogue". *Art AsiaPacific* 27 (2000).

Clark, John. "Panel Report on Commodification/Patronage/Censorship". In *Beyond the Future: Conference Proceedings, The Third Asia-Pacific Triennial of Contemporary Art*, ed. C. Turner and M. Low. Brisbane: Queensland, 2000.

Dale, Robert. "Reviews: The Third Asia-Pacific Triennial of Contemporary Art". *Eyeline* 41 (1999/2000).

Fink, Hannah. "Fizzle". *Art AsiaPacific*, 27 (2000).

Foley, Matt. Ministerial Statement. Queensland Parliamentary Hansard, 26 August 1999.

Gibson, Jeff. "Third Asia-Pacific Triennial of Contemporary Art". *Artforum International* 38, 5 (January 2000).

Green, Charles. "Beyond the Future: The Third Asia-Pacific Triennial". *Art Journal* 58, 4 (1999): 81–7.

Hall, Doug. *The Courier-Mail* (23 April 1999).

________. "Foreword". In *Beyond the Future: The Third Asia-Pacific Triennial of Contemporary Art*. Exhibition catalogue. Brisbane: Queensland Art Gallery, 1999.

________. *The Age* (10 September 1999).

Holder, Jo and Catriona Moore. "Going Glocal — APT 3: Beyond the Future". *Realtime*, 34: 24.

Jackson, Beth. "Improbable Architectures". *Art AsiaPacific* 27 (2000).

Low, Morris. "Hybrid transplants at the Queensland Art Gallery". *Artlink* 20, 2 (July 2000).

McNamara, Andrew. "The Third Asia-Pacific Triennial of Contemporary Art: To the point of distraction! Entertaining Diversity". *Eyeline* 42 (Autumn/Winter, 1999/2000): 31–3.

Miki Akiko. "Evaluating the Asia-Pacific Triennial". *Artlink* 20, 2 (July 2000).

Taylor, Roger. "A dynamic of cultures". *Asian Art News* 9, 6 (1999).

Turner, Caroline. "Introduction". In *Beyond the Future: Conference Proceedings, The Third Asia-Pacific Triennial of Contemporary Art*, ed. C. Turner and M. Low. Brisbane: Queensland, 2000.

________. "Journey Without Maps: The Asia Pacific Triennial". In *Beyond the Future: The Third Asia-Pacific Triennial of Contemporary Art*, exhibition catalogue. Brisbane: Queensland Art Gallery, 1999.

Turner, Caroline and M. Low., ed. *Beyond the Future: Papers from the Conference of the Third Asia-Pacific Triennale of Contemporary Art*. Brisbane: Queensland Art Gallery & Griffith University, 1999.

Turner, Caroline and Rahna Devenport. *Beyond the Future: The Third Asia-Pacific Triennial of Contemporary Art*. Exhibition catalogue. Brisbane: Queensland Art Gallery, 1999.

Turner, Caroline et al. "On Understanding the Asia-Pacific Triennial', *Artlink* 20, 2 (July 2000).

Ushiroshôji Masahiro. "The APT and Fukuoka: a comparison". *Artlink* 20, 2 (July 2000).

APT IV 2002

Eastburn, Melanie. "A Decade Of Challenges". APT4 Review. *Asian Art News* 12, 6 (November/December 2002).

Gibson, Jeff. "Asia-Pacific Triennial of Contemporary Art". *Artforum International* 41, 1 (September 2002).

Grace, Helen. "Asia-Pacific Triennial of Contemporary Art 2002: Islands of Promise in the Dark Waters of a New World Order". *Eyeline* 50 (2002/2003): 24–7.

Ng, Elaine W. "Queensland Looks East". *ArtAsiaPacific* 45 (2005). [Regarding APT4 and New Queensland Art Gallery.]

Sambrani, Chaitanya. "Austerity – Excesss – Invention: the Asia-Pacific Triennial 2002". *Art Monthly Australia* 155 (November 2002).

Seear, Lynne, ed. *Asia-Pacific Triennale of Contemporary Art*. Brisbane: Queensland Art Gallery, 2002.

Thomas, Morgan. "Asia-Pacific Triennial 2002: We are Not the World". *Eyeline* 50 (2002–03): 32–3.

Wu Hung. *"Mapping Contemporaneity" in APT 2002: Asia Pacific Triennial of Contemporary Art*. Exhibition catalogue. Brisbane: Queensland Art Gallery, 2002.

APT V 2006

Fairlie, Gina. "Connections and the Future". *Asian Art News* 17, 1 (Jan–Feb 2007). [Review of the Fifth Asia Pacific Triennale, Brisbane.]

Seear, Lynne and Suhanya Raffel. *The 5th Asia Pacific Triennial of Contemporary Art*. Brisbane: Queensland Art Gallery Publishing, 2006.

## Fukuoka: various names

Overall

[Fukuoka Ia] *Asian Artists Exhibition Part I: Contemporary Asian Art Show*. Fukuoka: Fukuoka Fine Arts Museum, 1980.

[Fukuoka Ib] *Asian Artists Exhibition Part I: India, China & Japan*. Fukuoka: Fukuoka Fine Arts Museum, 1979.

[Fukuoka II] *2nd Asian Art Show, Fukuoka; Special Section: Art of Bali*. Fukuoka: Fukuoka Fine Arts Museum, 1985

[Fukuoka III] *3rd Asian Art Show, Fukuoka*. Fukuoka: Fukuoka Fine Arts Museum, 1989.

Fouser, Robert. "Asia as a state of mind". *Art AsiaPacific* 24 (1999).

Fukuoka Asian Art Museum Art Exchange Programs. *Annual Report 01-02*. Fukuoka: Fukuoka Asian Art Museum, 2002.

________. *Annual Report 00-01*. Fukuoka: Fukuoka Asian Art Museum, 2001.

________. *Annual Report 99-00*. Fukuoka: Fukuoka Asian Art Museum, 2000.

Fukuoka Asian Art Museum. *Asian Collection 50*. Fukuoka: Fukuoka Asian Art Museum, 2000.

Matsuura Jin. *"Notes on Artist in Residence Program": Winds of Artists in Residence 2001*. Fukuoka: Fukuoka Asian Art Museum, 2001.

Murata Makoto. "Asia as an Art Museum". *Art AsiaPacific* 24 (1999).

### 1994 4th Asian Art Show

Fukuoka Art Museum, ed. *4th Asian Art Show Fukuoka*. Fukuoka: Fukuoka Art Museum, 1994.

*4th Asian Art Show Fukuoka: Realism as an Attitude*. Fukuoka: Fukuoka Art Museum, 1994.

### 1999 1st Fukuoka Asian Art Triennale

Kuroda Raiji. *The First Fukuoka Asian Art Triennale*. Fukuoka: Fukuoka Asian Art Museum, 1999.

Matsuura Jin and Kamachi Masae. *The First Fukuoka Asian Art Triennale [The 5th Asian Art Show] Seminar: "Asian Art – Towards the 21st Century"*. Fukuoka: Fukuoka Asian Art Museum, 1999.

________. *The First Fukuoka Asian Art Triennale 1999 [The 5th Asian Art Show]: Document of Art Exchange Programme*. Fukuoka: Fukuoka Asian Art Museum, 1999.

Ushiroshôji Masahiro. "The APT and Fukuoka: a comparison". *Artlink* 20, 2 (July 2000).

### 2002 2nd Fukuoka Asian Art Triennale

Fouser, Robert J. "2nd Fukuoka Asian Art Triennale". *ART AsiaPacific* 36 (2002).

Kuroda, Raiji. "Ajibi no 5-nen – kôryûjigyô wo chûshin ni". *In Fukuoka Asian Art Museum Collection Now: Soul of Asia*. Sapporo: Hokkaidôritsu Kindaibijutsukan, 2004.

Kondo Kazuyo, Nakao Tomomichi, and Yamaki Yuko, ed. *Imagined Workshop: The 2nd Fukuoka Asian Art Triennale 2002*. Fukuoka: Fukuoka Asian Art Museum, 2002.

Matsuura Jin. "Note son the artist-in-residence programme". In *Artisto in rejidensu seikaten*. Fukuoka: Asian Art Museum, 2002.

Nakao Tomomichi. *Hoka hen, Dai 2 kai Fukuoka ajia bijutsu toriennare 2002: The 2nd Fukuoka Asian Art Triennale 2002*. Fukuoka: Fukuoka Ajia Bijutsukan, 2002.

Turner, Caroline. "Imagined Workshop". 2nd Fukuoka Asian Art Triennial Review, *IIAS Newsletter* 29 (November 2002).

Ushiroshôji Masahiro. "'Ajia Bijutsukan' to iu arikata – sono imi, hôhô, shisutemu". *Ritsumeikan Gengo Bunka Kenkyû* 13, 4 (28 February 2002).

### 2005 3rd Asian Art Triennale

Igarashi Rina, ed. *The 3rd Fukuoka Asian Art Triennale 2005*. Fukuoka: Fukuoka Asian Art Museum, 2005.

Nagoya Satoru. "Yokohama and Fukuoka Triennials Report". *Flash Art* XXXIX, 246 (January–February 2006).

Rawanchaikul, Toshiko. "How were the artists selected?". In *The 3rd Fukuoka Asian Art Triennale 2005*, ed. Igarashi Rina. Fukuoka: Fukuoka Asian Art Museum, 2005.

## Guangzhou: Guangzhou Triennale

### 2002

Wu Hung with Wang Huangshang and Feng Boyi. *1st Guangzhou Triennial: Re-interpretation: a decade of Experimental Chinese Art (1990–2000)*. Guangzhou: Guangdong Museum of Art, 2002.

2005

Clark, John. "A Spectacle of Questions". *Asian Art News* 16, 1 (2006).

Goodbody, Bridget. "Beyond the Delta". *ArtAsiaPacific* 46 (2005).

Koegel, Eduard. "How to Urbanise a Special Economic Zone? The 2005 Biennale of Urbanism and Architecture in Shenzhen". *Yishu: Journal of Contemporary Chinese Art* 5, 2 (June 2006).

Pi Li. "The Second Guangzhou Triennial". *Flash Art* XXXIX, 246 (January–February 2006).

Spalding, David. "Second Guangzhou Triennale". *Artforum* 44, 8 (2006).

Vine, Richard. "Cities on the make: reflecting China's runaway building boom, the second Guangzhou Triennial examined the forces driving today's urban development and globalized art". *Art in America* 94, 8 (September 2006).

________. "Through a Chinese Lens". Review. *Art in America* 93, 6 (June–July 2005).

2006

Hou Hanru, Hans Ulrich, and Guo Xiaoyan, curators. *D-Lab/The Second Guangzhou Triennial BEYOND: an extraordinary space of experimentation for modernization*. Guangzhou: Lingnan Chubanshe, 2006.

________, curators. *The Second Guangzhou Triennial BEYOND: an extraordinary space of experimentation for modernization*. Exhibition catalogue. Guangzhou: Lingnan Chubanshe, 2006.

________, curators. *The Second Guangzhou Triennial BEYOND: an extraordinary space of experimentation for modernization*. Exhibition guide. Guangzhou: Lingnan Chubanshe, 2006.


## Gwangju/Kwangju Biennale


1995

Heartney, Eleanor. "Into the International Arena". *Art in America* 84, 4 (April 1996): 50(5).

Jin Young-sun and Chung Joon-mo, ed. *The First Kwangju International Biennale — International Exhibition of Contemporary Art: Beyond the Borders*. Volume I. Seoul: Life & Dream Publishing, 1995. [Director General of Visual Arts: Lee Yongwoo.]

Kim Hwan et al. "95 Kwang-ju International Contemporary Art Festival Catalogue". Kwang-ju: Kwang-ju City Gallery, 1995.

Lee, James B. "Pursuing global stature". Asia: Korea, *ARTnews* 94, 9 (November 1995): 224(2).

________. "The call to globalization: a booming economy has meant a proliferation of artists, galleries, and museums. But when will the West catch on? (Korea '95) (includes related articles on artists Lee Bul and Lee Sang-Hyun)". *ARTnews* 94, 4 (April 1995): 126(4).

1997

Kim Su-ki, ed. *97 Kwangju Biennale: Unmapping the Earth*. Kwangju: Kwangju Biennale Press, 1997. [Artistic director: Lee Young-chul.]

1998

Jay, Martin. "Kwangju: From Massacre to Biennale". *Salmagundi* I, 20 (Fall 1998): 15–26.

Vine, Richard. "Asian futures: status of South Korea in art world". *Art in America* 86, 7 (July 1998): 34–43.

2000

Cho Sung-kwan, ed. *Kwangju Biennale 2000 Man + Space*. Kwangju: Kwangju Biennale Press, 2000. [Artistic Director: Oh Kwang-su.]

________, ed. *Kwangju Biennale 2000 Man + Space: The Special Exhibition*. Kwangju: Kwangju Biennale Press, 2000. [Artistic Director: Oh Kwang-su.]

*Kwangju Biennale 2000 Man + Space*. Exhibition Guide.

2002

Chung Guyon, ed. *Gwangju Biennale 2002 Project4 Connection*. Curated by Chung Guyon. Gwangju: Gwangju Biennale Press, 2002.

*Gwangju Biennale 2002 Project 1 PAUSE, Project 2: THERE, Project 3 Stay of Execution*. Exhibition Guide. Gwangju: Gwangju Biennale Press, 2002.

Hou Hanru. "Event city and pandora's box: curatorial notes on the 2002 Gwangju Biennale". *Yishu* 1, 2 (2002).

Kee Joan. "2002 Gwangju Biennale". *ART AsiaPacific* 36 (2002);

Kim Youngna. "Let's Pause & Talk, Let's Pause & Drink". *IIAS Newsletter* 28 (July 2002)

Lee Weng Choy. "Biennale time and the specters of exhibition". *FOCAS 4* (2002).

Min Yong Soon, ed. *Gwangju Biennale 2002 Project2:THERE: Sites of Korean Diaspora*. Gwangju: Gwangju Biennale Foundation 2002. [Artistic Director: Sung Wan-kyun.]

Napack, Jonathan. "Alternative Visions". Gwangju Biennial Review. *Art in America* 90, 11 (November 2002).

Park Manu, ed. *Gwangju Biennale 2002 Project 1 PAUSE: Conception*. Curated by Sung Wan-kyung, Charles Esche, and Hou Hanru. Gwangju: Gwangju Biennale Press 2002.

Sung Wan-kyung, curator and ed. *Gwangju Biennale 2002 Project3 Stay of Execution*. Gwangju: Gwangju Biennale Press 2002.

Sung Wan-kyung, Charles Esche, and Hou Hanru, curators. *Project 1 Pause: Conception & Project 1 Pause: Realization*. Gwangju: Gwangju Biennale Press, 2002.

2004

Gwangju Biennale 2004. *Viewer-Participants Discission Papers: The Audience, Who Are They?* Gwangju: Gwangju Biennale Foundation, 2004.

________. *Press Open*. Press briefing for Biennale Opening, In Korean. Gwangju: Gwangju Biennale Foundation, 2004.

________. *A Grain of Dust, A Drop of Water*. Gwangju: Gwangju Biennale Press, 2004.

Gwangju, *Biennale Ecometro*.

## Busan Contemporary Art Exhibition, Busan Sea Art Festival

Breuvart, Valerie. "Gwangju Biennale 2004". Review. *Artforum* 46, 5 (January 2005).

*Busan Sculpture Project.* São Paolo 26th Biennial.

Clark, John. "Three Recent Biennales in Asia: Gwangju, Busan and Shanghai". *Art and Australia* 42, 3 (2005).

Heartney, Eleanor. "Report from Korea I: Biennial Anxiety". *Art in America* 93, 5 (May 2005) [Gwangju and Busan Biennials.]

Jheon Soocheon. *Social landscape: 2004 Gwangju Biennale.* Seoul: Jheon Soocheon, 2004.

Judd, Craig. "Gwangju Biennale 2004: A Viewer-Participant Memoir". *Eyeline* 56 (Summer 2004–5).

Kim Hyun-do, ed. *Gwangju Biennale 2004: A Grain of Dust. A Drop of Water.* Gwangju: Gwangju Biennale Foundation 2004. [Artistic Director: Lee Wong-yu.]

________. *Gwangju Biennale 2004: A Grain of Dust. A Drop of Water. — Korea Express Site 2.* Curated by Shim Jae-wook and Jung Gun-ho. Gwangju: Gwangju Biennale Foundation 2004.

### 2006

Clark, John. "A Narrowing of Horizons: The Shanghai and Gwangju Biennales 2006". *Art Monthly Australia* 196 (December 2006–February 2007).

Fenner, Felicity. "Gwangju Biennale". *Art and Australia* 44, 3 (2006).

Gwangju Biennale 2006. "Fever variations: Press Release". *Gwangju Biennale Foundation* (2006).

________. *Open Forum: World Contemporary Art and International Biennales.* Gwangju: Gwangju Biennale Foundation, 2006.

Han Kyung ah, ed. *Gwangju Biennale 2006: Fever Variations.* Curated by Wu Hung et al. Seoul: Designhouse Co., 2006). [Artistic Director: Kim Hong-hee.]

Lee, Pamela M. "2006 Singapore Biennale/6th Gwangju Biennale". *Artforum* 45, 3 (2006).

Lee Weng-Choy. "Eastern Front". *Artforum* 45, 1 (2006). [Singapore, Shanghai and Gwangju Biennales.]

## Istanbul: International İstanbul Biennial

### 2001 7th Biennial

Atagök, Tomar and Susan Plate. "The Istanbul Biennial: the digestible other". *Third Text* 55 (2001): 103.

Hori Motoaki. "Between East and West: The 7th International Istanbul Biennial". *ART AsiaPacific* 35 (2002).

Istanbul Biennale review. *Art in America* (March 2002).

Schwabsky, Barry. "Istanbul Biennial". *Artforum International* 40, 1 (September 2001).

Shawa, Wendy. "Art among the myths of globalism: the Istanbul Biennial". *Third Text* 16, 1, 58 (2002).

**2003 8th Biennial**

Heartney, Eleanor. "Mending the Breach". *Art in America* (January 2003): 74–9.

Kent, Rachel. "2003 Istanbul Biennial: Poetic Justice". *Art & Australia* 41, 3 (Autumn 2004): 278–9.

Nahas, Dominique. "Preview: The 8th International Istanbul Biennial". *Art Asia Pacific* 38 (Fall 2003): 25–6.

## Kassel: Documenta

**General Texts**

Block, René et al. *Das Lied von der Erde / The Song of the Earth*. Kassel: Museum Fridericianum, 2000.

Glasmeier, Michael and Karin Stengel, ed. *50Jahre/Years documenta, Archive in Motion*. Bilingual retrospective catalogue and texts. Göttingen: Steidi Verlag, 2005.

1992

*Documenta IX*

Galloway, David. "Documenta 9 The Bottom Line". *Art in America* 81, 9 (September 1993): 55.

1997

*Documenta X* artistic director Catharine David.

2002

*Documenta XI* artistic director Okwui Enwezor.

Downey, Anthony. "The Spectacular Difference of Documenta XI". *Third Text* 17, 1 (March 2003): 85–92.

Enwezor, Okwui et al. *Créolité and creolization: Documenta 11_Platform 3*. Kassel: documenta und Museum Fridericianum-Veranstaltungs Gmbh, 2003.

________. *Documenta IX: Platform Five*. Exhibition catalogue. Ostfildern-Ruit: Hatje Cantz Verlag, 2002.

Heartney, Eleanor. "A 600-hour Documenta". *Art in America* 90, 9 (September 2002): 86(10).

Lee Weng Choy. "Biennale time and the specters of exhibition". *FOCAS 4* (2002).

Lopez, Sebastian. "Starting Points: 'Documenta". *IIAS Newsletter* 25 (July 2001).

Nochlin, L. et al. "Platform Muse: Documenta 11". *Artforum International* 41, 1 (September 2002): 160(10).

## Johannesburg

**1997 Johannesburg 2nd Biennale**

Becker, Carol. "The second Johannesburg Biennale". *Art Journal* 57, 2 (Summer 1998): 86(15).

Diawara, Manthia. "Moving company, the Second Johannesburg Biennale". *Artforum International* 36, 7 (March 1998): 86.

Enwezor, Okwui. Interview by Carol Becker. *Art Journal* 57, 2 (Summer 1998): 101–8.

Heartney, Eleanor. "Mapping the postcolonial". *Art in America* 86, 6 (June 1998): 51(4).

*Hong Kong, etc.* Curated by Hou Hanru and organized by the Johannesburg Biennale.

## Kitakyushu Biennale

### 2003

Inaga Shigemi et al. *7th Kitakyushu Biennale: Art for Sale: Intimacy between Aesthetics and Economy*. Curated by Makiko Matake. Kitakyushu: Kitakyushu Municipal Museum of Art, 2003.

## Liverpool Biennale

### 2000

Bond, Antony, curator. *Trace: The International Exhibition*. Liverpool: Liverpool Biennial of Contemporary Art, 2000.

### 2002

Biggs, Lewis, ed. *International 2002*. Liverpool: Liverpool Biennial of Contemporary Art, 2002.

### 2004

Domela, Paul, ed. *international 04*. Liverpool: Liverpool Biennial of Contemporary Art, 2004.

### 2006

Domela, Paul, ed. *international 06*. Liverpool: Liverpool Biennial of Contemporary Art, 2006.

## Lyon Biennial

### 2001

Budge, Andrew. "'Partage d'exotismes': do 'magicians' grow wise or just old". *Third Text* 16, 1, 58 (2002).

Prat, Thierry & Thierry Raspail, artistic directors. *Partage D'Exotismes, Volume*. 5th Lyon: Biennale d'Art Contemporrin de Lyon, 2000.

## Manifesta [site varies]

Domela, Paul, ed. *Manifesta: Coffee Break*. Liverpool: Liverpool Biennial, 2005.

## New Delhi: India Triennale

### 1991

Nakamura Hideki. *JAPAN, Triennale India 1991- Yoshio Kitayama, Mio Shirai, Miran Fukuda*. Tokyo: The Japan Foundation, 1991.

## Osaka Triennale

### 1995

Osaka Prefectural Government, ed. *Osaka Triennale 1995. Sculpture. 6th International Contemporary Art Competition*. Curated by Hiroyuki Nakatsuka et al. Osaka: Osaka Prefectural Government 1995.

## *São Paulo: São Paulo Bienal*

### 1994

Leffingwell, Edward. "The Extraterritorial Zone: the 26th Sao Paulo Bienal". *Art in America* (February 2005).

### 1998

Leffingwell, Edward. "Cannibals All — 24th Sao Paulo Bienal". *Art in America* (May 1999).

## Singapore

### 2006

*Artstrings: National Arts Council Annual Report 2005/06*. Singapore: National Arts Council, 2006.

Chang, T.C. "Renaissance Revisited: Singapore as a 'Global City for the Arts'". *International Journal of Urban and Regional Research* 24, 4 (December 2000).

Cruikshank, Alan. "Interview: Fumio Nanjo Artistic Director Singapore *Biennale* 2006". Broadsheet 35, 3 (2006).

Gill, Simryn. *Guide to the Murals at Tanjong Pagar Railway Station, Singapore*. Singapore: Simryn Gill and Singapore Biennale 2006.

Hill, Jo Martin. "A Tale of Two Biennales: Singapore and Shanghai". *Yishu: Journal of Contemporary Chinese Art* 5, 4 (December 2006).

Kendzulak, Susan. "Interview with Fumio Nanjo, Artistic Director of the Singapore Biennale". *Yishu: Journal of Contemporary Chinese Art* 5, 4 (December 2006).

Kirker, Anne. "Decentralisation Works: Singapore Biennale 2006". *Eyeline*, 62 (Summer 2006–7).

Lee, Pamela M. "2006 Singapore Biennale/6th Gwangju Biennale". *Artforum* 45, 3 (2006).

Lee Weng Choy. "Calibrated Expectations: A Roundtable on the Inaugural Singapore Biennale 2006". *Broadsheet* 35, 3 (2006).

________. "Eastern Front". *Artforum* 45, 1 (2006). [Singapore, Shanghai and Gwangju Biennales.]

________. "The public remainder: Singapore goes to Venice, the Biennale comes to Singapore". *Broadsheet* 32, 2 (June–August 2005).

Slater, Ben, ed. *belief: Exhibition Short Guide*. Singapore: National Arts Council, 2006.

Thompson, Jonathan. "A Willingness to Engage". *Asian Art News* 16, 6 (November–December 2006) [Review of First Singapore Biennale.]

Yap, June. "Hope: [Regarding Belief]". *Eyeline* 62 (Summer 2006–7). [Singapore Biennale.]

## Shanghai

### 1998

*'98 Shanghai Art Biennale Exhibition Catalogue (in Chinese)*. Shanghai: Shanghai Art Museum, 1998.

### 2000

Chen Long, ed. *Shanghai Biennale 2000: Shanghai Spirit*. Curated by: Fang Zengxian et al. Shanghai: Shanghai Shuhua Chubanshe, 2000.

Hou Hanru. "A naked city". *Art AsiaPacific* 31 (2001).

Hou Hanru et al. *2000 Shanghai Biennale, Shanghai*. Shanghai: Shuhua Chubanshe, 2000.

*Shanghai Biennale 2000 Exhibition Guide*. Shanghai: Shanghai Art Museum, 2000.

Wu Hung. "The 2000 Shanghai Biennale". *Art AsiaPacific* 31 (2001).

### 2002

Genocchio, Benjamin. "Letter from Shanghai". *Art Monthly Australia* 157 (March 2003).

Withers, Rachel. "Shanghai Biennale". *Artforum International* 41, 1 (September 2002).

Wu Changfu and Lu Yongyi. *Urban Creation: Selected Works of International Students' Exhibition*. Shanghai: Shanghai Biennale 2002.

Xu Jiang and Li Xiangyang, ed. *2002 Shanghai Biennale: Urban Creation*. Curated by Fan Di-an et al. Shanghai: Shanghai Art Museum 2002.

### 2004

Fang, Zengxian and Xu Jiang, ed. *2004 Shanghai Biennale: Techniques of the Visible*. Curated by Xu Jiang et al. Shanghai: Shanghai Fine Art Publishers, 2004.

### 2006

Clark, John. "A Narrowing of Horizons: The Shanghai and Gwangju Biennales 2006". *Art Monthly Australia* 196 (December 2006–February 2007).

Fang Zengxian and Xu Jiang, ed. *2006 6th Shanghai Biennale: HyperDesign*. Curated by Zhang Qing et al. Shanghai: Shanghai Fine Art Publishers, 2006.

Hill, Jo Martin. "A Tale of Two Biennales: Singapore and Shanghai". *Yishu: Journal of Contemporary Chinese Art* 5, 4 (December 2006).

Koop, Stuart. "A Busy Week in a Frantic Century: Shanghai Biennale". *Eyeline* 62 (Summer 2006–07).

Lee Weng-Choy. "Eastern Front". *Artforum* 45, 1 (2006). [Singapore, Shanghai and Gwangju Biennales.]

Slater, Ben, ed. *Belief: Exhibition Short Guide, Singapore Biennale 2006*. Singapore: National Arts Council Singapore, 2006. [Artistic Director: Fumio Hanjo.]

Tinari, Philip, "6th Shanghai Biennale". *Artforum* 45, 3 (2006).

Zhang Qing. "The Undesignable". *Yishu: Journal of Contemporary Chinese Art* 5, 4 (December 2006).

## Sharjah, Sharjah International Biennial

### 2003

Lewis, Peter, ed. *Sharjah International Biennial 6 Guide*. United Arab Emirates: Sharjah International Biennial, 2003. [Director: Hoor Al-Qasimi.]

Turner, Grady. "Fast Forward in the Persian Gulf (Report from the U.A.E.)". *Art in America* (November 2003): 86–91.

## Sydney: Biennale of Sydney

### Overall

Paroissien, Leon. "Australian art and biennial and triennial exhibitions". *In Twenty: Sherman Galleries 1986–2006*, ed. Laura Murray Cree. Sydney: Craftsman House, 2006.

### 2002

Chen, Elsa Hsiang-chun. "Identity Politics? Allegorical Existence? On the way to the fantastic". *Yishu* 1, 2 (2002).

Duncan, Michael. "Self-created worlds". Sydney Biennale Review. *Art in America* 90, 10 (October 2002).

### 2006

Macdonald, Ewan and Luke Parker, ed. *2006 Biennale of Sydney: Zones of Contact*. Sydney: Biennale of Sydney, 2006.

Merewether, Charles. "Zones of Contact". *Art and Australia* 43, 4 (Winter 2006).

________. "Interview". *Broadsheet: Contemporary Visual Arts + Culture* (June–August, 2006).

________. "Taking Place: acts of survival for a time to come". In *2006 Biennale of Sydney: Zones of Contact*, ed. Ewan Macdonald and Luke Parker. Sydney: Biennale of Sydney, 2006.

________. "Cultural Chameleon". Interview by Mark Mordue. *The Weekend Australian* (20–21 May 2006): R6.

## Taipei Biennial

### 1996

Lee Yulin, chief ed. *1996 Taipei Biennial: The Quest for Identity (Essays)*. Taipei: Taipei Fine Arts Museum, 1996. [Executive Curator: Alice B.H. Lin.]

Lin, Alice B.H. *1996 Taipei Biennial: The Quest for Identity 11 Exhibition Catalogue*. Taipei: Taipei Fine Arts Museum, 1996. [Curator in Chief: Yulin Lee.]

1998

Chang Fangwei and Akikio Miki, ed. *Site of Desire 1998 Taipei Biennial Exhibition Catalogue*, Taipei: Taipei fine arts museum, 1998.

2000

*The Sky is the Limit 2000 Taipei Biennial exhibition Catalogue*. Curated by Jérôme Sans and Manray Hsu. Taipei: Taipei Fine Art Museum, 2000.

2002

*Taipei Biennial Great Theatre of the World Exhibition Guide*. Curated by Bartomeu Mari and Chia Chi Jason Wang. Taipei: Taipei Fine Art Museum 2002.

Yu, Sharleen, ed. *2002 Taipei Biennial Great Theatre of the World Exhibition Catalogue*. Curated by Bartomeu Mari and Chia Chi Jason Wang. Taipei: Taipei Fine Art Museum 2002.

2004

Huang, Andrew. "Art into Life". *Asian Art News* 15, 1 (2005).

Kendzulak, Susan. "Do You Believe in Reality". *Flash Art* XXXVIII, 240 (January–February 2005).

Vanderlinden, B., ed. *Do You Believe in Reality Taipei 2004 Exhibition Catalogue*. Curated by Barbara Vanderlinden and Amy Huei-hua Cheng. Taipei: Taipei Fine Art Museum, 2004.

2006

Clark, John. "Global Intentions". *Asian Art News* 17, 1 (January–February 2007).

Yu, Sharleen and Freya Chou. *Dirty Yoga 2006 Taipei Biennial Exhibition Catalogue*. Curated by Dan Cameron and Jun-jeh Wang. Taipei: Taipei Fine Art Museum, 2006.

## Venice: La Biennale di Venezia

Overall:

Alloway, Lawrence. *Venice Biennale, 1895–1968: from Salon to Goldfish Bowl*. London: Faber & Faber, 1969.

Di Martino, Enzo. *The History of the Venice Biennale 1895–2005*. Venezia: Italy Papiro Arte, 2005.

Jachec, Nancy. *Politics and painting at the Venice Biennale, 1948–1964, Italy and the Idea of Europe*. Manchester: Manchester University Press, 2007.

Rizzi, Paolo and Enzo Di Martino. *Storia della Biennale 1895–1982*. Milano: Electa, 1982.

*1974–78 Cronache della nuova Biennale*. In dialogue with Alberto Moravia and photographs by Lorenzo Capellini. Milano: Electa, 1978.

## Main catalogues and general texts by year

### 1993 45th Biennale

Blackall, Judith. "The Transit of Venice". Art & Text 46 (September 1993).

McEvilley, Thomas. "1993 Venice Biennale: Venice the Menace". *Artforum International* 32, 2 (October 1993).

*New Chinese Painting*, Advised by Francesca dal Largo for overall curator Achille Bonita Oliva. Also with catalogue text on Chinese avant-garde by Li Xianting in Aperto: Difference/Indifference, curated by Kong Chang'an and Lau-k'ung Chan.

Verzotti, Giorgio. "'Aperto 93': The better biennale". *Artforum International* 32, 2 (October 1993).

### 1995 46th Biennale

Lasschuyt, Helga. "The Venice Biennale Game". *Asian Art News* 5, 5 (September/October 1995).

Nanjô Fumio et al., ed. *La Biennale di Venezia 1995:TransCulture [Bilingual].* Curated by Nanjô Fumio and Dana Frijs-Hansen. Tokyo: The Japan Foundation and Fukutake Science and Culture Foundation, 1995.

### 1997 47th Biennale

Bryson, Norman and Gilbert Rolfe. "XLVII Venice Biennale". *Art & Text* 59 (November 1997–January 1998).

Kent, Rachel. "The Venice Biennale: Japan, Korea and Taiwan". *Art AsiaPacific* 18 (1998).

Cai Guoqiang [overall curator Germano Celant]; As People's Republic of China: Chao Ge, Chen Yifei, Hong Ling, Hu Jiancheng, Liu Gang, Liu Xiaodong, Shen Ling, Sun Weimin, Wan Jiyuan, Weng Yuping, Yu Hong, Yuan Yunsheng, Xie Dongmin [commissioners Sun Weimin & Giovanni Iovane, organiser unclear from Biennale catalogue]

### 1999 48th Biennale

Huang Yong Ping and Jean-Pierre Bertrand. *French Pavilion Catalogue, 48th Biennale di Venezia.* Commissioned by Hou Hanru and Denys Zacharopoulos. Association Francaise d'Action Artistique, 1999.

Schwabsky, Barry. "48th Venice Biennale". *Art & Text* 67 (November 1999–January 2000).

Stringa, N. *Terrecotte Cinesi dalla 48th Biennale di Venezia (Cai Guoqiang).* Cornuda: Garfiche Edizioni, 2003.

Szeeman, Harald. *d'APERtutto / APERTO over ALL.* 1999.

Withers, Rachel. "Allied Forces". Venice Biennial Review. *Artforum International* 37, 9 (May 1999).

### 2001 49th Biennale

Birnbaum, Daniel. "More is less". Venice Biennial Review. *Artforum International* 40, 1 (September 2001).

Lee Weng Choy. "Biennale Time and the Specters of Exhibition". *FOCAS* 3 (January 2002).

Clark, John. "Asian Artists at the 2001 Venice Biennale" *IIAS Newsletter* 26 (November 2001).

_______. "Review of Asian Art at the Venice Biennale". *IIAS Newsletter* (November 2001).

Chua, Kevin. "In Venetian Waters: Singapore at the 49th Venice Bienale". *FOCAS* 3 (January 2002).

Pijnappel, Johan. "Asia at Venice". *Asian Art News* 12, 1 (2002).

Siegel, Katy. "Human, all too human". Venice Biennial Review. *Artforum International* 40, 1 (September 2001).

Szeeman, Harald. *Plateau of Humanity*. 2001.

### 2003 50th Biennale

*Clandestine: Liu Zheng*. Curated by Francesco Bonami.

Clark, John. "Venice in Full Flow", in *Asian Art News* 13, 5 (September/October 2003): 46–50.

*Dreams and Conflicts: the Dictatorship of the Viewer: La Biennale di Venezia: 50th International Art Exhibition, La Biennale di Venezia 50th: 2003*. Venezia: Marsilio, 2003. (Director: Francesco Bonami.)

Genocchio, Benjamin. "The Big One Venice – Conflicting Agendas: No Buzz at Venice 2004" in *Art Asia Pacific* 38 (Fall 2003): 42–7.

Lenzi, Iola. "The Pioneering Sprit". *Asian Art News* 13 (September/October 2003): 51–53.

Li Luming, ed., *Guangdong Kuaiche / Canton Express*. Changsha: Hunan Meishu Chubanshe, 2003.

Obrist, Hans-Ulrich, Molly Nesbit and Tiranvanija Rirkrit. *Utopia Station*. 50th Biennale di Venezia, 2003.

Vetrocq, Marcia E. "Venice Biennale: "Every Idea But One". *Art in America* (September 2003): 76–87.

_______. "Venice Biennale takes shape". *Art in America* 91, 2 (February 2003).

_______. "New curator for the Venice Biennale". *Art in America* 90, 5 (May 2002).

*Zones of Urgency*. Curated by Hou Hanru.

### 2005 51st Biennale

*Always a Little Further: La Biennale di Venezia, 51st International Art Exhibition: La Biennale di Venezia 50th: 2003*. Dir. Rosa Martinez. Venezia: Marsilio, 2003.

Nagy, Peter. "The Home and the World". *Art India* X, iii (quarter iii, 2005). [Regarding the unofficial Indian pavilion.]

*Participating Countries/Collateral Events: La Biennale di Venezia, 51st International Art Exhibition: La Biennale di Venezia 50th: 2003*. Venezia: Marsilio, 2003.

Raza, Sara. "West and Center: An Asian presence at 51st Venice Biennale". *Art Asia Pacific* 45 (2005).

*The Experience of Art: La Biennale di Venezia, 51st International Art Exhibition: La Biennale di Venezia 50th: 2003*. Dir. Maria de Corral. Venezia: Marsilio, 2003.

## Yokohama: Yokohama Triennale

### 2001

Makabe Kaori, Mikami Yutaka, Yokohama Triennale office, ed. Yokohama 2001. Curated by Nakamura Nobio et al. Yokohama: The Organizing Committee of the Yokohama Triennale, 2001.

Statements from the Triennale's curators. http://www.jpf.go.jp/yt2001/2/info.html.

"Yokohama Toriennaare 2001 kôki – sono tenmatsu no kojinteki memorandamu". *aica Japan Newsletter* 2 (November 2001).

### 2005

Cash, Stephanie. "Yokohama Triennale Trouble". *Art in America* 93, 2 (February 2005).

Isozaki Arata. "Statement on the Yokohama Triennale". www.jpf.go.jp/yt2005/e/inquiry.htm, accessed on 13 October 2004.

Kondo Ken'ichi. "Yokohama 2005: International Triennale of Contemporary Art". Review. *ArtAsiaPacific* 48 (2006).

Koplos, Janet. "On the Waterfront: the second Yokohama Triennale, set in warehouses in an active port zone, had a subtext of international movement". *Art in America* 94, 4 (April 2006).

Nagoya Satoru. "Yokohama and Fukuoka Triennials Report", *Flash Art* XXXIX, 246 (January–February 2006).

Shinoda Takatoshi, Koyama Naomi, and Tabata Mikiko. *The Second Yokohama Triennale, Yokohama*. Yokohama: The Organizing Committee for Yokohama Triennale, 2005.

Tama Bijutsudaigaku Geijutsugakuka Tatehatazemi Shimpojiumu kikaku et al. *Yokohama Kaigi 2004: Naze Kokusaiten ka?*. Yokohama: BankART1929, 2005.

# National Exhibitions at Biennales:

## China:

### São Paolo:

Chang Tzong-zung. *Ho Siu-kee*. Hong Kong Arts Development Council. At 23rd São Paolo Biennial. 1996.

________. *Special Exhibition: Qiu Shi-hua*. Fundação de São Paolo. Curated by Chang Tsong-zung. At 23rd São Paolo Biennial. Hong Kong: Hanart TZ Gallery, 1996.

________. *Chinese Contemporary Art at São Paulo: 1 – The remaking of Mass Culture; 11 – Wakefulness and the Weightless Present*. At the 22nd Biennial of São Paolo. Hong Kong: Hanart TZ Gallery, 1994.

________. *Catalogue of Five Chinese artists in 22nd Biennial of São Paolo*. 1994.

Fan Di'an and Pi Li, ed. *The 25th São Paulo Biennial: Here and now: Chinese art in the process of urbanization*. Curated by Fan Di'an with assistant Pi Li. Beijing: China International Exhibition Agency, 2002.

Huang Du. *The 26th São Paolo Biennial: Chinese Pavilion: Landscape of Deterritorialization*. Art by Qu Yan. Beijing: China International Exhibition Agency, 2004.

Pong, Melanie et al., ed. *The Other Face: Three Chinese Artists at the Centenary Exhibition*. Curated by Chang Tsong-zung. Milan: Zanzibar 1995.

## Venice:

Chang Tsong-zung. "The Other Face". In *Catalogue 46th Biennale di Venezia*. 1995.

Dal Largo, Francesca. "Chinese Art at the Venice Biennale". In Chinese Art at the End of the Millennium, ed. John Clark, 158–166. Hong Kong: New Art Media, 2000.

________. "New Chinese Painting". In *Catalogue 45th Biennale di Venezia*. 1993.

Fan Di'an and Wang Yong, with assistant Huang Du. *China National Pavilion, 50th Biennale di Venezia*. Beijing: International Exhibitions Agency; Guangzhou: Guangdong Museum of Art, 2003.

Goodbody, Bridget. "No Introductions Necessary". *ArtAsiaPacific*, 45 (2005). [Regarding the China pavilion at Venice Biennale, 2005).

Hou Hanru. *Canton Express*. Project for *"Z.O.U – Zone of Urgency", 50th Biennale di Venezia*. Changsha: Hunan Arts Publishing House, 2003.

________. *One Man, Nine Animals: Huang Yong Ping's project for the French pavilion in Venice Biennale*. Paris: Association Française d'Action Artistique, 1999.

Huang Du, ed. *Synthi-Scapes, 50th Venice Biennale 2003, Chinese Pavilion*. Curated by Fan Di'an and Wang Yong. Exhibition Guide. Beijing: China International Exhibition Agency, 2003.

Huang Du and Van Dong, ed. *Synthi-Scapes, 50th Venice Biennale 2003, Chinese Pavilion*. Beijing: China International Exhibition Agency, 2003.

Lu Jie. "About the Chinese Presentation at the 2005 Yokohama Triennale". *Yishu: Journal of Contemporary Chinese Art* 4, 4 (December 2005).

*Regular • Fragile – Liu Jianhua. Project for the 50th Biennale Di Venezia – China Pavilion*. Shanghai: ShangHART, 2003.

Szeeman, Harald. *d'APERtutto / APERTO over ALL*, 1999. Including Venice's Collection Courtyard; organized by Cai Guoqiang. [Later published as Stinga, Nico. *Terrecotte Cinesi dalla 48A Biennale di Venezia*. Nove: Antiga Edizioni, 2003.]

________. "Harald Szeeman talks to Chinese artists about Venice, CCAA and curatorial strategies". In *Chinese Art at the Crossroads: Between Past and Future, Between East and West*, ed. Wu Hung. Hong Kong: New Art Media, 2001.

*Yishu: Journal of Contemporary Chinese Art* 4, 3 (September 2005). [Issue focusing on artists from PRC, Hong Kong, Taiwan and Singapore at the Venice Biennale/ Chinese presence at other biennale/triennial event.]

## China-HongKong:

Chang Tsong-zung. *Hong Kong pavilion*. At 49th Biennale di Venezia. Hong Kong: Hong Kong Arts Development Council, 2001.

________. *Venice Hong Kong, Magic at Street Level*. Hong Kong pavilion, at 49th Biennale di Venezia. Hong Kong: Hong Kong Arts Development Council, 2001.

*investigation of a journey to the west by micro+polo: artists from hong kong china*. At 51st Biennale di Venezia. Hong Kong: Hong Kong Arts Development Council, 2005.

*Navigating the Dot, Artists from Hong Kong, China*. At 50th Biennale di Venezia. Commissioned by Darwin Chen and curated by Para/Site Collective. Hong Kong: Hong Kong Arts Development Council, 2003.

Para Site Collective. *Navigating the Dot, artists from Hong Kong, China*. Curated by Para Site. Hong Kong: Arts Development Board, 2003.

Thompson, Jonathan. "Challenges and Questions" (Hong Kong Art Biennial). *Asian Art News* 16, 2, 2006.

## Indonesia:

Pruss, Jaana and Alexander Ochs, ed. *Arahmaiani I 11 June 2002*. Catalogue for 50th Biennale di Venezia with essay "About Arahmaiani" by Werner Kraus. Berlin: Pruss & Ochs Gallery, 2003.

Review of CP Biennale 2006, Indonesia. *Asian Art News* 15, 6 (2005).

Review of Yogyakarta Biennale. *Asian Art News* 16, 1 (2006).

## Iran:

Aghdashiou, A., *H. Khosrojerdi, Dreams & Conflicts*. Pamphlet. Venice Biennale, 2002.

*Ahmad Nadalian: Dreams and Conflicts*. Brochure. 50th Biennale di Venezia, 2003.

*Behrooz Daresh*. Brochure for 50th Biennale di Venezia, 2003.

## Japan:

### Bangladesh:

Kuroda Raiji, commissioner. *Document: Japanese Artists in the 7th Asian Art Biennial Bangladesh 1995*. Exhibition Catalogue. Tokyo: The Japan Foundation, 1995.

Mitsuda Yuri, commissioner and ed. *Embracing Life, Japan at the 10th Asian Art Biennale Bangladesh*. Exhibition Catalogue. Tokyo: The Japan Foundation, 2002.

Mori Tsukasa, Tsubaki Noboru, Kitayama Yoshio, and Domoto Yuum. *Report on Japan's Participation, 11th Asian Art Biennale, Bangladesh 2003*. Tokyo: The Japan Foundation, 2003.

Nakamura Makoto, commissioner. R*eport on Japan's participation in the 9th Asian Art Biennale Bangladesh 1999*. Tokyo: The Japan Foundation, 1999.

Nakamura Makoto and Kuriyama Masayuki, ed. Japan, *Asian Art Biennale Bangladesh 1999*. Exhibition Catalogue. Tokyo: The Japan Foundation, 1999.

Tsubaki Noboru, Kitayama Yoshio, and Domoto Yuum. *Japan at the 11th Asian Art Biennale, Bangladesh, 2003*. Exhibition Brochure. Tokyo: The Japan Foundation, 2003.

### São Paolo:

Motoe Kunio. *Masato Kobayashi: The Art of Luminosity*. Tokyo: The Japan Foundation, 1996.

Tadayasu Sakai. *Japan at the 10th Sao Paulo Bienal: Akira Kamiyama, Katsura Funakoshi, Kanji Wakae*. Tokyo: The Japan Foundation, 1989.

Takatori Shuji. *Toshihiro Kuno. 24th Sao Paulo Bienal*. Tokyo: The Japan Foundation, 1998.

Yamawaki Kazuo. *Kimio Tsuchiya: After the Deluge, 25th Sao Paulo Bienal*. Tokyo: The Japan Foundation, 2002.

Venice:

*City of Girls — Japanese pavilion, Venice Biennale: 7th International Architecture Exhibition, 2000.*

*Giappone — XLVIII Biennale di Venezia 1999, Dove Va L'Arte? Whither the Arts.* Exhibition Catalogue. Tokyo: The Japan Foundation, 1999.

*Giappone, La Biennale di Venezia 1996: VI Mostra Internazionale di Architettura.* Exhibition Brochure. Tokyo: The Japan Foundation, 1996.

Harumi Miwa, ed. *The Venice Biennale: 40 Years of Japanese Participation.* Tokyo: The Japan Foundation; Tokyo: The Mainichi Newspapers, 1995). [Bilingual.]

Hasegawa Yuko and The Japan Foundation, ed. *Heterotopias, Japanese Pavilion, the 50th Venice Biennale 2003.* Organised by the Japan Foundation and commissioned by Yuko Hasegawa. Tokyo: The Japan Foundation, 2003.

Osaka Eriko, ed. *Giappone — XLVIIII Biennale di Venezia 2001: Fast and Slow.* Tokyo: The Japan Foundation, 2001.

Korea:

Kee, Joan, ed. *Landscape of Differences, The Korean Pavilion, the 50th Venice Biennale 2003.* Commissioned by Kim Hong-hee. Seoul: Korean Culture & Arts Foundation, 2003.

Kim Sunjung, Kim Heejin, and Kim Jang Un, ed. *Secret beyond the door, The Korean Pavilion, the 51st Venice Biennale.* Commissioned by Kim Sunjung. Seoul: Korean Culture & Arts Foundation, 2005.

Kim Yoon-Soo and Li Guang-Jun, organisers. *Korean Painting at the Beijing International Art Biennale, China 2003.* Seoul: The Korean Culture & Arts Foundation, 2003.

*La Biennale di Venezia, The 49th International Art Exhibition, Korean Pavilion: Do-Ho Suh.* Commissioned by Park Kyung-Mee. Seoul: The Korean Culture and Arts Foundation, 2001.

*La Biennale di Venezia, The 49th International Art Exhibition, Korean Pavilion: Michael Joo.* Commissioned by Park Kyung-Mee. Seoul: The Korean Culture and Arts Foundation, 2001.

## Malaysia

Zhang Wubin. "The Ascent of the Image". *Asian Art News* 15, 6 (2005). [Review of First Kuala Lumpur International Photography Biennale.]

________. "Setting New Goals". Asian Art News 15, 6 (2005). [Interview regarding First Kuala Lumpur International Photography Biennale.]

## Philippines:

Flores, Patrick D. *Going for a Ride. M201: In God We Trust, 50th Biennale di Venezia*, 2003. Exhibition Catalogue.

## Singapore:

Chua, Kevin. "Singapore in the 49th Venice Biennale". *FOCAS* 3 (January 2002): 274.

Clark, John. "Venice Biennale". *Asian Art News* 13, 5 (September 2003).

Khor Koh Wah, commissioner. *Mike (Lim Tzay Chuen)*. Singapore: National Arts Council and Singapore Art Museum, 2005.

Langenbach, Ray. "Garlands of Love: Socialist Realist Aesthetics in Singapore". In *Eye of the Beholder*, ed. John Clark, Maurizio Peleggi, and T.K. Sabapathy. Sydney: Wild Peony Press, 2006.

________. *Hidden Things*. On the occasion of the exhibition "A work by Lim Tzay Chuen". Singapore: LaSalle-SIA, 2005.

Lee Weng Choy and Ray Langenbach. "Athens, Singapore" [a dialogue]. In *Kunst aus Megastädten Asiens — Art from Asia Pacific Megacities*, ed. Claus Friede and Ludwig Seyfarth. Hamburg: Kunsthaus Hamburg, 2000.

*Singapore*. Singapore: Singapore Art Museum and National Heritage Board, 2001.

*Singapore, Tan Swie Hian, Francis Ng, Heman Chong*. Singapore: National Arts Council and National Heritage Board, 2003.

## China-Taiwan:

Arttaiwan. *46th Biennale di Venezia*. Commissioned by Tsai Chin-fen and Paolo De Grandis. Taipei: Taipei Fine Arts Museum, 1995.

Kao Chien-hui. *Taiwan pavilion at 49th Biennale di Venezia*. Taipei: Taipei Fine Arts Museum, 2001.

Lei Yi-ting, ed. *Limbo Zone: organized by Taipei Fine Arts Museum, 50th Biennale di Venezia*. Guest curator Lin Shu-min. Taipei: Taipei Fine Arts Museum, 2003.

*Limbo Zone: organized by Taipei Fine Arts Museum, 50th Biennale di Venezia*. Guest curator Lin Shu-min. Exhibition Guide. Taipei, Taipei Fine Arts Museum, 2003.

Yang We-I and Odile Chen. *VOC: Handle With Care, Huang Yong-ping & Yang Mao-lin*. 48th Biennale di Venezia. Taiwan: Lin & Keng Gallery, 1999.

Yang Wen-i and Enrico Pedrini. *VOC: Handle with care, Huang Yongping & Yang Maolin*. As part of the 1997 Taiwan Pavilion curated by Shih Ju-Jen. 1999.

## Thailand:

Poshyananda, Apinan, commissioner. *Dreams Those Dying Wishing to Stay, Those Living Preparing to Leave, Montien Boonma & Araya Rasdjarmrearnsook, Thai Pavilion, 51st Biennale di Venezia*. Curated by Panya Vijinthanasarn, Luckana Kunavichayanont, and Sutee Kunavichayanont. Office of Contemporary Art & Culture and Ministry of Culture, Thailand, 2005.

________. *Dreams and Conflicts: The Dictatorship of the Viewer, Thai Pavilion, 5oth Biennale di Venezia*. Coordinated by Somsak Chowtadapong and Samart Chansoon. Office of Contemporary Art & Culture and Ministry of Culture, Thailand, 2003.

## United Kingdom:

Bowness, Sophie and Clive Phillpot, ed. *Britain at the Venice Biennale*. London: The British Council, 1995

*Britain and the São Paulo Bienal 1951–1991 / A Grã-Bretanha e a Bienal de São Paulo 1951–1991*, with essays by Margaret Garlake and Guy Brett. The British Council Brazil, 1991.

Furlong William, et al. *International; Venice Agendas 2003, a series of three breakfast meetings*. Wimbledon: Wimbledon School of Art Research Centre in association with Audio Arts Magazine, 1999.

________. *Venice Biennale 1999*. Wimbledon: Wimbledon School of Art Research Centre in association with Audio Arts Magazine, 1999.

________. *Venice Biennale 2001: Research Symposium March 2000*. Wimbledon: Wimbledon School of Art Research Centre in association with Audio Arts Magazine, 2000.

## Biennales from an Asian perspective

Burke, Gregory. "Distance Up Close: The Asian Biennials". *ArtAsiaPacific* 50 (2006).

Maerkle, Andrew. "Curating by Committee: Behind Asia's Biennials". *ArtAsiaPacific* 50 (2006).

Sinha, Gayatri. "Locating Biennales, Revising Frameworks". *Art India* X, ii (Quarter ii, 2005).

## Other Catalogues Consulted by Year of Publication

### 1968

*When Attitudes Become Form*. Curated by Harald Szeeman. Bern: Kunsthalle, 1968.

### 1985

Joachimides, Christos M., Normal Rosenthal, and Wieland Schmied, ed. *German Art in the 20th Century, Painting and Sculpture 1905–1985*. London: Royal Academy of Arts; Munich: Prestel Verlag, 1985.

*Reconstructions: Avant-Garde Art in Japan 1945–1965*. Curated by Kaido Kazu and David Elliott. Oxford: Museum of Modern Art, 1985.

### 1987

*Beyond the Open Door: Contemporary Paintings from the People's Republic of China*. Mostly chosen Waldemer A. Nielsen. Essay by Richard L. Strassberg. Organized by Pacific Asia Museum, Pasadena, 1987.

Pierquin Tian, Odile. *Peintres et Sculpteurs Chinois à Paris*. Typescript catalogue of exhibition. Paris: Centre de Recherches et de Documentation sur la Chine contemporaine and L'École des hautes études en sciences sociales, 18 May to 3 June 1987.

## 1989

*Against Nature: Japanese Art in the 1980s*. Curated by Kathy Halbreich, Kômoto Shinji, Nanjô Fumio, and Thomas Sokolowski. New York: New York University Grey Art Gallery, 1989. [Toured the USA from 15 June 1989–12 February 1991.]

*Magiciens de la terre*. Overall curator Jean-Hubert Martin. Paris: Centre Georges Pompidou, 1989.

Nakahara Yûsuke et al. *Europalia 89: Japan in Belgium*. Gent: Museum van Hedenndaagse Kunst, 1989. [Exhibited in Belgium from 28 October 1989–7 January 1990.]

## 1990

*Art Chinois 1990 Demain pour Hier*. Curated by Fei Dawei. Organized by Association Française d'Action Artistique & Les Domaines de l'Art, Pourrières & Editions Carte Segrete.

Hara Toshio and Howard T. Fox. *A Primal Spirit*. Tokyo: Hara Museum of Contemporary Art; Los Angeles: Los Angeles County Museum of Art, 1990. [Toured USA, 10 March 1990–22 September 1991.]

Kondô Yukio, Nanjô Fumio, and Peter Weiermaier. *Japanischer Kunst der Achtziger Jahre*. Frankfurt: Frankfurter Kunstverein, Edition Stemmle, 1990. [Frankfurter Kunstverein, 15 February–7 April 1991, Museum moderner Kunst, Wien.]

Namba Hideo and Okada Takahiko. *Japan Art Today*. Tokyo: Sezon Museum of Modern Art, 1990. [Sent to Scandinavia from 24 January 1990–25 August 1991.]

Tezuka Osamu et al. *Tezuka Osamu ten = Osamu Tezuka*. Tokyo: Tokyo Kokuritsu Kindai Bijutsukan, 1990.

## 1991

Annear, Judy and Tatehata Akira. *Zones of Love*. Sydney: Museum of Contemporary Art, 1991. [Exhibited in Australia from May 1991–September 1992.]

*Exceptional Passage*. Curated by Fei Dawei. Fukuoka: Fukuoka Art Museum.

Köppel-Yang, Martina, Peter Schneckman, and Ernst R. Schneider. *Gebrochene Bilder, Junge Kunst aus China: Selbstdarstellungen*. Heidelberg: Gesellschaft für Kulturaustausch mit Asien, 1991.

*"I don't want to play cards with Cézanne" and other works. Selections from the Chinese "New Wave" and "Avant-Garde" art of the eighties*. Curated by Richard L. Strassberg with essays by Zheng Shengtian, Tang Qingnian, and Lee Ou-fan. Organized by Pacific Asia Museum.

## 1992

*Artists Regional Exchange, Perth, April 1992: Four Views*: Vivienne Binns, "Culture as Transformation"; Ian Howard, "Towards a Legitimate Interest"; Anne Kirker, "A Dialogue with Thailand"; and Adrian Jones, "Managing ARX". *Artlink* 12, 3 (Spring 1992).

*New Art From China*. Curated by Claire Roberts. Art Gallery of New South Wales, 1992.

## 1993

*China's New Art, Post 1989, with a retrospective from 1979–1989.* Curated by Chang Tsong-zung and Li Xianting. Organized by Hanart TZ Gallery, Hong Kong.

*Fragmented Memory: The Chinese Avant Garde in Exile.* Curated by Julia F. Andrews and Gao Minglu. Organized by Wexner Center for the Arts.

Pöhlmann, Wolfger et al. *China Avant-Garde: Counter-currents in Art and Culture.* Berlin: Haus der Kulturen der Welt & Editions Braus, 1993. [Exhibited in Berlin from 20 January–16 May 1993, then Oxford 4 September–24 October 1993.]

*Silent Energy.* Curated by David Elliott and Lydie Mepham. Organized by Museum of Modern Art, Oxford.

## 1994

*Out of the Centre: Chinese Contemporary Art.* Curated by Hou Hanru. Pori, Finland: Pori Art Museum.

*Scream against the sky: Japanese Art after 1945.* Curated by Alexandra Munro. New York: Harry N. Abrams, 1994.

## 1995

*Contemporary Art of the Non-Aligned Countries 1995, Jakarta, Indonesia: Programme Book.* 1995.

*Contemporary Art of the Non-Aligned Countries 1995, Jakarta, Indonesia: Catalogue.* 1995.

*Contemporary Art of the Non-Aligned Countries 1995, Jakarta, Indonesia: Contemporary Balinese Art: Continuity in Change.* 1995.

*Contemporary Art of the Non-Aligned Countries 1995, Jakarta, Indonesia: Unity in Diversity in International Art, Seminar Proceedings.* 1995.

Huang Zhuan et al. *New Asian Art Show.* Tokyo: Japan Foundation Forum; Osaka: Kirin Plaza, 1995.

Ronte, Dieter and Walter Smerling. *"Quotation Marks": Chinese Contemporary Paintings.* Singapore: Singapore Art Museum, 1995. Also published as Dieter Ronte, Walter Smerling, Evelyn Weiss; mit Beiträgen von Chang Tsong-zung, et al. *China: zeitgenössische Malerei.* Köln: DuMont, 1996.

*Sengo bunka no kiseki / Japanese culture of the Postwar Years, 1945–1995.* Meguro-ku: Bijutsukan henshû; Tokyo: Asahi Shinbum, 1995.

Yang Wen-I and Jose Nicholas, ed. *Art Taiwan.* Taipei: Taipei Fine Arts Museum; Sydney: Museum of Contemporary Art, Sydney, 1995.

## 1996

*Inklusion/Exklusion: Kunst im Zeitalter von Postkolonialismus und Globaler Migration.* Curated by Peter Weibel. Graz: Neue Galerie, 1996.

*Reckoning with the past.* Curated by Chang Tsong-zung. With essays by John Clark and Yan Shanchun. Organized by The Fruitmarket Gallery, Edinburgh.

## 1997

*Another Long March: Chinese Conceptual and Installation Art in the Nineties.* Curated by Marianne Brouwer and Chris Driessen. With texts by Fei Dawei, Hou Hanru, and Tang Di. Organized by Fundament Foundation Breda.

*Parisien(ne)s.* Included Chen Zhen, Huang Yongping, Shen Yuan. Curated by Hou Hanru. Organized by Camden Arts Centre.

*Secession: Cities on the Move.* Curated by Hou Hanru and Hans-Ulrich Obrist. Organized by Wiener Secession and capc Musée d'art contemporain de Bordeaux.

*The Birth of Modern Art in Southeast Asia: Artists and Movements.* With Ushiroshôji Masahiro as supervising curator. Fukuoka Art Museum, 1997.

## 1998

*Chinese Contemporary, 96–98.* Curated by Julia Colman, Ludovic Bois. Organized by Chinese Contemporary Limited.

*Cream: Contemporary Art and Culture.* London and New York: Phaidon, 1998.

*Die Hälfte des Himmels.* Curated by Chris Werner, Qiu Ping, and Marianne Pitzen. Organized by Frauenmuseum Bonn.

Gao Minglu, curator and writer. *Inside Out: New Chinese Art.* New York: Asia Society; Berkeley: University of California Press, 1998.

*Großschwanzelefant / Big Tail Elephant.* Curated by Bernard Fibicher. Bern: Kunsthalle 1998.

Menzies, Jackie, ed. *Modern Boy, Modern Girl: Modernity in Japanese Art, 1910–1935.* Co-curated by Ajioka, Clark, Menzies, and Mizusawa. Sydney: Art Gallery of New South Wales, 1998.

Keusen, Elle, Inge Schmidt, and Helge Weihs. *Per Video.* Köln: Museum Ludwig, 1998.

## 1999

*Art at the Turn of the Millennium.* Burkhard Riemschneider and Uta Grosenick, ed. Köln: Taschen, 1999.

*ARX 5.* Iola Lenzi. "Process and Politics". *Art AsiaPacific* 23 (1999).

*ARX 5.* Lee Weng Choy. "Misunderstanding art". *Art AsiaPacific* 23 (1999).

*China 1999.* Organized by Limn Gallery, San Francisco.

*Cologne-Beijing, Beijing-Cologne Exchange Exhibition.* Curated by Tang Xin and U. Urle. Organized by Gothaer Kunstforum, Köln.

*Logan Collection.* Organized by Limn Gallery, San Francisco.

*Melbourne Biennale.* China curated by Huang Du.

*Modern Chinese Art.* Curated by Hans van Dijk. With essay by John Clark. Organized by Modern Chinese Art Foundation.

*Representing the People.* Curated by Karne Smith and Pi Li. Organized by The Courtyard Gallery & Newcastle, Tyne, and Weir Museums.

*Toi Toi Toi, Kassel 1999.* Louise Garrett. "Toi Toi Toi". *Art AsiaPacific* 23 (1999).

*Transience: Chinese Art at the End of the 20th Century*. Curated by Wu Hung. Chicago: Smart Museum of Art, University of Chicago.

*Truths from the Open Door: Chinese Conceptual Photography*. Curated by Wu Meichun and Zheng Shengtian. Art Gallery of Chulalongkorn University.

*Vielfaches echo (manifold echoes), Stuttgart, 1998*. Victoria Hynes. "Manifold Echoes". *ArtAsiaPacific*, 22 (1999).

## 2000

*Exhibiting Experimental Art in China*. Curated by Wu Hung. Organized by Smart Museum, University of Chicago.

*Fresh Cream: Contemporary Art and Culture*. London and New York: Phaidon, 2000.

*Paris pour escale*. Curated by Hou Hanru and Evelyne Jouanno. Organized by Musée d'Art Moderne de la Ville de Paris.

Perkins, Hetti and Hannah Fink, ed. *Papunya Tula: Genesis and Genius*. Sydney: Art Gallery of New South Wales in association with Papunya Tula Artists, 2000.

*Shanghe Meishuguan / Upriver Gallery*. Tianjin: Tianjin Shehui Kexueyuan Chubanshe, 2000.

Williams, Gilda, ed. *Fresh Cream*. London: Phaidon, 2000.

## 2001

Huang Zhuan and Pi Li. *Tuxiang jiushi liliang / Image is Power*. At He Xiangning Art Museum. Changsha: Hunan Meishu Chuban she, 2001.

Jay, Sian E. "Emerging visions". *Asian Art News* 11, 2 (2001). [Nokia Art Awards.]

*Living in Time 29 zeitgenössische Künstler aus China*. Curated by Hou Hanru, Fan Di'an, Gabriele Knapstein. Organized by Nationalgalerie im Hamburger Bahnhof Museum für Gegenwart in cooperation with the Ministry of Culture of PRC and China International Exhibition Agency.

Makabe Kaori, Mikami Yutaka, Yokohama Triennale Office, ed. *Yokohama Triennale 2001*. Yokohama: 2001.

## 2002

Chen Tong. *Look*. Exhibition Catalogue. Guangzhou: The Gallery of Guangzhou Fine Art Academe, 2002.

Jewyo Rhii. *Warming and Humidifying*. Korea: 2002.

*Landscape of Sur-consuming*. Curated by Hu Fang. Exhibition Catalogue. Guangzhou: Vitamin Creative Space, 2002.

*Paris-Pékin*. Curated by Chang Tsong-zung. Organized by Gallery Enrico Navarra. Chinese Century.

*Stay in Shanghai 2002*. Exhibition Catalogue. Shanghai: EastLink Gallery, 2002.

*The Shine of the City Contemporary Art Exhibition 2002*. Exhibition Catalogue.

Yasuko Furuichi. "Asia in Transition: Representation and Identity". In *Report of the International Symposium 2002*. Japan: The Japan Foundation Asia Centre, 2002.

## 2003

*Alors, la Chine?*. Curated by Chantal Béret, Alain Sayag, Pi Li et al. Organized by Centre Pompidou Paris.

*Art/34/Basel/18-23/6/03, Media Documents*. Basel, 2003.

*Basel 2003*. John Clark, "Art 34 Basel". *Art Asia Pacific* 38 (Fall 2003): 48–9.

*Cream 3: Contemporary Art and Culture*. London and New York: Phaidon, 2003.

Gao Minglu. *Chinese Maximalism/ Zongguo jiduo zhuyi*. Beijing: Millenium Art Museum; Buffalo: State University of New York at Buffalo Art Gallery. Catalogue published by Chongqing: Chongqing Chubanshe, 2003.

*How Latitudes Become Forms*. Curated by Philippe Vergne, Chinese Advisor, and Hou Hanru. Organized by Walker Art Center of contemporary art at the Today Art Gallery. Curated by Gu Zhenqing. Hong Kong: China Today Gallery Publishing House, 1993.

*Shanghart 2003*. Catalogue of artists represented by ShangART. Shanghai, 2003.

*A Strange Heaven: Contemporary Chinese Photography*. Curated by Petr Nedoma and Chang Tsong-zung. Organized by Hong Kong: Asian Art Archive; Paris: Galerie Enrico Navarra.

Zhang Baoquan & Gu Zhenqing, ed. *Second hand Reality: Post-Reality – an exhibition of contemporary art at the Today Art Gallery*. Curated by Gu Zhenqing. Hong Kong: China Today Gallery Publishing House Ltd, 1993.

## 2004

*Contemporary Taiwanese Art in the Era of Contention*. Curated by Pan An-yi. With catalogue essays by Yan Chuan-ying, Hsiao Chong-ray. Taipei: Taipei Fine Arts Museum; Ithaca: Herbert F. Johnson Museum of Art, 2004.

Ham Jin. Catalogue in conjunction with the exhibition *Aewan*. Essay by Iris Moon. Seoul: pkm Gallery, 2004.

*The Monk and the Demon: Contemporary Chinese Art*. Fei Dawei et al. Milan, 5 Continents Editions, 2004. [Exhibition in Lyon and Guangdong.]

Rawanchaikul, Toshiko and Lisa Horikawa, ed. *China Dream: Another Flow in Chinese Modern Art*. Fukuoka: Fukuoka Asian Art Museum, 2004.

Wu Hung and Christopher Phillips. *Between Past and Future: New Photography and Video from China*. Göttingen: Steidl Publishers, 2004.

## 2005

Fibicher, Bernard and Matthias Frehner, ed. *Mahjong: Contemporary Chinese Art from the Sigg Collection*. Ostfildern-Ruit: Hatje Cantz, 2005.

Jung Yeondoo. *Dreams Come True, Almost*. Seoul: Kukje Gallery, 2005.

Murakami Takashi, ed. *Little Boy: The Arts of Japan's Exploding Subculture*. New York: Japan Society; New Haven: Yale University Press, 2005.

Tatehata Akira et al. *Cubism in Asia: Unbounded Dialogues*. Tokyo: The Japan Foundation, 2005.

## 2006

Gong Mingguang, ed. *Entry Gate: Chinese Aesthetics of heterogeneity, 2006 MoCAEnvisage*. Bilingual Catalogue. Shanghai: Shanghai Shuhua Chubanshe, 2006.

*Second Shanghai Duolun Exhibition of Yong Artists*. Curated by Biljana Ciric, Huang Yuelin, and Tang Dixin. Bilingual catalogue. Shanghai: Duolun Museum, 2006.

# Index